Official
Advanced
PowerBuilder® 6

The Definitive Guide

Kouros Gorgani

Publisher
Keith Weiskamp

Acquisitions
Jeff Duntemann
Stephanie Wall

Project Editor
Jeff Kellum

Production Coordinator
Jon Gabriel

Cover Design
Anthony Stock

Layout Design
April Nielsen

CD-ROM Development
Robert Clarfield

The Coriolis Group, Inc.
An International Thomson Publishing Company
14455 N. Hayden Road, Suite 220
Scottsdale, Arizona 85260

602.483.0192
FAX 602.483.0193
http://www.coriolis.com

Library of Congress Cataloging-In-Publication Data

Gorgani, Kouros.
Official advanced PowerBuilder 6 : the definitive guide / by Kouros Gorgani.

     p. cm.
     Includes index.
     ISBN 1-85032-919-2
     1. Application software--Development.   2. PowerBuilder.   I. Title.

QA76.76.A65G67   1998
005.2'76--dc21   98-11495
                                                                  CIP

Printed in the United States of America
10 9 8 7 6 5 4 3 2 1

an International Thomson Publishing company

Albany, NY • Belmont, CA • Bonn • Boston • Cincinnati • Detroit
Johannesburg • London • Madrid • Melbourne • Mexico City
New York • Paris • Singapore • Tokyo • Toronto • Washington

Dedicated to my wife and best friend, Mojgan. Thank you for your loving patience throughout this project and thank you for our love-filled life and all the happiness I feel just because of you.

Acknowledgments

I would like to first thank God and then my parents, without whom I would not be here. Next, my special thanks goes to Mitchell Kertzman for this book's Foreword, and to Doug Hern and Mike Paola for their kind words.

Now, a book is never the work of a single individual, as writing a book takes so much more than simply putting words together. This book is the result of many people's diligent efforts that I would like to mention here.

I'd like to thank everyone at The Coriolis Group involved with this project, especially Jeff Kellum, Bart Reed, Bob LaRoche, and Jon Gabriel. Thank you Jeff and Bart for turning my words into English.

My humble thanks goes to four of Sybase's Senior Technical Consultants and good friends that have assisted me with specific areas of this book. I'd like to thank Chris Keating, Stephen Rice, and David Carson for Chapters 13, 22, and 23. These chapters are invaluable and would not be in this book without these knowledgeable individuals. I'd also like to thank my good friend and technical reviewer Jarek Siuda for bringing me up to date with object-orientation and for correcting my silly mistakes throughout this book.

Next, I'd like to thank a number of my close friends that have helped me throughout my life and career. I'd like to thank Homayoun Amir-Behboudi, Aboulfazl Esmailpour, Reza Fattahi, and Ebbi Shahani for their continuous encouragement. I would also like to thank Craig Smith for getting me started in the computing industry many years ago right after graduation, and Sue Boshoff for motivating me to excel when I needed it the most.

I would like to also thank John Kastrinos of PowerCerv, Yves de Montcheuil of CYRANO, and Heather Swanson of GreenBrier & Russel for their input into Chapter 33 and the demo material on accompanying CD-ROM.

Finally, I would like to thank everyone at Sybase Waterloo for being such a great gang to work with. You are the best I've ever worked with. A few names that I want to mention here are Mark DeLaFranier, Jamie Buchanan, Tunde Abiodun, David Loop and Bill Allison.

There are undoubtedly people I have forgotten to mention. To all of those who have helped me along the way so far, a heartful thanks.

About The Author

Kouros Gorgani has worked with the Sybase Technical Support group in Waterloo, Ontario, Canada, since 1995, where he has become a senior specialist with the PowerBuilder product. He quickly became a key resource for technical questions for the PowerBuilder product and is currently a member of its Alliance group, whose goal is to supply a relationship-focused, escalated-level of customer service. Kouros enjoys working with PowerBuilder and lets people know about it. Like a parent with his child, Kouros is tough but fair with the product. Like a savvy veteran, Kouros always stays fit by keeping up with the latest technology and evaluating the competition. He is also a certified PowerBuilder developer, has extensive experience in client/server development, and has worked with DBMSs on mainframes and PC networks for several years.

Kouros is a contributing writer for the *PowerBuilder Developer's Journal.* Kouros is also a speaker at the Powersoft annual user conference and often provides technical sessions for local user groups. He continues to be a willing mentor to others and retains a keen interest in educating and keeping people up to speed on product information. Kouros has dedicated himself to the proactive side of the business, contributing well to such things as technical documents, white papers, and technical talks. Writing a book on the subject seems to be a natural evolution for him.

Foreword

Personal computing has come a long way from being a part-time hobby to a multibillion dollar industry. In the early days, software carried with it an aura of history in the making, of a revolution that would alter not only the business world but the fabric of society as well. Network computing technologies such as client/server, Internet, and Java are now revolutionizing the world of corporate computing and in the personal computer, we have found a new vehicle for the exchange of ideas and the formation of a global community

As the face of computing is changing at an astounding rate, Sybase is responding. For example, Sybase is the first DBMS vendor to deliver a multitier framework to manage and deploy components across the distributed computing environment. This gives you the choice to design, develop, and deploy your mission-critical business applications on any tier depending on your requirements. This also provides a multitier platform, which makes the development and deployment of Internet applications an easier task.

PowerBuilder has also changed significantly. Version 6 is a leap forward in technology, and if you are a PowerBuilder developer, you should be very excited. The author of this book has brought PowerBuilder to a newer and greater height by covering almost everything that PowerBuilder 6 has to offer, putting it all into one complete, easy-to-read book. He has done a nice job of anticipating user confusions and has packed this book with valuable information.

On a final note, I would also like to take this opportunity to thank each one of you for using Sybase products. It is your support that has made Sybase the success it is today. We are committed to getting to the future as fast as our customers are, and we will deliver the products and services to make the transition as easy as possible.

Mitchell Kertzman
President and CEO
Sybase Inc.

Table Of Contents

Introduction   xxiii

PART I   The Overview Guide   1

Chapter 1   Overview Of PowerBuilder   3

The Evolution Of PowerBuilder   3

Component Architecture   4

What's New In PowerBuilder 6.0   4

Moving On   7

Chapter 2   The Technology   9

Client/Server   9

Object Orientation   13

COM, DCOM, And ActiveX   18

OLE DB   20

CORBA   21

Java   23

JavaBeans   24

Moving On   25

PART II *The Development Guide* 27

Chapter 3 DataWindows 29

DataWindow Objects 29

DataWindow Controls 36

DataWindowChild 46

Database Communication 48

Generating HTML 49

New In DataWindows 52

Moving On 57

Chapter 4 Windows 59

Types Of Windows 59

Instantiating Windows 63

Creating Objects 64

Window Events 65

Window Functions 69

Calling Window Functions And Events 70

Executing Events 71

Executing Functions 72

Events Or Functions? 74

Moving On 74

Chapter 5 Window Controls 75

Control Events And Attributes 76

The Control Array 78

Controls And Instantiation Of Windows   79

ListBox And PictureListBox   79

DropDownListBox And DropDownPictureListBox   80

TreeView   81

ListView   84

RichTextEdit   85

Tab Control   88

Moving On   90

Chapter 6   Multiple Document Interface   91

MDI Frames   91

MDI Sheets   94

MDI Menus   96

MicroHelp   97

MDI Toolbars   98

Moving On   101

Chapter 7   Menus   103

The Menu Architecture   103

Types Of Menus   104

Menu Inheritance   107

Menu Events And Functions   108

Menus In MDI   109

Menu Performance Issues   111

Moving On   111

Chapter 8 User Objects 113

User Objects And Object-Oriented Programming 113

Types Of User Objects 115

C++ Class 131

Moving On 133

Chapter 9 Drag-And-Drop 135

Drag-And-Drop In PowerBuilder 135

Moving On 140

Chapter 10 Printing 141

The Basics 141

Printing Functions 142

Printing And DataWindows 146

Print Properties 147

Using Fonts 151

Moving On 153

Chapter 11 Structured Query Language 155

Database Objects 155

SQL Statements 156

Referential Integrity 161

Transactions 162

Stored Procedures 162

Embedded SQL 164

Dynamic SQL 166

Moving On 169

Chapter 12   Debugging Your Application   171

The New PowerBuilder Debugger   171

The Debug Window   172

PowerBuilder Debug Trace   178

Profiling And Tracing   182

Moving On   194

PART III   The Advanced Guide   195

Chapter 13   Version Control   197

Version Control Benefits   197

PowerBuilder Version Control Interfaces   199

PowerBuilder Library Configuration   200

Working With Version Control   203

Version Control Support   213

Moving On   214

Chapter 14   Advanced DataWindows   217

Dynamic DataWindows   217

Query Mode   220

Sharing Result Sets   221

Changing The SQL SELECT Statement   223

DataStores   224

Moving On   227

Chapter 15 Transaction Object 229

Using Transactions 229

Extending Transaction Objects 235

Moving On 240

Chapter 16 MAPI 241

MAPI—Simple And Extended 241

MAPI In PowerBuilder 242

PowerBuilder Library For Lotus Notes 250

Moving On 250

Chapter 17 External Functions 251

Writing External DLLs 252

C To PowerBuilder 255

Declaring External Functions 257

Passing Arguments To DLLs 258

Passing Structures To DLLs 258

Windows API 264

Moving On 269

Chapter 18 Object Linking And Embedding (OLE) 271

OLE Essentials 272

OLE Controls 275

Programmable OLE Objects 282

OLE Enhancements 284

Moving On 288

Chapter 19   PowerBuilder Automation Server   291

PowerBuilder As An Automation Server   291

A User Object As An Automation Server   295

Named Automation Server   297

Objects And The Registry   299

Moving On   303

PART IV   The Database Connectivity Guide   305

Chapter 20   Database Connectivity   307

Powersoft Native Drivers   307

Preparing To Use Your Database   309

New Connectivity Features   314

Troubleshooting Your Connection   325

Porting Your Application   326

Moving On   328

Chapter 21   ODBC   329

Advantages Of ODBC   329

The ODBC Architecture   330

The Driver Architecture   334

ODBC Conformance Levels   336

ODBC Initialization Files   342

PowerBuilder And ODBC   346

Troubleshooting   350

Moving On   351

Chapter 22   Sybase SQL Anywhere   353

System Requirements   353

Architecture   355

Connecting To SQL Anywhere   358

Advanced Configurations   365

Development Practices   372

Deploying SQL Anywhere   377

Moving On   379

Chapter 23   Adaptive Server Enterprise   381

Server Installation   382

Sybase Server Architecture   383

Connecting To Your Database   392

System Tables   396

Logins, Users, And Other Security Issues   398

Creating New Databases   401

Stored Procedures And Triggers   401

Database Administration Tools   404

Other Information Sources   405

Moving On   406

PART V   The Deployment Guide   407

Chapter 24   Creating A Project   409

Application Project   409

Proxy Library   415

C++ 416

Moving On 417

Chapter 25 Deployment 419

The Deployment Kit 419

PowerBuilder Deployment DLLs 419

Database Connectivity 422

OLE And OCX/ActiveX Deployment 425

Automating Your Deployment 427

PBSync Synchronization 427

Troubleshooting 431

Moving On 432

PART VI The Administration Guide 433

Chapter 26 Performance And Fine-Tuning 435

Performance Issues 435

Garbage Collection 443

Moving On 444

Chapter 27 The Data Pipeline 445

Creating A Data Pipeline Object 445

Pipeline In Your Applications 448

Moving On 451

Chapter 28 Creating Help Files 453

Windows Help Files 453

Context-Sensitive Help 464

Help Compilers   465

Moving On   465

PART VII   *The Comprehensive Guide*   467

Chapter 29   Distributed PowerBuilder   469

The Architecture   469

The Client Application   471

The Server Application   478

Shared Objects   480

Server Push   484

Asynchronous Processing   485

DataWindow Synchronization   487

Q&A   493

Moving On   495

Chapter 30   Internet Development   497

The Internet Tools   497

Web.PB Wizard   504

Window ActiveX Control   505

Secure Mode For Plug-Ins And ActiveX   509

The Context Object   510

Web Jumps   514

Choosing A Strategy   514

Moving On   515

Chapter 31   Internationalization   517

Unicode   517

Japanese Double-Byte
  Character Support   519

Arabic And Hebrew   519

Design Issues   521

Translation Toolkit   522

Moving On   523

Chapter 32   PowerBuilder Foundation Class Library   525

The PFC Architecture   525

The Application Manager   533

Programming With PFC   535

Using PFC Services   536

New PFC 6.0 Features   540

Moving On   549

Chapter 33   CODE Partners   551

PowerCerv   552

CYRANO   554

Greenbrier & Russel   558

Moving On   561

Chapter 34 Other Sybase Design And Development Tools 563

Power++ 563

PowerJ 565

PowerDesigner 6.1 567

Jaguar Component Transaction Server (CTS) 568

Other Sybase Design And Development Tools 578

Visual Components 579

Moving On 579

Chapter 35 Looking Into The Future 581

Future Directions 581

Java, Java, And More Java 583

Moving On 584

Index 585

Introduction

Official Advanced PowerBuilder 6: The Definitive Guide is a new and different approach to this powerful program. I have tried to construct this book in a fashion that provides a comprehensive look into the features of PowerBuilder 6. It was not my intention to offer a replacement for the PowerBuilder documentation, but rather to provide an additional resource to help you extend your knowledge base, become more proficient, and even exceed your goals.

PowerBuilder has so many features and so much potential for enhancing your applications that it can be quite overwhelming to try to master them all at once. Therefore, in this book I have tried to cover PowerBuilder's features in a way that allows you to focus specifically on information most appropriate and timely for your particular needs. I am assuming that you are somewhat familiar with PowerBuilder. However, if you are a newcomer to the program, this book will introduce you to the concepts behind client/server development and to the most efficient ways of using PowerBuilder to develop and deploy GUI applications. On the other hand, if you are an advanced developer, you'll probably be particularly interested in finding solutions to problems and scenarios you've frequently encountered in your applications.

I have divided this book into seven parts. Part I basically provides an overview on PowerBuilder and defines some of the industry buzzwords. Part II gets into the development phase; I've covered some of the most common objects and classes used during development, including windows, controls, DataWindows, User objects, printing, SQL, and debugging. Part III discusses more advanced topics such as external interfaces, dynamic DataWindows, OLE, MAPI, and version control. In Part IV, I have described database connectivity in detail. You'll learn about ODBC, PowerBuilder's database interfaces, Sybase SQL Anywhere, and the Adaptive Server Enterprise. Part V covers creating executables, as well as deploying and executing your applications. Part VI is all about administration: you'll learn performance and fine-tuning tips, how to use Data Pipeline objects, and how to create Help files. Part VII, the final part, is a comprehensive section, focusing on distributed computing, building Web servers, PFCs, internationalization, other class libraries, and various third-party and Sybase tools. In a nutshell, most PowerBuilder features are explored in great detail.

I wanted this book to be a technical session between you and me, so I have tried to get straight to the point and have skipped some of the basics. I have also had the benefit of input from four of Sybase's Senior Technical Consultants, who assisted with various chapters of the book.

All in all, I think you'll find this book friendly, readable, filled with juicy tidbits, and packed with information that can be used in a real enterprise application. I hope you enjoy reading it as much as I have enjoyed writing it.

PART I
The
Overview
Guide

Overview Of PowerBuilder

The need for an easy-to-use, yet powerful development tool has increased tremendously in the last few years because corporations have begun migrating their conventional mainframe-based or DOS-based applications to LAN-based GUI client/server environments. In a relatively short time, PowerBuilder has become one of the leading client/server development tools in the industry. PowerBuilder's object orientation, its ability to efficiently handle large-scale databases and distributed processing, its Internet development capabilities, its overall improvement over previous releases, and, most important of all, Sybase's vision into the future have set PowerBuilder far above other tools currently available in the marketplace.

The Evolution Of PowerBuilder

It all started in 1991, with the release of version 1.0. In a short period of time, PowerBuilder has established itself as one of the leaders in the client/server industry with the reengineering of most business processes. Within a few years, PowerBuilder has become the most widely used client/server tool available. Every new release has been a giant leap toward the future of computing, making PowerBuilder a pacesetter for all other contenders. I remember how excited I was when menu toolbars were introduced in version 3.0. Well, things have changed quite a lot since then. In June 1995, with the release of version 5.0, Sybase impressed every PowerBuilder user. We were introduced to application partitioning and the multitier architecture, compiled code, Object Cycle, OLE 2.0 and the OCX technology, runtime servers, PFCs, and more.

Today we have version 6.0, and I am extremely excited. I think we should all be. This version should meet all your needs when creating business applications in any of the architectures used in today's computing enterprises. PowerBuilder 6.0 supports the

3

development of applications in traditional client/server, multitiered, Web-based or distributed component-based architectures. By pairing PowerBuilder with Sybase's Adaptive Component Architecture, you are given the ability to use familiar and proven technologies to create robust business applications for today and tomorrow.

Component Architecture

Let me tell you a little about this new concept everybody is talking about. Sybase's Adaptive Component Architecture anticipates that reusable standard components will be the fundamental building blocks of all business applications. Components will be in compliance with industry standards such as ActiveX, CORBA, and JavaBean specifications. These components will then be distributed onto all application tiers, executing on client machines, middle-tier application servers, and back-end database servers. They will also interact with one another using one or more standard protocols, including COM/DCOM and CORBA. Powerful transaction servers will manage the execution of application logic components. The distributed component-based applications of the future will operate in heterogeneous platform environments and access a wide variety of database servers. They will also run over a LAN, WAN, intranet, the Internet, and perhaps other Internet-based networks. Doesn't this sound just awesome?

However, let me warn you that creating components for various middle-tier environments can be quite a cumbersome job. Fortunately, the good news is that PowerBuilder 6.0's component architecture removes all the complexity of developing these components—by automatically generating common PowerBuilder objects as standard components. PowerBuilder supports the generation of multiple component types from PowerBuilder objects, enabling the easy transition from one component model to another. These components can then be deployed into a variety of middle-tier server environments, including distributed PowerBuilder servers, Microsoft's Transaction Server, and the Sybase Jaguar Component Transaction Server. I find it a privilege to be working with PowerBuilder as well as being part of a company such as Sybase that has the technological edge over its competitors. Sybase has done an excellent job with version 6.0 of PowerBuilder.

Now without further ado, let's get to the new features of this great release.

What's New In PowerBuilder 6.0

In this version, Sybase has enhanced most of the existing features of PowerBuilder and added many new features that fall into the categories of Internet deployment, open technology, and developer productivity, all of which are discussed in the following sections.

Internet Deployment

If you need to deploy your application on Web-based clients, you'll be glad to know that PowerBuilder 6.0 Enterprise is now bundled with the Internet Developer Tools (IDT). Here are some of the features of the IDT:

- Web.PB for CGI, ISAPI, and NSAPI Web servers

- The Web.PB class library for generating HTML and managing the state of a browser connection

- The Web.PB Wizard for creating the HTML elements required to invoke the services of distributed objects

- The PowerBuilder window plug-in DLL

- Windows ActiveX

- The DataWindow plug-in DLL

- The O'Reilly WebSite Web server

To further facilitate the deployment of PowerBuilder's runtime environment, many of the PowerBuilder deployment DLLs have now been combined to form what is called the PowerBuilder *Virtual Machine (VM)*. You have also been given a synchronization tool called *PBSynch*, which verifies that any set of files includes the latest versions of all DLLs or that these DLLs will be automatically updated as needed. To facilitate Web deployment, Sybase has future plans for a JavaBean proxy generator for PowerBuilder. *Proxies* allow distributed PowerBuilder objects to communicate with distributed PowerBuilder server objects. The JavaBean proxy is a form of a PowerBuilder proxy that is written as a Java bean, which allows it to be downloaded and run on any Java VM. Also, support exists for the future creation of multiple standard components, including ActiveX, CORBA, and JavaBeans.

Open Technology

PowerBuilder 6.0 fully supports the move toward open, distributed, component-based application architectures, providing you with application scalability, code reusability, flexibility, and maintainability. Unix platform support has been extended for IBM AIX and HP-UX. PowerBuilder can also act as both a consumer and a producer of objects for transaction servers, including the Sybase Jaguar CTS and the Microsoft Transaction Server.

To facilitate the open technology, PowerBuilder 6.0 is now available in several new language versions, significantly expanding language support. For example, it's available in both 32-bit Arabic and 32-bit Hebrew right-to-left language versions. To add to this, a new Unicode version of PowerBuilder Enterprise is also available for the Windows NT 4.x platform. To facilitate internationalization even more, the PowerBuilder Translation Toolkit package (previously known as the Translation Assistant) is also bundled with PowerBuilder Enterprise.

Developer Productivity

For you, the developer, Sybase has added many new functional capabilities to make PowerBuilder easy to use and to increase your productivity. Here's a brief description of some of these features:

- **Enhanced distributed PowerBuilder.** Includes asynchronous application server processing, server push, named server utility, and shared objects.

- **A class definition interface.** Added to PowerBuilder to enable you to obtain information about PowerBuilder's class definitions via PowerScript.

- **A new source control interface.** Complies with the Microsoft Common Source Code Control (SCC) interface specification.

- **An enhanced PBTest interface.** This is an OLE interface to the existing testing tools interface to simplify and standardize access.

- **An excellent new debugger.** Includes a new pane-based interface that facilitates the viewing of different types of information simultaneously. *Just-In-Time debugging* is included, as well. This allows you to break into the debugger at runtime. You are also given access to the following:

  - Conditional breakpoints

  - Call stack

  - Objects in memory

  - Source

  - Source browser

  - Source history

  - Variables

  - Watch variables

- **Application profiling and tracing.** Allows you to collect, trace, and analyze information about the execution of your PowerBuilder applications.

- **Redesigned toolbars.** Toolbars now have a "flat" Microsoft Office 97 style.

- **Greatly enhanced database connectivity.** Extended to include Informix 7.2 and Sybase SQL 11.1. Also, the version of ODBC support has been upgraded to level 3.0.

- **Extension of the DataWindow.** Allows you to save to Excel 5 format as well as ASCII. The ASCII save option now includes saving computed columns and headings rather than just column names. You are also given device support for the IntelliMouse pointing device, which enhances DataWindow scrolling and navigation through any Windows control, such as ListViews and TreeViews. The DataWindow now has support for Button objects, which can have predefined or custom actions associated with them. In addition, new GroupBox objects can be used to frame and label sets of objects on a DataWindow. Scrollable support is now provided in print preview and the **RowFocusChanging** event.

- **Added capabilities for client-side DataWindows and DataStores.** They can now exchange data from a server-side DataStore object.

- **Enhanced PowerBuilder foundation class library.** Here's what's new in PFCs:

  - Calendar

  - Calculator

  - Progress bar

  - Splitbar

  - Application preference service

  - Windows' most recently used service

  - Linked list service

  - Broadcaster service

  - MetaClass service

  - Timer service

  - Many new objects

Moving On

As you are well aware, the technology industry is changing rapidly. As the industry changes, PowerBuilder is also changing. In this chapter, I have listed PowerBuilder 6.0's new features. The list is long, and I might have missed a feature or two. I know that becoming proficient with every new feature requires hard work and lots of resources. In order to be successful in what we do, this extra effort is required. The learning curve is steep, and that's where this book comes in handy. I hope that what you learn in the following chapters will guide you on the road ahead.

In Chapter 2, I explain some of the mysterious buzzwords you've heard and read about so often and take you behind the basic mechanics of these technologies.

The Technology

Keeping pace with the rapid changes in computer technology has become a challenge. The purpose of this chapter is to define and describe the processes behind some of the buzzwords you're hearing and reading about. In some cases, the specifications covered in the chapter do not necessarily apply to PowerBuilder; but who knows what the future holds, so let's be prepared. As we go through the rest of this book, you'll learn more about these specifications; however, this chapter will at least give you a head start.

Client/Server

Before the Internet stole the spotlight, client/server technology was the hottest topic in the computer industry. Today, client/server technology is as popular as ever. Most application-development vendors are targeting this client/server market, and many traditional mainframe-based application software companies are migrating their products to this remarkable environment.

So what is *client/server* anyway? In a nutshell, client/server is a computational architecture that involves client processes requesting services from server processes. From a programmer's perspective, client/server computing is a logical extension of the old modular programming, where most of the intelligence is placed on the server. The fundamental logic of modular programming is the separation of large pieces of code into constituent modules, which facilitates both development and maintenance. Client/server computing takes this one step further by recognizing that not all of those modules need to be executed within the same process. With this architecture, the calling procedure becomes the client that requests the service, and the called procedure becomes the server that provides the service. Simple, huh? Figure 2.1 shows a typical client/server architecture.

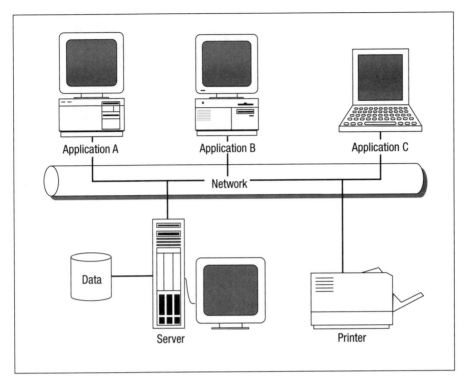

Figure 2.1
A typical client/server architecture.

The Client Process

A client process sends a message to a server process requesting that a task be performed. The client application is sometimes referred to as the *front end*. Client applications usually manage the user-interface portion of the application; they validate data entered by the user, dispatch requests to server programs, and sometimes execute business logic. The front end also manages the local resources the user interacts with, such as the monitor, the keyboard, the local CPU, and other peripherals that may be hooked up locally.

The Server Process

A server process, sometimes known as the *back end*, fulfills the client request by performing the given task. Server programs generally execute database retrieval and updates, manage data integrity, and dispatch responses to client requests. Sometimes, server programs execute common or complex business logic and may run on another machine on the network. The server process also acts as a software engine that manages shared resources such as databases, printers, communication links, or high-powered processors. In other words, the server process performs the tasks that are common to similar applications.

The simplest form of server is a *file server*. The client passes requests for files or file records over a network to the file server. This form of data service requires large bandwidth and can cause considerable slowdowns on a network with many users. Traditional local area network (LAN) computing allows users to share resources, such as data files and peripheral devices, by moving them from standalone computers onto a networked file server (NFS). The more advanced types of servers are database, transaction, and application, which are discussed here:

- **Database servers.** A client passes an SQL request as a message to the server. The database engine executes the SQL query, and the result is returned over the network back to the client. The code that processes the SQL request and its data resides on the server. With this method, the server uses its own processing power to find the requested data, rather than passing all the rows back to the client and letting it find its own data, as is the case with the file server.

- **Transaction servers.** A client invokes a remote procedure that resides on a server. This server also contains an SQL database engine and procedural commands that execute a group of SQL statements. The applications that are based on transaction servers handle what is called *online transaction processing (OLTP)*. Usually OLTP involves mission-critical applications that require extremely fast response times and tight control over the security and integrity of the database. The communication overhead in this approach is kept to a minimum because the exchange typically consists of a single request/reply.

- **Application servers.** These servers are not necessarily database centered, but they do serve various user needs. An example is a fax server, where faxes are regulated and sent. Basing resources on a server allows users to share data, while security and management services, which are also based in the server, ensure data integrity and security.

The most significant benefit of client/server technology is its flexible architecture. Some of the other advantages of this environment include:

- Adaptability
- Cross-platform capability and affordability
- Incorporation of business rules into the RDBMS
- Interoperability
- Effective use of CPU cycles
- Faster applications development
- Scalability

Distributed Processing

Distributed processing allows you to get the most out of your investment in the client/server architecture. It allows processing to occur on more than one processor in order for a transaction to be completed. In other words, processing is distributed across two or more machines, and the processes are totally independent of each other, as seen in Figure 2.2. Often, the data used in a distributed processing environment is also distributed across platforms.

Distributed applications introduce a whole new kind of design as well as deployment issues. For this extra effort to be worthwhile, there has to be a notable payback, which I'll get to next.

Many applications nowadays are also distributed, in the sense that they have at least two components running on different machines. Your company's email system is an example. Thinking of these applications as distributed applications and running the right components in the right places benefits the user and optimizes the use of network and computer resources. The application designed with distribution in mind can accommodate different clients with

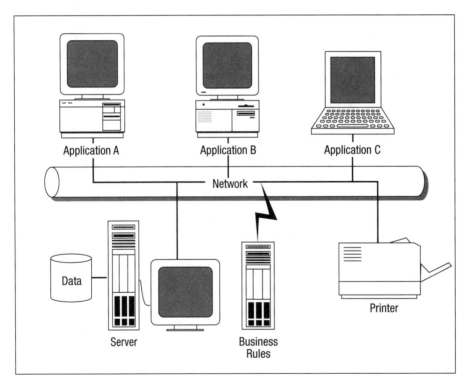

Figure 2.2
A typical distributed processing environment.

different capabilities by running components on the client side when possible and running them on the server side when necessary.

Designing applications for distribution gives you a great deal of flexibility in deployment. Distributed applications are also much more scalable than their monolithic counterparts. If all the logic of a complex application is contained in a single module, there's only one way to increase the throughput without tuning the application itself—with faster hardware. Today's servers and operating systems scale very well, but it's often cheaper to buy an identical machine than to upgrade to a server that is twice as fast. With a properly designed distributed application, a single server can start out running all the components. When the load increases, some of the components can be deployed to additional lower-cost machines.

Clearly, distributed processing offers a natural way to separate user interface components from the business logic required by an application. In a distributed application, a client can invoke services provided by remote objects. A client can invoke methods (functions and events) that are associated with a remote object as if they were defined in a local object.

PowerBuilder gives you the ability to build applications that run in a distributed computing environment. This feature was first introduced in version 5.0, and it has been improved by a large margin in the latest release. Chapter 29, "Distributed PowerBuilder," covers PowerBuilder's distributed computing in more detail.

Object Orientation

This is an exciting subject—it has become the talk of the town for the past few years, and for some it has become almost a religion. *Object-oriented programming (OOP)* is a relatively new programming concept that differs from traditional processing-oriented computer programming. Because of the proliferation of object-oriented approaches in recent years, it's very difficult to give a general definition for object orientation. Nevertheless, any programming language that provides a mechanism to exploit packaging of objects can be categorized as "object oriented."

One of the most important benefits of object orientation is its ability to reuse code and designs. Everything is structured in objects, and the definition of an object can be easily altered with minimum consequent effects on other objects. You can make extensions or modifications to a system's behavior without modifying existing code—rather, you add new code to it. This results in code that is easier to understand. Overall, object-oriented programming allows faster development, better quality, and easier maintenance of programs.

PowerBuilder implements the OOP concepts as follows:

- **Classes.** Objects such as windows, menus, and User objects

- **Properties.** Object variables and instance variables

- **Methods.** Events and functions

Fortunately, PowerBuilder does not force you into object-oriented programming, and you don't have to know all about OOP in order to take advantage of some of its features. However, without learning OOP and applying what you have learned, you won't harvest the full benefits of what I am about to discuss with you. As we go through the rest of this book, you'll learn more about OOP, but I feel it's absolutely necessary to briefly discuss some of its essential concepts.

Objects And Messages

An *object* is an abstract entity that understands and executes a well-defined set of commands. These commands are called the *methods* of the object. Objects can interact by sending messages to each other. Such a message is a request to execute a certain method. When a message is sent to an object, the corresponding method is looked up and invoked, and sometimes a result is returned.

Inheritance

Inheritance is the architecture that allows an object to be derived from existing objects and to obtain its attributes and behaviors from another object, which then becomes the ancestor object (see Figure 2.3).

In other words, inheritance allows for the development of a basic set of objects, known as *base classes* (or *superclasses*), that contain a set of attributes reusable by descendant objects. The descendant objects can also be called *subclasses*. True inheritance allows the descendant object to both extend and override the properties of its ancestor. When inheriting, code is passed to the descendant objects instead of being copied, and a descendant class can change some of the attributes or behaviors of its ancestor while maintaining the core set of functionality built into the ancestor.

In PowerBuilder, you can inherit from windows, menus, and User objects. You cannot inherit from anything else. When you inherit these objects, you actually inherit their attributes, instant and shared variables, controls, user-defined events, object-level functions, and scripts.

> **Note:** *You cannot remove anything in the descendant that has been inherited from an ancestor.*

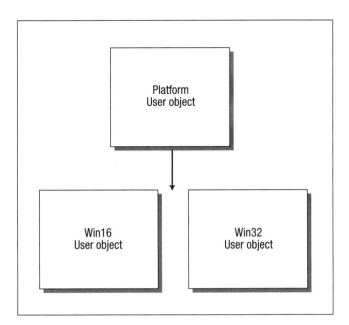

Figure 2.3

A basic inheritance architecture.

Inheritance works differently for attributes than it does for events and scripts. All the attributes of a descendant are inherited from an ancestor. You cannot remove these attributes, but you can override the values of the ancestor's attributes. You can also add new attributes to the descendant. When events are inherited, the scripts behind those events are extended by default. This means that the code in any ancestor is executed first, then the code for the descendants. You can choose to extend or override the script.

> **Note:** There are times when you won't want to execute the functionality of the ancestor in your descendant objects. When there's a need to do this, you'll want to override the ancestor object.

Extending an ancestor event or function results in execution of the ancestor code plus the execution of any code defined for the event in the descendant object. Overriding an ancestor event or function results in execution of only the code defined in the descendant object.

A natural extension of inheritance is *multiple inheritance*. Multiple inheritance occurs when a subclass can inherit from more than one parent class. Another interesting variation on class-based inheritance is what is called *partial inheritance*. In this case, some properties are inherited and others suppressed. Partial inheritance is therefore convenient for code sharing, but it can create a mess of a class hierarchy. This functionality is not available in PowerBuilder, but the PFCs (see Chapter 32, "PowerBuilder Foundation Class Library," for more discussion on this) have introduced a neat method to implement a workaround for multiple inheritance.

Encapsulation

Encapsulation is the process of hiding all the details of an object that do not contribute to its essential characteristics. The only thing that is really essential to an object is the set of methods it can execute. Consequently, encapsulation hides the implementation details of the object, and the only thing that remains externally visible is the interface of that object. Once an object is encapsulated, its implementation details are not immediately accessible anymore. Instead, they are packaged and are only indirectly accessible via the object's interface. The only way to access such an encapsulated object is via *message passing*. When the object receives a message, the object selects the method by which it will react to the message.

Various kinds of encapsulation exist, but the one we're concerned with is *object-based encapsulation*. Object-based encapsulation means that an object is free to use private resources to comprehend its behavior, where the senders of messages to the object have no access to these private resources. Another way to describe this is that an object can only understand its behavior by making use of its own attributes and private resources. With object-based encapsulation, an object has no direct access to the implementation details of any of its acquaintances, even if it has itself as an acquaintance. The acquaintances of an object are all the objects it has knowledge of or can directly refer to.

PowerBuilder supports the encapsulation of variables, events, and functions at the object level for windows, menus, and User objects. By using instance variables, user-defined events, and object-level functions, all the data and behaviors of an object can be encapsulated into a single package.

Instantiation

One of the most important mechanisms for code reuse in OOP is *instantiation*. A first approach to instantiation is through the use of *object classes*. A *class* is a number of things considered together as a group because they have similar characteristics. Within an object class, objects in a set share a common structure and a common behavior. Through defining object classes, you can define your own kinds of objects and instantiate them as you need them. An instance of a class is an object that is described by that class. In simple words, instantiation of a class is the creation of a new instance of that class.

Delegation

The term *delegation* refers to the assignment of responsibility. It allows the behavior of an object to be defined in terms of the behavior of another object. The primary emphasis of delegation is on message passing, where an object can delegate responsibility of a message it can't handle to objects that potentially can handle the message.

With delegation, an object associates itself with a service object designed specifically for that object. To give you an example, you might create a service object that handles multitable updates for your DataWindows. In this case, you would simply call the multitable update service to update your DataWindows.

Polymorphism

In Greek, *poly* means "many" and *morph* means "forms," hence the word *polymorphism*. In object-oriented programming, polymorphism refers to the ability of an object to become different forms of objects.

Polymorphism can be both parametric and ad hoc. Please note that there is an important distinction between parametric polymorphism and ad hoc polymorphism. Parametric polymorphism is obtained when an operation works uniformly on a range of objects that exhibit some common structure. This kind of polymorphism is also referred to as *genericity*. Ad hoc polymorphism, on the other hand, is obtained when the operation works on several unrelated objects and behaves in entirely different ways for each object. In terms of implementation, a generic function will execute the same code for arguments of any admissible type, whereas an ad hoc polymorphic function may execute different codes for each type of argument. An example of ad hoc polymorphism would be a case where two objects accidentally have a method with the same name but an entirely different body (for example, a **uf_Sort**() function that exists on two objects but has totally different behaviors).

Notice that class-based inheritance is also closely related to polymorphism. The same operations that apply to instances of a parent class also apply to instances of its subclasses. This kind of parametric polymorphism is sometimes called *subclass polymorphism*. Of course, it's possible to have support for polymorphism without class-based inheritance. Thus, polymorphism enhances software reusability by making it possible to implement generic software that will work not only for a range of existing objects, but also for objects to be added later.

PowerBuilder supports polymorphism in the form of overloaded functions and the capability to override ancestor functions and events as seen in Figure 2.4. This allows you to define generic types of functionality that behave differently depending on the referenced object.

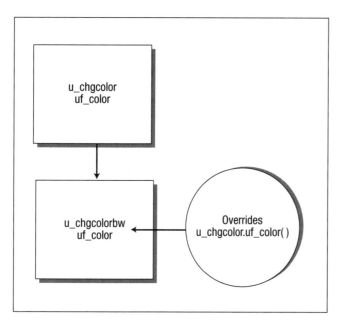

Figure 2.4
An example of polymorphism in PowerBuilder.

Function Overloading

In *function overloading*, the descendant function (or an identically named function in the same object) has different arguments or argument data types. PowerBuilder determines which function to execute based on the arguments or argument data types specified in the function call.

> **Note:** *PowerBuilder events cannot be overloaded. They just can't!*

PowerBuilder overloads many of the prebuilt functions. For example, **MessageBox()** exemplifies function overloading:

```
int  li_number
MessageBox( "Function Overloading", String( li_number) )
MessageBox( "Function Overloading", li_number )
```

COM, DCOM, And ActiveX

The *component object model (COM)* is the underlying framework that makes OLE, and more recently ActiveX, possible. It's an object-based framework for developing and deploying software components. I like to refer to COM as a specification on how applications interoperate and the technology that lets developers like you capture abstractions as

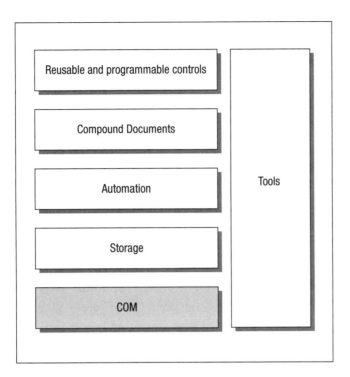

Figure 2.5
The common object model.

component interfaces and then provide binary classes that implement those interfaces. Figure 2.5 illustrates the COM architecture.

COM comprises several basic fundamentals that provide the architecture of the object model. The binary standard allows components written in different languages to call each other's functions. Interfaces are logical groups of related functions that provide some well-defined capability. A COM interface defines the behavior or capabilities of a software component as a set of methods and properties. An interface has a responsibility to guarantee consistent semantics from objects that support it. Each COM object must support at least one interface, which is called the *Iunknown*—although they can support many interfaces simultaneously. A *globally unique identifier (GUID)* is assigned to each interface to eliminate any ambiguity that might arise from name collisions. Iunknown is the interface that COM defines to allow components to control their own life spans and to dynamically determine another component's capabilities. One capability a component object does not provide is direct access to its data. The common object library, implemented as part of the operating system (OS), provides the legwork associated with finding and launching component objects.

Distributed COM (DCOM) extends COM to support communication among objects on different machines networked via a LAN, a wide area network (WAN), or even the Internet. With DCOM, your application can be distributed at locations that make the most sense to your customer and for the application.

ActiveX is the technology that brings interactivity to the Internet. ActiveX is supported by many different languages and tools; because of this, it enables developers with different backgrounds and levels of expertise to bring innovation and creativity to the Web. The specification for ActiveX is based on a refinement of the existing COM standards, which makes it much simpler for the development community to get involved without a steep learning curve.

OLE DB

OLE DB, which I believe will be the replacement of ODBC in the near future, gives you a whole new look at the methods you use to access your data. OLE DB can access all kinds of data via a standard COM interface, regardless of where and how that data is stored (see Figure 2.6). This includes storage media such as relational databases, documents, spreadsheets, files, and electronic mail. With the OLE technology, the database as we know it today becomes a component called a *data provider*. In fact, any component that directly exposes functionality through an OLE DB interface over a native data format is an OLE DB data provider. This includes everything from a full SQL DBMS to an ISAM file to a text file or data stream.

Individual OLE DB component objects can be built to implement advanced features on top of simple data providers; such components are called *service providers*. Through service providers such as query processors, specialized applications—for example, report writers—can take advantage of providers that interconnect and offer different combinations of data presented as tables. Reports can span different data storage types without bringing data locally to a client, as in the typical case of heterogeneous joins. Just as there are different types of data providers, there are different types of OLE DB *data consumers*. Data consumers can be custom programs written to one data provider, or generic consumers written to work with a variety of data providers. Future versions of software packages could become data consumers as well as data providers. In that case, one software program could directly access data in another software program's format, and so on.

You may be worried about whether your current applications can use ODBC, but there's no need to be concerned. Microsoft is supplementing the ODBC driver manager with an OLE DB provider to allow you access to your current ODBC data. This component

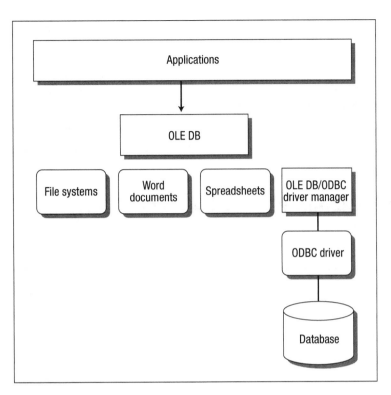

Figure 2.6
The architecture of OLE DB.

immediately provides OLE DB data consumers access to SQL data, while at the same time broadening the class of applications accessing ODBC drivers. I'm willing to bet that there will not be an ODBC 4.0, so watch out for OLE DB!

CORBA

The *Common Object Request Broker Architecture (CORBA)* is an emerging and open infrastructure for distributed object computing. CORBA specifies a system that provides interoperability between objects in a heterogeneous distributed environment and does so in a way that's transparent to the programmer. Its design is being standardized by the Object Management Group (OMG) and is based on the OMG object model.

The OMG is a nonprofit consortium created in 1989 with the purpose of promoting theory and practice of object technology in distributed computing systems. In particular, it aims to reduce the complexity, lower the costs, and hasten the introduction of software applications. Originally formed by 13 companies, OMG membership has grown to more than 500 software vendors, developers, and users.

CORBA automates many common network programming tasks such as object registration, location, and activation. As a CORBA developer, you can create your objects in a specific programming language and then create proxy objects called *stubs* and *skeletons*. A stub is compiled into the language of the client application. It contains the interface for a remote object but not the behavior. A skeleton is compiled in the language of the target application and is installed on a server.

The Object Management Architecture (OMA)

OMA is a high-level vision of a complete distributed environment. It consists of four components that can be roughly divided into two parts: system-oriented components (object request brokers and object services) and application-oriented components (application objects and common facilities).

Of these parts, the object request broker is the one that constitutes the foundation of OMA and manages all communication among its components. It allows objects to interact in a heterogeneous, distributed environment, independent of the platforms on which these objects reside and the techniques used to implement them. In performing its task, it relies on object services that are responsible for general object management, such as creating objects, access control, keeping track of relocated objects, and so on.

Common facilities and application objects are the components closest to the end user, and in their functions they invoke services of the system components. The CORBA design is based on the OMG object model.

The OMG Object Model

The OMG object model defines common object semantics for specifying the externally visible characteristics of objects in a standard and implementation-independent way. In this model, clients request services from objects, which can also be called *servers*, through a well-defined interface. This interface is specified in OMG IDL (Interface Definition Language). A client accesses an object by issuing a request to the object. The request is an event, and it carries information including an operation, the object reference of the service provider, and actual parameters. The object reference is an object name that defines an object reliably. The primary components in the OMG reference model architecture are illustrated in Figure 2.7.

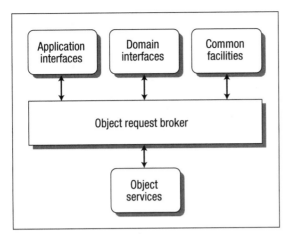

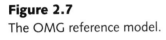

Figure 2.7
The OMG reference model.

Java

Sun Microsystems' Java programming language is an object-oriented third-generation programming language with roots primarily in Smalltalk and Objective-C, which has a built-in graphics API. The Java syntax is derived from ANSI C, with some intentional differentiations. Java is advertised to be simple, portable, object oriented, and secure; it has built-in thread support and garbage collection to reclaim unused memory.

The Java compiler creates a platform-independent set of byte codes that the Java interpreter reads and converts to native machine language at runtime. This makes Java suitable for distributed application development on a heterogeneous set of machines (for example, the Internet).

Java may be the most intriguing among the many new Web technologies. Code written in Java can be securely downloaded from a Web server to a Web client; Java code can be run on virtually any client platform, and it cannot harm the client computer (these are required features for successful Web implementations). Singular in its capabilities, Java's power comes from both the programming language and the execution environment. The Java programming language includes security features that make it an excellent language choice in which to write application code (called *Java applets*) that will be executed on a Web client. Using Java, you cannot access local machine resources. For example, you cannot code a "file save" or "disk format" command into a Java program. This allows Web clients to rest assured that any Java applets they download and execute will not harm their machines. These limitations are only for applets—Java applications have no security restrictions.

Java also specifies the use of the Java Virtual Machine (VM) to verify the integrity of downloaded Java code and to interpret or compile that code for runtime execution. A Java VM must be loaded and run on each end-user machine. Although they are platform specific, versions of the Java VM are available for all significant user platforms today and, in fact, are bundled with the corresponding platform versions of the most popular Web browser software. The ready availability of Java VMs ensures Java developers that their code can be securely downloaded to and executed on any Web client machine.

JavaBeans

JavaBeans components, or *beans*, are reusable software components that can be manipulated visually in a builder tool. Beans can be combined to create traditional applications or applets. In addition, applets can be designed to work as reusable beans. The Java bean is a complete component model. It supports the standard component architecture features of properties, events, methods, and persistence. In addition, Java beans provide support for introspection and customization.

Java beans bring the power of Java to component development, offering the ideal environment for you to extend the concept of reusable component development beyond one platform and one architecture to embrace every platform and every architecture in the industry. Java beans work with any network model, including CORBA and DCOM. Also, they integrate well with CORBA IDL, which is an excellent solution for customers in a heterogeneous distributed computing environment with platform-independent components.

Individual beans will function quite differently, but typical unifying features that make up a bean are:

- **Introspection.** Enables a builder tool to analyze how a bean works.

- **Customization.** Enables you to use an application builder tool to customize the appearance and behavior of a bean.

- **Events.** Enables beans to communicate and connect together.

- **Properties.** Enables you to customize a bean.

- **Persistence.** Enables you to customize a bean in an application builder and then retrieve that bean, with customized features intact, for future use.

Moving On

Well, I think we have covered enough to give you a head start on what exists and what is yet to come in the near future. However, we know from past experience that as each new specification is introduced, another is likely to become obsolete!

Now that you have a foundation in the various specifications, it's time to move on to the development part. In Chapter 3, "DataWindows," I'll cover the patented DataWindow object. Information data has become a key asset these days, and for your corporation to be successful, you'll need accurate and timely access to your data. The DataWindow object, which I can confidently say is the most powerful feature of PowerBuilder, is used to retrieve, present, and manipulate data from various data sources. Let's begin.

PART II
The
Development
Guide

DataWindows

Most business applications that you build these days are centered around your organization's data. The DataWindow is the most powerful feature of PowerBuilder: It enables you to retrieve, present, manipulate, validate, and update your data from various sources. These sources can include a relational database such as a Sybase SQL Server, an Oracle database, an IBM DB/2 mainframe, or even a single file such as an ASCII text file or an Excel spreadsheet. So what does the DataWindow consist of? The DataWindow has two basic parts: the *object* and the *control*.

Internally, the DataWindow object is used to retrieve, format, present, and manipulate data. It can hold information about the actual formatting of the data, validations used against the data, and the datasource of the object. A DataWindow object cannot be displayed to your users and cannot be used by itself. It has to be plugged into a DataWindow control or a User object inherited from **DataWindow** or **DataStore**. The DataWindow control, on the other hand, provides the program interface for your DataWindow objects. The DataWindow control has a set of encapsulated events and properties that provide you with a great deal of flexibility to control and manipulate your DataWindow objects.

DataWindow Objects

In this chapter, I'll cover DataWindow objects, controls, their use, working with your database, and more. I won't get into too much about creating a DataWindow, but instead I'll cover the internals of how a DataWindow works.

Datasources

As shown in Table 3.1, there are five datasources you can select from when building your DataWindows.

Table 3.1 Creating a new DataWindow.

Datasource	Description
Quick Select	Used when choosing columns from one or more tables related by foreign keys. This source has an easy interface but gives you less control over the **SELECT** statement.
SQL Select	Used when choosing columns from one or more tables. Gives you more control over the **SELECT** statement.
Query	This data source is based on a predefined **SELECT** statement that has been saved as a query.
External	Used when selecting your data to come from a source other than a database (for example, importing from a text file).
Stored Procedure	Uses the result set of a stored procedure from your database.

Note: Once a DataWindow has been built, you cannot change its datasource or its presentation style. However, if you were to use a query, you wouldn't need to rebuild your SQL syntax over and over again.

Presentation Styles

After you've selected your desired datasource, you then have 11 presentation styles from which to choose, as shown in Table 3.2.

Table 3.2 Presentation styles.

Presentation Style	Description
Composite	Displays data from multiple DataWindow objects. Used for reporting purposes only.
Crosstab	Two-dimensional analysis of data presented in a spreadsheet grid. Used for reporting purposes only.
Freeform	Displays columns in a nontabular layout. Used to display one row at a time.
Graph	Displays data in a graphical form. Used for reporting purposes only.
Grid	Displays data in a row-and-column format with grid lines. Your users can reorder and resize the columns.
Group	Displays grouped presentations.
Label	Used for mailing or other label types. Used for reporting purposes only.
N-Up	Presents two or more rows of data on the same line. Similar to "newspaper" columns.

(continued)

Table 3.2   Presentation styles *(continued).*

Presentation Style	Description
OLE 2.0	Supplies data to an OLE 2.0 server such as an OCX/ActiveX or Microsoft Graph.
RichText	Displays data via fields in a formatted rich text document.
Tabular	Organizes columns in row-and-column format.

Referencing Object Properties

The DataWindow object has a set of properties that can be accessed directly from scripts using dot notation. The following syntax is used to refer to a property of the DataWindow object:

```
<dwcontrol>.Object.DataWindow.<property>
```

For example, to refer to the **RetrieveAsNeeded** property of your DataWindow object and to set it on, you would use the following script:

```
dw_customer.Object.DataWindow.Retrieve.AsNeeded='YES'
```

Using the same notation, you can refer to a property of a component of the DataWindow object, such as a column:

```
<dwcontrol>.Object.<component>.<property>
```

The following script assigns a tag to the customer_id column:

```
dw_customer.Object.customer_id.Tag='Customer ID'
```

> **Note:** In a DataWindow object, all properties are stored as strings, but the value returned is of the data type **Any** and must be cast properly before being used— or else!

You could also set and get the previous properties using the **Describe**() and **Modify**() functions, as seen here:

```
dw_customer.Modify("DataWindow.Retrieve.AsNeeded=Yes")
dw_customer.Modify("customer_id.Tag='Customer ID'")
```

> **Note:** Using DWsyntax (a utility used to report on and manipulate attributes of DataWindow objects and objects within a DataWindow object) or PowerBuilder's

Object Browser, could save you a lot of time that you would otherwise spend figuring out the correct syntax for setting/getting DataWindow properties.

Now you can also conditionally set a column property or a band property of your DataWindow object at design time. This is done by right-clicking on the desired column or band and selecting Properties from the Expressions tab page. Here's the syntax for an expression:

```
IF(<Boolean expression>, <true value>, <false value>)
```

For example, to change the background color of the salary column to red whenever a salary is greater than $100,000 (not mine for sure!) or to change the background color of a row when it's a newly inserted one, you would use the following code:

```
IF( salary > 100000, 255, 0 )
IF( IsRowNew( RGB(255,255,0), 16777215 )
```

Generating SQL

PowerBuilder determines the type of SQL statement it needs to generate by looking at the status of each row in the buffers. Table 3.3 lists the status of rows and columns in your DataWindows.

When a row is first retrieved into your DataWindow, it and all its columns have the **NotModified!** status. As soon as an item is changed either by your users or by assigning a value to it from a script, the column and row status changes to **DataModified!**. Please note that changing a column's status to **Modified!** changes the row's status to **Modified!** as well. When you insert a new row into your DataWindow, the row gets a **New!** status, but all its columns have the **NotModified!** status. After a column in this new row is changed, the column status changes to **DataModified!**, thereby changing the row status to **NewModified!**. The DataWindow engine generates an **INSERT** statement for **NewModified!** and an **UPDATE** for **DataModified!**.

Table 3.3 Buffer status in DataWindows.

Status	Applies To
NotModified!	Rows and columns
DataModified!	Rows and columns
New!	Rows
NewModified!	Rows

To determine the status of a specific row or column, you would use the **GetItemStatus**() function. Here's the syntax for this function:

```
<dwcontrol>.GetItemStatus( row, column, buffer )
dwItemStatus l_colstat, l_rowstat

//get the status of fname column in row 1
l_colstat = dw_customer.GetItemStatus(1,"fname",Primary!)

//get the status of the entire row, substitute 0 for column
l_rowstat = dw_customer.GetItemStatus(1,0,Primary!)
```

Now if you were to set the status of a column or a row, you would use the **SetItemStatus**() function. Here's the syntax for this function:

```
<dwcontrol>.SetItemStatus ( row, column, buffer, status )
//change the status of fname column in row 1
dw_customer.SetItemStatus(1,"fname",Primary!,NotModified!)
//change the status of the entire row 1
dw_customer.SetItemStatus(1,0,Primary!,NotModifed!)
```

Update Properties

The **UPDATE** SQL statement sent to your database for a specific DataWindow can be specified by setting its update properties at design time. The selections set in this window, shown in Figure 3.1, are quite important because based on these selections, PowerBuilder determines the table to update, how to build its **WHERE** clause for **UPDATE** and **DELETE** statements, and how to perform key modifications when a unique key column is modified.

WHERE Clause For UPDATE/DELETE

PowerBuilder provides you with three ways to construct the **WHERE** clause of an **UPDATE** or **DELETE** statement:

- **Key columns.** This option builds an SQL statement that compares the values of the originally retrieved key column for the row against the value of the key column for that row in the database. If the key values match, then the update takes place as seen here:

```
UPDATE customer SET city = 'Waterloo'
   WHERE customer_id = 1009
```

- **Key and updatable columns.** This option builds an SQL statement that compares the value of the originally retrieved key column and the values of any originally retrieved columns that are updatable in the row with the same values in the database.

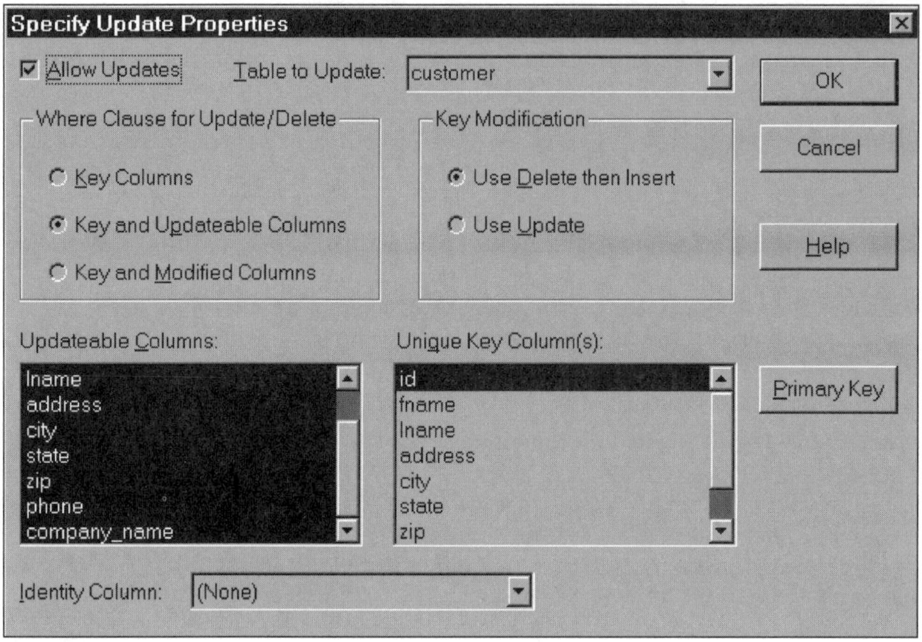

Figure 3.1
Update properties of a DataWindow.

If the values match, then the update takes place. This option provides maximum concurrent update checking and is probably the safest in a multiuser environment as seen here:

```
UPDATE customer SET city = 'Waterloo'
   WHERE customer_id = 1009
      AND fname = 'Kouros'
        AND lname = 'Gorgani'
```

- **Key and modified columns.** This option builds an SQL statement that compares the value of the originally retrieved key column and the values of the originally retrieved columns that have since been modified with the same values in the database. If the values match, then the update takes place, as seen here:

```
UPDATE customer SET city = 'Waterloo'
   WHERE customer_id = 1009
      AND city = 'Toronto'
```

Key Modification

PowerBuilder generates one of two SQL statements whenever a key column is modified. The two statements are:

- **DELETE and INSERT.** This option is the default. It deletes the row with the modified key and inserts a new row with a new key value.

- **UPDATE.** This option updates the row with the modified key by replacing the value in the columns with the new key values.

Previewing DataWindow's SQL

After your DataWindow generates an SQL statement and just before it is sent to the database, the **SQLPreview** event on the control gets triggered. You can code this event to see what the SQL statement is, or even overwrite it if necessary. Note that the **SQLPreview** event triggers once upon a **Retrieve()** and once for each row updated with an **Update()** function call.

The following arguments for this event give you full access to the SQL statement and additional information:

- **request.** The **SQLPreview** function that caused the event to be triggered

- **sqltype.** The **SQLPreview** type (the type of SQL statement being built)

- **sqlsyntax.** The actual syntax of the SQL statement

- **buffer.** The buffer containing the row involved

- **row.** The number of the row involved in the database activity

The following script in the **SQLPreview** event populates a MultiLineEdit with the SQL statement of your DataWindow:

```
mle_sql.Text = sqlSyntax
```

You could overwrite the SQL statement sent to your database. The next statement in the **SQLPreview** event sets the current SQL string for the DataWindow **dw_data:**

```
dw_data.SetSQLPreview( &
   "INSERT INTO d_fin_data VALUES(1997,Q1,e1,101)" )
```

> *Note: If **sqlSyntax** contains question marks instead of data values, you'll need to disable binding. For this purpose, you set the **DisableBind dbparam** parameter to 1 upon connecting to your database.*

Constructing A DataWindow

You've selected your datasource and your presentation style, and you have a DataWindow object. So how does the DataWindow engine construct a view of your DataWindow? Well, this task is handled in the following four phases:

1. The DataWindow design is first loaded into memory. This is done by loading the design settings into a details structure. Each band in the DataWindow is given its own band information structure. Furthermore, each band is also given an array of graphical object structures. Now, if any of these graphical objects is a nested DataWindow, it is allocated a nest details structure, which in turn is given its own DataWindow details structure, and then the nested DataWindow is loaded to its own array of structures.

2. The data is then loaded into memory. Each DataWindow's details structure is addressed in turn to issue its **SELECT** statement. A data detail structure is set up to point to the data buffers of the DataWindow. A row detail structure is then set up for each row of data in the data buffers to hold row processing information. Also, any data sets for groups, page counts, numbers, and the like, must be predefined before any displaying is done.

3. The loaded data is then paginated. However, before the rows can be arranged into pages, page sizes must be calculated as the physical page size, less any space that needs to be reserved for headers and footers. The number of rows that can fit into a page size determines the number of report pages required. This is done by examining each row and then examining each graphical object. If a row does not fit within the remainder of a page size, the row will start in the next page.

4. Finally the DataWindow is painted. Header bands are painted first, then each detail row in a page, followed by trailers and footers. If you're printing this DataWindow, each page is cycled through and painted to the printer device.

DataWindow Controls

As I mentioned earlier, a DataWindow control is a PowerBuilder custom control that lets you display, manipulate, and update your data. The DataWindow is a container control and must be associated with a DataWindow object either at design time or at runtime in order to be used. When this is done, you are actually setting the initial value of the control's DataObject attribute. When you run your application, PowerBuilder creates an instance of the DataWindow object and uses it in the control.

DataWindow controls can be minimized or maximized in script. This requires that you enable the title bar as well as the minimize and maximize attributes of your DataWindow control, as seen in the following code:

```
// minimize
Send(Handle(dw_customer), 274, 61472, 0)
```

```
//maximize
Send(Handle(dw_customer), 274, 61488, 0)
//restore back to normal
Send(Handle(dw_customer), 274, 61728, 0)
```

You can change the DataObject property of your DataWindow dynamically at runtime by using dot notation, as seen here:

```
dw_report.DataObject = "d_customer"
```

> **Note:** If you change your DataWindow objects dynamically, you must include the DataObject's name in a PBR file. This is done to include the object in the executable or the dynamic link library. Here's the syntax:
>
> ```
> <computer code> mysample.pbl( d_customer )
> ```

The DataWindow control has a series of events that you can use in order to have more control over your DataWindow. These events are listed in Table 3.4.

> **Note:** The **RETURN** statement lets you control how an event behaves. See your DataWindow object reference guide for the effect of a **RETURN** in various events.

In PowerBuilder, every object has a series of system events that are mapped to various Windows messages. You can map your own user events to these system events if they have not been mapped already.

> **Note:** Windows messages that do not map to a particular PowerBuilder event ID can usually be trapped by checking the value of **message.number** in an object's **Other** event.

Table 3.4 DataWindow control events.

Event	Description
ButtonClicked	Occurs when a Button object is clicked
ButtonClicking	Occurs just before a Button object is clicked
Clicked	Occurs when a user clicks anywhere in a DataWindow control
Constructor	Occurs when the control is created and just before the **Open** event for the window that contains the control
DBError	Occurs upon a database error in a DataWindow

(continued)

Table 3.4 DataWindow control events *(continued)*.

Event	Description
Destructor	Occurs when the control is destroyed and right after the **Close** event of a window
DoubleClick	Occurs when the DataWindow control is double-clicked
DragDrop	Occurs when an object is dragged onto a control and the mouse button is released
DragEnter	Occurs when a drag object is entering a control
DragWithin	Occurs when a drag object is dragged within a control
EditChanged	Occurs for each keystroke a user types in an edit control
Error	Occurs when an error is found in a data or property expression for a DataWindow object
GetFocus	Occurs when a DataWindow gets focus
ItemChanged	Occurs when an item in a DataWindow control has been modified and loses focus
ItemError	Occurs when data in a field does not pass the validation rules for its column
ItemFocusChanged	Occurs when a current item changes
Other	Occurs when a non-PowerBuilder system message is fired
PrintEnd	Occurs when the printing of a DataWindow ends
PrintPage	Occurs before each page of a DataWindow is formatted for printing
PrintStart	Occurs when the printing of the DataWindow starts
RbuttonDown	Occurs when the right mouse button is pressed
Resize	Occurs when the control is opened or resized
RetrieveRow	Occurs after a row has been retrieved
RetrieveStart	Occurs when the current row focus changes
RowFocusChanged	Occurs after the current row focus has changed
RowFocusChanging	Occurs just before the current row focus changes
ScrollHorizontal	Occurs when a user scrolls left or right in a DataWindow
ScrollVertical	Occurs when a user scrolls up or down in a DataWindow
SQLPreview	Occurs just before an SQL statement is sent to the database
UpdateStart	Occurs after a script calls the **Update** function and just before changes in the DataWindow are sent to the database
UpdateEnd	Occurs when all the updates to a database from a DataWindow are complete

An example of this is to change the Enter key to act as a Tab key in your DataWindow. This requires you to create a user event to be mapped to the **pbm_dwnprocessenter** event on your DataWindow. You then need to add the following code in that event:

```
//send a message for processing the Tab key
Send( Handle(This),256,9,Long(0,0))
//ignore processing the Enter key
RETURN 1
```

As your users add or change data, the data is first handled as text in an *edit control.* If the data is accepted after going through four levels of validation routines, it is placed as an item in a DataWindow data buffer.

DataWindow Buffers

As shown in Figure 3.2, four data buffers are associated with each DataWindow. They are as follows:

- **Primary buffer.** Contains data that has been inserted into it either via an **InsertRow()** command or by a retrieval being performed on a table. This is the only data that is visible to your users.

- **Filter buffer.** Contains data that has been filtered out of the primary buffer.

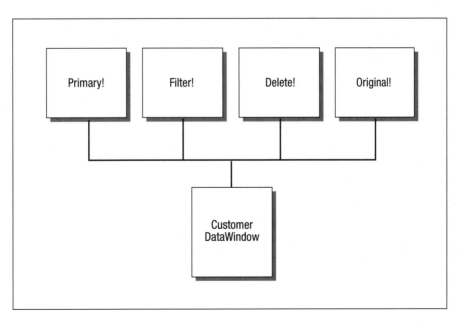

Figure 3.2
The four DataWindow buffers.

- **Delete buffer.** Contains data that has been deleted from the primary buffer and has not yet been applied to the database. The **DeleteRow**() command places rows into this buffer.

- **Original buffer.** Contains the original values prior to them being modified in the primary buffer.

   Note: Having an original buffer does not mean that you have duplicate copies of your data in memory. The original buffer becomes populated as items are changed.

Validating Data

As soon as you begin to enter text in the edit control, PowerBuilder begins to validate your data. By entering text in the edit control and then pressing Enter, tabbing away, or calling the **AcceptText**() function, the **EditChanged** event is fired. Once this event is triggered, four levels of validation occur on the text in the edit control:

- The first level checks to see if the data type of the entry in the edit control matches the data type of the item. If not, the **ItemError** event is fired.

- The second level checks the contents of the edit control against a validation rule that you might have defined for a column. If the validation fails, the **ItemError** event is fired.

- The third level compares the contents of the edit control to the item. If the two are the same, there's no change and validation stops; if they're not, the **ItemError** event is fired.

- Finally, the **ItemChanged** event fires. You use this event for further script validation and to code a **RETURN** value to force the validation to fail, which would in turn cause the **ItemError** event to fire.

To prevent your users from entering invalid data, you have to use validation rules. Validation rules can either be at the DataWindow level or at the server level. Server-based validation in the forms of referential integrity, stored procedures, constraints, and triggers are easier to maintain because they are centralized in one place. You definitely need to perform important validation at the server level in case you forget to do so at the client level. Now, if you were to validate data at the DataWindow level, you would do so with the following methods:

- Using code tables

- Using a validation rule

- Using script to validate user input

Code Tables

Using code tables for validation ensures that the data entered by your users is in a pre-defined table. As you can see in Figure 3.3, code tables in a DataWindow consist of a data value and a display value, shown in the DataWindow. Code tables can be defined for the following edit styles:

- CheckBox

- DropDownDataWindow

- DropDownListBox

- Edit Style

- EditMask

- RadioButtons

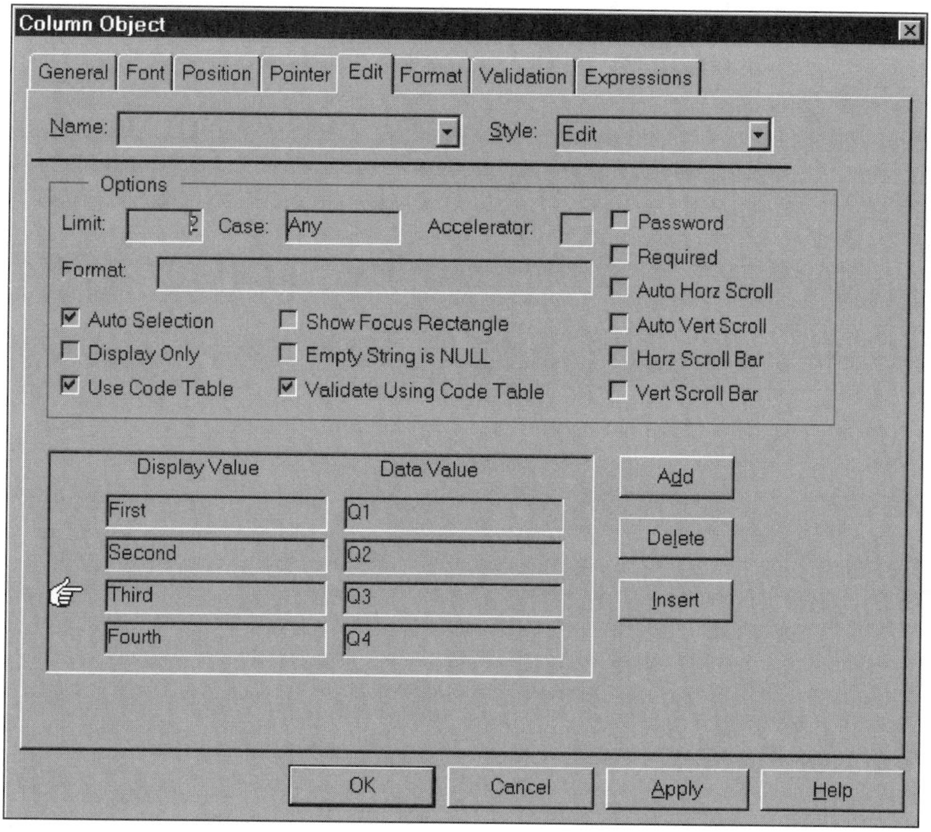

Figure 3.3
DataWindow code tables.

You may need to change the values in your code tables. To achieve this, you need to change the **values** attribute of the column that has the code table:

```
dw_data.Object.quarter.values = "First Quarter~tQ1/Second Quarter~tQ2"
```

Validation Rule

In PowerBuilder, you can create your own custom validation rules. The validation rule placed in the DataWindow object at the column level is a Boolean expression that's defined using the database painter or the DataWindow painter. Rules defined in the database painter are stored in the PowerBuilder system tables and are part of the extended attributes. The benefit of these rules is that they are reusable by any DataWindow that goes against your database. Validation rules defined at the DataWindow level are stored in the DataWindow itself and cannot be used elsewhere. Figure 3.4 illustrates a simple validation rule set to ensure that a numeric value entered is greater than 0.

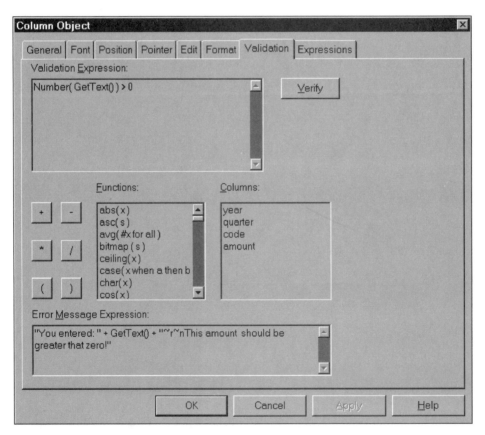

Figure 3.4
Defining a DataWindow validation rule.

PowerBuilder gives you the ability to get and set validation rules dynamically during runtime by using the **GetValidate()** and **SetValidate()** functions:

```
dw_data.Object.amount.validation =  "Number(GetText()) > 0"
dw_date.Object.amount.validationmsg = "You entered: " +&
GetText() + "~r~nThis amount must be greater than 0"
```

Script Validation

Whenever a column's data changes and the column loses focus, the **ItemChanged** event is triggered. This event is usually used to validate any rules that may apply to a particular column.

> **Note:** It's quite important that the **ItemChanged** event does not trigger another **ItemChanged** event, which can result in an endless loop and a big headache. Therefore, avoid **AcceptText()**, **SetColumn()**, and **SetRow()** functions inside an **ItemChanged** event.

The following code in the **ItemChanged** event checks for a particular column in order to validate the data entered by the user:

```
//obtain the column name

string ls_colname
ls_colname = dwo.Name

IF ls_colname = "amount" THEN
   IF Integer( data ) < 50000 THEN
      MessageBox( "Validation Error", &
            "Item must be less than 50000" )
      //reject the data, don't allow focus to change
      RETURN 1
   END IF
END IF
```

You can also validate your users' input through an *edit mask*. An edit mask specifies the format of a field, making it easier for your users to enter values with a fixed format. An edit mask consists of special characters that enforce correct input. For example, the mask ##,### allows numeric input only.

Accessing Data

Using data expressions, you can access data directly in the primary, filter, and delete buffers and differentiate between current and original values. The basic syntax for DataWindow expressions begins with **<dwcontrol>.Object** and can be followed by a column name or the **Data** keyword. The column name can then be followed by brackets and a row number, a buffer, or a datasource. The following examples all refer to the first row and the customer_id column that is positioned at column 1:

```
dw_customer.Object.customer_id[1]
dw_customer.Object.Data[1,1] dw_customer.Object.customer_id.Current
dw_customer.Object.customer_id.Primary[1]
```

You can refer to a block of data by specifying the row and column numbers of the upper-left corner and the lower-right corner of the block. For example, to refer to a block of data from row 1, column 1 to row 10, column 5, use the following code:

```
dw_customer.Object.Data[1,1,10,5]
```

You can also refer to an entire row, the selected row, or the entire data in a buffer:

```
dw_customer.Object.Data[2] // entire row 2
dw_customer.Object.Data.Selected //the selected row
dw_customer.Object.Data //the entire primary buffer
```

> **Note:** Your DataWindow object's **Data** can be directly assigned to the following items:
>
> - An array of structures with matching columns
>
> - An array of nonvisual objects with instance variables with matching columns
>
> - Any variable

The DataWindow control functions listed in Table 3.5 can be used as alternative methods for accessing data in your DataWindow buffers.

Table 3.5   DataWindow control functions.

Function	Description
GetItemString()	Gets the value of a string item
GetItemNumber()	Gets the value of a numeric item
GetItemDecimal()	Gets the value of a decimal item
GetItemTime()	Gets the value of a time item
GetItemDate()	Gets the value of a date item
GetItemDateTime()	Gets the value of a date/time item
SetItem()	Assigns a value to an item of any data type

Using these functions gives you an advantage over direct notation access only when the column names or numbers are not known. With dot notation, you must know the column name or number; however, functions allow you to reference columns dynamically using a string or an integer variable.

If you need to copy rows from one DataWindow buffer to another, you can use the **RowsCopy()**, **RowsMove()**, and **RowsDiscard()** functions. For example, to copy rows from one DataWindow to another, use the following code:

```
dw_1.RowsCopy(dw_1.GetRow(),  &
dw_1.RowCount(), Primary!, dw_2, 1, Primary!)
```

> **Note:** *Make sure that your DataWindows' tab orders are not set to 0. You may use the **Protect** attribute though!*

Handling Errors

The **DBError** event is triggered in a DataWindow when a database error occurs after an **Update()** function. When this event is triggered, PowerBuilder uses a default message box to display the error code and message to you. If you don't want to see this default error message, you need to change the return value of the **DBError** event:

```
//DBError event
RETURN 1
```

Now, in order to display a more meaningful error message to your users, you can get more information from the arguments of the **DBError** event. The **DBError** event has the following arguments:

- **sqldbcode.** DBMS-specific error code
- **sqlerrtext.** DBMS-specific error message
- **buffer.** The DataWindow buffer where the error occurs
- **row.** The number of the row within the buffer

The **Error** event of a DataWindow triggers whenever you refer to a nonexistent object or misspelled property name, or if you have referenced nonexistent data. The arguments of the **Error** event give you more information about the error. By reading these arguments, you can find out the cause and location of your error. The arguments are listed in Table 3.6.

Table 3.6 Arguments of an **Error** event.

Argument	Type
ErrorNumber	UInt
ErrorText	String
ErrorWindowMenu	String
ErrorObject	String
ErrorScript	String
ErrorLine	UInt
Action	ExceptionAction
ReturnValue	Any

You can return three enumerated values for the **ExceptionAction** type that let you control your error. Here are the values:

- **ExceptionFail!** Allows the error to occur.

- **ExceptionIgnore!** Ignores the error and continues processing.

- **ExceptionSubstituteReturnValue!** Substitutes the return value.

The following example displays information about the error that occurred and allows the script to continue on:

```
MessageBox("Error Number: " + String(errornumber)  &
   + " Occurred", "Error text: " + String(errortext))
//ignore the error message
action = ExceptionIgnore!
```

DataWindowChild

A *DropDownDataWindow (DDDW)* in a DataWindow object is an object within an object. It's called the *DataWindowChild object*. DDDWs also provide an excellent way of validating user input, where the data entered can be chosen from another DataWindow. For example, you may want your users to select a valid department ID when adding a new employee to the employee table. This is done by selecting a DDDW edit style for your required column. Another example would be when you want to display a DDDW of all employees for the department selected in the dept_id column. Now, to achieve this, you have three options:

- Build a DDDW with a retrieval argument

- Use the **SetFilter**() and **Filter**() functions

- Dynamically change the **WHERE** clause of the DDDW object

Establishing A Reference

In order to use any of the aforementioned options, you must obtain a reference to your DDDW by using the **GetChild**() function, assign it a transaction object, and then populate it using the **Retrieve**() function. Remember that the data type of a DDDW is DataWindowChild.

The following example in the **RowFocusChanged** event populates a DDDW:

```
DataWindowChild ldwc_employees
integer li_rc, li_deptid
//obtain the current dept_id
li_deptid = This.Object.dept_id[currentrow]
//obtain a reference to the DDDW
li_rc = This.GetChild( "dept_id", ldwc_employees )
//retrieve
ldwc_employees.SetTransObject( SQLCA )
ldwc_employees.Retrieve (li_deptid )
```

> **Note:** If your DDDW requires a retrieval argument, you'll be prompted for one, as per the **RowFocusChanged** event code example given. In order to avoid the RetrievalArgument dialog box, you must either insert a blank row into your DDDW at runtime or store a blank row in your DDDW object using the Rows|Data menu options in the DataWindow painter.

When a nested report is placed in a DataWindow, you cannot use **GetChild**() on it to use its handle. **GetChild**() would return −1. However, you can use dot notation to reference the nested report. For example, let's says that you have placed a nested report in DataWindow **d_dept_emp** and have named your report dept_employee_report. In order to access its data, use the following code:

```
Any lany_empdata
lany_empdata = d_dept_emp.Object.dept_employee_report.Data
```

Now, if your nested report dept_employee_report had a DDDW on the emp_id column, to access its data you would use this code:

```
Any lany_empdata
lany_empdata = dw_dept_emp.Object.dept_employee_report. &
    Object.emp_id.Object.Data
```

In a composite DataWindow, each DataWindow is a child, and you can use the **GetChild**() function on any of them. However, if you were to refer to a DDDW that existed on one of the DataWindows in your composite, you would have to use dot notation.

Note: *You cannot use **GetChild()** on external DataWindows in a composite report.*

If you need to get the display value of your DDDW, you can use the following script:

```
string ls_row, ls_displayvalue

ls_rownumber = String( dw_customers.GetRow() )
ls_isplayvalue = dw_customers.Describe("Evaluate( &
    "LookUpDisplay(dept_id) ", " + rownumber + ")")
```

Optimizing Performance

When dealing with large result sets, the **SetItem()** function can affect the performance of your application. To avoid this problem, you should use functions such as **ImportString()** and **ImportFile()** for external source DataWindows or **Retrieve()** for DataWindows with an SQL Select datasource instead of using **SetItems**. The performance hit is even more apparent when using the **SetItem()** function on nested DataWindows. This is because using **SetItems** against nested reports requires a considerable code path internally (because PowerBuilder has to recalculate the positions of everything). If you're using multiple **SetItems** in a loop, PowerBuilder has to do all that recalculating for every single **SetItem()** function.

Filtering and sorting can also have a performance impact on your nested DataWindows. Both of these functions reorder row numbers in the internal table representation, forcing PowerBuilder to rebuild all the nested reports so that they know which row they are associated with. Once again, I strongly recommend that you either design nested DataWindows without any sorting or filtering or else use separate DataWindows instead of nested ones.

Database Communication

A *transaction object* is used to provide communication between your application and your database. I cover transaction objects in Chapter 15, "Transaction Object," in detail, but to give you a brief overview, the transaction object is used to connect to your database and receive status information from your database. The default transaction object in PowerBuilder is a global nonvisual object named the *SQL communication area (SQLCA)*.

Once you have successfully connected to your database, you have to set the transaction object for a DataWindow control. To do this, you use the following functions:

- **SetTrans()**. This function copies the values from a transaction object to the DataWindow control's internal transaction object. The DataWindow uses its own transaction object and automatically connects and disconnects as needed. All errors that occur will cause an automatic rollback.

- **SetTransObject().** This function tells the DataWindow control to use a user-defined transaction object. With this function, you have more control over the database processing and are responsible for managing the transaction. An example is seen here:

```
//constructor event of a DataWindow control
Long ll_rows
This.SetTransOBject( SQLCA )
ll_rows = This.Retrieve()
IF ll_rows < 1 THEN MessageBox( "Database Error", &
    "No rows were retrieved!" )
```

If your DataWindow retrieves too many rows, you may want to manage this potentially expensive database operation. In an ideal client/server architecture, you should not be retrieving thousands of rows into your DataWindows. However, you can manage your retrievals via the following methods:

- Using a predefined query. This way you know the number of rows that will be retrieved. But then again, what happens when the database grows?

- Using the Retrieve Rows As Needed option of the DataWindow. This option only retrieves rows that can be displayed in a control; as your user pages down through the data, PowerBuilder continues to retrieve only as needed. Note that specifying a sort order or using any aggregate function such as **Sum()** will override the Retrieve Rows As Needed option.

- Using **Count()** and disallowing retrieval if too many rows are being retrieved.

- Using the **RetrieveRow** event and counting the number of rows being retrieved. You can cancel the retrieval if too many rows are being retrieved. However, because this event is fired for every row, it may slow down the execution of your retrieval. If you do decide to go this route, I recommend placing a **Yield()** in the **RetrieveRow** event to yield control to other graphic objects.

Your applications should include error tests after each database operation. When using the **Retrieve()** or **Update()** function, you should check to see the function's return code to ensure that the activity was successful. With **Retrieve()** and **Update()**, all you need to check is the return code. With SQL statements such as **CONNECT**, **COMMIT**, and **DISCONNECT**, you should always check the **SQLCode** attribute of your transaction object.

Generating HTML

You can use the data in your DataWindows to generate HTML syntax. Once the HTML has been created, you can display it in any Web browser. To generate HTML, assign the

Data.HTMLTable property of the DataWindow to a string variable. Once you have created this HTML string, you can modify the HTML by using string manipulation operations. You can also use the **FileOpen()** and **FileWrite()** functions to save your HTML to a file.

HTML can also be created by using the **SaveAs()** function to save the contents of your DataWindows directly to a disk file.

> **Note:** Crosstab, freeform, group, grid, and tabular DataWindows generate better HTML than others.

Creating An HTML String

The following example creates an HTML string from the data in the customer DataWindow by assigning the **Data.HTMLTable** property to a string variable. After the HTML has been constructed, a header is added to the HTML string and is saved to a file:

```
string ls_html, ls_file
integer li_fileno, li_bytes
//generate the HTML
ls_html = This.Object.DataWindow.Data.HTMLTable
IF IsNull( ls_html ) or Len( ls_html ) <=1 THEN
    MessageBox( "Error", "HTML was not created!" )
    RETURN
ELSE
    ls_html = "<H1>Sample HTML generated from PowerBuilder" &
        + "</H1><P>" + ls_html
END IF
//now create the file
ls_file = filename + ".htm" //filename is an argument
li_fileno = FileOpen( ls_file, StreamMode!, Write!, &
    LockReadWrite!, Replace! )
IF li_fileno >- 0 THEN
    li_bytes = FileWrite( li_fileno, ls_html )
    FileClose( li_fileno )
    MessageBox( "HTML", "HTML file was created!" )
END IF
```

Creating An HTML Form

PowerBuilder can create HTML form syntax for DataWindow objects that use the freeform or tabular presentation styles. You can create an HTML form that displays a specified number of columns for a specified number of rows. You create HTML form syntax by calling the **GenerateHTMLForm()** function. This function creates HTML form syntax for the detail band only. If you have any embedded, nested DataWindows, they will display as HTML tables within the form.

The following Web.PB example calls the **SaveAsHTMLPage()** function, creates a complete HTML page, and returns it to the browser:

```
String ls_html, ls_syntax, ls_style, ls_action
Integer   li_return

ls_action =  &
   "/cgi-bin/pbcgi060.exe/myapp/uo_customers/f_customers"

li_return = ds_customers.GenerateHTMLForm  &
   (ls_syntax, ls_style, ls_action)

IF li_return = -1 THEN
   ls_html = "Unable to create HTML form."
ELSE
   ls_html = "<HTML>"
   ls_html += ls_style
   ls_html += "<BODY>"
   ls_html += "<H1>Customer Listing</H1>"
   ls_html += ls_syntax
   ls_html += "</BODY></HTML>"
END IF
RETURN ls_html
```

To use the syntax returned by the **GenerateHTMLForm()** function, you must write code to merge the syntax into an HTML page. A complete HTML page requires **<HTML>** and **<BODY>** elements to contain the style sheet and syntax. One way to do this is to create a global or object function that returns a complete HTML page, taking as arguments the form and style elements generated by the **GenerateHTMLForm()** function. Here's an example:

```
/··· uf_MakeHTMLPage
      Arguments: string   as_syntax
                 string   as_style
      Returns:   string
···/

string   ls_html
//return if arguments are empty
IF as_syntax = "" OR as_style = "" THEN
   Return ""
END IF
```

```
ls_html = "<HTML>"
ls_html += as_style
ls_html += "<BODY>"
ls_html += "<H1>Employee Information</H1>"
ls_html += as_syntax
ls_html += "</BODY></HTML>"
//return the formatted string
Return ls_html
```

New In DataWindows

In PowerBuilder 6.0, the DataWindow has been enhanced tremendously. For example, a new Button object has been included that can have predefined or custom actions associated with it. In addition, a new GroupBox object can be used to frame and label a set of objects on your DataWindow.

The scrollbars used for viewing DataWindow objects in print preview mode now scroll through the complete DataWindow object. The DataWindow border painting has been refined to apply zooming and device units conversion to border sizes. Device support is provided for the IntelliMouse pointing device, which enhances DataWindow scrolling and navigation. Also, N-Up row selection has been enhanced to select only the specified row instead of all rows in the same level.

Other examples include a new event, **RowFocusChanging**, that fires when the current row is about to change. Also, rows in a DataWindow can now be saved to Excel 5 format and to ASCII; checkboxes without text can be centered; and the upper limit on the length of DataWindow object syntax strings that can be saved has been extended from 32K to an unknown large number. Now, let's go over a few of these new features.

The Button Object

The Button object is a command-style or picture-style button that can be placed in a DataWindow object. When clicked, the Button object can activate either a built-in or user-defined action. These objects make it easy to provide command button actions in your DataWindows without additional coding. Also, in keeping with the object-oriented "religion," using buttons in the DataWindow object ensures that the actions appropriate to the DataWindow object are encapsulated within the object.

When a button is clicked, the new **ButtonClicking** event is fired. If script exists in the **ButtonClicking** event, it will be executed. If the return code is 0, the action assigned to the button is then executed. After the action is executed (or if the return code from the **ButtonClicking** event is 1), the **ButtonClicked** event is then fired. You have the ability to suppress event processing for the button when it is clicked—via its property sheet. When this option is selected and the button is clicked, only the action assigned to the button is executed. The **ButtonClicking** and the **ButtonClicked** events are not triggered. Actions that can be assigned to a Button object are listed in Table 3.7.

*Note: The **Clicked** event is triggered before the **ButtonClicking** event.*

Table 3.7 Actions for the Button object.

Action	Description	Value	Value returned to ButtonClicked event
User-defined	Allows you to script the action.	0	The return code from the user's coded event script.
Retrieve (Yield)	Retrieves rows from the database with Yield turned on.	1	The number of rows retrieved. Upon failure, returns -1.
Retrieve	Retrieves rows from the database.	2	The number of rows retrieved. Upon failure, returns -1.
Cancel	Cancels a retrieval that has been started with Yield.	3	0.
Page Next	Scrolls to next page.	4	The row is displayed at the top of the control when scrolling is done. Upon failure, returns -1.
Page Prior	Scrolls to prior page.	5	The row is displayed at the top of the control when scrolling is done. Upon failure, returns -1.
Page First	Scrolls to first page.	6	Returns 1 if successful, -1 if not.
Page Last	Scrolls to last page.	7	The row is displayed at the top of the control when scrolling is done. Upon failure, returns -1.
Sort	Displays the Sort dialog box to sort the DataWindow.	8	Returns 1 if successful, -1 if not.
Filter	Displays the Filter dialog box to sort the DataWindow.	9	Returns 1 if successful, -1 if not.
Delete Row	Deletes the current row or the row associated with the button in the detail band.	10	Returns 1 if successful, -1 if not.
Append Row	Inserts a row at the end.	11	The row number of the new row.
Insert Row	Inserts a row.	12	The row number of the new row.
Update	Saves changes to the database. **COMMIT** and **ROLLBACK** operations are done appropriately.	13	Returns 1 if successful, -1 if not.

(continued)

Table 3.7 Actions for the Button object *(continued).*

Action	Description	Value	Value returned to ButtonClicked event
SaveRowsAs	Displays the Save As dialog box.	14	The number of rows filtered.
Print	Prints one copy of the DataWindow.	15	0.
Preview	Toggles between preview and print preview modes.	16	0.
Preview With Rulers	Toggles rulers on and off.	17	0.
Query Mode	Toggles query mode on and off.	18	0.
Query Sort	Allows users to specify sorting criteria.	19	0.
Query Clear	Removes the **WHERE** clause from a query.	20	0.

Figure 3.5 shows the property sheet of the new Button object. Now, to prevent the button from displaying when print previewing or printing, two new properties have been added to the DataWindow object. You can toggle them on and off via the property sheet of your DataWindow object or dynamically at execution time. By default, the Button object does not display during print preview or when printed, as seen here:

```
dw_data.Object.Print.Button - YES
dw_data.Object.Preview.Buttons - YES
```

GroupBox Object

You now have the ability to place a GroupBox object in your DataWindows. The GroupBox object is a static frame used to group and label a set of objects in a DataWindow object. The group box is a visual enhancement that improves the layout of information in a DataWindow object.

> **Note:** Make sure that the Send To Back property of the GroupBox object is checked; otherwise, your controls within a group box will not be visible.

Centered Checkboxes

Checkboxes without text can now be centered. The CheckBox feature makes it easy to create a neat layout of checkboxes in DataWindow objects. An easy way to take advantage of checkbox centering is to first work with the column header text object and the column object being

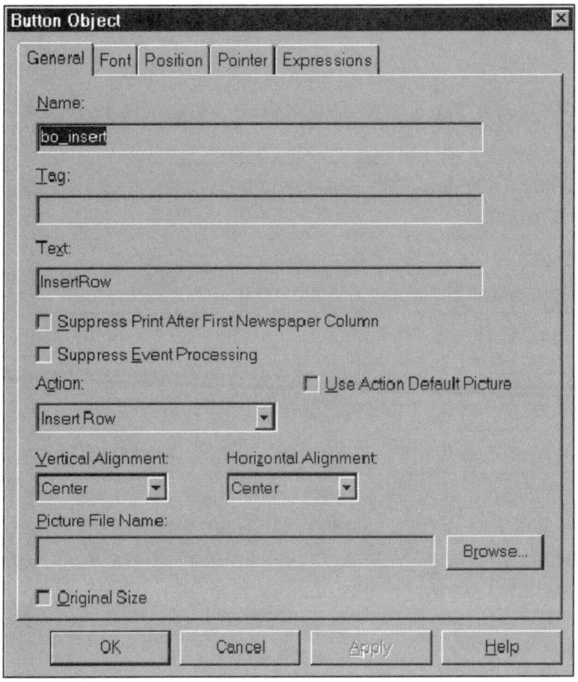

Figure 3.5
The property sheet of the Button object.

displayed as a checkbox. Make these two objects the same size and specify "left aligned." Then, center both the column header contents and the column object being displayed as a checkbox using the style bar or the objects' property sheets. The checkboxes will be centered under the centered column header text with no fussy movement of the checkbox and header text objects. For centering to work, the Left Text checkbox option in the Edit Style property page must not be checked, and the checkbox must not have associated text.

Scrollbars In Print Preview Mode

The scrollbars used for viewing DataWindow objects in print preview mode now scroll through the complete DataWindow object. To sweeten this even further, support for changing pages, as well as for moving to particular pages easily, has also been added. This feature improves the behavior of print preview. The scrolling behavior is described in Table 3.8.

IntelliMouse Pointing Device

The IntelliMouse pointing device is a new piece of hardware that can be used as a standard two-button mouse on 16-bit operating systems, or as a three-button mouse with

Table 3.8 Scrollbar behavior in print preview mode.

Action	Description
Line Down	The display goes down by a line. If it goes beyond the print page, the top of the next page displays.
Line Up	The display goes up by a line. If it goes beyond the print page, the bottom of the previous page displays.
Page Down	The display goes down by the screen height until it reaches the bottom of the page. The following Page Down goes to the top of the next page.
Page Up	The display goes up by the screen height until it reaches the top of the page. The following Page Up goes to the top of the previous page.
Top	The display goes to the top of the first page of the DataWindow object.
Bottom	The display goes to the top of the last page of the DataWindow object.
Dragging	While the cursor is being dragged, the display is unchanged. The page number corresponding to the current location of the cursor displays on the MicroHelp bar and in a small window next to the thumb in the scrollbar. The display changes to a new page when the cursor is released.

the added capability of a scroll wheel on 32-bit operating systems. Using the IntelliMouse, users can scroll a DataWindow object by rotating the wheel. They can also zoom a DataWindow object larger or smaller by holding down the Ctrl key while rotating the wheel. This functionality is also available in TreeViews or ListViews.

RowFocusChanging Event

The **RowFocusChanging** event occurs when the DataWindow's current row is about to change. This event has two arguments:

- **currentrow.** The number of the current row. If the DataWindow object is empty, **currentrow** is 0 to indicate that there is no current row.

- **newrow.** The number of the row that is about to become current. If the new row is going to be an inserted row, **newrow** is 0 to indicate that the row does not yet exist.

The Return codes are either 0 (to continue processing) or 1 (to prevent the current row from changing).

SaveAs

The **SaveAs** function for DataWindows and DataStores has a new value for the **saveas** type argument (which is the Excel 5 format). The new function **SaveAsAscii()** has also been added to allow more control over how the contents of a DataWindow are saved. The following example saves the contents of **dw_fin_data** to the file FINDATA.TXT. The saved file is in ASCII format, with the ampersand (&) as the separator character, the single quote (') as the character used to wrap values, and ~r~n as the default line ending. Computed columns are included with the saved information.

```
dw_fin_data.SaveAsAscii("FINDATA.TXT","&","'")
```

Moving On

In this chapter, we talked about DataWindow objects, controls, and their mechanics. We also covered DataWindowChilds, database communication, generating HTML, HTML pages, and finally, the new 6.0 features. As you can see, the power of the DataWindow is awesome. It makes data presentation fun and your applications more robust. However, there's even more to learn about the DataWindow—when we get to Chapter 14, "Advanced DataWindows," it will get even more interesting.

Usually after you've created your DataWindows, you'll want to preview them to see how they work or test them in an application. One method of doing so is to place your DataWindow controls on a window. The next chapter, "Windows," covers the PowerBuilder Window object.

Windows
4

This chapter focuses on PowerBuilder windows. The Window object is the most visual object in the development environment, and almost every application utilizes some type of window. Windows form the interface between your users and your application. They display information, request information from users, and respond to user input. In PowerBuilder, a basic window is inherited from the Window object, which in turn is inherited from the Graphic object. A Window object is one of the three "real" objects, along with menus and User objects. You can create a window in two ways: you either build a new one or inherit from an existing one.

PowerBuilder allows you to create five different types of windows. Let's go over them quickly, and then we'll concentrate more on window instantiation and creation, events, calling events, and functions, as well as food for thought on the question of using functions versus events.

Types Of Windows

PowerBuilder allows you to create five different types of windows. Each window has a special purpose that may differ in functionality based on the type of application interface used. In PowerBuilder, you can create a *single document interface (SDI)* or a *multiple document interface (MDI)*. An SDI allows you to use one set of windows, whereas an MDI allows you to manipulate multiple windows. The main difference is that in an SDI, windows are not related to each other, as is the case with frame windows in an MDI. The window type can be changed in the properties page of the window, as shown in Figure 4.1.

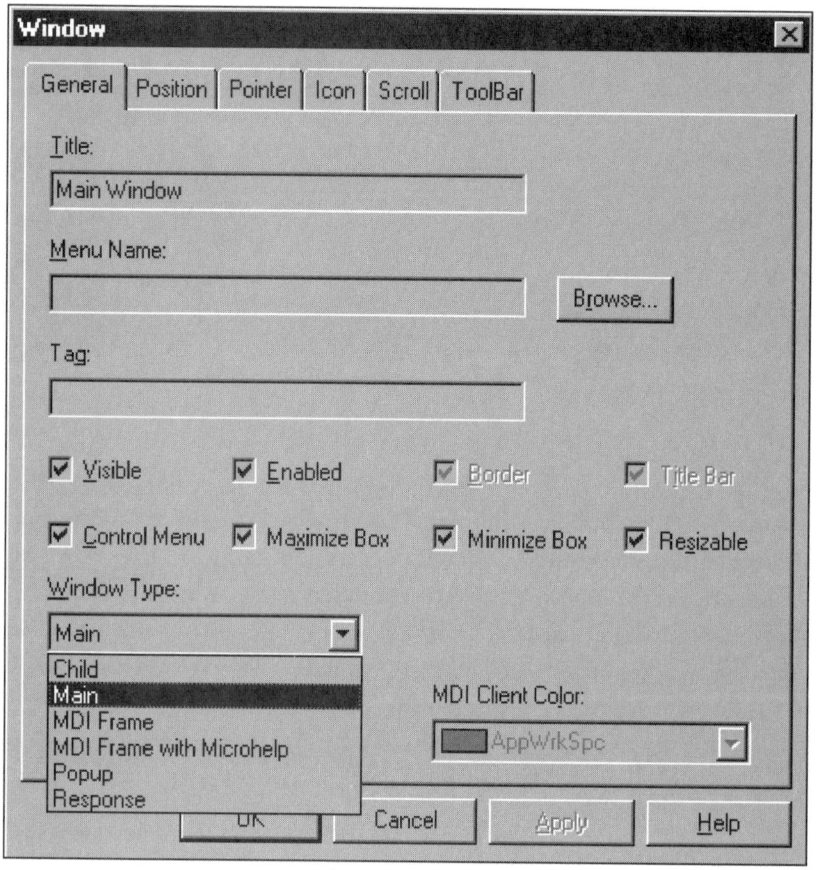

Figure 4.1
Selecting window types.

Main Windows

The main window type is a totally independent window. It overlaps other windows and can be overlapped by other windows. In an SDI, a main window serves as the base of the application; in an MDI, it serves as a sheet. A main window can have a title bar, a menu, and a control menu, and it can be minimized, maximized, and resized. Any other type of window that is opened from a main window is subservient to the main window. If a main window is minimized, all other windows associated with it are also minimized. Please note that this does not apply to response windows, which are modal windows and will be explained later in this chapter.

In Figure 4.2, a main window is used as a base window in an SDI application to display customer information from the customer table.

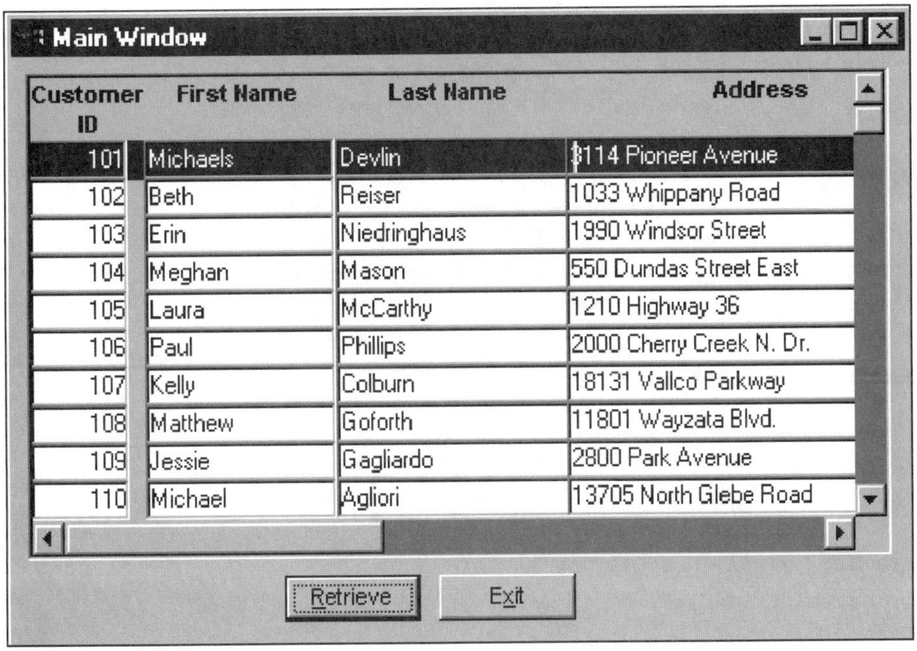

Figure 4.2
A main window in an SDI application.

Child Windows

Child windows must always be opened from a main window or pop-up window. Child windows are always subservient to the window that has opened them, and the caller window becomes its parent. Child windows only exist within the boundaries of the parent; when you move the parent around with your mouse, PowerBuilder clips the child to the boundaries of the parent so that only a portion of the parent window space is visible. Also, when you move the parent, the child moves with the parent and maintains its position relative to the parent.

A child window can have a title bar and can be minimized, maximized, and resized. When maximized, the child window fills the space of its parent. A child window cannot have a menu associated with it and will never have focus.

Pop-Up Windows

A pop-up window behaves the same as a child window except that its boundaries can extend beyond the boundaries of its parent. Unlike a child window, a pop-up window can have an associated menu. A pop-up window can display outside its parent window, and it cannot be overlaid by its parent. A pop-up window is hidden when its parent is

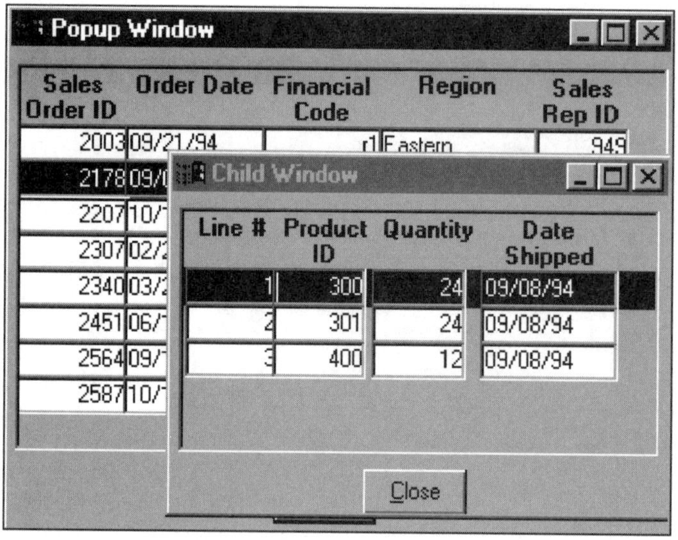

Figure 4.3
A pop-up window and a child window.

minimized and is closed when its parent is closed. When a pop-up window is minimized, it is shown as an icon on your MS Windows desktop.

In Figure 4.3, a pop-up window is used to display sales order information, and once a row has been double-clicked, line ID information is displayed in a child window.

Response Windows

Response windows behave in a manner that's totally different from other windows. A response window is modal: when it is opened, it does not allow access to other windows until your user has responded to it. Note that other applications are accessible. I usually use response windows to force my users to respond to an action.

One method of communicating between the response window and the calling script is to use the **CloseWithReturn**() function to pass information back.

> **Note:** *The next line of script after opening a response window isn't executed until the response window has been closed.*

Sometimes you want to prevent your users from choosing the control menu to close a response window—you want to force them instead to use your "close" command button. The following script in a user-defined event mapped to the **pbm_syscommand** prevents that action:

```
IF Message.WordParm = 61536 THEN RETURN 1
```

MDI Frame And MDI Frame With MicroHelp Window

MDI frame windows are used with MDI applications and are the base for that interface. Any window type opened in an MDI window becomes subservient to this window. This topic is covered in detail in Chapter 6, "Multiple Document Interface."

Instantiating Windows

When an application is executed, an instance of a **Window** class provides the interface for your user to interact with your application. In PowerBuilder, instances of **Window** classes are instantiated by using one of the following functions:

- **Open()**

- **OpenWithParm()**

- **OpenSheet()**

- **OpenSheetWithParm()**

When an instance of a **Window** class is instantiated, memory is required to store the scripts and values of its properties. Because of this requirement, an instance has to be destroyed when it is no longer needed so that memory is freed up. Physically destroying window instances is not normally required because this task is usually taken care of either by the user or by the frame window. However, window instances can be destroyed within script with the following functions:

- **Close()**

- **CloseWithReturn()**

    *Note: The **Close()** function may be used to close any type of window. However, the **CloseWithReturn()** function can only be used to destroy response windows where a value is to be returned to the script that has created that window.*

Because a window is actually a data type, you can also declare variables of this data type. You can then refer to these variables in your code:

```
w_main lmain
Open( lmain )
```

You can also create an array of windows. This is achieved by declaring an array of the window data type:

```
w_main lmain[3]
Open( lmain[1] )
```

Creating Objects

When PowerBuilder creates objects, four basic resources are used:

- **Class pool.** An area of memory where a class definition is kept until after the last instance of that class is destroyed. This area of memory contains events, function scripts, and shared variables.

- **Instance pool.** An area of memory where each instance has storage allocated for its instance variables.

- **Global memory pool.** An area of memory where global variables are kept.

- **Reference variables.** An area of memory to reference object instances.

When the **Open()** function is called using the class name as its argument, PowerBuilder first checks to see if a global reference variable exists for that class; if not, it creates one. It then checks to see if the class definition is in the class pool. If this is so, it uses the existing definition. If the class definition does not exist in the class pool, it retrieves the class definition from the PBLs (PowerBuilder Library) listed in the applications library search path and places it in the class pool. The next step is to create an instance of that class and assign the address of the new instance to the value of the global reference variable. The final step is to create a visual display of the object. Figure 4.4 illustrates this point.

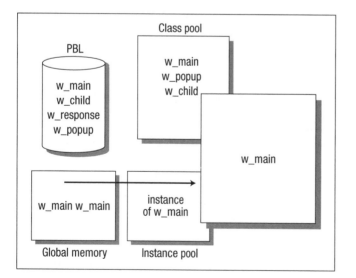

Figure 4.4
Creating an instance.

To instantiate an inherited window, all user-defined ancestors of that window must also be loaded into the class pool.

Note: Ancestors are loaded as needed. They remain in memory until the last instance that references their definitions is destroyed.

Window Events

The Window object has 29 predefined events that allow you to write scripts to perform various functions based on your users' actions. These events are described in Table 4.1.

Table 4.1   Window object events.

Event	Event Description
Activate	Occurs just before the window becomes active. When this event occurs, the first control in the tab order gets focus. If there are no visible objects in the window, the window gets focus.
Clicked	Occurs when a user clicks in an unoccupied area on the window.
Close	Occurs just before the window is removed from display to the user.
CloseQuery	Occurs when a window is closed, before the **Close** event.
Deactivate	Occurs when the window becomes inactive.
DoubleClicked	Occurs when the user double-clicks in an unoccupied area of the window.
DragDrop	Occurs when a dragged control is dropped on the window.
DragEnter	Occurs when the user is dragging an object and enters the control.
DragLeave	Occurs when the user is dragging an object and leaves the control.
DragWithin	Occurs when the user is dragging an object within the control.
Hide	Occurs just before the window is hidden.
HotLinkAlarm	Occurs after a DDE server application has sent new/changed data and the client DDE application has received it.
Key	Occurs when the user presses a key and the insertion point is not in a line edit.
MouseDown	Occurs whenever the left mouse button is pressed in an unoccupied area of the window.
MouseMove	Occurs whenever the mouse is moved within the window.
MouseUp	Occurs whenever the user releases the left mouse button.
Open	Occurs after a window is opened and before it's displayed.

(continued)

Table 4.1 Window object events *(continued)*.

Event	Event Description
Other	Occurs when a system message occurs that is not a PowerBuilder message.
RbuttonDown	Occurs when the right mouse button is pressed in an unoccupied area of the window.
RemoteExec	Occurs when a DDE client application has sent a command.
RemoteHotLinkStart	Occurs when a DDE client wants to start a hot link.
RemoteHotLinkStop	Occurs when a DDE client wants to stop a hot link.
RemoteRequest	Occurs when a DDE client requests data from a DDE server.
RemoteSend	Occurs when a DDE client application sends data.
Resize	Occurs when the user or a script opens or resizes a window.
Show	Occurs just before the window is displayed.
SystemKey	Occurs when the insertion point is not in a line edit and the user presses Alt or Alt plus another key.
Timer	Occurs when a specified number of seconds elapses after the **Timer()** function has been called.
ToolbarMoved	Occurs in an MDI frame window when the user moves any FrameBar or SheetBar.

Viewing Events

Some of these predefined events allow you to access their predefined arguments and specify different return codes to perform different actions. An excellent way of viewing them is by using the Object Browser (see Figure 4.5).

You can also view an event's declaration from the Window Painter menu by selecting the Declare|User Events|Args next to each listed event. The event declaration for the **Clicked** event is shown in Figure 4.6. One of my favorite Window events is **CloseQuery** event. If this event returns a value of 1, the closing of the window is aborted and the **Close** event that usually follows **CloseQuery** does not occur. This event is particularly useful when your users close a window but have not saved their work. The following code prevents this:

```
integer li_return

//accept the last data entered into your DataWindow
dw_customer.AcceptText()

//Check to see if any data has changed
IF dw_customer.DeletedCount()+dw_customer.ModifiedCount() &
```

```
> 0 THEN
li_return = MessageBox("Window Closing", &
   "Do you wish to save your changes?", Question!, &
   YesNoCancel!, 3)

//your user chooses to save then close the window.
IF li_rc = 1 THEN
   Window lw_sheet
   lw_sheet = w_mdi_frame.GetActiveSheet()
   lw_sheet.EVENT POST ue_update()
   RETURN 0

//your user chooses to close the window but not save
ELSE IF li_return = 2 THEN
   RETURN 0
//your user wishes to cancel
ELSE
   RETURN 1
END IF
ELSE
//no processing, simply close the window
   RETURN 0
END IF
```

Note: *These standard events cannot be modified.*

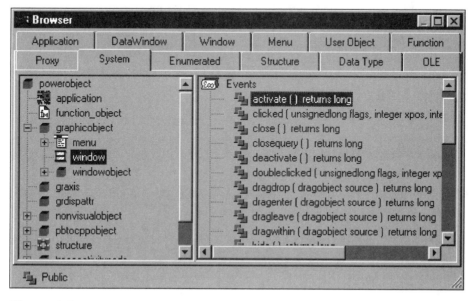

Figure 4.5
Using the Object Browser to view events.

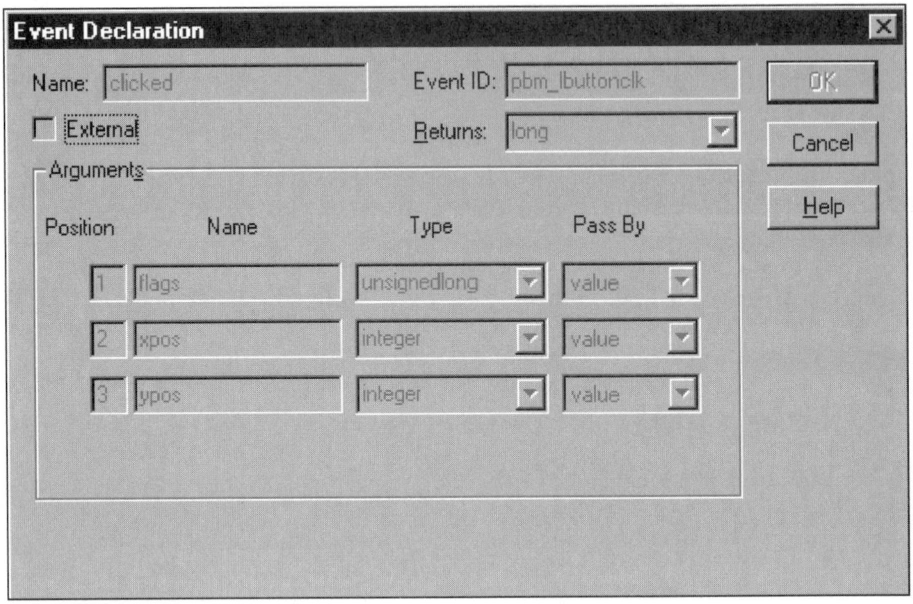

Figure 4.6
Event declaration for the **Clicked** event.

To give you an example, the **Clicked** event for the window takes three arguments and returns a long. Two very useful arguments are **xpos** and **ypos**, which contain the X and Y coordinates of the area on the window that your user clicks on:

```
MessageBox( "Clicked Event", "You clicked on:~r~t X: " + &
          String(xpos) + "~r~t Y: " + String(ypos)  )
```

Custom User Events

Sometimes, you may want to create your own user-defined events for a window or window control to perform tasks. The tasks could vary from calling functions or other events to performing a specific process. These must be user-defined events that are explicitly triggered by you, the developer. User-defined events can have arguments and return types and can be posted or triggered. You can create a user-defined event in Window Painter by selecting Declare|User Events menu items as seen in Figure 4.7.

A good example of user-defined events is a post-open event. Every time a window is opened, the **Open** event is triggered before the window is actually displayed to your users. The **Open** event usually holds large scripts, and as this script is executed, your users may perceive that the application is slow. This can be avoided by creating a user-defined event and posting it in the **Open** event so that its script is executed after the

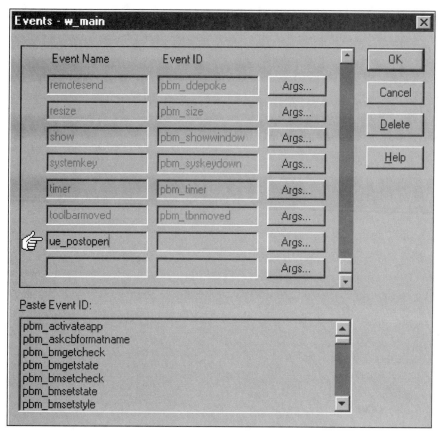

Figure 4.7
Declaring a user-defined event.

window has been displayed to the user. Here's a simple example of posting a user-defined event in the **Open** event of a window:

```
This.EVENT POST ue_postopen()
```

Window Functions

PowerBuilder also allows you to create user-defined functions for a window class; they are defined using the Declare|Windows Functions menu item. Like an event, a Window function can have arguments and return types, and it can be posted. So, if both windows and events can have arguments and return types and can be posted or triggered, then why would you use functions?

Unlike events, functions can be overloaded. Also, if there are multiple levels of inheritance for the class, the execution process for a function is very different from that of an event—you'll learn more about this in the next section.

Calling Window Functions And Events

The general syntax for calling both events and functions is:

```
{ref_var}.{TIRGGER|POST}{STATIC|DYNAMIC}{FUNCTION|EVENT} Method_Name({args})
```

The order of the keywords is not important, but they must precede the method name. If the **EVENT** keyword is not specified, PowerBuilder treats the method as a function. Therefore, you must include the **EVENT** keyword if the method you're calling is an event. The keyword **STATIC|DYNAMIC** specifies whether PowerBuilder will attempt to find the event or function at compile time. These keywords give you the ability, without getting a compile error, to include calls to an event or a function that may not exist until runtime. Here are some examples of calling events and functions:

```
This.EVENT POST ue_postopen()
This.of_Retrieve()
This.POST of_Retrieve(101)
```

Here are some alternate ways to invoke events only:

```
objectname.TriggerEvent(Enumerated-Event, {word,long} )
objectname.TriggerEvent(string, {word,long} )
objectname.PostEvent(Enumerated-event, {word,long} )
objectname.PostEvent(string, {word,long} )

This.TriggerEvent( Clicked! )
This.PostEvent( "ue_postopen", 101, 0 )
```

> **Note:** Messages that are triggered bypass the message queue and are executed synchronously, which means immediately. Messages that are posted join the message queue and execute in the order in which they are received (or asynchronously).

Another important point to note is that **TriggerEvent/PostEvent** and dot notation are completely different. Dot notation and parameterized events were first introduced in version 5.0 to provide support for OLE 2.0 controls. Some veteran PowerBuilder programmers still like to use the old method, but bear in mind that **TriggerEvent/PostEvent** is a function that takes the event name as its argument. You can pass information to the event script only with the two word and long arguments. The information is stored in the Message object.

Dot notation *calls* the event as if it were a function, and it can therefore add arguments if the event is unmapped and parameterized. When writing applications, you need to be consistent in your coding where arguments are stored. Dot notation and **TriggerEvent/PostEvent** do not mix because their arguments are stored in different places.

Executing Events

The best way I can describe how scripts are executed in a class hierarchy is to refer you to Figure 4.8. Let's say that you want to execute the following:

```
w_sheet_employee.EVENT ue_Retrieve()
```

When a script executes, PowerBuilder builds the script. This process begins at **w_sheet_employee**. A call is made to the ancestor, and its script is placed in front of **w_sheet_main**; this process completes when **w_anc_sheet** is reached. The final script, which is **w_anc_sheet** + **w_sheet_main** + **w_sheet_employee**, is then executed. Because the script is built from the bottom up, the executed script runs from the top down. However, if you were to override the script, this process would take a different turn.

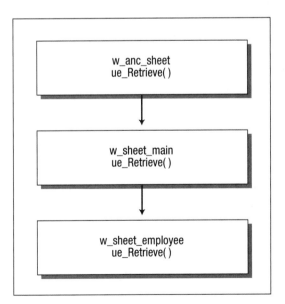

Figure 4.8
Event execution in a class hierarchy.

Overriding an event directs PowerBuilder to deviate from its normal execution sequence to execute an alternative script. To override an event script, select the Design|Override Ancestor Script menu item from the Powerscript Painter. If Override Ancestor Script is selected for **ue_Retrieve()** in **w_sheet_main**, when the event is executed, the script's build will be for **ue_Retrieve()** in **w_sheet_main**, followed by **w_sheet_employee**.

By default, events are extended and PowerBuilder internally puts the following line of code in a descendant event, where **Clicked** is the extended **Clicked** event:

```
Call Super::Clicked
```

When PowerBuilder executes the descendant event, the first line it executes is **Call Super::Clicked**, and then control is transferred to the ancestor script. In an application with multiple levels of hierarchy, **Call Super::Clicked** will be the first line of code in the **Clicked** event of all levels, except for the topmost level of the hierarchy chain. Once control is transferred to the topmost ancestor, the script is executed by falling through the hierarchy chain all the way to the lowest descendant. The exception to this is overriding the script in the descendant.

When overriding, during the execution process PowerBuilder travels up the hierarchy chain and executes the **Call Super::Clicked** line of code until it comes to the first override script. This is the cutoff point for the script to be built further, and all higher-level ancestors are cut off. The script then executes top-down from the level that had the override ancestor script on.

Executing Functions

When executing user-defined functions, here are some things to remember:

- Functions with the same name can exist at multiple levels of an ancestor hierarchy.

- A function name can be defined many times within one class. Note that in this case, the number or type of arguments must be different.

- PowerBuilder first takes a look at the current object to determine which function to execute. If a match is found, the function is executed. If not, PowerBuilder searches up the ancestor chain until it finds the match it needs.

Look at Figure 4.9. When the following command is issued, the method **w_sheet_main** is executed because the function name and its argument type are matched:

```
w_sheet_employees.of_Retrieve(101)
```

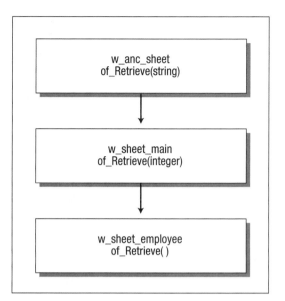

Figure 4.9
Function execution in a class hierarchy.

> **Note:** *PowerBuilder overrides functions by default. Descendant scripts extend ancestor scripts by default and execute after the ancestor script.*

To understand *extending* and *overriding* functions, it's important to know how functions are executed in a class with multiple levels of inheritance. Functions with the same name and signature can exist at multiple levels of an ancestor hierarchy. The signature of a function consists of the function name, the number of arguments, and the argument types. If a function with the same signature exists at various levels of the hierarchy, PowerBuilder first looks in the class definition of the current object. If it doesn't find the function there, it travels to the next level of ancestry in the hierarchy and keeps going up the hierarchy chain until it finds the function and executes it. To *extend* an ancestor function, you redefine the function using the same signature in the descendant class, code as the first line a call to the ancestor script using the pronoun **Super**, and then code the rest of the script. A **Return** statement in the ancestor script will transfer control to the descendant script, and the rest of the script in the function will then execute. To give you a quick example, let's say you have an ancestor function called **of_retrieve**(). You would declare **of_retrieve**() in the descendant and use the following code as the first line of script:

```
Super::of_retrieve()
```

Overriding an ancestor function takes place by default when a function with the same signature is declared in the descendant. As mentioned earlier, PowerBuilder first looks for the function in the current object and then moves up the hierarchy chain if it doesn't find the function. Therefore, redefining the function with the same signature in the descendant enables PowerBuilder to find the function, thus traversing up the chain is not required.

Events Or Functions?

Because both events and functions can have arguments and return values, both can be called statically and dynamically and both can be triggered and posted—so which should you use?

This question has been an interesting discussion topic among support staff, consultants, and instructors. I won't go into debating the pros and cons here, but I'll leave you with the following summary and let you decide for yourself:

- **Accessibility.** Functions can have access levels; events are public.

- **Extendibility.** Events can be easily extended or overridden by a descendant. To override a function, you must redefine it in the descendant. To extend a function, you must override the ancestor and then call the ancestor from the descendant first.

- **Usage.** Events are only associated with objects. Functions can be both local and global.

- **Performance.** PowerBuilder uses two different ways to look for events and functions. Functions are faster.

- **Errors.** Events fail silently; functions don't.

- **Overloading.** Events cannot be overloaded; functions can.

Moving On

Now that we have talked about PowerBuilder's Window object, the next step is to begin working with window controls. Window controls handle, primarily, the interaction between your application and your users, and the next chapter describes how to use these controls. Stay tuned!

Window Controls

As your users run your applications, they interact primarily with the controls you have placed on your windows. PowerBuilder's window controls can be categorized into two basic groups:

- Descendants of the DragObject

- Descendants of the DrawObject

The following controls are inherited from the DragObject and have events:

- CheckBox
- CommandButton
- DataWindow
- DropDownListBox
- DropDownPictureListBox
- EditMask
- Graph
- HScrollBar
- ListBox
- ListView
- MultiLineEdit
- OLEControl

- Picture
- PictureButton
- PictureListBox
- RadioButton
- RichTextEdit
- SingleLineEdit
- StaticText
- Tab
- TreeView
- User object
- VScrollBar

And these are inherited from the DrawObject, which has no events:

- Line
- GroupBox
- Oval
- Rectangle
- RoundRectangle

Figure 5.1 illustrates the window controls hierarchy as shown in the Object Browser.

I won't talk about every single control, as that would probably fill an entire book. However, in this chapter I'll discuss some of the controls that are used the most. But first, let's talk a little about control events, the control array, and a few performance issues. Note that I have dedicated full chapters to DataWindows (Chapter 3), the OLEControl (Chapter 18), and User objects (Chapter 8), all of which need to be covered extensively.

Control Events And Attributes

Most controls in the PowerBuilder environment have events. The only controls that do not have events are the descendants of the DrawObject, which are used for drawing purposes. Table 5.1 lists the standard events that each control has.

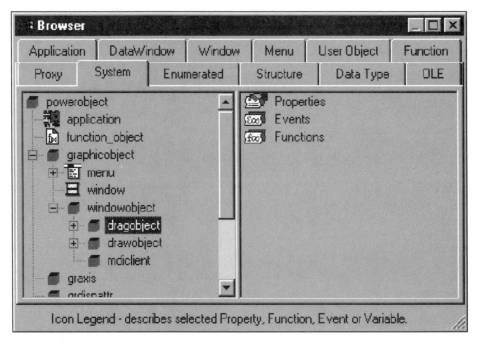

Figure 5.1
The window controls hierarchy.

Table 5.1 Standard control events.

Control Event	Description
Clicked	Occurs when a control is clicked or selected and the Enter key is pressed.
Constructor	Occurs when the control is created, just before the **Open** event for the window that contains the control.
Destructor	Occurs when the control is destroyed, immediately after the **Close** event of the window.
DragDrop	Occurs when an object is dropped on a control.
DragEnter	Occurs when an object is dragged into a control.
DragLeave	Occurs when an object is dragged out of a control.
DragWithin	Occurs when an object is dragged within a control.
GetFocus	Occurs when a control receives focus.
LoseFocus	Occurs when a control loses focus.
Other	Occurs when an event other than a PowerBuilder event occurs.
RbuttonDown	Occurs when the right mouse button is pressed.

Some controls have additional events that are listed in the event list for that control. Controls also have a number of different attributes that you can change during development or allow your users to change during runtime. For example, a control's text size is specified in the control's **TextSize** property. PowerBuilder saves the text size in points, using negative numbers. If you define the text for a CommandButton control, say, **cb_ok**, to be 12 points, PowerBuilder sets the value of **cb_ok**'s **TextSize** property to -12. Negative numbers are used for compatibility with previous releases, which saved text sizes in pixels as negative numbers. Here's an example:

```
cb_ok.TextSize = -10  //10 points
cb_ok.TextSize = 10   //10 pixels
```

PowerBuilderUnits (PBUs) are based on the size of the average character in the system font of the user's machine (for example, width/32; height/64). In order to properly calculate PBU conversions, you need the following:

- Height (in pixels) of a system font character

- Average width (in pixels) of the system font characters

- Number of pixels per horizontal inch according to the screen device driver

- Number of pixels per vertical inch according to the screen device driver

The Control Array

When a window is created in PowerBuilder, an internal array called the *control array* is also created with that window. This array contains a listing of all the controls on that particular window. Figure 5.2 shows the control list of a window within the PowerBuilder development environment.

The following example is in the **Open** event of a window that has been opened by **OpenSheetWithParm**(), and an object has been passed to it for further processing:

```
GraphicObject    lgo_object
object  lo_type

lgo_object = Message.PowerObjectParm
lo_type = lgo_object.TypeOf( )

CHOOSE CASE lo_type
   CASE DataWindow!
   // do your processing on DataWindow
   CASE    SingleLineEdit!
   // do your processing on a SingleLineEdit
CASE ELSE
   // display a messagebox
END CHOOSE
```

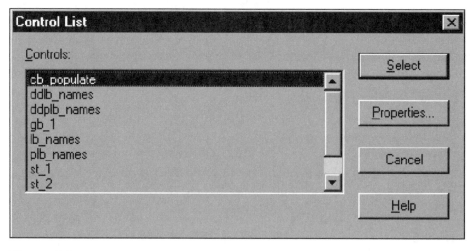

Figure 5.2
A control list.

Controls And Instantiation Of Windows

Part of the instantiation process for a window is creating each control that has been placed on that window. Because these controls are created dynamically during execution, the fewer you use, the faster your window opens and is displayed to your users.

Each standard window control requires its own resource. Although a DataWindow may contain many text objects and columns, its use of the window's resources is quite low and far more efficient. A DataWindow control uses one resource for itself, one for the edit control, and maybe one for the columns that have multiple EditMasks. This represents significant savings, especially if multiple rows of data are involved. Also, using validation and code tables in a DataWindow is much faster than writing scripts yourself. All of these factors contribute to faster instantiation of window controls.

ListBox And PictureListBox

You use a ListBox to list information and a series of choices. You can present this information as simple text in a ListBox, or you can display it with text and pictures in a PictureListBox. Once you've placed these controls on your window, obviously you need to present the information to your clients. If your ListBox already contains items, **AddItem** adds a new item to the end of the list. If the list is sorted, then PowerBuilder re-sorts the list after the item is added. A list can have duplicate items. Items in the list are tracked by their position in the list, not by their text. **InsertItem** inserts a new item before the item identified by an index. **AddItem** and **InsertItem** do not update the Items property array. You can use **FindItem** to find items added during execution. Figure 5.3 illustrates a few simple lists.

The following code populates a ListBox and PictureListBox from a DataStore:

```
long ll_rows
SetPointer( Hourglass! )

ll_rows = ids_customer.Retrieve( )

IF ll_rows > 0 THEN
FOR li_loop = 1 TO  ll_rows
   lb_names.AddItem( ids_customer.Object.Data[li_loop,2] )
   plb_names.AddItem(ids_customer.Object.Data[li_loop,2],1 )
END IF
```

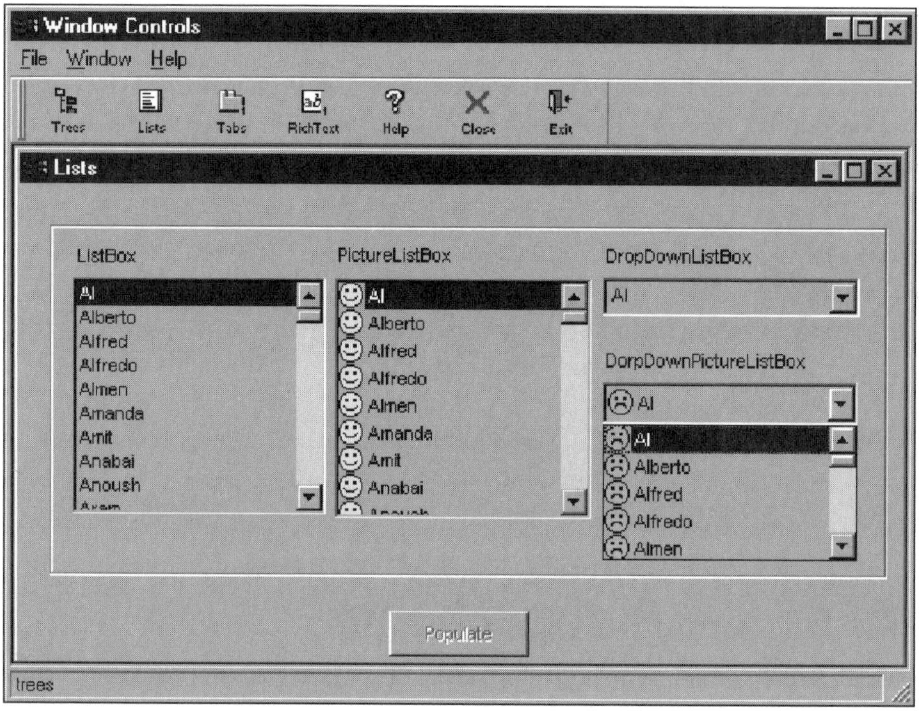

Figure 5.3
Various lists.

You can use the **AddPicture**() function to add pictures to your PictureListBox dynamically. You can also change the image or image size at will before adding the picture. The following example sets the size of the picture and adds a bitmap file to a PictureListBox:

```
plb_names.PictureHeight = 75
plb_names.PictureWidth = 75
plb_names.AddPicture( "employee.bmp" )
plb_names.AddItem( "John Doe", 1 )
```

DropDownListBox And DropDownPictureListBox

A drop-down list box (or *drop-down*) is another way in which you can present a simple list of information and choices to your users. Drop-downs basically consist of a SingleLineEdit and a ListBox/PictureListBox. Drop-downs come in two basic types: editable and noneditable.

Noneditable drop-downs allow you to choose from a fixed set of selections for a field. The cursor does not appear in the SingleLineEdit. However, you can change the **AllowEdit** attribute statically at development time or dynamically at execution time:

```
ddlb_names.AllowEdit = TRUE
```

Editable drop-downs allow your users to type in data for a particular item. You can write script to validate this entry, add it to the list, and so on.

TreeView

A TreeView provides hierarchical relationships in lists. The Windows Explorer is an excellent example of a TreeView, where directories, files, and other items of information are listed graphically. The TreeView control assigns a handle to each of its items. This handle can be used to get and set any attribute for an item. The handles are also used when inserting new items or deleting existing items. Each TreeView item can have a normal image, a selected image, a state image, or an overlay image. Each of these images can be constructed from bitmaps, icons, or cursors.

You can use four functions to add items to a TreeView control:

- **InsertItem()**. Inserts the item at a specified location
- **InsertItemFirst()**. Inserts the item at the first position of the TreeView level
- **InsertItemLast()**. Inserts the item at the last position of the TreeView level
- **InsertItemSort()**. Inserts a child item in sorted order under the parent item

When adding items to a TreeView with **InsertItem()** or **AddItem()**, you can supply two levels of information. First, you can add an item by supplying a picture index and a label, as seen here:

```
Long ll_tvi, ll_tvparent
ll_tvi = tv_1.FindItem( CurrentTreeItem!, 0 )
ll_tvparent = tv_1.FindItem( ParentTreeItem!, ll_tvi )
tv_1.InsertItem( ll_tvparent, ll_tvi, "Item 1", 2 )
```

Or, you can add your items by supplying the TreeView item itself:

```
Long ll_handle, ll_roothandle
TreeViewItem l_tvi

ll_handle = tv_1.FindItem( CurrentTreeItem!, 0 )
ll_roothandle = tv_1.FindItem( RootTreeItem!, 0 )
```

```
tv_1.GetItem( ll_handle, l_tvi )
tv_1.InsertItemLast( ll_roothandle, l_tvi )
```

The following example populates a TreeView from two DataStores. The items in the last level of the TreeView are clicked on; a ListView in Report mode is then populated.

```
long ll_rowcount, ll_index, ll_row
TreeViewItem ltvi_customer

//instantiate your datastores
ids_views[1] = create datastore
ids_views[1].DataObject = "d_customer"
ids_views[1].SetTransObject(SQLCA)
ll_rowcount = ids_views[1].Retrieve()

ltvi_customer.PictureIndex = 1
ltvi_customer.SelectedPictureIndex = 2

//populate customer information from the datastore
FOR ll_index = 1 TO ll_rowcount
   ltvi_customer.Label = String( &
      ids_views[1].object.fname[ll_index] ) &
      + ", " + String( ids_views[1].object.lname[ll_index] )
   ltvi_customer.Data = Integer( &
      ids_views[1].object.id[ll_index] )
   ltvi_customer.Children = TRUE
  tv_1.InsertItemLast( 0, ltvi_customer )
NEXT

//script for the itempopulate event of the TreeView
TreeViewItem ltvi_child, ltvi_parent
Integer   ll_count, ll_index, li_rc

//item information for  the current item
This.GetItem( handle,ltvi_parent )

CHOOSE CASE ltvi_parent.Level
   CASE 1 // level 1, customer
       ll_count = ids_views[2].Retrieve(ltvi_parent.Data)
       ltvi_child.PictureIndex = 3
       ltvi_child.SelectedPictureIndex = 4
       ltvi_child.Children = TRUE
       //populate the items
       FOR ll_index = 1 to ll_count
          ltvi_child.Label = String( &
          ids_views[2].object.id[ll_index] )
          ltvi_child.Data = Integer( ltvi_child.Label )
           li_rc = This.InsertItemSort( handle,ltvi_child )
```

```
        NEXT
CASE 2          //   level 2, sales orders
        ll_count = ids_views[3].Retrieve(ltvi_parent.Data)
        FOR ll_index = 1 to ll_count
            ltvi_child.Label = String( &
            ids_views[3].object.line_id[ll_index])
            ltvi_child.Data = Integer( &
            Integer(ids_views[3].object.id[ll_index])
            ltvi_child.Children = FALSE
            ltvi_child.PictureIndex = 5
            ltvi_child.SelectedPictureIndex = 5
            This.InsertItemSort( handle,ltvi_child )
        NEXT

END CHOOSE

//script for the selectionchanged event of the treeview
TreeViewItem ltvi
long ll_rows
Integer li_loop
string ls_liststring

//item information for  the current item
This.GetItem( newhandle, ltvi )

IF ltvi.Level = 2 THEN
    //delete the current listview items
    lv_1.DeleteItems()
    ll_rows = ids_views[3].Retrieve( Integer( ltvi.Label ) )
    //repopulate the listview from the datastore
    FOR li_loop = 1 TO ll_rows
        ls_liststring = String( &
          ids_views[3].Object.Data[li_loop,2])+"~t"+ &
        String(ids_views[3].Object.Data[li_loop,3])+"~t"+ &
        String(ids_views[3].Object.Data[li_loop,4]) +"~t"+ &
        String(ids_views[3].Object.Data[li_loop,5], &
        "MMM/DD/YYYY")
        lv_1.AddItem( ls_liststring, 1)
    NEXT
END IF
```

Finally, don't forget to destroy your DataStores, or you'll be leaking…(drop, drop!):

```
Integer   li_cnt
FOR li_cnt = 1 TO 3
    DESTROY ids_views[li_Cnt]
NEXT
```

ListView

A ListView control allows you to display graphical information as well as text in a variety of arrangements. You can display your information as large icons, small icons, small icon freeform list, or vertical list. You can also display additional information about each list item by associating additional columns with each list item. You can allow your users to add, delete, edit, and rearrange ListView items, or you can use these items to invoke specific actions.

ListView controls consist of items that are stored in an array. Each item consists of the following components:

- **Label.** The name of the item

- **Index.** The position of the item

- **Picture index.** The number that associates the item with an image

- **Overlay picture index.** The number that associates the item with an overlay image

- **State picture index.** The number that associates the item with a state picture

You use the **AddItem()** or **InsertItem()** function to add items to a ListView dynamically during execution. The following code adds an item to ListView **lv_1**:

```
ListViewItem     l_lvi
l_lvi.Label = "Item Number 1"
lv_1.AddItem( l_lvi )
```

If you want your ListView to be in Report view, more information is required. To enable Report view, you must write a script to establish columns with the **AddColumn()** and **SetColumn()** functions. You then populate the columns using the **SetItem()** function. Here is an example:

```
This.AddColumn("Line ID" , Left! , 300)
This.AddColumn("Product ID" , Left! , 300)
This.AddColumn("Quantity" , Left! , 300)
This.AddColumn("Date Shipped",Left!,400)

This.SetItem( 1, 1, "1" )
This.SetItem( 1, 2, "300" )
This.SetItem( 1, 3, "12" )
This.SetItem( 1, 4, "Sep/26/1997" )
```

Or, you could use the following code instead:

```
String ls_string
ls_string = "1" + "~t" + "300" +"~t" + "Sep/26/1997"
lv_1.AddItem( ls_liststring, 1)
```

RichTextEdit

Rich text format (RTF) is a standard for specifying formatting instructions and document contents in a single ASCII document. Many word processors and text editors that support RTF interpret the formatting instructions and display the text with the formatting. If you were to look at an ASCII file that contains RTF, you would see nothing but unrecognizable characters with your text embedded in the formatting—for example:

```
{\b\f1\fs32\cf0\up0\dn0 Advanced PowerBuilder 6.0, }
```

However, the RichTextEdit control lets your users view or edit formatted text. You can provide your users with toolbars, editing keys, print preview, and pop-up menus for formatting. PowerBuilder also provides you with functions to insert text, get text, insert and manage input fields, and set properties of all or some of the contents. In other words, everything you need to create simple word processor-formatted reports or mail-merge applications is available to you. Figure 5.4 shows the various properties of an RTE that you can set in your applications.

> **Note:** *PowerBuilder's RTE control supports version 1.2 of the RTF standard, except for formatted tables, drawing objects, and double underlines.*

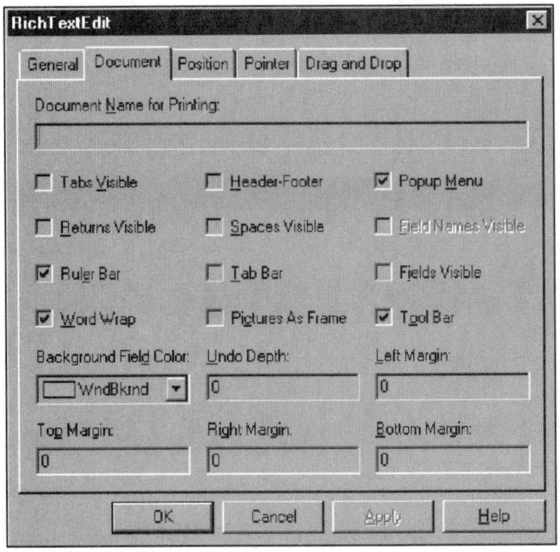

Figure 5.4
Various properties of an RTE.

Saving An RTE's Contents

The RTE control has many features that you can utilize in your applications. The following example demonstrates saving the contents of an RTE:

```
integer li_rtn, li_value
string ls_docname, ls_named

//popup a dialog box to get the desired file name
li_value = GetFileSaveName("Select File",  &
   ls_docname, ls_named, "rtf",  &
   "RichText Files (·.RTF),·.RTF,")

IF li_value = 1 THEN rte_demo.SaveDocument( &
   ls_docname, & FileTypeRichText!)
```

If the file you're trying to save already exists, PowerBuilder provides you with the **FileExists** event on the RTE that is triggered in such cases. You could code the following script in such an event:

```
integer li_rc
//prompt the user for overwrite
li_rc = MessageBox("SaveDocument","File already exists! &
   OverWrite?",Exclamation!, OKCancel!, 2)
//if not, return
IF li_rc = 2 THEN RETURN 1
```

You could also save the contents of an RTE to a database. The following example gets the text of an RTE via the **CopyRTF()** function and sets it to a DataWindow column. You could use the **PasteRTF()** function to paste from a retrieved column, like this:

```
String ls_richtext
Long ll_row

//store the text in a string
ls_richtext = rte_demo.CopyRTF( FALSE )

//get current row & assign the RT to the desired column.
ll_row = dw_1.GetRow()
dw_1.Object.contract[ll_row] = ls_richtext
```

Remember that a string in a DataWindow column can only hold 32K of text. If your rich text is more than 32K, you must use the **SELECTBLOB** and **UPDATEBLOB** embedded

SQL commands to retrieve and save your rich text. Note that you're still limited to 60,000 characters, because that's the maximum a string can hold. Here is an example:

```
String ls_richtext
Blob   b_contract
//embedded SQL using SELECTBLOB
SELECTBLOB contract_will_no
   INTO    :b_contract
   FROM documents
   WHERE documents.contract_will_no = 1001
   USING  SQLCA;

//cast your blob into a string
ls_richtext = String( b_contract )
//past the string into the RTE control
rte_demo.PasteRTF( ls_richtext )
```

Sharing Data With A DataWindow

Another very useful function that allows a RichTextEdit control to share data with a DataWindow and display the data in its input fields is **DataSource**. If input fields in the RichTextEdit control match the names of columns in the DataWindow, the data in the DataWindow is assigned to those input fields. The document in the RichTextEdit control is repeated so that there's an instance of the document for each row in the DataWindow.

The following example inserts a document called CONTRACT.RTF into the RichTextEdit control **rte_demo**. The names of the document's input fields match the columns in a DataWindow object **d_customer**. The example creates a DataStore, associates it with **d_customer**, and retrieves the data. Then it inserts the document in **rte_demo** and sets up the DataStore as the datasource for the control. Here's an example:

```
//declare a data type of datastore
DataStore lds_customer

//instantiate the object
lds_customer = CREATE DataStore
lds_customer.DataObject = "d_customer"
lds_customer.SetTransObject( SQLCA )
lds_customer.Retrieve( )

//insert the contract document into the RTE
rte_demo.InsertDocument("contract.rtf", TRUE)
rte_demo.DataSource( lds_customer )
```

Tab Control

A *Tab control* is a container for tabbed property pages that can display other controls. Tab controls present information that can logically be grouped together but may be divided into distinct groups. One page at a time fills the display area of the Tab control, and each page has a tab-like index that can display a label for that tab page.

A *tab page* is nothing more than a User object. You can define tab pages either statically at development time, by adding pages to the control, or dynamically, by creating custom visual User objects. The two methods mentioned here can be mixed and matched. The Tab control has settings for controlling the position and appearance of the tabs. In addition, each tab page can have its own label, picture, and background color. The properties of a Tab control are shown in Figure 5.5.

In script, you must fully qualify the controls on a Tab control by specifying the Tab control name, the tab page, and then the control, as seen here:

```
tab_1.tabpage_1.dw_1.retrieve( )
```

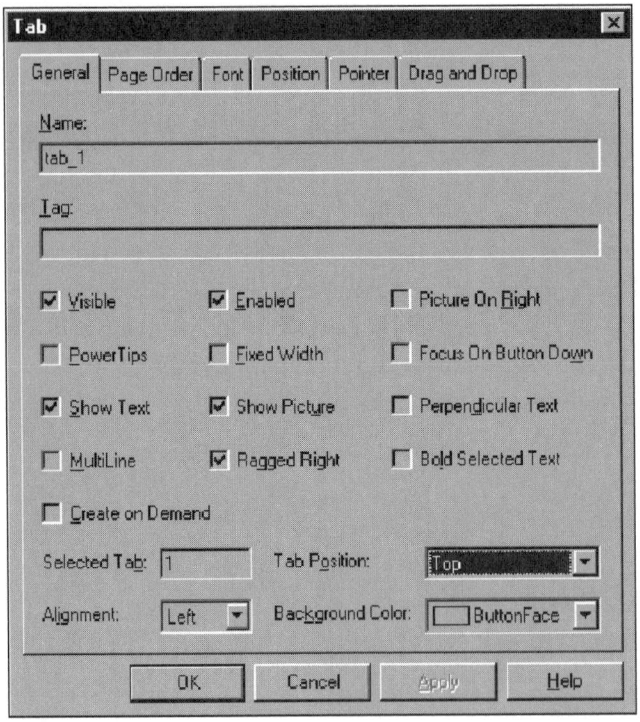

Figure 5.5
Various properties of a Tab control.

The following code opens an instance of a User object named **u_orders** as a tab page in the Tab control **tab_1** and the code that follows closes that instance of the User object:

```
Integer li_rc
li_rc = tab_1.OpenTab(u_orders, 0)

//close the tab page
CloseTab( u_orders )
```

You can use **OpenTab**() and **OpenTabWithParm**() to dynamically add tab pages to a Tab control. Because the control array for the Tab control is only updated when tab pages are created in Painter, any tab pages that are created dynamically must be tracked by you in another array and referred to from there. The control array—**control**[ ]—is a property of the Tab control that specifies the array of tab pages within the Tab control. It's important to remember that any tab pages you create dynamically will not be destroyed when the Tab control is destroyed, because they're not included in the **control**[] array for the Tab control. Therefore, you must issue a **CloseTab**() on all dynamically created tab pages; otherwise, a memory leak will occur.

Here's how to reference User object tab pages dynamically created in script:

```
//Declare another array of User objects to track tab pages
UserObject uo_array[]
Ii_tabindex++ // Instance variable

/*Open Tab where tab_1 is the Tab control name,
 u_array contains the reference to the opened User object,
 u_page is name of the User object, which is opened as a tab page
*/

tab_1.OpenTab(uo_array[ii_tabindex],"u_page", ii_tabindex)
uo_array[ii_tabindex].Text="Tab Page 1"
```

> **Note:** When you dynamically create a tab page, to get the handle of each tab page and assign a label value, keep an array of **uo_tabpages** and use **OpenTab(uo_tabpages[index],0)** to keep track of the tab pages.

Let's say you have a User object called **uo_tab** with a Tab control on it. On one of the tab pages you have a DataWindow, and, in one of the DataWindow events, you want to reference a User object function called **uf_view**(), like this:

```
uo_tab luo_tab
luo_tab = GetParent( ).GetParent( ).GetParent( )
luo_tab.uf_change( )
```

The first **GetParent()** references the tab page, the second **GetParent( )** references the Tab control, and the third **GetParent()** references the User object. (In Chapter 8, "User Objects," I'll walk you through creating a generic function that always returns the parent window of an object.)

> **Note:** I don't recommend using Tab controls for navigational purposes. The information you display on the tab pages should not be related to each other. You should avoid this type of GUI design because it's hard to code and confuses your users. Use a Tab control to display information that doesn't have one-to-many relationships.

Moving On

This chapter discussed window controls, the control array, and some of the more popular controls that are used regularly. As you can see, controls play an important role in your applications, and hopefully this chapter has provided insight for you.

Now that we've covered windows and window controls, I'll concentrate a little more on the multiple document interface (MDI) and the MDI frame window. The MDI provides a friendly and flexible user interface—most of the applications you build these days are probably MDI.

Multiple Document Interface

In Chapter 4, "Windows," I covered PowerBuilder windows; however, one of those window types—the MDI frame window—deserves special attention, so now we'll revisit it in this chapter. Before we jump into that, though, let's talk a little about the paradigm this window type represents.

The *multiple document interface (MDI)* is a Windows application style that you can use to open and interact with multiple instances of windows (better known as *sheets*) in a single window, as shown in Figure 6.1. Most large-scale applications built today are MDI applications. When developed properly, MDI can provide a friendly and flexible user interface. To give you some examples, Microsoft Word, Excel, and, yes, even PowerBuilder are MDI applications. In PowerBuilder, MDI is often selected because it's the only interface that allows you to associate toolbars and MicroHelp with your menus and windows.

In this chapter, we'll concentrate on MDI frames, sheets, menus, toolbars, and MicroHelp.

MDI Frames

An *MDI frame* is simply an application shell that contains a client area (**MDI_1**), sheets, menus, and MicroHelp. I recommend keeping MDI frames to a minimum in size and complexity because the majority of the work is done in sheets.

When building application interfaces, you can create two types of MDI frames: standard and custom. A s*tandard* MDI frame window contains a menu bar, MicroHelp, and a toolbar; the client area is empty. Sheets are opened in the client area, and they may have their own menus. Sheets use the menu bar to display their own menus when activated, or they inherit their menus from the frame menu. A *custom* frame is created when you add controls to a standard frame window. When you create an MDI frame window, PowerBuilder creates a control named **MDI_1**, which it uses to identify the client area of

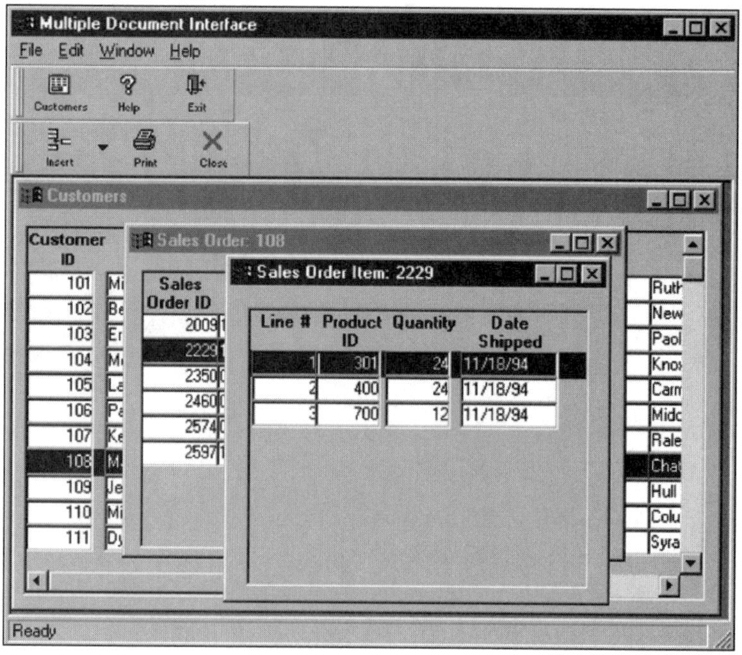

Figure 6.1

A multiple document interface application.

the frame window (see Figure 6.2 for an example of a custom MDI application). In standard frames, PowerBuilder manages **MDI_1**, but in custom frames, you have to write code for the frame's **Resize** or **Open** event in order to size **MDI_1** appropriately.

The Object Browser is an excellent tool for displaying information about **MDI_1**, as shown in Figure 6.3.

As I mentioned earlier, if you place any controls on your MDI frame, you must resize the client area. If you don't resize this area, the sheets will open but might not be visible at all. In the following example, I have added a rectangle to an MDI frame. Here's the script that must be in the frame's **Resize** or **Open** event:

```
int li_width, li_height

// obtain the width and height of the workspace
li_width = This.WorkSpaceWidth( )
li_height = This.WorkSpaceHeight( )
// calculating the workspace between my rectangle and the MicroHelp.
li_height = li_height - ( r_white.y + r_white.height )
li_height = li_height - MDI_1.MicroHelpHeight
li_height = li_height + WorkSpaceY( )
```

```
// Moving the client area to begin below my control
MDI_1.Move( WorkSpaceX( ), r_white.y + r_white.height )
// Resize the client area
MDI_1.Resize( li_width, li_height )
```

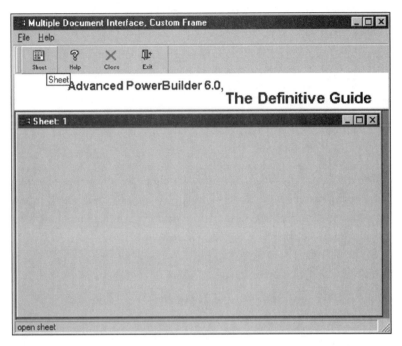

Figure 6.2

A custom MDI application.

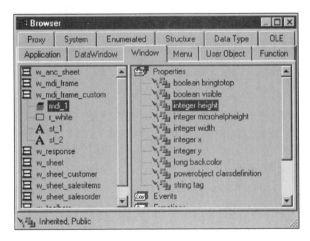

Figure 6.3

MDI_1 properties.

MDI Sheets

Sheets are the most important part of your MDI application, because that's where your users do the majority of their work. When you open a sheet, it becomes the active sheet, and if the opened sheet has an associated menu, that menu becomes the menu at the top of the frame.

To open sheets in the client area of your MDI frame, PowerBuilder provides two functions:

```
OpenSheet ( sheetrefvar {, windowtype }, mdiframe &
{, position {, arrangeopen } } )

OpenSheetWithParm ( sheetrefvar, parameter {, windowtype }, &
mdiframe {, position {, arrangeopen } } )
```

The data type of *sheetrefvar* is usually **Window**, from which all windows are inherited, but it can be any ancestor of *windowtype*. When you specify *windowtype*, the Window object specified in *windowtype* must be the same data type as *sheetrefvar*. The following example illustrates two methods of opening a sheet window:

```
// method 1
Window  lw_sheet
OpenSheet(lw_sheet, "w_sheet_customer", ParentWindow, 0, Original!)

//method 2
W_sheet_customer lw_sheet
OpenSheet(lw_sheet, ParentWindow, 0, Original!)
```

> **Note:** PowerBuilder doesn't automatically copy objects that are dynamically referenced through string variables into your executable. To include the Window object specified in **windowtype** in your application, you must list it in a PBR file.

OpenSheet() opens a sheet and appends its name to the item on the menu bar, specified in **position**. If **position** is 0 or greater than the number of items on the menu bar, PowerBuilder appends the name of the sheet to the next-to-last menu item in the menu bar. In most MDI applications, the next-to-last menu item on the menu bar is the Window menu, which contains options for arranging sheets as well as the list of open sheets. If the sheets don't appear on the menu, PowerBuilder can't append the sheets to a menu that doesn't have any other menu selections. You must ensure that the menu you specify (or, if you leave out **position**, the next-to-last menu) has at least one other item.

> **Note:** Sheets in a frame cannot be made invisible. When you open a sheet, the value of the **Visible** property is ignored. However, you can use API commands to change this property so that a sheet becomes invisible.

When you use the **OpenSheetWithParm**() function, you can pass arguments to the sheets. This passing of arguments is done by the *Message object*. The Message object is used to process events that are not PowerBuilder-defined events, to communicate parameters between windows when you open and close them, and to specify whether optional parameters are used in **TriggerEvent** or **PostEvent**.

The system Message object has three properties for storing data. Depending on the data type of the parameter specified for **OpenSheetWithParm**(), scripts for the opened sheet check one of the following properties:

- **Message.DoubleParm.** A numeric variable

- **Message.PowerObjectParm.** Any PowerBuilder object, including user-defined structures

- **Message.StringParm.** A string variable

The following script in the **DoubleClicked** event of a DataWindow control opens the sales order sheet and passes it a variable called **li_id**:

```
//script in the doubleclicked event
w_sheet_salesorder  lw_sheet
integer li_id
//obtain the sales order id which is column 1
li_id = This.Object.Data[row,1]
//open an instance of the window and pass it the variable
OpenSheetWithParm( &
lw_sheet,li_id,w_mdi_frame,0,Original! )
```

In the opened window, you should access the value passed in the Message object right away, because some other script may use the Message object (which is a global object) for another purpose. The following script extracts an integer variable from the Message object:

```
integer li_sales
li_sales = Message.DoubleParm
This.Title = "Sales Order Item: " + String( li_sales )
dw_1.Retrieve( li_sales)
```

> **Note:** When you pass a PowerObject as a parameter, you're passing a reference to the object. The object must exist when you refer to it later; otherwise, you'll get a null object reference, which causes an error. For example, if you pass the name of a control on a window that is being closed, that control will not exist when a script accesses the parameter.

To manage your MDI sheets, PowerBuilder provides four functions to assist you:

- **mdiframeWindow.GetFirstSheet()**

- **mdiframeWindow.GetNextSheet(sheet)**

- **mdiframeWindow.GetActiveSheet()**

- **mdiframeWindow.ArrangeSheets(arrangetype)**

GetFirstSheet() obtains the top sheet in an MDI frame, which may or may not be active. Don't forget to use the **IsValid()** function to find out if the return value is valid. If it's not, no sheet is open. **GetNextSheet()** obtains the sheet that's behind a specified sheet in the MDI frame. The following examples use both of these functions to loop through the open sheets and add their titles to a ListBox control:

```
boolean lb_valid
Window  lw_sheet
//get the first sheet
lw_sheet = ParentWindow.GetFirstSheet()
IF IsValid( lw_sheet )  THEN
   //add title to the ListBox.
lb_sheets.AddItem( lw_sheet.Title )
   DO
      lw_sheet = ParentWindow.GetNextSheet( lw_sheet )
      lb_valid = IsValid ( lw_sheet)
      IF lb_valid THEN &
      lb_sheets.AddItem( lw_sheet.Title )
   LOOP WHILE lb_valid
END IF
```

The **GetActiveSheet()** function returns the currently active sheet in your MDI frame window, and **ArrangeSheet()** simply rearranges your sheets in the MDI frame window. The following script accesses the active sheet and closes it:

```
Window lw_sheet
lw_sheet = ParentWindow.GetActiveSheet( )
IF IsValid( ls_sheet ) THEN Close( lw_sheet )
```

MDI Menus

A popular reason for creating MDI applications is the use of menus and toolbars. Menus are usually used for navigation purposes, and there are a couple of things that you should know about MDI menus. (Menus are covered in more detail in Chapter 7, "Menus.")

When you open and display a window, after the window itself and all of its controls have been created, the window's associated menu is constructed. This involves retrieving the menu class and any ancestor classes into memory and creating the menu items, each of which is a separate object. When multiple instances of a window are created, PowerBuilder creates a global variable for the menu and an instance of the menu for each window instance. Because this global variable points to the last menu instance that was created, the pointer can sometimes point to the wrong menu. To avoid incorrect referencing, the code for the menu should not be hard-coded.

Placing a noun/pronoun reference in your script ensures that your code references the current instance of the menu. To give you an example, suppose in your MDI application that several sheets are opened. Your user selects Window|Vertical to rearrange all the open sheets. You can use the pronoun **This** or the noun **Parent** instead of hard-coding the menu name to provide a checkmark next to the arrangement style of your sheets. Here is an example:

```
This.check()
Parent.m_horizontal.Uncheck()
Parent.m_layer.Uncheck()
Parent.m_cascade.Uncheck()
```

> **Note:** When you use **Parent** in a menu script, it refers to the menu item on the level above the menu the script is for.

The term **ParentWindow** can be used only in scripts for menus; it refers to the window that a menu is associated with at execution time. Technically, **ParentWindow** is a property of the Menu object, not a pronoun. However, you can use it as you would a pronoun to refer generically to the Menu object's parent window. For example, the following statement in a script for a menu closes the window the menu is associated with at execution time:

```
Close( ParentWindow )
```

> **Note:** You cannot use **ParentWindow** to qualify a reference to a control on a window. A workaround is to get a reference to the sheet using the **GetActiveSheet()** function.

MicroHelp

MicroHelp displays information to your users in the status area at the bottom of a frame. Generally, it's used to enhance an MDI application by offering additional text for key items. It's also a good tool for providing visual representation to your users as to what your application is doing—for example, displaying retrieval information as your user clicks the Retrieve button.

If you have the need to provide MicroHelp for controls on objects, you can use the **Tag** attribute in conjunction with the **SetMicroHelp** function. The **Tag** attribute allows you to tag values to columns, fields, Graphic objects, and User objects. You can provide MicroHelp for controls in several ways—the one that I like best is implemented with the **MouseMove** event. Follow these steps:

1. Assign your text to the **Tag** attribute of your control.

2. Create a user-defined event and map it to the **pbm_mousemove** event. Next, add the following code for this newly created event:

```
Parent.SetMicroHelp( this.Tag )
```

3. Place the following script in the **mousemove** event of the window:

```
This.SetMicroHelp( "ready" )
```

MDI Toolbars

Toolbars simply make your MDI application more attractive and easier to use. As you might have noticed already, toolbars are only available to you in an MDI application and cannot be used in a non-MDI environment unless you write them yourself. There's no magic to using toolbars—they behave the same as the window or the DataWindow Painter toolbar icon. Toolbars are created in the Menu Painter and are mapped directly to a specified menu item.

As shown in Figure 6.4, you can provide your users with the ability to display text in toolbars, use PowerTips, and float the toolbar or move it around the frame.

Note that if both your frame and your sheet have toolbars, once you've opened your sheet, the menu displayed is the Sheets menu; however, both toolbars are visible and functional. Also, if your current sheet does not have a menu, the menu and the toolbar of the frame are displayed. In your scripts, you refer to a toolbar item the same way you refer to a menu item:

```
m_frame.m_file.m_close.ToolBarItemVisible = TRUE
```

A menu can have a drop-down toolbar (see Figure 6.5). When your user clicks a button in the drop-down toolbar, that button becomes visible and is moved to the top.

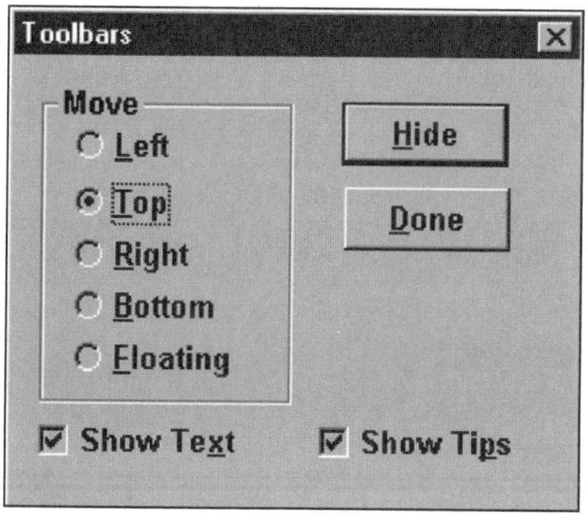

Figure 6.4
Managing toolbars.

You can specify properties for the toolbars or toolbar items by setting the properties listed in Table 6.1.

Whenever a toolbar moves in an MDI frame window, PowerBuilder triggers the **ToolbarMoved** event for that window. You can check to see which toolbar has moved as

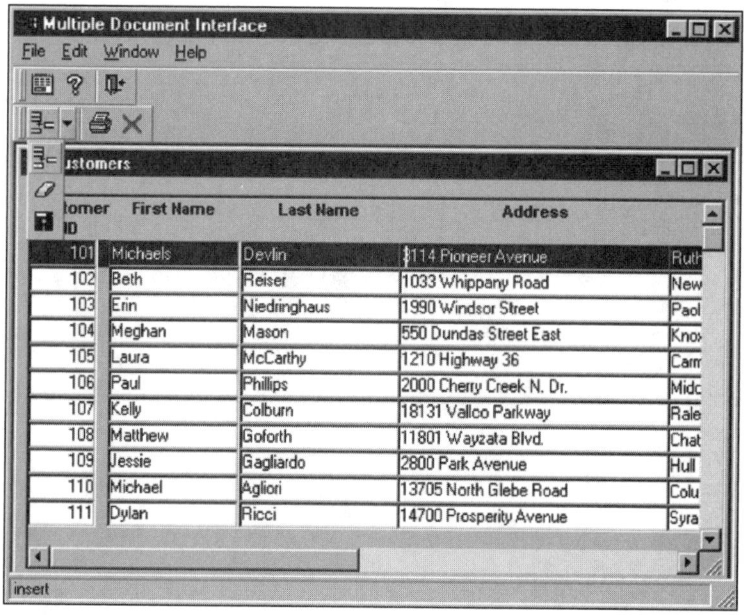

Figure 6.5
A drop-down toolbar.

Table 6.1 Properties for toolbars and toolbar items.

Attribute	Data Type	Description
ToolbarAlignment	Enumerated	Specifies where the toolbar is located
ToolbarItemDown	Boolean	Specifies the appearance of the toolbar
ToolbarItemName	String	Specifies the name of the toolbar item bitmap
ToolbarItemDownName	String	Specifies the name of the toolbar item when depressed
ToolbarItemOrder	Integer	Specifies the number of the order of the toolbar item
ToolbarItemSpace	Integer	Specifies the amount of space in front of a toolbar item
ToolbarPopMenuText	String	Specifies the text on the pop-up menu
ToolbarSheetTitle	String	Specifies the title for the sheet bar
ToolbarUserControl	Boolean	Specifies that the toolbar pop-up menu can be used
ToolbarText	String	Specifies the text for the toolbar
ToolbarTip	String	Specifies the text for the toolbar tip
ToolbarItemText	String	Specifies the text of an item.
ToolbarItemVisible	Boolean	Specifies the visibility of a toolbar item
ToolbarItemTitle	String	Specifies the title of the MDI sheet toolbar when floating
ToolbarHeight	Integer	Specifies the height of the toolbar when floating
ToolbarFrameTitle	String	Specifies the title of the toolbar item that is created in an MDI floating toolbar

PowerBuilder populates the **Message.WordParm** and **Message.LongParm** properties with the following values:

- **Message.WordParm:** Frame bar has moved (0); sheet bar has moved (1).

- **Message.LongParm:** Moved to the left (0); moved to the top (1); moved to the right (2); moved to the bottom (3); floating (4).

Moving On

I hope this chapter has given you a better understanding of MDI and MDI applications. Almost every application that you'll write or debug will use this interface, and I could get into some interesting examples if time and space permitted. But, it's time to move on.

You have built your windows and controls, and you may have decided on your interface by now. Next, you need to create the object that serves as a means of initiating actions. In the next chapter, we'll do that by focusing on PowerBuilder menus.

Menus 7

In most applications that you develop, the menu serves as a means of initiating actions. In PowerBuilder, menus are objects, possessing certain characteristics not shared by any other objects. Using the Menu Painter, you can create menus that have scripts and object functions. PowerBuilder menus can also benefit from inheritance.

In this chapter, I'll cover the menu types available to you, menu events and functions, toolbars, and some performance issues that you should be aware of when creating menus. First, however, I'll begin by telling you a little about the architecture of PowerBuilder menus.

The Menu Architecture

In PowerBuilder, unlike any other third-level languages you may have used in the past, each menu item is a separate object. Each menu consists of multiple Menu objects or items that are related to each other by pointers. (To learn more about pointers, refer to Chapter 17, "External Functions.") One could say that the **MenuItem** class is a secondary class or an embedded class within a parent class. Some PowerBuilder developers call this architecture the *link list*. Each MenuItem object has its own **Clicked** and **Selected** events that allow you to have separate and distinct implementations for these events. Because each MenuItem object is a separate instance, it has its own **Enable** and **Visible** properties that can be enabled or disabled.

Because of this architecture, the following statement could be used to reference the **Enable** property of the MenuItem **m_close** from any script within an application:

```
m_frame.m_file.m_close.Enable = FALSE
```

As you can see, PowerBuilder menus have some extraordinary attributes, including the following:

- An instance of the **Menu** class is created when your window is created. Note that this is not a descendant class, as is the case with the control objects.

- The **Menu** class name is used when it's associated with a window.

- The window uses its **MenuId** property for a reference pointer and not the class name of the menu.

- Menus can be instantiated dynamically via **ChangeMenu()** or by using the **CRE-ATE** command and **PopMenu()**.

As mentioned in previous chapters, when you open and display a window, the window's associated menu is constructed after the window itself and all its controls have been created. This involves retrieving the **Menu** class and any ancestor classes into memory and creating the menu items, each of which is a separate object. When multiple instances of a window are created, PowerBuilder creates a global variable for the menu and an instance of the menu for each window instance. Because this global variable points to the last menu instance that was created, the pointer can sometimes point to the wrong menu. To avoid incorrect referencing, the code for the menu should not be hard-coded. Placing a noun/pronoun reference in your script ensures that your code references the current instance of the menu.

Let's say your user has opened several windows and then selects Window|Vertical to rearrange all the open sheets. You can use the pronoun **This** or the noun **Parent** instead of hard-coding the menu name to provide a checkmark next to the arrangement style of your sheets. The pronoun **ParentWindow** can only be used in scripts for menus and refers to the window that a menu is associated with at execution time.

Types Of Menus

All new menus that are created for your application are inherited from the PowerBuilder **Menu** class, which in turn are inherited from the GraphicObject. Figure 7.1 illustrates the inheritance tree for **m_frame**.

These new menus can be divided into two groups: menu bars and pop-up menus.

Menu Bars

The *menu bar*, which is the most common menu used, is a horizontal row of MenuItem objects. This row appears below the title bar of your window, and each menu item offers

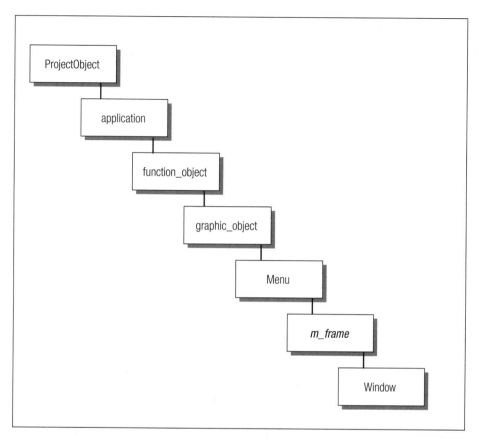

Figure 7.1
The inheritance tree from **m_frame**.

further choices by displaying cascading or drop-down menus. Menu instances cannot exist on their own like controls. Instead, they must be associated with a Window object either directly as property values, or you can use the **ChangeMenu**() function. So, once you've created your menu, you must associate it with the window of your choice. However, keep in mind that child and response windows cannot have menus associated with them because they are opened from a parent window. Child windows are never active, and response windows are application modal.

Pop-Up Menus

Pop-up menus can be invoked from a MenuItem object or when a user chooses to do some work within a specific work area. Usually pop-up menus are invoked by clicking the right mouse button, just as you would right-click a window or a control in

PowerBuilder. To display a pop-up menu that is already associated with your window, you can simply call the MenuItem directly with the **PopMenu()** function. This function requires you to use the current cursor position or supply the X and Y coordinates yourself. Figure 7.2 illustrates the use of the pop-up menu via the following code in the **RbuttonDown** event:

```
m_frame.m_edit.PopMenu( xpos, ypos )
```

Remember that **xpos** and **ypos** designate the distance of the mouse pointer from the left edge of the window and the top of the window, respectively. If you want to pop up the menu right where your user clicks, use **PointerX()** and **PointerY()** instead of **xpos** and **ypos**.

> **Note:** If your MenuItem is not visible, you must make it visible before using **PopMenu()** on it.

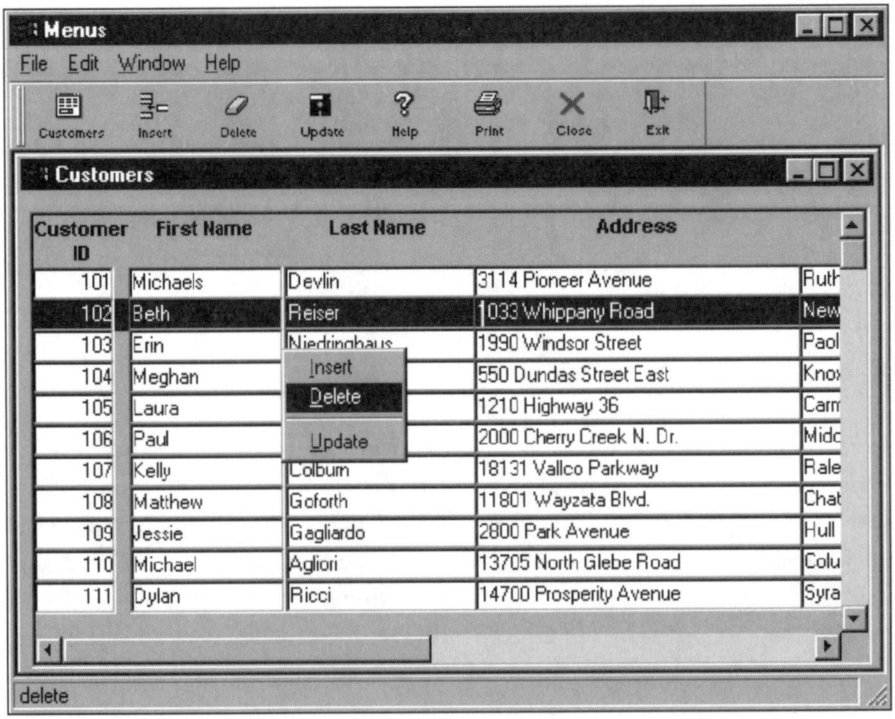

Figure 7.2
An example of a pop-up menu.

Menu Inheritance

Menus can be inherited, thus allowing object methods and properties to be reused. Although inherited menus have some disadvantages, inheritance is the simplest method for implementing and maintaining menus within your application's life cycle.

> **Note:** *Ancestor menus help you to develop applications with a common look and feel. Develop standards to ensure consistency across your applications and apply them to the ancestor objects.*

PowerBuilder's support of inheritance for Menu objects is similar to that of any other object, allowing you to do the following:

- Modify MenuItem objects

- Add new MenuItem objects to the inherited menu

- Add scripts

- Extend and override ancestor scripts

- Declare functions, structures, and variables

PowerBuilder uses the following syntax to show names of inherited Menu objects:

```
ancestorMenu::Menu Object
```

For example, in a menu derived from **m_frame**, you'll see the following for the **m_insert** Menu object:

```
m_frame::m_insert
```

MenuItems in a descendant cannot be inserted between inherited MenuItems. However, their apparent positions can be controlled with the Shift Over\Down property. This property controls where the MenuItems appear when your Menu object is instantiated and made visible. **Over** shifts the item on a menu bar all the way to the right, and **Down** shifts the item all the way to the bottom of a list of items. (See Figure 7.3.)

> **Note:** *The more levels of inheritance used, the longer it takes for the menu to be instantiated due to the extra processing required to establish all the relationships between the various link lists.*

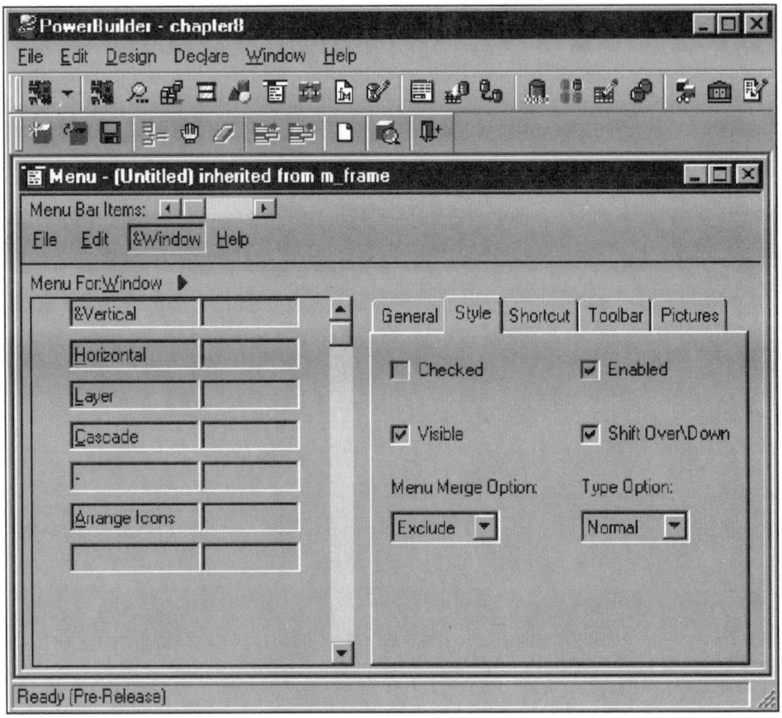

Figure 7.3
The Shift Over\Down property.

Menu Events And Functions

Like windows, menus have events and can have user-defined object functions. The two events associated with a MenuItem object are:

- **Clicked.** Occurs when the left mouse button is released and when both the **Enable** and **Visible** properties of the item are set to True.

- **Selected.** Occurs when the user highlights the MenuItem.

The following script to close a sheet can be in the **Clicked** event of a Close menu item:

```
Window lw_sheet
lw_sheet = ParentWindow.GetActiveSheet()
IF IsValid( lw_sheet ) THEN Close( lw_sheet )
```

Now menus can have object-level functions—for example, enabling or disabling the Close menu item. You can encapsulate this functionality right into the menu itself, as seen here:

```
//function declaration: of_enableClose(boolean switch)
IF  switch THEN
   m_frame.m_file.m_close.Enabled = TRUE
ELSE
   m_frame.m_file.m_print.Enabled = FALSE
END IF
```

Note: Use menus as a means of initiating actions. Route messages to their associated windows to perform specific tasks.

Menus In MDI

When designing your MDI applications, you can set up your menus in two ways: with only one menu and no others in the frame, or with separate menus for each sheet.

Note: In an MDI application, the frame menu can act as the menu for both the frame and the active sheet.

In the first method, you create only one menu, which contains all your needed menu items. As sheets are opened, you'll have to make related menu items optionally visible/invisible or enabled/disabled. Making menu items enabled/disabled is a better method—they will be grayed but still visible. This way, your users can see all the options available in your application. If you're building some sort of security system, this is not a very good method. The second method involves having a separate menu for each sheet. This way, every time a sheet opens, its associated menu replaces the frame menu and becomes visible. You may want to use inheritance if your menu items are repeated across your sheets.

In an MDI application, sheets are opened with the **OpenSheet**() and the **OpenSheetWithParm**() functions. These functions contain a position argument that specifies the number of the MenuItem object to which you want to append the names of the open sheets. Menu bar MenuItems are numbered from the left, beginning with 1. The default value, 0, lists the open sheets under the next-to-last menu item.

If you're going to use several menus in your application, you might as well use a design approach that makes the most sense for your requirements. No single design method optimizes both flexibility and performance, and your design should be chosen carefully. Here are two recommendations for designing menus:

- Use a common ancestor for application frame and sheets

- Use a base menu with extension classes for the frame and sheets

In the first approach, an ancestor menu, being the abstract class, contains all the generic items needed for the frame and the sheets. You then create another menu inherited from the ancestor menu. This menu is the application extension and the extension class. All the menu items that are application-specific and common to both the frame and the sheets, will be added to this layer. You then inherit the frame and sheet menus from the same ancestor and add your sheet-specific menu items. This method uses only three layers of inheritance, but you would have a larger frame.

The second design approach requires four levels of inheritance, but extension levels are totally flexible. You create an ancestor menu with all the items needed for the frame and the sheets: Inherit an ancestor common extension menu from the base menu. Inherit an extension ancestor sheet from the common extension class. Inherit an extension ancestor frame menu from the common extension class. Inherit the application frame menu from the frame menu extension class. Inherit the sheet menus from the sheet menu extension class. The disadvantage of this approach is that the frame will contain invisible items. Figure 7.4 illustrates both methods.

Note: Don't forget the **Visible** property of a window. This property is particularly useful when you're inheriting menus with ToolbarItems but not showing any in the descendant. To get rid of the empty bar, check this property.

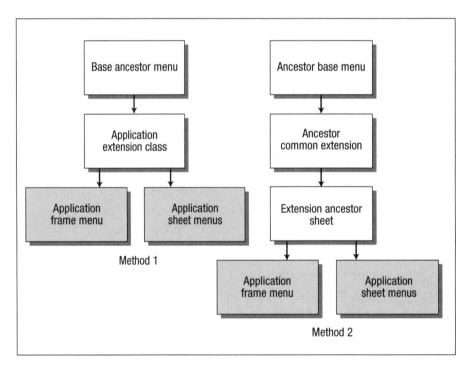

Figure 7.4
Menu design approaches.

Menu Performance Issues

When designing the menus for your application, try to create them in such a way that you never need to alter a MenuItem object to make it visible or invisible. Changing the **Visible** attribute is costly to performance, because PowerBuilder has to destroy the menu completely and then rebuild it. This is a very important issue to bear in mind when designing your menus.

You need to consider some other design issues. Let's go over a few important ones:

- For any window, only show menu items that are applicable to that particular window and no other windows. This way, you don't confuse your users. Also, when it comes to maintenance, you'll thank yourself for avoiding potential problems.

- Keep your ancestor hierarchy short, and minimize the number of your menu items.

- Use the **Enable** property instead of **Visible** whenever possible. As I mentioned earlier, making a menu invisible forces PowerBuilder to rebuild the entire menu. You don't want to do that in a large enterprise application.

- Use ancestor menus to ensure consistency across your applications. This way, your applications have the same look and feel, making them more user friendly.

Moving On

In this chapter, we discussed the PowerBuilder Menu object, which basically is implemented for navigational purposes. With the use of menus and tools such as toolbars and MicroHelp, you can develop an application that is uncomplicated to use and a lot of fun to develop.

Now, as you're building your PowerBuilder applications, you'll often have features you would like to use multiple times. To avoid recoding the same functionality over and over again, why not recycle? You can build a User object, encapsulate all your functionality within that object, and use it as many times as you like within your applications. (Remember, one of the tenets of our OOP religion is reusing objects and components as much as possible.) In the next chapter, I'll discuss this important feature of PowerBuilder.

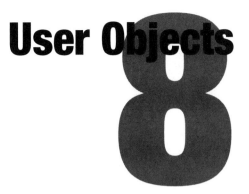

User Objects

PowerBuilder provides you with many mechanisms to create reusable objects and share your code. Some of the objects you need repeatedly in your applications can be developed using a User object, which can then be used as many times as needed. For example, you might want all your DataWindow controls to perform the same type of error checking. Instead of reinventing the wheel each time you use a DataWindow control, you can simply create a DataWindow type of User object that encapsulates all your error checking and then use it throughout your application.

In this chapter, I'll discuss the various types of User objects, the interface between User objects and windows, and dynamic User objects.

User Objects And Object-Oriented Programming

In Chapter 2, "The Technology," I talked about object-oriented programming (OOP) and its architecture. One of the primary objectives of designing object-oriented applications is to build objects that are reusable. Defining behavior once and using it subsequently when needed results in saving development time and maintenance. PowerBuilder's User objects assist in incorporating OOP into your applications.

Inheritance

Using inheritance to build User objects is similar to building a menu or a window. If your application needs many different implementations of **u_ExternalFunctions** for various platforms, an inheritance hierarchy can be established. You can code all your basic functions for all platforms in the ancestor level and then create descendants to perform platform-specific functions.

Remember that when you create a standard visual User object (UO), all the attributes, events, and functionality of the base PowerBuilder classes are inherited. When you're creating a custom visual UO, the events for the UO are predetermined and are *not* inherited from any base PowerBuilder classes.

Polymorphism

Polymorphism is basically the ability of an object to take many different forms. In polymorphism, functions with the same name can behave differently depending on the referenced object. Polymorphism in User objects can be implemented with events and functions. Taking the **u_dw** example (discussed later in the chapter), you could write a script in the **DBError** event and interrupt the database error handling, thus displaying your own error window. Once you've implemented inheritance, this custom error processing is also inherited, extending the error processing to descendant-level events. Polymorphism can also be implemented with functions in the same manner. However, functions cannot be *extended*, they can only be *overridden*. Take a look at Figure 8.1.

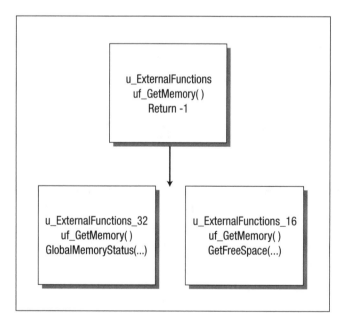

Figure 8.1
Declaring a function in multiple places in a User object hierarchy.

Function **uf_GetMemory**() exists at the base ancestor level. However, it does not contain code and simply *does* nothing. Both the two inherited descendants have the very same function name and signature, but the functions contain different scripts. Once you have instantiated either of the two descendants, upon execution, the function at the ancestor level is ignored, and only the local **uf_GetMemory**() function is executed. Now, if **u_ExternalFunctions_16** did not have the function **uf_GetMemory**() and a call was made to this function, the ancestor's function would be executed.

You can take advantage of this neat technique to build reusable components and minimize the use of scripts written for your objects.

Encapsulation

Encapsulation in PowerBuilder allows you to protect your objects' data, thus restricting access by declaring instance variables as "private" or "protected." You can also write object functions to provide selective access to these instance variables.

One method of encapsulating data is to define instance variables as "public," "private," or "protected," depending on the degree of outside access. If you want to have complete encapsulation, you should define instance variables as either "private" or "protected." You then define functions to perform your processing and provide access to the object's data.

Another method is to have a single entry point in which you can specify actions to be performed. You define instance variables as "private" or "protected." You then define private or protected object functions to perform your processing. Finally, you need a single public function with arguments that indicate the type of processing to be performed.

Types Of User Objects

There are two main types of User objects: visual and class (nonvisual). The *visual* User object type includes standard, custom, and external. The *class* type of User object includes standard, custom, and C++, if you have Class Builder installed. Figure 8.2 illustrates the available PowerBuilder User objects.

Standard Visual User Objects

Standard visual User objects (SVUO) are inherited from the standard PowerBuilder controls; they allow you to extend the definition of the ancestor controls in the User Object Painter. You can extend the class definitions in any of these ways:

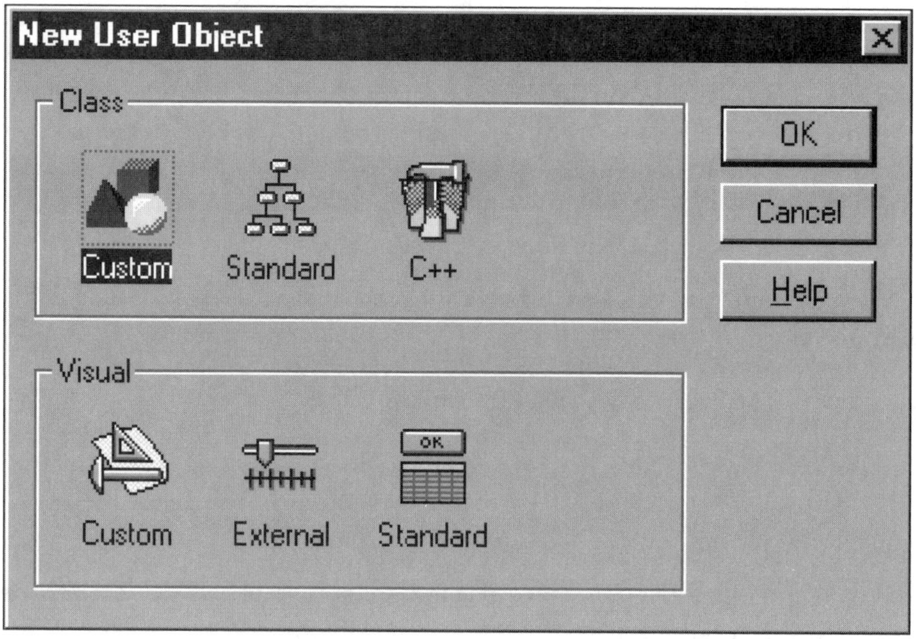

Figure 8.2
Creating a new User object.

- Declare new properties

- Change property settings

- Declare new events

- Code scripts for events

- Declare new object-level functions

- Declare local external functions

Not all controls can be used as ancestors for SVUOs. For example, the descendants of the DrawObject are out of the picture, but any of the following 23 PowerBuilder window controls that are descendants of the DragObject can be subclassed:

- CheckBox
- CommandButton
- DataWindow
- DropDownListBox
- DropDownPictureListBox

- EditMask
- Graph
- HScrollBar
- ListBox
- ListView

- MultiLineEdit
- OLEControl
- Picture
- PictureButton
- PictureListBox
- RadioButton
- RichTextEdit

- SingleLineEdit
- StaticText
- Tab
- TreeView
- User Object
- VScrollBar

Remember that the DragObject is four levels deep in the PowerBuilder system class hierarchy. When you declare an SVUO, such as **u_close**, it becomes a descendant of the CommandButton control, which in turn is a descendant of the DragObject, as shown in Figure 8.3.

Taking this Close CommandButton as an example, let's say that the Close button may be used many times in your application to close a window. Instead of placing a separate CommandButton on every window and coding its **Clicked** event, you can simply create

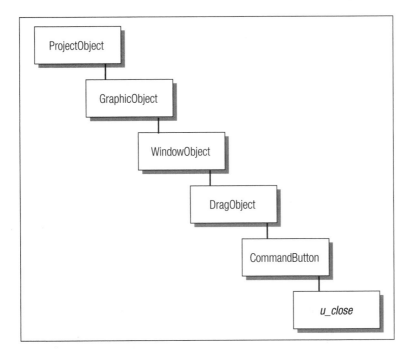

Figure 8.3
DragObject in PowerBuilder system class hierarchy.

a User object and use it instead. For example, if your CommandButton is to close only a window it's placed on, you can use the following code:

```
Close( parent )
```

If your CommandButton is to close only sheets in MDI applications, you can use this code:

```
Window lw_Window
lw_Window = <MDI_frame_Window>.GetActiveSheet( )
IF IsValid( lw_Window ) THEN Close( lw_Window )
```

Now, what happens if you want to build a CommandButton that might be placed on a sheet or a response window or a tab control? This is possible; however, you'll have to know how many levels deep your button is going to be buried and then write your script appropriately, as seen here:

```
Window    lw_parentWindow
//object function to return the parent window
lw_parentWindow = of_GetParentWindow()

IF IsValid(lw_parentWindow) THEN
   Close( lw_parentWindow )
END IF

/*This is code for of_GetParentWindow function. */
PowerObject    lpo_parent
lpo_parent = This.GetParent()

// Loop getting the parent of the object until it is of type Window!
DO WHILE IsValid (lpo_parent)
   IF lpo_parent.TypeOf() <> Window! THEN
      lpo_parent = lpo_parent.GetParent()
   ELSE
      EXIT
   END IF
LOOP

//return the parent window
RETURN lpo_parent
```

Another good use of an SVUO is the DataWindow: You can code generic DataWindow-related functionality, such as drag-and-drop, retrieval, or error checking, and then reuse it throughout your application. To give you an example, let's say you want all your

DataWindows to have their own **DBError** error checking. The **DBError** event has several arguments that can provide you with a more descriptive explanation of what has gone wrong:

- **sqldbcode.** Database-specific error code
- **sqlerrtext.** Database-specific error message
- **sqlsyntax.** The full text of the SQL statement being sent to the DBMS when the error occurred
- **buffer.** The buffer containing the row involved in the database activity that caused the error
- **row.** The number of the row involved in the database activity that caused the error

The **RETURN** code can either be 0 (displays the error message) or 1 (does not display the error message).

First, you must create the structure **str_error** with the following elements defined:

- **sqldbcode.** long
- **sqlerrtext.** string
- **sqlsyntax.** string
- **buffer.** dwbuffer
- **row.** long

You then add the following code in the **DBError** event of your SVUO DataWindow:

```
str_error   ErrorStr

//populate the error structure
ErrorStr.sqldbcode = sqldbcode
ErrorStr.sqlerrtext = sqlerrtext
ErrorStr.sqlsyntax = sqlsyntax
ErrorStr.buffer = buffer
ErrorStr.row = row

//open the error Window
OpenWithParm ( w_error , ErrorStr )

//do not display the error message
RETURN 1
```

The following script goes in the **Open** event of a response window acting as your user-defined error display window:

```
//Open Event
str_error ErrorStr

//structure passed, in the Message object
ErrorStr = Message.PowerObjectParm

//display error message in a user-defined response window
sle_buffer.text = String( ErrorStr.buffer )
sle_row.text    = String( ErrorStr.row )
sle_code.text   = String( ErrorStr.sqldbcode )
mle_sqlsyntax.text = ErrorStr.sqlsyntax
mle_errtext.text   = ErrorStr.sqlerrtext
```

Custom Visual User Objects

A *custom visual User object (CVUO)* is an encapsulated single object that consists of one or more controls. If you find yourself frequently grouping controls in a window and using them to perform the same task many times, a CVUO is what you should be using.

> **Note:** When an object is encapsulated in an interface, it's called a component.

Previously, you learned that an SVUO consists of one control with associated scripts and that it inherits its definition from a standard control. A CVUO, on the other hand, consists of many controls and scripts that function as a unit—and a CVUO does not inherit its definition from a standard control. The inheritance hierarchy tree of a CVUO is also different from that of an SVUO. All new custom visuals are inherited from the PowerBuilder system class **UserObject**. Therefore, if you were to create **u_login**, its hierarchy would look like Figure 8.4.

> **Note:** The total number of controls in a CVUO is the number of standard controls on this object, plus an additional one for the custom object itself.

A CVUO also has a set of predefined events associated with it that you can use. These events are listed in Table 8.1.

The process of instantiating a CVUO with embedded controls is very much the same as instantiating a window control. For each control in a CVUO, the following occurs:

- A reference variable is declared.

- An instance of the control is created with the CVUO.

- The instances of the controls are destroyed when the CVUO is destroyed.

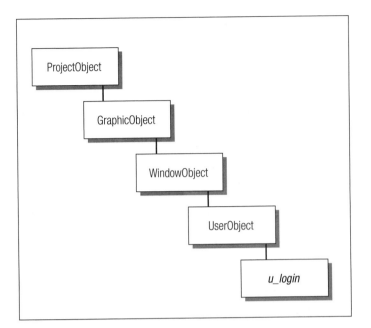

Figure 8.4.
Inheritance hierarchy tree for a CVUO.

Table 8.1   Predefined events for custom visual User objects.

Event	Description
Constructor	Occurs when the object is created, just before the **Open** event for the window that contains the control
Destructor	Occurs when the object is destroyed, immediately after the **Close** event of the window
DragDrop	Occurs when an object is dropped on this object
DragEnter	Occurs when an object is dragged into this object
DragLeave	Occurs when an object is dragged out of this object
DragWithin	Occurs when an object is dragged within this object
Other	Occurs when an event other than a PowerBuilder event occurs
RbuttonDown	Occurs when the right mouse button is pressed

To reference a control in a CVUO, use dot notation. For example, to reference **cb_close** in **u_toolbars**, use this code:

```
u_toobars.cb_close
```

Personally, I don't like to use too many CVUOs unless I have to group a few controls together and use them repeatedly in my applications. An appropriate use for a CVUO, as shown in Figure 8.5, is for creating a custom VCR toolbar to handle DataWindow scrolling.

Let's go through this example together. First, you create your CVUO with all your controls. This UO has encapsulated functionality to scroll the rows and pages of any DataWindow bound to it. You create two instance variables on this UO. The first variable is the instance pointing to the bound DataWindow, and the second specifies row or page scrolling:

```
DataWindow idw_scroll
Boolean ib_row
```

The **Constructor** event of **rb_row** needs to be coded to set **ib_row** to True when checked:

```
IF This.Checked THEN ib_row = TRUE
```

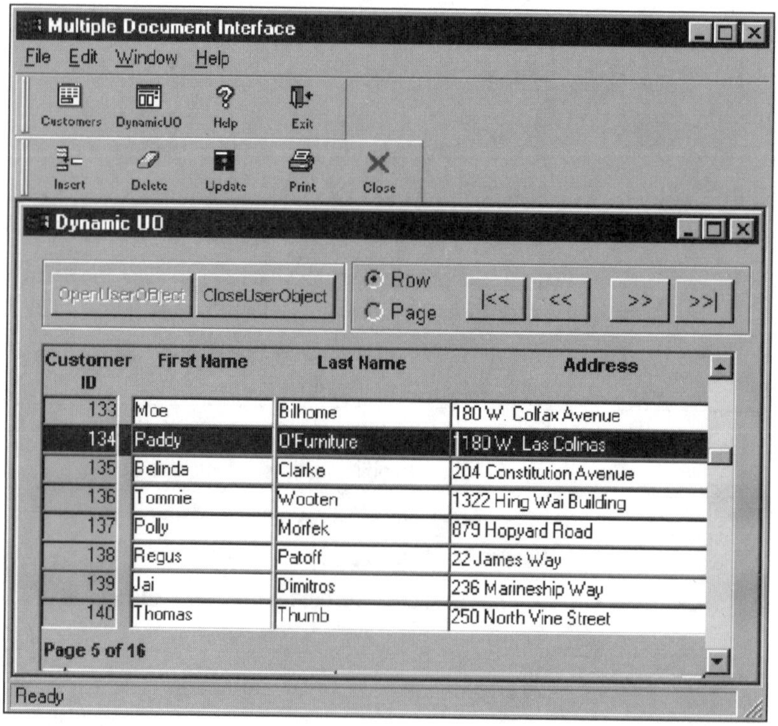

Figure 8.5

A VCR custom visual User object.

You also need to set the **ib_row** to True when it's clicked:

```
ib_row = TRUE
```

Similarly, you need to do the same for **rb_page**:

```
//Constructor event
IF This.Checked THEN ib_row = FALSE
//Clicked event
ib_row = FALSE
```

The next task is to code the UO-level functions to perform scrolling:

```
Private function uf_ScrollNext()
/*check our Boolean variable to determine scrolltype */
IF ib_row THEN
    //next row
    idw_scroll.ScrollNextRow( )
ELSE
    //next page
    idw_scroll.ScrollNextpage( )
END IF

Private function uf_ScrollPrior()
/*check our Boolean variable to determine scroll type */
IF ib_row THEN
    //prior row
    idw_scroll.ScrollPriorRow( )
ELSE
    //prior page
    idw_scroll.ScrollPriorpage( )
END IF

Private function uf_goFirst()
/*check our Boolean variable to determine scroll type */
IF ib_row THEN
    //first row
    idw_scroll.ScrollToRow( 1 )
ELSE
    //first page
    idw_scroll.ScrollToRow( 1 )
END IF

Private function uf_golast()
long ll_page, ll_currentpage, ll_counter
string ls_currentrow, ls_currentpage
```

```
//get the page count
ll_page = Long(idw_scroll.Describe &
    ("Evaluate('PageCount()',0)"))

IF ib_row THEN
    //go to last row
    idw_scroll.ScrollToRow(idw_scroll.RowCount())
ELSE
    //go to last page
    ls_currentrow=idw_scroll.Object.DataWindow.FirstRowOnPage
    ls_currentpage=idw_scroll.describe &
        ("Evaluate('Page()'," + ls_currentrow+")")
    ll_currentpage=Integer(ls_currentpage)
    idw_scroll.SetReDraw( FALSE )
    IF ll_page > ll_currentpage THEN
        FOR ll_counter = 1 TO  ll_page - 1 //ll_currentpage
            idw_scroll.ScrollNextPage()
        NEXT
    ELSEIF ll_page < ll_currentpage THEN
        FOR ll_counter = 1 TO  ll_currentpage - 1 //ll_page
            idw_scroll.ScrollPriorPage()
        NEXT
    END IF
    idw_scroll.SetReDraw( TRUE )
END IF
```

Finally, you need a function that binds your DataWindow to this UO—public function **uf_scrollInit()**, which takes an argument of type DataWindow by reference:

```
idw_scroll = idw_passed
```

Based on the selected radio button, these functions scroll to the next/prior row or page and also jump directly to the first/last row or page. One thing that you have to do in your calling object is to register your DataWindow with the UO, and that's done with the following script:

```
u_scrollbar.uf_scrollInit( dw_customer )
```

Dynamic Visual User Objects

When placing visual User objects on a window, the Window Painter is used. Both standard and custom visual User objects can also be dynamically created at runtime. This is particularly useful when the number of controls needed for the window is not known until runtime. Now, instead of adding a lot of unnecessary controls to your windows, you can instantiate them as needed, thus saving resources.

Earlier, you learned that **CREATE** instantiates a nonvisual User object. For visual User objects, you must use the **OpenUserObject()** and **OpenUserObjectWithParm()** functions. Here's an example of the syntax:

```
<WindowName>.OpenUserObject(UOvar {, x, y } )
<WindowName>.OpenUserObjectWithParm(UOvar, parameter {, x, y } )
```

Here's another syntax example:

```
<WindowName>.OpenUserObject( UOvar, UOtype {, x, y } )
<WindowName.OpenUserObjectWithParm(UOvar,parameter,UOtype {, x, y } )
```

The following example creates an instance of the class **u_dw**, which associates a DataObject with it and then populates that DataObject:

```
//declare a variable of appropriate type
u_dw iu_dw
This.OpenUserObject( iu_dw, 10, 100 )
iu_dw.DataObject = "d_customer"
iu_dw.SetTransObject( )
iu_dw.Retrieve( )
```

Here's a second method, which opens a User object when the data type of the UO is not known until execution:

```
DataWindow iu_dw //could also be DragObject
This.OpenUserObject( iu_dw, "u_dw", 10, 100 )
iu_dw.DataObject = "d_customer"
iu_dw.SetTransObject( )
iu_dw.Retrieve( )
```

The following example passes a numeric parameter, **li_custID**, to the User object **u_dw** (used earlier):

```
DataWindow iu_dw
Integer li_custID
This.OpenUserObjectWithParm(iu_dw, li_custID, &
   "u_dw", 10, 100)
```

The parameter **li_custID** will be stored in **Message.DoubleParm**.

Because PowerBuilder does not destroy a dynamically created User object, it is your responsibility to do so. Here's an example that shows you how:

```
CloseUserObject( iu_dw )
```

*Note: When using the second syntax, keep in mind that the object specified in **UOtype** is not automatically included in your EXE. To include it, you must save it in a PBD file.*

External Visual User Objects

The last type of visual User object is the *external visual User object (EVUO)*. The EVUO allows you to write your own custom control DLL to be used as an external User object or to use DLLs that have been written by third-party vendors. One way of measuring a software's success is by counting the number of third-party vendors that write libraries and software add-ons. PowerBuilder has a long list of partners and nonpartners that are constantly coming up with new add-ons for PowerBuilder. One example is Blaise Computing, Inc., developers of CPALETTE.DLL. This DLL has a number of different class objects that can be declared as PowerBuilder EVUOs. I won't go into too much detail on EVUOs because I think for the most part you should be using an OCX/ActiveX instead of EVUOs.

Standard Class

PowerBuilder includes many nonvisual objects as part of the system class hierarchy. These are classes that do not have visual components and are not visible to your users. All nonvisual User objects are inherited from the PowerBuilder System class **NonVisualObject**. The transaction object is a very good example of a nonvisual User object that is used in every application but has no visible representation. The standard class User object allows you to build nonvisual User objects of the PowerBuilder nonvisual classes and to customize them to your requirements. With this functionality available to you, you can add extra variables to the Message object, or you can track additional error information in the Error object. Here's a list of the classes available to you:

- Connection
- ContextInformation
- ContextKeyword
- DataStore
- DynamicDescriptionArea
- DynamicStagingArea
- Error
- Inet
- InternetResult

- MailSession
- Message
- OleObject
- OleStorage
- OleStream
- Pipeline
- Service
- Transaction
- Transport

One of my favorite Standard classes is **Transaction**, because I can add all my RPC, stored procedure, and ODBC API calls to it. This topic is discussed further in Chapter 15, "Transaction Object." However, to give you a quick example, let's say you want to encapsulate an ODBC API call in your transaction object. Here's what you need to do:

1. Select New in the User Object Painter.

2. Select Standard and then select Transaction from the list.

3. Declare a local external function call:

```
Function Int SQLGetInfo(ulong hdbc, uint infooption, ref string infostr, &
    int maxlen, ref int ilength)  Library "odbc32.dll"
```

4. Declare the User object function **uf_GetDriverVersion**(), which returns a string:

```
//function script
ulong   lul_hDB
uint lui_infotype
int li_value, li_maxlen, li_strlen, li_retcode
string ls_info

//get the current handle of the transaction object
lul_hDB = DBHandle( SQLCA )
//SQL_DRIVER_VER, defined in sqltext.h
lui_infotype = 7

ls_info = space(10)
//local external function to ODBC32.DLL
li_retcode = SQLGetInfo(lul_hDB, lui_infotype, &
    ls_info, Len(ls_info), li_strlen)

IF li_retcode >= 0 THEN
    return ls_info
ELSE
    RETURN ""
END IF
```

5. Finally, you can call your UO function from anywhere within your application:

```
String ls_version
ls_version = SQLCA.uf_GetDriverVersion()
```

Well, I've left something out. Can you guess what it is? You have to replace the current Transaction object with your own SCUO **u_transaction** first. This is done in the Application

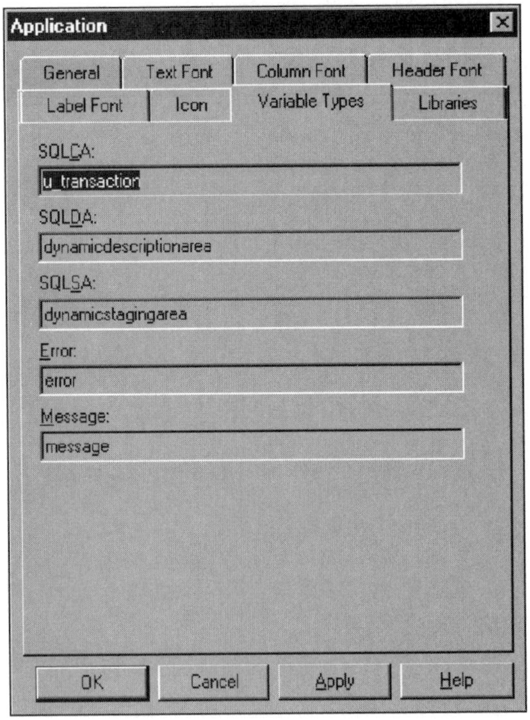

Figure 8.6
Changing PowerBuilder default global variables.

object by selecting the Entry|Properties menu item and then selecting the Variable Types tab page, as shown in Figure 8.6.

Now, if you need several instances of your nonvisual, you have to *instantiate* them. All non-visual objects in PowerBuilder are instantiated using the **CREATE** statement; to remove instances of your nonvisuals, you must use the **DESTROY** statement. Here's an example:

```
Transaction itrans_sybase
Itrans_sybase = CREATE Transaction
...
DESTROY itrans_sybase
```

> *Note: Every **CREATE** must have a **DESTROY**, or else you'll be leaking!*

Custom Class User Objects

A *custom class User object (CCUO)*, better known as a *nonvisual object (NVO)*, is an object used to encapsulate behaviors independent of the user interface. NVOs are similar to classes in lower-level object-oriented languages that perform processes. NVOs have many uses—here are some of the most popular ones:

- Providing services to extend the functionality of other classes

- Encapsulating business rules

- Implementing multiple inheritance

You've learned that when a nonvisual object has been created, it must be instantiated in order to be used. NVOs can be instantiated in one of many ways. For example, this first method declares a variable and creates the NVO into that variable:

```
Ulong lul_mem
NonVisualObject lu_func
lu_func = CREATE  u_externalfunctions_32
lul_mem = lu_func.uf_GetFreeMemory()
DESTROY lu_func
```

This second method creates the NVO onto itself:

```
Ulong lul_mem
u_externalfunctions_32 = CREATE u_externalfunctions_32
lul_mem = u_externalfunctions_32. uf_GetFreeMemory()
DESTROY u_externalfunctions_32
```

Another method is to set the **AutoInstantiate** property of the NVO. By using this method, the NVO is created before the first time it is called and destroyed automatically by PowerBuilder.

The following method passes a class name as a string or the value of a string to the **CREATE** statement. This is particularly useful when the class name is unknown until execution time or when generic code needs to be instantiated without changing ancestor logic. In the following example, **u_externalfunctions_win16** and **u_externalfunctions_win32** are descendants of **u_ExternalFunctions**, and they need to be instantiated based on the correct environment:

```
string ls_userobject
//this is the ancestor UO
u_externalfunctions luo_extfunc
Environment le_env
long ll_memory
//get environment
GetEnvironment( le_env )

/*
If 16bit, instantiate the UO that makes 16bit calls, and if 32bit,
```

```
     instantiate the UO that makes 32bit calls. */
IF le_env.Win16 = TRUE THEN
    ls_userobject = "u_externalfunctions_win16"
ELSE
    ls_userobject = "u_externalfunctions_win32"
END IF

//create using the class name
luo_extfunc = CREATE USING ls_userobject

ll_Mem = luo_extfunc.uf_GetFreeMemory()
DESTROY luo_extfunc
```

This last method demonstrates a really neat use of NVOs. Let's say your application makes many API calls and you want to deploy to both Win16 and Win32 environments. You can simply have two NVOs—one for the 16-bit world and the other for the 32-bit environment.

Now, let's say you have an application that uses OLE automation for Microsoft Word. However, some of your clients are using Word 95 and others are using Word 97. As you probably know, Microsoft has changed the Word.Basic macro language in Word 97 to VBA. Although Word 97 is supposed to be backward-compatible, some commands may perform slowly or even not work at all. To work around this problem, you can have two NVOs—one that uses Word.Basic for Word 95 and the other that uses VBA for Word 97. The following code queries the Registry to find out what the version of Word is and then instantiates the correct NVO:

```
Integer li_rc
String ls_wordver, ls_RegistryGet, ls_word

/*Search the Registry for the version of Word installed.*/
ls_RegistryGet = &
"HKEY_CLASSES_ROOT\Word.Document\CurVer"
li_rc = RegistryGet( ls_RegistryGet, "", ls_wordver)

CHOOSE CASE ls_wordver
    //office 95
    CASE "Word.Document.6"
        ls_word = "u_office95"
    //office 97
    CASE "Word.Document.8"
        ls_word = "u_office97"
    CASE ELSE
        ls_word = ""
END CHOOSE
```

```
IF ls_word = "" THEN MessageBox("Error", "Cannot find Microsoft Word!")

/*
Now instantiate the correct NVO for your OLE automation purposes.
And don't forget the DESTROY command!
*/
```

Controlling Access To Instance Variables

To gain control over how other objects' scripts access your instance variables, use instance variable *access rights*. In your application, you can specify whether a variable is:

- **Public.** Accessible to any other object

- **Protected.** Accessible only in scripts for the object and its descendants

- **Private.** Accessible in scripts for that object only

You can further qualify access to public and protected variables with the following so-called modifiers:

- **PrivateRead**

- **PrivateWrite**

- **ProtectedRead**

- **ProtectedWrite**

For example, you can use the following code:

```
Private integer ii_custID
Public PrivateWrite ii_deptID
protected PrivateWrite string is_fname
```

Note that private variables allow you to encapsulate your object's functionality. This is a very good object-oriented technique—it enables an object's data and code to be part of the object itself. The object determines the interface it should represent to other objects.

C++ Class

If you were a C++ developer in the past and wish you could do things in PowerBuilder like you used to in the old days, this class is for you. The C++ ClassBuilder, based on the Watcom compiler, allows you to compile PowerScript UO functions into a Windows DLL from PowerBuilder. With ClassBuilder, you can create UO functions and variables with PowerBuilder, generate the corresponding C++ classes and code, and then do the actual function logic writing in C++. If you need to learn more about DLLs, please refer to Chapter 17, "External Functions."

If you've never used the C++ ClassBuilder, I recommend going through the "getting started" manual, which provides an excellent tutorial.

I'm not going to get into too much detail on ClassBuilder. Setting it up can sometimes be tricky, so hopefully the following information will shed some light if you're having configuration problems. Most of the problems encountered while trying to run ClassBuilder are environment related. Here's a checklist to go through in case of problems:

- Ensure that the settings of the environment variables in your AUTOEXEC.BAT or the PowerBuilder app path in the Registry are correct. Under Windows NT, the following Registry key is checked:

    HKEY_LOCAL_MACHINE/Software/Microsoft/Windows/CurrentVersion/App Paths/PB050.EXE

- Double-click PB050.EXE and confirm that you have the following strings:

    - **Value name.** Value data

    - **Path.** C:\pwrs\wantcnt\binnt;pwrs\watcnt\binw;C:\pwrs\sys32

    - **Edpath.** C:\pwrs\watcnt\eddat

    - **Include.** C:\pwrs\watcnt\h;c:\pwrs\watcnt\h\nt

    - **Watcom.** C:\pwrs\watcnt

- If you're a Windows 95 user, add these strings to your AUTOEXEC.BAT by using **SET** commands. ClassBuilder also requires temporary storage for file placements. Be sure you have both TEMP and TMP set to a temporary directory.

Business Rules

NVOs are most useful in separating business rules from the user interface logic. Your front-end application should be making calls to different business object NVOs to perform various business tasks. For example, a law firm may have a generic contract document, a wills document, and a real estate document inherited from the generic contract document. These NVOs are to be kept separate from the user and only used when needed. To give you another example, let's use the PowerBuilder demo database layout. In order for an employee to sell a product, that product must exist in the Product table and have a quantity greater than 0. In this case, you could simply create an NVO that invokes this validation rule as needed.

Moving On

In Chapter 2, you learned that distributed processing offers a natural way to separate user interface components from the business logic required by your applications. PowerBuilder gives you the ability to build applications that run in a distributed computing environment, but the only objects that can take full advantage of distributed environments are nonvisual User objects. In this chapter, you've discovered how User objects allow you to encapsulate specific functionality into reusable components that can be plugged into your programs as needed, making them more powerful and robust. In the applications you build, you should use NVOs and implement object-oriented techniques into them as much as possible. You'll definitely thank yourself when it comes to maintenance and reusability.

Next, we move on to drag-and-drop, a feature that can enhance your application's graphical interface.

Drag-And-Drop

Drag-and-drop is a type of graphical interface feature that makes your applications more intuitive and user friendly. In the old days, the most widely used method for transferring data between controls was the Clipboard. With the Clipboard method, your users had to use Copy in the source object, move to the target, and then use Paste to place the data in the target object. This worked fine, but a quicker, more natural way is to exchange data simply by clicking on the source and dragging it to the target.

There are two ways to use drag-and-drop:

- **Interobject dragging.** Objects within objects can be dragged out of their containers to other windows or objects.

- **Dragging over icons.** Objects can be dragged over to a resource icon such as a printer.

In this chapter, I'll introduce you to PowerBuilder's drag-and-drop feature. I'll first cover the drag-and-drop properties and the available functions. Then, to help you understand drag-and-drop even better, we'll go through an example together.

Drag-And-Drop In PowerBuilder

Drag-and-drop in PowerBuilder involves at least two controls: the *drag control* that is being dragged, and the *drag target* (the drop zone). In PowerBuilder, all controls except for the drawing objects can be dragged. When a control is being dragged, it is in Drag mode. You can define a control so that PowerBuilder puts it automatically in Drag mode whenever a **Clicked** event occurs on that control. You can also write a script to put a control into Drag mode when a specific event occurs on your window or application. You can associate an icon with your control when in **Drag** mode, and this can be done statically at design time or at runtime. This icon will appear when a control is dragged over a valid drop target.

In PowerBuilder, all objects and all controls, except for the drawing objects, have events that occur when they are drag targets. When a dragged control is within the target or dropped on a target, these events are fired.

Drag-And-Drop Properties

The drag-and-drop properties of a control allow you to define a *drag icon*. A drag icon can be selected from a number of predefined icons, or you can specify your own customized icon. The drag icon is displayed when the control goes into Drag mode while being dragged.

Another control property is Drag Auto. When you select Drag Auto, PowerBuilder puts the control into Drag mode automatically when your user clicks the control.

> **Note:** Clicking the control while it is in Drag Auto mode triggers the **DragDrop** event, not the **Clicked** event.

By default, Drag mode is disabled, and you have to call the **Drag** function to put your control manually into Drag mode. Figure 9.1 shows the drag-and-drop property sheet for a control, where you can select Drag Auto or assign a drag icon to your control.

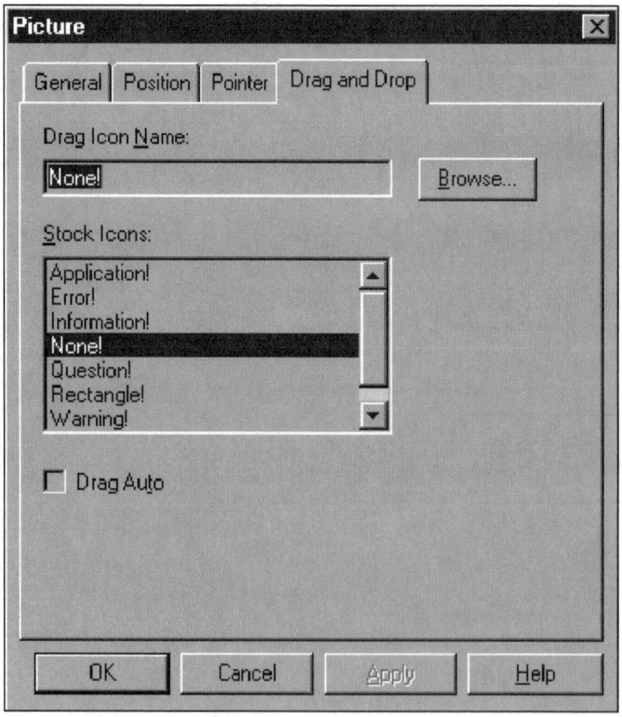

Figure 9.1
Drag-and-drop properties of a control.

*Note: When Drag Auto is enabled for any of the graphic controls, the **Clicked** event for that control is disabled. If you've coded your **Clicked** event, you must think of another way to place your control in Drag mode, such as mapping a user event to **pbm_lbuttondown**.*

Drag-And-Drop Events

Table 9.1 lists the standard drag-and-drop events that you get with most controls. The **BeginDrag** and **BeginRightDrag** events apply to ListViews and TreeViews only.

Drag-And-Drop Functions

Three functions are used in PowerBuilder in relation to drag-and-drop: **Drag()**, **DraggedObject()**, and **TypeOf()**, all of which are discussed next.

Drag()

The **Drag()** function starts or ends the dragging of a control. This function applies to all controls except for the drawing controls. Here's the syntax used:

```
Object.Drag(dragmode)
```

Object is the name of the control that you want to place in Drag mode. *Dragmode* is a value of the **DragMode** data type indicating the action you want to take on your control. Here are the valid actions:

- **Begin!** Puts the control in Drag mode

Table 9.1   Drag-and-drop events.

Event	Description
BeginDrag	Occurs when your user presses the left mouse button in a ListView or TreeView control and begins dragging.
BeginRightDrag	Occurs when your user presses the right mouse button in a ListView or TreeView control and begins dragging.
DragDrop	Occurs when the hot spot of a Drag icon is over a target and the mouse button is released.
DragEnter	Occurs when the hot spot of a drag icon enters the boundaries of a target.
DragLeave	Occurs when the hot spot of a drag icon leaves the boundaries of a target.
DragWithin	Occurs when the hot spot of a drag icon is moved within the boundaries of a target.

- **Cancel!** Stops dragging the control but does not cause a **DragDrop** event

- **End!** Stops dragging the control and, if your control is over a target object, causes a **DragDrop** event

DraggedObject()

The **DraggedObject()** function returns a reference to the control that triggered a **Drag** event. The return data type from **DraggedObject()** is a special data type called **DragObject** that includes all controls that can be dragged.

TypeOf()

The **TypeOf()** function is a general function that can be applied to any object to determine the type of that object or control. The return data type is an object enumerated data type.

Identifying The Dragged Control

The **DragDrop** event has an argument source whose type is **DragObject**. This argument allows you to identify the type of dragged object by using the **TypeOf()** function. Here's an example:

```
//DragDrop event of a picture control
CHOOSE CASE TypeOf( Source )
    CASE DataWindow!
        MessageBox( "dragdrop", "DataWindow" )
    CASE SingleLineEdit!
        MessageBox( "dragdrop", "SingleLineEdit" )
    CASE StaticText!
        MessageBox( "dragdrop", "StaticText" )
    CASE ELSE
        MessageBox( "dragdrop", "Invalid control was dragged!" )
END CHOOSE
```

The following code, located in the **Clicked** event of a DataWindow, places the DataWindow in Drag mode and assigns a drag icon to it:

```
This.Drag( Begin! )
This.DragIcon = "Row.ico"
```

This code, located in the **DragDrop** event of DataWindow **dw_sales**, retrieves sales orders for a specific customer ID that has been dragged over from **dw_customer**:

```
long ll_row
integer li_sales
```

```
//get currentrow of dw_customer, then the sales order number
ll_row = dw_customer.GetRow()
li_sales = dw_customer.Object.Data[ll_row, 1]

This.Retrieve( li_sales )
This.Object.st_title.Text = "Customer ID: " &
   + String( li_sales )
```

Now, if you want to delete rows dragged over to a PictureButton from one particular DataWindow, you must identify that DataWindow by using the **ClassName**() function. Here's an example:

```
string ls_name
long ll_custid
//determine the type of source
IF TypeOf( source ) = DataWindow! THEN
  //get its name
  ls_name = source.ClassName ()
  IF ls_name = "dw_customer" THEN
     ll_custid = dw_customer.object.id[dw_customer.getrow()]
     IF MessageBox( "Delete", "Delete customer: " +  &
     String( ll_custid), Exclamation!, OKCancel!, 2  ) = 1 THEN
     //delete from desired DataWindow
     dw_customer.DeleteRow( dw_customer.GetRow() )
   END IF
  END IF
END IF
```

Drag-and-drop events on a DataWindow have additional parameters you can use:

- **Source.** The dragged object.

- **Row.** The number of the row the pointer was over when the user dropped the object. If the pointer wasn't over a row, the value of the row argument is 0. For example, the row is 0 when the pointer is outside the data area, in text or spaces between rows, or in the header, summary, or footer area.

- **Dwo.** A reference to the object under the pointer within the DataWindow when the user dropped the object.

The following example for the **DragDrop** event for a DataWindow checks whether the source object is a DataWindow control and then finds the current row in the source and moves it over to the target:

```
DataWindow ldw_source
```

```
IF source.TypeOf() = DataWindow! THEN
   ldw_source = source
   IF row > 0 THEN
      ldw_source.RowsMove( row, row, Primary!, &
         This, 1, Primary!)
   END IF
END IF
```

Moving On

The drag-and-drop feature allows your users to initiate various activities by dragging a control and dropping it on another control. It's a simple way to make your applications highly graphical as well as easy to use. As you can see, drag-and-drop is really not that difficult to implement, and you can get as creative as you like.

In the next chapter, we'll explore printing. Most business applications developed these days produce reports, and these reports have to be printed at some point. PowerBuilder provides several print methods that I'll discuss in the next chapter.

Printing

Because most applications written these days are business related, the ability to print data in the form of reports, graphs, and so on, is now an important part of your applications. In this chapter, I'll cover some of the things you need to know about printing from PowerBuilder.

The Basics

In the Windows environment, your applications do not talk directly to the printer. These applications first obtain information such as the printer model, device driver, and printer port from the operating system. This information is used to create a device context for the current printer. When you issue a print command, the output is sent to the device context, and, in turn, Windows activates the print spooler to manage the print job.

In the old days, applications used printer escape sequences to communicate with the printer's device driver. Today, current Windows applications, including PowerBuilder, interface only with the standard print interface during printing. This interface then communicates with the printer driver to translate the printer commands and thus print your data.

In PowerBuilder, all printing is defined in terms of the *print area*. The print area is the physical page size less any margins. For example, if a page size is 8.5 inches by 11 inches, and the top, bottom, and side margins are all half an inch, the print area is 7.5 inches by 10 inches. Also, all measurements in the print area are in thousands of an inch. For example, if you have a print area of 7.5 inches by 10, then:

- The lower-left corner is 0,0
- The lower-right corner is 0,7500

- The upper-left corner is 0,10000

- The upper-right corner is 7500,10000

When printing, PowerBuilder uses a *print cursor* to keep track of the print location. The print cursor stores the coordinates of the upper-left corner of the location at which printing will occur. PowerBuilder updates the print cursor after each print command, except for specific functions such as **PrintBitMap()**, **PrintLine()**, **PrintRectangle()**, and **PrintRoundRect()**.

Printing Functions

PowerBuilder provides you with many functions that enable you to print your objects. These functions are listed in Table 10.1.

Table 10.1   Print functions.

Function	Definition
Print()	Prints a string in the current font.
PrintBitmap()	Prints a bitmap image at a specified location in the print area.
PrintCancel()	Cancels printing.
PrintClose()	Closes the print job and sends the page to the printer.
PrintDataWindow()	Prints a DataWindow with other DataWindows in a print job.
PrintDefineFont()	Defines a font for the print job. PowerBuilder supports eight fonts for each print job.
PrintLine()	Prints a line of a specified thickness at a specified location.
PrintOpen()	Starts the print job and assigns it a print job number.
PrintOval()	Prints an oval (or circle) with a specified line thickness at a specified location.
PrintPage()	Sends the current page to the printer and sets up a new blank page.
PrintRect()	Prints a rectangle with a specified line thickness at a specified location.
PrintRoundRect()	Prints a round rectangle with a specified line thickness at a specified location.
PrintScreen()	Prints the screen image as part of a print job.

(continued)

Table 10.1   Print functions *(continued).*

Function	Definition
PrintSend()	Sends a specified string directly to the printer.
PrintSetFont()	Sets the current print job font to one of the defined fonts.
PrintSetSpacing()	Sets the spacing factor that will be used to determine the space between lines.
PrintSetup()	Calls the Printer Setup dialog box for the printer driver.
PrintText()	Prints specified text at a specified location.
PrintWidth()	Returns the width (in 1/1000s of an inch) of the specified string in the current font.
PrintX()	Returns the X coordinate of the cursor.
PrintY()	Returns the Y coordinate of the cursor.

Before giving you a few simple examples, let me first say that PowerBuilder manages print jobs by opening a job, sending the data, and then closing the job. When you use a simple **Print()** function, print job management is done automatically for you. Here's an example of this:

```
//print the customer DataWindow
dw_customer.Print( )
```

The **Print()** function also has a Boolean argument value that controls whether or not you want to display a nonmodal dialog box that allows your users to cancel printing. An example of this is shown here:

```
//print the customer DataWindow, allow cancel
dw_customer.Print( TRUE )
```

> **Note:** The **Print()** function for DataWindow controls or DataStores triggers a **PrintStart** event just before any data is sent to the printer or spooler. Next, it triggers a **PrintPage** event for each page break and, finally, a **PrintEnd** event when printing is completed. The **PrintPage** event has return codes that let you control the printing of that particular page. For example, you can skip the printing of the upcoming page by returning a value of 1 in the **PrintPage** event.

Now, if you want to print a visual object other than a single DataWindow, you have to manage the print job manually. This is done by using a job number that the **PrintOpen()** function returns to identify the print job in all subsequent print functions.

*Note: Make sure you have defined the job as a Long or else **Print()** may hang your system.*

You then issue all your print commands. Finally, you send your output to the printer and close the print job. This is done by issuing a **PrintClose()**. Note that a new print job always begins on a new page, the font used is set to the default font of the printer, and the print cursor is at the upper-left corner of the print area. Depending on the printer, you may be able to change margins using **PrintSend()** and printer-defined escape sequences.

The following example opens a print job and sends an escape sequence to an HP LaserJet printer to change the left margins to 20:

```
long Job
Job = PrintOpen( )
//Send a escape sequence to set left margins to 20
PrintSend(Job,"~027~038~09720~076")
PrintDataWindow( job, dw_customer )
PrintClose(Job)
```

Note: Refer to your printer's documentation for more on escape sequences.

The printed output uses the same fonts and layout that appear on screen for the visual object. Line spacing in PowerBuilder is proportional to character height. The default line spacing is 1.2 times the character height. When **Print()** starts a new line, it sets the X coordinate of the cursor to 0 and increases the Y coordinate by the current line spacing. You can change the line spacing with the **PrintSetSpacing()** function, which lets you specify a new factor to be multiplied by the character height. Here's an example:

```
long Job
Job = PrintOpen( )
// Set the spacing factor to 1 and a half.
PrintSetSpacing(Job, 1.5)
```

The following example opens a print job that defines a new page and then prints a title. A graph on the first page is printed and, finally, the actual window on the second page is sent to the print job:

```
long Job
//obtain a print job
Job = PrintOpen( )
//send a title to the print job
Print(Job, "Customer Report")
gr_customer.Print(Job, 1000,PrintY(Job)+500,6000,4500)
//print a page
```

```
PrintPage(Job)
//print the customer window
w_customer.Print(Job, 1000,500, 6000,4500)
//close the print job and print the job
PrintClose(Job)
```

Printer Setup

Good application design dictates that you should give your users the ability to call the Print Setup dialog box provided by the system printer driver to let them change their printers or specify settings for their printers. In PowerBuilder, this is achieved by calling the **PrinterSetup()** function. Note that under Windows NT and 95, the settings that the user sets only have effect for the duration of the application. After the application is terminated, printer settings revert to their previous values. In Win16, these settings become the new settings for the printer driver and affect subsequent print jobs for all applications.

Changing Printers Dynamically

Sometimes you may need to print a specific DataWindow or a report to a different printer than your current printer. Currently, the only way to change your default printer in your applications is to use the **PrintSetup()** function and pop up a dialog box to let your users change printers. In the Win16 environment, this task is achieved by changing the WIN.INI settings. A **SetProfileString()** command and a **Send()** command are used to change the printer and when the print job is completed, another **SetProfileString()** command and a **Send()** command are needed to reset the printer back to what it was before the change. However, in Win32 (Windows NT, for example), this is another story. You have to use a Windows SDK command to set the INI in the Registry and then notify the operating system of the change.

The following example illustrates how the default printer can be changed programmatically via SDK commands in PowerBuilder. The SDK functions used are **GetProfile StringA()** to get the name of the default printer and **WriteProfileStringA()** to change the default printer:

```
//local external functions
FUNCTION boolean WriteProfileStringA(string section,string &
    key, string newprinter) LIBRARY "kernel32.dll"

FUNCTION int GetProfileStringA(string section,string key, &
    string defaultstring , REF string currentprinter, ulong &
    buffersize) LIBRARY "kernel32.dll"

//script to change printers
boolean lb_rc
ulong lul_buffsize, lul_rc
```

```
string ls_section, ls_key, ls_newprinter, ls_orgprinter
string ls_default

ls_section = "windows"  // address of section name
ls_key = "device"       // address of key name
lul_buffsize = 255
ls_orgprinter = Space( lul_buffsize )

lul_rc = GetProfileStringA( ls_section,ls_key, ls_default, &
    ls_orgprinter, lul_buffsize )
// you could do some error checking here…

ls_newprinter = "\\PRINT- Server\ LJ4si,winspool,Ne00:"

lb_rc = WriteProfileStringA(ls_section,ls_key,ls_newprinter)
IF lb_rc THEN
    // let the OS know of your change
    Send(65535,26,0,0)
    dw_customer.Print()
    //reset printer back to the original one
    lb_rc = WriteProfileStringA(ls_section,ls_key, &
            ls_orgprinter )
ELSE
  MessageBox( "Error!","Can not assign new printer" )
END IF
```

Printing And DataWindows

As shown in the examples used earlier, you can print your DataWindows using basic print functions, such as **Print()** or **PrintDataWindow()**, that PowerBuilder provides for you. Now, you may need to print your DataWindows in landscape mode or print to a different bin, and so on. PowerBuilder gives you this ability. Select the Print Specifications tab page from the property sheet of the DataWindow object, as shown in Figure 10.1. From here, you are able to print in multicolumn format (newspaper-style columns), specify how many columns you want to print across the page, and how wide you want the columns to be. You can also specify the following:

- The document name, if any, that you want to display in the print queue.

- The top, bottom, and side margins in the unit of measurement specified for the DataWindow object. You can set margin values in PowerBuilder units.

- A print orientation from the list in the drop-down list box.

- A paper size from the list in the drop-down list box.

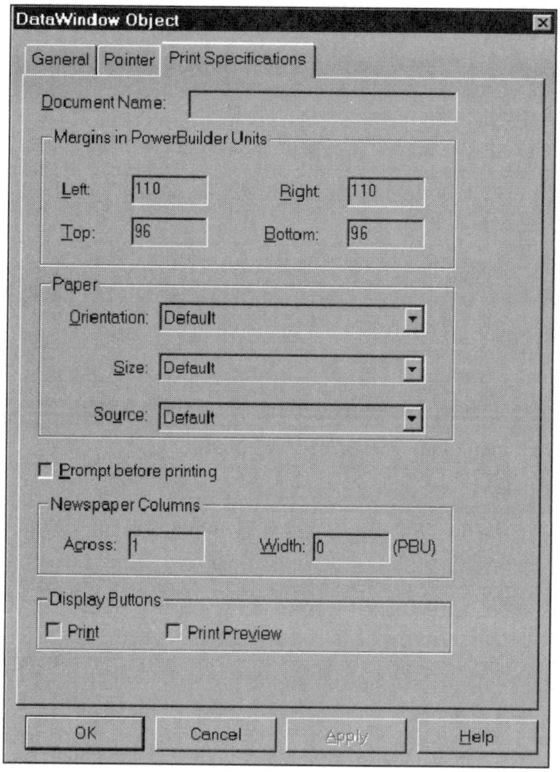

Figure 10.1
The Print Specifications tab page of the DataWindow object.

- A paper source from the list in the drop-down list box.
- A display of the Printer Setup dialog box before the job prints (click the Prompt Before Printing option).

  Note: When you select Prompt Before Printing, the user can cancel the print job by pressing Esc when the Printer Setup window displays.

Print Properties

The DataWindow also has a set of print properties that you can manipulate to give you more control over your print jobs. These properties are listed in Table 10.2.

Here is some code that shows some of the properties being used:

```
dw_customer.Object.DataWindow.Print.Paper.Size = 3
dw_customer.Object.DataWindow.Print.Margin.Top = 500
```

Table 10.2 DataWindow print properties.

Property	Definition
Collate	Specifies whether printing is collated. Collating is usually slower because the print is repeated to produce collated sets.
Color	Indicates whether the printed output will be color or monochrome.
Columns	Specifies the number of newspaper-style columns the DataWindow will print on a page. For purposes of page fitting, the whole DataWindow is a single column.
Columns.Width	Specifies the width of the newspaper-style columns in the units specified for the DataWindow.
Copies	Indicates the number of copies to be printed.
DocumentName	Contains the name that will display in the print queue.
Duplex	Indicates the orientation of the printed output. You can specify 1 for simplex, 2 for horizontal, or 3 for vertical.
Filename	Contains the name of the file to which you want to print the report. An empty string sends your job to the printer.
Margin.Bottom	Indicates the width of the bottom margin on the printed page in the units specified for the DataWindow.
Margin.Left	Indicates the width of the left margin on the printed page in the units specified for the DataWindow.
Margin.Right	Indicates the width of the right margin on the printed page in the units specified for the DataWindow.
Margin.Top	Indicates the width of the top margin on the printed page in the units specified for the DataWindow.
Orientation	Indicates the print orientation. You can set 0 for the default orientation, 1 for landscape, or 2 for portrait.
Page.Range	Contains the numbers of the pages you want to print, separated by commas.
Page.RangeInclude	Indicates what pages to print within the desired range. You can set 0 to print all, 1 to print all even pages, or 2 to print all odd pages.
Paper.Size	Indicates the size of the paper that will be used for the output.
Paper.Source	Indicates the bin that will be used as the paper source. You can set 0 for Default, 1 for Upper, 2 for Lower, 3 for Middle, 4 for Manual, 5 for Envelope, 6 for Envelope Manual, 7 for Auto, 8 for Tractor, 9 for Smallfmt, 10 for Largefmt, 11 for Large Capacity, or 14 for Cassette.

(continued)

Table 10.2 DataWindow print properties *(continued)*.

Property	Definition
Preview	Indicates whether the DataWindow object is displayed in preview mode. You can set Yes to display in preview mode or No to not display in preview mode.
Preview.Rulers	Indicates whether the rulers display when the DataWindow object displays in preview mode. You can set Yes to display the rulers or No to not display the rulers.
Preview.Zoom	Indicates the zoom factor of the print preview.
Prompt	Indicates whether a prompt will display before the job prints so that your users can cancel the print job. You can set Yes to display a prompt before the job prints or No to not display a prompt before the job prints.
Quality	Indicates the quality of the output. You can set 0 for Default, 1 for High, 2 for Medium, 3 for Low, 4 for Draft.
Scale	Specifies the scale of the printed output as a percent. The scaling percentage is passed to the print driver. If you have problems with scaling, you may be using a driver that does not support scaling.

As illustrated in Figure 10.2, you can always write a custom, user-friendly Window object that provides your users the choice to set these various DataWindow print options and manipulate its properties. This Window object takes the DataWindow via the Message object, where its print options can be changed graphically, as desired.

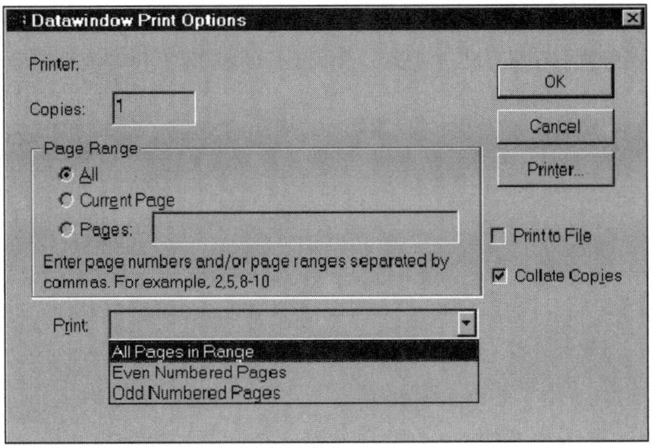

Figure 10.2
A user-defined Print dialog box.

```
//opening the print options window, pass it the DataWindow
OpenWithParm ( dw_customer )
```

In the **Open** event of the receiving Window object, the DataWindow in the Message object is assigned to an instance variable of type DataWindow. Here is an example:

```
//assign DataWindow to an instance variable
idw_dw = Message.PowerObjectParm
sle_printer.Text = idw_dw.Describe("Datawindow.Printer" )
is_page_range = "a"
```

The following script changes the print options of the DataWindow:

```
string ls_range, ls_command
long ll_row
string   ls_file, li_filename
int    li_rc

// determine the rangeinclude (all,even,odd)
CHOOSE CASE Lower(Left(ddlb_range.Text,1))
    CASE 'a' // all
       ls_range = '0'
    CASE 'e' // even
       ls_range = '1'
    CASE 'o' //odd
       ls_range = '2'
END CHOOSE

ls_command="Datawindow.print.page.RangeInclude="+ls_range
// collate output
IF cbx_collate.checked THEN
    ls_command=ls_command+ "Datawindow.print.collate=yes"
ELSE
    ls_command=ls_command+"Datawindow.print.collate=no"
END IF

// page range
CHOOSE CASE is_page_range
    CASE "a" // all
       ls_range = ""
    CASE "c" // current page
       ll_row = idw_dw.GetRow()
       ls_range = idw_dw.Describe("Evaluate("Page()","+String(ll_row)+")")
    CASE "p" // range
       ls_range = sle_page_range.text
```

```
END CHOOSE
IF len(ls_range) > 0 THEN ls_command=ls_command+ &
    " Datawindow.print.page.Range='"+ls_range+"'"

// number of copies
IF Len(em_copies.Text) > 0 THEN ls_command=ls_command+ &
    " Datawindow.print.copies="+em_copies.Text

IF cbx_print_to_file.checked THEN
    // print to file
    li_rc = GetFileSaveName("Print To File", ls_file, &
        li_filename, "PRN", "Print (*.PRN),*.PRN")
    IF li_rc = 1 THEN
        ls_command=ls_command+" Datawindow.print.filename= &
            '"+ls_file+"'"
    ELSE
        // user has cancelled
        RETURN
    END IF
END IF

// change the DataWindow properties
ls_range = idw_dw.Modify(ls_command)
IF len(ls_range) > 0 THEN
    MessageBox("Error","Error message = " + ls_range + &
        "~r~n ls_command = " + ls_command)
    RETURN
END IF

//print
idw_dw.Print(TRUE)
//close the window
CloseWithReturn(Parent,1)
```

Using Fonts

PowerBuilder enables you to designate a font to be used for text printed with the **Print()**
functions. You specify the font by number. This is done first by using the **Print
DefineFont()** function to associate a font number with a desired font, size, and a set of
properties. You can use as many as eight fonts in one print job. If you require more than
eight fonts in one job, you can call **PrintDefineFont()** again to change the settings for a
font number.

The following example starts a new print job and specifies that font number 2 is Courier,
18 point, bold, default pitch, in modern font with no italic or underline. The

PrintSetFont() function then sets the current font to font number 2, which the **Print**() statement uses to print a line of text.

```
long Job
Job = PrintOpen( )

// Define the font for Job.
PrintDefineFont(Job, 2, "Courier 10Cps",  &
    250, 700, Default!, Modern!, FALSE, FALSE)

// Set the font for Job.
PrintSetFont(Job, 2)

// Print some text in the specified font.
Print(Job,"PowerBuilder 6.0, The Definitive Guide")
PrintClose( Job )
```

Now, in an ideal operating system, when you choose a font and point size in an application, your video driver should display that font and your printer should print with that same font. But this is not always so.

Sometimes a printer may not have the font you send to it. If this is so, the printer substitutes what it considers an equivalent font. This may cause the print in a column to expand, which results in the text wrapping to the next line, or the print could shrink and look undersized. It's also possible for text fields to fall off the edge of the printed page. Sometimes, even if the printer does have the same font, there may be small variations between what you see on the screen and what's actually printed. Also, sometimes the font you've chosen for your application does not exist on your users' machines. In that case, Windows also substitutes fonts. So, what's the solution?

When choosing fonts for your application, the fonts you use should be available to the printers and video drivers of all your users. If your users run the same operating system you do, the fonts needed should be there. However, there's no guarantee for this. The Windows TrueType fonts—Arial, Courier New, Times New Roman, Symbol, and Wingdings—are on every Windows machine. They are made to print in graphics mode to any printer. They represent the five typeface families: Swiss, Modern, Roman, Symbol, and Decorative. These are the fonts you should use to ensure availability to all users in all environments.

> *Note:* Make sure you always have the latest and greatest printer drivers for your printer because old and out-of-date printer drivers have caused the space-time continuum to burst!

Moving On

As I mentioned earlier, printing is an important feature of your applications. The applications that you build should be flexible enough to print to various sources. This can be done programmatically, or you may prompt your users to specify a desired datasource. In this chapter, I covered PowerBuilder's print functions, various methods for printing DataWindows, and the print properties of DataWindows, which you can tweak as you need them.

In the next chapter, I cover SQL—the industry standard database access language. SQL provides a wide variety of commands for querying, manipulating, and maintaining your data. Fortunately, PowerBuilder includes an excellent SQL builder that will help ease your SQL learning curve.

Structured Query Language 11

Structured Query Language (SQL) is the industry standard database access language. SQL provides a wide variety of commands for querying, manipulating, and maintaining data. It also provides commands for managing database security and enforcing data integrity. SQL is not exactly the same on every DBMS platform; therefore, you should become familiar with the syntax and features of your specific DBMS.

PowerBuilder does not force you into SQL, but if you're a series developer, you should know this underlying language that is used to communicate with various PowerBuilder-supported databases. When you issue a DataWindow **Retrieve**() or **Update**(), the DataWindow automatically generates the SQL statements needed to maintain the data for you. Going a step further, you can also enter SQL statements directly into your scripts via embedded SQL.

In this chapter, I'll cover SQL in more detail. Note that I've mostly used Sybase SQL Anywhere as well as System 11 for my examples.

Database Objects

In a relational DBMS, there are many different types of objects that form the logical structure of your database. All SQL statements work on data from these objects, and this data is organized into sets called *tables*. Tables in a multiuser environment are associated with an owner. These objects can be organized in the following hierarchical structures:

- Databases
- Objects (tables)
- Attributes (columns)

155

When you reference a database object, you can qualify it by one or more of each of these elements so that you determine which object is used. If you don't qualify it completely, the DBMS will try at runtime to resolve which object you are using. Generally, you reference objects in the following format:

```
<DatabaseName>.<Owner>.<Table>.<Column>
```

When referring to tables in a database you're connected to, the database name does not have to be specified. If you do not qualify an owner, the default owner name will be the login name you are currently using. For example, if you're connected to the PSDEMODB database as DBA, you do not need to qualify the owner name when referring to the customer table. Instead, you can simply use the following code:

```
SELECT   customer.id,
         customer.fname,
         customer.lname
FROM     customer;
```

You can create a short alias name to save typing when writing SQL scripts. For example, the previous **SELECT** could be this:

```
SELECT   c.id,
         c.fname,
         c.lname
FROM     customer c;
```

> **Note:** In PowerBuilder, once you qualify a column in an SQL statement, every column owned by that table in the SQL statement has to be qualified as well.

Each column in a table has a data type that specifies what kind of data it must hold. Each database has it own set of data types, and most of these types will map between various back ends. However, there are exceptions—for example, special unique data types for a given DBMS or numeric precisions or even DateTimes.

When you've created your table, you need to specify the data types for each column. Once a table has been created, you cannot change any of the column data types without "dropping" the table and re-creating it.

SQL Statements

Four main statements in SQL deal with manipulating data in your tables: **SELECT**, **INSERT**, **UPDATE**, and **DELETE**. These are all the DataWindow needs to do its processing. Let's take a look at these statements in more detail.

Figure 11.1
The PowerBuilder SQL Painter.

> **Note:** To build your SQL statement, you can always use PowerBuilder's SQL Painter (shown in Figure 11.1).

SELECT

A **SELECT** statement is used to retrieve data. It must always contain the keywords **SELECT** and **FROM**. For example, to retrieve all the columns from the customer table, you issue the following command:

```
SELECT * FROM customer;
```

The asterisk character returns all the columns in the table in the order they are created. Your result set can be sorted by using the **ORDER BY** clause. Here's an example:

```
SELECT   *
FROM     customer
ORDER BY customer.lname ASC;
```

> **Note:** When using **ORDER BY**, sorting is done at the server. This is faster than sorting at the client side.

Narrowing Down Your Result Set

To narrow down your result set, you can add a conditional phrase in your **WHERE** clause. The phrases are usually built by using a comparison operator. Some of the most common operators are listed in Table 11.1.

Orphan records are those records that should reference a foreign key, but a row with that key is missing. The following SQL statement is used to find orphan records:

```
SELECT emp_id, emp_lname, emp_fname
FROM    employee
WHERE   NOT exists
        (SELECT *
         FROM    department
         WHERE   employee.emp_id = department.dept_id);
```

Table 11.1 SQL comparison operators.

Operator	Description
=	Equal to
>	Greater than
<	Less than
>=	Greater than or equal to
<=	Less than or equal to
!=, <>	Not equal to
!>	Not greater than
!<	Not less than
LIKE	Pattern matching, wildcard '%', '_'
IS NULL	Null value
BETWEEN	Range of values

Sorting

One of the best ways developers can manage large amounts of data is through *sorting* (or *grouping*). The **GROUP BY** clause directs your DBMS to search through specified rows and treat all the rows in which the contents of the specified column are identified as one row. Therefore, only the contents of the specified rows and aggregate functions can be included in the **SELECT** list for an SQL statement using the **GROUP BY** clause.

Aggregate functions work on groups of information. The following five functions are supported on most back ends:

- **COUNT()**. Number of rows in a result set
- **MAX()**. Maximum value in a result set
- **MIN()**. Minimum value in a result set
- **AVG()**. Average value in a result set
- **SUM()**. Numeric sum of values in a result set

The following example uses both a **GROUP BY** and an aggregate function:

```
SELECT    id, count(id)
FROM      customer
GROUP BY id
ORDER BY id;
```

SELECT statements can contain only columns included in the **ORDER BY** clause, plus any aggregate functions. If you want to include a customer name and you know that the customer name is unique for each group, you can use the following aggregate function:

```
Max(cust_name)
```

Joins

Relational databases give you the ability to join information located in more than one table into a single result set. Joining tables is usually done in tables that are most related to each other through reference columns. The primary/foreign key relationship is the most efficient way of joining two tables together; but even when columns are not foreign keys, you can use similar columns as the means of joining tables together in a **SELECT** statement. Here's an example of a simple join:

```
SELECT   department.dept_name
         employee.emp_lname,
         employee.emp_fname
FROM     employee, department
WHERE    (employee.dept_id = department.dept_id)
```

> **Note:** Because the number of rows to be compared in the join is equal to the number of rows in each table multiplied together, a join of three or four large tables will slow down your query somewhat. Unless you have a very fast and powerful server, avoid joins for more than four or five large tables.

A *left outer join* refers to a **SELECT** statement where two of the tables involved have a relationship such that a column in the first table references a column in the second table, but the corresponding value in the second table might not exist. The first table appears on the left side of the equal sign in the **WHERE** clause, hence the name "left outer join." Note that not all back ends support left outer joins.

For example, let's take the following SQL statement. It provides a list of all the departments in the department table along with the names of their employees. Now, if a department has no employees, it would not be displayed. However, with a left outer join, you're allowed to list all the departments regardless of whether or not they have employees associated with them.

```
SELECT   department.dept_name,
         employee.emp_fname,
         employee.lname
FROM     {oj department LEFT OUTER JOIN employee ON
         department.dept_id = employee.dept_id};
```

INSERT

The **INSERT** statement inserts rows of data into a table. When inserting rows, you must make sure you include all the required columns. If you don't include a column list, the column list will include all your table's columns by default. Also, if you have any column constraints that exist for your table, they must be satisfied. Here is an example:

```
INSERT INTO department
        ( dept_id,
          dept_name,
          dept_head_id )
VALUES  ( 600,
          'Systems',
          501 )  ;
```

> **Note:** To copy the entire contents of one table into another table that has an identical structure, use the following code:
>
> ```
> INSERT INTO tableA
> SELECT * FROM tableB;
> ```

DELETE

The **DELETE** statement is used to delete sets of rows from a table based on given criteria in the **WHERE** clause. If you don't include a **WHERE** clause, all the rows in the table will be deleted. To delete one specific row, you use that row's primary key. Here's an example:

```
DELETE FROM department
WHERE department.dept_id = 600;
```

To delete a group of rows, your **WHERE** clause should identify those rows as shown in the following example:

```
DELETE FROM department
WHERE  department.dept_id IN (100,200,300);
```

The following line simply deletes the entire contents of the department table:

```
DELETE FROM department;
```

UPDATE

The **UPDATE** statement is used to modify data. This statement can be used on one or more columns in a table, but you can only use it on one table at a time. You specify the columns to be updated with the **SET** clause. Here is an example:

```
UPDATE customer
SET    state = 'NY'
WHERE  city = 'New York';
```

Note that if you don't use a **WHERE** clause, all the columns in your specified table are updated.

Referential Integrity

In a relational database, columns often refer to data in other tables. When that reference is to a *primary key* in another table, you can declare the column as a *foreign key*. The following describes both the primary key and the foreign key:

- **Primary key.** A unique column (or columns) that identifies a row. A table can have only one primary key of which no part can be null. If a primary key is made up of more than one column, it's known as a *compound key*.

- **Foreign key.** A column (or columns) in one table that is the same as the primary key in another table and references that table.

Columns that are foreign keys can only contain values that are already stored in the related primary key. For example, let's say that dept_id in the employee table is a foreign key for the dept_id in the department table. If you enter a value in employee.dept_id that does not exist in department.dept_id, a database referential integrity error will occur.

Sybase SQL Anywhere allows for some referential integrity extension for managing dependent rows when a primary key is deleted. As shown in Figure 11.2, these options can be set in the Foreign Key Definition dialog box of the Database Painter by selecting one of the following radio buttons in the On Delete Of Primary Table Row section:

- **Disallow If Dependent Rows Exist (RESTRICT).** Does not allow **DELETE** if any dependent rows exist.

- **Delete Any Dependent Rows (CASCADE).** Deletes along with any dependent rows that may exist.

- **Set Dependent Columns To NULL (SET NULL).** Sets dependent columns to **NULL**.

In the example, the third option is selected. This means that when a department row is deleted, any columns in other tables that reference the deleted department's dept_id will be set to **NULL**. Now, what if any one of those columns has a constraint of **NOT NULL**? You guessed it, a database error will occur.

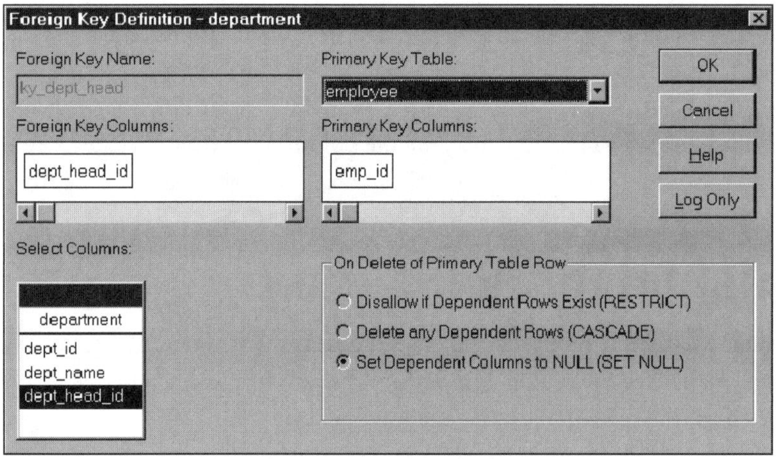

Figure 11.2
Foreign Key Definition dialog box.

Transactions

A *database transaction* is one or more SQL statements that form a logical unit of work. This means that if one part of your logical unit fails, the entire unit may be invalid. Whenever an error that violates a logical transaction occurs, the entire transaction has to be undone. Databases do not usually make data manipulation changes permanent until a **COMMIT** is executed. In order to undo a transaction, a **ROLLBACK** is executed. Here's an example:

```
Integer li_rc
li_rc = dw_customer.Update( )

IF li_rc = 1 AND SQLCA.SQLNRows > 0 THEN
   COMMIT USING SQLCA;
ELSE
   ROLLBACK USING SQLCA;
END IF
```

Stored Procedures

Stored procedures are sets of SQL code that have been compiled and stored on your database server. Stored procedures can be called from your applications or from within triggers. A stored procedure can return no result or one or more result sets. Arguments can be used when calling stored procedures. Stored procedures are particularly useful for minimizing the amount of network traffic required to send a series of SQL statement to your server. Stored procedures are optimized before they are stored on your server; therefore, they take very little time to load and do not require any syntax checking or optimizing.

> **Note:** *The syntax for creating and calling stored procedures varies between databases. Refer to your database's manuals for correct syntax. In order to use a stored procedure as the datasource of a DataWindow, the stored procedure must contain a **SELECT** statement.*

The following stored procedure returns a result set to PowerBuilder:

```
CREATE Procedure sp_department_list()
Result(dept_id integer,dept_name char(40))
   Begin
      SELECT dept_id,dept_name
      FROM   department
   End
```

This next stored procedure has two arguments. It takes an integer as an **IN** parameter and a decimal as an **OUT** parameter.

```
CREATE Procedure sp_getsalary
(IN empid Integer, OUT empsalary Decimal)
Begin
   SELECT salary
   INTO   empsalary
   FROM   employee
   WHERE  emp_id = empid
End
```

> **Note:** *If possible, use referential integrity, column constraints, and triggers to enforce business rules on your database.*

Triggers

Triggers are SQL scripts that automatically execute before or after a row is inserted, updated, or deleted in a table.

Triggers are used whenever referential integrity and other declarative constraints are not sufficient. For example, you may want to enforce a more complete form of referential integrity involving more detailed checking, or you may want to enforce checking on new data but allow legacy data to violate constraints. Another use for triggers is in logging activities on database tables, independent of the applications using the database.

Triggers can be defined as *row-level* triggers or *statement-level* triggers. Row-level triggers can execute *before* or *after* each row modified by the triggering **INSERT**, **UPDATE**, or **DELETE** operation is changed. Statement-level triggers execute *after* the entire operation is performed.

The following trigger is an example of a row-level **INSERT** trigger; it checks that the dept_id inserted for a new department is not less than 100:

```
CREATE TRIGGER check_dept_id AFTER INSERT ON department
REFERENCING NEW AS new_dept
FOR EACH ROW
   BEGIN
      DECLARE err_dept_error EXCEPTION FOR SQLState '99999';
      IF new_dept.dept_id < 100 THEN
         SIGNAL err_dept_error;
      END IF;
   END
```

AutoCommit

The setting of the **AutoCommit** property of the transaction object determines whether your application should issue SQL statements inside or outside the scope of a transaction. When **AutoCommit** is set to False, SQL statements are issued inside the scope of the transaction. When you set **AutoCommit** to True, SQL statements are issued outside the scope of a transaction.

Some databases, such as Sybase SQL Server, require you to execute Data Definition Language (DDL) statements outside the scope of a transaction. If you execute a database stored procedure that contains DDL statements within the scope of a transaction, an error message is returned and the DDL statements are rejected. Now, to execute SQL Server-stored procedures containing DDL statements, you must set **AutoCommit** to True so that PowerBuilder issues the statements outside the scope of a transaction. However, if **AutoCommit** is set to True, you cannot issue a **ROLLBACK**. Therefore, you should set **AutoCommit** back to False immediately after completing the DDL operation. When you change the value of **AutoCommit** from False to True, PowerBuilder issues a **COMMIT** statement by default.

Embedded SQL

When you write scripts for your applications, you can use embedded SQL statements in these scripts to perform various database operations. The features supported when you use embedded SQL depend on the DBMS to which you are connecting. For example, if you're using Sybase SQL Server System 11, you can embed the following types of SQL statements in your scripts:

- Transaction management statements

- Cursor statements

- Noncursor statements

- Database stored procedures

Let's go though a couple of examples of using embedded SQL. The first example updates rows from the customer table where the column ID is equal to the value entered in a SingleLineEdit object (**sle_custNumber**):

```
Integer li_custID

li_custID = Integer( sle_custNumber.Text )

UPDATE customer
   SET lname = :sle_lastName.Text
   WHERE customer.id  = :li_custID
   USING SQLCA;

//if no errors, makes changes permanent
IF SQLCA.SQLNRows > 0 THEN
   COMMIT USING SQLCA;
END IF
```

The next example uses a cursor to populate a list box:

```
Int li_deptid
String ls_deptname

//cursor declaration
DECLARE dept_cur CURSOR FOR
   SELECT department.dept_id,
          department.dept_name
   FROM   department  ;

//open the cursor
OPEN dept_cur;

//loop through the cursor
DO WHILE SQLCA.SQLCode = 0
   //fetch values into our variables
   FETCH NEXT dept_cur INTO :li_deptid, :ls_deptname;
   //no rows left
```

```
    IF SQLCA.SQLCode <> 100 THEN
        //populate the ListBox
        lb_dept.AddItem( string(li_deptid)+" "+ls_deptname )
    END IF
LOOP

//close the cursor
CLOSE dept_cur;
```

The previous example can be done via a stored procedure, as seen here:

```
Int li_deptid
String ls_deptname

//declare our stored procedure
DECLARE dept_proc PROCEDURE
FOR sp_department_list ;

//run the stored procedure
EXECUTE dept_proc;

//loop through our result set
DO WHILE SQLCA.SQLCode = 0
    FETCH dept_proc INTO :li_deptid, :ls_deptname;
    IF SQLCA.SQLCode <> 100 THEN
        //Populate the Listbox
        lb_dept.AddItem( string(li_deptid)+" "+ls_deptname )
    END IF
LOOP

//close the procedure
CLOSE dept_proc;
```

Dynamic SQL

PowerBuilder gives you the ability to dynamically build SQL statements in your applications. There are four basic formats to dynamic SQL. However, before we go any further, you should know what SQLSA and SQLDA are.

DynamicStagingArea (SQLSA) is a PowerBuilder data type that is used to store information for use in dynamic SQL statements. DynamicStagingArea is the only connection between the execution of a statement and a transaction object, and it's used internally by PowerBuilder. You cannot access information in DynamicStagingArea, and there are no properties associated with it.

DynamicDescriptionArea (SQLDA) is a PowerBuilder data type that is used to store information about the input and output parameters used in Format 4 of dynamic SQL.

Format 1

Format 1 of dynamic SQL is used to execute SQL statements that do not produce a result set and do not require input parameters. This format is generally used to execute all forms of DLL statements. Here's the syntax:

```
EXECUTE IMMEDIATE SQLStatement {USING TransactionObject} ;
```

This example creates a database table named SeeMee; the statements use the string **ls_sql** to store the **CREATE** statement:

```
String ls_sql

ls_sql = "CREATE TABLE SeeMee "&
    +"(id Integer Not NULL,"&
    +"first_name char(15) Not NULL, "&
    +"last_name  char(25) Not NULL)"

//run the
EXECUTE IMMEDIATE :ls_sql ;
```

Format 2

Format 2 is used to execute SQL statements that do not produce a result set but do require input parameters. This format is also used to execute all forms of DDL statements. Here's the syntax:

```
PREPARE DynamicStagingArea FROM SQLStatement {USING TransactionObject} ;
EXECUTE DynamicStagingArea USING {ParameterList} ;
```

In this example, a **DELETE** is prepared with one parameter in SQLSA that is populated during execution from **ls_empid**:

```
Integer ls_empid = 56

PREPARE SQLSA
    FROM "DELETE FROM employee WHERE emp_id = ?" ;

EXECUTE SQLSA USING :Emp_id_var ;
```

Format 3

Format 3 is used to execute an SQL statement that produces a result set in which the input parameters and result set columns are known at compile time. Here's the syntax:

```
DECLARE Cursor | Procedure  DYNAMIC CURSOR | PROCEDURE
FOR DynamicStagingArea ;
PREPARE DynamicStagingArea FROM SQLStatement {USING TransactionObject} ;
OPEN DYNAMIC Cursor {USING ParameterList} ;
EXECUTE DYNAMIC Procedure {USING ParameterList} ;
FETCH Cursor | Procedure INTO HostVariableList} ;
CLOSE Cursor | Procedure ;
```

In this example, a cursor named **my_cursor** is associated with SQLSA, a **SELECT** statement is prepared with one parameter in SQLSA, the cursor is opened, and the value of the variable **li_custid** is substituted for the parameter in the **SELECT** statement. The **company_name** in the active row is returned into the PowerBuilder variable **ls_company**.

```
DECLARE my_cursor DYNAMIC CURSOR FOR SQLSA ;

Integer li_custid
String ls_sql, ls_company

ls_sql= "SELECT company_name FROM customer "&
   +"WHERE id = ?"

PREPARE SQLSA FROM :ls_sql;
OPEN DYNAMIC my_cursor using :li_custid;
FETCH my_cursor INTO :ls_company ;
CLOSE my_cursor ;
```

Format 4

Format 4 is used to execute an SQL statement that produces a result set in which the number of input parameters or the number of result set columns (or both) are unknown at compile time. Here's the syntax:

```
DECLARE Cursor | Procedure DYNAMIC CURSOR | PROCEDURE
FOR DynamicStagingArea ;
PREPARE DynamicStagingArea FROM SQLStatement {USING TransactionObject} ;
DESCRIBE DynamicStagingArea  INTO DynamicDescriptionArea ;
OPEN DYNAMIC Cursor | Procedure USING DESCRIPTOR DynamicDescriptionArea} ;
EXECUTE DYNAMIC Cursor | Procedure USING DESCRIPTOR DynamicDescriptionArea ;
FETCH Cursor | Procedure USING DESCRIPTOR DynamicDescriptionArea ;
CLOSE Cursor | Procedure ;
```

The following script uses dynamic SQL format 4 to retrieve company_name where id is not known until runtime:

```
String ls_Sql

ls_sql = "SELECT company_name FROM employee " &
    +"WHERE id = ?"

PREPARE SQLSA FROM :ls_sql ;
DESCRIBE SQLSA INTO SQLDA ;

DECLARE my_cursor DYNAMIC CURSOR FOR SQLSA ;

SetDynamicParm(SQLDA, 1, 101)

OPEN DYNAMIC my_cursor USING DESCRIPTOR SQLDA ;
FETCH my_cursor USING DESCRIPTOR SQLDA ;
CLOSE my_cursor ;
```

> **Note:** *Now, how do you fine-tune your SQL statements to speed up data retrieval? Well, you just simplify them. Here are some hints:*
>
> - *Avoid the use of **LIKE** in **SELECT** statements*
> - *Break larger SQL statements into several simpler, smaller queries*
> - *Avoid excessive, complex table joins*

Moving On

As you can see, SQL is a pretty powerful language. Its use is mainly for communication in relational databases, but it's also widely used in database applications. In this chapter, I covered some of the essentials of SQL. Because SQL is a full-featured language, and the SQL dialect may vary from one RDBMS to another, I strongly recommend that you take a quick look at your RDBMS's manuals for further information.

In the next chapter, I cover debugging. PowerBuilder 6.0 has a brand new debugger that provides a number of different tools and options for debugging your applications. I'll discuss these tools and options with you in the next chapter.

Debugging Your Application

Sometimes your application might not behave the way you think it should. Perhaps a variable isn't getting its proper assignment, or a script isn't executing exactly the way you expected it to. If this is the case, then some form of debugging is required for your application.

A number of different tools are currently available for debugging your applications: the Debug window, runtime debugging, tracing and profiling debuggers, database trace debugging, and a number of third-party debugging tools. The PowerBuilder debugger is a brand new tool that supports new breakpoint, watchpoint, and stepping capabilities, and it displays multiple views of your application in panes that you can move, resize, and overlap for a customized layout. You can also use Just-In-Time debugging to open the Debug window if a system error occurs or you notice problems while running your application from the Run button.

In this chapter, I'll first cover the new PowerBuilder debugger; then, I'll go over some other useful debugging methods. So, put your safari clothes on, get your backpack, your rifle, and let's go debugging!

The New PowerBuilder Debugger

The latest PowerBuilder debugger is a new beast altogether. It's by far one of the best debuggers available in the market today. You can do so much now that you were not able to do in previous releases. Now, when you run your applications in the debug mode, you can use conditional and occasional breakpoints, and you have the ability to set a breakpoint when a variable changes to fine-tune where you suspend execution. You can then set variables and expressions that you want to watch, and step through your code examining variables and memory objects. You can step into, over, and out of functions, run to the location where you set the cursor, and set the next statement you want executed. Wow, isn't that fantastic?

When you run your application in debug mode, PowerBuilder stops execution before it executes a line containing a breakpoint. You can then step through your applications and examine your code. Here are the steps to debugging an application:

1. Open the Debug window.

2. Set your breakpoints.

3. Run your applications in the debug mode.

4. When execution is suspended at a breakpoint, you can look at the values of variables, the properties of objects in memory, and the call stack, or you can change the values of variables.

5. If needed, step through the code line.

6. If needed, add or modify your breakpoints.

The Debug Window

The Debug window contains several views. Each of these views displays as a separate pane and shows you different kinds of information about the current state of your application or the debugging session. The following list summarizes what each view shows and explains the things you can do from that view:

- **Breakpoints.** A list of breakpoints with indicators showing whether the breakpoints are currently active or inactive. You can set, enable, disable, and clear breakpoints, set a condition for a breakpoint, and show the source for a breakpoint in the Source view.

- **Call Stack.** The sequence of function calls leading up to the function that was executing at the time of the breakpoint, shown as the script and line number from which the function was called. You can examine the context of the application at any line in the call stack.

- **Objects In Memory.** An expandable list of objects currently in memory. You can view the names and memory locations of the instances of each memory object and property values of each instance.

- **Source.** The full text of a script. You can go to a specific line in a script, find a string, open another script (including ancestor and descendant scripts), and manage breakpoints.

- **Source Browser.** An expandable hierarchy of objects in your application. You can select any script in your application and display it in the Source view.

- **Source History.** A list of the scripts that have been displayed in the Source view. You can select any script in the Source History view and display it in the Source view.

- **Variables.** An expandable list of all the variables in scope. You can select which kinds of variables are shown in the view, change the value of a variable, and set a breakpoint when a variable changes.

- **Watch.** A list of variables you have selected to watch as the application proceeds. You can change the value of a variable, set a breakpoint when a variable changes, and add an arbitrary expression to the Watch view.

Managing The Debug Window

When you first open the Debug window, you'll see two rows of panes, some of them tabbed. Each tab shows a different view. All the available views are included in the default layout, including five different views for variables, one for each variable type, as shown in Figure 12.1.

Each pane that you see in the Debug window has the following features:

- A title bar that you can display temporarily or permanently

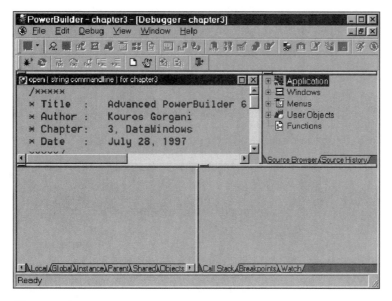

Figure 12.1
The Debug window.

- A handle in the top-left corner you can use to drag the pane to a new location

- Splitter bars between the pane and each adjacent pane

The layout of the Debug window can be changed as you like, and all your settings can be changed for various debugging tasks.

Displaying The Title Bars

When you're debugging, the kind of information displayed in each pane and your familiarity with the layout of the Debug window usually makes title bars unnecessary. However, you can display a title bar for any pane either temporarily or permanently. The default layout always displays the title bar for the Source view permanently because it shows the name of the script being displayed.

To display a title bar for a Debug window pane, place your cursor on the splitter bar at the top of the pane. Notice that your cursor changes to an arrow with a bar and the title bar displays. Click on the push pin at the left of the title bar. The title bar remains visible when you move the cursor. Click the push pin again to hide the title bar.

Moving A Pane

A window pane can be moved to any location. Place your cursor on the handle in the top-left corner of the pane and hold down the left mouse button. A gray outline appears in the pane. You can now drag the outline to a new location. The outline changes size as you drag it. When your cursor is over the middle of a pane, the outline fills the pane. As you drag the cursor towards any border, the outline becomes a narrow rectangle adjacent to that border. When the cursor is over a splitter bar between two panes, rows, or columns, the outline straddles the splitter bar.

Once you've found a new home for a pane, release the mouse button to drop the outline in the new location. The following list should assist you in moving your panes around:

- **Between two panes.** Drop the outline on the splitter bar between the panes

- **Between a border and a pane.** Drop the outline at the side of the pane nearest the border

- **Onto a new row.** Drop the outline on the splitter bar between two rows or at the top or bottom of the Debug window

- **Onto a new column.** Drop the outline on the splitter bar between two columns or at the left or right edge of the Debug window

- **Onto a stack of panes.** Drop the outline on the middle of the pane

Note: If you moved some tabbed panes using the handle in the top-left corner of the top pane, all the panes in the stack move. To move one of the panes out of the stack, drag the tab for the pane you want to move instead of the handle.

Adding And Removing Panes

To add a new pane to the Debug window, select the view you want from the View menu. The new pane displays as a new row. Then, move the pane to where you want it. To remove a pane, simply select Close from the pane's pop-up menu.

Changing Variable Views

The default Debug window contains a separate Variables view for each variable type. If you choose, you can combine two or more variables in a single view. This is achieved by first displaying the pop-up menu for a tabbed Variables view that you want to change. Then, click the names of the variable types you want to display.

Saving Your Layout

Once you've finished rearranging the panes in your Debug window, PowerBuilder saves the layout in your PB.INI file and restores it next time you open the Debug window. You can also save customized layouts yourself so that you can switch from one layout to another for various debugging tasks.

To save customized layouts, select the Debug|Options menu item, select the Layout tab page, and then click the Save As command button.

Breakpoints

A *breakpoint* is a point in your application code where you want to interrupt the normal execution of the application while you're debugging. If you suspect a problem is occurring in a particular script or function call, set a breakpoint at the beginning of the script or at the line where the function is called. When you close the Debug window, any breakpoints you set are written to your PB.INI file and are available when you reopen the Debug window.

Setting Breakpoints

To set a breakpoint on a line in a script, display the script in the Source view and place your cursor where you want to set the breakpoint. Then, simply double-click the line. PowerBuilder sets a breakpoint and a red circle displays at the beginning of the source line. If you select a line that does not contain executable code, PowerBuilder sets the breakpoint at the beginning of the next executable statement.

Breakpoints can be triggered when a statement has been executed a specific number of times (an *occasional* breakpoint), when a specified expression is true (a *conditional* breakpoint), or when the value of a variable changes. If you need to check the progress of a loop without interrupting execution in every iteration, you can set an occasional breakpoint that is triggered only after a specific number of iterations. To specify that execution stops only when conditions you specify are met, set a conditional breakpoint. Both occasional and conditional breakpoints can be set at the same time. To set a breakpoint, select the Variables tab page in the Edit|Breakpoints menu item dialog box; then, specify the script and line number where you want the breakpoint.

You can also specify an integer occurrence, a condition, or both. Remember that the condition must be a valid Boolean PowerScript expression. When PowerBuilder reaches the location where the breakpoint is set, it evaluates the breakpoint expression and triggers the breakpoint only when the expression is true.

Now, you can interrupt execution every time the value of a variable changes. To do this, drag the variable from the Variables view or Watch view to the Breakpoints view. PowerBuilder watches the variable during execution and interrupts execution when the value of the variable changes.

Running In Debug Mode

When all your breakpoints have been set, you can run the application in debug mode. The application executes normally until it reaches a statement containing a breakpoint. After examining your application, you can single-step through it, continue execution until another breakpoint is reached, or stop the debugging run so that you can start a new debugging run or close the Debug window.

When your application is suspended at a breakpoint, use the Variables, Watch, Call Stack, and Objects In Memory views to examine its state. When you have stopped execution at a breakpoint, you can use several commands to step through your application code and then use the views to examine the effect of each statement. As you step through your code, the Debug window views change to reflect the current context of your application, and a yellow arrow cursor indicates the next statement to be executed.

To continue execution from a breakpoint, click the Continue button in the debugger toolbar. Execution begins at the statement indicated by the yellow arrow cursor and continues until the next breakpoint is hit or until the application terminates normally. Now, to terminate a debugging run at a breakpoint, select Debug|Stop from the menu bar. PowerBuilder resets the state of the application and all the Debug window views to their state at the beginning of the debugging run. You can now begin another run in debug mode, or you can close the Debug window.

Examining Variable Values

Each Variables view shows one or more types of variables in an expandable outline. Click the plus or minus signs next to the variable names to expand and contract the hierarchy.

Watching Variables And Expressions

The Watch view lets you watch selected variables and expressions as the application runs. If your variable or expression is in scope, the Watch view shows its value if it has been initialized. An X in the Watch view indicates that the variable or expression is not in scope. This is how you would add variables or expressions to the Watch view:

- To add a variable to the Watch view, select the variable in the Variables view. Then, drag it to the Watch view.

- To add an expression to the Watch view, select Insert from the pop-up menu and then enter any valid PowerScript expression in the New Expression dialog box.

Monitoring The Call Stack

The Call Stack view shows the sequence of function calls leading up to the script or function that was executing at the time of the breakpoint. Each line displays as the script and line number from which the call was made. The yellow arrow shows the script and line where the execution is stopped.

Objects In Memory

The Objects In Memory view shows an expandable list of objects currently in memory. Click the plus sign next to an entry to view the names and memory locations of instances of each object and property values of each instance.

Source View

The Source view displays the full text of a script. As you step through your application, the Source view is updated to show the current script with a yellow arrow indicating the next statement to be executed. You can open more than one Source view. Remember that if multiple Source views are open, only the first one opened is updated to show the current script when the context of your application changes.

Now, when you have stopped execution at a breakpoint, you can use several commands to step through your application code. Let's quickly take a look at these commands.

You can use either Step In or Step Over to step through an application one statement at a time. They have the same result, except when the statement contains a call to a function. You can use Step In if you want to step into a function and examine the effects of each statement. Use Step Over to step over the function, executing it as a single statement.

If you step into a function that you don't want to single-step through, use Step Out to continue execution until the function returns.

As you step through your application, you may reach sections of code that you don't care much about. You can use Run To Cursor to select a statement further down in a script where you want execution to stop.

You can also use the Set Next Statement command to bypass a section of code that contains a bug, or to test part of an application using specific values for variables. Execution continues from the statement where you place the cursor.

Just-In-Time Debugging

If you're running your application in regular mode using the Run button and you notice that the application is behaving incorrectly, Just-In-Time debugging lets you switch to debug mode without terminating the application.

When you open the Debug window while running an application, the application does not stop executing. The Source, Variables, Call Stack, and Objects In Memory views are all empty because the debugger does not have any context. To suspend execution and examine the context in a problem area, open an appropriate script and set your breakpoints; then, initiate the action that calls the script. If Just-In-Time debugging is enabled and a system error occurs while an application is running in regular mode, the Debug window opens automatically, showing the context where the error occurred.

Remember that you must enable Just-In-Time debugging before you run your application to take advantage of this feature. To enable Just-In-Time debugging, select System Options from the toolbar. Check the Just In Time Debugging checkbox and then click OK. You can also use the **DebugBreak()** function to break into the debugger.

When PowerBuilder encounters the **DebugBreak()** function, the Debug window opens showing the current context. The following code tests whether a variable is null and opens the Debug window if it is:

```
IF IsNull(g_env) THEN DebugBreak()
```

PowerBuilder Debug Trace

If you want to generate an activity log with no timing information in a text file, you can turn on PBDebug tracing in the System Options dialog box. The PBDebug trace file contains a log showing which object functions, instructions, and system DLL functions were executed in a chronological order. You can generate the same kind of trace file when you run a PowerBuilder executable.

To generate a trace file, select Enable PBDebug Tracing in the General tab of the System Options dialog box. You can optionally specify a path name for the PBDebug output file. If you don't specify an output file path, PowerBuilder creates an output file with the name PB60.DBG in the same directory as the PowerBuilder executable file. When you turn PBDebug tracing on, PowerBuilder writes the following entries in your PB.INI file:

```
DebugOutFile=<debug file path>
PBDebug=on
```

Now, each time you run your application with PBDebug on, PowerBuilder appends the new trace output to the same trace file as before. A long session with PBDebug turned on can produce a large trace file, so beware!

Also, each time the PowerBuilder development environment is started with PBDebug on, the trace file is overwritten. If you want to save the data in the existing trace file, rename the output file when you start PowerBuilder.

> **Note:** Running your application with PBDebug on will affect its performance.

Runtime Trace

When you've created your executable, you can run create a trace file by including the **/PBDebug** command line switch when running your executable. This creates a trace file that's the same name as your executable but with the extension .DBG. For example, if your executable is named SALES.EXE, you would run the following:

```
Sales.exe /PBDebug
```

> **Note:** For machine-code executable files, tracing is only enabled if you check the Trace Information checkbox when you build the executable.

The following is a small trace file. It contains the creation and execution of each event and function for all the Window, Menu, and User objects. This file is well indented, so following the trace should be straightforward. This is a good way of tracking your application to ensure that your created User objects are destroyed, and so on. It also tells you what line your code fails at, if that is the case.

```
Executing object function +CREATE for class CHAPTER12, lib entry CHAPTER12
   Executing instruction at line 2
   Executing instruction at line 3
   Executing object function +CREATE for class MESSAGE, lib entry _TYPEDEF
   End object function +CREATE for class MESSAGE, lib entry _TYPEDEF
```

```
  Executing instruction at line 4
  Executing object function +CREATE for class TRANSACTION, lib entry _TYPEDEF
  End object function +CREATE for class TRANSACTION, lib entry _TYPEDEF
  Executing instruction at line 5
  Executing object function +CREATE for class DYNAMICDESCRIPTIONAREA,lib entry _TYPEDEF
  End object function +CREATE for class DYNAMICDESCRIPTIONAREA, lib entry _TYPEDEF
  Executing instruction at line 6
  Executing object function +CREATE for class DYNAMICSTAGINGAREA, lib entry _TYPEDEF
  End object function +CREATE for class DYNAMICSTAGINGAREA, lib entry _TYPEDEF
  Executing instruction at line 7
  Executing object function +CREATE for class ERROR, lib entry _TYPEDEF
  End object function +CREATE for class ERROR, lib entry _TYPEDEF
End class function +CREATE for class CHAPTER12, lib entry CHAPTER12
Executing event +OPEN for class CHAPTER12, lib entry CHAPTER12
  Executing instruction at line 8
  Executing instruction at line 10
  Executing instruction at line 11
  Executing instruction at line 13
  Executing instruction at line 15
  Executing instruction at line 20
  Executing class function OPEN for class SYSTEMFUNCTIONS, lib entry _TYPEDEF
  End class function OPEN for class SYSTEMFUNCTIONS, lib entry _TYPEDEF
  Executing instruction at line 20
End event +OPEN for class CHAPTER12, lib entry CHAPTER12
Executing object function +CREATE for class DWOBJECT, lib entry _TYPEDEF
End object function +CREATE for class DWOBJECT, lib entry _TYPEDEF
Executing object function +DESTROY for class DWOBJECT, lib entry _TYPEDEF
  Executing instruction at line 2018
  Executing object function DESTROY_OBJECT for class DWOBJECT, lib entry _TYPEDEF
  Executing system dll function
  End class function DESTROY_OBJECT for class DWOBJECT, lib entry _TYPEDEF
End class function +DESTROY for class DWOBJECT, lib entry _TYPEDEF
Executing event +CLOSE for class CHAPTER12, lib entry CHAPTER12
  Executing instruction at line 8
End event +CLOSE for class CHAPTER12, lib entry CHAPTER12
Executing object function +DESTROY for class CHAPTER12, lib entry CHAPTER12
  Executing instruction at line 2
  Executing object function +DESTROY for class TRANSACTION, lib entry _TYPEDEF
  End object function +DESTROY for class TRANSACTION, lib entry _TYPEDEF
  Executing instruction at line 3
  Executing object function +DESTROY for class DYNAMICDESCRIPTIONAREA, lib entry _TYPEDEF
  End object function +DESTROY for class DYNAMICDESCRIPTIONAREA, lib entry _TYPEDEF
  Executing instruction at line 4
  Executing object function +DESTROY for class DYNAMICSTAGINGAREA, &
      lib entry _TYPEDEF
  End object function +DESTROY for class DYNAMICSTAGINGAREA, lib entry _TYPEDEF
```

```
Executing instruction at line 5
Executing object function +DESTROY for class ERROR, lib entry _TYPEDEF
End object function +DESTROY for class ERROR, lib entry _TYPEDEF
Executing instruction at line 6
Executing object function +DESTROY for class MESSAGE, lib entry _TYPEDEF
End object function +DESTROY for class MESSAGE, lib entry _TYPEDEF
End class function +DESTROY for class CHAPTER12, lib entry CHAPTER12
```

Database Trace

PowerBuilder provides you with two tracing tools to troubleshoot your database connections:

- **Database Trace.** Traces any database connection
- **ODBC Driver Manager Trace.** Traces ODBC connections only

You can use the ODBC Driver Manager Trace tool in PowerBuilder to trace connections to ODBC datasources through the Sybase database interface. To start and stop ODBC Driver Manager Trace for your connection in the development environment, you'll have to edit your database profile as shown in Figure 12.2.

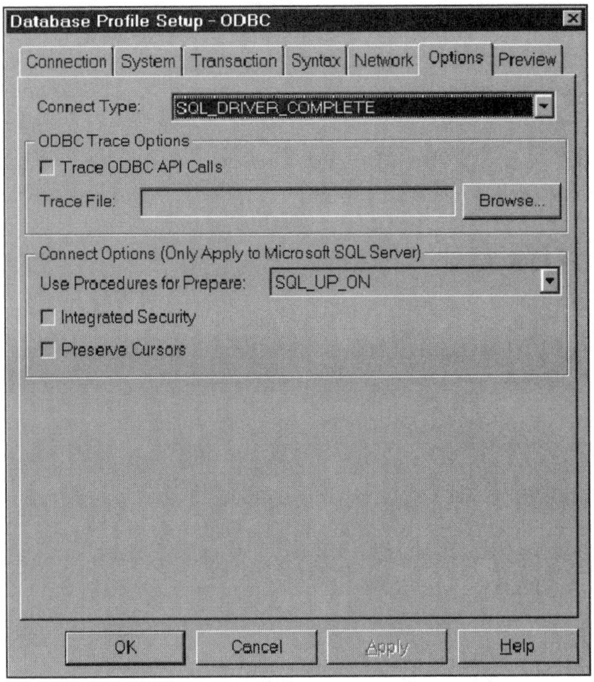

Figure 12.2
Enabling ODBC Driver Manager Trace.

To start ODBC Driver Manager Trace in the development environment, on the Options tab in the Database Profile Setup—ODBC dialog box for your connection, select the Trace ODBC API Calls checkbox. You can optionally specify a file where you want to send the output of ODBC Driver Manager Trace. By default, if the Trace ODBC API Calls checkbox is selected and no trace file is specified, PowerBuilder sends ODBC Driver Manager Trace output to a file named PBTrace.LOG.

Once you've checked this checkbox, the next time you connect to the database with this profile, PowerBuilder starts tracing your connection. To enable a database trace for other database interfaces such as Oracle or Sybase, select the Generate Trace option on the Connection tab in the Database Profile Setup dialog box of your connection.

After you've generated your trace file, stepping through it is not that difficult. Usually, the trace file gives you a more meaningful error message than the ones reported in your application. A sample trace file might look something like this:

```
DIALOG CONNECT TO TRACE SYC:
LOGID=sa
SERVER SYS11SERVER
DATA=master
SRV 10  #5701  Changed database context to 'master'.
 (0 MilliSeconds)
SRV 10  #5701  Changed database context to 'master'.
 (0 MilliSeconds) (4517 MilliSeconds)
 DISCONNECT: (1021 MilliSeconds)
 SHUTDOWN DATABASE INTERFACE: (0 MilliSeconds)
```

Profiling And Tracing

Profiling and tracing is a new feature in PowerBuilder 6.0. Tracing allows you to run your applications and generate execution trace files. Then, you can use profiling to learn which functions called which other functions and how long each activity took to execute. This information will help you identify areas that you should rewrite to improve performance and find errors in the application's logic. The PowerBuilder documentation is quite clear on this, but let me just provide a brief overview.

When you run an application with tracing turned on, PowerBuilder records a timer value in a data file every time a specific activity occurs. You control when logging begins and ends and which activities are recorded. Once you have generated a trace file, you can create several different profiles or views of the application by extracting different types of information from the trace file. Examining these profiles tells you where the application is spending the most time. You can also find routines that are being called too many times or that are being called from classes or routines that you didn't expect to call them, and you may find routines that aren't being called at all. You'll probably use the Application Profiler tool to do most of your profiling, but you can also create your own analysis tools.

PowerBuilder provides three sets of objects and functions to analyze trace files:

- Performance analysis objects and functions let you build a *call graph model* from the trace file and then get the information you want from the model. A call graph model contains information about all the routines in the trace file: how many times each routine was called, which routines called it and which routines it called, and the execution time taken by the routine itself and any routines it called.

- Trace tree objects and functions let you build and get information from a *nested trace tree model.* A nested trace tree model lists all recorded activities in the trace file in chronological order with the elapsed time for each activity.

- Trace file objects and functions access the data in the trace file sequentially.

New Objects

A number of new system objects have been added to PowerBuilder to support tracing and profiling. The following objects provide the functions and properties needed to create a performance analysis model from your trace file and to extract information from that model:

- **ProfileCall.** Provides information about the calls in the performance analysis model, including information about the called routine and the calling routine, the number of times the call was made, and the elapsed time. You use the ProfileCall object in conjunction with the ProfileRoutine and Profiling objects. No events are associated with this object.

- **ProfileRoutine.** Provides information about the routines in the performance analysis model. It includes the time spent in the routine, any called routines, the number of times each routine was called, and the class to which the routine belongs. You use the ProfileRoutine object in conjunction with the Profiling and ProfileCall or ProfileLine objects.

- **ProfileClass.** Provides information about the classes in the performance analysis model, including the routines that exist within a class. You use the ProfileClass object in conjunction with the Profiling object.

- **Profiling.** Analyzes the performance of a PowerBuilder application. It provides a performance analysis model listing all the routines (both functions and events) logged in a given trace file. It includes the functions you call to name the trace file to be analyzed, build the model, and list the classes and routines included in the model. You use the Profiling object in conjunction with the ProfileCall, ProfileClass, ProfileLine, and ProfileRoutine objects.

- **ProfileLine.** Provides information about the lines in each routine in the performance analysis model, including the number of times the line was hit, any calls made from the line, and the time spent on the line and in any called functions. You use the ProfileLine object in conjunction with the ProfileRoutine and Profiling objects.

The following objects provide the functions and properties to create a nested tree model from your trace file and to extract information from that model:

- **TraceTree.** Used to analyze the performance of a PowerBuilder application. It provides a tree model listing all the nodes logged in a given trace file. It includes the functions you call to name the trace file to be analyzed, build the tree model, and list the top-level entries in the tree model. You use the TraceTree object in conjunction with the TraceTreeNode, TraceTreeError, TraceTreeESQL, TraceTreeGarbageCollect, TraceTreeLine, TraceTreeObject, TraceTreeRoutine, and TraceTreeUser objects.

- **TraceTreeNode.** Provides information about the nodes in the tree model, including the type of activity represented by the node. You use the TraceTreeNode object in conjunction with the TraceTree object.

- **TraceTreeError.** Provides information about a tree model node identified as an occurrence of a system error or warning, including the error message and severity level. To access the extra properties of the TraceTreeError object, you assign a TraceTreeNode object whose activity type is **ActError!** to the TraceTreeError object.

- **TraceTreeObject.** Provides information about a tree model node identified as an occurrence of an object. To access the extra properties of the TraceTreeObject object, you assign a TraceTreeNode object whose activity type is **ActObjectCreate!** or **ActObjectDestroy!** to the TraceTreeObject object.

- **TraceTreeESQL.** Provides information about a tree model node identified as an occurrence of an embedded SQL (ESQL) statement. To access the extra properties of the TraceTreeESQL object, you assign a TraceTreeNode object whose activity type is **ActESQL!** to the TraceTreeESQL object.

- **TraceTreeRoutine.** Provides information about a tree model node identified as an occurrence of a routine. To access the extra properties of the TraceTreeRoutine object, you assign a TraceTreeNode object whose activity type is **ActRoutine!** to the TraceTreeRoutine object.

- **TraceTreeGarbageCollect.** Provides information about a tree model node identified as an occurrence of garbage collection, including the children or classes and routines called by that node. To access the extra properties of the TraceTreeGarbageCollect object, you assign a TraceTreeNode object whose activity type is **ActGarbageCollect!** to the TraceTreeGarbageCollect object.

- **TraceTreeUser.** Provides information about a tree model node identified as an occurrence of an activity you selected for logging, including the activity argument and message. To access the extra properties of the TraceTreeUser object, you assign a TraceTreeNode object whose activity type is **ActUser!** to the TraceTreeUser object.

- **TraceTreeLine.** Provides information about a tree model node identified as an occurrence of a routine line hit. To access the extra properties of the TraceTreeLine object, you assign a TraceTreeNode object whose activity type is **ActLine!** to the TraceTreeLine object.

The following objects provide the functions and properties to access the data in your trace file sequentially:

- **TraceActivityNode.** Provides information about the nodes in a trace file, including the type of activity represented by a node. You use the TraceActivityNode object in conjunction with the TraceFile object.

- **TraceGarbageCollect.** Provides information about a node in a trace file identified as an occurrence of garbage collection. To access the extra properties of the TraceGarbageCollect object, you assign a TraceActivityNode object whose activity type is **ActGarbageCollect!** to the TraceGarbageCollect object.

- **TraceBeginEnd.** Provides information about a node in a trace file identified as an occurrence of a logging start or finish. To access the extra properties of the TraceBeginEnd object, you assign a TraceActivityNode object whose activity type is **ActBegin!** to the TraceBeginEnd object.

- **TraceLine.** Provides information about a node in a trace file identified as an occurrence of a routine line hit. To access the extra properties of the TraceLine object, you assign a TraceActivityNode object whose activity type is **ActLine!** to the TraceLine object.

- **TraceError.** Provides information about a node in a trace file identified as an occurrence of a system error or warning, including the error message and severity level. To access the extra properties of the TraceError object, you assign a TraceActivityNode object whose activity type is **ActError!** to the TraceError object.

- **TraceObject.** Provides information about a node in a trace file identified as the creation or destruction of an object. To access the extra properties of the TraceObject

object, you assign a TraceActivityNode object whose activity type is **ActObjectCreate!** or **ActObjectDestroy!** to the TraceObject object.

- **TraceESQL.** Provides information about a node in a trace file identified as an occurrence of an ESQL statement. To access the extra properties of the TraceESQL object, you assign a TraceActivityNode object whose activity type is **ActESQL!** to the TraceESQL object.

- **TraceRoutine.** Provides information about a node in a trace file identified as an occurrence of a routine. To access the extra properties of the TraceRoutine object, you assign a TraceActivityNode object whose activity type is **ActRoutine!** to the TraceRoutine object.

- **TraceFile.** Accesses the contents of a trace file created from a PowerBuilder application. Unlike the Profiling and TraceTree objects, the TraceFile object does not provide properties and functions to create an analysis model. You use the TraceFile object in conjunction with the TraceActivityNode, TraceBeginEnd, TraceError, TraceESQL, TraceGarbageCollect, TraceLine, TraceObject, TraceRoutine, and TraceUser objects.

- **TraceUser.** Provides information about a node in a trace file identified as an occurrence of an activity you selected for logging, including the activity argument and message. To access the extra properties of the TraceUser object, you assign a TraceActivityNode object whose activity type is **ActUser!** to the TraceUser object.

The following functions enable you to collect data in a trace file:

- **TraceBegin()**
- **TraceEnd()**
- **TraceClose()**
- **TraceError()**
- **TraceDisableActivity()**
- **TraceOpen()**
- **TraceUser()**
- **TraceUser()**

The following example opens a trace file and then begins logging the enabled activities for the first block of code to be traced:

```
END CHOOSE

TraceOpen("MyTrace",Clock!)
```

```
TraceEnableActivity(ActESQL!)
TraceEnableActivity(ActGarbageCollect!)
TraceEnableActivity(ActObjectCreate!)
TraceEnableActivity(ActObjectDestroy!)

TraceBegin("Trace_block_1")
```

These functions enable you to build models or extract information for your trace file:

- **BuildModel()**
- **NextActivity()**
- **ClassList()**
- **Open()**
- **Close()**
- **OutgoingCallList()**
- **DestroyModel()**
- **Reset()**
- **EntryList()**
- **RoutineList()**
- **GetChildrenList()**
- **SetTraceFileName()**
- **IncomingCallList()**
- **SystemRoutine()**
- **LineList()**

Collecting Trace Information

You can collect trace information for an entire application or for specific parts of an application. To trace an entire application run in the development environment, use the Profiling tab on the System Options dialog box and select Enable Tracing (see Figure 12.3).

To trace an entire application run or specific parts of an application, you can insert trace calls at the beginning and end of the code you want to trace, or you can add a window to the application that lets you turn tracing on and off as you run the application. With any of these methods, the following information can be specified:

- **The name and location of the trace file and optional labels for blocks of trace data.** The default name of the trace file is the name of the application with the extension .PBP. The trace file is saved in the directory where the PBL or executable file resides, and it overwrites any existing file of the same name. If you run several different tests on the same application, you'll want to change the trace file name for each test. You can also associate a label with the trace data. If you're tracing several different parts of an application in a single test run, you can associate a different label with the trace data for each part (called a *trace block*).

- **The kind of timer used in the trace file.** By default, the time at which each activity begins and ends is recorded using the clock timer, which measures an absolute time with reference to an external activity, such as the machine's startup time. The clock timer measures time in microseconds. Depending on the speed of your machine's central processing unit, the clock timer can offer a resolution of less than one microsecond. A timer's resolution is the smallest unit of time the timer can measure. You can also use process or thread timers, which measure time in microseconds with reference to when the process or thread being executed started. Use the thread timer for distributed applications. Both process and thread timers exclude the time taken

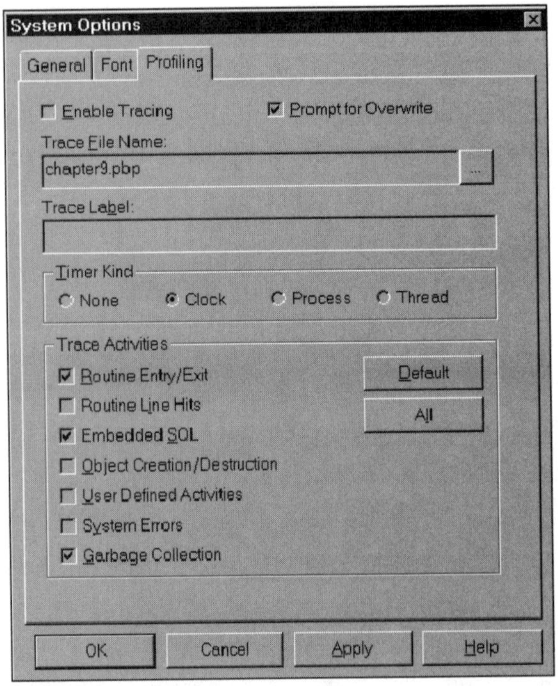

Figure 12.3
Enable tracing for profiler.

by any other running processes or threads so that they give you a more accurate measurement of how long the process or thread is taking to execute, but both have a lower resolution than the clock timer.

- **The activities you want recorded in the trace file.** You can choose to record in the trace file the time at which any of the following activities occurs. If you're using PowerScript functions to collect trace information, use the TraceActivity enumerated type to identify the activity.

  - **ActRoutine!** Routine entry or exit

  - **ActLine!** Execution of any line in any routine

  - **ActESQL!** Use of an embedded SQL verb

  - **ActObjectCreate!** Object creation or destruction

  - **ActObjectDestroy!** Object creation or destruction

  - **ActUser!** An activity that records an informational message

  - **ActError!** A system error or warning

  - **ActGarbageCollect!** Garbage collection

  - **ActProfile!** Routine entry and exit, embedded SQL verbs, object creation and destruction, and garbage collection

  - **ActTrace!** All except **ActLine!**

Analyzing Trace Information

PowerBuilder provides three ways for you to analyze your generated trace information:

- Analyze performance by building a call graph model and extracting information about specific classes and routines

- Build a trace tree model showing the sequence of activities executed and the time elapsed for each activity and for the activities resulting from it

- Access the data in the trace file directly

Analyze Performance

You use the functions and objects listed in Table 12.1 to analyze the performance of your applications. Please note that each of these functions returns a value of type **ErrorReturn**. It is good practice to check the return before doing further processing. These return values may vary from function to function and the PowerBuilder function reference manual lists them all. The objects listed in Table 12.1 contain information such as the

Table 12.1 New functions and objects to analyze application performance.

Function	Object	Description
SetTraceFileName()	Profiling	Sets the name of the trace file to be analyzed.
BuildModel()	Profiling	Builds a call graph model based on the trace file.
RoutineList()	Profiling, ProfileClass	Gets a list of routines in the model or in a class.
ClassList()	Profiling	Gets a list of classes in the model.
SystemRoutine()	Profiling	Gets the name of the routine node that represents the root of the model.
IncomingCallList()	ProfileRoutine	Gets a list of routines that called a specific routine.
OutGoingCallList()	ProfileRoutine, ProfileLine	Gets a list of routines called by a specific routine or from a specific line.
LineList()	ProfileRoutine	Gets a list of lines in the routine in line order.
DestroyModel()	Profiling	Destroys the current performance analysis model and all its associated objects.

number of times a line or routine was executed as well as the amount of time spent in a line or routine and in any routines called from that line or routine.

Trace Tree Model

You can use the functions and objects listed in Table 12.2 to build a nested trace tree model of your applications. Each of these functions returns a value of type **ErrorReturn**. Each TraceTreeNode object returned by EntryList and GetChildrenList represents a single node in the trace tree model and contains information about the parent of the node and the type of activity it represents.

Accessing Trace Data

The functions and objects listed in Table 12.3 can be used to access the data in the trace file directly so that you can develop your own analysis tools. With the exception of NextActivity, each of these functions returns a value of type **ErrorReturn**. Each TraceActivityNode object includes information about the category of the activity, the timer value when the activity occurred, and the activity type. The category of the activity is either In or Out for activities that have separate beginning and ending points, such as routines, garbage collection, and tracing, itself. Each such activity has two timer values associated with it: the time when it began and the time when it completed.

Table 12.2 New functions and objects used to build a trace tree model.

Function	Object	Description
SetTraceFileName()	TraceTree	Sets the name of the trace file.
BuildModel()	TraceTree	Builds a trace tree model.
EntryList()	TraceTree	Gets a list of the top-level entries in the trace tree model.
GetChildrenList()	TraceTreeRoutine, TraceTreeObject, TraceTreeGarbageCollect	Gets a list of the children of the routine object.
DestroyModel()	TraceTree	Destroys the current trace tree model.

Table 12.3 New functions and objects to access data in a trace file directly.

Function	Object	Description
Open()	TraceFile	Opens the trace file.
NextActivity()	TraceFile	Returns the next activity.
Reset()	TraceFile	Resets the next activity to the beginning of the trace file.
Close()	TraceFile	Closes the open trace file.

The Profiler

The Application Profiler is a PowerBuilder sample application that performs most common profiling and analysis tasks for you. You can view and analyze the output of a trace file (.PBP) to learn which functions and events called which other functions and events and how long each activity took to execute. This information can help you find errors in your application logic as well as bottlenecks that are somewhat slow and should be rewritten to improve performance.

The Profiler provides you with three views on your trace information—Class view, Routine view, and Trace view—which we'll take a look at in more detail.

Class View

Class view uses the call graph model to display statistics for PowerBuilder objects as well as their functions and events. The Class view contains only those classes that executed while tracing was enabled. Figure 12.4 shows you the bar graph generated by the Profiler to display statistical information in the **w_main** window.

Now, you might be asking what all the metrics mean. Altogether, five metrics are displayed in Class view:

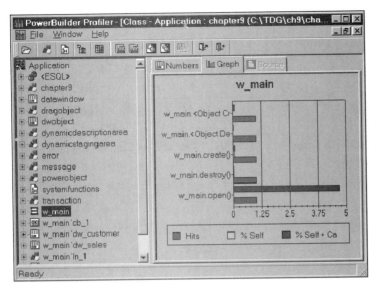

Figure 12.4
Graph statistics in a bar graph.

- **Hits.** The number of times a routine is executed in a particular context

- **Self.** The time spent in the routine or line itself

- **%Self.** Self as a percentage of the total time the calling routine was active

- **Self+Called.** The time spent in the routine or line and in routines or lines called from the routine or line

- **%Self+Called.** Self+Called as a percentage of the total time tracing was enabled

Routine View

Routine view uses the call graph model to display statistics for a routine, all routines that called that routine, and all routines called by that routine. The Routine view contains only those routines that executed while tracing was enabled. This view uses three main DataWindows to display information for a specific routine (see Figure 12.5):

- **Calling routines.** The top DataWindow, which lists functions and events that call the routine displayed in the middle DataWindows

- **Current routine.** The middle DataWindow, which highlights the current routine along with its detailed statistics

- **Called routines.** The bottom DataWindow, which lists functions and events called by the current routine

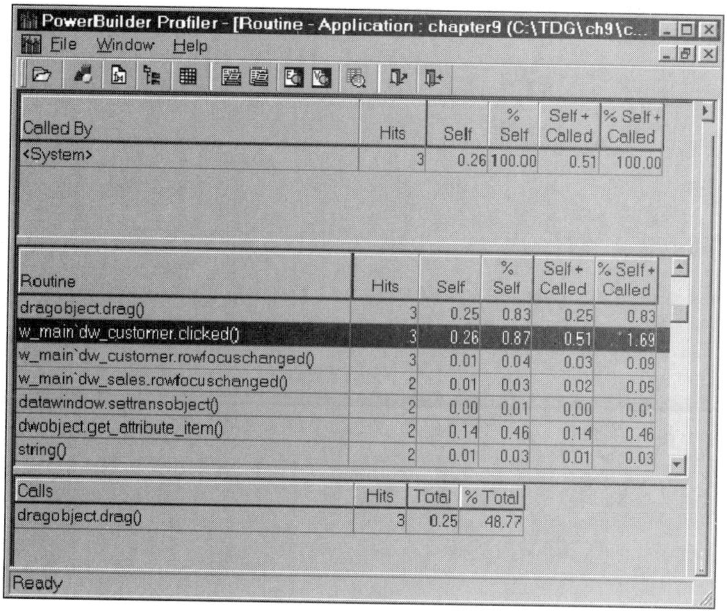

Figure 12.5
Routine view statistics.

The metrics displayed in Routine view are the same as the ones for the Class view, with the addition of the following:

- **Self Min.** The shortest time spent in the routine or line itself

- **Self Max.** The longest time spent in the routine or line itself

- **Self+Called Min.** The shortest time spent in the routine or line and in called routines or lines

- **Self+Called Max.** The longest time spent in the routine or line and in called routines or lines

- **Total.** The total time spent in the routine

- **%Total.** Total as a percentage of the total time tracing was enabled

Trace View

Trace view uses a TreeView control to display the events and functions in your trace file. The initial display shows all top-level routines. Then, each level expands to show you the sequence of routine execution. Once this is fully expanded, you'll see the complete sequence of executed instructions for your trace file. Figure 12.6 shows the Trace view window.

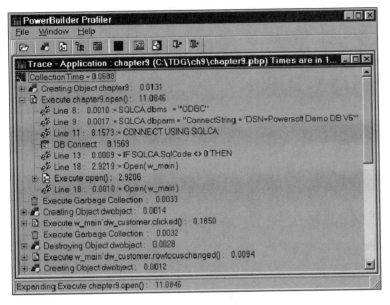

Figure 12.6
Trace view window.

The Routine metric represents the routine or line number that was executed. The Execution Time metric is the total execution time for the Tree view entry. This is total time from the start of the entry to the end of the entry.

Moving On

As you can see, PowerBuilder provides you with many tools for debugging your applications. You have a new debugger, and you have the ability to run both a database trace and an application trace. You now have the Profiler tool to analyze your application trace to find errors and performance bottlenecks as well as to print various statistical reports. Not that you need to use these tools, right?

Next, we'll get into the advanced development part of PowerBuilder. I'll begin with version control. As you get involved in various development projects, you should be using some sort of version control to manage changes that occur in your development phases. This is where we have to check in.

PART III
The
Advanced
Guide

Version Control

Version control provides a tracking mechanism for changes to the objects in your development project. As objects are changed and the changes are recorded, the version control system creates a version of the object in an archive. The archive contains a complete history of the changes made to an object. As a result, you can get any revision of an object at any point in the development process. Most version control systems offer recovery methods and provide a secondary backup mechanism. These tools also offer management functions that enable you to manage your complex development environment.

Every development project should be using a version control tool of some kind. The complexity and dynamics that exist in development require careful management. A version control tool will allow you to manage the coding effort more effectively. Version control can help manage changes that occur at any point in the development life cycle, including, but not limited to, requirements, design, and documentation.

This chapter emphasizes the use of version control in the development of your PowerBuilder applications. You can version any PowerBuilder object directly in the development environment using the Source menu option of the Library Painter. Other version control requirements will need to be undertaken in the version control tool.

Version Control Benefits

Version control offers many critical benefits to development projects:

- When used in a team development environment, version control prevents developers from overwriting each other's work by granting modify access to an object to only one developer.

- Version control eases the complexity of creating the necessary project files. You can select any revision of the objects to build the files. By default, the most current versions are used to create these files. You can access any version of an object that has been checked into the version control tool. You can also create a complete Change History that includes changes to the source.

- Version control offers a complete back-up and recovery mechanism for the development team. However, as Steve McConnell mentions in the book *Code Complete* (ISBN: 1-55615-484-4), you shouldn't completely rely on version control as a back-up strategy. Back up the version control data files on a regular basis.

The following scenarios illustrate the use of version control in real development environments. The complexity of the environment, which increases in each example, determines the sophistication level of the version control tool required. As the complexity of the environment increases, the version control requirements increase. As a result, increasingly sophisticated version control tools are needed.

Scenario 1

When in college, I was working on a term assignment that involved the creation of an application that managed the ticket sales for a film festival. The project included complicated pointer manipulation. On project due date, I discovered that my application had a minor error in one of the pointer functions. I set forth to correct the error, but had neglected to create a backup of the files. Once I had identified the suspected problem code, I began to modify the code to correct the error. After recompiling the application, I began to experience additional errors. Again, I identified the suspected problem code and made changes to correct the error. After several iterations, my application no longer worked. Without a backup, I was not able to submit the program with the initially minor error. More important, I was no longer able to submit an application that functioned!

Now, if I had used version control, I would have been able to get copies of the source files at the point in which the minor error existed and submit that version of the application. Here, a good backup strategy would have prevented the problems that occurred later on when I made more changes to my application.

Scenario 2

You are working with a project team and are responsible for making modifications to a function contained in a window. The modification of the layout for the same window is assigned to a colleague. After completing the changes, you save the window into a shared set of libraries. Shortly after completing this work, your colleague saves some changes to the window to the same location. The changes that you have made have been overwritten by your colleague.

Using version control, your colleague would not be able to overwrite the changes you made. When assigned to the task, you would "check out" the object. Your colleague would not be able to modify the same object until you have "checked in" your changes. He would be able to access the object in read-only mode, thus enabling him to plan his changes given the current state of the object. This functionality is critical in team-development environments. It ensures that only one developer can have modify access to an object at any given point in time.

In such a scenario, you could use the PB Native version control functionality to prevent one developer from overwriting the changes of another. When an object is checked out using this technique, the object is locked, and other users cannot access the object for modification. A full-featured version control tool will allow for future growth in the version control requirements without impacting the basic requirements.

Scenario 3

An application has been assigned to multiple development teams. One of the teams is assigned to the development of version 1.0 of the application, and another team is assigned to the development of version 2.0, which will be started at a milestone in the version 1.0 development process. Now, how do you separate version 2.0 from version 1.0 as one of the teams still needs work on version 1.0?

Most version control tools provide mechanisms to create multiple projects to represent the application versions. Furthermore, the new project can be populated easily with the version 1.0 objects that existed at the time the version 2.0 team started development efforts. In this example, you'll need a full-featured tool to support the version control requirements of the environment.

The conclusion is that a development environment consisting of more than one developer should implement a full-featured version control tool.

PowerBuilder Version Control Interfaces

PowerBuilder offers minimum version control functionality in the PB Native interface. This interface prevents multiple developers from accessing an object at the same time. This level of version control is sufficient in development environments in which there is no interest in being able to backtrack to earlier versions of objects.

To achieve full version control, you may need to use a version control tool such as Object Cycle, INTERSOLV PVCS Version Manager, or MKS Source Integrity. Full version control support includes the ability to provide phased implementations, revision histories, and reporting. Prior to PowerBuilder version 5.0.03, there was limited support for third-party version control tools.

The introduction of the SCC API interface in the PowerBuilder 5.0.03 maintenance release has allowed for a broader range of version control tools to be implemented in the PowerBuilder development process. The SCC API allows you to access any version control tool that complies with the Microsoft Common Source Control Code specification. Most version control vendors have adopted this standard into their tools.

Version control is a necessary component of a development project. At minimum, you should use PB Native to ensure there's no conflict in the development efforts. If you need to track the evolutionary changes of the development project, you need to use a full-featured version control tool. In this case, choose a tool that has a native interface such as Object Cycle, PVCS Version Manager, MKS Source Integrity, or a tool which is SCC API-compliant. Because PowerBuilder offers only basic version control support within the development environment, you'll need to evaluate the advanced functionality you want to use and select a tool that meets those needs.

PowerBuilder Library Configuration

The problems encountered by PowerBuilder developers when working with a version control tool are primarily caused by the inappropriate configuration of libraries. In the sections that follow, the components that make up an appropriate configuration are defined. The components are the work library, the archived libraries, and the shared libraries. Figure 13.1 illustrates the configuration of the libraries to support version control.

Work Library

The work library is the workhorse for version control activities in PowerBuilder. You check out objects from the archived libraries into this library for modification. Any new objects you create for the PowerBuilder application will initially be created in your work library prior to being archived in the version control environment. Because the work library will have objects being added and removed frequently, there's a greater risk of corruption of the library. The library should be optimized periodically as a preventative measure. If the application begins to exhibit unusual behavior that cannot be explained, library optimization should be performed.

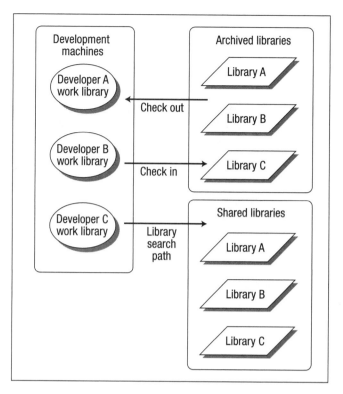

Figure 13.1
The PowerBuilder library configuration.

The work library is a private library used by individual developers. The library is normally stored on your computer or a private network drive. The library can be stored in a shared network directory, but it's recommended that a suitable naming standard be adopted to ensure that the library is not used by other developers. For example, you can use your network logon ID for the name standard of the working library.

The work library should have a current version of the application object whose library search path includes the shared libraries. The application object should be configured for the version control tool. This is accomplished by connecting to the version control tool and selecting the configuration file that has been defined for the archived libraries. The inclusion of the application object in the work library allows you to perform testing and debugging for the objects that are being created or modified without impacting the registered libraries. The configuration to the version control tool helps to ensure that the check-in function archives the changes within the proper version control tool. A check-in that occurs when not connected to a version control tool will use PB Native. When you check in objects while connected to PB Native, the object is not archived.

Archived Libraries

The archived libraries, which consist of the PowerBuilder project libraries, contain the objects that have been registered with the version control tool. The objects contained in these libraries will have the drum icon, which defines its current state in the version control environment. A drum icon indicates that the object has been registered with the version control tool and is available for check-out. A drum icon with a lock indicates that the object is currently checked out. You can only access these objects in read-only mode. An object without a drum icon has not been registered with the version control tool. Objects in this state in the archived libraries should be awaiting registration to the version control tool. Any new objects that are being added to the project should be registered when the object is added to an archived library.

Shared Libraries

The shared libraries are created periodically based on the state of the archived libraries. These libraries are included in the library search path for the application object that's contained in the work library. The version control manager should create the shared libraries frequently to ensure that each developer has access to a recent version of the objects. If the shared library contains objects that are not current, any testing conducted is suspect.

Many environments do not include the shared libraries. Rather, they use the archived libraries in the library search path of the work library. Developers working in this environment will experience frequent PowerBuilder I/O errors when performing version control activities. The cause of the I/O error is related to the need to provide a constant state to the objects during a debugging session. Periodically during a debugging session, the libraries are locked so as to prevent changes to the objects that they contain. This prevents PowerBuilder from updating the library file during many version control processes.

The shared libraries are normally stored on a network drive so that each developer can access the libraries. In some environments, these files are copied locally to obtain improved performance during development and testing. Under this scenario, you should make sure the libraries are synchronized with the shared libraries.

The creation of the shared libraries requires the creation of a set of libraries that duplicates the libraries contained in the archived libraries. The shared libraries can be updated by using the Take Functionality option of the Registration Directory dialog box. This technique requires that the administrator know the owner library of each object. An alternative is to use the Library Painter Entry|Copy function. The version control administrator copies each object from the archived libraries to the shared libraries. The use of Windows Explorer, File Manager, or some other file-copying method cannot be used.

When these techniques are used, the objects retain the drum status icon, and it's more difficult to differentiate between archived and shared libraries.

Working With Version Control

Once your application is configured properly, you can begin to work with your version control tool. In the next section, let's go through using version control together.

Connecting To The Version Control Tool

Prior to using any version control activities, you should connect to a version control tool from the Library Painter's Source|Connect menu item. In the Connect dialog box, select the desired version control tool. In the sample connection shown in Figure 13.2, the PowerBuilder SCC API is being used for version control. This function establishes a connection to the version control tool. The title bar of the Library Painter indicates the source control tool that is currently connected.

The message shown in Figure 13.3 is displayed if PowerBuilder is not able to locate the source management DLL. Two common reasons exist for not being able to connect to the source control tool. First, the PowerBuilder interface file for the version control tool has not been installed. This file is located in the PowerBuilder system directory. The PowerBuilder documentation contains the name of the interface file for your tool. Second, if the interface file exists, the version control tool has not been installed correctly or the required paths have not been defined.

> **Note:** If you're not able to connect using the SCC API, you might need to install the Microsoft IDE option for the version control tool. For example, Object Cycle has a checkbox for this option. PVCS, however, uses a separate installation option.

PowerBuilder, during the connection process, confirms that the necessary interface file exists and ensures that the necessary version control tool files have been installed. The PB.INI initialization file contains an entry for each application that has an associated

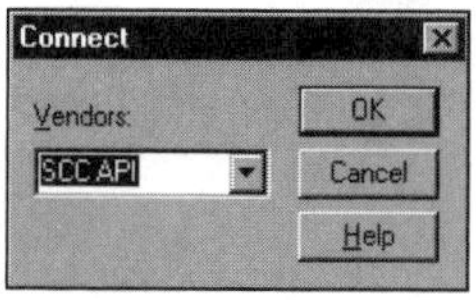

Figure 13.2
The Connect dialog box.

Figure 13.3
Unable to locate source management DLL.

configuration. If an entry exists for the current application, PowerBuilder initializes the connection using the information contained in the configuration file. Otherwise, the interface prompts you to create one or select an existing one, after which it creates the entry in the initialization file.

Creating The Configuration File

The first time you connect your application, you'll be prompted to create a new configuration file or use an existing one. To create a new configuration file, use the Save Configuration File dialog box to select the desired directory to locate the file and enter the file name. If you are using an existing configuration file, select the file using the dialog box shown in Figure 13.4.

> *Note: You may want to use an existing configuration file to ensure consistency between the archived libraries and your work.*

The configuration file is associated with the application object. The PowerBuilder initialization file has an entry in the Library key for each application configured. The configuration file contains configuration information specific to the version control tool. In the example shown in Figure 13.5, a configuration is being defined for the SCC API for Object Cycle. You can change the settings for the file using the Source|Configuration option in the Library Painter.

> *Note: For specific information regarding the configuration for your version control tool, refer to PowerBuilder's version control documentation.*

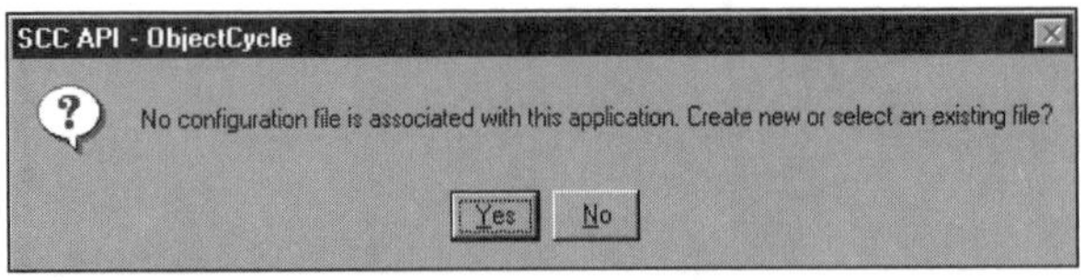

Figure 13.4
Using an existing configuration file.

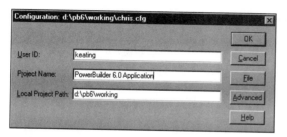

Figure 13.5
SCC API configuration Object Cycle.

Registering The PowerBuilder Objects

The archived libraries contain the objects that are registered with the version control tool. When an object is registered, the version control tool creates the initial version of the object and places the object under version control.

The version control manager should be responsible for registering PowerBuilder objects. To register objects, select the desired objects in the Library Painter and then select Source|Register. When prompted, you should provide a useful comment that identifies the object's purpose. The Registration dialog box is shown in Figure 13.6. During the registration process, an internal flag in the library file that is used to indicate the version control status of the object is set to Registered. The flag is also used to determine the drum icon that is displayed in the Library Painter.

Objects that are registered will have a drum icon displayed to the right of the object-type icon in the Library Painter. As indicated previously, the drum icon may have a lock that indicates that the object is checked out. The object is locked and cannot be accessed by other developers for modification. See Figure 13.7 for an example of how a registered library looks in a version control environment.

Figure 13.6
The ObjectCycle Registration dialog box.

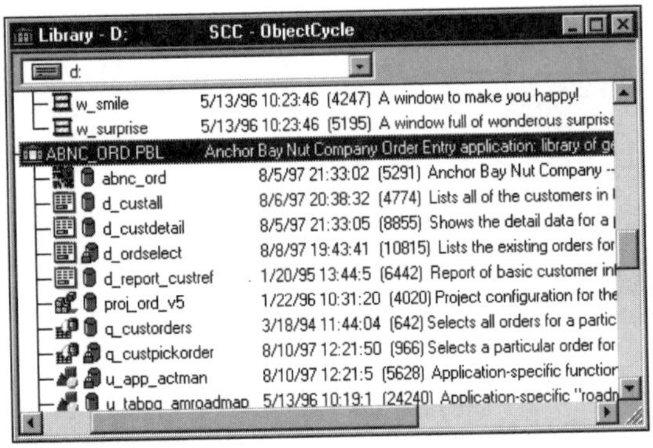

Figure 13.7
A registered library in a version control environment.

To ensure that you are able to get objects at any point in the development cycle, it's best to introduce version control prior to any development work. This does not mean you cannot version existing applications. You need to cease any new development work until the application is successfully registered. The creation of the archived libraries should be managed carefully. Make sure that only the desired objects are included. Once the libraries have been verified as being correct, you can register the objects. When the archive libraries have been registered successfully, your development work can recommence.

When adding new objects to an application, you create these objects in the working library. When your object is at a state where it should be registered, move it to the desired archived library and then register it.

Checking Out The Desired Objects

Once the objects have been registered, you're able to start development work. You need to check out the object to your working library in order to make modifications. Select the desired object in the archived library and then select Source|Check Out from the Library Painter. In the Check Out Library Entries dialog box, shown in Figure 13.8, select your working library to store the checked-out object.

Objects that have been checked out cannot be checked out by other developers. Modifications to an object that has not been checked out cannot be saved or checked in. This ensures that only one developer can have modification access at any given time.

The PowerBuilder check-out process queries the version control tool for the tip (or last revision) of the object. The version control tool then returns the revisions using an import-like function to create the object in the working library. If the object is successfully created in the working library, the internal flag is set to represent a checked-out object. Using this flag, PowerBuilder displays a drum icon that has an arrow pointing to the left.

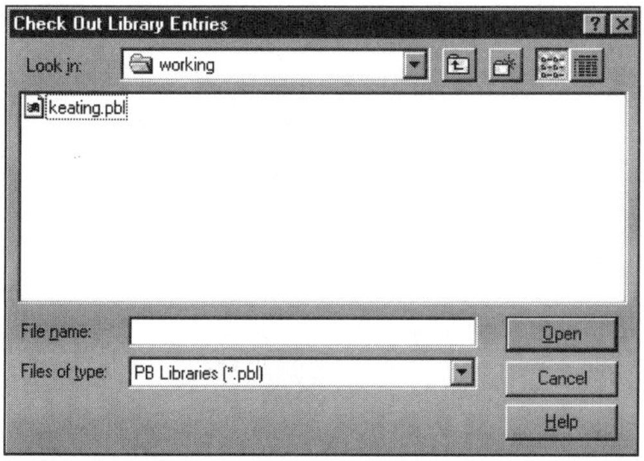

Check Out Library Entries

Look in: working

keating.pbl

File name:

Files of type: PB Libraries (*.pbl)

Open

Cancel

Help

Figure 13.8
The Check Out Library Entries dialog box.

The archived library status flag is set to indicate that the object has been checked out, resulting in a drum icon with a lock.

Checking In The Modified Objects

An object that has been checked out and modified needs to be checked in to create a new revision in the archive history of the object. Once the changes have been made and the required testing is completed, it is recommended that the object be checked in. This will allow other developers to have access to the object. You'll be asked to provide a comment for the object during the check-in process. Make sure that the comment describes the modifications made to the object. You may also want to include other relevant information such as who made the changes, when they were made, and why they were made. The Check In Object(s) dialog box is shown in Figure 13.9. Prior to any major builds, your development team should check all relevant objects into the version control system. This ensures that the most current versions of the objects are available for that build. The administrator may also want to refresh the shared library directory at this time.

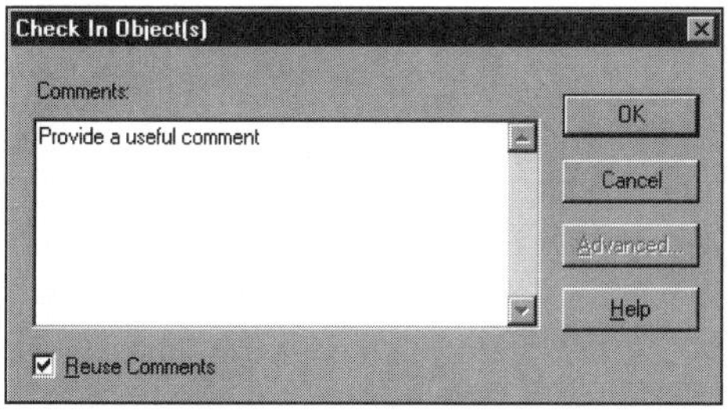

Check In Object(s)

Comments:

Provide a useful comment

OK

Cancel

Advanced

Help

☑ Reuse Comments

Figure 13.9
The Check In Object(s) dialog box.

The check-in process creates a temporary file that is similar to an exported file without the export header. This file is then passed to the version control tool that creates a version in its archive. Once this is done, the object is removed from the working library. The archived library status flag for the object is set to indicate that the object is registered but not checked out. The drum icon is changed from the locked image to the standard drum. The archived library object is updated with the current version.

Clearing The Check-Out Status Of An Object

Have you ever worked on a development project in which you were experimenting with the implementation of a solution? You may have experienced occasions in which this experimentation has resulted in an object that is no longer usable.

If the object is under version control, you can recover the object by getting the last revision from the archive. You can also clear the check-out status and then check out the object again. To do this, select the object in your working library and select Source|Clear Check Out Status from the Library Painter. Only the owner of the checked-out object can perform this task in the PowerBuilder environment. As shown in Figure 13.10, you'll be prompted for a confirmation of clearing the check-out status. Once this is confirmed, PowerBuilder queries the archived library or the version control tool to determine the ID of the user who originally checked out the object. It compares this information with the user ID entry in the Library section of the initialization file. If these values match, PowerBuilder requests that the version control tool reset the check-out status. The archived library status flag and drum icon are reset to indicate a registered object. Once this is done, PowerBuilder asks whether the object should be deleted from the working library. If you do not delete the file, the drum icon is removed from the working library object. The removal of the drum indicates that the object is no longer under version control.

The need to clear check-out status is critical in situations in which the developer is not able to come to work for a period of time. An administrator of the version control system should be contacted to perform this task. Under this scenario, it may be necessary to implement this function using the version control tool directly.

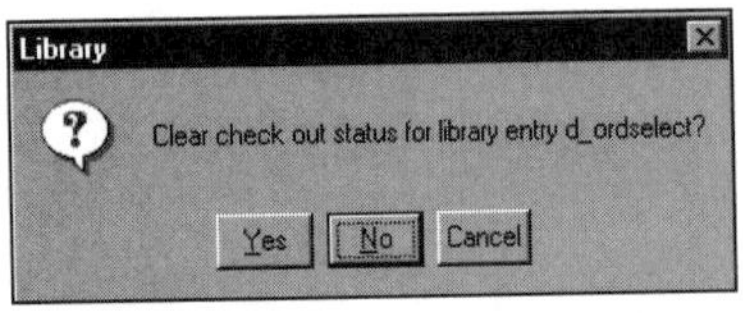

Figure 13.10
Clearing check-out status.

Note: *Do not clear the check-out status of objects that are not yours without good reason. A developer who is taking a sick day should not pay the penalty of losing changes made to the object resulting from someone clearing the check-out status indiscriminately. If your environment requires many developers to work on the same object in similar time frames, you should recommend that objects be checked in on a daily basis. However, one of the problems with this technique is that objects are checked out in a first-come-first-served strategy. Daily check-ins may prevent the completion of work by a developer on the next day because a colleague has already checked out the object.*

Viewing The Check-Out Status Of Registered Objects

You can also see which objects have been checked out from the archived libraries. Select Source|View Check Out Status from the Library Painter. The dialog box (see Figure 13.11) contains valuable information, including the following:

- The developer who has the object checked out

- The archived library (indicated as the source) that owns the object

- The working library (indicated as the destination) where the object resides for modification

Figure 13.11
Check-out status.

This information may be for informative purposes only. However, you might need to find out who has the object checked out if you've been assigned to immediately fix an error in that object. Without this information, you have to contact each member of the development team to find out who has the object checked out. If the developer who has the object is not in the office, it may take time to get access to that object.

Viewing The Registration Directory

The registration directory displays a complete listing of registered objects. Selecting objects in the list enables the Report, Take, and Label functions. A report provides information regarding the archive history, including the revisions in the archive. The Take function is used to get copies of the objects. The objects that are obtained in a Take are not under version control. You cannot modify these files and create a revision in the source archive. When the shared library was discussed earlier in the chapter, the use of the Take function was offered as a means to populate the shared libraries. The Label function provides a method to name a revision of an object. You may want to label an object to simplify the selection of a group of objects that are related in some fashion. The SCC API does not support labeling in PowerBuilder. If you're using this interface, access the labeling feature directly from the version control tool.

You can also get a list of revisions for an object by double-clicking the desired object in the Registration Directory dialog box. This feature is not available to all version control tools. For example, the SCC API connected to Object Cycle uses the Report button for this information. In the Registration dialog box shown in Figure 13.12, the **d_custall** object has three revisions.

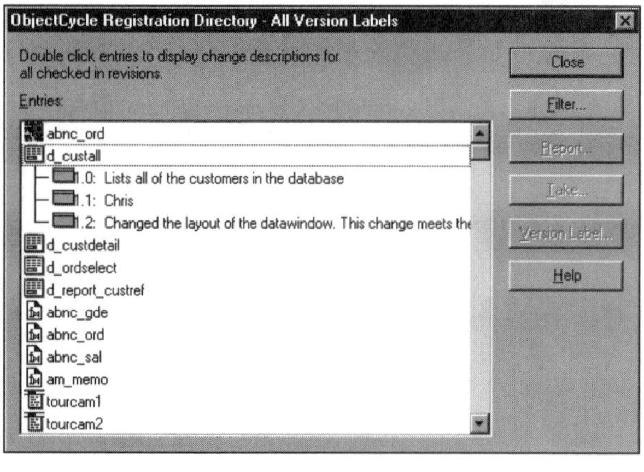

Figure 13.12
Registration directory.

Creating New Releases Of Your Application

You can create a new release at any point. Typically, a new release is created at a project milestone. In a staged release environment, a new release is created at the end of each stage. If you begin to work on the next version of your application, you create a new release to identify the starting point of the next version. The creation of a new release should be handled by your version control administrator.

To create a new release, select Source|Create New Release from the Library Painter. In the dialog box shown in Figure 13.13, enter the name of the new project. You may want to identify the version in this project name. The starting revision number should reflect the version of the project. For example, the starting revision for the version 2.0.2 release could be set to 2.0.02. Select the location to store the archive files in the archive or folder section of the dialog box. You should create new directories for the archives if the version control tool stores the archives as files. There's no need to change the folder names for an Object Cycle project. Do not use the old libraries to store objects for the new release. New libraries should be defined.

Restoring Libraries For A Project Build

When you build an executable, PowerBuilder stores information about the application in the project object. This information enables the restoration of the project libraries. Each time the executable is built, PowerBuilder updates the project object with the new information. The management of the build process is an important component in

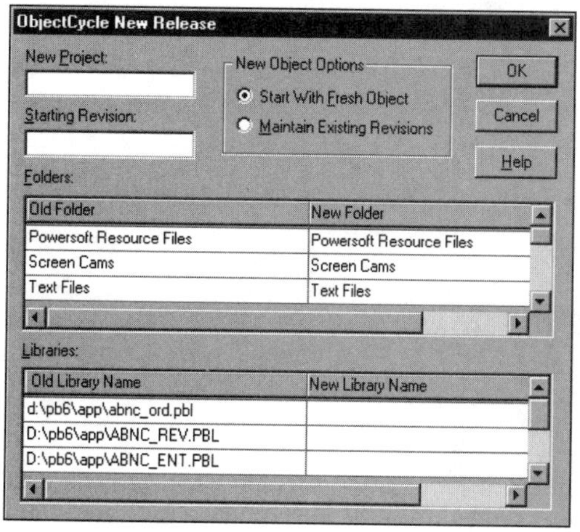

Figure 13.13
Creating a new release.

allowing you to re-create libraries that match the project libraries. PowerBuilder stores the following items:

- The object name, the object type, and the library in which the object was stored

- Archive names and revision details

- Revision labels (if defined)

The first piece of information can be accessed directly by selecting Design|List Objects from the Project Painter, as shown in Figure 13.14. The remaining information is reserved for use by PowerBuilder and is hidden.

You can re-create the libraries that existed for a project build by selecting Design|Restore Libraries, as shown in Figure 13.15. Prior to restoring libraries, you should create a directory to store the restored libraries. If you restore libraries in the same location as the archived libraries, you might lose registration information. In the new library column, enter the path to the new directory and the library name.

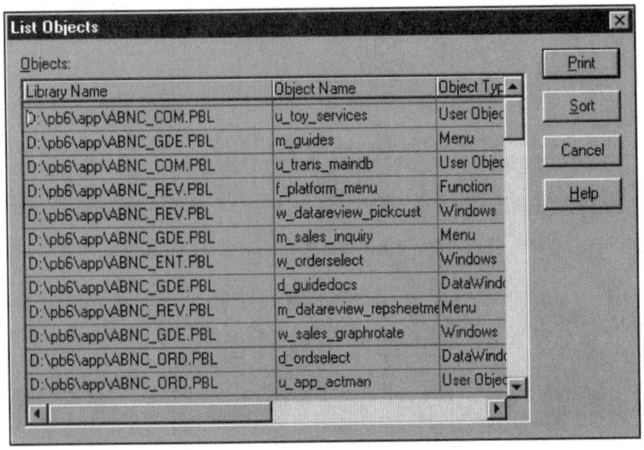

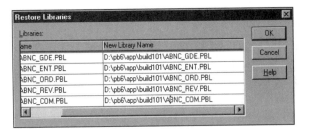

Figure 13.14
List of objects.

Figure 13.15
Restoring libraries.

Note: Create a project object for each build. The comment or project name should include a build identifier for reference purposes. You'll then be able to re-create any build version of your executable.

Version Control Support

Suppose you have been assigned to a PowerBuilder development project. The following section describes the activities that would be necessary to support version control for this project.

The development team should assign two or more individuals who will act as administrators. Multiple administrators ensure that the development team has a backup administrator. These administrators will provide support functions for the version control environment that include:

- The creation of user IDs for each developer
- The creation of version control projects
- The registration of objects
- The creation of the shared libraries

The administrator creates the archived libraries by registering the objects in the version control tool. In the process of creating the archives, the administrator will need to create the configuration file for the application. The administrator should use the registration directory to create the shared libraries on a periodic basis. During the initial development period, the rate of change in the project files will require frequent updating of these libraries. As the project nears completion, the updating of the shared libraries will be less frequent. It's the responsibility of the administrator to ensure that these libraries reflect the current state of the project.

When the project reaches a milestone that requires the creation of a new release, the administrator should ensure that all objects are checked in. Once this task is complete, the creation of a new release can be undertaken. If the project libraries need to be restored to match a specific build, the administrator should restore the libraries from the project object for the build.

The administrator should be responsible for clearing the check-out status of objects that are checked out by another developer after careful examination of the justifications for such a request. An example that justifies this action is when a developer who has left for vacation has forgotten to check in an object. The clearing of the registration of an object should be solely an administrative task. The administrator can take precautions to ensure that the archive history for the object can be recovered, should it be necessary.

As a developer using version control, you'll need to create a working library that has a copy of the application object for the project. This application object should be updated periodically to ensure that it is kept in sync with the project. Initially, you'll need to create or select an existing configuration file to support your version control activities. You'll check out the objects needed to complete your assigned tasks to your working library as they are needed. Once the modifications to the objects have been made and tested, you should check the objects back in so that other developers can have access to them. During check-in, you should provide meaningful comments that describe the changes made to the objects. If you're creating new objects, you may also be expected to register the objects or notify the administrator that a new object needs to be registered.

The check-out and check-in of objects are the most common activities that you'll use to interact with the version control tool. Other version control functions will be used periodically. For information regarding these functions, refer to the discussion for the desired function that appears earlier in this section.

Version Control For Common Libraries

Class libraries, such as the PowerBuilder Foundation Class library, have some special considerations in a version control environment. These libraries typically consist of base libraries and extension libraries. The problems encountered with class libraries are related to the fact that the base libraries are constant, whereas the extension layer is subject to change. Common libraries are sets of libraries that provide common functionality to a variety of applications within an organization. These libraries typically are modified frequently.

You should take the same approach to version control of an application for class and common libraries. These special libraries should not be registered as a part of an application in which they are used. Instead, register these libraries in separate projects in the version control tool. Although the extension layer may be application-specific, these libraries also should be registered in a separate project. You may want to have multiple extension layers—one layer for corporate standards and one application-specific layer. In this case, the application-specific layer is included with the application project.

Moving On

Development projects that involve more than one developer require some level of version control. All aspects of your development life cycle can benefit from the use of version control. The dynamics and complexity of software development these days demand the ability to be able to mange versions. This management enables the development team to review the historical changes systematically.

PowerBuilder provides support for basic source control management. This ensures that multiple developers cannot work on the same object. For more sophisticated version control requirements, PowerBuilder provides the ability to connect to tools from leading version control vendors either though native interfaces or the SCC API.

This chapter described the recommended configuration of your project. It also described the application of each of the critical version control functions within the PowerBuilder environment. PowerBuilder offers basic version control functionality directly in the development environment. For other functions, refer to the documentation for the version control tool used in your environment.

As promised in Chapter 3, "DataWindows," we're going to cover the topic of DataWindows again—only this time, we'll discuss some of its advanced features.

Advanced DataWindows

In Chapter 3, "DataWindows," I covered the basics of DataWindows. In this chapter, I'll cover DataWindows, but from a different perspective. During the execution of your applications, you may have to dynamically create DataWindow elements or objects. You may also want to give your users the ability to query a DataWindow, or you may want to change the SQL **SELECT** statement of your DataWindows. These are more advanced topics, and they will be covered in this chapter. I'll also cover the DataStore object, which is your next-best friend, right after the DataWindow object. So, fasten your seat belt; here we go!

Dynamic DataWindows

A DataWindow object that is modified or created at runtime is called a *dynamic* DataWindow object. Using dynamic DataWindows, you can allow your users to change the appearance of a DataWindow or create an ad hoc report based on a given datasource. These dynamically created DataWindow objects can then be printed or saved as needed.

In order to create a DataWindow at runtime, you need to use the **Create()** function:

```
DataWindowControl.Create( syntax-string {, error-buffer } )
```

The **Create()** function creates a DataWindow object using the source code in syntax-string. It substitutes the new DataWindow object for the DataWindow object currently associated with your control. DataWindow source code syntax is quite complex. However, you can use the **Describe()** and **LibraryExport()** functions to obtain the source code of existing DataWindows to use as models. Another source of DataWindow code is the **SyntaxFromSQL()** function, which creates DataWindow source code based on an SQL

217

statement. The **ErrorBuffer** argument of the **Create()** function is optional. It's the name of string that you want to fill with any error messages that may occur. Note that if you do not specify an error buffer, a message box will display the error message.

SyntaxFromSQL()

SyntaxFromSQL(), when applied to your transaction object, returns the complete syntax for a DataWindow object, which is based on a given SQL **SELECT** statement. This function takes the following parameters:

- A string containing the **SELECT** statement that PowerBuilder will use to create the DataWindow object

- A string identifying the desired presentation style

- The name of the string that you want to fill with any error messages that may occur

  *Note: If you can call **SyntaxFromSQL()** directly as the value for the **Create()** syntax, you are not given the chance to check whether errors have been reported in its error argument. Before you use **SyntaxFromSQL()** in **Create()**, make sure the SQL syntax is valid.*

The following example uses the **SyntaxFromSQL()** function to create a dynamic DataWindow object:

```
string ls_style, ls_syntax, ls_sql, ls_errors

//sql statement
ls_sql = "SELECT customer.id, customer.fname," + &
    "customer.lname,customer.company_name,customer.phone" + & " FROM customer"
```

Also, you can always use a query object for your SQL statement:

```
//sql statement
ls_sql = LibraryExport("chapter3.pbl","q_customer", &
        ExportQuery!)
```

Here's the rest of the code:

```
//create syntax
ls_style = "style(type=grid)"

ls_syntax= SQLCA.SyntaxFromSQL(ls_sql, ls_style, ls_errors )
```

```
IF len( ls_errors ) > 0 THEN
   MessageBox( "Error", ls_errors )
   RETURN
END IF


//create the object
dw_customer.Create( ls_syntax, ls_errors )

//check for errors
IF Len( ls_errors ) > 0 THEN
   MessageBox( "Create Error", ls_errors )
ELSE
   //retrieve
   dw_customer.SetTransObject( SQLCA )
   dw_customer.Retrieve( )
END IF
```

> **Note:** If your database is SQL Server or Oracle and you call **SyntaxFromSQL()**
> when transaction processing is on, PowerBuilder cannot determine whether or
> not the indexes are updateable, so it assumes they are not. Therefore, you should
> set **AutoCommit** to True before you call **SyntaxFromSQL()**.

LibraryExport()

You can use the **LibraryExport()** function to export the syntax for a DataWindow object
and store the syntax in a string. This string can then be used to create the dynamic
DataWindow object. Here's an example:

```
string ls_syntax, ls_errors

//get syntax from an existing DataWindow
ls_syntax = LibraryExport( "chapter3.pbl", &
   "d_customer_temp", ExportDataWindow! )

//create
dw_customer.Create( ls_syntax, ls_errors )

//check for errors
IF Len( ls_errors ) > 0 THEN
   MessageBox( "Create Error", ls_errors )
ELSE
   //retrieve
   dw_customer.SetTransObject( SQLCA )
   dw_customer.Retrieve ( )
END IF
```

Creating And Destroying Elements

You can use **CREATE** to add elements such as text and graphic objects dynamically to your DataWindows. If you're not sure about the syntax, use the DWSyntax utility to create the syntax and then paste it into your script. The DWSyntax utility is bundled with PowerBuilder enterprise and is used to learn how to report on and manipulate attributes of DataWindow objects and objects within a DataWindow object. Here's an example that creates a computed column:

```
string ls_syntax

ls_syntax = 'CREATE Compute (Expression = "'Page '+page)+' of '+pageCount()"
             band=footer alignment="1" x="2" y="16" height="77" width="261"
             background.mode="1" background.color="16777215")'

dw_customer.Modify( ls_syntax )
```

You can also dynamically delete elements. The following statement deletes the column named company_name from the DataWindow **dw_customer** and deletes data from the buffer. Not specifying the **column** keyword will keep data in the buffer.

```
dw_customer.Modify( "DESTROY column company_name" )
```

Query Mode

You can provide your users with the ability to specify what rows are retrieved into a specific DataWindow at runtime. This is done by putting the DataWindow into query mode. Once a DataWindow is in query mode, a user can specify selection criteria using Query by Example. A user's selection criteria is then added to the **WHERE** clause of the **SELECT** statement the next time data is retrieved.

> *Note: You cannot put a DataWindow in query mode when its datasource contains a **UNION** or a nested **SELECT** statement.*

In order to turn on query mode for a DataWindow, you either use a **Modify()** command or the following dot notation syntax:

```
dw_customer.Object.DataWindow.QueryMode = 'Yes'
```

When this statement is issued, all the data in the DataWindow is blanked out; however, it still exists in the primary buffer. A user can then type in some selection criteria where the data had been (28 rows are available for typing in the criteria).

Valid operators are:

- =
- <>
- <
- >
- <=
- >=
- LIKE
- IN
- AND
- OR

Selection criteria are specified using the same format as Quick Select when defining a DataWindow object's datasource. Criteria in one row are AND-ed together, and the criteria in different rows are OR-ed. Once the selection criteria have been entered, you have to recall another **Retrieve**() function and then turn off the query mode to display the rows. Here's an example:

```
dw_customer.Retrieve( )
dw_customer.Object.DataWindow.QueryMode = 'Yes'
```

If you have the need to clear up the selection criteria, you can use the following code:

```
dw_customer.Object.DataWindow.QueryClear = 'Yes'
```

You can also allow your users to sort rows in a DataWindow while entering criteria in query mode. By doing so, the first row in your DataWindow becomes dedicated to sort criteria. This can be achieved with the following syntax:

```
dw_customer.Object.DataWindow.QuerySort = 'Yes'
```

Sharing Result Sets

PowerBuilder gives you the ability to share a result set among two or more DataWindows or DataStores. This means that the contents of the buffers of one DataWindow can be shared with buffers of other DataWindows.

Note: Your data is the only thing that's shared. For example, the data's formatting isn't shared. This feature lets you present your data from the same buffer in different ways.

When you're sharing DataWindows, all the information stored in the buffers is shared. This includes the primary, delete, and filter buffers as well as the sort order. To share data, the result set description for the DataWindow object in the primary DataWindow must match that of the DataWindow object in the secondary DataWindow control. However, the **SELECT** statements may be different. For example, the following **SELECT** statements are valid:

```
SELECT  id, fname, lname FROM customer
SELECT id, fname, lname FROM customer WHERE id = 101
SELECT id from sales order
```

To share data, use **ShareData**() for each secondary DataWindow control. To turn off sharing, you have to call the **ShareDataOff**() function. When sharing is turned off for the primary DataWindow, the secondary DataWindows are disconnected and the data disappears. However, turning off sharing for a secondary DataWindow does not affect the data in the primary DataWindow or other secondary DataWindows.

When you call functions in either the primary or secondary DataWindow that change the data, PowerBuilder applies them to the primary DataWindow control and all secondary DataWindow controls are affected. For example, when you call any of the following functions for a secondary DataWindow control, PowerBuilder applies it to the primary DataWindow. Therefore, all messages normally associated with the function go to the primary DataWindow control. Such functions include:

- **DeleteRow**()
- **GetSQLSelect**()
- **ImportString**()
- **InsertRow**()
- **Reset**()
- **SetFilter**()
- **SetSQLSelect**()
- **Update**()

- **Filter**()
- **ImportFile**()
- **ImportClipboard**()
- **ReselectRow**()
- **Retrieve**()
- **SetSort**()
- **Sort**()

The following sample code shows you how to share data between two DataWindows. Dw_customer is the primary source of data. Dw_customer_detail simply feeds off the buffers of dw_customer:

```
dw_customer.SetTransObject( SQLCA )
dw_customer.Retrieve( )
dw_customer.ShareData( dw_customer_detail )

//sample code to share data off
dw_customer.ShareDataOff( )
```

> **Note:** *You cannot share data with crosstab DataWindows. Also, in a distributed application, you cannot share data between a client and the server.*

Changing The SQL SELECT Statement

PowerBuilder provides you with the ability to dynamically change the SQL **SELECT** statement of your DataWindows at runtime. Here are the two functions related to this subject:

- **GetSQLSelect()**

- **SetSQLSelect()**

The following example obtains the current SQL **SELECT** statement of a DataWindow, adds a **WHERE** clause, and then retrieves a new result set:

```
string ls_newsyntax, ls_where, ls_oldsyntax
ls_oldsyntax = dw_customer.GetSqlSyntax()
ls_where = " WHERE company_name = 'Sybase' "
ls_newsyntax = ls_oldsyntax + ls_where

dw_customer.SetSQLSelect( ls_newsyntax )
dw_customer.Retrieve()
```

If a DataWindow is updateable, PowerBuilder first validates the SQL **SELECT** statement against the database and DataWindow column specifications when you call the **SetSQLSelect()** function. Each column in the SQL **SELECT** statement must match the column type in the DataWindow object. If the new **SELECT** statement has a different table name in the **FROM** clause and the DataWindow object is updateable, PowerBuilder must change the update information for the DataWindow object. Be aware that PowerBuilder assumes that the key columns are in the same positions as in the original definition.

> *Note:* You must use the **SetTrans()** or **SetTransObject()** function to set the trans-
> action object on a DataWindow before the **SetSQLSelect()** function will execute.

Here are the conditions that will keep a DataWindow from being updateable:

- More than one table exists in the **FROM** clause.

- A DataWindow update column is a computed column in the **SELECT** statement.

If changing the **SELECT** statement makes the DataWindow object not updateable, the
DataWindow control cannot execute an **Update()** function call for the Data-Window
object.

> *Note:* Use **SetSQLSelect()** only if the datasource for the DataWindow object is
> an SQL **SELECT** statement without retrieval arguments and you want PowerBuilder
> to modify the update information for the DataWindow object.

If need be, you can also achieve this via dot notation or the **Modify()** command. Here's
the syntax:

```
<dwControl>.Modify("DataWindow.Table.Select = '<select_statement>' ")
<dwControl>.Object.DataWindow.Table.Select = <select_statement>
```

Note that using **Modify()** or dot notation will not verify the **SELECT** statement or
change the update information. This latter procedure is faster but also more susceptible
to errors. Although you can use **Modify()** when arguments are involved, it's not recommended because of the lack of checking. The following changes the SQL statement of a
nested DataWindow:

```
dw_composite.object.my_report.Object.DataWindow.Table.Select = ls_newsyntax
```

> *Note:* If you need to change the **SELECT** statement of a nested DataWindow, you
> must use dot notation.

DataStores

A DataStore is a nonvisual DataWindow control that behaves the same as a DataWindow
control, except it doesn't have any of the visual characteristic associated with DataWindows
controls. Looking at the PowerBuilder system class hierarchy in Figure 14.1, you can see
that a DataStore is inherited from the NonVisualObject with only three levels of inheritance involved.

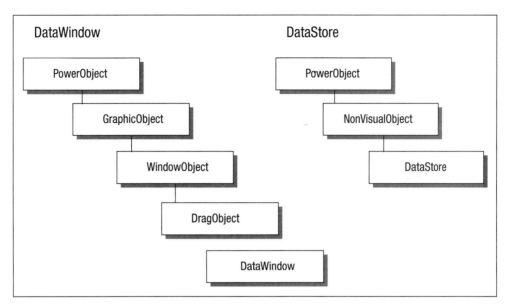

Figure 14.1
The system class heirarchy for a DataStore.

DataStores are particularly useful for the following tasks:

- DataWindow caching

- Performing background processing against the database without having to hide DataWindow controls on a window

- Manipulating table rows without having to use embedded SQL

- Performing database access on distributed servers

    Note: Because DataStores do not require any visual overhead, using them is more efficient than using invisible DataWindows.

DataStore Methods

Most of the events and functions available for DataWindows are also available for DataStores. However, some of the functions that require user interaction are not available. To give you an example, you can use **InsertRow()** and **DeleteRow()** on a DataStore, but you can't use **SetRowFocusIndicator()**.

You must also remember that because DataStores are nonvisual, the behavior of some of the functions is somewhat different than when they're used on DataWindows. Let's use the **SetSort()** and **SetFilter()** functions as an example. If you pass a null to these functions,

PowerBuilder will prompt you to enter information. When using a DataStore, this behavior is not present, and you'll not be prompted to enter your sort or filter information.

Now, to confuse you a bit, PowerBuilder has given DataStores some visual methods. Because you can print DataStores, support for the **SetBorderStyle()** and **SetSeriesStyle()** functions is present to control the presentation of data at print time. Also, DataStores support the **ItemError** event because the data imported from a string or a file that does not pass the validation rules for a column will trigger this event.

Using DataStores

Because a DataStore is a nonvisual object, in order to use it, you must first create an instance of the DataStore object in script and then assign a DataWindow object to it. Then, you need to set the transaction object for it. Once you have done this, you can retrieve data, share data, and perform other processing.

*Note: To keep your plumber away, remember to destroy every **CREATE**!*

The following script uses a DataStore to retrieve data into the **d_customer** DataWindow object:

```
Long ll_rows
DataStore lds_customer

//generate an instance of the DataStore object
lds_customer = CREATE DataStore

//set its transaction object
lds_customer.SetTransObject( SQLCA )

ll_rows = lds_customer.Retrieve()

IF ll_rows > 0 THEN
    //assign the data of the DataStore to a DataWindow
    dw_cache.Object.Data = lds_customer.Object.Data
ELSE
    MessageBox( "Error", "No customers were cached!" )
END IF
//do some house cleaning
DESTROY lds_customer
```

You may want to use a custom version of the DataStore object that performs specific processing. To define a custom DataStore, you have to define a standard class User object, as illustrated in Figure 14.2. You can customize your User object by scripting its event, or by defining functions, user events, and instance variables.

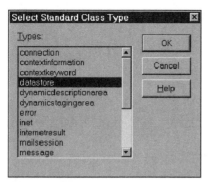

Figure 14.2
Selecting a standard class type.

Once you have created your custom DataStore, you can write code that uses your User object to perform the processing you've coded for. Here's an example:

```
long ll_rows
uo_customer lds_customer
lds_customer = CREATE uo_customer
lds_customer.SetTransObject( SQLA )
ll_rows = lds_customer.Retrieve()
dw_customer.Object.Data = lds_customer.Object.Data
DESTROY lds_customer
```

Moving On

In this chapter, we discussed some of the more advanced features of the DataWindow. As you can see, the DataWindow is truly a powerful feature of PowerBuilder. If used correctly, it can boost your application's performance tremendously.

In the next chapter, I cover the transaction object, which is a nonvisual object that functions as the communications area between your application and your database.

Transaction Object

This chapter covers the transaction object—a PowerBuilder nonvisual object that functions as the communications area between your application and your database. The transaction object specifies parameters that PowerBuilder uses to connect to your database and to receive error and status information from your database.

When you start running your application, PowerBuilder creates a global predefined default instance of a transaction object called the SQL Communications Area (SQLCA). You can use this default transaction object, or you can define additional transaction objects if you need to connect to multiple databases. Each transaction object has 15 properties, 10 of which are used to connect to your database. The other five are used to receive status information from your database about the success or failure of each operation you perform. This chapter discusses the transaction object in detail.

Using Transactions

The transaction object specifies the parameters that PowerBuilder uses to connect to a database. If your applications communicate with a database, then you're most probably using a transaction object. Now, let's cover this object in more detail.

Working With The Transaction Object

PowerBuilder uses a basic concept of database transaction processing called a *logical unit of work*. This is synonymous with a transaction. Therefore, a *transaction* is one or more SQL statements that form a logical unit of work. PowerBuilder provides you with four transaction management statements:

- CONNECT
- DISCONNECT
- COMMIT
- ROLLBACK

A successful **CONNECT** begins a transaction, and a **DISCONNECT** ends it. When you issue a **COMMIT**, all changes to the database since the start of the current transaction are made permanent, and a new transaction is started. When you issue a **ROLLBACK**, all changes since the start of the current transaction are undone and a new transaction is started. You can issue a **COMMIT** or **ROLLBACK** only if the **AutoCommit** property of the transaction object is set to False. Figure 15.1 demonstrates how this is done.

*Note: When you disconnect a transaction, a **COMMIT** is issued by default.*

Transaction Properties

Table 15.1 lists the properties that are used to connect to and communicate with your database. Note that not all databases use every one of these properties. Refer to the *Connecting to Your Database* manual to determine which properties are used for your specific database.

Table 15.2 lists properties that return status information on your operations.

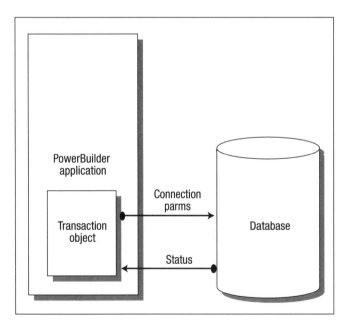

Figure 15.1
Use of a transaction object in PowerBuilder.

Table 15.1 Properties of the transaction object.

Property	Type	Description
DBMS	String	Name of your DBMS
Database	String	Name of your database
UserID	String	User ID for your database logon
DBPass	String	Password
Lock	String	Isolation level
LogID	String	User ID for your server logon
LogPass	String	Password
ServerName	String	Name of your server
AutoCommit	Boolean	Transaction processing "on" or "off"
DBParm	String	DBMS-specific settings

Table 15.2 Transaction object's properties that return status information.

Property	Type	Description
SQLCode	Long	Status code for the last SQL operation: 0 = OK 100 = No result set pending -1 = SQL error
SQLNRows	Long	Number of rows affected by the most recent SQL operation
SQLDBCode	Long	DBMS-specific error code
SQLErrText	Long	DBMS-specific error message
SQLReturnData	Long	DBMS-specific information

There are three ways to populate SQLCA:

- Hard code the values in the transaction object

- Prompt your users for the values

- Read the values from an INI file or the Windows Registry.

   Note: In general, you should not use hard-coded values because they limit the flexibility of your applications.

If you're going to populate your SQLCA from INIs or the Registry, PowerBuilder provides you with several functions to read your preferences. In order to read information from an INI file, you can use the **ProfileString**() and **ProfileInt**() functions. Here's an example:

```
SQLCA.DBMS        = ProfileString(ls_ini,"db","dbms","")
SQLCA.database    = ProfileString(ls_ini,"db","database","")
SQLCA.userid      = ProfileString(ls_ini,"db","userid","")
SQLCA.dbpass      = ProfileString(ls_ini,"db","","dbpass","")
SQLCA.logid       = ProfileString(ls_ini,"db","logid","")
SQLCA.logpass     = ProfileString(ls_ini,"db","logpass","")
SQLCA.servername= ProfileString(ls_ini,"db","servername","")
SQLCA.dbparm      = ProfileString(ls_ini,"db","dbparm","")
```

PowerBuilder also provides you with many functions to manipulate the Windows system Registry. The **RegistryGet()** function reads values from the Registry. For example, on Windows NT, this statement obtains the value for the name **ServerName** and stores it in the string **ls_servername**:

```
string ls_servername
RegistryGet( "HKEY_LOCAL_MACHINE\Software\TDG", &
    "ServerName",ls_servername)
```

> **Note:** If needed, you can enable a DBMS trace to create a log on the communications between PowerBuilder and your database. This is done with the **trace** keyword. For example, **SQLCA.DBMS="trace ODBC"** or **SQLCA.DBMS="trace SYC"**. This creates a PBTRACE.LOG file on your local drive.

The **DBParm** property of the transaction object contains DBMS-specific connection parameters that support particular DBMS features. It's simply a string that is sent to the DBMS. The DBMS examines the string and reacts to it appropriately. Again, it's very important that you take a look at the *Connecting to Your Database* manual and understand the parameters you can use with your database. Here's the general syntax for **DBParm**:

```
SQLCA.DBParm = "Async=1, StaticBind=0,DisableBind=1"
```

If you're using ODBC and a DataStore, make sure you place the **DBParm** parameters correctly, as seen here:

```
SQLCA.DBParm = &
    "ConnectString='DSN=MyDataSource;UID=dba;PWd=sql', Async=1"
```

> **Note:** When using **DBParm** parameters with ODBC, the parameters are supported by the Sybase ODBC interface only if both the ODBC driver you're using and the DBMS support the features.

Connecting To Your Database

Once you've populated your transaction object, you can begin connecting to your database. Once you have issued a **CONNECT** statement, make sure you check the return codes for any errors. The following code is a simple example:

```
CONNECT USING SQLCA;
IF SQLCA.SQLCode <> 0 THEN
   MessageBox( "Connection Error "+String(SQLCA.SQLCode)+ &
      SQLCA.SQLErrText )
   RETURN
END IF
```

> **Note:** As a good practice, always check the **SQLCode** property of your transaction object to ensure the success or failure of your **CONNECT**, **DISCONNECT**, **COMMIT**, or embedded and dynamic SQL statements.

Make sure you disconnect after your database processing has completed. This is done via the SQL **DISCONNECT** statement:

```
DISCONNECT USING SQLCA;
```

Multiple Transaction Objects

If you have to perform operations on multiple databases at the same time, you'll have to create new transaction objects. To create a transaction object other than SQLCA, you first have to declare a variable of type **Transaction** and then instantiate the new Transaction object. Here's how:

```
//declare and create the new transaction object
Transaction SybaseTrans
SybaseTrans = CREATE Transaction

//populate the new transaction object
SybaseTrans.DBMS = "SYC"
SybaseTrans.Database = "dev1"
SybaseTrans.ServerName = "gorgani1"
SybaseTrans.LogId = "kgorgani"
SybaseTrans.Logpass = "kgorgani"

//connect
CONNECT USING SybaseTrans;
IF SybaseTrans.SQLCode <> 0 THEN
   MessageBox( "Error: " + String(SybaseTrans.SqlCode), &
      SybaseTrans.SQLErrText )
```

```
        RETURN
END IF

INSERT INTO names
    VALUES ( "John", "Doe", 5198863700 )
        USING SybaseTrans;

//disconnect
DISCONNECT USING SybaseTrans;

//destroy the transaction object
DESTROY SybaseTrans
```

> **Note:** If you need to populate a second transaction object with the same property values as the default SQLCA, do not use **SybaseTrans=SQLCA**. This is not a one-on-one assignment. Both of these objects are reference variables, and therefore, **SybaseTrans** would point to SQLCA. Use property-by-property assignment instead of **SybaseTrans.DBMS=SQLCA.DBMS**, and so on.

Pooling Transactions

Transaction pooling maximizes database throughput while controlling the number of database connections that can be open at one time. This is an excellent method for reusing connection objects made to the same datasource.

When your applications connect to a database without using transaction pooling, PowerBuilder terminates each database transaction for which a **DISCONNECT** is issued. When transaction pooling is in effect, PowerBuilder logically terminates the database connections and commits any database changes, but it does not physically remove them. Instead, the database connections are kept open in the transaction pool so that they can be reused for other database operations.

To establish a transaction pool, use the **SetTransPool()** function. This function can be executed anywhere in your application, but it must occur before you connect to your database. Here's the syntax for **SetTransPool()**:

```
applicationname.SetTransPool ( minimum, maximum, timeout )
```

The three arguments are the minimum number of transactions to be kept open, the maximum number of transactions, and the number of seconds to allow a request to wait in a transaction pool. For example

```
server_app.SetTransPool(8,8,0)
```

specifies that up to eight database connections will be allowed through this server, and that all eight will be kept open once successfully connected. When the transaction pool is full, each subsequent connection request will immediately result in an error.

Before reusing a connection in the transaction pool, PowerBuilder checks to see that the database parameters specified in the incoming connection request match those specified by one of the connections in the pool. A match occurs when both transaction objects specify the same **DBMS**, **ServerName**, **LogID**, **LogPass**, **Database**, and **DBParm** values. Also, note that the minimum value specified in the **SetTransPool()** function must be less than or equal to the maximum value. When the minimum value is less than the maximum and the number of transactions in the pool is greater than the minimum, PowerBuilder physically terminates connections for which a **DISCONNECT** statement is issued until the minimum number is reached. The maximum value specified for a transaction pool limits the total number of database connections made by the application. When the transaction pool is full, each attempt to connect will fail after the timeout interval has been exceeded.

Extending Transaction Objects

PowerBuilder's SQLCA is a predefined global variable of type **Transaction** that can be used in all your applications. Now, you have the ability to define a customized version of SQLCA that does certain processing on your data. For example, you can specialize your SQLCA to execute remote procedure calls, or you can encapsulate specific methods into SQLCA for error processing or calling APIs. Let's look at these in more detail.

Remote Procedure Calls

If your database supports stored procedures, you may have already used remote procedures. Calling remote procedures can also be encapsulated into your transaction object. Let's go through an example:

1. Define a standard class User object of type **Transaction** in the User Object Painter.

2. Select the Declare|Local External Functions menu item. This brings up the Local External Functions dialog box. Notice the additional command button for procedures.

3. As illustrated in Figure 15.2, by clicking the Procedures button, all your stored procedures are listed in the Remote Stored Procedures dialog box. In this example, we're going to select **sp_getsalary** from the list of remote stored procedures, as seen here:

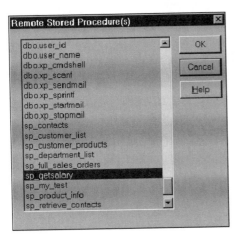

Figure 15.2
Selecting a remote stored procedure.

```
CREATE PROCEDURE
   sp_getsalary(IN empid Integer, OUT empsalary Decimal)
      Begin
         SELECT salary
         INTO empsalary
         FROM employee
         WHERE emp_id = empid
      End
```

4. Select the desired stored procedure. PowerBuilder automatically uses the **RPCFUNC** keyword to declare the stored procedure as an external function or a subroutine for the User object. Here's an example:

```
SUBROUTINE sp_getsalary(long empid,ref decimal empsalary) &
   RPCFUNC ALIAS FOR "~"dba~".~"sp_getsalary~"""
```

> **Note:** You cannot used a remote procedure call to access result sets returned by stored procedures. If you need to access a result set, you must use the embedded SQL **DECLARE** procedure statement.

5. Save your customized transaction object as **u_trans**.

6. Specify this User object as the default global variable type for SQLCA, as shown in Figure 15.3.

7. To call the remote procedure, use dot notation (object.function):

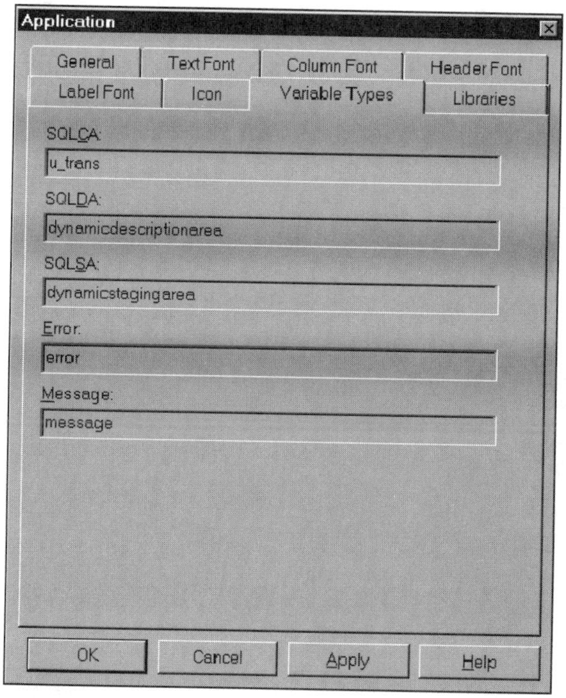

Figure 15.3
Specifying a User object as the default SQLCA.

```
Long ll_emp
Decimal ld_sal

//obtain the employee number from a SingleLineEdit
ll_emp = Long( sle_emp.Text )

//call the remote procedure
SQLCA.sp_getsalary( ll_emp, ld_sal )

//display salary
em_salary.Text =  String( ld_sal  )
```

Calling APIs

You can also extend your transaction object even further by encapsulating specific methods such as error routines and functions that call APIs. Calling APIs is a favorite of mine because it gives me access to the outside world—stuff that SQLCA does not provide. For example, you can call the ODBC SDK to get the driver version of your connection or change the isolation level for your database. Let's go through a couple of examples together. I'll use ODBC to illustrate my point.

Getting The ODBC Driver Version

SQLGetInfo() is an ODBC SDK function to ODBC32.DLL that returns general information about the driver and the datasource associated with a connection. You need to add the following external function to the local external declaration of the **u_trans** transaction object:

```
Function Int SQLGetInfo(ULong hdbc, UInt infooption, &
    REF String infostr, Int maxlen, REF Int ilength) &
    Library "odbc32.dll"
```

Once this has been done, you can simply call the function to get the driver version of the connection, as seen here:

```
ULong    lul_hDB
UInt lui_infotype
Int li_value, li_maxlen, li_strlen, li_retcode
String ls_info

//getting the handle of the transaction object
lul_hDB = DBHandle( SQLCA )

//SQL_DRIVER_VER, defined in sqltext.h
lui_infotype = 7

ls_info = space(10)
li_retcode = SQLCA.SQLGetInfo(lul_hDB, lui_infotype, &
    ls_info, Len(ls_info), li_strlen)

//display the current version
sle_version.text = ls_info
```

To get the various values **SQLGetInfo** uses (for example, **SQL_DRIVER_VER**), refer to SQLTEXT.H. The section you need is "extended definitions for SQLInfo." Here's a sample of what you'll find:

```
SQL_DRIVER_HDBC                  3
SQL_DRIVER_HENV                  4
SQL_DRIVER_HSTMT                 5
SQL_DRIVER_NAME                  6
SQL_DRIVER_VER                   7
SQL_ODBC_API_CONFORMANCE         9
SQL_ODBC_VER                    10
```

Changing The Isolation Level

When using SQLCA and ODBC, changing the isolation level on the database has to be done upon connecting. Your choices are to disconnect, change the isolation level, and then reconnect, or use SDK calls. The two SDK calls involved in this example are the **SQLGetConnectAttr()** and **SQLSetConnectAtr()** functions. You first have to add the following two functions to the local external function declaration of your transaction object. Here is an example:

```
Function Int SQLGetConnectAttr( ulong hdbc, uint foption,&
    REF Int ptr, Int buff, REF Int b1) Library "odbc32.dll"

Function Int SQLSetConnectAttr( ULong hdbc, UInt foption, &
    Int  ptr, Int sqlint) Library "odbc32.dll"
```

Now, let's call the functions to change the isolation levels in the midst of a running application during a valid connection. This script gets the current isolation level:

```
ULong   lul_hDB
Int li_level, li_len, li_retcode, li_buflen

//obtain the handle of our transaction object
lul_hDB = DBhandle( SQLCA )

//SQL_TXN_ISOLATION (109) from sqltext.h, connection //attributes
li_retcode = SQLCA.SQLGetConnectAttr( lul_hDB, 108, &
    li_level, li_buflen, li_len)

//display the current isolation level
sle_currentlevel.Text = String( li_level )
```

And now to change the isolation level:

```
ULong lul_hDB
Int li_retcode,  li_level_ptr, li_sqlint

lul_hDB = DBhandle( sqlca )

//value for the new isolation level. Level 1.
li_level_ptr = 1

//set the new isolation level
li_retcode = sqlca.SQLSetConnectAttr( lul_hDB, 108, li_ptr,&
    li_sqlint )
```

Once again, the "connection attributes" section of SQLTEXT.H contains all the necessary values you'll need to pass to the **SQLGetConnectAttr()** and **SQLSetConnectAttr()** functions. For example, **SQL_TXN_ISOLATION** is 108, as per the following information:

```
// connection attributes from sqltext.h
SQL_ACCESS_MODE              101
SQL_AUTOCOMMIT               102
SQL_LOGIN_TIMEOUT            103
SQL_OPT_TRACE                104
SQL_OPT_TRACEFILE            105
SQL_TRANSLATE_DLL            106
SQL_TRANSLATE_OPTION         107
SQL_TXN_ISOLATION            108
SQL_CURRENT_QUALIFIER        109
SQL_ODBC_CURSORS             110
SQL_QUIET_MODE               111
SQL_PACKET_SIZE              112
```

Different databases support different isolation levels. SQL Anywhere supports four isolation levels, numbered 0 to 3. (See Chapter 22, "Sybase SQL Anywhere," for more information.)

Moving On

As you can see, once again PowerBuilder has given you the ability to extend a simple object—in this case, the transaction object—into a robust, powerful object. Now you can get quite imaginative as the future is wide open!

In the next chapter, I'll cover MAPI. With PowerBuilder, you have the ability to incorporate email into your applications and to interact with any MAPI-compliant email system. For example, you may simply want to fire off an email to the system's administrator when an error occurs in your transaction. In this case, MAPI could be the answer you're looking for.

16 MAPI

Because of PowerBuilder's support for MAPI, you have the ability to incorporate email into your applications and interact with any MAPI-compliant email system. This can be very useful because sometimes the need exists to distribute a DataWindow or a report to other users directly from your applications, or maybe you need to build an error routine that notifies you when an error occurs during the runtime of your application.

In the Windows environment, the two dominant email standards are Microsoft's Messaging Application Programming Interface (MAPI) and Vendor Independent Messaging (VIM). In this chapter, I mostly concentrate on MAPI because PowerBuilder has a MAPI interface. It also provides you with many PowerScript functions to manipulate MAPI.

In this chapter, we'll discuss MAPI, the differences between Simple and Extended MAPI, and PowerBuilder's MAPI interface. Finally, I'll briefly talk about VIM and PowerBuilder's Library for Lotus Notes.

MAPI—Simple And Extended

MAPI is an architectural specification that defines a messaging subsystem. The entire idea behind MAPI is to push the characteristics of the underlying messaging systems down to the messaging back-end level and hide them from you behind a standardized API. This API specifies the functionality available to you and gives you an open, nonproprietary interface to talk to. You always see a consistent interface regardless of which messaging back-end you're connected to, and anything that is unique or proprietary to your messaging back-end is hidden from you. You communicate with the back-end system through the client interface of the MAPI subsystem, which acts as the middle layer between your applications and the messaging system.

Simple MAPI contains the 12 most common API calls and is designed to make it easy for you to build powerful custom messaging applications. Microsoft originally implemented a library of 12 functions that was called MAPI. This API was essentially a public version of the functions used by the Microsoft Mail client to communicate with Microsoft Mail post offices. That MAPI API is now called Simple MAPI, and it enables your applications to send, address, and receive messages. These messages can include data attachments and OLE objects.

Extended MAPI provides more complex messaging capabilities. For example, it will allow your applications to manage the generation and handling of complex messages, large numbers of received messages, message stores, and complex addressing information. Extended MAPI application functionality includes data collection, work flow, message management, unattended message filtering, and agent-based retrieval applications. Also, the Extended MAPI client interface returns OLE COM objects to the client, which the client then uses to request services from the MAPI subsystem.

> **Note:** PowerBuilder's MAPI interface is based on Simple MAPI, which is included with Windows SDK and provides basic email services.

MAPI In PowerBuilder

To support MAPI in PowerBuilder, you are provided with a nonvisual system object (mailSession), a series of mail-related structures, object level functions, and enumerated data types.

The nonvisual system object mailSession establishes your MAPI session with your MAPI-compliant messaging system and has the following attributes:

- **MessageID.** Contains the IDs of the messages in a user's mail inbox
- **SessionID.** Contains the handle of the current messaging session

Reading Mail

In order to read mail from your mailbox, you first have to instantiate a mailSession object. Because the mailSession object is a nonvisual, in order for it to be instantiated, it must be created. Also, don't forget to destroy it after you've finished with it. Here is an example:

```
//instantiate a mailSession object
mailSession mSession
mSession = CREATE mailSession

//destroying the mailSession object
DESTROY mailSession
```

Now, here are the three PowerBuilder-defined mail structures that provide you with more information about your messages:

- **mailFileDescription object.** A system structure containing information about an attachment file to a mail message. Table 16.1 lists mailFileDescription's properties.

- **mailMessage object.** A system structure containing information about a specific mail message. Table 16.2 lists mailMessage's properties.

- **mailRecipient object.** A system structure containing information about the recipient of a mail message. This structure is populated with the **mailAddress**() function. Table 16.3 lists mailRecipient's attributes.

> **Note:** None of the structures in these three lists has events.

PowerBuilder has encapsulated 14 functions into the mailSession object that you can use. However, only 11 of these functions are mail related. Table 16.4 lists these functions.

> **Note:** Don't mix and match 16-bit and 32-bit together. PowerBuilder 32-bit talks to 32-bit MAPI, and PowerBuilder 16-bit with 16-bit MAPI only.

Table 16.1 Properties of the mailFileDescription object.

Attribute	Data Type	Description
FileType	Enumerated, mailFileType	Specifies the name of the attachment file.
FileName	String	Name of the attachment file.
PathName	String	Full path of the attachment file.
Position	Ulong	Position of the attachment file within the message body.

Table 16.2 Properties of the mailMessage object.

Attribute	Data Type	Description
AttachmentFile[]	mailFileDescription	Contains information about the attachment file.
ConversationID	string	Specifies the conversation thread ID for the current message.
DateReceived	string	The date on which the message was received.
MessageSent	String	The date on which the message was sent.
MessageType	String	Indicates the type of the current message.
NoteText	String	Contents of the message.

(continued)

Table 16.2 Properties of the mailMessage object *(continued)*.

Attribute	Data Type	Description
ReceiptRequested	Boolean	Specifies whether or not a receipt needs to be returned.
Recipient	mailRecipient	Specifies the current recipient of the message.
Subject	String	Subject of the message.
Unread	Boolean	Specifies whether or not the message is read.

Table 16.3 Attributes of the mailRecipient object.

Attribute	Data Type	Description
Address	String	Specifies the email address of the current recipient.
EntryID	Blob	Binary entry identifier information that is used internally.
RecipientType	mailRecipientType	Specifies the type of the current recipient.
Name	String	Name of the current recipient.

Table 16.4 PowerBuilder mailSession object functions.

Function	Data Type Returned	Description
mailAddress()	mailReturnCode	Updates a mailRecipient array for a mail message.
mailDeleteMessages()	mailReturnCode	Deletes a mail message from the inbox.
mailGetMessages()	mailReturnCode	Populates the messageID array with the message IDs from the user's mail inbox.
mailHandle()	Ulong	The handle of the mailSession object.
mailLogOn()	mailReturnCode	Logs into a mail session.
mailLogOff()	mailReturnCode	Ends the mail session.
mailReadMessage()	mailReturnCode	Opens a mail message in the mail session's message array.
mailRecipientDetails()	mailReturnCode	Recipient's address information.
mailResolveRecipient()	mailReturnCode	Validates the recipient's name.
mailSaveMessage()	mailReturnCode	Create a new message in the inbox.
mailSend()	mailReturnCode	Sends the mail message.

The following script logs you into an instantiated mailSession object. Note that if you don't provide a login ID and a password, you'll be prompted for one by your default mail software.

```
mailReturnCode    mRet
//establishes a mail session, create a new session
mRet = mSession.mailLogon ( mailNewSession! )
IF mRet <> mailReturnSuccess! THEN
   MessageBox ("Mail Logon", 'Could not login.' )
   RETURN
END IF

//and this code ends your mailSession
mailReturnCode mRet
mRet = mSession.mailLogoff ( )

IF mRet <> mailReturnSuccess! THEN
    MessageBox ("Mail Logoff", 'Could not Logoff!' )
   RETURN
END IF
```

> **Note:** If you're using Microsoft Exchange or Windows Messaging System upon login, you may be prompted for a profile name, as shown in Figure 16.1. You can prevent this by doing the following:
>
> - Replacing the current MAPI.DLL with a 16-bit MAPI.DLL
>
> - Specifying a profile name instead of a user ID in **MailLogOn()**
>
> - In Exchange, making sure your profile name is the same as your mail user ID

The following script populates an external DataWindow from your mail inbox. The external DataWindow has a computed column with the expression **bitmap(IF (unread = 1, "pack.bmp", ""))** to display a bitmap next to a message if it has not been read. Figure 16.2 illustrates the result of this code.

```
int       li_numattached, li_index, li_row, li_msgs
string    ls_ret

mailReturnCode       mRetCode
mailMessage          mMessage[]

//reset the dw and set redraw off
dw_inbox.Reset()
dw_inbox.SetRedraw( FALSE )
```

```
//get the list of mail message IDs in the mailbox
mRetCode = mSession.mailGetMessages( )

li_msgs = UpperBound( mSession.MessageID )

//loop through and read messages
FOR li_index = 1 TO li_msgs
    mRetCode = mSession.mailReadMessage ( &
        mSession.MessageID[li_index], &
            mMessage[li_index], mailEnvelopeOnly!, FALSE )

    //insert messages into the dw
    li_row = dw_inbox.InsertRow ( 0 )
    dw_inbox.object.Sender[li_row] = &
        mMessage[li_index].Recipient[1].Name
    dw_inbox.object.Subject[li_row] = &
        mMessage[li_index].Subject
    dw_inbox.object.datesent[li_row] = &
        mMessage[li_index].DateReceived
    dw_inbox.object.MessageId[li_row] = &
        mSession.MessageID[li_index]
    //if unread, set a computed column to 1
    IF mMessage[li_index].unread THEN
        dw_inbox.object.unread[li_row] = 1
    ELSE
        dw_inbox.object.unread[li_row] = 0
    END IF
NEXT

//reset redraw back to on
dw_inbox.SetRedraw( TRUE )
```

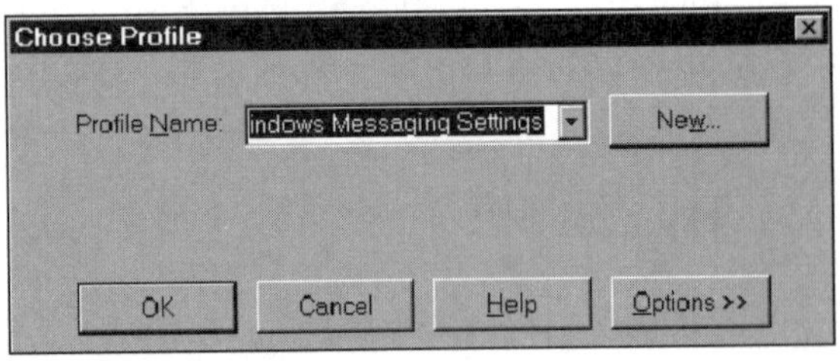

Figure 16.1
The profile selection screen.

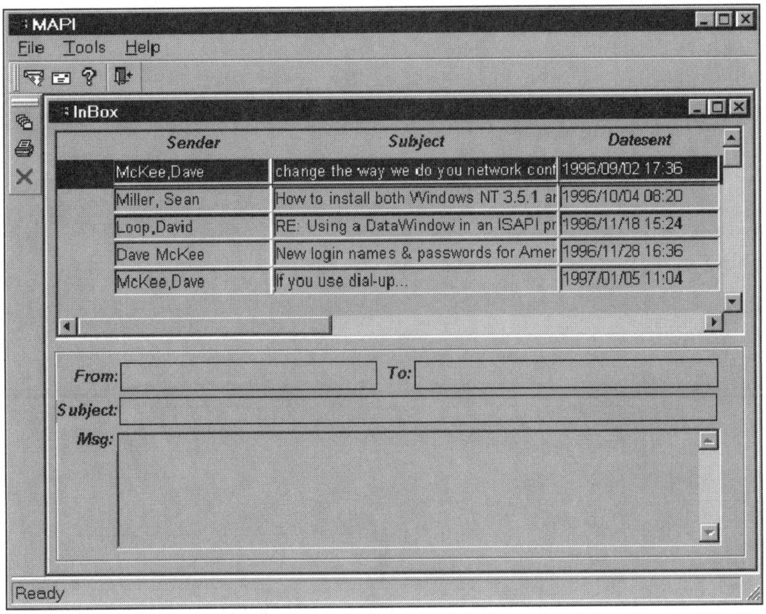

Figure 16.2
Populating a DataWindow from your inbox.

The following script, located in the **Clicked** event or the **RowFocusChanged** event of the DataWindow, displays more information about your message when it has been selected in the DataWindow:

```
mailReturnCode    mRet
mailMessage    mMessage[]

int      li_ret, li_recips, li_index
string   ls_messageid,ls_ret, ls_syntax,ls_name

//get mail message ID
ls_messageid = This.object.MessageID[row]

mRet = mSession.mailReadMessage( ls_messageid,mMessage[1], &
        mailEntireMessage!,TRUE )
li_recips = Upperbound(mMessage[1].Recipient)
//loop through the recipients and display them
FOR li_index = 1 TO li_recips
   IF mMessage[1].Recipient[li_index].RecipientType = &
        mailOriginator! THEN
      sle_from.text = mMessage[1].Recipient[li_index].name
   END IF
```

```
    //get to and cc names, format them
    IF mMessage[1].Recipient[li_index].RecipientType = &
    mailTo! OR & mMessage[1].Recipient[li_index].RecipientType &
        = mailCC! THEN
       IF mle_to.text = "" THEN
          mle_to.text = mMessage[1].Recipient[li_index].name
       ELSE
          mle_to.text = mle_to.text + "; " + &
             mMessage[1].Recipient[li_index].name
       END IF
    END IF
NEXT

//set subject and message text
sle_subject.text = mMessage[1].subject
mle_msg.text = mMessage[1].NoteText
```

Sending Mail

The following script demonstrates sending emails out with a DataWindow PSR attachment:

```
mailReturnCode        mRet
mailMessage           mMsg
mailFileDescription mFile

string    ls_text, ls_n, ls_attachment = 'report.pst'
int       li_index, li_recipients, li_ctr
boolean   lb_noerrors
long      ll_pos

SetPointer(HourGlass!)

//do we want to attach the report? If so, a checkbox is checked
IF cbx_attach.checked THEN
    //save our DataWindow in PSR format
    dw_customer.SaveAs(ls_attachment,PSReport!,TRUE)
    mFile.FileType = mailAttach!
    mFile.PathName = ls_attachment
    mFile.FileName = ls_attachment
    //place the attachment at the end the message
    mFile.Position = Len(mMsg.notetext) - 1
    mMsg.AttachmentFile[1] = mFile
END IF

//Copy user's email subject to the mail message.
mMsg.Subject   = sle_subject.text
mMsg.notetext = mle_msg.text +"~n~r "
```

```
IF sle_to.text = "" THEN
   mRet = mSession.mailAddress ( mMsg )
END IF

// Resolve recipient email addresses
SetPointer(HourGlass!)
Do
   lb_noerrors = TRUE
   ls_text = sle_to.text
   ll_pos = Pos( ls_text, ";" )
   //parse the string
   DO WHILE ll_pos <> 0
      ls_n = left( ls_text,ll_pos - 1 )
      li_ctr = li_ctr + 1
      mMsg.Recipient[li_ctr].Name = ls_n
      ls_text = right( ls_text, Len(ls_text) - ll_pos )
      ll_pos = Pos( ls_text, ";" )
   LOOP

   IF ls_text <> ""   THEN
    ls_n = ls_text
    li_ctr = li_ctr + 1
    mMsg.Recipient[li_ctr].Name = ls_n
   END IF

   li_recipients = UpperBound( mMsg.Recipient )
    FOR li_index = 1 TO li_recipients
      mRet = mSession.mailResolveRecipient( &
         mMsg.Recipient[li_index].Name)
      IF mRet <> mailReturnSuccess! THEN lb_noerrors = False
   NEXT

   IF NOT lb_noerrors THEN
      Messagebox("Mail Error","Error Resolving Name(s)")
      mRet = mSession.mailAddress(mMsg)
   END IF

LOOP UNTIL lb_noerrors

//Now, send the mail message, including the attachment.
IF UpperBound ( mMsg.Recipient ) < 1 THEN
   messagebox("Mail Error","Your mail have at least 1 recipient")
   RETURN
END IF

mRet = mSession.mailsend ( mMsg )
```

PowerBuilder Library For Lotus Notes

The PowerBuilder Library for Lotus Notes allows you to access Notes databases in your PowerBuilder applications. This library has the following components:

- A set of Notes API libraries

- The Notes DataWindow Builder

- A sample application

For more information about this library, refer to the PowerBuilder Library for Lotus Notes manual. Versions 4.51 and later of Lotus Notes are now MAPI-compliant, meaning that you can use PowerBuilder's MAPI interface with them.

Moving On

Incorporating email into your application used to mean including a series of API calls, making for a hard task. Well, it's not that way with PowerBuilder. The examples I've used in this chapter are simple ones. They are meant to provide you with a jump start. Sybase has done a great job in wrapping MAPI APIs within PowerBuilder objects and functions, because calling these APIs directly could be quite a cumbersome job.

Talking about APIs, in the next chapter I'll cover external functions. *External functions* are functions that are written in languages other than PowerScript, and they are stored in dynamic link libraries that can be called directly from your applications.

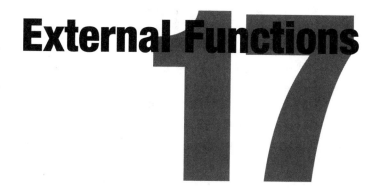

External Functions

External functions are functions that are written in languages other than PowerScript and stored in dynamic link libraries (DLLs). A *DLL* is a file containing executable Windows code. This code can be called from a PowerBuilder program even though it is written in another language such as C or Pascal or in any other language that supports the Pascal 16-bit calling convention or the Standard 32-bit calling convention. DLLs are dynamically loaded and linked at runtime, and the code can be shared among several applications. DLLs can be moveable or fixed in memory, preloaded or loaded on demand, and discarded or permanently loaded.

PowerBuilder offers hundreds of functions for use in developing applications, and with so many various functions easily available, there may not be a need for external functions. However, there may be times when you want to provide your users with functionality that is not available within PowerBuilder itself; in this case, you'll have to refer to external functions. The Windows Application Programming Interface (API) includes over a thousand functions that can be called from within PowerBuilder. However, the real value of external function calls comes with extending PowerBuilder in new directions. For example, reusing existing C or Pascal code, getting closer to the operating system to program low-level DOS and Windows functions, building protective layers between PowerScript and APIs, replacing scripts with faster code, and much more.

The two general guidelines for using an external DLL in PowerBuilder are that the DLL must be written using the correct calling convention, and the data types required to pass to and from the DLL must have an appropriate counterpart in PowerScript.

> **Note:** *My platform of choice is Windows NT 4.0; therefore, most of the examples in this chapter have been written for the Win32 platform.*

Writing External DLLs

As I mentioned earlier, a DLL is an executable module with export functions that an application calls to perform certain tasks. A DLL's primary purpose is to provide a library of callable functions. This library must be loaded into memory in order to call the functions. A DLL remains in memory until the last application referencing it has been unloaded from memory. Note that DLLs function differently in 16-bit and 32-bit environments. In the 16-bit environment, only one copy of the DLL is loaded into memory, and it doesn't have its own stack, so it uses the stack of the task that calls it. In the 32-bit environment, each DLL is mapped to the address space of the application that calls it, and each process that calls the DLL has its own local copy of that DLL's data.

A DLL must contain an entry point. Usually, 16-bit DLLs have a **LibMain()** function where as 32-bit DLLs have a **DllMain()** function. These functions are called by the system to initialize the DLL and are called only once, when the first program that requires the DLL is loaded. The following list shows you the parameters passed to **LibMain()**:

- **HANDLE.** A handle to the instance of the DLL

- **WORD.** The library's data segment

- **WORD.** The heap size

- **LPSTR.** Command-line parameters

Here is an example of **LibMain()** code:

```
#include <stdio.h>    //standard io
#include <windows.h> //windows header

int FAR PASCAL LibMain( HANDLE hInst,WORD WDataSeg,
    WORD WheapSize, LPSTR lpszCmdLine )
{
return( 1 );          /* indicate success */
/* returning 0 indicates initialization failure */
}
```

Here is an example of **DllMain()** code:

```
int WINAPI DllMain( HINSTANCE hInst, DWORD fdwReason,
     PVOID pvReserved )
 {
            return TRUE;

 }
```

Now, you can write your functions. Remember that your DLL functions must be prototyped with the correct calling convention.

Compiler Calling Conventions

A *calling convention* tells the compiler how the function expects to receive its arguments and how it will store the return value. A particular calling convention could push the arguments onto the program stack, for example, whereas another calling convention might pass them in processor registers instead.

Calling conventions are important in two situations: when calling a function through a function pointer, and when exporting or importing a function from a DLL. You must declare an exported function with a portable calling convention if you want to be able to call it from applications built with different compilers.

There are only two calling conventions you need to know about when writing DLLs for PowerBuilder: Pascal and Standard. Windows API functions are all declared using these conventions, and any functions imported or exported from a DLL should also be declared with them.

> **Note:** Use the Pascal calling convention for 16-bit DLLs and Standard for 32-bit DLLs, or you can simply prototype your functions with the WINAPI macro.

To specify that a function uses the Standard (**stdcall**) convention, use the keyword **__stdcall**, starting with two underscores. In the **stdcall** calling convention, function names are preceded by an underscore (_) and followed by "@*nnn*," where "*nnn*" is replaced by the number of bytes to push on the stack. The number of bytes per parameter is rounded up to a multiple of four. This name changing is called *decoration*, and it's separate from *name mangling*, which is done in C++ to implement overloaded functions.

PowerBuilder Enterprise is bundled with the Class Builder, which is based on the Watcom 11.0 compiler. In Class Builder, you'll find PBDLL.H. This header file consists of a definition for the macro PB_EXPORT. In a 32-bit environment, this macro uses a pragma to change the calling convention to Standard, and in a 16-bit environment, to Pascal. You must include this header file in your source code to ensure that the correct calling convention is used with your function. Note that this file will only be recognized by Power++ and Watcom C/C++ compilers. Other compilers might not recognize the pragma parameters used, so make sure you're using equivalent commands. Here are the contents of the PBDLL.H:

```
// pbdll.h
#ifdef __NT__
        //32bit
    #pragma aux __fortran "*" parm [] modify [eax ecx edx];
    #define  PB_EXPORT    __export __fortran
#else
        //16bit
    #define  PB_EXPORT    __pascal __export
#endif
```

Using Other Compilers

When using other C/C++ compilers, once you have used the correct calling convention, as discussed earlier, your function name is decorated. You can either call your function from PowerBuilder with its decoration or use a definition file to ensure that your function name is properly exported without any decorations. Here's an example:

```
// MSVC++ .CPP file
extern "C" int __declspec( dllexport ) __stdcall AddNums( int iNum1, int iNum2 )
    {
     // take two integers and return their sum
     return iNum1 + iNum2;
    }
```

For example, the following module definition file (better know as a DEF file) ensures that the function remains **AddNums**, not **_AddNums@8**:

```
// DEF file
Library ch17ms.dll
EXPORTS AddNums = _AddNums@8
```

Watcom Library Manager: WLIB.EXE

The Watcom Library Manager is another great tool that ships with Class Builder in PowerBuilder Enterprise. It's an excellent utility for finding out more information about your DLLs and their contained functions.

Let's say you've been given the file CH17MS.DLL and have been instructed that the function **AddNums** takes two integers and returns another. However, upon calling this function, you run into errors. In this case, you can use the Watcom Library Manager to ensure that the function you're trying to call actually does exist and to verify its proper name.

> **Note:** You should not guess at a function's calling convention by simply looking at its name.

You first create an import library. Then, you create a list file that contains readable information about your DLL. Here is an example:

```
WLIB ch17ms.lib +'ch17ms.dll'
WLIB -l ch17ms

******* Ch17ms.lst *******
AddNums.......................................ch17ms.dll
_AddNums@8....................................ch17ms.dll
```

C To PowerBuilder

Moving between PowerBuilder and C is quite simple because the overall order and placement of the component pieces of both declarations are almost identical. The PowerBuilder declaration differs from the C declaration in the use of the prefix for the DLL function and the keyword **REF**. This indicates whether a return value is expected or the object or a pointer to the object is expected. The structural necessity is the library specification, which consists of the **LIBRARY** keyword followed by a quoted string with the DLL name. Here's an example:

```
void Foo(LPINT iVariable)
SUBROUTINE Foo(REF int iInteger) LIBRARY "ch17wat.DLL"

int Foo(char * lpzString)
FUNCTION int Foo(REF string sString) LIBRARY "ch17wat.DLL"
```

Table 17.1 lists some C/C++ data types and their PowerBuilder equivalents.

Table 17.1   Some C/C++ data types and their PowerBuilder equivalents.

C/C++ Data Type	PowerBuilder Data Type
UNSIGNED SHORT	UINT
LONG	LONG
BYTE, CHAR	CHAR
BOOL	BOOLEAN
WORD	UINT
DWORD	ULONG
LPSTR	STRING
LPBYTE	STRING
LPINT	INT

(continued)

Table 17.1 Some C/C++ data types and their PowerBuilder equivalents *(continued)*.

C/C++ Data Type	PowerBuilder Data Type
LPWORD	UINT
LPLONG	LONG
LPDWORD	ULONG
TLPVOID	STRING
DOUBLE	DOUBLE
FLOAT	REAL
DOUBLE	DECIMAL
HANDLE	UINT

A Note On Pointers

Every variable has a unique memory address that indicates the beginning of the memory area occupied by its value. The amount of memory used depends on the type of data involved. For example, in the case of an int, this area is 2 bytes, whereas a float uses 4 bytes. Because, in all cases, data is stored in an orderly, predictable way, it is possible to access data by manipulating a variable that contains the relevant address. Such a variable is called a *pointer*. Pointers allow you to access and manipulate structured data easily without having to move the data itself around in memory.

Memory is divided into segments, which can be no longer than 64K. To refer to data in these segments, two 16-bit values are used. These values are the segment and the offset of the data within the segment. When all the data is within a segment, the program can just use the offset, which is called a *near pointer* because it contains only an offset, with the segmented value assumed to be the same as the current data segment. When the data that you're referring to is not in the same data segment, the segment address is needed as well, resulting in a 32-bit far pointer. A *far pointer* contains not only the offset within the segment but also the segment address (as another 16-bit value), which is then left-shifted and added to the offset. By using far pointers, you can have multiple code segments; that, in turn, allows you to have programs larger than 64K.

> *Note: If you add values to a far pointer, only the offset is changed. This means that if you add enough to cause the offset to exceed FFFF (maximum), the pointer just wraps around back to the beginning of the segment. If you add 1 to 5031:FFFF, the result is 5031:0000, not 6031:0000; likewise, if you subtract 1 from 5031:0000, you get 5031:FFFF, not 5030:000F.*

Declaring External Functions

Before you can use an external function in any script, you must declare it. You can declare two types of external functions: *global* external functions, which are stored in the application object and are available from anywhere in the application, or *local* external functions, which are available only within the declared object (for example, a Window or a User object). Using local external functions somewhat encapsulates the object's functionality and is more object-oriented.

The syntax for declaring external functions in PowerBuilder is quite simple. It begins with one of two keywords: **FUNCTION**, for routines that return values, or **SUBROUTINE**, for routines that do not return values. For functions, the returned data type is then listed next. Both methods are followed by the function name and then parentheses containing the data types and names of the parameters. The optional keyword **REF** in front of a data type declaration specifies that the function can modify the data. Finally, the keyword **LIBRARY** is followed by the name of the DLL containing the routine you're calling.

Here's the declaration syntax

```
{ Access-Level } FUNCTION ReturnDataType FunctionName
( {REF} {DataType1 Arg1, ..., DataTypeN ArgN} )
LIBRARY LibName
```

or:

```
{ Access } SUBROUTINE SubroutineName
( {REF} {DataType1 Arg1, ..., DataTypeN ArgN} )
LIBRARY LibName
```

Specifying an access level for an external function or subroutine *only* applies to local external functions and is optional. A function's access can be public, protected, or private. *Public* external functions are available from within any script in the application. *Private* functions are available in scripts in the object for which the function is declared. This does not apply to the descendants. *Protected* functions are available in scripts for the object for which the function is declared and its descendants.

ReturnDataType is a valid PowerBuilder data type. It's not required for subroutines. *FunctionName/SubroutineName* is the name of a function or subroutine that resides in a DLL. *ArgumentDatatypes* are the valid PowerBuilder data types that correspond with the DLL's argument definition. *ArgumentNames* is a variable name for the argument. *DLLLibraryName* is a string containing the name of the DLL or EXE containing the function/subroutine. See Figure 17.1 for an external function declaration.

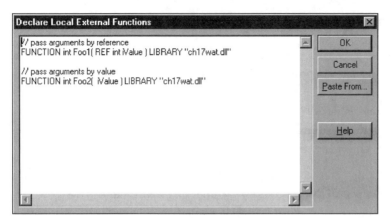

Figure 17.1
Declaring external functions.

Passing Arguments To DLLs

In PowerBuilder, you can define external functions that expect arguments to be passed by reference or by value. When you pass an argument by reference, the external function receives a pointer to the argument and you can change the contents of the argument. When you pass the argument by value, the external function receives a local copy of the argument and it can change the contents of the local copy. The changes affect only the local copy; the contents of the original argument are unchanged.

When passing strings to an external function by reference, PowerBuilder passes the actual string to the function, not a pointer to that string. You cannot pass a pointer to a string to PowerBuilder. Sometimes, however, you may want to pass strings by value. All memory management is done in PowerBuilder; therefore, if the function **Foo()** takes a name and replaces it with another name, the string variable must be long enough to hold the returned value.

> **Note:** *To ensure proper memory handling for strings, first declare the string variable and then use the **Space()** function to fill it with spaces equal to the maximum number of characters that you expect the function to return.*

Passing Structures To DLLs

You can also define external functions that expect structures to be passed as arguments by reference. The following example passes a PowerBuilder structure to a C DLL. The DLL calls a Windows API to get the current printer and populates the structure with new values; then, the structure's contents are displayed in PowerBuilder.

```
//******* str_to_pass *******
title     string
printer   string

//******* ch17wat.c *******
#include "ch17wat.h"
#include <windows.h>
#include <string.h>

void PB_EXPORT Ch17StrExample( void * pStructure )
{
char ptrBuff[80];
strFromPowerBuilder * PBStructure;
PBStructure = ( strFromPowerBuilder * )pStructure;

//get current printer from NT Registry. API command.
GetProfileString("windows","device","printer",ptrBuff,79);

// Copy new values into the structure elements
strcpy( PBStructure->strMsg, "Chapter 17" );
strcpy( PBStructure->strPrinter, ptrBuff" );
}

//DLL entry point
int APIENTRY LibMain( HANDLE hdll,DWORD  reason, LPVOID reserved )
{
   return( 1 );
}
```

Here's the source code for the header file:

```
//******* ch17wat.h *******
#include "pbdll.h"          // to ensure correct calling convention
#pragma pack( push, 1 );  // structure packing

/* create a new data type name*/
typedef struct strtag {
   char * strTitle;
   char * strPrinter ;
   } strFromPowerBuilder;

/* restore the previous alignment */
#pragma pack( pop );

/* function prototype */
void PB_EXPORT Ch17StrExample( void *pSructure );
```

Now you have to declare a local external function in PowerBuilder. Figure 17.2 illustrates this.

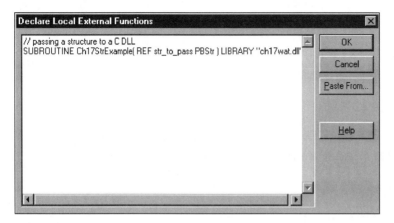

Figure 17.2
Passing a structure to a C DLL.

The following code then needs to be added to the script:

```
str_to_pass  sStr
sStr.title   = Space( 25 )
sStr.printer = Space( 80 )

Ch17StrExample( sStr )
sle_title.text   = sStr.title
sle_printer.text = sStr.printer
```

Passing Structures Within Structures

It's also possible to pass structures to C DLLs that contain arrays or other structures as their elements. This particular topic seems to be a problem for many developers, so let's go through a very simple example together.

First, you need to create a couple of simple structures in PowerBuilder:

```
//******* s_main_str *******
myfname      string
mylname      string
myage      long
strwithin      s_embedded_str

//******* s_embedded_str *******
mycar      string
itsmodel      long
```

Now, let's code the DLL. First, you need to code the header file. Notice that both structures have to be defined in our header file.

```
//******* source1.h *******
//Header file to ensure correct calling convention & export
#include "pbdll.h"

//byte alignment
#pragma pack( push, 1 );

//defining the embedded structure
typedef struct my_str_embedded_tag{
  char * cpMyCar;
  int iModel;
} MyStrEmbedded;

typedef struct my_str_main_tag {
    char * cpMyFName;
    char * cpMyLName;
    int iMyAge;
    MyStrEmbedded StrEmbedded;
}  MainStrFromPB;

#pragma pack(pop);

int PB_EXPORT Ch17StrWithinStrFunc( void * pStructure );
```

Here's the main source code for the DLL:

```
//******* source1.c *******
#include "source1.h"
#include <string.h>
#include <windows.h>

int PB_EXPORT Ch17StrWithinStrFunc( void * pStructure )
{
  MainStrFromPB * pbStructure;
  pbStructure = (MainStrFromPB *) pStructure;
  strcpy( pbStructure->cpMyFName , "Kouros" );
  strcpy( pbStructure->cpMyLName , "Gorgani" );
  pbStructure->iMyAge = 33;
  strcpy( pbStructure->StrEmbedded.cpMyCar, "BMW 325is");
  pbStructure->StrEmbedded.iModel = 1996;

    //returning a dummy number
    return 1;
}
```

```
//DLL entry point
int APIENTRY LibMain( HANDLE hdll,DWORD  reason, LPVOID reserved )
{
   return( 1 );
}
```

In PowerBuilder, you first need to declare a local external function call
and then call the DLL from the script:

```
//******* local external function *******
FUNCTION int Ch17StrWithinStrFunc(REF s_main_str mystr) &
         LIBRARY "ch17wat2.dll"

//******* PowerScript *******

//populate the structure
s_main_str mainStr
long li_rc

//preallocate space for structure
mainStr.myfname = Space(20)
mainStr.mylname = Space(20)
mainStr.myage = 1
mainStr.strwithin.mycar = Space(20)
mainStr.strwithin.itsmodel = 1

//call the external function
li_rc = Ch17StrWithinStrFunc( mainStr )

//display new elements of the structure
sle_fname.text = mainStr.myfname
sle_lname.text = mainStr.mylname
sle_age.text = string( mainStr.myage)
sle_car.text = mainStr.strwithin.mycar
sle_model.text = string(mainStr.strwithin.itsmodel)
```

> **Note:** *Remember to use the correct calling convention, structure packing (one
> byte alignment), and to preallocate memory for your strings.*

Structure Packing

The **pack()** pragma can be used to control the way in which structures are stored in
memory. The following form of the **pack()** pragma can be used to change the alignment
of structures and their fields in memory

```
#pragma pack ( push, n );
```

where *n* is 1, 2, 4, or 8 and specifies the method of alignment.

The alignment of structure members is described in Table 17.2. If the size of the member is 1, 2, 4, or 8, the alignment is given for each of the "zp" options. If the member of the structure is an array or structure, the alignment is described by the row X.

An alignment of 0 means no alignment, 2 means word boundary, 4 means double word boundary, and so on. If the largest member of structure "x" is 1 byte, then "x" is not aligned. If the largest member of structure "x" is 2 bytes, then "x" is aligned according to row 2. If the largest member of structure "x" is 4 bytes, then "x" is aligned according to row 4. If the largest member of structure "x" is 8 bytes, then "x" is aligned according to row 8. If no value is specified in the **pack**() pragma, a default value of 1 is used. Note that the default value can be changed with the "zp" Watcom C/C++ compiler command-line option. The following form of the **pack**() pragma can be used to restore the previous alignment amount from an internal stack:

```
#pragma pack ( pop ) ;
```

Functions Requiring Callbacks

Some of the Windows API functions require callbacks. A callback is a pointer to a user-defined function to which the Windows API functions should return information. This requires a lower-level language, and PowerBuilder is not capable of providing pointers to a user-defined function. Basically, you can call a Windows API function or other DLLs from your existing code, but a Windows API function or another DLL cannot call your code.

In order for a higher-level language such as PowerScript to interface with a Windows API function that requires a callback, a custom DLL must be developed that acts as a wrapper for that API function. This wrapper DLL sets up its own routine for the callback and then

Table 17.2 The alignment of structure members.

Sizeof(member)	zp	zp2	zp4	zp8
1	0	0	0	0
2	0	2	2	2
4	0	2	4	4
8	0	2	4	8
X	0			

calls the Windows API function for you. This function should then accept parameters from you and give back the data returned from the Windows API function. You'll want to become quite familiar with the structure of DLLs before taking on this task.

Windows API

The Application Programming Interface (API) is a set of operating system service calls for a particular product. It includes information about internal variables and ways to link into that product. Microsoft's set of Windows APIs, which is also known as the Windows SDK, provides over a thousand functions that can be called from within PowerBuilder.

The Windows SDK API functions are basically divided into three groups:

- **GDI.** The Graphics Device Interface functions. These functions handle the painting, drawing, plotting, printing, and color functions. The library to call is GDI32.DLL.

- **USER.** The Windows manager interface functions. These functions provide window creation, communications, hardware, and messaging. The library to call is USER32.DLL.

- **KERNEL.** System service interface functions. These functions handle memory management, multitasking, and resources. The library to call is KERNEL32.DLL.

You should refer to the Microsoft SDK manual or the Win32 API online Help to determine what functions are needed for certain tasks and how to use these functions. The Win32 API online Help is installed with PowerBuilder Enterprise and Class Builder, as well as with any major C/C++ compiler. The following subsections provide a few examples.

GetComputerName()

This call retrieves the computer name of the current system. The name is established at system startup when it is initialized from the Registry:

```
//******* API function as per SDK
BOOL GetComputerName(
    LPTSTR  lpszName,       //address of name buffer
    LPDWORD lpcchBuffer ); //address of size of name buffer

//******* External function declaration
FUNCTION boolean GetComputerNameA(REF string cName,REF &
    ulong lBuff) LIBRARY "kernel32.dll"
```

```
//******* PowerScript code to call the function
string ls_computer
ulong ll_buff
boolean lb_rc

ll_buff = 25
ls_computer = Space( ll_buff )

lb_rc = GetComputerNameA( ls_computer, ll_buff )
sle_comp.text = ls_computer
```

GetCurrentDirectory()

This function retrieves the current directory for the current path. You can use **SetCurrentDirectory**() to set a directory as the current path:

```
//******* API function as per SDK
DWORD GetCurrentDirectory( &
    DWORD  cchCurDir,   //size in char, of directory buffer
    LPTSTR lpszCurDir);         //address of buffer for current dir

//******* External function declaration
FUNCTION ulong GetCurrentDirectoryA( ulong buffLen, &
    REF string curDir) LIBRARY "kernel32.dll"

//******* PowerScript code to call the function
string ls_curdir
ulong lu_buff, lu_rc

lu_buff = 50
ls_curdir = Space( lu_buff )

lu_rc = GetCurrentDirectoryA( lu_buff, ls_curdir )
sle_curdir.text = ls_curdir
```

GlobalMemoryStatus()

This call retrieves information about both physical and virtual memory and populates a structure:

```
//*******  API function as per SDK
VOID GlobalMemoryStatus( LPMEMORYSTATUS
    LpmstMemStat); //address of memory status structure

//******* External function declaration
SUBROUTINE GlobalMemoryStatus( REF str_mem PBstrMem ) &
    LIBRARY "kernel32.dll"
```

```
//******* PowerScript code to call the function
str_mem memgetstr
memgetstr.length = 32

GlobalMemoryStatus( memgetstr )
```

GetProfileString()

The function retrieves the string associated with the specified key in the given section of
the Registry or the WIN.INI file:

```
//******* API function as per SDK
DWORD GetProfileString(
    LPCTSTR lpszSection,      //address of section name
    LPCTSTR lpszKey,          //address of key name
    LPCTSTR lpszDefault,      //address of default string
    LPTSTR  lpszReturnBuffer, //address of destination buffer
    DWORD   cchReturnBuffer); //size of destination buffer

//******* External function declaration
FUNCTION boolean GetProfileStringA(string sSection, string &
    sKey, string defVal, REF string secGet,  long lenVal ) &
    LIBRARY "kernel32.dll"

//******* PowerScript code to call the function
boolean lb_rc
string ls_section, ls_key, ls_default, ls_retbuff
long ll_len

ls_section = "windows"
ls_key = "device"
ls_default = "printer"
ls_retbuff = Space ( 80 )
ll_len = Len ( ls_retbuff )

lb_rc = GetProfileStringA( ls_section,ls_key,ls_default, &
    ls_retbuff, ll_len )

sle_printer.text = ls_retbuff
```

GetUserName()

This function retrieves the user name (the name of the current user logged onto the
system) of the current thread:

```
//******* API function as per SDK
BOOL GetUserName(
```

```
        LPTSTR  lpBuffer,      // address of name buffer
        LPDWORD lpcchBuffer); // address of size of name buffer

//******* External function declaration
FUNCTION boolean GetUserNameA(REF string cBuffer,REF long &
    nSize) library "advapi32.dll"

//******* PowerScript code to call the function
string ls_user
long li_len
boolean lb_rc

li_len = 25
ls_user = Space ( li_len )

lb_rc = GetUserNameA( ls_user, li_len )
sle_user.text = ls_user
```

GetSystemDirectory()

This function retrieves the path of the Windows system directory:

```
//******* API function as per SDK
UINT GetSystemDirectory(
    LPTSTR  lpszSysPath, //address of buffer for directory
    UINT cchSysPath);    //size of directory buffer

//******* External function declaration
FUNCTION uint GetSystemDirectoryA(REF string cBuff,uint &
    nSize) LIBRARY "kernel32.dll"

//******* PowerScript code to call the function
string ls_buff
uint lui_rc, lui_len

lui_len = 50
ls_buff = Space ( lui_len )

lui_rc = GetSystemDirectoryA( ls_buff, lui_len )
sle_systemdir.text = ls_buff
```

GetWindowsDirectory()

This function retrieves the path of the Windows directory:

```
//******* API function as per SDK
UINT GetWindowsDirectory(
```

```
    LPTSTR  lpszWinPath, // address of buffer for  directory
    UINT  cchWinPath);   // size of directory buffer

//******* External function declaration
FUNCTION uint GetWindowsDirectoryA(REF string cBuff,uint &
   nSize) LIBRARY "kernel32.dll"

//******* PowerScript code to call the function
string ls_buff
uint lui_rc, lui_len

lui_len = 50
ls_buff = Space ( lui_len )

lui_rc = GetWindowsDirectoryA( ls_buff, lui_len )
sle_windir.text = ls_buff
```

PlaySound()

This function plays a waveform file (.WAV):

```
//******* API function as per SDK
BOOL PlaySound(
   LPCTSTR lpszName,   // sound string
   HANDLE hModule,     // sound resource
   DWORD fdwSound);    // sound type

//******* External function declaration
FUNCTION boolean PlaySound(string fileName,long hModule, &
   ulong fSound)LIBRARY "winmm.dll"

//******* PowerScript code to call the function
string ls_filename
boolean lb_rc

ls_filename = "boomchin.wav"
lb_rc = PlaySound( ls_filename,0,0 )
```

Refer to your Win32 online Help to find out more about the various forms in which you can play a waveform file.

WinExec()

This function runs a specified application. It's similar to the PowerScript **Run**() function, but it has more functionality:

```
//******* API call as per SDK
UINT WinExec(
   LPCSTR  lpszCmdLine, // address of command line
   UINT  fuCmdShow);    // window style for new application

//******* External function declaration
FUNCTION uint WinExec(REF string fileName,uint fileShow) &
   LIBRARY "kernel32.dll"

//******* PowerScript code to call the function
uint lui_rc, lui_show
string ls_filename

ls_filename = "notepad.exe"
lui_show = 7 //run minimized

lui_rc = WinExec( ls_filename, lui_show )
```

Refer to your Win32 Help to learn more about its functionality.

Moving On

In this chapter, we covered external functions, which simply provide us with external functionality that may not be available within the PowerBuilder environment. We covered DLLs, calling conventions, parameter passing, and more. We also covered the Windows Application Programming Interface, which includes over a thousand useful functions that you can call from PowerBuilder via external functions.

In the next chapter, I cover object linking and embedding (OLE). OLE is the foundation for component solutions, allowing software components supplied by different vendors to work and communicate together.

Object Linking And Embedding (OLE)

OLE is a foundation for component solutions, allowing software components supplied by different vendors to work together. OLE provides an extensible set of component services that allows you to build business solutions using prefabricated solutions. One set of services that OLE provides is *OLE documents*.

OLE 2.0 is a major extension to the OLE 1.0 technology, which provided some compound document features. OLE 2.0 provides greatly enhanced document services with the introduction of OLE documents. OLE 2.0 provides a new level of application interoperability and offers substantial improvements in user-oriented features, providing a more powerful computing environment while being fully compatible with OLE 1.0. OLE 2.0 is built on the underlying OLE COM technology (see Chapter 2, "The Technology"), which makes OLE 2.0 a foundation for object services that extend well beyond document technologies. As such, OLE provides a single, integrated architecture that addresses your needs to build business applications.

PowerBuilder provides extensive support for OLE 2.0 in the form of OLE controls and containers. In addition, PowerBuilder provides support for OLE automation, OCX, and ActiveX controls. This chapter describes several ways of implementing OLE in your applications. I'll first give you an overview of OLE fundamentals and then we'll get into some juicier topics such as OLE controls, insertable and programmable objects, and OCX/ActiveX controls. Finally, I'll cover some advanced ways to manipulate OLE objects. (Instead of referring to both OCX and ActiveX controls, I'll simply use ActiveX, but the concept is the same.)

OLE Essentials

A question I'm often asked is, Why use OLE? Well, OLE is a mechanism that allows applications to interoperate, thereby allowing your users to work more productively. That, in a nutshell, should answer your question. Now to be verbose: Your end users of OLE container applications can create and manage OLE and compound documents. OLE documents can seamlessly incorporate data or objects of different formats. Spreadsheets, sound clips, text, and bitmaps are some simple examples of objects commonly found in OLE documents. Each object is created and maintained by its object application, but through the use of OLE, the services of the different object applications are integrated. Your end users don't need to be concerned with managing and switching between the various object applications; they can focus solely on the task being performed.

Linking And Embedding

When an object is incorporated into a document, it maintains an association with the object application that created it. *Linking* and *embedding* are two different ways to associate objects with their object applications in an OLE document. The difference between linking and embedding lies in how and where the actual source data that comprises the object is stored. This, in turn, affects the object's portability, its method activation, and the size of the OLE document.

When an object is linked, the source data (or *link source*) continues to reside physically wherever it was initially created. Only a reference (or a *link*) to the object and the appropriate presentation data are kept with the OLE document. Remember that linked objects cannot go with the documents to another machine. They must remain within the local file system or be copied explicitly.

Linking is efficient and keeps the size of the OLE documents small. Your users may choose to link when the source object is owned or maintained by someone else, because a single instance of the object's data can serve many documents. Changes made to the source object are automatically reflected in any OLE documents that have a link to that object.

With an embedded object, a copy of the original object is physically stored in the OLE document, as is all the information needed to manage the object. As a result, the object becomes a physical part of the document. An OLE document containing embedded objects will be larger than one containing the same object in a linked fashion. Embedding offers several advantages that may outweigh the disadvantages of the extra storage overhead. For example, OLE documents with embedded objects may be transferred to another computer and edited there.

Embedded objects can be edited "in place"—that is, all maintenance to the object can be done without ever leaving the OLE document. Because each user receives a copy of the object's source data, changes made to the embedded object by one user will not affect other users' OLE documents containing the very same embedded object.

OLE Automation

OLE automation refers to the ability of an application to define a set of properties and commands and make them accessible to other applications to enable programmability. OLE provides a mechanism through which this access is achieved. OLE automation increases application interoperability without the need for user intervention.

OLE automation also allows you to create applications that can interact with existing applications. OLE automation is powerful in that it allows OLE-enabled applications to function as components that can be combined into complete applications.

OLE As An Object-Oriented Design

Object-oriented design is a technique built around ideas that enable you to write code that can be easily maintained, reused, and executed. These ideas center around the *object class* or *type*, a structure consisting of member functions that define the behavior for the object class and the object data upon which the member functions operate. To promote reuse, an object class may contain other objects or inherit from other object classes, which means that both the data and the member functions become part of the new object class. In the latter case, the new object class may use just the member functions' names or their full implementation. When only the names are inherited, the new object class provides its own unique implementation of the member functions. A single instance of an object class is called simply an *object*.

The OLE architecture incorporates these design ideas through its own scheme of objects. The OLE libraries define interfaces, or sets of member functions, that describe object behavior in an abstract manner without providing an implementation.

Interfaces

An *interface* provides the means by which OLE applications access object services, such as drawing, saving, or visual editing. Interfaces are defined by OLE, but they can be implemented by OLE, by an object application, or by a container application, depending on the service provided by the interface. The services that are standard for all applications are implemented in interfaces provided by OLE. Services that are application, document, or object specific, such as pasting from the Clipboard, are supported by interfaces implemented by the application.

As illustrated in Figure 18.1, both the container and the object application implement interfaces that allow use of their services or functions. For example, when the user of the container application wants to edit an embedded object, the container makes calls to the appropriate interface implemented by the object application. The communication between the container and the object application is maintained through the OLE library. The library intercepts calls and provides a variety of services through its own interfaces. Services provided by OLE library interfaces include the packaging and sending of parameters between the different process spaces, providing storage for objects, and translation of object names. The services that are provided by interfaces fall into one of four general areas: communication between objects, infrastructure support, basic linking and embedding, or advanced features.

OLE Objects

Two levels of OLE objects exist. The more general OLE object, the *component object*, supports the communication interfaces. Component objects are used throughout OLE to provide applications with access to lower-level interfaces implemented by OLE.

The second level of OLE objects is the object that's used in OLE documents. *OLE document objects* support both the communication interfaces and at least one of the basic

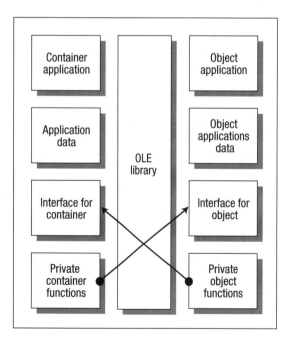

Figure 18.1
Interfaces in an OLE application.

linking and embedding interfaces. OLE associates two types of data with an OLE document object:

- **Presentation data.** Needed to render the object on display or other output devices

- **Native data.** Needed for an object application to edit the object

Interprocess Communication

OLE provides transparent communication. An application is unaware of whether a call to a member function remains within its process space or crosses into another process space. Messages and data are grouped so that multiple OLE requests are sent together and traffic between processes is reduced. This mechanism is not a protocol because there's no need for a conversation between the two processes. Data is simply sent to a predefined space on the disk where it is read by a process dedicated to that task.

Linking And Naming

The linking and naming services in OLE are implemented through the use of *monikers*, or *aliases*. Monikers are names of various types given to objects to maintain a tie between an object and its link source. OLE provides implementations of a set of interfaces and API functions used to manipulate and control monikers.

Where the user of an OLE document needs to access the link source, the application initiates a process known as *binding*. In order to locate the link source, the binding process parses the moniker and interprets each piece according to preestablished rules.

OLE Controls

You can add OLE objects and ActiveX controls to a Window or User object. To do so, you use one of the PowerBuilder OLE controls, which acts as an OLE container. You can associate two main types of OLE objects with your PowerBuilder Window objects:

- **An insertable OLE object.** A document associated with a server application. The object can be activated and the server provides its commands and toolbars for modifying the object.

- **An OLE custom control (ActiveX).** A server that processes user actions according to scripts in your program. You can write scripts for ActiveX events as well as for events that PowerBuilder provides for the OLE container.

Once you've placed an OLE control in a Window or User object, PowerBuilder displays the Insert Object dialog box, as shown in Figure 18.2. Using the three available tabs, you

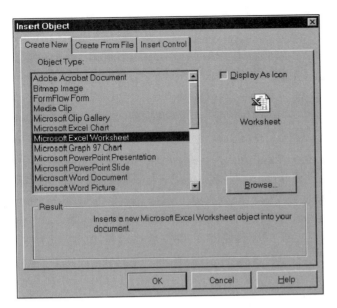

Figure 18.2
The Insert Object dialog box.

can choose a server application, a specific object for the control (which embeds or links an object in the control), or a custom control. Your choices then are:

- To create a new object that becomes embedded in your application, click the Create New tab.

- To select an existing object for the control, click the Create From File tab.

- To insert an ActiveX control, click the Insert Control tab.

- If you want to leave the control empty, click the Cancel button.

If you've inserted an object, PowerBuilder opens the server application so that you can view and edit that object. To link or embed an existing object in your OLE control, specify the file name in the File Name box. To insert an ActiveX in your control, select the Insert Control tab—you'll see a list of ActiveX controls installed on your system.

> *Note: Once an ActiveX control has been registered, PowerBuilder gets the property, event, and function information from the ActiveX itself via the Registry.*

OLE 2.0 Controls And Insertable Objects

The OLE 2.0 control that you use contains an insertable OLE object. The object can be assigned either at design time in the Painter or dynamically at runtime in your scripts. The following subsections describe the options that are unique to the OLE 2.0.

The Contents option specifies what you can insert in the control at runtime. Here are the values:

- **Any.** Inserts either a linked or embedded object
- **Embedded.** Inserts an embedded object
- **Linked.** Inserts a linked object

The Display Type option specifies what the control displays. You may choose the following values:

- **Contents.** Displays a representation of the object, reduced to fit within your control
- **Icon.** Displays the icon associated with the data

The Link Update option specifies when the object in the control is linked. Here are the methods for updating link information:

- **Automatic.** The link is automatically updated.
- **Manual.** The Link must be established via the **LinkTo**() or **UpdateLinksDialog**() function.

The Activation option specifies how the user activates the control. Here are the choices:

- **Double Click.** Activated when the control is double-clicked
- **Get Focus.** Activated when the control receives focus
- **Manual Only.** Activated programmatically with the **Activate**() function

To Link Or To Embed

As discussed earlier, an OLE object can be linked or embedded in your applications. The data for an embedded object is stored in your application's PBL. When you build your application, this data is stored in the EXE or PBD/DLL.

> *Note: To save your data at runtime, you can use the **SaveAs()** and **Open()** functions to save your user's data to a file or an OLE storage area.*

When you link an object, your application contains a reference to the data, not the data itself. The application also stores an image of the data for display purposes. The server application handles the actual data, which is usually saved in a file. Remember that the server, not PowerBuilder, maintains the link information. Information in the OLE object tells PowerBuilder what server to start and what data file and item within the file to use. If a link is broken because the file has been moved, the Update setting of the control determines how the problem is handled. When it is set to Automatic, PowerBuilder pops up a dialog box prompting you to find the file.

Offsite Or In-Place

When your users activate an object in an OLE control, PowerBuilder tries to activate the embedded object *in-place*. This means that your users interact with the object inside your Window object. The menus provided by the server application are merged with your application's menus. You can control how the menus are merged in the Menu Painter.

Offsite activation means that the server application opens up and the object becomes an open document in the server's window. Note that all the server's menus are available in this case.

> **Note:** OLE 1.0 objects cannot be activated in-place. OLE 2.0 standards dictate that linked objects are to be activated offsite.

Events For The OLE 2.0 Control

Several events let PowerBuilder know when actions take place in the server application that affect your OLE object. Here's a list of these events:

- **DataChanged.** The data has changed

- **Rename.** The object has been renamed

- **Save.** The data has been saved

- **ViewChange.** The view of the data has been changed

Changing The Object In Your OLE Controls

You can take advantage of several functions for changing the object in an OLE control:

- **InsertObject.** Lets your users choose an object

- **InsertClass.** Creates a new object for a specified server

- **InsertFile.** Embeds a copy of an existing object in your control

- **LinkTo.** Links to an existing object in the control

- **Open.** Opens an existing object from a file or a storage area

Accessing An OLE Object In An OLE Container

To refer to an OLE object in an OLE container, use the following syntax:

```
OleContainer.Object.{serverqualifiers}.propertyname
```

In the following example, Word 97 is the class associated with **ole_container**. This script inserts text from a MultiLineEdit into a Word document that has been activated in-place:

```
//Activate InPlace
ole_container.Activate( InPlace! )

//Inserts a new line
ole_container.Object.Application.Selection.TypeParagraph()

//Insert text into the document
ole_container.Object.Application.Selection.typetext( mle_text.text )
```

> **Note:** If a value is returned from an OLE control, its data type is **Any**. After the value has been captured, it has to be casted into the proper data type.

The following example retrieves a **Blob** data type—either an image or a document—from a database table and then displays it in an OLE 2.0 container:

```
Blob myblob
SELECTBLOB blob_column
    INTO :myblob
    FROM mytable
WHERE id_column = :ls_title;

IF SQLCA.SQLCode <> 0 THEN
    MessageBox("SQL error",SQLCA.SQLErrText,Information!)
END IF

//assign the Blob data to an OLE 2.0 data control
ole_1.ObjectData = myblob
```

OCX/ActiveX

The PowerBuilder OLE control gives you the option of inserting an OCX or an ActiveX control in an OLE container. I'm only going to refer to term ActiveX here, but the container is for both. An ActiveX is an embedded component, implemented as an in-process server DLL, that also supports in-place activation. As shown is Figure 18.3, this is done via the Insert Control tab. If you have registered your ActiveX, it will show up in the Control Types area. Otherwise, you have the option of registering an ActiveX via the Register New button.

An ActiveX usually has its own properties and its own property sheet for setting values that can be activated via the OCX Properties button on the OLE container's property sheet. An ActiveX also has its own set of events, which PowerBuilder merges with the event of the OLE container.

> **Note:** The PowerBuilder compiler does not know the correct syntax for accessing the properties and methods of an ActiveX. Therefore, it does not check any

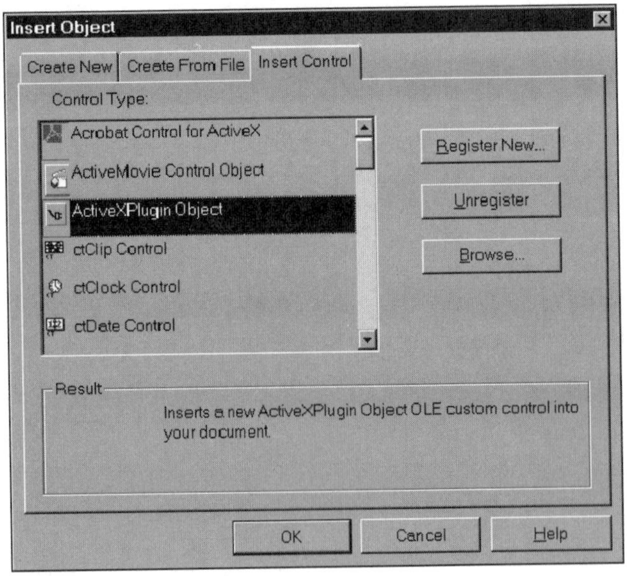

Figure 18.3
Selecting an OCX/ActiveX.

> syntax after the **Object** property. However, you can use **ExternalException** and
> **Error** events for handling OLE errors. These events allow you to intercept and
> handle errors without invoking **SystemError**, which terminates your application.

Now, remember that an ActiveX is always active. It does not contain an object that needs to be opened or activated. Your users don't need to double-click and start an OLE server. However, you can code the **DoubleClicked** event of the control or any other event to start ActiveX processing.

Accessing An ActiveX In Script

Programming an ActiveX is the same as programming OLE automation for insertable objects. You use the container's **Object** property to address the properties and functions of the ActiveX. Here's the syntax used to refer to an ActiveX's property or method:

```
OleControl.Object.ActiveXProperty
```

The following statements control date scrolling in the **ctDate** OCX from Visual Components, which is bundled with PowerBuilder:

```
ole_1.Object.LastYear()   //move to last year
ole_1.Object.NextYear()   //move to next year
ole_1.Object.LastDay()    //move to last day
ole_1.Object.NextDay()    //move to next day
```

The Object Browser

Your operating system stores information about the OLE server applications and ActiveX controls installed on your computer in the Windows Registry. PowerBuilder reads the Registry and displays the registration information for all registered OLE servers and ActiveX controls. To view this information in PowerBuilder, use the Object Browser.

The Object Browser is your second-best friend when developing applications. (The first is this book.) You can always use the Object Browser to see what events, properties, and functions your ActiveX has to offer, as shown in Figure 18.4. Here are the three categories of OLE objects shown in the Object Browser:

- Insertable controls

- Custom controls

- Programmable controls

> **Note:** If you have used an ActiveX in your application, note that when it comes to deployment, the ActiveX and its accompanying DLLs have to be deployed with your application and registered on your client's machines. Chapter 25, "Deployment," discusses this topic in more detail.

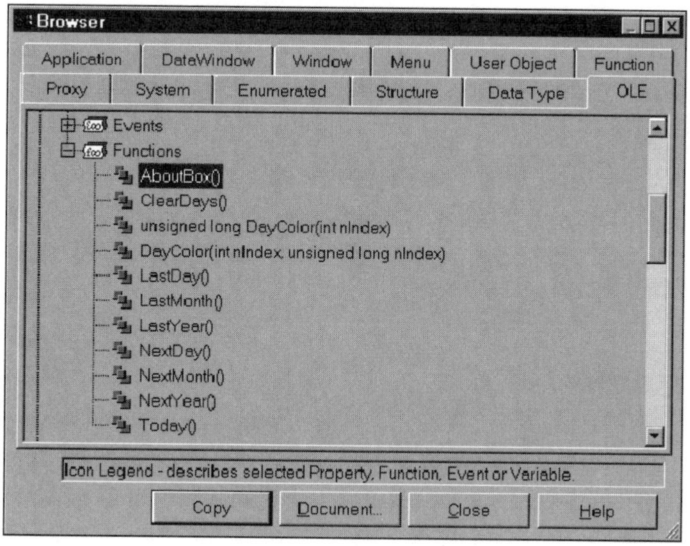

Figure 18.4
Using the Object Browser to view an ActiveX's functions.

Programmable OLE Objects

You don't need to place an OLE control on your Window or User object to use an OLE object. If the OLE object you want to use doesn't need to be visible, you can create an OLE object independent of a control, connect to the server application, and process your automation. To achieve this, PowerBuilder provides OLEObject, a dynamic object type. This means that the compiler will accept any property names, function names, and parameter lists for the object.

To work with OLEObject, you must follow these steps:

1. Declare the variable and instantiate it.

2. Connect to the OLEObject.

3. Manipulate the object, as desired, using the OLE server's properties and functions.

4. Disconnect from the OLEObject. Don't forget to destroy the variable.

The following example demonstrates using OLEObject to connect to Excel 97. A new workbook is then added, "worksheet1" is renamed, some values are inserted into the worksheet, and finally, the document is printed:

```
OLEObject myOleObject
int li_ret

//allocate memory
myOleObject = CREATE OLEObject

//connect to new object
li_ret = myOleObject.ConnectToNewObject( "Excel.Sheet" )

IF NOT IsValid( myOleObject ) THEN RETURN

//add a new workbook
myOleObject.Application.Workbooks.Add
myOleObject.Application.Visible = TRUE

//change sheet name
myOleObject.Application.ActiveWorkbook.Worksheets[1].name = "Test Sheet"

//set some values one cell at a time
myOleObject.Application.ActiveWorkbook.Worksheets[1].cells[1,1].value = 123.45
myOleObject.Application.ActiveWorkbook.Worksheets[1].cells[1,2].value = "Test 1"
myOleObject.Application.ActiveWorkbook.Worksheets[1].cells[1,3].value = "Test 2"
```

```
//set values in a range of cells
myOleObject.Application.ActiveWorkbook.Worksheets[1].Range("B2:E5").value = "Range"

//print the workbook
myOleObject.Application.ActiveWorkbook.Printout()

//disconnect and destroy
DisconnectObject( myOleObject )
DESTROY myOleObject
```

> **Note:** If you need to deploy an application that uses OLE but don't know ahead of time the version of Office your client has installed, you may want to encapsulate your OLE functions in two different User objects. Then, based on the version of Office, instantiate the correct object to issue automation commands. An example of this can be found in Chapter 8, "User Objects."

The following examples demonstrate OLE automation for two Office versions. This example shows you how to connect to a Word 95 document, insert some text, save the document, and then exit:

```
OleObject myOleobject
integer li_rc

//connect to Word
myoleobject = CREATE OLEObject

li_rc = myoleobject.ConnectToNewObject("Word.Basic")
myoleobject.FileOpen("ch18-95.doc")

//move the insertion point, and insert text
myoleobject.LineDown(1)
myoleobject.EndOfLine()
myoleobject.InsertPara()
myoleobject.InsertPara()
myoleobject.Insert("The Definitive Guide")

//save the file
myoleobject.FileSave()
myoleobject.AppShow(AsStatement!)

//disconnect
myoleobject.DisconnectObject()
DESTROY myoleobject
```

The following example is the same as the previous one, but with Word 97. Please note that Word 97 uses Visual Basic for Applications (VBA).

```
OleObject myoleobject

//connect to word
myoleobject = CREATE OleObject
myoleobject.ConnectToNewObject("Word.Application.8")

//insert a new line and text
myoleobject.Selection.TypeParagraph()
myoleobject.Selection.typetext("The Definitive Guide")

//save your document
myoleobject.ActiveDocument.Save()

//display the document
myoleobject.Application.Visible = TRUE

//disconnect from Word
myoleobject.DisconnectObject()
DESTROY myoleobject
```

With VBA, the syntax for calling Word macros has also changed. The following shows you both:

```
myoleobject.Application.Run(<macro_name>) //Word 95
myoleobject.ToolsMacro(<macro_name>,TRUE) //Word 97
```

Your next question would probably be on inserting values into bookmarks. Both methods are demonstrated here:

```
//Word 95
myoleobject.EditGoto(<book_mark_value>)
myoleobject.Insert(<book_mark_value>)

//Word 97
myoleobject.WordBasic.WW7_EditGoto(<book_mark_name>)
myoleobject.Selection.InsertAfter(<book_mark_value>)
```

OLE Enhancements

PowerBuilder 6.0's OLE interface has been enhanced immensely. First of all, you can now activate remote OLE servers via Distributed COM (DCOM). I, personally, have been waiting for this for a long time. Next, the OLE automation performance has been improved. Performance has been a major concern for many developers, but no longer. Also, the Object Browser can now display enumerated types for any OLE automation server. Let's take a look at some of these enhancements more closely.

SetAutomationPointer()

SetAutomationPointer() assigns the underlying automation pointer used by OLE into a descendant of OLEObject. Here's the syntax used for this function:

```
oleobject.SetAutomationPointer ( object )
```

Here, *object* is the name of an OLEObject variable that contains the automation pointer you want to use to set the pointer value in OLEObject.

The following example creates an OLEObject variable and calls **ConnectToNewObject**() to create a new Excel object and connect to it. It also creates an object of type OLEObjectChild, which is a descendant of OLEObject, and sets the automation pointer of the descendant object to the value of the automation pointer in the OLE object. Then, it sets a value in the worksheet using the descendant object, saves it to a different file, and then destroys both objects.

```
OLEObject    myole
OLEObjectChild myolechild
integer    li_rc

myole= CREATE OLEObject
li_rc = myole.ConnectToNewObject( "Excel.Application")

myoleChild = CREATE OLEObjectChild
li_rc = myoleChild.SetAutomationPointer( myole )

IF ( li_rc = 0 ) THEN
   myoleChild.WorkBooks.Open( "report1.xls" )
   myoleChild.Cells(1,1).value = 123.45
   myoleChild.ActiveWorkbook.SaveAs("report2.xls" )
   myoleChild.ActiveWorkbook.Close()
   myoleChild.Quit()
END IF

myole.disconnectobject()

DESTROY myoleChild
DESTROY myole
```

SetAutomationTimeOut()

SetAutomationTimeout() lets you set the timeout period for OLE procedure calls from your PowerBuilder client to an OLE server. The default timeout period is five minutes, but within this function you can set the number of milliseconds your PowerBuilder client waits before canceling an OLE procedure call to the server.

In most situations, you do not need to call **SetAutomationTimeout()**. The default time-out period of five minutes is usually appropriate. Use **SetAutomationTimeout()** to change the default timeout period if you expect a specific OLE request to take longer than five minutes.

> **Note:** If your OLE timeout period expires, a runtime error may occur. To handle this error, you may want to add appropriate code to your application.

The following example calls the **ConnectToObject()** function to connect to an Excel worksheet; it then sets a timeout period of 10 minutes (which is 600,000 milliseconds).

```
OLEObject myole
integer li_rc

myole = CREATE OLEObject

li_rc = myole.ConnectToObject( "Excel.Application")
li_rc = myole.SetAutomationTimeOut( 600000 )
```

ConnectToRemoteObject()

You learned that the OLEObject variable is used for OLE automation, in which your PowerBuilder applications ask the server application to manipulate the OLE object programmatically. **ConnectToRemoteObject()** uses DCOM to activate servers that support remote activation. Note that DCOM is not supported on all available platforms and, at the present time, is only available on Windows NT 4.x and Windows 95, assuming that the DCOM service pack is installed. Another thing you should be aware of is that DCOM on Windows 95 currently does not support secure remote activation. Windows 95 can therefore only be used for DCOM clients and not for DCOM servers.

Security on the server must be configured correctly to launch objects on remote hosts successfully. Security can be configured using Registry keys. You must specify attributes for allowing and disallowing the launching of servers and connections to running objects to allow client access. The Registry can be updated manually, or you can use graphical tools such OLE Viewer. Here's the syntax for using this function:

```
oleobject.ConnectToRemoteObject ( hostname, filename {, classname } )
```

Oleobject is the name of an OLEObject variable that you want to connect to an OLE object. *Hostname* is a string whose value is the name of the remote host where the COM server is located. *Filename* is a string whose value is the name of an OLE storage file. COM looks for the file name on the client machine. If it's located on the remote host, its location must be made available to the local host via sharing. Use the share name for the remote drive to specify a file on a remote host—for example, \\hostname \shared_directory\test.ext. *Classname* is an optional string whose value is the name of an OLE class, which identifies an OLE server application and a type of object that the server can manipulate via OLE.

As with any other function, you should always check the return code. The return for this function is 0 if it succeeds or one of the following negative values listed in Table 18.1 if an error occurs.

The following example declares and creates an OLEObject variable and connects to an Excel worksheet on a remote host named "LabPC". The drive where the worksheet resides is mapped as F:\files\excel on the local host.

Table 18.1 Return codes for **ConnectToRemoteObject()** function.

Value	Description
-1	Invalid call. The argument is the **Object** property of a control.
-2	Class name not found.
-3	Object could not be created.
-4	Could not connect to object.
-5	Could not connect to the currently active object.
-6	File name is invalid.
-7	File not found or could not be opened.
-8	Load from file not supported by server.
-9	Other error.
-10	Feature not supported on this platform.
-11	Server name is invalid.
-12	Server does not support operation.
-13	Access to remote host denied.
-14	Server unavailable.

```
integer li_rc
OLEObject myoleobject

myoleobject = CREATE OLEObject
li_rc = myoleobject.ConnectToRemoteObject( "LabPC", &
        "f:\files\excel\test.xls")
```

ConnectToNewRemoteObject()

ConnectToNewRemoteObject() creates a new OLE object in a specified remote server and associates the new object with a PowerBuilder OLEObject variable. **ConnectToNew-RemoteObject** starts the server application, if necessary. Here's the syntax:

```
oleobject.ConnectToNewRemoteObject ( hostname, classname )
```

Oleobject is the name of an OLEObject variable that you want to connect to an OLE object. *Hostname* is a string whose value is the name of the remote host where the COM server is located. *Classname* is a string whose value is the name of an OLE class, which identifies an OLE server application and a type of object that the server can manipulate via OLE.

Refer to **ConnectToRemoteObject**() for appropriate return code values. Now, the following example creates an OLEObject variable and calls **ConnectToNewRemoteObject**() to create and connect to a new Excel object on a remote host:

```
integer li_rc
OLEObject myoleobject

myoleobject = CREATE OLEObject

li_rc = myoleobject.ConnectToNewRemoteObject( "LabPC", &
    "Excel.Application")
```

Moving On

As you can see, OLE opens many new doors and enables you to extend your applications to new directions. In this chapter, we talked about OLE's general architecture. We then talked about displaying data from other applications and allowing your users to edit that data in an OLE control that can be placed on a Window or User object. We talked about adding a custom control to your applications and invoking its methods. We also covered programmable objects, where an OLE server application programmatically modifies its OLE object. Finally, we talked about some of the new features of OLE in PowerBuilder 6.0.

So far, you've learned to use PowerBuilder as a client to talk to OLE server applications. Well, how about getting other client applications such as a Visual Basic application or a Power++ application, or even another PowerBuilder application, to talk to an OLE server written in PowerBuilder. Yes, this is possible, and it will be the topic for the next chapter, "PowerBuilder Automation Server." If you're an OLE fan like I am, you'll definitely enjoy the next chapter.

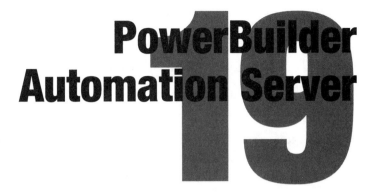

PowerBuilder Automation Server

The *PowerBuilder automation server* is an OLE server for programmable objects instead of insertable, visible objects. It provides access to nonvisual objects you've created in a PowerBuilder Library via OLE automation. You can start a server session, create one or more objects, and send commands to those objects via OLE automation syntax. Any User object that encapsulates functionality and provides information can be a useful OLE automation server.

Any client application that supports OLE automation and programmable objects can access your PowerBuilder automation server. For example you can create your client application in Visual Basic, Power++, or PowerBuilder itself. PowerBuilder automation servers can be accessed in the following three ways:

- You can access PowerBuilder itself as the automation server.

- You can access a nonvisual object that you have created and registered.

- You can access a named server that allows you to use a server name appropriate for your environment.

PowerBuilder As An Automation Server

When you install PowerBuilder on your machine, an entry is added to the Windows Registry for *PowerBuilder.Application*. This is a general purpose PowerBuilder automation server that allows you to create instances of any number of nonvisual objects and access their properties and methods.

To use PowerBuilder.Application as your automation server, you have to follow these steps:

- Create the User objects that you are going to use.

- Compile the libraries that contain the nonvisual objects.

- Write code for your client applications to connect to PowerBuilder.Application, create the objects, and then access their methods and properties.

When you connect to PowerBuilder.Application, you specify the libraries that you want to access. You can instantiate any number of nonvisual objects that you have in your libraries, as well as system objects. Each object you create in the client exists as an independent OLE object in the client, and you can address each one via OLE automation. If your client passes a server object reference back to another server object in the same runtime session, PowerBuilder has the smarts to recognize the PowerBuilder data type of the object. This allows two objects to interact in the server session, instead of being limited to OLE automation commands from the client.

Creating The NVO

Creating the nonvisual object really depends on your specifications and the type of application you are building. The object must be of type standard or a custom class User object; you can create instance variables and functions for your object. The object can declare and instantiate other objects for its own use, as needed.

The best way to describe this functionality is to go through a short example together. Let's create a custom class User object, called **u_abacus**, that contains a User object function called **uf_add**(). This function takes two numbers and simply returns their sum. Not exactly a business rule, but simple enough to demonstrate the procedure. You could expand on this as you like.

After you've created this nonvisual object, you have to use the Library or Project Painter to build a PowerBuilder Dynamic Library. Your dynamic library can be in the pcode (PBD) or machine code (DLL). Once you've done this, your dynamic library is ready to be used as an OLE server.

> **Note:** All libraries accessed in the same PowerBuilder.Application session must be of the same type. You cannot mix and match PBDs with DLLs.

Client Code

A PowerBuilder application that needs to establish a PowerBuilder.Application session must connect to the server, set properties for the server, instantiate the objects, and then

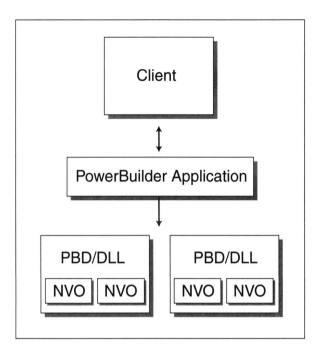

Figure 19.1
Using PowerBuilder as the automation server.

access those objects. Figure 19.1 illustrates how a client application communicates to PowerBuilder as the OLE server.

To call your nonvisual object from another PowerBuilder application, you could use code similar to this:

```
//declare our variables
OLEObject   lole_PBApplication,lole_PBUserObject
long        ll_Status
integer     li_Result

//create the ole object and connect to server
lole_PBApplication = CREATE OLEObject
ll_Status = lole_PBApplication.ConnectToNewObject( &
    "PowerBuilder.Application" )

IF ll_Status >= 0 THEN

    //generate an object instance
    lole_PBUserObject = CREATE OLEObject
```

```
//add the new PB library to the library search path
lole_PBApplication.LibraryList = "ch19oleserver.dll"
lole_PBApplication.MachineCode = TRUE

//create an instance of the PowerBuilder class
lole_PBUserObject = lole_PBApplication.CreateObject( &
    "u_abacus" )

IF IsNull( lole_PBUserObject ) THEN
    //failed
    MessageBox ("Error","Cannot create the nonvisual object " )
    RETURN

ELSE

    //call our adding machine
    li_Result = lole_PBUserObject.uf_add( 3, 4 )

    MessageBox ("uf_add( 3, 4 )", li_Result )
    MessageBox ("Status","Completed successfully.")

END IF

//do some housecleaning and disconnect from server
DESTROY lole_PBUserObject
lole_PBApplication.DisconnectObject()
ELSE
    MessageBox ("Status","Failed with Return Code: " + &
        String( ll_Status ))
END IF

DESTROY lole_PBApplication
```

You might have an information systems department in your corporation that codes in Power++ or Visual Basic. Well, with the OLE automation technology, they can have access to your business rules. The following example shows how your nonvisual object and its **uf_add**()function can be called in Visual Basic:

```
DIM ole_pb AS OBJECT
DIM ole_uo AS OBJECT
DIM li_result AS INTEGER

'connect to server
SET ole_pb = createObject( "PowerBuilder.Application" )
IF ole_pb IS NOTHING THEN
    MsgBox "Error!"
END IF
```

```
'set the proper library list
ole_pb.LibraryList = "ch19oleserver.dll"
ole_pb.MachineCode = TRUE

'create an instance of the class
SET ole_uo = ole_pb.CreateObject( "u_abacus" )
IF ole_uo IS NOTHING THEN
   MsgBox "Error!"
END IF

'call the adding machine
li_result = ole_uo.uf_add( 3, 4 )

MsgBox CStr(li_result), 48,"uf_add(3, 4)"

'release memory
SET ole_uo = NOTHING
SET ole_pb = NOTHING
```

A User Object As An Automation Server

With User objects as automation servers, you can create a nonvisual object and register it in the Registry. When you use your client's functions for accessing an external object, you have access to the nonvisual object's properties and functions. This is the preferred method because there's less complex code for accessing the object. Also, the Registry contains browsable information on your object. This makes it easy for others to program around your object. Security is also tighter here. Your clients can only access classes that you publish in the Registry.

You can pass your object references to other objects in the client application. These references are of type OLEObject, and your object can use OLE automation syntax to access properties and methods of the object. Figure 19.2 illustrates how a client application communicates with a registered nonvisual object as the automation server.

Here are the steps for using a registered nonvisual object as an automation server:

1. Create the nonvisual objects you want to use.

2. Compile the library that contains the nonvisual objects.

3. Create Registry information and then register your object.

4. Finally, write code for your client applications to connect to your registered server.

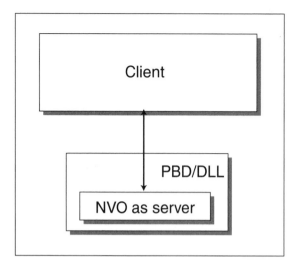

Figure 19.2
Using a registered nonvisual object as the automation server.

Creating Your Nonvisual Objects

For this example, we'll use **u_abacus** and **uf_add**() once again. Also, remember that creating the object really depends on your specifications and the type of application you're building. The object must be of type standard or a Custom Class User object, and you can create instance variables and functions for your object. The object can declare and instantiate other objects for its own use, as needed.

The next step is to register this object in the Windows Registry. Because this topic is very important and needs to be explained in great detail, I'll leave it until the end. For now, let's assume that you've registered the object as "Ch19NVO.Add."

Client Code

Writing client code to access a registered object is somewhat simpler than writing code to access PowerBuilder as the automation server. All you really need to do is simply connect to the object and use OLE automation commands to access its properties and methods.

If your client is another PowerBuilder application, you could use the following code:

```
//initialize our variables
OLEObject    lole_Pbuo
long         ll_rc
integer      li_Result
```

```
//create the object instance
lole_PBuo = CREATE OLEObject

//connect to the server
ll_rc = lole_PBuo.ConnectToNewObject("Ch19.NVO.Add" )

IF ll_rc >= 0 THEN

    //call our adding machine
    li_Result = lole_PBuo.uf_add( 3, 4 )

    MessageBox("uf_add( 3,4 )", li_Result )

    //disconnect from server
    lole_PBUserObject.DisconnectObject()
ELSE
    MessageBox("Status","Return Code: " + String(ll_Status))
END IF

//release memory
DESTROY lole_PBUserObject
```

Once again, the nonvisual object and its **uf_add**() function can be used in Visual Basic, as seen here:

```
DIM ole_uo AS OBJECT
DIM li_result AS INTEGER

SET ole_uo = CreateObject( "ch19.NVO.Add" )

IF ole_uo IS NOTHING THEN
      MsgBox "Error!"
END IF

li_result = ole_uo.uf_add( 3,4 )

ole_uo.Projection = TRUE

SET ole_uo = NOTHING
```

Named Automation Server

The final method for accessing PowerBuilder automation servers is via *named servers*. If you want to avoid references to PowerBuilder.Application but still want to access the additional functionality it provides, you can use a named server. You can create an entry in the Registry that serves as a second pointer to PowerBuilder.Application, thus allowing you to give the server a more meaningful name that better suits your organization.

Here are the steps for using a named server:

1. Create the nonvisual objects you'll be accessing.

2. Compile your library that contains the nonvisual objects.

3. Register your server in the Registry.

4. Write client code that connects to your named server, creates objects, and accesses their methods and properties.

Creating Nonvisual Objects

Once again, let's use **u_abacus** and **uf_add()**. The first step is to register the server. For now, let's assume that the server has been registered as "Ch19.Application."

To write client code to access a named automation server, you have to connect to the server, instantiate your objects, and then simply access those objects.

The following example calls the adding function via the named automation server from another PowerBuilder client:

```
//initialize our variables
OLEObject lole_NamedServer, lole_PBuo
long li_status
integer li_result

//connect to our named server
li_status = lole_NamedServer.ConnectToNewObject( &
    "Ch19.Application" )

IF li_status > 0 THEN

    //create an instance of the PB class
    lole_PBuo = lole_NamedServer.CreateObject( "u_abacus" )

    IF IsNull( lole_PBuo ) THEN
        MessageBox( "Error", "Cannot Create the nonvisual object" )
        RETURN
    ELSE

        //call our adding machine
        li_result = lole_PBuo.uf_add( 3,4 )
        MessageBox( "uf_add(3,4)", li_result )
```

```
        //release memory
        DESTROY lole_PBuo
    END IF

END IF

//disconnect and release memory
lole_NamedServer.DisconnectObject()
DESTROY lole_NamedServer
```

Objects And The Registry

The Windows Registry stores information your client applications need to access registered objects. The Registry is used by your client application to find the information it needs to access your object. The Registry includes information on where to find the files for the PowerBuilder runtime environment and runtime libraries. It can also contain a pointer to a type library file that lists the properties and methods of your object. The type library lets you examine your object in an OLE browser.

To add your object to the Registry, you need a Registry update file (.REG). This file contains information to be added to the system's registration database. Before I get into creating the REG file, let's talk about the information you have to add to the Registry.

GUIDs, IIDs, And CLSIDs

Every interface is defined by an *interface identifier*, or *IID*, which is a *universally unique identifier*, or *UUID*. The universally unique identifier is also known as a *globally unique identifier*, or *GUID*. The GUID is 128 bit. It's to be a unique value, and every interface and object class uses it for identification. OLE defines IIDs for every standard interface, along with *class identification*, or *CLSID*, for every standard object class. When you call any function that asks for an IID or a CLSID, a reference is passed to an instance of the GUID structure that exists in the process space.

Every component object class must have a unique CLSID associated with it in the registration database.

ProgIDs

OLE 2.0 object classes that are to be insertable objects must have a *programmatic identifier*, or *ProgID*. This string uniquely identifies a given class and is intended to be in a form that can be read by the environment. ProgIDs are not guaranteed to be universally unique; therefore, they can be used only where name collisions are manageable, such as in achieving compatibility with OLE 1.0.

The ProgID string must have no more than 39 characters and contain no punctuation; also, it must not start with a digit and must be different from the class name of OLE 1.0 applications. Because it's necessary to make a conversion between the ProgID and the CLSID, it's important to note that there are two kinds of ProgIDs—one depends on the version of the object application, and the other does not:

- The *version-dependent* ProgID includes a version number. It's the string used when OLE 1.0 is trying to contact OLE 2.0 using DDE.

- The *version-independent* ProgID doesn't include a version number. In this situation, the application can use the version-independent ProgID to determine the latest version of the needed object application.

Registering Your Object

PowerBuilder provides the following functions for generating Registry information:

- **GenerateGUID()**. Gets a valid globally unique identifier to serve as the CLSID of your object and its type library.

- **GenerateRegFile()**. Uses the properties of PowerBuilder.Application and other values to generate a Registry update file that the Registry editor can use.

- **GenerateTypeLib()**. Uses the information in the object to generate a type library and updates the Registry file with information about the type library.

- **CreateObject()**. Creates an instance of a PowerBuilder class in an OLE server session.

You can also take the easy route and use the PowerBuilder OLE Generate Registration Painter, which starts a utility that allows you to generate a GUID, a REG file, and a Type Library file (TLB). The Type Library file contains information about the objects, properties, and methods that are available for automation.

OLE Generate Registration (OLEGenReg)

To invoke the OLEGenReg utility, click the OLEGenReg button in the PowerBar. If for some reason you don't see this button in your PowerBar, add the following line to the PB section of your PB.INI file:

```
OleGenReg=pbgenreg,<path>\pbgenreg.pbd
```

The OLEGenReg utility is extremely user-friendly—it walks you through six steps to register your object. Let's go through these steps together and register the **u_abacus** non-visual object and its **uf_add()** function.

1. In the first screen, you need to specify your compiled library in the form of a PBD or a DLL, your nonvisual object in the library, its description, your object's version number, and whether or not your library is machine code. (See Figure 19.3.)

2. Next, you'll have to give your object a ProgID that identifies your object. Some developers like to stick to the format *<name>.Application*, but you can specify any name that makes the most sense to you. In this example, we'll use "Ch19.NVO.Add."

3. In the third screen, you need to generate a GUID for the object class and a target REG file that updates your Registry (see Figure 19.4). The REG file generated here can be used over and over again, but it contains information specific to your PC. If you're going to use this same file for deployment, you'll have to modify it so that it points to the correct location of files on your deployed PC.

4. In the fourth screen, you need to generate a GUID for your type library as well as a target type library file. If you want to skip the creation of a type library file, check the Skip Type Library checkbox. (See Figure 19.5.)

5. Click Proceed to generate your Registry and type library files.

6. Now you are done. To update the Registry, click Finish and exit OLEGenReg.

If you go to the Object Browser, you should be able to see the automation server in the OLE tab under Programmable Objects, as shown in Figure 19.6.

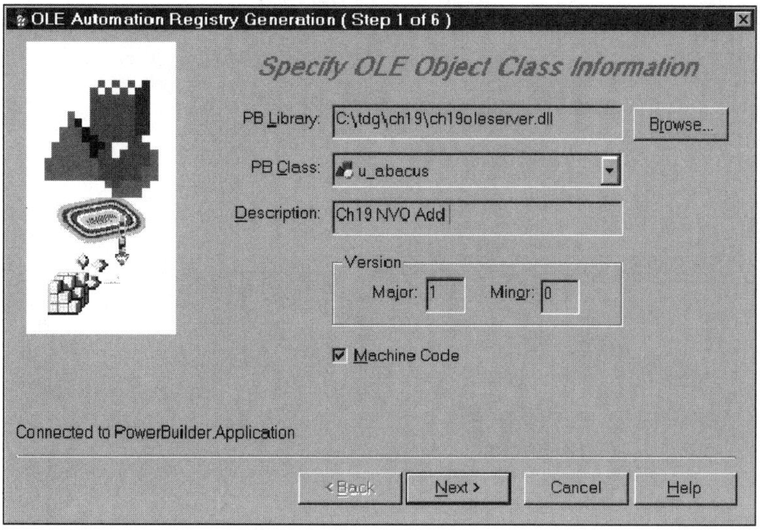

Figure 19.3
The first screen of OLEGenReg.

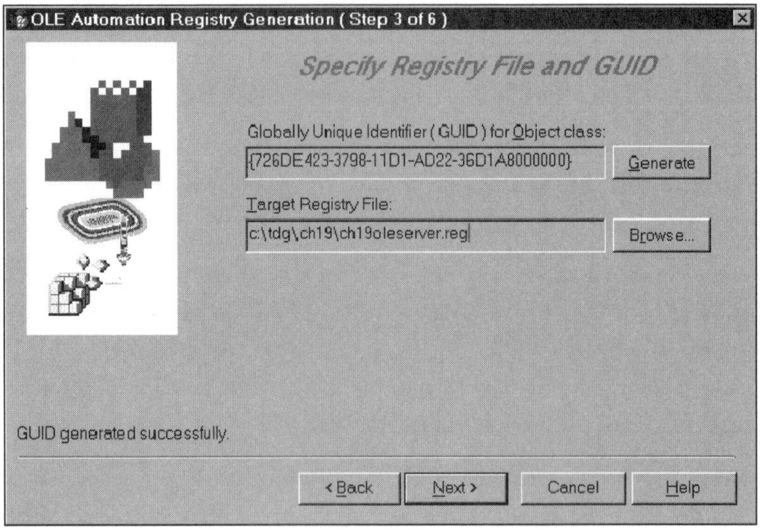

Figure 19.4
Specifying a GUID and generating a REG file.

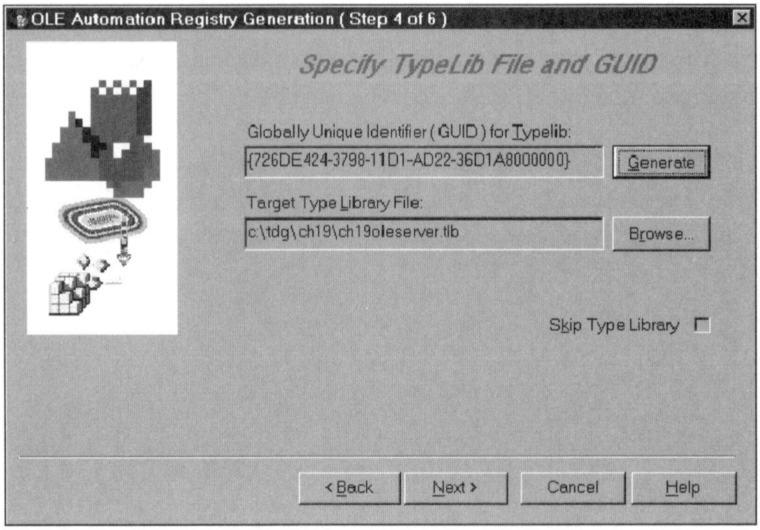

Figure 19.5
Specifying a GUID and generating a type library file.

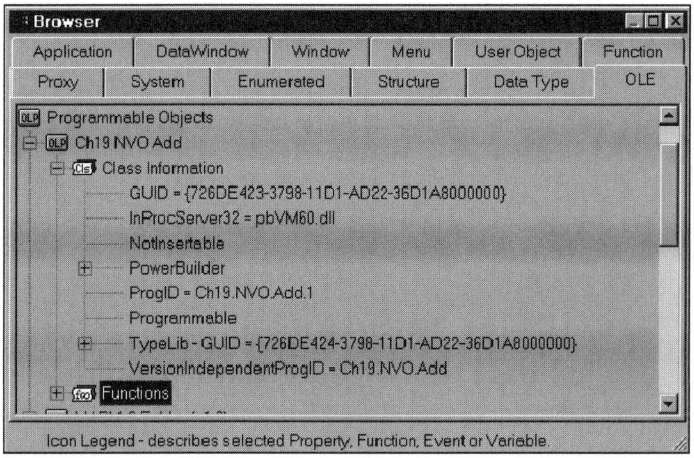

Figure 19.6
Viewing the nonvisual object automation server in the Object Browser.

Moving On

In this chapter, you learned about PowerBuilder's ability to become an inbound OLE automation server. This is a great technology because it enables client applications developed in any tool that supports OLE automation to access your PowerBuilder class User objects. Your business objects are no longer private to PowerBuilder, and they can be used throughout your organization. We also talked about the various methods of creating automation servers, registering them, and using them in client applications.

The next chapter begins Part IV of this book, which is the database connectivity guide. Most business applications that you build these days are centered around your organization's data and your datasources, thus making database connectivity an important element of PowerBuilder. In the next chapter, I'll discuss PowerBuilder's database connectivity.

PART IV
The
Database
Connectivity
Guide

Database Connectivity

Information has become a key asset in the corporate world. Nowadays, to be success-ful, corporations need accurate and timely access to information that has been reposited in database management systems. PowerBuilder provides you with two ways to access your data:

- Via ODBC and through Powersoft's ODBC interface

- Through one of the native Powersoft database interfaces supplied with PowerBuilder Enterprise

In the next three chapters, you'll learn in full detail about ODBC, Sybase SQL Any-where, and Adaptive Server Enterprise. However, before going on to those chapters, I'll cover a few brief points you should be aware of before making any database connections from PowerBuilder.

Powersoft Native Drivers

A Powersoft database interface, better known as a *native driver*, is a native connection to a database in PowerBuilder. If your site uses an RDBMS, and if you have the required network, database server, and database client software installed, you can access your data by installing the corresponding native driver.

Each native driver uses its own interface DLL to communicate with a specified database because each DLL must connect to the database through a different database vendor API. To give you an example, Powersoft's Oracle7.3 database interface uses the PBO7360.DLL.

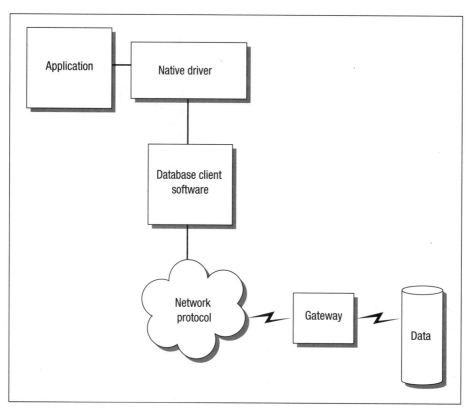

Figure 20.1
Components within a native connection.

> **Note:** *A database connection goes through several layers before actually reaching your data (see Figure 20.1). Each layer is a separate component of the connection and each of these components may come from different vendors.*

Here's a list of the native drivers supplied with PowerBuilder Enterprise:

- IBM databases
- Informix IN5 through Informix-Net 5.x and IN7 through Informix ESQL 7.2
- Microsoft SQL Server 4.x DB-Lib
- Microsoft SQL Server 6.x
- Oracle versions 7.1, 7.2, 7.3 and 8.0 beta.
- Sybase InformationCONNECT DB2 Gateway Interface
- Sybase Net-Gateway for DB2 Interface

- Sybase SQL Server 4.x DB-Lib

- Sybase SQL Server 10.x and System 11.x

  Note: I definitely recommend taking a good look at your Connecting to Your Database manual—it provides excellent information on various database connectivity issues. Also, several faxline documents are available from Sybase technical support on various database connections. You should look at these, as well.

Preparing To Use Your Database

Before connecting to your database, you must prepare to use the database. Preparing your database ensures that you'll be able to access and use your data in your applications. Preparing your database requires you to do so outside the PowerBuilder environment. These are some of the steps that you should take first:

- Make sure your database server is properly installed and configured. Confirm this with your database administrator. This is supplied by your database vendor.

- If network software is needed, make sure it's properly installed and configured and that your client machine can connect to your database server. This is supplied by your network/database vendor.

- Make sure your database client software is installed on your client machine. This is supplied by your database vendor.

- Make sure you've created the Powersoft repository tables outside of PowerBuilder. This is usually done by running an SQL script that is supplied with PowerBuilder. Refer to the *Connecting to Your Database* manual to see if your database requires one.

- Make sure you have a valid connection to your database outside of PowerBuilder first. Test your connection with a client utility that your database vendor has provided.

  Note: Make sure the database client software you use matches your operating system, PowerBuilder platform, and the version of database that you want to access. Trying to connect 32-bit PowerBuilder via 16-bit client software or vice versa is a common mistake that you should avoid, because it will not work.

Repository Tables

PowerBuilder stores application-based information you provide for a database table such as headings, validation rules, display formats, and so on, in a set of system tables in your database. These system tables are called the Powersoft *repository*. The following five system tables are created:

- **PBCatTbl.** Contains information about tables in your database

- **PBCatCol.** Contains information about columns in your database

- **PBCatFmt.** Contains information about display formats

- **PBCatVld.** Contains information about validation rules

- **PBCatEdt.** Contains information about edit styles

The first time you connect to your database, PowerBuilder creates these repository tables for you. Therefore, you must make sure you have proper access rights to make these repository tables available to all users. This means you should have sufficient authority to create tables and grant permission to PUBLIC.

> **Note:** *The first person connecting to your database must log on with the proper authority (that is, a database owner, database administrator, system user, system administrator, or a system owner).*

Database Preferences

Based on your database back end, PowerBuilder allows you to specify various database preferences. The following subsections cover the valid database preferences.

AutoCommit

The AutoCommit preference controls whether PowerBuilder issues SQL statements outside or inside the scope of a transaction. When AutoCommit is set to False, SQL statements are issued inside the scope of a transaction. When AutoCommit is set to True, SQL statements are issued outside the scope of a transaction, as seen here:

```
SQLCA.AutoCommit = TRUE
```

Keep Connection Open

PowerBuilder opens a database connection the first time it connects to your database and stays connected throughout the session until you exit. When you connect to your database in the PowerBuilder development environment without using a database profile, you can set the Keep Connection Open database preference to specify when PowerBuilder closes the database connection. Note that Keep Connection Open applies only when you're connecting in the PowerBuilder development environment without using a database profile.

Lock

The Lock preference sets the isolation level to use when connecting to your database. In multiuser databases, to prevent concurrent transactions from interfering with each other and compromising the integrity of your database, some DBMSs allow you to set the isolation level when you connect to the database. These isolation levels are defined by your DBMS, and they specify the degree to which operations in one transaction are visible to operations in a concurrent transaction.

You must set the Lock value before you connect to the database in the PowerBuilder development environment or in a PowerBuilder application. The Lock value takes effect only when the database connection occurs. Changes to the Lock value after the connection occurs have no effect on the current connection.

The following statement sets the Lock value to 3, which is a serializable transaction for a Sybase SQL Server System 11 database:

```
SQLCA.Lock = "3"
```

Read Only
The Read Only setting determines whether or not you can update the tables in your database.

Shared Database Profiles
This preference specifies the path name of the PowerBuilder initialization file containing the database profiles you want to share. To share database profiles contained in the file PB.INI, type the following in the Shared Database Profiles box in the Database Preferences property sheet:

```
F:\Shared\PB.INI
```

SQL Terminator
This preference specifies the SQL statement terminator character used by the Database Administration Painter in PowerBuilder. The default terminator character for the Database Administration Painter is a semicolon (;). If a semicolon conflicts with the terminator character used by your DBMS syntax, you can change the Painter's terminator character by specifying another character in the SQL Terminator Character box in the Database Preferences property sheet. A good choice for a terminator character is the backquote (') character. Changing the Database Administration Painter's terminator character is recommended when you're using the Painter to create or execute stored procedures, triggers, and SQL scripts.

Use Powersoft Repository
This preference controls access to the Powersoft repository by specifying whether you want PowerBuilder or InfoMaker to create the Sybase repository tables. The Sybase repository (also known as the Sybase *extended catalog* or *system tables*) consists of five tables that contain

default extended attribute information for your database. By default, the Use Powersoft Repository preference is selected in the Database Preferences property sheet. This setting creates the repository tables the first time you connect to a database using PowerBuilder or InfoMaker.

Table 20.1 shows each supported database interface and its connection-specific preferences that you can use:

Table 20.1 Connection-specific preferences for various database interfaces.

Database Interface	Connection-Specific Preferences
IBM	Keep Connection Open
	Read Only
	Shared Database Profiles
	SQL Terminator Character
	Use Powersoft Repository
Informix	AutoCommit
	Keep Connection Open
	Lock
	Read Only
	Shared Database Profiles
	SQL Terminator Character
	Use Powersoft Repository
Microsoft SQL Server 6.0	AutoCommit
	Keep Connection Open
	Lock
	Read Only
	Shared Database Profiles
	SQL Terminator Character
	Use Powersoft Repository
ODBC	AutoCommit
	Keep Connection Open
	Lock
	Read Only
	Shared Database Profiles
	SQL Terminator Character
	Use Powersoft Repository

(continued)

Table 20.1   Connection-specific preferences for various database interfaces *(continued)*.

Database Interface	Connection-Specific Preferences
Oracle	Keep Connection Open
	Read Only
	Shared Database Profiles
	SQL Terminator Character
	Use Powersoft Repository
SQL Server 4.x	AutoCommit
	Keep Connection Open
	Read Only
	Shared Database Profiles
	SQL Terminator Character
	Use Powersoft Repository
Sybase InformationCONNECT DB2 Gateway	AutoCommit
	Keep Connection Open
	Read Only
	Shared Database Profiles
	SQL Terminator Character
	Use Powersoft Repository
Sybase Net-Gateway for DB2	Keep Connection Open
	Read Only
	Shared Database Profiles
	SQL Terminator Character
	Use Powersoft Repository
Sybase SQL Server System 10/11	AutoCommit
	Keep Connection Open
	Lock
	Read Only
	Shared Database Profiles
	SQL Terminator Character
	Use Powersoft Repository

DBParm

As I mentioned in earlier chapters, the **DBParm** property contains DBMS-specific connection parameters that support particular DBMS features. **DBParm** is simply a string that's sent to the DBMS. The DBMS examines the string and reacts to it appropriately. The *Connecting to Your Database* manual lists all the supported DBMS-specific parameters that you can use with your database. You should review and understand all the parameters you might use with your database because they sometimes provide you with features that can be quite useful to you. I'll go through a couple of examples.

PBCatalogOwner

This parameter specifies a nondefault owner for the tables in the Powersoft repository. When you specify a **PBCatalogOwner** name that is different from the default repository owner for your DBMS, PowerBuilder creates a new set of repository tables with the owner name you specify. Here is an example:

```
PBCatalogOwner = 'SYSIBM'
```

DisableBind

This parameter is for those DBMSs that support bind variables. PowerBuilder binds input parameters to a compiled SQL statement by default. The **DisableBind** parameter allows you to specify whether or not you want to disable this default binding. When you set **DisableBind** to 1 to disable the binding, PowerBuilder or InfoMaker replaces the input variable with the value entered by the application user or the value specified in a script. Here is an example:

```
DisableBind = 1
```

New Connectivity Features

PowerBuilder version 6 has many new connectivity features and an enhanced user interface. In this section I would like to cover some of these enhancements.

New User Interface For Database Profiles

PowerBuilder provides you with an improved user interface for creating and managing your database profiles. As you well know, a database profile is a named set of parameters stored in your PowerBuilder INI file that defines a connection to a particular database in your development environment. As you can see in Figure 20.2, the database profile's user interface has been totally redesigned and is much easier to use now.

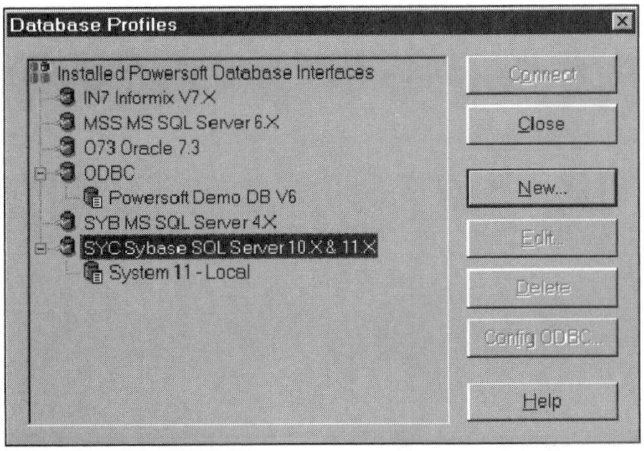

Figure 20.2
The Database Profiles dialog box.

This new interface makes it much easier for you to perform the following tasks:

- See a list of your database profiles, which is now organized by database interface.

- Access the Configure ODBC dialog box to create and manage ODBC datasources.

- Supply values for the connection options required by your database interface.

- Set **DBParm** parameters in the development environment without having to manually edit and set a **DBParm** string. (This is a great feature.)

- Generate correct PowerScript connection syntax in the PowerBuilder development environment for use in your PowerBuilder application script.

The following subsections describe the components of the new user interface.

Database Profiles Dialog Box

The main Database Profiles dialog box has been redesigned using a tree control format so that you can easily see each installed database interface and its database profiles. You can create, edit, and delete database profiles from this dialog box. In addition, when the ODBC interface or one of its profiles is selected, you can access the Configure ODBC dialog box to create, edit, or delete an ODBC datasource definition.

Database Profile Setup Dialog Box For Each Interface

Each database interface now has its own Database Profile Setup dialog box where you can set your interface-specific connection options and **DBParm** parameters. For example, if you select the SYC interface and click New in the Database Profiles dialog box, the Database Profile Setup—Sybase System 10/System 11 dialog box displays, containing settings only for those connection options that apply to the SYC interface. Figure 20.3 illustrates this point.

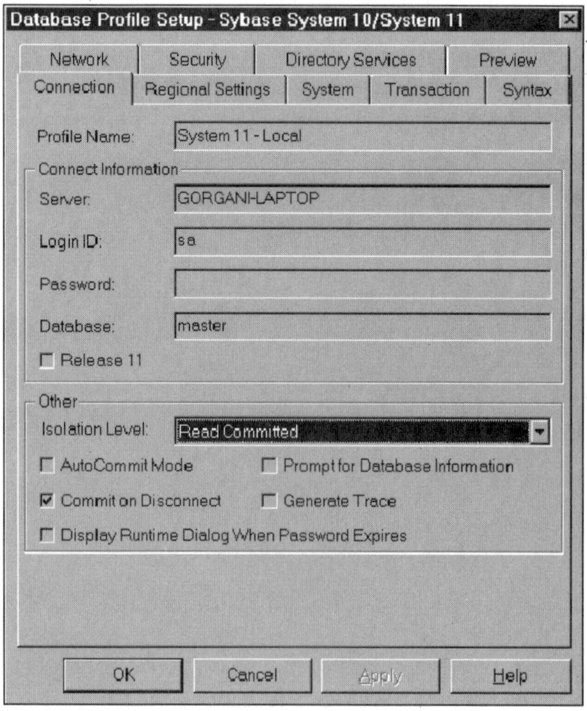

Figure 20.3
The Database Profile Setup—Sybase System 10/11 dialog box.

The Database Profile Setup dialog box groups similar **DBParm** parameters on the same tabbed page, and it lets you easily set values for **DBParm** parameters using checkboxes, drop-down list boxes, and text boxes. As you complete the Database Profile Setup dialog box in PowerBuilder, the correct PowerScript connection syntax for each selected option is generated on the Preview tab. You can then copy the syntax you want from the Preview tab into your PowerBuilder script.

Creating A New Database Profile

The new Database Profiles dialog box displays a listing of all your installed Powersoft database drivers in a tree control format. Those interfaces that are preceded by a plus sign have one or more database profiles already defined. To see a list of database profiles defined for your particular interface, click the plus sign to the left of the interface name or double-click the interface name to expand the list. When you run the Setup program, it updates the Vendors list in the [**Database**] section of your PowerBuilder INI file with the interfaces you install. The Database Profiles dialog box displays the same interfaces that appear in the Vendors list.

To create a new Profile, select an interface name and click New. The Database Profile Setup dialog box for the selected interface displays. For example, if you select the SYC interface, the Database Profile Setup—Sybase System 10/System 11 dialog box displays. On the Connection tabbed page, type the profile name and supply values for any other basic parameters your interface requires to connect.

> **Note:** You no longer need to specify the DBMS identifier in a database profile. When you create a new profile for any installed Powersoft database interface, PowerBuilder generates the correct DBMS connection syntax automatically.

Click OK to save your changes and close the Database Profile Setup dialog box. The Database Profiles dialog box displays with the new profile name highlighted under the appropriate interface. Note that the database profile values are saved in your PowerBuilder INI file.

Setting Additional Parameters

To tweak your connection and take advantage of your DBMS-specific features that your Powersoft database interface supports, you can set additional connection parameters in your database profile at any time. These additional connection parameters include **DBParm** parameters and SQLCA properties. This new improved interface allows you to perform the following tasks:

- **Supply values for connection options.** Similar parameters are grouped on the same tabbed page. The Database Profile Setup dialog box for all interfaces includes the Connection tab and Preview tab. Depending on the requirements and features of your interface, one or more other tabbed pages may also display.

- **Set DBParm parameters in the development environment.** Previously, you had to manually edit a **DBParm** string to set **DBParm** values in a database profile. You can now specify values with easy-to-use checkboxes, drop-down list boxes, and textboxes. PowerBuilder generates the proper **DBParm** syntax automatically when it saves your database profile in the initialization file.

- **Generate PowerScript connection syntax for use in your application script.** As you complete the Database Profile Setup dialog box in PowerBuilder, the correct PowerScript connection syntax for each selected option is generated on the Preview tab. PowerBuilder assigns the corresponding **DBParm** parameter or SQLCA property name to each option and inserts quotation marks, commas, and semicolons where needed. You can then copy the syntax you want from the Preview tab into your PowerBuilder script.

As you can see, creating a new database profile and setting various database parameters and options for your connection is now much simpler in version 6.0. Many functionalities have been added to the Database Profiles dialog box, and what I've covered is just the tip of the iceberg. You should experiment with this new interface and learn all about it.

ODBC 3.0

PowerBuilder version 6.0 now installs and uses ODBC 3.0 Driver Manager. The ODBC 3.0 Driver Manager supports access to a datasource through any level 1 or higher 32-bit ODBC 1.x, 2.x, or 3.0 driver obtained from Powersoft or another vendor. Note that PowerBuilder still provides the ODBC 2.x Driver Manager for accessing 16-bit ODBC drivers. To lean more about ODBC, specifically ODBC 3.0, refer to Chapter 21, "ODBC."

Informix 7.x Database Driver

PowerBuilder now provides a new Informix IN7 native database interface that accesses the following Informix database servers:

- Informix-OnLine versions 5.x, 6.x, and 7.x

- Informix-SE versions 5.x and 6.x

The Informix IN7 database interface goes through Informix ESQL version 7.2 client software to make the connection. Therefore, you must have Informix ESQL version 7.2 installed on your client machine to use the interface. To use the Informix IN7 database interface in PowerBuilder, make sure the following software is installed on the client machine as appropriate for your operating system platform:

- Informix ESQL version 7.2 (or ESQLC for the C language)

- PowerBuilder

- The Informix IN7 native database interface that comes with PowerBuilder

The DBMS identifier for Informix 7.x is "IN7." If you need to use this identifier in script, you can use the following code:

```
SQLCA.DBMS = "IN7"
```

Oracle7.3 And 8.0 Database Driver

PowerBuilder now provides a new Oracle7.3 and 8.0 native database interface that accesses Oracle7.3 and 8.0 database servers. Both Oracle7.3 and 8.0 database interfaces go through Oracle SQL*Net version 2.3 client software to make the connection. Therefore, you must have Oracle SQL*Net version 2.3 or higher installed on your client machine to use the interface.

The DBMS identifiers for Oracle7.3 and 8.0 are "O73" and "O80." To specify the O73 or O80 DBMS identifier in your scripts, type the following:

```
SQLCA.DBMS="073"
//Oracle 8
SQLCA.DBMS="080"
```

Oracle7.3 and 8.0 provide support for thread safety in their client libraries. To enable this feature in PowerBuilder, the Oracle7.3 and 8.0 database interfaces include a new **DBParm** parameter named **ThreadSafe**, which specifies whether or not your connection should take advantage of the Oracle7.3 or 8.0 thread-safe client libraries. In PowerBuilder, **ThreadSafe** is set to No, by default, to specify that your connection does not use the thread-safe client libraries. You should use this setting when you build nondistributed applications that require a single-threaded environment. To specify that your connection should use the thread-safe client libraries, set **ThreadSafe** to Yes.

```
SQLCA.DBParm = "ThreadSafe = 'Yes'"
```

Support For Sybase Open Client 11.1 Features

The Sybase SQL Server Systems 10 and 11 database interface has been enhanced to support new features in Sybase Open Client 11.1. This support includes several new **DBParm** parameters that enable Open Client 11.1 security and directory services in your applications.

Support for Sybase Open Client 11.1 features provides you with two important benefits:

- **Your applications can take advantage of security and directory services.** Open Client 11.1 provides support for network-based security and directory services. If you access an SQL Server 10.x or 11.x database server in PowerBuilder with one of the supported database interfaces, you can set several new **DBParm** parameters to take advantage of Open Client 11.1 security services and directory services in your application.

- **The Sybase Systems 10 and 11 distributed application interface works with the thread-safe version of Open Client 11.1.** This is for the Solaris platform only. The Sybase Systems 10 and 11 distributed application interface is the first Sybase SQL Server interface on the Solaris platform that works with the thread-safe version of the Open Client 11.1 libraries. This allows you to build distributed PowerBuilder applications on Solaris that access SQL Server 10.x or 11.x databases.

Release DBParm Parameter

When you're accessing a Sybase SQL Server 10.x or 11.x database on the Windows or Solaris platform, **Release** specifies whether your PowerBuilder application should use Sybase Open Client Client-Library (CT-Lib) 10.x or 11.x behavior. By default, **Release** is set to 10 to indicate that you want your application to use Open Client CT-Lib 10.x behavior. If you want your application to take advantage of Open Client 11.1 features, such as network-based security and directory services, you must set **Release** to 11 to specify that your application use Open Client CT-Lib 11.x behavior.

For example, to specify that your PowerBuilder application should use Sybase Open Client CT-Lib 11.x behavior, set Release to 11 in either of the following ways:

- Select the Release 11 checkbox on the Connection tab in the Database Profile Setup dialog box

- Type the following in a PowerBuilder script:

```
SQLCA.DBParm = "Release = '11'"
```

Directory Services

PowerBuilder 6.0 now provides several new **DBParm** parameters that enable Sybase Open Client 11.1 network-based directory services in your application. As with any other **DBParm** parameter, you can set the directory services **DBParm** values in the Database Profile Setup dialog box for your connection or in a PowerBuilder application script. Also, you must specify values for the directory services **DBParm** parameters before connecting to the database in PowerBuilder or InfoMaker.

Table 20.2 lists the **DBParm** parameters that have been added to PowerBuilder and InfoMaker to support Sybase Open Client 11.1 directory services. For each **DBParm**, the table lists the corresponding Sybase Open Client Client-Library (CT-Lib) 11.1 connection property.

Security Services

PowerBuilder 6.0 also provides several new **DBParm** parameters that enable Sybase Open Client 11.1 network-based security services in your application. Open Client 11.1 security services allow you to use a supported third-party security mechanism to provide login authentication and per-packet security for your application. Login authentication establishes a secure connection, and per-packet security protects the data transmitted across the network.

Table 20.2 The **DBParm** parameters that have been added to PowerBuilder and InfoMaker.

DBParm Parameter	CT-Lib Connection Property
DS_Alias	CS_DS_EXPANDALIAS
DS_Copy	CS_DS_COPY
DS_DitBase	CS_DS_DITBASE
DS_Failover	CS_DS_FAILOVER
DS_Principal	CS_DS_PRINCIPAL
DS_Provider	CS_DS_PROVIDER
DS_TimeLimit	CS_DS_TIMELIMIT

Two categories of **DBParm** parameters support Open Client 11.1 security services:

- Login authentication **DBParm** parameters in this category correspond to Sybase Open Client Client-Library (CT-Lib) 11.1 connection properties that allow an application to establish a secure connection.

- Per-packet security services **DBParm** parameters in this category correspond to CT-Lib 11.1 connection properties that protect each packet of data transmitted across a network. Note, however, that per-packet security services create extra overhead for communications between the client and server.

Also, the following **DBParm** parameters have been added to PowerBuilder to support Sybase Open Client 11.1 security services. Table 20.3 is a list of the login authentication **DBParm** parameters.

Table 20.4 lists the per-packet security **DBParm** parameters.

Table 20.3 The login authentication **DBParm** parameters.

DBParm Parameter	CT-Lib Connection Property
Sec_Channel_Bind	CS_SEC_CHANBIND
Sec_Cred_Timeout	CS_SEC_CREDTIMEOUT
Sec_Delegation	CS_SEC_DELEGATION
Sec_Keytab_File	CS_SEC_KEYTAB
Sec_Mechanism	CS_SEC_MECHANISM
Sec_Mutual_Auth	CS_SEC_MUTUALAUTH
Sec_Network_Auth	CS_SEC_NETWORKAUTH
Sec_Server_Principal	CS_SEC_SERVERPRINCIPAL
Sec_Sess_Timeout	CS_SEC_SESSTIMEOUT

Table 20.4 The per-packet security **DBParm** parameters.

DBParm Parameter	CT-Lib Connection Property
Sec_Confidential	CS_SEC_CONFIDENTIALITY
Sec_Data_Integrity	CS_SEC_INTEGRITY
Sec_Data_Origin	CS_SEC_DATAORIGIN
Sec_Replay_Detection	CS_SEC_DETECTREPLAY
Sec_Seq_Detection	CS_SEC_DETECTSEQ

CommitOnDisconnect

CommitOnDisconnect specifies whether PowerBuilder should commit or roll back all previously uncommitted database updates before disconnecting from a datasource. For example, to tell PowerBuilder to roll back uncommitted database updates instead of committing them when disconnecting from the database, set **CommitOnDisconnect** to No. There are two ways to do this:

- Clear the Commit On Disconnect checkbox on the Connection tab in the Database Profile Setup dialog box.

- Type the following in a PowerBuilder script:

```
SQLCA.DBParm = "CommitOnDisconnect = 'No'"
```

Support For PBCatalogOwner In Oracle

All Oracle database interfaces in PowerBuilder now support the **DBParm** parameter **PBCatalogOwner**, which allows you to specify a nondefault owner for the tables in the Powersoft repository, also known as the Powersoft extended catalog or the Powersoft system tables. When you specify a value for **PBCatalogOwner** that is different from 'SYSTEM', PowerBuilder creates a new set of repository tables with the owner name you specify.

Increased Limit For DBParm Strings

Strings containing **DBParm** parameters that you specify in your Database Profile Setup dialog box for your connection can now be up to 999 characters in length. Previously, the **DBParm** string could not exceed 499 bytes, and PowerBuilder ignored any **DBParm** settings in the string that were beyond this limit.

Print Statements In SQL Server Stored Procedures

When you access an SQL Server database in PowerBuilder with one of the Sybase Systems 10 and 11 interfaces, you can now use **PRINT** statements in your stored procedures for debugging purposes.

PWDialog

This **DBParm** parameter is for use with Sybase Systems 10 and 11 on all supported platforms and with Sybase Systems 10 and 11 distributed application interface on Solaris. When you're using one of these interfaces to access the database, **PWDialog** controls whether a Password Expired dialog box displays if necessary in your PowerBuilder or InfoMaker application at execution time.

When PWDialog is set to 1, the Password Expired dialog box prompts application users to change their passwords if they attempt to log in to the database with an expired password. By default, **PWDialog** is set to 0 to specify that the Password Expired dialog box will not display in your application at execution time. For example, to display the Password Expired dialog box when needed in your application at execution time, set **PWDialog** to 1 in either of the following ways:

- Use the database profile

- Type the following in a PowerBuilder script:

```
SQLCA.DBParm = "PWDialog = 1"
```

DateTimeAllowed

DateTimeAllowed controls whether columns having a DateTime data type can appear as unique key columns in the **WHERE** clause of an SQL **UPDATE** or **DELETE** statement. PowerBuilder generates an **UPDATE** statement or a **DELETE** statement followed by an **INSERT** statement, to update the database from a DataWindow object.

When you're working in the PowerBuilder DataWindow Painter, you specify which columns to include in the **WHERE** clause by selecting them from the Unique Key Columns list in the Specify Update Properties dialog box. By default, **DateTimeAllowed** is set to 0 to prohibit DateTime columns from displaying in the Unique Key Columns list and, consequently, from appearing in the **WHERE** clause of an **UPDATE** or **DELETE** statement. When you set **DateTimeAllowed** to 1, any DateTime columns in your database table display in the Unique Key Columns list and can therefore be selected to appear in the **WHERE** clause of an **UPDATE** or **DELETE** statement. For example, to allow the use of DateTime columns in the **WHERE** clause of an **UPDATE** or **DELETE** statement, set **DateTimeAllowed** to 1 in either of the following ways:

- Select the DateTime Data Type Allowed checkbox on the Syntax tab in the Database Profile Setup dialog box

- Type the following in your script:

```
SQLCA.DBParm = "DateTimeAllowed = 1"
```

Please note that this **DBParm** parameter only applies to Microsoft SQL Server 6.x, SQL Server 4.x DB-Lib, Sybase Systems 10 and 11 CT-Lib, Sybase Systems 10 and 11 CT-Lib distributed application, and Sybase SQL Server DB-Lib interface.

FormatArgsAsExp

This parameter controls whether PowerBuilder converts a DataWindow or a report retrieval argument of the decimal data type to scientific notation if the argument exceeds 12 digits. If **FormatArgsAsExp** is set to Yes, PowerBuilder performs this conversion. The setting of **FormatArgsAsExp** may affect the speed of data retrieval in your DataWindows and reports, especially if you're accessing large databases. To tell PowerBuilder to leave a retrieval argument exceeding 12 digits as a decimal and not convert it to scientific notation, set **FormatArgsAsExp** to No in either of the following ways:

- Clear the Format Arguments In Scientific Notation checkbox on the Syntax tab in the Database Profile Setup dialog box

- Type the following in your script:

```
SQLCA.DBParm = "FormatArgsAsExp = 'No'"
```

Note that this parameter applies to IBM, ODBC, Oracle, Sybase InformationCONNECT DB2 Gateway, and Sybase Net-Gateway for DB2.

AutoCommit Support In Sybase Net-Gateway

The Sybase Net-Gateway for DB2 interface in PowerBuilder now supports the AutoCommit SQLCA property. Note that this is supported only when you're using Sybase Net-Gateway version 3.0 or higher. To tell PowerBuilder to issue SQL statements outside the scope of a transaction, set AutoCommit to True in either of the following ways:

- Set AutoCommit in the Database Profile Setup dialog box by selecting the AutoCommit Mode checkbox on the Connection tab in the Database Profile Setup dialog box

- Set AutoCommit in your application by using the following code:

```
SQLCA.AutoCommit = True
```

UTF8

If you're using the Sybase System 11 interface in PowerBuilder for Unicode, the UTF8 **DBParm** parameter specifies whether the Sybase SQL Server database server you're accessing has standard ANSI or UTF8 installed as its default character set. By default, UTF8 is set to 0 to indicate that your database server uses a standard ANSI character set. If you set UTF8 to 1, this means that your database server uses the UTF8 character set as its default. To specify that the Sybase SQL Server database server you're accessing with PowerBuilder for Unicode uses UTF8 as its default character set, set UTF8 to 1 in either of the following ways:

- Select the UTF8 Character Set Installed checkbox on the Regional Settings tab in the Database Profile Setup dialog box

- Type the following in your script:

```
SQLCA.DBParm = "UTF8 = 1"
```

Troubleshooting Your Connection

If you're having problems connecting to your database, prepare a checklist for yourself to see if you've gone through all the necessary connectivity steps. A general list might look something like this:

- Make sure your database server software is installed and online. Also, make sure you can ping it.

- Make sure all your environment variables and paths, if any, are set up properly.

- Make sure you have installed your database client software on your machine and you have a valid connection to your database outside of PowerBuilder.

- Make sure you have the platform version of your database client software that matches the version of PowerBuilder you're using (32-bit to 32-bit, 16-bit to 16-bit).

- Make sure you've run any SQL scripts that PowerBuilder needs outside of the PowerBuilder environment. For example, with the System 10/11 and the Adaptive Server Enterprise, you need to run PBSYC.SQL, and so on, to create certain stored procedures that PowerBuilder uses.

- Make sure you've installed the correct Powersoft native driver that corresponds to your database. For example, you need PBSYC60.DLL to connect to System 10/11 and the Adaptive Server Enterprise via CT-Lib. If you are using ODBC, make sure you have the appropriate ODBC driver installed.

- Make sure you do not have duplicate DLLs or out-of-date DLLs on your machine. Having multiple ODBC drivers with different dates in paths may cause problems.

- Make sure the first time you log in to your database, you log in with an ID that has the proper authority to create the Powersoft repository tables and grant permission on them to all. For example, "sa", "DBA", or "system".

If you're still unsuccessful, take a break. Sometimes, minor things are overlooked when you're tired or frustrated. And, if all else fails, then panic! No, I don't recommend that at all. You can always post a message on various newsgroups, search the infobase folio, go to various Web sites, or call technical support.

Porting Your Application

If you have the need to port your application from one database to another, it's best to consider this before designing your application. I have talked to many developers who had built an entire application using SQL Anywhere because it's shipped with PowerBuilder and then, upon completion of the application, wanted to port it to a larger RDBMS. Well, this may cause a few problems. The owners of the tables, the database functions used, the syntax used for stored procedures, and the triggers and outer joins could all become potential problems. One of the most common problems with porting an SQL Anywhere application to a larger RDBMS is the "DBA" user ID, specifically if you've built your entire application while logging in with this user ID.

Let's go through an example together. In this example, we'll port an application that connects and uses a customer SQL Anywhere database to Oracle7.

First, create a table called Customer in SQL Anywhere. Afterwards, you'll need to create a user called "customer" and grant DBA permissions to it. In SQL Anywhere, "DBA" is a reserved word and should always have double quotes around it. Note that "DBA" is also a user ID.

```
GRANT CONNECT TO customer IDENTIFIED BY sql;
GRANT DBA TO customer;
```

You then need to modify PBODB060.INI and set **DelimitIdentifier** to No. This option allows the DataWindow syntax to be generated without the quotes around it. You also need to set **PBCatalogOwner** to "customer." By setting **PBCatalogOwner** to "customer," all your users will use the catalog tables that are created by customer upon a first connection to the database.

Now, let's start up PowerBuilder. Configure an ODBC connection for SQL Anywhere to connect to the customer database with the user ID customer. You need to create all your tables with this user ID. You should save all your SQL scripts so that you can use them later when porting to Oracle.

Next step is to create a group that all your user IDs will have membership in:

```
GRANT CONNECT TO developers IDENTIFIED BY sql;
GRANT GROUP TO developers;
GRANT ALL ON customer.table1 TO developers;
```

Create your user IDs and grant them membership in the developers group:

```
GRANT CONNECT to JohnDoe IDENTIFIED BY sql;
GRANT MEMBERSHIP IN GROUP developers to JohnDoe;
```

Reconnect to your database with the JohnDoe user ID and create all your DataWindows. The syntax generated for the DataWindow will be fully qualified with owner.table.column. Once your application is ready to be ported over, you need to export PBCatalog tables.

On the Oracle7 side, you need to create a new user ID for "customer" and grant it proper authority similar to "system." Once this is done, connect to Oracle as customer. Import the PBCatalog tables that you exported from SQL Anywhere into Oracle's PBCatalog tables. Next, create all your tables in your customer database using the SQL script that you saved previously. Make modifications to it as needed—for example, change data types as needed (using a PowerBuilder Pipeline object is also a very good choice here).

Create the appropriate users and groups similar to what you did in SQL Anywhere:

```
CREATE ROLE developers IDENTIFIED BY sql;
GRANT ALL ON customer.table1 TO developers;
CREATE USER JohnDoe IDENTIFIED BY sql;
GRANT ROLE TO JohnDoe;
```

Now connect to your Oracle7 database as JohnDoe, which is a member of "role developer," and complete any development you may have. Make any minor modifications as necessary.

Moving On

In this chapter, we covered database connectivity. Most business applications are centered around data and accessing the information it represents. This alone should give connectivity a high priority in your development phase. Most development shops have database and network administrators who take care of setting up networks, databases, and so on. However, because connectivity is so important, it's best to know all about the subject as it pertains to the databases you connect to.

Now that we've covered some of the basics, let's get ready to get into the juicy stuff. In the next three chapters, I'll cover ODBC, Adaptive SQL Anywhere, and the Adaptive Server Enterprise. First, we'll start with ODBC.

21 ODBC

One of the challenges of database connectivity is accessing multiple, heterogeneous datasources from within a single application. A second challenge is flexibility. Your applications should be able to directly access data from a variety of datasources without making any modifications to your source code. These challenges are common to you when getting off-the-shelf applications, and to some of you who may be attempting to provide solutions to your users for migrating data to new platforms. The problems of database connectivity are apparent in the differences among the programming interfaces, DBMS protocols, DBMS languages, and network protocols of diversified datasources. Even when datasources are restricted to relational DBMSs that use SQL, significant differences in SQL syntax and semantics must be resolved.

Several vendors have attempted to address the problem of database connectivity in a variety of ways, such as using gateways, a common programming interface, and a common protocol. The ODBC approach addresses the heterogeneous database connectivity problem using the common interface approach. You use one API to access all datasources. ODBC is based on a Call Level Interface (CLI) specification that was developed by a consortium of over 40 companies that are all members of the SQL Access Group. The result of this is a single API that provides all the functionality you need as well as the architecture you require to ensure interoperability.

In this chapter, we'll look inside ODBC PowerBuilder's interface to ODBC.

Advantages Of ODBC

ODBC provides many significant benefits to you and your industry by providing an open, standard way to access your data. Some of the many advantages of ODBC include the following:

- ODBC allows you to access data in more than one data storage location from within a single application.

- ODBC allows you to access data in more than one type of DBMS from a single application.

- ODBC simplifies your application development.

- ODBC is a portable API. By enabling the same interface and access, it's a cross-platform tool.

- ODBC insulates applications from changes to underlying network and DBMS versions.

- ODBC promotes the use of SQL, which is the standard language for DBMSs, as defined in the ANSI 89 standard.

Keep in mind that ODBC does have its disadvantages, too. Performance can be slower because of the additional layer that has been added between your DBMS and the client. Also, specific features of a DBMS may not always be used because ODBC does not support features of all DBMSs.

The ODBC Architecture

ODBC defines an API. Each application uses the same code, as defined by the API specification, to talk to many types of datasources through DBMS-specific drivers. As shown in Figure 21.1, a driver manager sits between the applications and the drivers. The application calls ODBC functions to connect to a datasource, send and receive data, and then disconnect.

The ODBC architecture has four main components:

- **Application.** Performs processing and calls ODBC functions to submit SQL statements and retrieve results.

- **Driver manager.** Loads drivers on behalf of your applications.

- **Drivers.** Processes ODBC function calls, submits SQL requests to a specific datasource, and returns the result to your application. If necessary, the driver also modifies an application's request so that the request conforms to syntax supported by the associated DBMS.

- **Datasource.** Consists of the data the users wants to access and its associated operating system, DBMS, and the network platform used to access the DBMS.

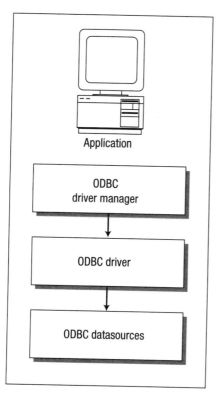

Figure 21.1
The ODBC architecture.

Application (SQL Processing)

To interact with a datasource, your application performs the following tasks:

- Connects to the datasource. It specifies the datasource name and any additional information needed to complete the connection.

- Processes one or more SQL statements. Your application places the SQL text string in a buffer. If the statement includes parameter markers, it sets the parameter values. If your statement returns a result set, your application assigns a cursor name for the statement or allows the driver to do so. Your application then submits the statement for prepared or immediate execution. If the statement creates a result set, the application can inquire about the attributes of the result set, such as the number of columns or the name and type of a specific column. Finally, it assigns storage for each column in the result set and fetches the results.

- Ends each transaction by committing it or rolling it back.

- Terminates the connection when it has finished interacting with the datasource.

In simpler words, memory for the ODBC environment is allocated and pointed to by an *environment handle*. Only one environment handle per application is possible. When an environment handle has been created, a *connection handle* is then obtained. This handle points to a memory location containing information about your connection. Note that multiple connection handles can exist for each environment handle. A lower-level handle is then created. This third handle, which is called a *statement handle*, is used for processing a query within your connection. Once again, note that there can be multiple statement handles for each connection.

Driver Manager

The main role of the driver manager is to load ODBC drivers. In addition, the driver manager also performs the following tasks:

- Processes several ODBC initialization and information calls

- Passes ODBC function calls from your application to the driver

- Performs error and state checking

- Logs function calls made by your application

Processing ODBC Initialization Calls

The driver manager processes all or a large part of the many ODBC functions before passing the call to the driver.

Information Functions

The **SQLDataSource()** and **SQLDriver()** functions are processed by the driver manager only. These calls are passed to the driver. For the **SQLGetFunction()** function, the driver manager processes the call if the driver does not support the **SQLGetFunction**.

Connection Functions

For **SQLAllocEnv()**, **SQLAllocConnect()**, **SQLGetConnectOption()**, **SQLFreeConnect()**, and **SQLFreeEnv()**, the driver manager processes the call. The driver manager calls **SQLAllocEnv()**, **SQLAllocConnect()**, and **SQLSetConnectOption()** in the driver when your application calls a function to connect to your datasource. The driver manager calls **SQLFreeConnect()** and **SQLFreeEnv()** in your driver when your application calls **SQLFreeConnect()**.

For **SQLConnect()**, **SQLDriverConnect()**, **SQLBrowseConnect()**, and **SQLError()**, the driver manager performs the initial processing and then sends the call to the driver that has been associated with your connection.

Passing Function Calls From Your Application To Your Driver

For any other ODBC function, the driver manager passes the call to the driver associated with your connection.

Error And State Checking

The driver manager checks function arguments and state transactions, and it checks for other error conditions before passing the call to the driver associated with your connection. This reduces the amount of error handling that a driver needs to perform.

Log Function Calls

If needed and if requested, the driver manager records each called function in a trace file after checking the function call for errors. The name of each function that does not contain errors detectable by the driver manager is recorded, along with the values of the input arguments and the names of the output arguments.

The ODBC Driver

An ODBC driver is a DLL that implements ODBC function calls and interacts with a datasource. The driver manager loads a driver when the application calls the **SQLBrowseConnect()**, **SQLConnect()**, and **SQLDriverConnect()** functions.

An ODBC driver performs the following tasks in response to ODBC function calls from your application:

- Establishes a connection to a datasource

- Submits requests to the datasource

- Translates data to or from other formats (if requested by the application)

- Returns the results to the application

- Formats errors into standard error codes and returns them to the application

- Declares and manipulates cursors if needed

- Initiates transactions if the datasource requires explicit transaction initiation

The Datasource

The datasource consists of the data you need to access, its associated DBMS, the platform on which the DBMS resides, and the network used to access that platform. Each datasource requires that a driver provide certain information in order to connect to it. At the core level, this is defined as the name of the datasource, a user ID, and a password. ODBC extensions allow drivers to specify additional information, such as a network address or additional passwords. The datasource is responsible for the following tasks:

- Processing SQL requests received from a driver

- Returning results to a driver

- Performing all other functions normally associated with a DBMS

The Driver Architecture

ODBC has two basic types of drivers: *single tier* and *multiple tier*. With single-tier drivers, the driver processes both ODBC calls and SQL statements. This way, the driver performs part of the datasource functionality. With multiple-tier drivers, the driver processes ODBC calls and passes SQL statements to the datasource.

Single-Tier Drivers

Single-tier drivers are basically intended for non-SQL databases. The database file is processed directly by the driver. The driver processes SQL statements and retrieves information from the database. SQL statements, once parsed and translated, are passed to the database as basic file operations. A driver that manipulates a dBase file is an example of such a driver.

A single-tier driver may limit the set of SQL statements that can be submitted. Single-tier drivers are generally slower than the native DBMS tools because they parse and translate the SQL statements into basic file operations. Figure 21.2 illustrates the architecture of single-tier drivers.

Multiple-Tier Drivers

Multiple-tier drivers send requests to a server that processes those requests, as shown in Figure 21.3. The requests may be SQL or a DBMS-specific format. Although the entire installation may reside on a single system, it's more often divided across platforms. In a typical system, the application, driver, and driver manager reside on one system, called the *client*. The database and the software that controls access to the database reside on another system, called the *server*. Multiple-tier drivers come in two types: *two-tier* and *three-tier*.

Two-Tier Drivers

Two-tier drivers have two variations. The variations are defined in terms of SQL functionality, being either SQL-based or non-SQL-based. Drivers for SQL-based DBMSs, such as Sybase and Oracle, have a straightforward implementation. The ODBC driver

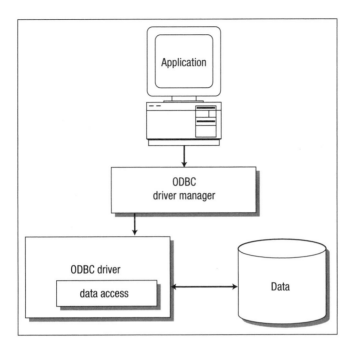

Figure 21.2
Single-tier drivers.

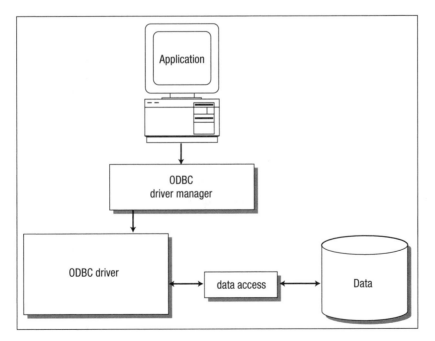

Figure 21.3
Multiple-tier drivers.

on the client side passes SQL statements directly to the server-based DBMS using the database's data stream. The DBMS handles all processing of the SQL statements.

DBMSs that are non-SQL-based require more work. The server side has to parse and translate the SQL to the native database format.

Three-Tier Drivers

Three-tier drivers, sometimes known as *gateways*, are another type of multiple-tier configuration. The driver passes SQL requests to a gateway process, which in turn sends the requests to the datasource residing on a host. Gateway drivers can support both SQL-based and non-SQL-based gateways.

Often, the gateway is simply a network communication-level gateway. In this case, SQL is passed all the way to the host. In other implementations, the gateway is parsed and translates the SQL into DBMS-specific SQL or a DBMS-specific format. Gateway code on the host is also typically required. Another architecture is the distributed relational database architecture (DRDA).

ODBC Conformance Levels

Conformance levels establish the amount of interoperability that a drive has with its corresponding datasource. ODBC defines conformance levels for drivers in two areas:

- The ODBC API
- ODBC SQL grammar

Conformance levels help both application and driver developers to establish standard sets of functionality.

API Conformance Levels

The API conformance level of a driver places limits on the functions that your application can call. Driver developers do not implement every ODBC function; they are encouraged to conform to one of four levels of functionality:

- Core API
- Extension level 1
- Extension level 2
- Extension level 3

These levels are general guidelines. Some drivers omit several functions from their claimed level of support. Almost all drivers implement functions belonging to a higher conformance level. Core API conformance is a bare minimum of functionality. The 23 functions that make up the core involve allocating and freeing environments, database connections, and SQL statements. They provide basic support for passing parameters into statements as well as accessing the returned results. Limited cataloging functions and error message retrieval functions are also available.

The core API conformance level suffices for very basic applications. This level is adequate only if the schema for each of your tables is known up front. If you must determine a table's schema at runtime, hold out for a more capable driver.

> **Note:** The best way to find out the API conformance level of a function is to look at the ODBC API online Help. Most versions of this file enable you to view functions by conformance level.

Extension level 1 adds 19 more functions for your use in your applications. Getting a table's schema is totally supported. You can learn what conceptual data types are available and what each is called. This ability is indispensable if your program is to work with several different drivers. You can also query the driver about support for different SQL conformance features. Note that the majority of drivers conform to this level.

Level 2 extends level 1 with 19 more functions. Most of the level 2 changes reflect support for advanced features found only in client/server databases. You can now get information about both primary and foreign keys. Among other additions, you can get information about table and column permissions as well as stored procedures in the your database. The most important features are the enhancements of cursor control and concurrency control.

Core API

The functionality of the core-level API can be summarized as follows:

- Allocates and frees environment, connection, and statement handles

- Connects to datasources

- Prepares SQL statements and executes them immediately

- Assigns storage for parameters in an SQL statement and result columns

- Retrieves data from a result set and information about that result set

- Commits or rolls back transactions

- Retrieves error information

Table 21.1 shows the core-level API functions.

Table 21.1 The core-level API functions.

Function	Description
SQLAllocConnect()	Obtains a connection handle.
SQLAllocEnv()	Obtains an environment handle. One handle is used for one or more connections.
SQLAllocStmt()	Allocates a statement handle.
SQLBindCol()	Assigns storage for a result column and specifies the data types.
SQLCancel()	Cancels an SQL statement.
SQLColAttributes()	Describes attributes of a column in the result set.
SQLConnect()	Connects to a specific driver by datasource name, user ID, and password.
SQLDescribeCol()	Describes a column in the result set.
SQLDisconnect()	Closes the connections.
SQLError()	Returns additional error or status information.
SQLExecDirect()	Executes a statement.
SQLExecute()	Executes a prepared statement.
SQLFetch()	Returns a result set.
SQLFreeConnect()	Releases the connection handle.
SQLFreeEnv()	Releases the environment handle.
SQLFreeStmt()	Ends statement processing and closes the associated cursor, discards pending results, and frees all resources associated with the statement handle.
SQLGetCursorName()	Returns the cursor name associated with the statement handle.
SQLNumResultCols()	Returns the number of columns in the result set.
SQLPrepare()	Prepares an SQL statement for later executions.
SQLRowCount()	Returns the number of rows affected by an insert, update, or delete request.
SQLSetCursorName()	Specifies a cursor name.
SQLSetParm()	Assigns storage for parameters in an SQL statement.
SQLTransact()	Commits or rolls back a transaction.

Level 1

The functionality of the level 1 API can be summarized as follows:

- Meets the core API functionality conformance level

- Connects to datasources with driver-specific dialog boxes

- Sets and inquires about values of statement and connection options

- Sends part or all of a result column value

- Retrieves part or all of a result column value

- Retrieves catalog information such as columns, special columns, statistics, and tables

- Retrieves information about driver and datasource capabilities, such as supported data types

- Supports both scalar functions and ODBC functions

Table 21.2 lists the level 1 API functions.

Table 21.2 The level 1 functions.

Function	Description
SQLColumns()	Returns the list of column names in specified tables.
SQLDriverConnect()	Connects to a specific driver via a connection string or requests that the driver manager and driver display connection dialog boxes for the user.
SQLGetConnectOption()	Returns the value of a connection option.
SQLGetData()	Returns part or all of one column of one row of a result set.
SQLGetFunctions()	Returns supported driver functions.
SQLGetInfo()	Returns information about a specific driver and datasource.
SQLGetStmtOption()	Returns the value of a statement option.
SQLGetTypeInfo()	Returns information about supported data types.
SQLParamData()	Returns the storage value assigned to a parameter for which data will be sent at execution time.
SQLPutData()	Sends part of a data value for a parameter.
SQLSetConnectOption()	Sets the transaction isolation level for a particular connection.
SQLSetStmtOption()	Sets a statement option.
SQLSpecialColumns()	Retrieves information about the optimal set of columns that uniquely identifies a row in a specified table and the columns that are automatically updated when any value in the row is updated by a transaction.
SQLSpecialColumns()	Retrieves statistics about a single table and the list of indexes associated with the table.
SQLTables()	Returns the list of table names stored in specific datasource.

Level 2

The functionality of the level 2 API can be summarized as follows:

- Meets the core and level 1 conformance levels

- Browses available connections and lists available datasources

- Sends arrays of parameter values and retrieves arrays of result column values

- Retrieves the number of parameters and describes individual parameters

- Uses a scrollable cursor

- Retrieves the native form of an SQL statement

- Retrieves catalog information

- Calls a translation DLL

Table 21.3 lists the level 2 API functions.

Table 21.3   The level 2 functions.

Function	Description
SQLBrowseConnect()	Returns successive levels of connection attributes and valid attribute values.
SQLColumnPrevileges()	Returns a list of columns and associated privileges for one or more tables.
SQLDataSources()	Returns a list of available datasources.
SQLDescribeParam()	Returns a list of available datasources.
SQLExtendedFetch()	Returns multiple result rows.
SQLForeignKeys()	Returns a list of column names that comprise foreign keys (if they exist).
SQLMoreResults()	Determines whether more result sets are available and, if so, initializes processing for the next result set.
SQLNativeSql()	Returns the text of an SQL statement as translated by your driver.
SQLNumParams()	Returns the number of parameters in a statement.
SQLPrimaryKeys()	Returns the list of column names that comprise the primary key.
SQLProcedureColumns()	Returns the list of input and output parameters as well as the columns that make up the result set for the specified procedures.
SQLSetPos()	Positions a cursor within a fetched block of data.
SQLSetScrollOptions()	Sets options that control cursor behavior.
SQLTablePrivileges()	Returns a list of tables and the privileges associated with each table.

Level 3

ODBC 3.0 has several new features. One of the major new features in level 3 is the use of descriptors. A *descriptor* is a data structure that holds information about either columns in a result set or dynamic parameters in an SQL statement. Descriptors streamline many application operations, providing a direct and uniform way to access column or parameter data. Many of the enhancements achieved in ODBC 3.0 are a result of using descriptors.

The connection and statement options in ODBC 2.0 have become attributes in ODBC 3.0, and the functions used to retrieve and set them have been changed. The concept of an *environment attribute* is introduced, and functions are provided to get and set these attributes. Note that the term *attribute* is a renaming of the term *option* that was used in ODBC 2.x.

New extensible functions are introduced to manipulate descriptor and diagnostic areas. New functions are introduced to get and set environment, connection, and statement attributes. Although these functions are very similar to those for setting connection and statement options in ODBC 2.x, they contain additional arguments to specify the buffer length and output string length.

Extensions For ODBC 2.x Features

ODBC 2.x had features that do not appear in the current CLI documents. To fit these features into ODBC 3.0, additional descriptor and diagnostics fields have been introduced. All connection and statement options in ODBC 2.x remain as connection and statement attributes in ODBC 3.0. The following is a list of ODBC 2.x features not yet in the standards that have been fit into the descriptor model:

- Multirow fetches

- Arrays of parameters

- Row-wise binding

- Positioned operations using **SQLSetPos**

- Fixed-length bookmarks

- ODBC cursor types—static, keyset driven, and dynamic

- Output and input/output parameters

- Support for stored procedures

SQL Grammar Conformance

The SQL conformance level of a driver determines which SQL grammar may be used in ODBC statements. It also specifies what data types are available. Here are the conformance levels defined for ODBC:

- Minimum SQL grammar

- Core SQL grammar

- Extended SQL grammar

Minimum Grammar

The minimum grammar contains most of the features that you need. You can create and drop tables and select, insert, update, and delete rows. There are some variations of the character field type. That type may correspond most closely with the standard data types **CHAR, VARCHAR,** or **LONG VARCHAR.**

The minimum grammar might be enough for many developers. The character data type alone, however, is not sufficient for most situations. You won't find many drivers of this SQL conformance.

Core Grammar

The core grammar adds a number of useful features for altering tables and creating and dropping indexes and views. It's possible to grant and revoke permission to create, read, and write rows to particular users. Several new data types are added. Integer types are introduced for both short and long integers. Floating-point types of both single and double precision are added, as well.

Extended Grammar

The extended grammar introduces some very sophisticated new features. The concept of cursor control is added. The extended grammar also adds the date field type, in addition to several other field types. DML now supports outer joins, and complex expressions are valid. Some of the extended grammar data types are **LONG VARCHAR, INT, TINYINT, BIGINT, BINARY, VARBINARY, LONG VARBINARY, DATE, TIME,** and **TIMESTAMP.**

ODBC Initialization Files

When you install and access ODBC, you need to know about two main initialization files:

- **ODBCINST.INI.** A list of ODBC drivers installed

- **ODBC.INI.** A list of defined datasources and associated drivers

In the 16-bit environment, these are actual files in your Windows directory. In Win32, they are subkeys of the Registry. When you access these keys in the Registry, the structure and content of the information is the same as what is contained in the physical files. For the examples in this chapter, I'll use Win32 and the Registry.

ODBCINST.INI

The OBCINST.INI file is mainly used by the ODBC installation program to install different ODBC drivers. When you install an ODBC-compliant driver supplied by Sybase or any other vendor, the ODBCINST.INI file or Registry subkey is automatically updated with a description of the driver. This description includes the following elements:

- The DBMS or datasource associated with your driver

- The drive and directory of the driver and setup DLLs

- Other information on driver-specific connection parameters

The Registry hierarchy looks like this: HKEY_LOCAL_MACHINE\Software\ ODBC\ODBCINST.INI

You should have two keys under ODBCINST.INI. The first is ODBC Drivers, which lists the installed drivers:

```
ODBC Drivers
                Name                     Data
                Sybase SQL Anywhere 5.0  Installed
```

The second is a separate key under ODBCINST.INI for each installed driver. The ODBCINST.INI architecture is illustrated in Figure 21.4.

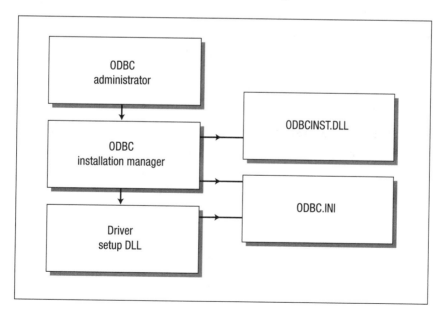

Figure 21.4
The ODBCINST.INI architecture.

```
Sybase SQL Anywhere 5.0
              Name            Data
              Driver          "WOD50T.DLL"
              Setup           "WOD50T.DLL"
```

ODBC.INI

The ODBC.INI file is the main ODBC initialization file. The ODBC driver manager uses this file to get the detail information about a datasource name to connect to the DBMS. This file includes all the ODBC DBMSs and their corresponding drivers, ODBC driver and datasource name mappings, and other information about the datasource.

When you define a datasource for a particular ODBC driver, the driver writes the values you specify in the ODBC Setup dialog box to the ODBC.INI file or Registry subkey. The [**ODBC Data Sources**] section of ODBC.INI lists the name of each defined datasource and its associated DBMS. ODBC.INI also includes a separate section for each datasource. This section contains the values specified for that datasource in the ODBC Setup dialog box. The values may vary for each datasource, but they generally include the following:

- Name

- Optional description

- DBMS-specific connection parameters

Once again, in the 16-bit environment, ODBC.INI is an actual file. In the 32-bit environment, the Registry hierarchy looks like this: HKEY_CURRENT_USER\ Software\ODBC\ODBC.INI\Powersoft Demo DB V6

Table 21.4 lists the values for this key. Figure 21.5 illustrates the ODBC.INI architecture.

Table 21.4 Values for ODBC.INI file's Registry key.

Name	Data
Autostop	"yes"
DatabaseFile	"c:\DB\PSDEMODB.DB"
Driver	"WOD50T.DLL"
PWD	"sql"
Start	"dbeng50"
UID	"dba"

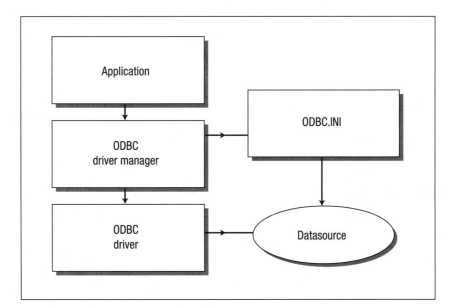

Figure 21.5
The ODBC.INI architecture.

If needed, you can get your 16-bit applications in a 32-bit environment to talk to 32-bit ODBC. Your 16-bit client talks to the 16-bit driver manager which is ODBC.DLL. As seen in Figure 21.6, the driver manager talks to the 16-bit generic thunking DLL (ODBC16GT.DLL) that, in turn, communicates with the 32-bit generic thunking DLL (ODBC32GT.DLL). This last DLL then talks to the 32-bit driver, which then communicates with the datasource. Here's an example of your INIs:

```
;ODBCINST.INI
[ODBC 32 bit Drivers]
Sybase SQL Anywhere 5.0 (32 bit)=Installed

[Sybase SQL Anywhere 5.0 (32 bit)]
Driver = ...<path>\WOD50T.DLL
Setup = ...<path>\WOD50T.DLL
32Bit = 1

;ODBC.INI
[Powersoft Demo DB V6]
Driver32 = ...<path>\WOD50T.DLL
```

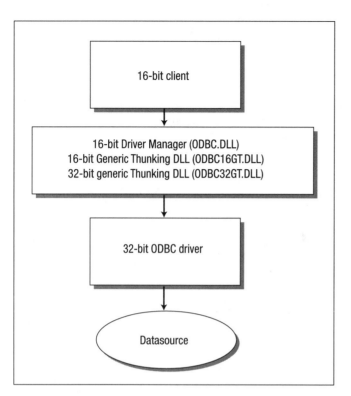

Figure 21.6
The thunking mechanisim.

PowerBuilder And ODBC

When you access an ODBC datasource from PowerBuilder, your connection goes through several layers before reaching your datasource, as shown is Figure 21.7. Note that it is PowerBuilder's ODBC file, PBODB60X.DLL, that talks to the ODBC driver manager, and so on.

PBODB60X.INI

PowerBuilder takes advantage of the extended capabilities of ODBC drivers by using PBODB60X.INI file entries in the datasource, DBMS driver, or DBMS section. If no section exists for a particular connection, PowerBuilder runs as an ODBC-compliant client, and any available extensions cannot be used.

Here's the search algorithm for the entries:

1. **IF** the section and entry are present for the current datasource

2. **THEN** use the entry value

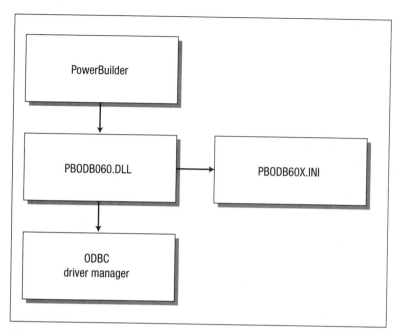

Figure 21.7

Illustration of how PowerBuilder communicates with ODBC.

3. **ELSE IF** the section corresponding to DBMS_name Driver_name exists

4. **THEN** use the entry value if it exists

5. **ELSE IF** the section corresponding to DBMS_name exists

6. **THEN** use the entry value if it exists

You shouldn't need to modify this INI file unless you need to use special data types or change the identifier case. In future releases of PowerBuilder, this file will probably become obsolete because you'll be able to set most of these parameters within the PowerBuilder development environment. Most of the parameters in this INI file can be set via **DBParm** parameters. Here's a small sample from the PBODB60X.INI.

```
[Sybase SQL Anywhere]
PBSyntax='WATCOM50_SYNTAX'
PBDateTime='STANDARD_DATETIME'
PBFunctions='WATCOM_FUNCTIONS'
PBSpecialDataTypes='WATCOM_SPECIALDATATYPES'
DelimitIdentifier='YES'
PBSpecialDataTypes='WATCOM_SPECIALDATATYPES'

[DB2/NT]
PBCatalogOwner='PBCATOWN'
PBSyntax='DB2CS_SYNTAX'
```

```
[WATCOM_SPECIALDATATYPES]
SpecialDataTypes='tinyint=DBI_TINYINT=-6'
;tinyint is native to the database, DBI_TINYINT is our DBI
;corresponding to the native, -6 is found in ODBC SDK

[WATCOM50_SYNTAX]
CreateTable='CREATE TABLE &TableOwner.&TableName
                   (::ColumnElement[, ::ColumnElement]...)'
ColumnElement='&ColumnName &DataType &NotNull ::Default'
Default='DEFAULT &default'
```

Isolation Levels

For those DBMSs that support the use of lock values and isolation levels, the Lock preference sets the isolation level to use when connecting to the database. In multiuser databases, transactions initiated by different users can overlap. If these transactions access common data in the database, they can overwrite each other or collide.

To prevent concurrent transactions from interfering with each other and compromising the integrity of your database, certain DBMSs allow you to set the isolation level when you connect to the database. Isolation levels are defined by your DBMS, and they specify the degree to which operations in one transaction are visible to operations in a concurrent transaction. Isolation levels determine how your DBMS isolates or locks data from other processes while it is being accessed.

PowerBuilder uses the Lock preference to allow you to set various database lock options. Each Lock value you can set corresponds to an isolation level defined by your DBMS. You must set the Lock value before you connect to the database in the PowerBuilder development environment or in your PowerBuilder application. The Lock value takes effect only when the database connection occurs. The following values can be set with ODBC:

- **RU.** Read Uncommitted

- **RC.** Read Committed

- **RR.** Repeatable Read

- **TS.** Serializable Transactions

- **TV.** Transaction Versioning

For example, to set the isolation level to Read Committed, use the following code:

```
SQLCA.Lock = "RC"
```

Cursor Support

You can specify various cursor scrolling options for cursors in an ODBC datasource. The location of a cursor indicates the current position in the result set produced by an SQL statement. Scrolling allows a cursor to move through the data in a result set one row at a time. Here are the different types of cursors you can use:

- **Forward.** The cursor only scrolls forward through the result set.

- **Static.** The data in the result set does not change.

- **KeySet.** The cursor is keyset driven. When a keyset-driven cursor is opened, the driver saves keys for the entire result set. As the cursor scrolls through the result set, the driver uses the keys in this keyset to retrieve the current values for each row.

- **Dynamic.** The driver saves and uses only the keys for the rows specified in the rowset.

The following code sets scrolling to Dynamic for cursors in an ODBC datasource:

```
//initialize variables and declare our cursor
int deptid
string deptname

DECLARE dept_cur CURSOR FOR
  SELECT "department"."dept_id",
         "department"."dept_name"
  FROM "department"  ;

//change the scroll options
SQLCA.Dbparm = CursorScroll = 'Dynamic'

//some examples of fetch directions in Dynamic scrolling
FETCH LAST dept_cur INTO :deptid, :deptnanme
MessageBox( "Last", String(deptid) + " " + deptname )

FETCH FIRST dept_cur INTO :deptid, :deptname;
MessageBox( "First", String(deptid) + " " + deptname )

FETCH NEXT dept_cur INTO :deptid, :deptname;
MessageBox( "Next", String(deptid) + " " + deptname )

FETCH PRIOR dept_cur INTO :deptid, :deptname;
MessageBox( "Prior", String(deptid) + " " + deptname )

//close our cursor
CLOSE dept_cur;
```

CursorLock

CursorLock, when used with the **CursorScroll** parameter, specifies locking options for cursors in your ODBC datasources. The values you can set for **CursorLock** control two aspects of cursor locking:

- **Concurrent access.** Ensures that multiple users can simultaneously access data that is accurate and current.

- **Collision detection.** Detects collisions that occur when multiple users update the same data at the same time.

Here are the various **CursorLock** values you can set:

- **Lock.** Uses the lowest level of locking sufficient to allow updates on table rows.

- **Opt.** Uses optimistic concurrency control. This means that table rows are not locked against updates by other users. To detect collisions, compare row versions or timestamps.

- **OptValue.** Uses optimistic concurrency control. This means that table rows are not locked against updates by other users. To detect collisions, compare selected values with their previous values.

- **ReadOnly.** Prohibits updates on table rows by any user.

The following code sets cursor scrolling to Dynamic and locking to OptValue:

```
SQLCA.DBParm = CursorScroll='Dynamic',CursorLock='OptValue'
```

Troubleshooting

If your application fails to connect to the database, the cause is probably one of the following:

- **Incorrect coding of the connection attributes of the transaction object.** This is most often the cause when your PowerBuilder development environment connects but your application fails to connect when you run it. When this happens, you need to carefully compare the settings in your transaction object with those coded in your database profile.

- **Incorrect ODBC configuration.** This can be either errors in completing the DBMS ODBC Configuration screen or errors in the ODBC installation. This is often seen either on initial configuration of an ODBC datasource or during deployment.

- **Incorrect DMBS client installation.** This is most often seen during deployment. You should only have one copy of any DMBS client file, and these files should all be of the same version.

Running a trace sometime provides you with more information on the type of problem you're having. You can enable a trace from your ODBC administrator, from your datasource via the **DBParm** parameter **ConnectOption**, from your database profile, or from PBODB60x.INI.

> **Note:** ODBC SDK provides ODBC Test and ODBC Spy—two great tools that you should definitely have.

Other Resources

Here's a list of some of the many other resources you can seek out for additional information or assistance:

- ODBC Help and ODBC SDK Help files.

- Microsoft Developer Network CD.

- The Microsoft Web site (www.microsoft.com).

- Microsoft KnowledgeBase.

- Sybase Electronic support and Infobases on the Web (www.sybase.com).

- Technical Information Library documents. These can be found in the Support section of the Sybase Web page.

Moving On

In this chapter, we covered ODBC. We talked about the architecture of ODBC, ODBC drivers, various conformance levels, and SQL grammar. We also talked about the ODBC initialization files, the Registry settings, and PowerBuilder's ODBC interface. As you can see, ODBC provides you with a single set of function calls that gives your applications transparent access to multiple datasources from multiple databases.

Now that we've covered database connectivity and ODBC, let's actually talk about an RDBMS or two. My favorite database of all time is Sybase SQL Anywhere. Why? Well, Sybase SQL Anywhere is a full-featured transaction-processing database that has been developed for personal computers. It has very small resource requirements and it delivers superior performance and full database functionality. In the next chapter, I'll discuss this great database with you.

Sybase SQL
Anywhere

22

Sybase SQL Anywhere is a full-featured transaction-processing database that was developed on personal computers for personal computers. Because it was developed specifically for the personal computer, it delivers superior performance and full database functionality while maintaining a small resource requirement.

Sybase SQL Anywhere has undergone two name changes since it was first developed in the late 1980s. The initial version was developed by Pace Systems and released under the name Pacebase. Shortly after its initial release, Pace Systems was acquired by Watcom International. All the employees of Pace joined Watcom at that time. The database was then released under the name Watcom SQL. Watcom SQL was bundled as part of the PowerBuilder development system from Powersoft. Watcom subsequently merged with Powersoft and then Sybase; the version 5.0 database was released as Sybase SQL Anywhere 5.0.

In this chapter, I'll cover SQL Anywhere—which is bundled with PowerBuilder—in detail. I'll also cover a few important points that you should know before starting to design and develop PowerBuilder applications utilizing SQL Anywhere.

System Requirements

Sybase SQL Anywhere supports all the major Intel x86 operating systems, including the following:

- DOS

- Windows 3.x

- Windows 95

- Windows NT

- OS/2

- NetWare

- QNX (a real-time Unix kernel)

In addition, versions of SQL Anywhere are available for the Macintosh, Sun Solaris, HP/UX, RS6000/AIX, and SGI platforms.

In general, a full SQL Anywhere install requires less than 15MB of disk space, and the version you receive with PowerBuilder requires considerably less. When running, the SQL Anywhere database uses approximately 1MB of RAM. In addition, an engine requests the cache memory specified on the command line.

Compliance To Standards

Generally, SQL Anywhere conforms to the ANSI SQL-89 standard. Some ANSI SQL-92 functionality is supported, most notably the syntax for persistent stored methods (PSM), which are commonly referred to as *stored procedures* or *triggers*.

SQL Anywhere also supports a significant subset of the Sybase SQL Server System 11 Transact SQL syntax. This subset is complete enough to allow you to develop a PowerBuilder application that can be connected to either an SQL Anywhere or SQL Server database transparently.

Where To Get Help

If you have questions about SQL Anywhere, there are many sources available. The more active of these are listed here:

- The technical support section of the Sybase Web site (www.Sybase.com) contains a wealth of information about SQL Anywhere. From this site, you can access the latest patches for SQL Anywhere and all of the current technical notes. You can also search all issues closed by the Technical Support department.

- The Sybase faxline system allows you to order any of the current technical notes for SQL Anywhere and have them faxed directly to you. These documents are also available from the Technical Information Library of the Sybase Web site.

- The SQL Anywhere newsgroups (found on forums.Sybase.com) are very active, moderated newsgroups where you can post your questions and have them answered by other users.

- The Workplace Database InfoBase CD contains all the closed technical support issues as well as all the current technical notes in an easy-to-search format.

- The SQL Anywhere technical support hotline is available between 8:00 A.M. and 8:00 P.M. EST Monday through Friday to answer your questions.

Architecture

Figure 22.1 presents a system block diagram that illustrates all the major components of SQL Anywhere.

Database And Transaction Log Files

Starting at the bottom, we have the database (.DB) and transaction log (.LOG) files. These files, like all files used by SQL Anywhere, are operating system files that are marked as read-only to prevent accidental alteration or deletion. When SQL Anywhere is not running, these files can be copied using the operating system file-handling utilities.

The database file is divided into pages and contains the system and user tables as well as data and indexes for the database.

The database file is expanded, as required, to add additional space to the database. This expansion is always done 32 pages at a time to keep the amount of time spent allocating and initializing file space to a minimum.

The database file is restricted to the largest file size supported by the operating system. For FAT file systems, this is 2GB. For NTFS, the limit set by NT 4.0 is 4TB (terabytes).

A user database can be extended to include additional files, which are referred to as DBSpaces. SQL Anywhere supports a maximum of 11 DBSpaces, which, when combined with the main database file, give a largest database size of 24GB on a FAT file system and 48TB on NTFS. Tables and indexes cannot span DBSpaces. This makes the largest table size slightly less than 2GB on FAT file systems and 4TB on NTFS.

The SQL Anywhere transaction log file contains a record of all operations executed against the database. The name and location of the log file is recorded in the main database file. When SQL Anywhere is started, it creates a transaction log if no log currently exists. The transaction log is expanded, like the database files, 32 pages at a time.

The transaction log is referred to as a *forward log* because all operations are written to the log whether they are committed or rolled back. This means that if you keep a copy of every log file used since the database was created, you would be able to re-create your database by translating the log file into SQL and executing it against a newly created database.

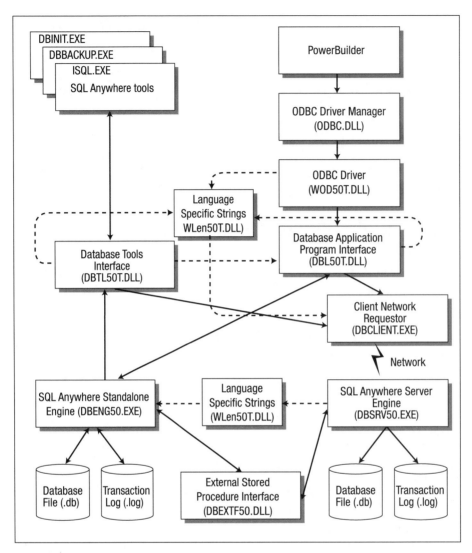

Figure 22.1

A SQL Anywhere System block diagram.

We'll examine the log file in more detail when we discuss backup and recovery in the section titled "Recovery From Failure" later in this chapter.

The Database Engine

The database engine provides all services required for executing SQL statements for multiple requestors. These requestors may be either local, on the same machine as the database engine, or remote, across the network.

The term *database engine* is used to refer interchangeably to the Standalone and Server versions of SQL Anywhere. The only difference between the Standalone and Server versions is that the Server version has a network requestor layer that allows DBClient processes to connect. The core database functions such as SQL processing, file handling, cache management, and so on, are identical between the two versions.

The database engine makes use of two supporting files. The *language module* provides the text strings displayed by SQL Anywhere in specific languages. By default, this is in English. The languages available include French, German, Spanish, and Dutch. If a language other than English is to be used, it can be specified.

The second supporting file is the *external function interface file*. This file provides the functions necessary for supporting external function calls from the database engine. The external function interface file allows you to program your own functions, which can then be called as part of an SQL statement or as a stored procedure. The database engine is the only process that accesses the database files. The database engine makes use of several other resources while executing. The most significant of these are cache and the temporary file.

By default, the database engine allocates 2MB of memory for the cache. This size can be altered with a command-line switch. The cache is divided into pages and is primarily used to hold database pages in an attempt to reduce physical disk I/O. Cache pages are flushed back to disk following a least recently used (LRU) algorithm.

The temporary file is used to hold pages that are not permanently part of the database but need to be swapped from cache. These pages are usually temporary table pages. The temporary file can normally be found in the directory pointed to by the TEMP or TMP environment variables. If you encounter "disk full" errors, it's often because the engine has exhausted the temporary file space.

The DBClient Process
DBClient provides network connectivity services for the Database API. The DBClient process provides all the functionality necessary to connect the Database API to one or more database servers.

DBClient accesses network services through the interfaces provided by the operating system. In Windows, this is the Windows Socket or Winsock API. The protocols supported are TCP/IP, IPX, and NetBIOS. DBClient also makes use of the language module.

The Database API
The main database API, DBLib, provides the only interface between the SQL programs accessing the database and the database engine. All other interfaces access the database through this interface.

DBLib is the component that understands how to connect to database engines, and it will connect to either a local engine or network server based on the connection parameters provided to it. DBLib is normally accessed via Embedded SQL (ESQL) programs written in C. The SQL Anywhere ISQL utility is an example of a program that accesses DBLib directly. DBLib also makes use of the language module.

The Database Tools API

The Database Tools API (DBTools) provides access to all the functionality of the SQL Anywhere tools. All database tools use this API. Examples of tools include the backup utility, the log file manager, the database creation utility, and the database unload utility.

User programs can access DBTools by making use of dbtools.h and linking to the appropriate library. DBTools also makes use of the language module.

The ODBC Driver

The SQL Anywhere ODBC is the primary API used by application programs to access the database. ODBC provides a standard API that allows the careful programmer transparent access to multiple databases.

> **Note:** The SQL Anywhere ODBC driver is version 2 and level 2 compliant. This means it implements all functionality required by ODBC.

The SQL Anywhere ODBC driver is very efficient. The API defined by ODBC and the SQL Anywhere DBLib are very similar in functionality; therefore, the ODBC driver does not need to implement much additional code. The ODBC driver also makes use of the language module.

Connecting To SQL Anywhere

SQL Anywhere provides transparent client/server architecture. You don't need to be concerned about whether deployment will be against a Standalone or Server version of SQL Anywhere. This is possible because all programs eventually access SQL Anywhere through the Database API (DBLib). DBLib is the only module that needs to know if it is connecting to a server or a standalone engine.

A connection is the *channel* through which all database requests are funneled. Each connection must log in to a database and acts independently of any other connection. An application can have a number of connections active at once, to either the same database or different ones.

Connection parameters are used to define where DBLib connects. These parameters are specified on the command line for tools and in the connection string for ODBC and ESQL applications. The SQL Anywhere documentation discusses these connection parameters in detail. Table 22.1 lists the most common ones.

As implied by Table 22.1, every SQL Anywhere engine and every database has a name. These names are used to resolve connections. By default, a database name is the same as the file name of the database with no path or extension. The default engine name is the same as the name of the first database started on that engine. For example, consider the following command line:

```
DBENG50.EXE "c:\pwrs\pb6\demodb\psdemodb.db"
```

This command line syntax starts the standalone engine running the sample database that comes with PowerBuilder. The database name is not specified, so the engine has defaulted to the file name, which is psdemodb. Likewise, the engine name is not specified, so the engine will default to the first database name, which is also psdemodb. You can override the default names by using the -n switch on the engine command line, as follows:

```
DBENG50.EXE -n myserver "c:\pwrs\pb6\demodb\psdemodb.db" -n demodb
```

Again, the command line starts the standalone engine, but this time both the engine and database names are explicitly specified. The database engine name is myserver and the database name is demodb.

The remainder of this section examines connecting from ODBC and from the SQL Anywhere tools. This is followed by a discussion about exactly how SQL Anywhere uses these parameters to connect.

Table 22.1   DBLib Connection Parameters.

Keyword	Description
DatabaseFile	The file name of the database to which you want to connect
DatabaseName	The name of the database to which you want to connect
EngineName	The name of a running database engine or server to which you want to connect
Password	Your database password
Start	A command-line parameter to start a database engine
UserID	The user ID with which you log on to the database

Connecting From ODBC

When you connect PowerBuilder to SQL Anywhere, you connect through ODBC. The PowerBuilder database profile, or the *transaction object*, defines SQL Anywhere as type ODBC and specifies a **ConnectString** in the **DBParm**. As a minimum, this connect string must provide a datasource name (DSN). This DSN corresponds to the datasource name already specified through the ODBC Administrator.

The ODBC Administrator can be launched directly from PowerBuilder. It presents a screen that allows you to edit existing datasources or add new ones. If the datasource being added or edited is for SQL Anywhere, the screen shown in Figure 22.2 is presented.

The SQL Anywhere ODBC Configuration screen allows you to specify every connection parameter. Table 22.2 lists the fields you will normally use.

Every value specified on this configuration screen can also be specified and overridden by including it as part of the PowerBuilder connect string following the DSN. This method is commonly used for providing the user ID and password.

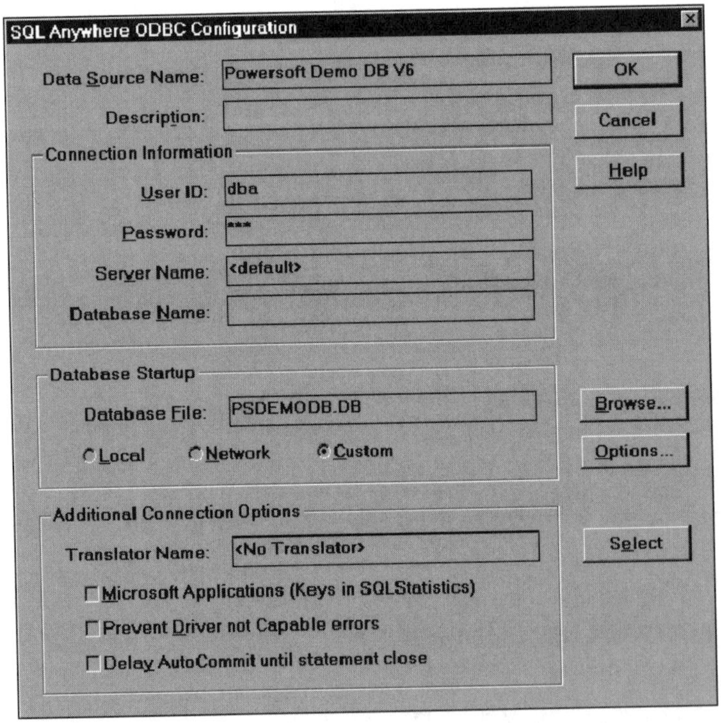

Figure 22.2
Configuring ODBC.

Table 22.2 List of connection parameters used when configuring ODBC.

Field	Description
Datasource Name	The name of the datasource. This is the same name that is specified in the PowerBuilder **ConnectString** as the **DSN=**.
Description	A longer description of the data source.
User ID	(Optional) The username to be used when connecting.
Password	(Optional) The password for the supplied user ID. Because the password supplied is stored in ODBC.INI, setting the password here may be a security risk.
Server Name	The name of an SQL Anywhere database engine or server. If this is not specified, the default engine is used. This field corresponds to the **EngineName** connection parameter.
Database Name	If specified, this field corresponds to the name of a database already running on an SQL Anywhere database engine or SQL Anywhere network server. This field corresponds to the **DatabaseName** connection parameter.
Database File	If specified, this field contains the name of a database file—for example, C:\sqlany50\sademo.db. You can use the Browse button to locate a database file name to place in this field. This field corresponds to the **DatabaseFile** connection parameter.
Local, Network, Custom	The command used to run the database software when the named database engine or server is not already executing. You can select Local or Network, as appropriate, if the default settings are satisfactory. Otherwise, select Custom and enter the command, including any command-line parameters, by pressing the Options button.
Microsoft Applications (Keys In SQLStatistics)	Not required for PowerBuilder.
Prevent Driver Not Capable Errors	Not required for PowerBuilder.
Delay AutoCommit Until Statement Close	Not required for PowerBuilder.

Connecting From SQL Anywhere Tools

All SQL Anywhere tools accept connection parameters following the -c command-line switch. For example, to connect ISQL to a database engine named myserver running a database named demodb, you would use the following command line:

```
ISQL -c "EngineName=myserver;DatabaseName=demodb;UserID=DBA;Password=SQL"
```

Connection Parameter Cross-Reference

Connection parameters can be specified using either their full name or short name. Table 22.3 lists the long names and then the short names:

How SQL Anywhere Resolves Connections

As indicated earlier, all SQL Anywhere connection parameters, with the exception of **UserID** and **Password**, are optional. SQL Anywhere will always attempt to find and connect to some database. It's important to understand how SQL Anywhere resolves connections when you're diagnosing connection problems or attempting to connect in an environment with many databases running.

SQL Anywhere uses the following steps to connect. These steps are identical whether from ODBC or from an ESQL application:

- **Step 1—find a database engine (local or server).** The first step is to locate a database engine to connect to. This is usually determined by the value specified by the **EngineName** parameter, as follows:

  - If **EngineName** is specified, look for a local database engine with that name. If one is found, connect to it. If no local engine is found, then look for an SQL Anywhere client (DBClient). If it is found, then look on the network for a server with the specified name. If one is found, connect to it.

Table 22.3 The long name and short name of connection parameters.

Long Name	Short Name
DatabaseFile	DBF
DatabaseName	DBN
DatabaseSwitches	DBS
DatasourceName	DSN
EngineName	ENG
Password	PWD
Start	Start
UserID	UID

- If **EngineName** is not specified, connect to the default local engine. (If only one engine is running, it's the default—otherwise, the default choice is operating system specific.)

- If no matching local database engine is found and the SQL Anywhere client is not running, the application starts a database engine or an SQL Anywhere client using the Start parameter.

- If no **Start** parameter is specified but **DatabaseFile** is specified, the application attempts to start a database engine on the named file using a default Start parameter.

If no engine has been found by this point, the attempt to connect fails.

- **Step 2—connect to a database.** Once the engine has been located, the next step is to connect (or log in) to a specific database. The database is specified by the **DatabaseName** or **DatabaseFile** parameter and the connection authority is specified by the **UserID** and **Password** parameters. Here's what happens next:

  - If neither a **DatabaseName** nor a **DatabaseFile** parameter is given, an attempt is made to connect to the default database on the engine using the specified **UserID** and **Password** parameters. The default database is the first database started on the engine.

  - If the database named by the **DatabaseName** parameter is running, an attempt is made to connect to the database using the specified **UserID** and **Password** parameters.

  - If the **DatabaseName** parameter is not specified but the **DatabaseFile** parameter is, an attempt is made to connect to a database whose name is the root of **DatabaseFile**. The root is defined as the file name without any path or extension.

  - If no running database is found but a database specified by the root of the **DatabaseFile** parameter is running, an attempt is made to connect to the database using the specified **UserID** and **Password** parameters.

  - If the database corresponding to the **DatabaseFile** parameter is not running, a request is sent to the engine or network server to start a database using the **DatabaseFile**, **DatabaseName**, and **DatabaseSwitches** parameters. (The **AutoStop** parameter determines if the database automatically stops when the last connection to the database is disconnected.) An attempt is made to connect to the database using the specified **UserID** and **Password** parameters.

If no connection is made, the attempt fails at this point.

Troubleshooting Connections

If your PowerBuilder application fails to connect to the database, it could be due to one of the following causes:

- **Incorrect coding of the connection attributes of the transaction object.** This is most often the cause when your PowerBuilder development environment connects but your application fails to connect when you run it. When this happens, you need to carefully compare the settings in your transaction object with those coded in your database profile.

- **Incorrect ODBC configuration.** This can be either errors in completing the SQL Anywhere ODBC Configuration screen or errors in the ODBC installation. This is often seen either on initial configuration of an ODBC datasource or during deployment. First, carefully review the settings in the ODBC configuration, paying particular attention to the **EngineName**, **DatabaseName**, **DatabaseFile**, and **Start** parameters. If you believe all these values are correct, use ISQL and substitute the values from the ODBC Configuration screen into the -c argument on the command line. If ISQL connects successfully, then verify that the SQL Anywhere directory is on the path and that there's one copy of the ODBC deployment DLLs on the system. These DLLs are listed in the PowerBuilder documentation.

- **Incorrect network configuration.** This is often seen during deployment when some systems or the target systems will not connect, but the development environment will. Diagnosing network connection problems is difficult because so many components are involved. Both DBClient.EXE and Server support the -Z switch, which outputs detailed network diagnostics. Using this switch often isolates the specific problem. In addition, the -x switch allows you to limit communications to specific protocols. A number of communications parameters associated with the -x switch allow you to deal with specific situations. Consult your SQL Anywhere Help file for more information because the switches available vary with each release.

- **Incorrect database installation.** This is most often seen during deployment, or during a system upgrade or recovery. As indicated in the section titled "Architecture" later in this chapter, the SQL Anywhere database records the file name of the transaction log file and any DBSpaces in the main database file. It's not unusual for these file names to contain explicit path information. If the specified path does not exist, the database will fail to start. The DBINFO utility can be used to display the transaction log location, and the SYS.SYSFILE table will display the location of any DBSpaces. The DBLOG utility allows you to modify the transaction log location. The **ALTER DBSPACE** SQL statement does the same for DBSpaces.

- **Incorrect SQL Anywhere installation.** This is most often seen during deployment or on systems that already have SQL Anywhere installed on them. You should only have one copy of any SQL Anywhere file on the system. All these files should be from the same version.

Advanced Configurations

The most basic SQL Anywhere configuration is a local engine running a single database. This is the configuration used by the PowerBuilder sample database. A single server running a single database is an equivalent configuration, although the introduction of DBClient and a network increases the complexity somewhat. These are both "simple" configurations, because the default connection logic will always connect you to the correct database.

There are three common advanced configurations—multiple databases on the same engine, multiple servers on the same network, and databases that are dynamically started.

Multidatabase Environments

It's common for an installation to require more than one SQL Anywhere database to be running against the same engine. Starting more than one database is accomplished by specifying the additional database file names and any associated switches on the engine command line. For example, consider the following command:

```
DBENG50 -n myserver c:\pwrs\pb6\demodb\psdemodb.db -n demodb
c:\sqlany50\sademo.db -n sademo
```

This command starts the local engine named myserver with two database files psdemodb.db and sademo.db, which are named demodb and sademo, respectively. To connect to psdemodb.db, you specify **EngineName=myserver** and **DatabaseName=demodb**. Similarly, to connect to sademo.db, you specify **EngineName=myserver** and **DatabaseName=sademo**.

> **Note:** Under most circumstances, it's preferable to run a single engine with multiple databases as opposed to multiple engines on the same computer, each with one database, because resources such as CPU, memory, and disk space are shared according to the usage of the database.

Multiserver Environments

In some environments, it's common to have multiple SQL Anywhere servers, each on different computers. Each server will have a unique name.

As you may recall from "Connecting To SQL Anywhere" earlier in this chapter, DBClient is the client network requestor and is capable of serving connections to multiple database servers. This means that only one DBClient process is required on an SQL Anywhere client computer.

Connection to a specific server is accomplished by specifying both the **EngineName** and **DatabaseName** parameters for the server/database combination required.

For example, if you have two different servers on two different computers, started with the command lines

```
//Server #1
DBSRV50 -n onesrv c:\sqlany50\sademo.db -n sademo

//Server #2
DBSRV50 -n twosrv c:\ pwrs\pb6\demodb\psdemodb.db -n demodb
```

then the ISQL command line to connect to the database running on Server #1 would be this:

```
ISQL -c "ENG=onesrv;DBN=sademo;UID=DBA;PWD=SQL;START=DBCLIENT.EXE"
```

Similarly, here's the ISQL command line to connect to the database running on Server #2:

```
ISQL -c "ENG=twosrv;DBN=demodb;UID=DBA;PWD=SQL;START=DBCLIENT.EXE"
```

Both of these commands could be executed on the same computer, starting two different ISQL sessions. The second invocation of ISQL will not start a separate DBClient.exe; instead it will use the one that is currently running.

Dynamically Starting Databases

SQL Anywhere has the ability to start and stop databases dynamically. If you review the section "How SQL Anywhere Resolved Connections" earlier in the chapter, you'll notice that if you provide **DatabaseFile** and **DatabaseName** parameters and the database name is not found running, the engine will attempt to start the database identified by **DatabaseFile**. This functionality is often used to allow infrequently accessed databases to be run when required without incurring the overhead of keeping them online at all times.

A database can be automatically shut down, or stopped, after the last user has disconnected from it if the **AutoStop=Yes** parameter is specified when the database is started.

It's important to remember that the **DatabaseFile** parameter specifies the path and file name of the database file that needs to be started. This parameter is passed to the operating system **FileOpen**()function, and therefore, must make sense to the operating system on which the engine is running. For example, suppose you have a server already running that was started with this command line:

```
DBSRV50 -n mysrv c:\<powersoft dir>\psdemodb.db -n demodb
```

Now, suppose you want to use ISQL to connect to the sample database that came with SQL Anywhere (sademo.db) and have the database shut down when you're done using it. (SQL Anywhere was installed onto the C: drive in the default directories.) The ISQL command line would be this:

```
ISQL -c "ENG=mysrv; DBF=c:\sqlany50\sademo.db; START=dbclient; UID=DBA;
PWD=SQL; AutoStop=Yes"
```

SQL Dialects

SQL Anywhere's default SQL dialect is Watcom SQL. Watcom SQL is based on the ANSI SQL standards. In addition, SQL Anywhere supports a large percentage of the Sybase SQL Server SQL dialect, which is called *Transact SQL*. Transact SQL is also highly compatible with Microsoft's SQL Server, because the initial release of the Microsoft database was a port to Windows NT of the Sybase code.

This compatibility allows you to develop a PowerBuilder application that will run unchanged on Sybase SQL Server 11, Microsoft SQL Server 6.x, and SQL Anywhere.

Mixing these dialects can also cause unexpected behavior, including runtime errors. This problem is especially common in stored procedures and triggers.

Object Ownership And Database Security

SQL Anywhere's primary security is provided through user IDs and permissions. Each connection to the database must provide a user ID and password that has already been defined in the database. Each user ID is also granted permissions that define what activities the user ID can perform on the database.

Each object in the database is owned by a user ID. When you create a table it is automatically owned by the user ID you're connected on. Unless you own the object, you must include the owner name in any reference. For example, suppose you're connected on the user ID DBA and execute the following statement:

```
CREATE TABLE seeMe (col1 int);
```

This statement has created a table named seeMe which is owned by DBA. If you had a second user ID defined in the database, it would have to refer to the table as DBA.seeMe.

Only the owner of a database object and the DBA have permission to access it. If any other user ID requires access, it must have permission. Table objects have the following permissions:

- **ALTER.** Permission to alter the structure of a table or create a trigger on a table.

- **DELETE.** Permission to delete rows from a table or view.

- **INSERT.** Permission to insert rows into a table or view.

- **REFERENCES.** Permission to create indexes on a table and to create foreign keys that reference a table.

- **SELECT.** Permission to look at information in a table or view.

- **UPDATE.** Permission to update rows in a table or view. (This may be granted on a set of columns in a table only.)

- **ALL.** All the previously mentioned permissions.

There's also the **EXECUTE** permission for stored procedures, which gives permission to call, or execute, the procedure.

It is also possible to grant a user ID permission to grant, or pass along, the permission to other users. This is done with the **WITH GRANT** clause, which is fully described in the SQL Anywhere Help files.

Three special permissions exist—**DBA**, **REMOTE DBA**, and **RESOURCE**. These permissions must be explicitly granted to a user ID and cannot be inherited.

The **DBA** permission has complete, unrestricted access to the database. This permission should not be given out lightly. By default, the only user ID with **DBA** permission is DBA. Throughout the remainder of this section, we'll assume that the user ID DBA has **DBA** permission, and I'll use DBA as a short form for any user ID with **DBA** permission.

Only the DBA can create user IDs or grant **DBA** permission to another user ID.

REMOTE DBA is only used by the SQL Remote replication technology and gives a user ID **DBA** permission only when the User ID is being used by SQL Remote.

The **RESOURCE** permission allows a user ID to create database objects, such as tables, views, stored procedures, and triggers. Resource authority may be granted only by the DBA to other users.

In most installations, groups are used to help manage permissions. A group is a special user ID that allows other user IDs to become members of the group. Most of a group's permissions are inherited by the members.

A user ID can belong to zero or more groups. Groups can also belong to zero or more groups.

Members of a group inherit the permissions explicitly granted to the group. Permission implicitly given to a group, such as access to all objects owned by the group, is *not* inherited.

If a user ID belongs to more than one group that grants different permission on the same database object, the most permissive, or highest level, permission is granted.

Members of a group do not need to specify the owner ID for objects owned by the group.

Stored procedures and triggers have special rules for permissions. A stored procedure always executes with the permission of the creator. This allows you to encapsulate functions that require elevated permissions, such as creating a user ID in a stored procedure owned by DBA, and to call that procedure from a user ID with significantly fewer permissions.

Triggers always execute with the permissions of the creator of the table on which they are declared.

User IDs, groups, and permissions are managed with the **GRANT** statement. The SQL Anywhere Help files contain a full description of the syntax; also, SQL Central provides an easy-to-use graphical interface.

Transactions And Locking

Every operation performed against SQL Anywhere is part of a transaction. A *transaction* is defined as a logical unit of work that either succeeds or fails entirely.

Transactions start with one of the following events:

- The first statement following a connection to a database

- The first statement following the end of a transaction

Transactions complete with one of the following events:

- A **COMMIT** statement makes the changes to the database permanent.

- A **ROLLBACK** statement undoes all the changes made by the transaction.

- A statement with the side effect of an automatic commit is issued. (Database definition commands, such as **ALTER**, **CREATE**, **COMMENT**, or **DROP** all have the side effect of an automatic commit.)

- A disconnection from a database occurs (implicit rollback).

> **Note:** SQL Anywhere's transaction processing ensures that each transaction is processed in its entirety or not at all.

Transaction processing is fundamental in ensuring that a database contains correct information. It addresses two distinct, yet related problems: data recovery and database consistency in the face of concurrent usage. When several users are connected to the database at once, they are said to be *concurrent*. As soon as a database has concurrent users, it's possible to introduce inconsistency into the application's view of the data.

Three types of inconsistencies can occur during the execution of concurrent transactions:

- **Dirty read.** Transaction A modifies a row; transaction B then reads that row before transaction A performs a **COMMIT**. If transaction A then performs a **ROLLBACK**, transaction B will have read a row that was never committed.

- **Nonrepeatable read.** Transaction A reads a row; transaction B then modifies or deletes the row and performs a **COMMIT**. If transaction A then attempts to read the same row again, the row will have been changed or deleted.

- **Phantom row.** Transaction A reads a set of rows that satisfy some condition. Next, transaction B executes an **INSERT** or **UPDATE** that generates one or more rows that satisfy the condition used by transaction A and then performs a **COMMIT**. Transaction A then repeats the initial read and obtains a different set of rows.

SQL Anywhere uses row-level locking to prevent inconsistencies.

The SQL Anywhere locking scheme restricts access to the information that a particular transaction is working with to ensure that other transactions do not see information that might not be committed to the database and do not alter information on which the transaction is relying.

When a transaction is reading or writing a row in a database table, the database engine automatically locks the individual row to prevent other transactions from interfering with the data or from obtaining unreliable data. The transaction that has access to the row is said to *hold the lock*. Depending on the type of lock, other transactions may have limited access to the locked row, or none at all.

All locks for a transaction are held until the transaction is complete (**COMMIT** or **ROLLBACK**), with the single exception when a transaction becomes blocked by another transaction. There are three distinct types of locks:

- **Read lock.** A read lock can be set when a transaction reads a row. A read lock is a nonexclusive lock; therefore, several transactions can acquire one on the same row. However, once a row has been read locked, no other transaction may obtain a write lock on it.

- **Write lock.** Whenever a transaction inserts, updates, or deletes a row, a write lock is set. A write lock is an exclusive lock; therefore, no other transaction can obtain a lock on the same row when a write lock is set.

- **Phantom lock.** A phantom lock is a read lock that prevents phantom rows. Phantom locks for lookups using indexes require a read lock on each row that is read, and one extra read lock to prevent insertions into the index at the end of the result set. Phantom rows for lookups that do not use indexes require a read lock on all rows in a table to prevent insertions from altering the result set; therefore, they can have a bad effect on concurrency.

The degree to which the operations in one transaction are visible to the operations in a concurrent transaction is defined by the *isolation level.* SQL Anywhere has four different isolation levels that prevent some or all inconsistent behavior. The isolation level is a database option that can be different for each connection. Database options are changed by using the **SET** command; the default setting is isolation level 0.

All isolation levels guarantee that each transaction will execute completely or not at all and that no updates will be lost. SQL Anywhere, therefore, ensures recoverability at all times, regardless of the isolation level.

The isolation levels are different with respect to dirty reads, nonrepeatable reads, and phantom rows. The following illustrates these relationships (an X means that the behavior is prevented, and a space means that the behavior may occur):

Isolation Level	0	1	2	3
Dirty reads		X	X	X
Nonrepeatable reads			X	X
Phantom rows				X

If your application is using cursors to perform retrievals and updates, an additional level of isolation called *cursor stability* is available. Cursor stability guarantees that any row that is the current position of a cursor will not be modified by another transaction until the cursor leaves the row. No row fetched through a cursor yields uncommitted data. SQL Anywhere automatically provides cursor stability at isolation levels 1, 2, and 3.

Write locks are employed at all isolation levels. This ensures that once data is modified by a transaction, no other transaction can modify it until the transaction is either committed or rolled back. As long as the transaction completes, no danger exists of its database update being interfered with by any other user.

Read locks are applied differently depending on the isolation level:

- At isolation level 0, no read locks are applied.

- At isolation level 1, a read lock is put on the current row of a cursor. The read lock is removed when the cursor is moved. This technique ensures cursor stability.

- At isolation level 2, a read lock is applied to each row as it is read and is maintained until the end of the transaction.

- At isolation level 3, a phantom lock is employed to prevent phantom rows. If your application looks up data in tables without using an index, concurrency can suffer considerably under isolation level 3.

When a locking conflict occurs, one transaction must wait for another transaction to complete. This means that a transaction becomes blocked on another transaction. If two transactions simultaneously have a read lock on a row, the behavior when one of them attempts to modify that row (acquire a write lock) depends on the database setting **BLOCKING**.

If **BLOCKING** is on (the default setting), the transaction that attempts to write is blocked until the other transaction releases its read lock. At that time, the write goes through. If **BLOCKING** is off, the transaction that attempts to write receives an error.

Blocking is more likely to occur with higher isolation levels because more locking and more checking is done. Higher isolation levels provide less concurrency.

Development Practices

This section outlines recommended practices when developing applications targeted for deployment against SQL Anywhere. These practices may also apply to systems targeted for other databases.

Identify A DBA

Having a single DBA (either a person or a group) responsible for maintaining the database gives you a better opportunity to understand and control the physical design of your database. It also ensures that at least one person is responsible for the routine administration, such as backups, of your databases. The DBA should also design the production procedures for your database. These will include, but may not be restricted to, backup practices, recovery procedures, log file management, and security design.

Use A Group To Own All Database Objects

You should create a group that will be the owner of all database objects used by the application. This group should have a name that reflects the nature of the owner application—for example, SALES. This group should allow logins and be used to create all objects for the project. The group should be explicitly given the **ALL** permission on all objects it creates so that members of the group can fully access the object.

Each developer should have his or her own user ID and be given membership in the group. This will allow the developer to access all objects in the group without explicitly specifying the owner ID. This enhances portability between database vendors because all databases do not support the concept of owners.

Give Every Table A Primary Key

SQL Anywhere uses the primary key to increase efficiency in several areas. These areas are:

- The transaction log records the primary key and the data that has changed. If no primary key exists, the entire row must be written to the transaction log.

- A primary key index is created. This can significantly speed up access.

Use The Built-In Referential Integrity Actions

SQL Anywhere supports a full set of built-in referential integrity actions. These actions are **Cascade**, **Restrict**, **Set Null**, and **Set Default**. They are declared when a foreign key is defined and you save the coding of triggers to perform the same action. Watch out for some database modeling tools that may create these triggers.

Test Your Stored Procedures And Triggers

SQL Anywhere does not compile stored procedures or triggers when they are created—it just parses them for syntactical correctness. This means that errors in references to other database objects will not be caught until the procedure or trigger is executed. Therefore, it is essential that you execute every stored procedure and trigger to catch runtime errors.

Stored procedures and triggers are compiled when they are first invoked, and the compiled form is stored in the database cache. This compiled form is lost when the database is shut down.

Consider Using User-Defined Data Types

SQL Anywhere allows you to create your own data types, or *domains*. Defining your own data type allows you to enforce consistency in your database. For example, you could create a data type for the autoincrement column used to uniquely identify rows in tables. This is created with the following statement:

```
CREATE DOMIAN uniqueId INT NOT NULL DEFAULT AUTOINCREMENT;
```

Consider Using User-Defined Functions

Similar to domains, user-defined functions allow you to define functions that are frequently used. For example, if you frequently concatenate names or addresses, a user-defined function that performs the operation may save you coding and will enforce consistency.

Use Integrity Constraints Instead Of Stored Procedures Or Triggers

Constraints, or *check conditions*, are declared when a table is created. They can be applied to a single column or to an entire table.

Check conditions applied to a single column allow you to ensure that the data in the column meets some defined criteria. For example, ensuring that an employee start date is not before the company was formed or that a telephone number is always in the form "(XXX)XXX-XXXX".

Check conditions applied to the entire table allow you to compare the values of several columns. For example, you can check that a loan's date_advanced value is greater or equal to the date_approved value.

Match Your Transaction Size To Your Isolation Level

Because SQL Anywhere maintains locks until a transaction completes, it's important that transactions size reflect the isolation level. Long read-only transactions at isolation level 0 introduce no concurrency issues because read locks are not taken at level 0. On the other hand, a long update transaction at isolation level 3 could conceivably reduce concurrency to almost zero.

Recovery From Failure

SQL Anywhere uses the following three logs to protect your data from system and media failure:

- **Checkpoint log.** This log holds a "before" copy of each database page. Before a page is updated (made dirty), a copy of the original is always made. The copied pages compose the checkpoint log. Dirty pages are not written immediately to the disk. For improved performance, they are cached in memory and written to disk when the cache is full or the server has no pending requests. A checkpoint is a point at which all dirty pages are written to disk. Once all dirty pages are written to disk, the checkpoint log is deleted.

- **Rollback log.** This log is kept for the purpose of canceling, or *rolling back*, changes. It's used for processing the **ROLLBACK** statement and for recovering from system failure. Each transaction has a separate rollback log. When a transaction is complete, its rollback log is deleted.

- **Transaction log.** All changes to the database are stored in the transaction log in the order in which they occur. Inserts, updates, deletes, commits, rollbacks, and database schema changes are all logged. The transaction log is called a *forward log file*.

Recovery from a system failure (which may occur, for example, during a power loss) is automatic. When you restart the SQL Anywhere database, the engine will detect that the database did not shut down cleanly. Upon detecting a "crashed" database, SQL Anywhere will perform the following tasks:

1. Apply the checkpoint log to the database file, restoring the database to the point of the last checkpoint. This is the last point where the database file was consistent because no dirty pages existed in cache.

2. Locate the last checkpoint marker in the transaction log and start applying transactions to the database from that point until the end of the transaction log. The last checkpoint marker in the transaction log corresponds to the state the database was in when the checkpoint log was applied. As transactions are applied from the transaction log, they are committed or rolled back as recorded in the transaction log.

3. Roll back any outstanding transactions. This is done because none of these transactions had completed before the system failed.

4. Checkpoint the database.

Protecting from media failure requires that you have a backup copy of your database. The two types of SQL Anywhere backups are *offline* and *online*. Within each of these types, there are full and incremental backups. A *full backup* backs up both the database and the transaction log. An *incremental backup* just backs up the transaction log so that it can be applied to a previously backed up database file.

Prior to performing a backup, you should perform a database validation using the DBValid database tool. DBValid checks all internal database pointers to ensure that they point to the correct type of object. In some cases, the database is too large or busy to perform a DBValid against the running database. In these cases, you should perform the DBValid operation against a *copy* of the backed up database. If you start the backed up copy of the database, you change the contents of the transaction log and make the database useless for recovery. This will become obvious during the discussion of recovery in the section titled "Recovery From Media Failure."

Offline backups are the simplest form of backup because they involve using only the operating system file management software. They require that you disconnect all users and stop the database engine. For a full backup, you copy the database file and any DBSpaces to a different device, usually a tape. For an incremental backup, you just copy the transaction log.

Online backups are performed while the database is still running and processing transactions. An online backup should be performed during a period of relatively low processing to ensure that it completes in a timely manner.

Online backups are made using the SQL Anywhere DBBackup utility. This utility forces a checkpoint of the database cache and then makes a copy of the database file transaction log in a directory that is specified on the command line. A full backup requires that the database file and transaction log be backed up. An incremental backup just requires that the transaction log be backed up.

Recovery From Media Failure

Recovery from media failure requires you to keep the transaction log on a separate device from the database file. The information in the two files is redundant.

The first step in recovering from a media failure is to clean up, reformat, or replace the device that failed. The steps to take in recovery depend on whether the media failure is on the device holding your database file or on the device holding your transaction log. When your transaction log is still usable, but you have lost your database file, the recovery process depends on whether you keep or delete the transaction log on incremental backup.

If you have not deleted or restarted the transaction log since the last full backup, the transaction log contains everything since the last backup. Recovery involves four steps:

1. Make a backup of the transaction log immediately. The database file is gone and the only record of the changes is in the transaction log.

2. Restore the most recent full backup (the database file).

3. Use the database engine with the apply transaction log switch (-a) to apply the transaction log and bring the database up to date.

4. Start the database in the normal way. The database engine will come up normally and any new activity will be appended to the current transaction log.

If you have archived and deleted the transaction log since the last full backup, each transaction log since the full backup needs to be applied in sequence to bring the database up to date. Here are the required steps:

1. Make a backup of all transaction logs immediately. The database file is gone and the only record of the changes is in the transaction logs.

2. Restore the most recent full backup (the database file).

3. Starting with the first transaction log after the full backup, apply each archived transaction log by starting the database engine with the apply transaction log switch (-**a**). For example, the last full backup was on Sunday and the data-base file is lost during the day on Thursday. SQL Anywhere does not allow you to apply the transaction logs in the wrong order or to skip a transaction log in the sequence.

4. Start the database in the normal way. The database engine will come up normally and any new activity will be appended to the current transaction log.

If your database file is still usable but you have lost your transaction log, the recovery process is as follows:

1. Make a backup of the database file immediately. The transaction log is gone and the only record of the changes is in the database file.

2. Restart the database with the -**f** switch. Without the switch, the database engine will "prompt you" about the lack of a transaction log. With the switch, the database engine will restore the database to the most recent checkpoint and then roll back any transactions that were not committed at the time of the checkpoint. A new transaction log will be created.

Deploying SQL Anywhere

Depending on your license, you may be deploying part or all of SQL Anywhere with your application. The actual files required for deployment are documented in an SQL Anywhere white paper available from the Sybase Web page (www.sybase.com) and will not be detailed here. The three deployment scenarios to consider are the runtime engine, the standalone engine, and the DBClient. In addition, we'll examine some of the optional components you may need to deploy.

In each case, you have the following two options:

- **Using the standard SQL Anywhere distribution to install the software.** This requires that you deploy a copy of the SQL Anywhere distribution and the appropriate instructions for installing it. This is common for servers where the customers are highly aware they are running SQL Anywhere.

- **Including the appropriate SQL Anywhere files into your own installation utility.** This method is common for applications where SQL Anywhere is embedded or for applications that use the DBClient interface.

Runtime

The Runtime version of SQL Anywhere is the lowest-cost deployment option. This version comes with a royalty-free right to deploy. The runtime engine has a number of limitations that may be significant under some circumstances. Specifically, the runtime engine:

- Does not support a transaction log.

- Does not support stored procedures.

- Does not support triggers.

- Does not support any data definition language (DDL), such as Create Table, except for the **GRANT** statements, which are required to manage user IDs and permissions.

The runtime engine is perfect for those applications that are introducing a relational database for the first time. It will introduce your customers to most of the advantages of a full-featured RDMS without any of the cost.

Standalone

Deploying a standalone, or *local,* engine gives your customers all the functionality and features of SQL Anywhere. Standalone engines are frequently embedded in a standalone application and installed as part of the application installation.

DBClient

Deploying DBClient implies that your customers will also have installed a server. The only issue specific to a DBClient deployment is to ensure that your customers' systems are configured to connect to the network correctly.

Optional Components

As part of your application design, you need to determine what components beyond the engine and interface you'll be deploying. Here are some components that are commonly included:

- **DBBackup.** To backup the database

- **DBValid.** To validate the database

- **DBLog.** To manage log files

- **DBTran.** To translate log files into SQL

- **DBRemote.** For replication

Moving On

A great database, huh? As you can see, Sybase SQL Anywhere is by all means a full-featured transaction-processing database. It has been developed for the PC and delivers superior performance and full database functionality while maintaining a small resource requirement. Now, for larger shops, a larger RDBMS may be required.

Next, we'll talk about Adaptive Server Enterprise—a leading high-performance relational database.

Adaptive Server Enterprise 23

Sybase Adaptive Server, previously known as Sybase SQL Server, has long been the leading high-performance relational database in the market. It's in use in thousands of sites worldwide and continues to expand its position in the database market, meaning you'll eventually have to develop an application using Sybase Adaptive Server as a back-end database engine. In this chapter, I'll introduce the primary concepts and features of the Sybase Adaptive Server, to allow you to successfully work with and develop applications for a Sybase Adaptive Server environment.

Currently, three primary versions of the Sybase SQL Server are available:

- **Version 4.x.** The original version of the server. This version is quickly disappearing.

- **Version 10.x.** The midlife version. Still in heavy use, but destined for migration to 11.x.

- **Version 11.x.** The current release of the server. Contains more features and better performance.

In this chapter, you'll be introduced to the various concepts that are unique to the Adaptive Server, such as Sybase's unique page-level locking architecture, and several of the newer features of the Adaptive Server. I'll specifically indicate differences in areas where the original pre-11.5 SQL Server product differs from the Adaptive Server 11.5 product. Although I'll try to cover the information, you'll need to develop applications for a Sybase database, the scope of this chapter does not allow me to provide a great depth of information. Therefore, I recommend acquiring additional information from any or all of the resources outlined at the end of this chapter.

Server Installation

Sybase Adaptive Server and the original SQL Server are currently available to run on five primary Unix platforms, several other lesser-used Unix platforms, and the Microsoft Windows NT operating system on both the Intel and DEC Alpha platforms. I'll highlight the installation requirements for both the Unix and NT environments, but I'm not going to cover the vendor-specific details for each flavor of Unix and NT. Therefore, I highly recommend reading the release notes and the installation guide for each specific environment you'll be installing.

Prior to beginning the installation, you must be sure you're logged in to the system with a user account that has sufficient permissions to read, write, and allocate various system resources needed by the Adaptive Server.

Under Unix, an account can be created by the *root* login called *sybase*. Give this account sufficient permissions to use devices and create directories (usually root permissions). You can use the root account, but creating a separate Sybase account provides better accountability and audit tracking for more secure environments.

If you're installing to an NT environment, you need to determine if the machine you're installing on is a member of an NT domain or simply in a workgroup. If the machine is in a domain, you may need to have an account that has domain administrator privileges to install successfully; otherwise, the local administrator account or a user account with administrative privileges will suffice. Under NT, the **LocalMachine** Registry entry needs to be updated, and in some domains, this component of the Registry is under the domain administrator's control.

Once you have established the correct user account for running the installation, you need to unload the software onto your machine. Under Unix, this is a two-stage process, where you unpack the software from the supplied installation media (tape or CD) and then run the installation program to do the actual installation. SQL Server installs using a program called *sybinit*, found in the $SYBASE/install directory. This is a non-GUI, command-line type utility that allows you to specify all the required information for your server installation; it then actually creates the base server databases, and so on. Adaptive Server changed this for the Unix environment by supplying an X-Windows GUI installation, called *srvbuild*.

NT users will only need to run the setup program found on the root directory of the CD.

You may run the srvbuild or setup program as often as required to reconfigure your system or to add new options if they are available on the CD. In the NT environment, you need to run the syconfig program to reconfigure your server. Many of the server performance and tuning parameters can be configured using the Sybase Central program, which for the Adaptive

Server is the primary administration tool. Sybase Central can also be used against older 11.0.x versions of SQL Server on both Unix and NT.

Two items prompted for during both installations are the character set and the default sort order. If you're configuring a new server, be sure to select these items, keeping in mind that they need to be the same for all servers you intend to move data between with bcp or backup dump/loads. Also, bear in mind that once the databases are created with a particular character set and sort order, it is *very* difficult to change them.

Once you have your server installed and running, you need to modify the default installation configuration to provide better performance. The initial configurations are intended to be sufficient to install the server and start it, but they are rarely sufficient to run it in a multiuser environment.

Sybase Server Architecture

Now that you have an installed and running server, what all did you get? The installation should have created a directory, usually called *Sybase*, with several subdirectories, as seen in Figure 23.1. The primary directories created are outlined in the following list. They represent a System 11 installation, as opposed to an older System 10 or 4.x installation. However, most of the structures are similar. Other directories exist, but their use is less important to this discussion.

The directory that we are most interested in is the *data* directory, because this is where the actual database files are stored. I'll give a brief outline of what is in the remaining directories here, but the primary discussion will be on the actual structure of the database files:

- The *bin* directory contains all the executables used to administer the server, the server executable itself, and the backup and monitor server executables.

- The *dll* directory contains all the support DLLs or the server and the connectivity libraries used to connect the server to the rest of the world.

- The *ini* directory contains the sql.ini file, which is used by the server to tell the server how to communicate with the rest of the world. It also contains a couple of additional configuration files, depending on the version of Open Client being used.

- The *install* directory contains the default error logs and some batch files to start the server manually.

- The *lib* directory is usually only installed as part of the Open Client or Open Server development environment, because most of the files are used to static link an Open Client/Open Server application.

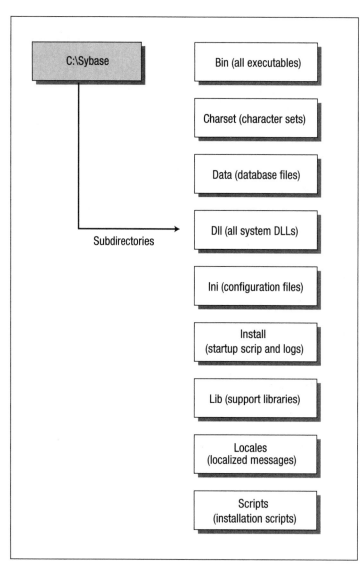

Figure 23.1
The Sybase directory structure.

- The *locales* directory works in conjunction with the default character and language set to provide localized messages for the various languages supported by the server.

- The *scripts* directory contains various scripts used to build or rebuild the master database, the system stored procedures, and some default test databases (for example, pubs2).

Now, back to the data directory. As I stated before, this is where the installation creates the primary databases for the server. These files can be placed elsewhere during the installation, but a good many sites do not change these particular file placements.

A Sybase database is created on an object known as a *device*. A device can be a file on Unix or NT or a "raw" device on Unix. I'll discuss devices as they relate to files in particular, but raw devices are similar in concept. A device is simply preallocated space in which the System Administrator can place a database. Usually, for performance purposes, each device file is placed on a separate physical disk drive if possible. Then, when a database is accessed, the drive controller does not have to run all over a disk drive to read data—it just pulls it from a physical drive.

Each database consists of a group of system tables, a log table (the log), and the user tables. When the System Administrator or you create a new database, you should first create two or more new devices, big enough to hold the new database and its future growth (as much as possible). This allows for better performance and recovery, by letting the data reside on one device and the log for the database reside on another. You can create a database with the data and log on the same device, but it's generally not recommended because it makes disaster recovery extremely difficult, if not impossible. Also, you can lose everything if the physical device that the database device is on fails. Figure 23.2 shows the relationship between devices and databases. Databases can span multiple

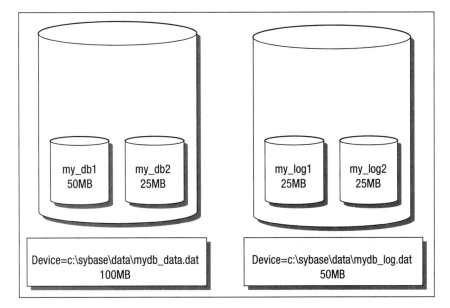

Figure 23.2
The relationship between devices and databases.

devices and can have new devices added to them as they grow; however, a device's size is specified when it is created, and it cannot be enlarged after the fact.

The figure shows two devices: mydb_dat.dat and mydb_log.dat. Mydb_dat.dat contains the data portion of two databases, my_db1 and my_db2. The mydb_log.dat device contains the logs for my_db1 and my_db2. Notice that the "data" device for the databases is 100MB in size and that 75MB have been used for the two databases. Another database could be added here, or the remaining space could be allocated to either database data segment at a later date. The log device, mydb_log.dat, is now full, and any further log expansion for either database would have to be done on a new device.

The Master Device

The first device created during an install is the *master* device, usually called *master.dat*. All but a small portion of the device is used for the three primary system databases. The three databases are *master, model*, and *tempdb*.

The model database is the template for all new databases created after the server is created. It contains the various default system tables and configurations required for any new database. Generally, you don't need to concern yourself with this database, other than to know that it's there, and that if it gets corrupted for any reason, all new databases will also be corrupted. If you get strange behavior or errors during the creation of a new database that are not related to disk space or other common problems, have the System Administrator validate the model database.

The tempdb database is the initial version of the temporary database, where temporary tables are created by users or system processes such as sorts and joins. Under most normal circumstances, the default tempdb database is too small. One of the first things an administrator should do is extend tempdb onto a new, larger device, so that you don't run into problems such as insufficient space to do sorts, and so on. Note that tempdb is re-created every time the server is shut down; therefore, don't create any tables or other objects there that you need to keep, unless you intend to re-create them each time the server restarts. If you ever experience corruption in tempdb, restart the server to try to clear it up, because tempdb will be dropped and re-created. Based on the information regarding the model database, you can assume that tempdb will look exactly like the model except for its size, right after the server restarts.

The most important database you have is the master database. Everything regarding your server, the databases managed by the server, the devices and their sizes and locations, and the users who can log in to the server is held here. Also, be sure to back it up—and keep it backed up any time you make any changes to your system. This database is usually the first target for an administrator to set up in his or her daily backup scripts. On a very active system, the normal process is to keep the log for this database backed up continually and the database backed up daily.

The master device is also the last place you want users creating databases. By default, all user logins place a user into the master database. When setting up new logins, be sure to set the default database to some database other than master. See the section "Logins, Users, And Other Security Issues" later in this chapter for more information.

As an administrative note, whenever you create a new device or database, keep the scripts you used to create them somewhere safe so that if the master database ever needs to be re-created, you can easily re-create your device mappings in the database. This will get you back online very quickly after a disaster recovery.

> **Note:** *Some place safe is not the same physical drive the master device is on!*

The sybprocs Device

During the installation, one other device is created, usually in the same directory as the master device. This device is called *sybprocs.dat*, and it contains nothing but the default system stored procedures. These procedures are used for everything from adding logins and users to managing databases and devices. Depending on the version of the server you're running, the size of the sybprocs device will be from 15MB to over 60MB.

The scripts to create the system stored procedures are located in the scripts directory, so if for some reason a particular procedure is dropped or the database is damaged, it can be recovered by rerunning the scripts after the device or database is checked out.

This is also the database that the administrator, and sometimes users, can add their own procedures to if they want to create a stored procedure that is global to the server and visible to all databases. Do not get carried away with adding procedures to this database. If the procedure really needs to be global, then put it here; otherwise, keep it local to the database it's related to. Also, be aware that during upgrades and some disaster recovery scenarios, the sybsystemprocs database will be rebuilt. All of your nice, handy stored procedures in this database are *gone*, so keep the scripts and be prepared to add them again if the server is upgraded, and so on. This is one of the reasons why only the administrator should add procedures here—it is his or her responsibility to be sure that the server is recovered to its original state after an upgrade or system restoration.

Sybase Page-Level Locking Mechanism

Now that a database server and a few databases are in place, it's probably a good time to explain one of the most debated issues with the Sybase server products.

A common concept in the database industry is to see data as rows within a table. Because of this concept, people generally tend to think of their data sets in terms of rows. When data is being manipulated during inserts, updates, and deletes, the server needs to lock the data rows being acted upon to prevent two sessions from modifying the data at the same time. This is considered *row-level locking*. Therefore, at any given time, a particular session could have one or many rows locked.

During the initial design phase of the first Sybase SQL Server, a design decision was made to manage data sets in a less granular mode—rather than try to handle lock management at the row level, it would be managed at the *page level*. One of the primary reasons for this is performance. The overhead associated with managing page locks versus row locks tends to be lower. Therefore, Sybase implemented a *page-level locking* scheme. This scheme has several pros and cons associated with it, just like any other scheme; however, the design decision is still valid, even though it tends to go against the current industry trend to support row-level locking.

Basically, Sybase's page-level locking will lock a page of data at a time, as opposed to a row, during inserts, updates, and deletes. A page is a 2K (2048 bytes) entity that allows, after space is used for page management and logging, a maximum row size of 1980 bytes. No single row of data can exceed this limit, because rows cannot span pages. This may seem like an odd restriction, but few cases exist in properly designed databases where individual rows of data need to be much larger. The only exception to this would be text or image data, which is handled somewhat differently by the server and is not limited by this restriction. You can have several rows on a page, or just one, but to access any row on the page, the entire page will be locked.

For most database environments, locking a particular page containing several rows will not cause a huge performance problem, because statistically, data is being manipulated all over the database and generally not from the same place at the same time. The primary times when this is a serious problem are cases where the database is taking a lot of inserts into one or more tables from several users at the same time. A "hot" page exists on the end of the table and an additional "hot" page on the end of the log file for the database.

Sybase addressed this issue in System 11 by providing you the ability to partition a table onto several devices, thus providing several "last" pages. This reduced hot page contention dramatically.

During the execution of a query or data manipulation, the server can read the required table data into the server's data cache in 2K blocks, which also turns out to be either the same size or a multiple of the operating system's disk I/O buffer. This helps to speed up the query by reducing the number of physical reads against the disk drive. Once in the cache, the data will stay there for future reads, as long as the space is not required for another data set. If a data cache is large enough, the number of physical reads against a disk drive can be quite low, and overall server performance can be quite high.

The page-level locking scheme used by the Sybase servers has rarely been a reason not to use the server, whereas its superior performance has always been a reason to use it. A little preliminary thinking with Sybase's locking process in mind is required to avoid any potential problems in your design that may be specifically related to row- versus page-level locking. The *Performance and Tuning Guide* that is part of the server documentation will aid you in the design process.

Server Configuration And Tuning

The Sybase Adaptive Server and previous versions have well over a hundred configuration parameters that can be used to configure the server for optimum performance for the type of database environment you're working in—for example, a decision support system (DSS) or an online transaction processing (OLTP) environment. Like all types of database configurations and tunings, there are tradeoffs between query response times for DSS and data manipulation or transaction rates for OLTP. Adaptive Server has the ability to tune its operating parameters to handle mixed-load environments or to provide optimum performance for one particular type of environment.

Due to the extensive number of parameters involved, I'll cover the main parameters that are usually modified to support the two types of server workloads. The *Performance and Tuning Guide* for Adaptive Server covers the process of tuning the server fairly extensively, and it makes a good reference for handling special types of performance issues.

I'll list the common tuning parameters and explain the use and restrictions with each; also, I'll attempt to keep them in order of importance. The primary tool for changing configuration parameters is the Sybase Central administration tool. It only runs on Windows 95 and NT, but can administer any server from across the network. You can also modify most parameters with a text editor—the 11.x servers use a text file, usually called <server name>.cfg, to hold the server configuration. This is another file that should be kept reasonably secure, because modifying this file improperly can cause your server to fail to start or to perform very poorly.

Memory

Memory is the first parameter any DBA needs to configure by setting the actual memory resources that the server needs to allocate on startup. This memory is used by the server for the kernel (the server engine itself), the data cache (where all database objects get read into for processing), and procedure cache (for all stored procedure execution).

Note: The basic method for calculating the memory available to Adaptive Server is to take the overall system memory and subtract the operating system's required memory. Then, subtract the memory required by any monitor and backup servers running on the machine and any overhead required for other programs that must run at the same time as Adaptive Server. Take whatever is left over and assign this to Adaptive Server.

Once the available memory has been calculated, you need to figure out the *required* memory for Adaptive Server. This formula is covered in the troubleshooting guide for Adaptive Server. Note that the configuration file sets memory in 2K pages, so be sure to divide the required memory by 2048 before entering the value into the configuration file. Generally, you don't need to do this calculation right after an installation. If you're having performance problems later on, you might have to look up the calculation and tune your system a little better. Figure 23.3 illustrates the Adaptive Server's memory map.

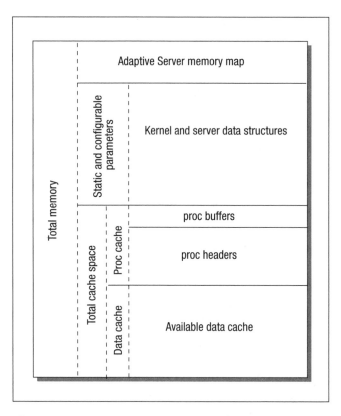

Figure 23.3
The Adaptive Server memory map.

Physical Resources

On a dedicated database server that runs Adaptive Server as the main executable on the system, approximately 80 percent of the overall system memory can be allocated to Adaptive Server, depending on the operating system requirements. This is a general rule of thumb, so be aware that many environments can't operate properly with this much memory dedicated to the server, but it's a good starting point.

The intent is to have as much physical memory, as opposed to *virtual* or *disk-based* memory, allocated to the database server as possible, without impacting the operating system. The Adaptive Server memory allocations should *never* be acquired from virtual or swapped memory, because this will severely degrade server performance.

One must also be careful not to run other memory-intensive applications on the same machine that is running the database server, as these could cause the Adaptive Server's resources to get swapped to disk. The allocated physical resources are:

- Parameter: Total memory

- Unit of Measure: 2K Pages

- Default: 7500 (15MB)

Network Communications

This parameter limits the number of users or other servers that can connect to Adaptive Server. Each user connection requires 75K of memory, which is taken from the pool of memory configured by the Total Memory parameter. This memory is allocated on startup. This value is also restricted by the license agreement with Sybase, which is based on total user connections. If your site purchases more user licenses, this parameter will need to be adjusted upwards and will therefore reduce the memory available to the default data cache. Recalculating the Total Memory value is usually required. The network communications defaults are:

- Parameter: Number of user connections

- Unit of Measure: Users and other connections

- Default: 25

SQL Server Administration (Objects)

Under most conditions, the default value is sufficient. You'll get an error message from the server if you begin to exceed this value, and you'll need to adjust it accordingly. Chapter 11 of the *System Administration Guide* covers tuning this parameter very well. The defaults are:

- Parameter: Number of open objects

- Unit of measure: Objects (tables/indexes/stored procedures, and so on)

- Default: 500

SQL Server Administration (Databases)

Most sites modify this value at installation to around 25, but if you're tight on resources, you may need to be a little more judicious and calculate how many databases you really have or require on the system. The quickest way to check the number of databases currently on your system is to use Sybase Central and check the databases folder or just check the error log file, because each database is recorded there as it comes online when the server starts up. The defaults are:

- Parameter: Number of open databases

- Unit of measure: Databases

- Default: 12

Backup/Recovery

This parameter basically drives the checkpoint process, which dictates the maximum amount of server processing time that's needed to recover should the server go down without writing the data cache to disk. In other words, by default, about five minutes of work would be rolled back or forward should the server go down suddenly.

Adaptive Server estimates that 6,000 rows in the transaction log require about 1 minute of recovery time. However, different types of log records can take more or less time to recover. If you set the recovery interval in minutes to 3, the checkpoint process writes changed pages to disk only when syslogs contains more than 18,000 rows. Depending on your environment and the type of transactions you're processing, you may want to lengthen or shorten this interval. The defaults are:

- Parameter: Recovery interval in minutes

- Unit of measure: Minutes

- Default: 5

Connecting To Your Database

One of the many great features of PowerBuilder is the ability to "hide" most of the database connection processes from the user. As a feature for the developer, it's a real time-saver, but sometimes things don't always work out the way you planned. In this section, I'll describe the basic connection structure to a Sybase server and point out areas where you might run into problems so that you can concentrate on programming.

Sybase, like all other database vendors, has its own proprietary mechanism for connecting to the server. System 10 and System 11 servers all use the Open Client Library network libraries and connection protocols. Earlier DB Library network libraries, originally designed to support the 4.x servers, can be used against the 10.x and 11.x servers, if required, but generally the newer 10.x or 11.x Open Client network libraries are the way to go. These have more features and will be supported into the next generation of servers.

You also have the ability to connect using an ODBC interface, but the ODBC interface relies on a properly functioning Open Client interface. Figure 23.4 shows the overall structure of the Open Client interface, including the ODBC layer.

Your application connects to the Sybase server either through the PowerBuilder ODBC layer and a Sybase ODBC driver to the Open Client or through the PowerBuilder native Sybase driver to the Open Client layer. See the PowerBuilder *Connecting to Your Database* manual for the description of these interfaces.

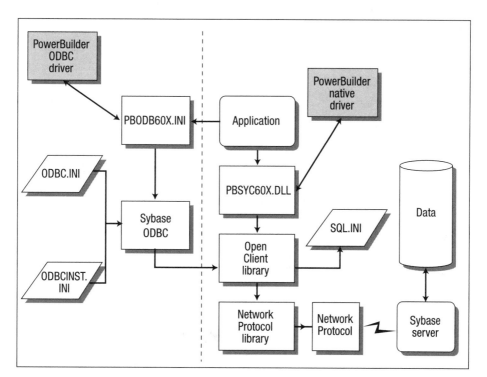

Figure 23.4
Connection diagram.

The Sybase Open Client layer relies on a system environment variable called **SYBASE**, which is set to point to the directory where the Sybase Open Client product is installed. If this variable is not set, you receive errors such as "Cannot Load NWNLSWCK net lib." The Open Client uses this variable to locate other support DLLs and network libraries. You'll also want to be sure that your **PATH** variable contains references to the bin and dll directories underneath your Sybase Open Client installation directories. Here are examples:

```
SYBASE=C:\Sybase
PATH=%PATH%;%SYBASE%\bin;%SYBASE%\dll
```

The next item that needs attention is the sql.ini file found in the ini directory under your **SYBASE** environment variable path. This is a text file that can be edited with any editor as long as you save it as a TXT file. Any other format can cause the Open Client layer to fail to locate your server. The best way to modify the file is to use the tools supplied with your Open Client installation. If you're using the 10.0.x version of the Open Client, you should have a program called sqledit.exe in your $SYBASE\bin directory. If you're using the 11.1.x version, you should have a program called dsedit.exe in the $SYBASE\bin directory. Use these tools to create an entry for the server to which you'll be connecting. You need to know the machine name if you're using a named pipes connection, or the TCP/IP name (host name) if you're using TCP/IP to connect. Once these entries are complete and correct, you should be able to "ping" the server using the **ping** functionality of the editing tool. Here's a sample sql.ini file:

```
;; Sybase Interfaces file
;;
;; [<database_server_name>]
;; <link_type>=<network_driver>,<connection_info>
;;
;; Examples:
;; [JUPITER]
;; QUERY=NLMSNMP,\\JUPITER\pipe\sybase\query
;; WIN3_QUERY=WNLNMP,\\JUPITER\pipe\sybase\query
;;
[ASE_B2]
$BASE$00=NLMSNMP,\\bigbox_pc\pipe\sybase\query
$BASE$01=NLWNSCK,bigbox_pc,5000
master=$BASE$00;$BASE$01;
$BASE$02=NLMSNMP,\\bigbox_pc\pipe\sybase\query
$BASE$03=NLWNSCK,bigbox_pc,5000
query=$BASE$02;$BASE$03;
```

The file shows connection information for a named pipes connection using the nlmsnmp DLL found in the $SYBASE\dll directory, and a TCP/IP connection using the nlwnsck DLL found in the same directory. Also, bigbox_pc is the machine name that the Sybase server is running on. The value 5000 for the TCP/IP connections is the port number that the Sybase server uses to listen for connections. This port is specified in the server's sql.ini file, and the entry on your machine needs to match it.

Once one sql.ini file is set up on a client machine and is working correctly, you should be able to install the Open Client on all other machines connecting to the Sybase server and then simply copy the working sql.ini file to all these new installations. Remember that *all* clients connecting to the Sybase server must have a copy of the Sybase Open Client installed, and your site will have to purchase a license for each client machine. Be sure to include this as part of the cost of deploying your application to the end users, because it is often forgotten and will cause plenty of complaints from the end users if you surprise them with this little detail.

On the same line of thought, if you're using ODBC to make your connections to the Sybase server, you'll also need to license a copy of the Sybase ODBC driver, in addition to the Open Client licenses.

The decision of whether to use an ODBC client connection or use the native client connection is always an issue. The ODBC client offers, if the application's SQL is designed correctly, the ability to point the application to any database vendor's product and run the application. The tradeoff, of course, is performance. A native client connection can be significantly faster, and even easier to deploy and maintain. If you need portability, then you can use ODBC, or be prepared to code for the various idiosyncrasies of each vendor's specific connection layers and SQL by using native drivers. Use native connections if you're building an application for internal use and know that you'll always be talking to a specific vendor's server.

Once you have a working connection to the Sybase server, the first PowerBuilder connection to the database will cause PowerBuilder to attempt to build its catalog tables used during development. Prior to connecting to a Sybase database with PowerBuilder, be sure to run the supplied SQL scripts for the particular version of the Sybase server you are connecting to. They are usually found on the PowerBuilder installation CD under the same directory as the deployment kit. Log in to the Sybase server with an account that has SA (System Administrator) permissions using Sybase's ISQL, change to the development database, and run the script. If you're using more than one database for development, you'll probably need to run the scripts while in the master database so that they're visible to all databases.

System Tables

In this section, I'll outline the use of each server-wide system table held in the master database, as well as the common database base system tables kept in each database. These tables are the heart of any server, and doing anything more than selecting against them is a potentially dangerous process. You should not modify the system tables manually except in extreme circumstances, and under the guidance of a knowledgeable Sybase server DBA or support person.

Table 23.1 lists the tables that occur in *all* databases.

Table 23.1 Common tables that are in all databases.

Table Name	Description
sysalternates	One row for each Adaptive Server user mapped to a database user.
sysattributes	One row for each object attribute definition.
syscolumns	One row for each column in a table or view and for each parameter in a procedure.
syscomments	One or more rows for each view, rule, default, trigger, and procedure, giving the SQL a definition statement.
sysconstraints	One row for each referential and check constraint associated with a table or column.
sysdepends	One row for each procedure, view, or table that is referenced by a procedure, view, or trigger.
sysindexes	One row for each clustered or nonclustered index; one row for each table with no indexes, and an additional row for each table containing text or image data.
syskeys	One row for each primary, foreign, or common key. Set by user (not maintained by Adaptive Server).
syslogs	Transaction log.
sysobjects	One row for each table, view, procedure, rule, trigger default, log, and (in tempdb only) temporary object.
syspartitions	One row for each partition (page chain) of a partitioned table.
sysprocedures	One row for each view, rule, default, trigger, and procedure, giving an internal definition.
sysprotects	User permissions information.
sysreferences	One row for each referential integrity constraint declared on a table or column.
sysroles	Maps server-wide roles to local database groups.

(continued)

Table 23.1 Common tables that are in all databases *(continued)*.

Table Name	Description
syssrvroles	Maps system and user-defined role names and passwords to server role IDs.
syssegments	One row for each segment (named collection of disk pieces).
systhresholds	One row for each threshold defined for the database.
systypes	One row for each system-supplied and user-defined data type.
sysusermessages	One row for each user-defined message.
sysusers	One row for each user allowed in the database.

Table 23.2 lists the tables that occur in the master database only.

Table 23.3 lists the tables that occur in the sybsecurity database only.

All these tables, as well as the column information for each, can be located in the appendixes of the *Server Administration Guide* or the supplement.

Table 23.2 Common tables that are within the master database only.

Table Name	Description
syscharsets	One row for each character set or sort order.
sysconfigures	One row for each configuration parameter that can be set by users.
syscurconfigs	Information about configuration parameters currently being used by Adaptive Server.
sysdatabases	One row for each database on the Adaptive Server.
sysdevices	One row for each tape dump device, disk dump device, disk for databases, and disk partition for databases.
sysengines	One row for each Adaptive Server engine currently online.
syslanguages	One row for each language (except U.S. English) known to the server.
syslisteners	One row for each type of network connection used by the current Adaptive Server.
syslocks	Information about active locks.
sysloginroles	One row for each server login that possesses a system-defined role.
syslogins	One row for each valid Adaptive Server user account.

(continued)

Table 23.2 Common tables that are within the master database only *(continued)*.

Table Name	Description
syslogshold	Information about the oldest active transaction and the Replication Server truncation point for each database.
sysmessages	One row for each system error or warning.
sysmonitors	One row for each monitor counter.
sysprocesses	Information about server processes.
sysremotelogins	One row for each remote user.
sysresourcelimits	One row for each resource limit.
syssecmechs	Information about the security services for each security mechanism available to Adaptive Server.
sysservers	One row for each remote Adaptive Server.
syssrvroles	One row for each server-wide role.
systimeranges	One row for each named time range.
sysusages	One row for each disk piece allocated to a database.

Table 23.3 Common tables that are within sybsecurity database.

Table Name	Description
sysauditoptions	One row for each global audit option.
sysaudits_01-8	The audit trail. Each audit table contains one row for each audit record.

Logins, Users, And Other Security Issues

The Sybase servers, by default, use a login/password and a Discretionary Access Control (DCA) type security mechanism within the server to secure access to the various databases and objects within them. The server implements two stages of security—one at the server login level and another at the database level.

A user is required to log in to the Adaptive Server to gain access to any of the databases managed by the server. The user is also required to be given user access to specific databases, prior to accessing them. The user may also be restricted as to what operations he or she can execute on a specific database. A user who can log in to a server is usually assigned a default database with which his or her application normally operates. Once logged in, the user may be limited to accessing this database only and performing only certain operations against this database.

Roles

Sybase servers also use the concept of *roles* to manage security and resource access. Three primary roles are available for assignment to a login: the *System Administrator* role (SA_ROLE), the *System Security Officer* role (SSO_ROLE), and the Operator role (OPER_ROLE).

A login that has been assigned SSO_ROLE may make the required changes for a particular user to assign him or her a default database, access to other databases, and limits on his or her operations on any given database. On a default installation, the user who is the System Administrator also carries the SSO role. SA_ROLE may access any resource or object on the server, unless the SSO has specifically denied access to the object. An example of such a case is restricting access to a payroll table so that only specified users can modify it. The SSO role does not have any specific access rights to system databases and objects, but it does have rights to manage access to these databases, system objects, and so on.

With this information in mind, I'll outline some basic processes to help you in administering your server and preventing security access problems while developing and deploying your applications.

Secure The SA Password

The first thing that needs to be done on a fresh installation is to give the sa login a password. At installation, it is set to null and should be changed as soon as possible. The **sp_password** stored procedure is used to change any login's password. Here's the basic syntax:

```
sp_password <old password>, <new password>
```

Once a server is up and running and you're ready to begin creating databases, you should assign SA_ROLE to specific users and then disable the default 'sa' account. This allows for better auditing of 'sa'-type activities such as configuration changes. If auditing is enabled, you can identify the user who executed a particular 'sa'-type command, as opposed to just knowing that the System Administrator executed it. Use the **grant role** and **revoke role** commands to modify roles for various logins to give another login SA_ROLE. It may also be a good time to decide who will be the System Security Officer, so that he or she can take responsibility for the security of the system. Here's the syntax:

```
grant role role_granted [{, role_granted}...]to grantee [{, grantee}...] revoke
role role_name [{, role_name}...]from grantee [{, grantee}...]
```

Note: *To use the 'sa' account later for a server upgrade, you must unlock the account. After completing the upgrades, you can lock the account again. The 'sa' account must be unlocked for upgrades to proceed successfully.*

Add New Logins And Users

Once the SSO has been established and the required logins have been given their SA_ROLE authorities, you may now add new logins and users to the system. Use the **sp_addlogin** stored procedure to create new logins and to specify their initial passwords and default databases. Giving each login a default database is usually a good idea, because, generally, most users or developers are working against one database, and the default database setting prevents them from having to worry about being in the correct database or accidentally dropping or deleting objects from the wrong database. Here's the syntax:

```
sp_addlogin loginname, passwd [,default db] [, default language [, fullname
or comment]]
```

Note that passwords *must* be longer than five characters and enclosed in quotes if it contains characters outside A to Z, a to z, and #, or if it begins with a number. After you specify the default database, add the user to the default database with **sp_adduser** so that he or she can log in directly to his or her default database.

Alias To DBO During Development

Another option, especially for sites that have many developers adding and modifying database objects, is to alias the logins to the database's dbo user. This allows all objects created in the database to be owned by 'dbo', a user created by default on all databases, which will prevent a particular user from owning an object. It also means that all SQL created during development can use the 'dbo' owner when referencing an object, which allows everyone a common object owner reference. Once deployed to another site, the dbo user exists and all of your SQL will work. If a particular user owns an object, it must be accessed using that user's name as part of the object qualifier, which creates major problems in a development environment where several thousand lines of SQL are generated using an object owner name that might not exist in a deployed site. For example, if table A is created by user bob, it must be referenced as *<Database>.bob.A*. Now, if table B is created by user 'dbo', it may be referenced as *<Database>.B*. All users aliased to 'dbo' can then access the table without an owner qualifier.

Nondevelopment users may be granted various permissions on objects as required by the object owner so that they may access the database as a user added by the **sp_adduser** procedure. A very good procedure is to have a separate machine set aside that replicates what the end user's environment is going to look like. Have a login created that has the "usual" permissions of an end user; then, test your applications against the server using this machine and login. This prevents some nasty permission and SQL execution problems from showing up as you start to deploy.

Creating New Databases

Only a System Administrator can grant permission to use the **create database** command. The **grant** command for permission on **create database** must be issued from master. In many installations, the System Administrator maintains a monopoly on **create database** permission in order to centralize control of database placement and database device space allocation.

The System Administrator can create new databases on behalf of other users and then transfer ownership to the appropriate user. If creating a database that is to be owned by another user, the System Administrator issues the **create database** command and then switches to the new database with the **use <database>** command. He or she then executes the system procedure **sp_changedbowner**.

Many possibilities exist for managing security on your server, and a careful analysis of the various options needs to be done prior to beginning a lot of application development against it. Spending some time up front configuring the system security and laying out the rules for development can save you many hours of reconfiguring the systems and searching through code to change nonportable SQL statements. Read the various sections on managing the security for your server in the server documentation.

Stored Procedures And Triggers

One of the original features of the Sybase SQL Server products was the implementation of stored procedures and triggers, which has since been included in all current database vendor's products. The use of stored procedures and triggers can enhance the performance of your applications by moving some database-related processing over to the database server. Processes such as large table sorts, filtering large result sets, expensive calculations based on database data, and some referential integrity management can be handled at the server as opposed to attempting them on the client.

Sybase Adaptive Server allows for the creation of an unlimited number of stored procedures and triggers, of more or less unlimited size. When creating procedures and triggers, attempt to keep their sizes down by not trying to write your entire application in a single procedure. Building procedures and triggers that encapsulate specific functionality will allow you to build PowerBuilder applications more efficiently and clearly.

Adaptive Server allows you to nest stored procedures and triggers up to 16 levels deep, including nested transactions. Just be aware that all the nested procedures and triggers need to be in the procedure cache at the same time. Several very large sets of nested procedures running at the same time can cause the procedure cache to fill, generating an execution error. Check the error log and increase the procedure or data cache to resolve the problem if it happens frequently. Sometimes, just reexecuting the procedure will allow it to succeed again. There are a few rules that apply to nested procedures and triggers and some system environment variables that can be checked to monitor your procedures as they execute. The following variables, related to transactions and stored procedure nesting, are available to the programmer:

- **@@nestlevel.** Contains the nesting level of the current execution with the user session, initially 0. Each time a stored procedure or trigger calls another stored procedure or trigger, the nesting level is incremented. If the maximum of 16 is exceeded, the transaction aborts.

- **@@trancount.** Contains the nesting level of the transactions in the current user session. Each **begin** transaction in a batch increments the transaction count. When you query **@@trancount** in chained transaction mode, its value is never 0 because the query automatically initiates a transaction.

- **@@error.** This global variable is commonly used to check the error status—whether it succeeded or failed—of the most recently executed batch in the current user session. **@@error** contains 0 if the last transaction succeeded; otherwise, **@@error** contains the last error number generated by the system.

- **@@transtate.** Contains the current state of a transaction after a statement executes in the current user session. However, unlike **@@error**, **@@transtate** is not cleared for each batch.

- **@@transtate.** May contain the following values:

  - **0.** Transaction in progress. An explicit or implicit transaction is in effect; the previous statement executed successfully.

  - **1.** Transaction succeeded. The transaction completed and committed its changes.

  - **2.** Statement aborted. The previous statement was aborted; no effect on the transaction.

- **3.** Transaction aborted. The transaction aborted and rolled back any changes.

- **@@sqlstatus.** Contains status information resulting from the last **fetch** statement for the current user session. **@@sqlstatus** may contain the following values:

  - **0.** The fetch statement completed successfully.

  - **1.** The fetch statement resulted in an error.

  - **2.** There is no more data in the result set. This warning occurs if the current cursor position is on the last row in the result set and the client submits a **fetch** command for that cursor.

You can usually display the text of a stored procedure with the system procedure **sp_helptext**. Some procedures, for security reasons, may have had their "text" removed from the syscomments table and are therefore not viewable. Here's an example:

```
Eg:  sp_helptext sp_count

# Lines of Text
-----------------

              1

(1 row affected)

text
---------------------------------------

create procedure sp_count as

select count(*) from sysusers

(1 row affected, return status = 0)
```

New with the Adaptive Server is the ability to call external stored procedures (for example, functions from a DLL) that further extend the ability to add functionality to your applications and share common code among all your clients. External stored procedures rely on the installation of the XP Server, which is installed by default as part of the Adaptive Server installation. This functionality exists for most Unix platforms and all NT platforms (Intel and Alpha). The use of external stored procedures allows you to code very fast routines in C/C++ or other languages and to access them from your Adaptive Server. It also allows you to use third-party DLLs if you want to invoke other functions from them. Also, as a side effect of being able to call external stored procedures from the server, the use of the Microsoft Mail API (MAPI) is also available and can be used by the

Adaptive Server to mail server information or query results to an end user or application. The MAPI functionality only exists on NT-based servers at this time and has been fully integrated with built-in procedure calls, and so on, to manage the interface for you.

Database Administration Tools

Several very good administration and backup tools are available for administering Sybase Adaptive Server and earlier versions of SQL Server. Sybase has supplied two such tools that can be used against its servers, and both are shipped as part of the package for most environments.

SSM—SQL Server Manager

The first of these tools is the Sybase SQL Server Manager (SSM)—a GUI tool capable of managing most of your server needs. It was first introduced and shipped with the 10.0.2 Open Client product and has since gone through a couple of minor revisions. It will work fine for any System 10 or System 11.0.x server but will not function properly against Adaptive Server. Several schema and stored procedure enhancements that cause the SSM to behave badly—such as rudely terminating with an exception—have been made for Adaptive Server.

SSM is available to run on Windows 3.1.x clients, Windows 95, and NT Intel platforms. It relies on the Microsoft Win32 API, and can be somewhat version dependent. It's currently, and most likely to continue to be, the only 16-bit management tool from Sybase that will continue to run on Windows 3.x. As Microsoft pushes the world into a 32-bit environment, requirements for 16-bit tools become fewer and fewer. SSM is currently not shipping with any new releases of the Open Client or bundles of Sybase products. It will most likely cease to be supported in the near future as demand wanes and newer tools replace it.

If you need 16-bit administration tools, SSM may fit the bill, but you won't get much in the way of bug fixes or long-term support.

Sybase Central

Sybase Central, or *SQL Central* as it was known in a previous life, is the latest in server administration tools from Sybase. It currently ships with most of the bundled Sybase Server products, including the SQL Anywhere database servers. It's a 32-bit GUI tool that runs on Windows 95 and Windows NT Intel platforms. A version based on Java exists that will allow it to be used as an administration tool for environments that are purely Unix. Windows 3.x is not, and will never be, supported because there's a dependency on the Win95 API for some of the visual components on-screen.

Sybase Central relies on *plug-ins* or *providers*, which allow the tool to be used with several flavors of the Sybase servers at the same time—from System 10.x, System 11.0.x, Adaptive Server, and SQL Anywhere. It also supports, within the same window, the NetImpact Dynamo Web Server product, and it allows for managing Web sites and their components stored in various Sybase databases.

The tool allows you to do most anything you have the permissions to do with your login—from one window. You can create devices, databases, stored procedures, triggers, and tables. You can modify the server's configuration file, add logins and users, and even generate schema DDL.

Sybase intends to continue to enhance the supported list of providers in order to provide support for other Sybase products such as Omni Services (Component Integration Layer) and Monitor Client (to monitor your server performance), and possibly even a Replication Server provider.

Sybase Central will continue to be for the foreseeable future, the primary tool from Sybase for performing basic server administration. It does not at this time, however, provide much support for Enterprise Server Management (ESM). However, several very good ESM products are available from third-party vendors.

Other Information Sources

Now, if you need additional resources or research material, here is a list of sources that I would definitely recommend having:

Sybooks

If you're doing serious development work against Sybase servers, I highly recommend that you acquire a copy of the latest Sybooks on CD. This will provide you with the entire online documentation set for the Sybase server products. There are several versions of Sybooks, each compiled as a resource for specific product groups. The Sybooks for almost any server platform should provide you with the required information for such things as configuration parameters, T-SQL commands, and basic server information. If you need specific information about your environment, such as NT or a Pyramid Nile Unix server, you'll want to be sure you get the correct one. Features on each platform are covered in the installation guides and manual supplements that only show up on certain Sybook packages.

The entire Sybooks information library for all products is also available on the Sybase Web site at www.sybase.com.

WWW

The World Wide Web has several good sites dedicated to Sybase products and support. Also, you can sign up for any of the Sybase Web-based technical support offerings, which allow you to open technical support cases, search for known problems and workarounds, access bug fixes for most products, and generally get fast support without waiting in a phone queue.

You can also find some good offerings on the Sybase product site, at www.Sybase.com. Currently, several hundred tech notes and other documents exist that deal with Sybase server, PowerBuilder, and others. Also, you can go to a free EBF download site for the Workplace products group, where you can acquire the latest fixes for PC-based Open Client, Server, and ODBC drivers.

Moving On

In this chapter, we discussed Sybase's Adaptive Server and the various concepts that are unique to it—for example, Sybase's page-level locking architecture. Note that there's lots more to the Adaptive Server Enterprise, and I've not done it justice by covering it in one chapter. If you want to learn more about Adaptive Server Enterprise, refer to its documentation. I hope this chapter has opened the doors to what is a great RDMS.

In the next chapter, I'll discuss the Project Painter. The Project Painter is the entry point to PowerBuilder's generator engines, which generate application projects as well as components.

PART V
The
Deployment
Guide

Creating A Project

The first step for deploying your application is to create a target project. PowerBuilder 6.0 has a totally new project generator that enables you to create various targets from the Project Painter. If you select *Application*, the Project Painter allows you to generate executable files and dynamic libraries. The other project types (depending on which generators you have installed) are *Proxy*, (which lets you generate proxy objects for distribution with the client application in a distributed application) or *C++*, which lets you generate a C++ header and source file with the same methods and arguments as a class User object.

Open interfaces to PowerBuilder NVOs will also be supported in the future. For this purpose, additional component generators will be added to support the creation of CORBA, DCOM, JavaBean, and ActiveX components. These generated components can be deployed into a variety of middle-tier server environments.

In this chapter, I'll cover the three project generators. I'll emphasize creating an application project, generating executables and dynamic libraries, and troubleshooting common problems. Then, I'll cover the other generators.

Application Project

To create an application target, click the Project Painter and then double-click Application in the New Project dialog box, as shown in Figure 24.1.

The application generator lets you create an executable file and its related dynamic libraries. The next screen, shown in Figure 24.2, gives you the various options to specify for your target. This is where you specify whether to generate Pcode or machine code,

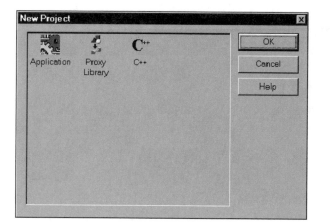

Figure 24.1
Selecting an application project.

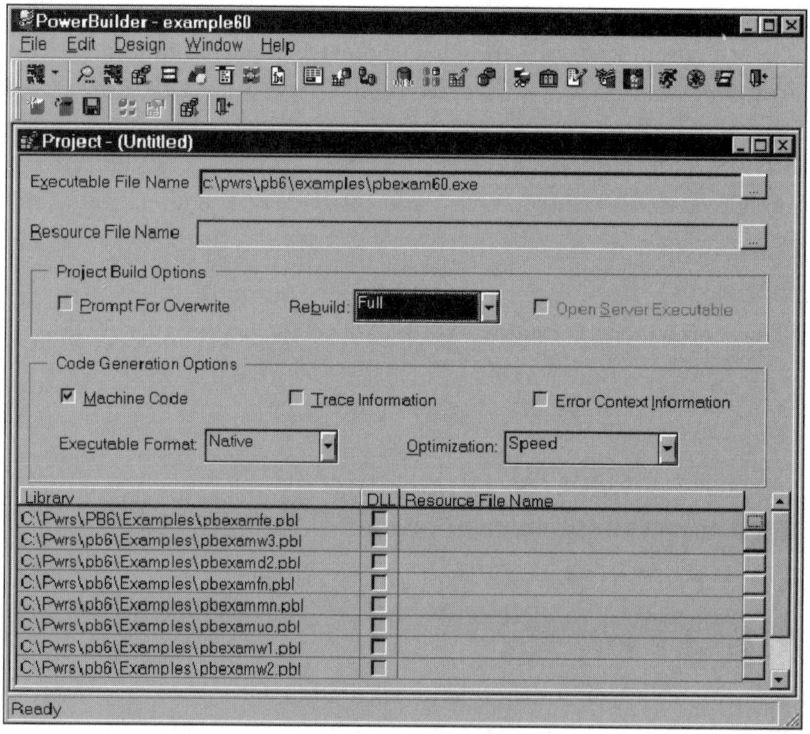

Figure 24.2
The application generator screen.

the bit level of your target (either 32 bit or 16 bit), the optimization format, and whether to include tracing and error information in your target. Let's take a closer look at these options:

- **Executable File Name.** This is the name of your executable file. You now have a Browse button to specify a location.

- **Resource File Name.** This is where you specify your PowerBuilder resource file (PBR). You have a new Browse button to search for a PBR file.

- **Prompt For Overwrite.** If you check this option, PowerBuilder displays a message box asking for confirmation before overwriting the executable file and each dynamic library.

- **Rebuild.** Specify either Full or Incremental to indicate if you want to regenerate all your objects or only objects that have changed. The incremental rebuild inspects the last-saved and last-compiled timestamps that PowerBuilder maintains for each object. For a given object, it compares that object's last-compiled timestamp with the last-saved timestamp of all its ancestors, and any object that it references. If PowerBuilder finds an object in either category that was saved after the current object was last compiled, it recompiles the current object.

- **Open Server Executable.** Check this option if you want to build a distributed server application that uses the OpenClientServer driver.

- **Machine Code.** Check this option if you want to generate compiled code instead of Pcode. The remaining code generation options are only applicable when Machine Code is selected.

- **Trace Information.** Check this option if you want to create a trace file when you run your executable. You can use the trace file to troubleshoot or profile your application. (See Chapter 12, "Debugging Your Application," for a more detailed discussion of this.)

- **Error Context Information.** Check this option if you want PowerBuilder to display context information such as object, event, and script line numbers for runtime errors.

- **Executable Format.** This option allows you to build either a 32-bit (native) executable or a 16-bit executable.

- **Library.** All your PBLs in your library search path are listed here. Check each one if you want to compile them into a dynamic library. These libraries are given the name of the PBL with the extension .PBD for Pcode or .DLL for machine code. You can also specify a PBR file for each of your PBLs. To search for one, click the small browse button.

Once you've selected all your options, select the Design|Build Project menu item to create your executable.

> **Note:** In PowerBuilder 6.0, you can now create 16-bit Pcode as well as 16-bit machine code targets from 32-bit PowerBuilder.

Pcode Vs. Machine Code

The executable file format that you can build from PowerBuilder can be either Pcode or machine code. Pcode is interpretive. Some developers refer to this format as a "virtual engine that interprets byte code."

Pcode substitutes for a number of machine code instructions, reducing the size of the executable at the price of performance. Pcode is generally slower than a compiled executable, but it's fairly compact and makes function calls into highly optimized PowerBuilder DLLs as it runs.

> **Note:** Machine code targets are considerably larger than Pcode targets.

So, how is a machine code target created? During development, your script is translated to Pcode. This Pcode is present when you begin your compilation. When you create a Pcode executable, PowerBuilder performs a link step and then copies the objects into the destination executable or PBD. Pcode is then translated into C code. This step resolves the Pcode into a series of C language statements. The C code is then compiled and linked to create a machine code executable and DLLs.

> **Note:** The creation of a machine code executable takes considerably longer than the creation of a Pcode executable. For speed of testing, you may want to create Pcode executables until your application is close to being completed for delivery or have a dedicated build machine that you can use to build executables without affecting your development time.
>
> Machine code does tighter checking on variables. If you don't cast your variables properly, you may get away with it in Pcode, but not in machine code. Make sure that your dot notations, your use of the **Any** variable, and so on, are properly casted.

When To Use Machine Code

Use compiled code when your application is very script-intensive (that is, code that contains many loops or scripts that perform a lot of calculations). Function calls are much faster in machine code than Pcode, so scripts that call functions or events are good candidates, especially in a loop. Here are the areas in which machine code provides better performance over Pcode:

- Loops

- Floating-point arithmetic

- Integer arithmetic

- Function calls

Some areas will not be any faster than in Pcode. These areas are window painting, database access, decimal math, and string handling. Also, a number of areas exist in which the internal code is identical between Pcode and compiled code, so you'll see no difference in execution speed for them. These areas include resources, classes, and DataWindow code.

Note: You cannot have DLLs and PBDs in the same application. Do not mix them.

Reducing The Size Of Dynamic Libraries

When PowerBuilder builds a dynamic library, it copies the compiled versions of all objects from the PBL into the dynamic library. The easiest way to specify source libraries is to simply use your standard PowerBuilder libraries as source libraries. However, your dynamic libraries will be larger than they need to be because they include all objects from the source library, not just the ones used in your application. You might want to create a PowerBuilder library that contains only the objects that you want to be in a dynamic library.

Note: Optimize your libraries prior to building an executable.

Using Resources

If you use resources such as pictures, pointers, and icons in your application, you can either distribute them separately with your compiled application or include them in your executable file or dynamic library.

If a resource has not been included in the executable file or in a dynamic library, PowerBuilder looks in the search path for the resource when that resource is referenced at execution time. Because of this, you must make sure you distribute your resources with your application. As long as the resource files are on the PC's search path at execution time, your application can load them when they are needed. Your application first looks in the current directory; then, it proceeds to the Windows and Windows\System directories. Finally, it searches other directories listed in your Windows search path.

Now, instead of distributing resources separately, you can create a PBR that lists all dynamically assigned resources.

Note: If you're assigning DataWindow objects to DataWindow controls dynamically in scripts, you must create a PowerBuilder resource file and include the objects in the executable or dynamic library file, or you can include the DataWindow objects themselves in a dynamic library file. You cannot distribute them separately as you can with bitmaps and cursors.

A PBR file is an ASCII text file in which you list resource names such as BMP, CUR, ICO, RLE, WMF files and DataWindow objects. To create a PBR file, use any text editor, list the names of each resource (one resource on each line), and then save the list as a file with the extension .PBR. For example, the following line adds the **d_customer** DataWindow from customer.pbl to your executable:

```
customer.pbl(d_customer)
```

Troubleshooting

Every now and then when generating an executable, you may run into errors. In this section, I'll cover some of the most common problems that developers encounter and offer possible solutions.

64K Segment Violation Error

This error is usually encountered when generating 16-bit machine code targets. The 16-bit platform has a size limitation of 64K for data and code segments. If you have a function or event that generates compiled object code exceeding this segment size, you'll receive an error during EXE creation. The only way to fix this error is to note the object and script and then reduce the script size by breaking it into smaller modules. This is a good practice anyway, because it increases performance and simplifies maintenance.

Disk Space

In order to generate a machine code executable, PowerBuilder creates a series of C files that are dumped in your TEMP directory. These file are removed when your executable is created. Make sure you have enough disk space available for these files to be successfully created. Also, if for some reason the process of generating an executable fails, make sure you delete any C files left over in your TEMP directory. (Obviously you must have a TEMP directory to begin with.)

Running Trace With Machine Code

If you run into a strange error during the execution of your program or your application does not behave the way it should, you may want to create a trace file and analyze your application. The question of how to create a trace file with a machine code executable has come up many times. To do so, make sure you check the Error Context Information and Trace Information options when generating your executable.

Error Opening DLLs

If you get an error message "Error Opening DLLs" when trying to run your executable, make sure your DLL and EXE names are not the same. Windows does not allow for this because an error will occur.

Library File Is Damaged

The "Library File Is Damaged" error message is related to your executable not having the correct deployment DLLs. Make sure your 16-bit target uses the PowerBuilder 16-bit deployment DLLs and your 32-bit target uses the PowerBuilder 32-bit deployment DLLs. Always create a shortcut and point this shortcut to start in the correct deployment DLL's directory.

Various Link Errors

If you run into various link errors when trying to create an executable, make sure you delete all the header files (.H) and precompiled header files (.PCH) from the CGEN directory. Then, try to recompile your application.

Proxy Library

The Proxy generator lets you build a proxy object that you can deploy with your client application in a distributed PowerBuilder application. The distributed client has a proxy object, which is a class User object that mirrors the functions and properties of a remote object on the distributed server. To create a proxy library, click the Project Painter and then double-click Proxy Library in the New Project dialog box (refer back to Figure 24.1).

The properties for the proxy library can be set by selecting the Edit|Design menu item. These properties, as shown in Figure 24.3, are described in the following list:

- **Output Library.** The name and location of the generated proxy library. Click the browse button to browse the file system.

- **Comment.** Comments that will be associated with your generated objects.

- **Prompt For Overwrite.** Specifies that you want PowerBuilder to prompt you before overwriting the output file if a library with the same name already exists.

- **Clear Output Library For Each Build.** Check this option if you want PowerBuilder to delete the existing PBL and create a new one that contains the generated proxy objects. If you clear this checkbox, PowerBuilder will add the generated proxy objects to the existing library if one with the same name already exists.

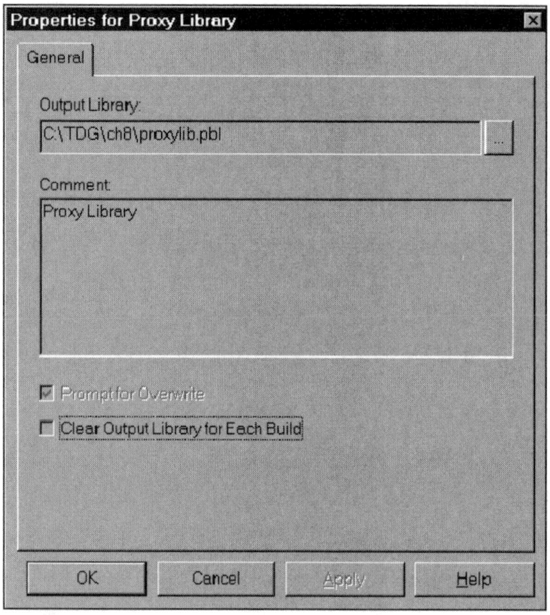

Figure 24.3
Properties for the proxy library.

To select objects for a proxy library, use the Edit|Select Options menu item. You'll be prompted with the dialog box shown in Figure 24.4 to select an object. The PBLs in your library search path will be listed in the Libraries section of the dialog box. To select a PBL, check the checkbox next to it. This will list all the User objects contained in that PBL in the Objects section of the dialog box. Check the checkbox next to each object that you want in your proxy library. Finally, select Design|Build Project to create the library.

C++

The C++ generator lets you build C++ files for a custom class User object. To create C++ files, click the Project Painter and then double-click the C++ icon in the New Project dialog box (refer back to Figure 24.1).

The C++ project generates C++ header files and source or binary files that are equivalent to the NVOs you specify. If you generate C++ files for an NVO, you'll need to write C++ code to access the object's methods. The properties for the proxy library can be set by selecting the Edit|Design menu item. Here's a list of the properties:

- **Header.** Lets you specify the name and location of the generated header file.

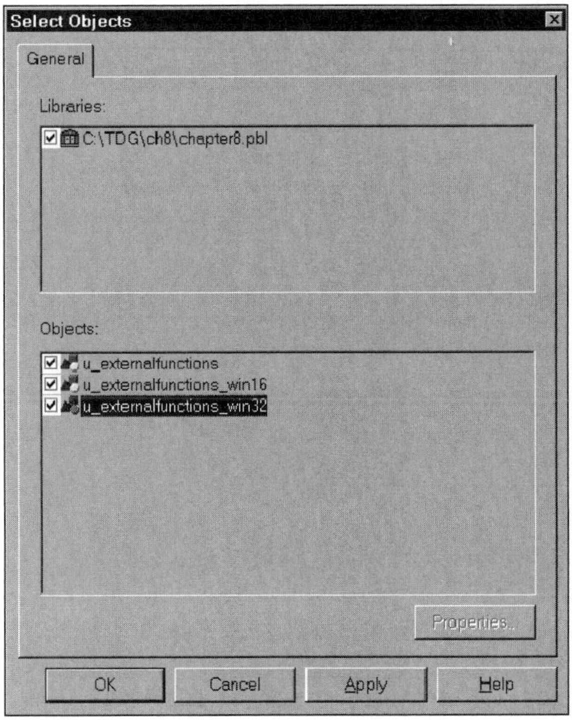

Figure 24.4
Selecting objects for a proxy library.

- **Create Binary.** This option generates a binary file. The default is to generate a C++ source file.

- **Source Or Binary.** This options lets you specify the name and location of the generated source or binary file.

- **Use Exceptions.** Check this option to generate code that supports C++ exceptions.

- **Comments.** You can specify comments that will be associated with the generated objects.

The procedure to generate C++ files is very much the same as the steps taken to generate a proxy library.

Moving On

PowerBuilder 6.0 includes a new project generator infrastructure that enables you to create various targets. The most common target created is the application target, which compiles your programs into Pcode or machine code targets. The project generator allows you to build proxy objects and C++ files from your NVOs. In this chapter, we discussed these targets.

You should note that support for component generators that create CORBA, DCOM, and other standard object types from your PowerBuilder-developed objects will be available in the future. These generators are simply plug-ins. Once installed, they will appear in the Project Painter. Now that you've built an executable, we'll cover deployment next.

Deployment 25

Your development is over, you've successfully created the executable version of your application, and now it's time to deliver your masterpiece to your users. This phase of your project simply involves installing all the right pieces in the right places.

In this chapter, I'll cover some of these pieces to assist you in better organizing your deployment process. I'll start with the deployment kit, the new deployment DLLs, and some of the issues surrounding them. I then talk about ODBC drivers, native drivers, client database software, and OCX/ActiveX components. I'll also suggest a few methods for automating your deployment. Finally, I'll discuss the new PowerBuilder synchronization tool.

The Deployment Kit

The deployment kit consists of four different components that you can install from your PowerBuilder CD-ROM onto your users' PCs:

- The deployment DLLs
- ODBC database drivers
- PowerBuilder database interfaces (native drivers)
- Sybase SQL Anywhere (if this database is used)

Let's take a closer look at each one of these components.

PowerBuilder Deployment DLLs

Good news! The deployment DLLs are now much smaller than they used to be. In PowerBuilder 6.0, several of the DLLs have been combined and reduced in size. For some applications, the deployment DLLs may consist of only one file—PBVM60x.DLL—the PowerBuilder virtual machine.

As you use specific features of PowerBuilder in your application, you need to deploy other needed DLLs for those features. Remember that in 6.0, deployment DLLs have different names for different environments. In Table 25.1, the "x" in the file name is replaced with a letter for deployment platforms other than the ANSI version of Windows 95 and NT. For example, if your application uses DataWindows, PBDWE60x.DLL is needed. You'll need to deploy PBDWE60.DLL on 32-bit Windows platforms, PBDWE60w.DLL on 16-bit platforms, and PBDWE60U.DLL if you developed your application with PowerBuilder for Unicode and are deploying on a version of Windows NT that supports the Unicode standard.

If your application uses ODBC, you need PowerBuilder's ODBC interface PBODB60x.DLL and PBODB60x.INI as well as the ODBC driver for your particular database. If you're connecting to your database via a native driver, you need to deploy the associated native DBMS driver. For example, the native driver for Sybase System 11 CT-Lib is PBSYC60x.DLL.

Table 25.1 Deployment DLLs.

Purpose	File Name	Windows 3.x	Windows 95/NT
For all	PBVM60x.DLL	Yes	Yes
DataWindow	PBDWE60x.DLL	Yes	Yes
RichText	PBRTC60x.DLL	Yes	Yes
OLE	PBOUI60w.DLL	Yes	No
OLE Server	PBAEN60.tlb	No	Yes
For all	PBBGR60w.DLL	Yes	No
For all	PBTYP60w.DLL	Yes	No
For all	PBVBX60w.DLL	Yes	No
DataWindow plug-in	NPDWE60x.DLL	Yes	Yes
Window lug-in	NPPBA60x.DLL	Yes	Yes
Secure Window plug-in	NPPBS60x.DLL	Yes	Yes
Window ActiveX	PBRX60x.OCX	No	Yes
Secure Window ActiveX	PBRXS60x.OCX	No	Yes
Synchronizer	PBSYNCx.DLL	Yes	Yes
Winsock	PBWSD60w.DLL	Yes	No

Note: Make sure you have the correct set of deployment DLLs installed. If your application is 16 bit, you need the 16-bit deployment DLLs. Also, if you want to install 16-bit and 32-bit applications on the same machine, make sure the executables point to the correct deployment DLLs (the 16-bit DLLs have a "W" appended to them—for example, PBVM60w.DLL).

After installing the runtime DLLs, you need to make sure your operating system is able to locate these files when your application is launched. This generally requires you to update your AUTOEXEC.BAT or the Windows Registry.

The Registry

The directory for the deployment DLLs should be added to your application's App Path path in the Registry. Every executable should have an App Path entry. For example, here's the App Path for SALES.EXE: HKEY_LOCAL_MACHINE\Software\Microsoft\Windows\CurrentVersion\App Path\sales.exe.

Let's go through adding an App Path entry to the Windows Registry:

1. Run REGEDIT.EXE. This file is the Registry editor; it's usually located in the Windows directory. Select the following hives: HKEY_LOCAL_MACHINE\Software\Microsoft\Windows\CurrentVersion\App Path.

2. Create a new key by right-clicking App Path. Select New from the pop-up menu and then select Key. This adds a new key, named New Key #1, to your App Path.

3. Rename this key to the name of the application executable file name (for example, SALES.EXE).

4. Click the new key that you just renamed. To the right of this key in a window you'll see a series of subkeys. Double-click Default. Change Value Data to be the path to your executable file. Here's an example:C:\app\sales.exe.

5. Select the menu item Edit|New|String Value; then, change the name of the string value to "Path".

6. Double-click Path. Change Value Data to be the listing of all directories needed by your application, separated by semicolons. Here is an example of this: c:\app\;c:\sqlany50\win32;c:\pwrs\shared.

   Note: To save time, space, and to centralize your application, you could always install your application, the deployment DLLs, and other files on a network. However, you still require proper Registry entries for your components.

Database Connectivity

If your application makes connections to a database, you need to install your database software client and configure it right away. For example, if your application needs a connection to Sybase System 11, you need to install and configure Open Client. Here are the steps to follow:

1. Install your database client software. Make sure you're at the correct bit level. This means that if your application is 32 bit, you need the 32-bit database client software.

2. Configure your database client software. Configure any host, services, and INI files, as needed.

3. Make sure you can ping your database.

4. Make sure you can connect to your database from outside of PowerBuilder. Usually, most database client software provides a tool for querying the database. For example, Open Client provides Sybase Central.

5. Make sure you have deployed the correct PowerBuilder database driver or ODBC database driver. If you're using ODBC, make sure you perform the following tasks:

   • Install Microsoft's ODBC files.

   • Set up your datasources appropriately. This involves making entries to the ODBCINST.INI and ODBC.INI files.

   • Deploy PowerBuilder's ODBC interface.

6. Make sure you have deployed any INI files that populate your transaction object's properties.

ODBC

As I just mentioned, if your application uses ODBC to connect to your database, you need PBODB60x.DLL and PBODB60x.INI. It makes sense to place these files with the rest of your deployment DLLs in the C:\pwrs\shared directory. You also need the Microsoft ODBC files and your ODBC database driver; then, you need to configure your ODBC driver.

Microsoft ODBC Files

The Microsoft ODBC files are usually installed in the Windows\System directory. When deploying, try to stick to the same default directory structure. Table 25.2 lists these files for both the 32-bit and 16-bit platforms. This table also lists the ODBC drivers for both platforms.

Table 25.2 Microsoft ODBC files.

Windows 3.x	Windows 95/NT
CPN16UT.DLL	DS16GT.DLL
ODBC16UT. DLL	DS32GT.DLL
ODBC.DLL	MSVCRT40.DLL
ODBCCURS DLL	ODBC32.DLL
ODBCINT.DLL	ODBC16GT.DLL
ODBCINST. HLP	ODBC32GT.DLL
ODBCADM. EXE	ODBCCP32.DLL
	ODBCCCP32.CPL
	ODBCCR32.DLL
	ODBCINT.DLL
	ODBCINST.CNT
	ODBCINST.HLP
	ODBCTRAC.DLL
	ODBCAD32.EXE

ODBC Database Drivers

Next, you'll need the ODBC DBMS driver your application uses to connect to your database. These drivers are usually from third-party or DMBS-specific vendors. PowerBuilder includes Sybase SQL Anywhere, its ODBC driver, and a few of Intersolv's ODBC drivers. (Refer to the *Connecting to Your Database* manual for more information on these drivers.)

The deployment kit's installation lists all the drivers bundled with PowerBuilder you can install and use. If you need a specific driver that's not bundled with PowerBuilder, you'll have to contact your DBMS vendor. For example, you'll need to get in touch with IBM if you need its ODBC database driver for DB2.

> *Note: Sometimes, having an ODBC database driver is not enough. You may still require your DBMS's client software. For example, if you need to connect to Oracle via Intersolv's ODBC driver, you still are required to have Oracle client software. Refer to your DBMS's manual for additional information on this.*

Configuring ODBC

Finally, you'll need to configure your ODBC driver. To use an ODBC datasource in your application, the ODBC configuration must include the following:

- An entry for the DBMS driver in ODBCINST.INI

- An entry for the datasource in ODBC.INI with instructions on how to start the database

In Windows 3.x, ODBCINST.INI and ODBC.INI are physical files located in your Windows directory. In the 32-bit environment, these files are entries in your Windows Registry. (See Chapter 21, "ODBC," for more information.)

When you install an ODBC database driver from the deployment kit, the necessary adjustments are made to your ODBCINST.INI file. You can examine this by looking at the following Registry keys: HKEY_LOCAL_MACHINE\Software\ODBC\ODBCINST.INI.

All you have to do is configure ODBC.INI. You can use the ODBC Administrator (ODBCAD32.EXE) to do this (see Figure 25.1).

Once you've created your ODBC.INI entries, you can examine them by looking at the following Registry key:HKEY_CURRENT_USER\Software\ODBC\ODBC.INI.

For example, here's what your Registry key would be if your 32-bit application connects to Sybase SQL Anywhere and the name of your datasource is "sales": HKEY_CURRENT_USER\Software\ODBC\ODBC.INI\Sales.

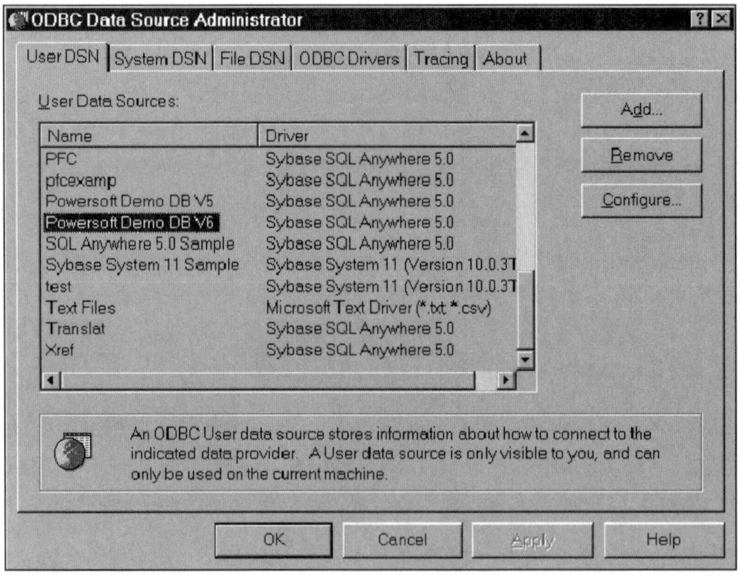

Figure 25.1
The ODBC Administrator.

Here are the values for this key:

- Autostop: yes
- DatabaseFile: C:\DB\PSDEMODB.DB
- Driver: WOD50T.DLL
- PWD: sql
- Start: dbeng50
- UID: dba

> **Note:** *Make sure that the datasource you create on your users' PCs has exactly the same name as the one in your application.*

Sybase Native Drivers

If your application connects to a larger scale RDBMS via a PowerBuilder native driver, you'll need to deploy that native driver. The deployment kit's installation lists all the drivers that you can select and install, as needed.

Once again, it's crucial for you to install your database client software first, test your connection outside of PowerBuilder, and then install your application.

OLE And OCX/ActiveX Deployment

If your application uses OLE automation or an OCX/ActiveX control, the OLE servers have to be installed on the deployed PC. For example, if you use OLE automation to Word or Excel, you have to ensure that these servers are installed.

> **Note:** *Incorporate some sort of error checking in your application to ensure that your OLE server is installed. You can always query the Registry.*

If you use an ActiveX control in your application, you'll need to deploy your ActiveX and all its related files. (These files are usually installed to the Windows\System directory.)

The next step is to register your custom control. If you fail to do so, the container for your control shows up blank. You can use two methods to register your custom control:

- **Use REGSVR32.** This utility registers and unregisters files in the Registry. Here's the syntax used to register or unregister a control:

```
REGSVR32 <activex_name>              //to register
REGSVR32 /U <activex_name>           //to unregister
```

- **Use an external function call.** All custom controls are supposed to be self-registering and contain a method called **DllRegisterServer()**. You can always query the Registry to see if your ActiveX control is installed. If it's not, simply call this external method for the control to Register itself. Here's an example:

```
//external function declaration
FUNCTION long DllRegisterServer() LIBRARY "myactivex.ocx"

//PowerScript to register the server
Long ll_reg
Ll_reg = DllRegisterServer()
//do some error checking…
```

> **Note:** An OCX/ActiveX control usually needs OLE2 system DLLs to be installed and registered. Make sure your users have MFC40.DLL, OLEPRO32.DLL, and MSVCRT40.DLL on their PCs.

If you encounter any error messages while trying to register your ActiveX control, make sure CTL3D32.DLL, MFC40.DLL, MFC40.DLL, MFC42.DLL, OLEPRO32.DLL, MSVCRT40.DLL, STDOLE2.TLB, and WININET.DLL on the deployment PC match the ones on your development PC. (Remember OC25.DLL in the Windows 3.x. environment)

If your ActiveX control is registered properly, it should be at HKEY_LOCAL_ MACHINE\Software\Classes in your Registry. (For Win16, see HKEY_LOCAL_ROOT /CLSID.)

If you're deploying on a Windows 3.x machine, make sure the following DLLs are present in the Windows/System directory:

- COMOBJ.DLL
- OLE2NLS.DLL
- CTL3DV2.DLL
- OLE2PROX.DLL
- OLE2.DLL

- STORAGE.DLL
- OLE2CONV.DLL
- TYPELIB.DLL
- OLE2DISP.DLL

For Windows 95 and Windows NT, the OLE DLLs are part of the system and do not need to be installed separately.

Automating Your Deployment

If your application has to be installed on many PCs, you may want to automate your deployment process. This way, you can compress all your deployment files on diskettes or on a CD-ROM that can be sent to your users.

> **Note:** I usually install my CD image on a network, where my users can run its setup and install the application.

A good installation program usually takes care of the application installation, as well as setting up your ODBC entries (if you're using them) and registering your ActiveX controls. This is the route I recommend you take.

In the previous version of PowerBuilder, InstallBuilder was used for this purpose. If you're used to this program, you may continue to use it. However, PowerBuilder 6.0 Enterprise now ships InstallShield 5. This new installation program provides the most powerful and versatile setup creation technology available today, and it's widely used in the industry.

InstallShield 5 includes a "getting started" document that describes the building blocks of a setup and walks you through the creation of a complete setup. In just a few minutes, you'll be able to create setups that include uninstall functionality and Start|Programs menu access. Also, you'll be able to build disk images optimized for your distribution media. I strongly recommend that you spend a few minutes learning either InstallBuilder or InstallShield—they are both useful tools when it comes to deployment.

PBSync Synchronization

Synchronization refers to keeping your users' application files up-to-date by giving your application the ability to automatically refresh itself with the latest files (which we'll call the *master set*). This means you don't need to deploy maintenance releases. When users run the target application, updated master files are copied to the appropriate locations.

PBSync is the new tool. It consists of an executable, an ActiveX control, and a development environment. PBSync looks immediately for a command-line instruction or a reference to a synchronization data file containing instructions. It then looks at the master files in a location you've specified. It compares the master files to the target files in the locations you specify by checking date/time stamps, sizes, and version information embedded in your executables and dynamic libraries. Finally, it copies or downloads the changed or nonexistent master files to the specified locations.

Your sources for a download can be the following:

- An FTP site

- A local driver

- A network driver

Let's take a look at the PBSync components.

PBSync Data File

The PBSync data file is a text file that gives PBSync its synchronization instructions. Although you can create this text file yourself, you should use the PBSync tool to create it so that the file's structure is maintained by the tool itself.

Most lines of a synchronization data file provide a source and a target. Here's an example of a sync file:

```
[log]
file=
replace=0
verbose=2
[sync]
syncop0=/src C:\dpb\client.pbd /dest C:\Program Files\sales\client.pbd /d /s /v
syncop1=/src C:\dpb\common.pbd /dest C:\Program Files\sales\common.pbd /d /s /v
[variables]
[start]
show=1
cancel=0
```

PBSync Editor

PBSYNC.EXE, the PBSync editor, can be used to create a synchronization data file. As shown in Figure 25.2, to add a new Sync command to the editor, right-click anywhere in the editor and then select New|Sync Command.

In the Command Properties dialog box, you can select a source file from a local driver, network driver, or an FTP site, as well as its destination. (See Figure 25.3.)

Finally, to test your command, click Run.

> **Note:** You can add the PBSync editor to PowerBuilder's PowerBar. To do so, in the [PB] section of the PB.INI file, add a line that points to the location of your PBSYNC.EXE file: **PBSync=C:\pwrs\pb6\sync\pbsync.exe**.

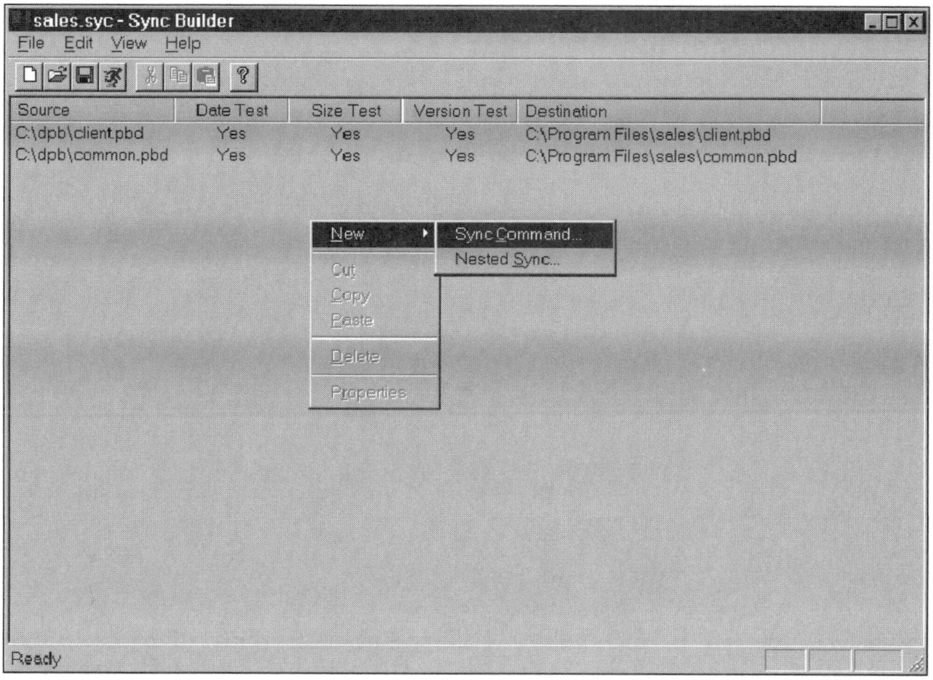

Figure 25.2
The PBSync editor.

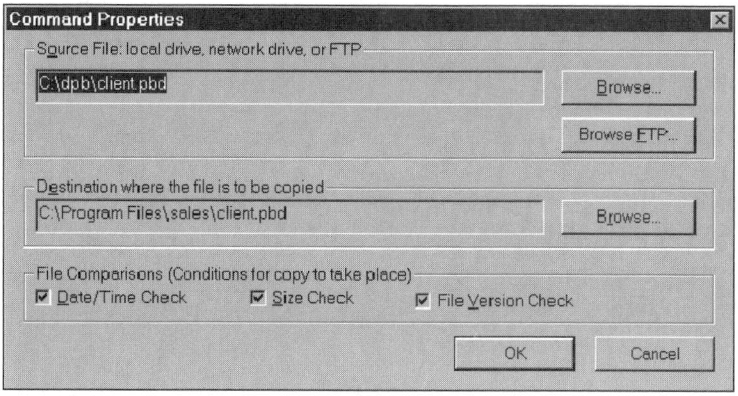

Figure 25.3
Synchronization command properties.

PBSync Runtime Executable

PBSYNCRT is a deployable runtime executable that starts synchronization. When you run PBSYNCRT, it executes the instructions in a synchronization data file and displays a status screen that indicates that file transfer is occurring.

You can run the PBSync runtime executable directly in either of two ways:

- Passing to PBSYNCRT.EXE a command-line argument with one synchronization instruction:

```
c:\pwrs\pb6\sync\pbsyncrt.exe /SRC \\myserver\app\sales.exe /DEST
c:\app\sales.exe
```

- Associating with PBSYNCRT.EXE a synchronization data file that contains synchronization instructions:

```
C:\pwrs\pb6\SYNC\pbsyncrt.exe c:\dpb\sales.syc
```

You can also execute the instructions in a synchronization data file by using the PBSync editor, loading a data file, and running it.

PBSync ActiveX

PBSYNC.OCX, the PBSync ActiveX control, runs a synchronization data file the same way PBSYNCRT.EXE does. However, the PBSync ActiveX control runs either in a PowerBuilder window or in an HTML page.

When you use the PBSync ActiveX control in a window or on a Web page, you'll be using the properties and methods of the ActiveX control. The ActiveX properties are:

- **ShowStatus.** A Boolean specifying whether a status window should display when the data file is run.

- **SyncFileName.** A string specifying the name and location of the PBSync data file.

The ActiveX methods are:

- **AboutBox().** A dialog box displaying information about the ActiveX control.

- **Execute().** Executes the instructions in the data file.

After you insert the ActiveX control in a window or HTML page, you specify the ActiveX control properties by naming the synchronization data file and specifying whether or not to show a status dialog box. Then, you call the **Execute()** method. Now, to use the PBSync ActiveX control in a PowerBuilder window, you need to add an OLE container to your window, associate the container with the PBSync ActiveX control, and then write the script for the control.

Now, if you want to insert the PBSync ActiveX control in an HTML page, here's some sample HTML:

```
<HTML>
<HEAD>
<TITLE>Testing PBSync ActiveX</TITLE>
</HEAD>
<OBJECT ID="synccocx1" WIDTH=0 HEIGHT=0
CLASSID="CLSID:EAE95FC6-A6Ec-11D0-A5D1-00CE3109FF">
        <PARAM NAME="_Version" VALUE="65536">
        <PARAM NAME="_ExtentX" VALUE="0">
        <PARAM NAME="_ExtentY" VALUE="0">
        <PARAM NAME="_StockProps" VALUE="0">
        <PARAM NAME="SyncFileName" VALUE="http://mydomain.com/kgorgani.syc">
</OBJECT>
<BODY OnLoad="Synccocx1.Execute()">
</BODY>
</HTML>
```

Note: If the PBSync ActiveX control does not run in your browser, you may need to lower some browser security settings. This is done by finding the security options of your browser and reducing the security level to medium or even none.

Troubleshooting

You've deployed your application and you can connect to your database. All is fine, but you're having a problem running your application. What do you do, where do you go, who do you call? Well, here's another checklist:

- If you're having database problems, refer to the "Database Connectivity" section, earlier in this chapter. There, you'll find a checklist. Make sure you have followed all the guidelines. If all else fails, run a database trace. A trace file sometimes provides useful information that you can use to troubleshoot your connectivity problem.

- Sometimes, a deployed application will run fine on all PCs except one. If this is the case, you'll have to put your thinking hat on and go through the process of elimination to find the cause of the problem. Ask yourself the question "What is different about this PC?" Here are some things to check:

  - Make sure your problem PC has the correct version of your application.

  - Make sure all the deployment DLLs are in sync.

- Make sure your system DLLs match the ones on other PCs.

- Check your software and hardware configuration. Sometimes, various video drivers and resolution settings may cause problems. Make sure you have the latest video driver installed and that it's the correct one for your video board.

- Make sure all your PCs are running at the same service pack level

- Disable any virus scanners or any other resident programs that may be running in the background temporarily.

- Make sure your problem PC has enough resources. Being low on system resources causes problems.

- If all your applications fail at runtime, run an application trace. Then, analyze the trace file to see where you've gone wrong. Here are some things to check:

  - Make sure all **CREATE** statements are destroyed

  - Make sure all data types are cast correctly

  - Make sure you've checked for return codes

- If you're seeing a specific error message, then find out if it's reproducible and always at the same address. Query the InfoBase databases on Sybase's Web page (www.Sybase.com—Support section, then the Electronic Support Services link) to see what the error message is and if any suggestions are available.

- And, finally, you can always call technical support.

Moving On

We've just covered deployment. As you can see, deployment is quite a considerable task and needs to be given careful considerations. In this chapter, we talked about the deployment kit, the deployment DLLs, issues surrounding database connectivity, and PowerBuilder's new PBSync tools.

The next chapter begins the administration section of the book. We'll start by discussing the topics of performance and fine-tuning your applications.

PART VI
The
Administration
Guide

Performance And Fine-Tuning

PowerBuilder developers generally have questions about performance and managing performance. For instance, you may have been asked by your users to improve the performance of your applications, or you've been meaning to somehow modify your existing applications to enhance their performance.

Users generally want a faster response to the commands they execute. This is performance from their point of view. They demand faster access to their data. You and I both know that a number of factors have an impact on the performance of applications—the load of the server, the network bandwidth, the amount of resources available on the client's PC, the configuration of the client's PC, the database design, and even the application design, itself, might all be important factors in poor performance.

In this chapter, we'll look at some of the most common performance issues and discuss possible solutions and tips that can help change a user's perception of the performance of an application.

Performance Issues

In my experience, the most common performance-related complaint concerns the speed at which an application or a window is opened and the data in a DataWindow is retrieved. Here are the factors that play a role in this issue:

- **Instantiating objects.** This is the time it takes to retrieve an object's class definition, instantiate that object and its related controls, and then execute any scripts.

- **Executing script.** This is the time it takes to actually execute coded methods.

- **DataWindow retrieval.** This is the time it takes to retrieve data from a datasource.

- **Local configuration.** Hardware and software setup on your client and server PCs, as well as your network, plays an important role in performance.

Let's take a closer look at each of these issues.

Instantiating Objects

We'll start by discussing how objects are loaded into memory at runtime. I'm often asked if an entire executable is loaded into memory. This is not so. At runtime, PBSTUB (the Windows bootstrap) is run. It's around 10K. This bootstrap starts off the creation of the Application object, which, in turn, creates the system nonvisuals such as SQLCA and the Error object. Then, the application's **Open** script opens a window or performs other processing based on your code. From that point on, objects are loaded into the class and instance pools, as needed.

PowerBuilder does not load all the objects contained within an executable when you start the application. It loads them when they are needed, because objects are merely resources, not true executable code. Therefore, no matter where you store an object, PowerBuilder is not going to load it until it's needed. Your compiled libraries (PBDs and DLLs) are not loaded into memory when the application opens; however, their search order is. When an object is needed, PowerBuilder searches the executable file first and then the compiled libraries in the order in which they are specified in your library search path. During this search, the index of each compiled library is loaded into memory to be searched. If the object is found, that segment is loaded into memory. The location of the compiled library and the loaded object are recorded in memory as well.

> **Note:** *Place your frequently used PBLs first on your library search path.*

When the object is destroyed and no other instances exist, it is marked for removal from memory. However, it might not be removed immediately. When the memory is needed, it will be overwritten. If the class definition is still in memory when it is needed again, it will be reused rather than reloaded. Classes are removed from the class pool when the last instance is destroyed (or at least marked for deletion) and then deleted if the memory is needed.

> **Note:** *Do not put your objects in your executable. Compile each of your PBLs to PBDs or DLLs.*

Now, let's take a look at some other causes for slow instantiation of objects.

Too Many Controls

When a window is instantiated, it has to construct your menu items and create each control on that window; therefore, too many controls on a window can slow down the instantiation of that window.

> **Note:** *Reduce the number of controls on your windows. Controls are dynamically created during execution—the fewer there are, the faster your windows will open. Use an external DataWindow instead of many window controls.*

Avoid having more than 20 controls on a window. By having too many controls, not only do your windows open slower, they also look crowded and quite confusing to the users.

Create Objects As Needed

Instead of using all static objects, create them as your application needs them. Here are a couple points to consider:

- If you tend to hide and show controls on your windows, use a visual User object for your controls and then use the **OpenUserObject()** function to create them on demand.

- In a Tab control, use the **CreateOnDemand** property of the control to instantiate objects. When you set this property, controls in a tab page instantiate the first time a user selects that page.

Resources

Include your bitmaps, pointers, and cursors and dynamically reference DataWindows in the actual executable file. By doing so, you reduce the number of places your executable has to search for your resources.

> **Note:** *Use a PBR file to include your resources in your executable.*

Also, you should leave your bitmaps at their original size. Do not adjust their size, because Windows does a lot of calculating to scale your bitmaps.

Release Memory

It's important that you release resources that are no longer needed. Your system will run much slower as memory is chewed up by unused resources. In previous versions of PowerBuilder, if you dynamically created User objects using **OpenUserObject()** or **OpenUserObjectWithParm()**, you had to destroy those objects with the **CloseUserObject()** function. Also, if you dynamically created a tab page using **OpenTab()**, you had to close it using **CloseTab()**. In 6.0, however, you no longer need to perform these tasks because they are all part of the control array—you just have to make sure you destroy any **CREATE** statements you use on NVOs.

Screen Redrawing

Screen redrawing is quite a costly operation in terms of time. If you're making many changes to a visual object, consider turning off the redrawing option by using the **SetRedraw()** function. This function controls the automatic redrawing of an object or control after each change to its properties. For example, to turn off redrawing for dw_customer, you would use the following code:

```
dw_customer.SetRedraw(FALSE)
```

> **Note:** If you turn off redrawing, you must turn it on again. Otherwise, you may run into unexpected painting problems. Also, if redrawing is off and you change the **Visible** or **Enabled** property of an object in the window, the tabbing order might be affected.

Regenerate And Optimize

If your application is slow during development time, you should regenerate and optimize your PBLs. As you make changes to your ancestor and descendant objects, regeneration of the ancestor and all the descendants is required. Also, over time, your libraries will become fragmented. Optimizing defragments your PBLs and alters how your objects are organized in the PBLs.

Executing Scripts

Another performance buster is script execution. If you code a script that takes a long time to execute that affects the instantiation of an object, you should consider moving it to a posted event. Let's take a look at some of the events that affect instantiation:

- The **Open** event for a window occurs when the window is instantiated. Your window isn't painted until the script for its **Open** event is completed. Consider moving the script in the **Open** event to a user-defined event and posting this user-defined event from the **Open** event.

- The **Activate** event occurs when a window opens and receives focus for the very first time. The opening of a window could be slow if you have a script in this event that takes a long time to execute.

- The **Constructor** events for the controls on your windows occur when they are instantiated. Having a script in the **Constructor** event that takes a long time to execute slows down the painting of the objects.

- The **GetFocus** event for each control on your window occurs when a control receives focus. Once again, having a script that takes a long time to execute in this event can affect performance.

- The **Resize** event occurs before a window can display. Avoid having a slow script in this event.

- Pass strings and date times as read-only, if possible. This is faster than passing them by reference, because it eliminates the need for PowerBuilder to make a copy. In turn, passing by reference is faster than passing by value.

- Local variables are faster to access than global or shared variables because they are allocated off the physical stack.

Object Functions

An object function executes much faster than a global function; therefore, you should use object functions instead of global functions. By doing so, not only will you get better performance, but you also obey the rules of our object-oriented programming religion.

Another thing to remember is that object functions execute faster than events. If possible, use object functions instead of events. If you need to post an event, you can post an object function instead.

> **Note:** Static functions result in better performance than static events. This is because the existence and location of the static methods are known at compile time. Triggering an event is faster than using dynamic functions, and dynamic functions are faster than dynamic events.

DataWindow Retrieval

If a window opens slowly, look for data retrievals in its **Open** and **Constructor** events. Retrieving data in these events can affect the instantiation of objects and can cause your system to run more slowly. The data has to be retrieved regardless of which event it is in, but you can code the event in such a way that your users actually think the performance of the application has improved. Here are a few techniques to consider when coding retrievals that give your users the impression that your application is performing faster:

- Create a user-defined event and code your retrieval in that event; then post this event to do your retrieval. This way, the window is displayed while the data is being retrieved in the background.

- Use the **Retrieve.As.Needed** property of your DataWindow object to display enough data to fill one DataWindow control; then, retrieve the rest of the result set as needed.

- Avoid coding the **RetrieveRow** event. This event can slow your application down tremendously because it's fired for every row retrieved.

Because the DataWindow object is used quite often, let's go over a few of its performance issues.

Changing Properties Of A DataWindow

To access and change a property of a DataWindow, you can use the **Describe()** and **Modify()** functions, or you can use dot notation to access the property directly. If you're going to modify a single property, use **Modify()** instead of a direct reference. This results in better performance. To modify multiple properties, the **Modify** function's performance is still a little faster than direct reference.

Sharing Data

If you have to view similar data in multiple DataWindows, try to use the **ShareData()** function to take advantage of the data sharing functionalities of the DataWindow. This way, you use one instance of the data instead of multiple instances.

Copying Data

To copy data or blocks of data from one DataWindow to another, use dot notation to directly access the data. This is much faster than using functions such as **RowsCopy()** or **RowsMove()**.

For example, to copy the entire data from one DataWindow to another, use the following code:

```
dw_2.Object.Data = dw_1.Object.Data
```

As another example, to copy selected rows from one DataWindow to another, use the following code:

```
dw_2.Object.Data = dw_1.Object.Data.Selected
```

Computed Fields

Having a large number of complex computed fields in a DataWindow can cause your data retrieval to be slow because the computations of your computed fields are performed every time a row is retrieved. Also, these calculations are recalculated when any value that affects a calculation changes. If your DataWindow is slow, avoid using too many complex computed fields.

Slide Columns And AutoHeight

Using slide columns and AutoHeight sizing creates additional computations for the DataWindow. If many columns use these features, the DataWindow paints slowly. Once again, if your DataWindow performance is poor, don't use these properties.

Database Design

Data retrievals can also be enhanced by sharpening your physical database design. Having too few indexes on a table slows down the retrieval process.

> **Note:** Indexing columns that appear repeatedly in your **WHERE** clauses improves data retrieval.

Bear in mind that having too many indexes slows down your update process. Therefore, the use of indexes must be balanced. Consult with your database administrator to see what best suits your needs.

Using SQL Cache

For the DBMSs that support SQL caching, the **DBParm** parameter **SQLCache** lets you specify the number of SQL statements that PowerBuilder should cache. By default, this value is set to 0, indicating an empty SQL cache. You can use cache for SQL statements in DataWindows-embedded SQL statements.

For example, to specify an SQL cache of 25, use the following code:

```
SQLCA.DBParm = 'SQLCache=25'
```

If you want to determine an appropriate size for your SQL cache, you can check the value of the **SQLReturnData** property of your transaction object. When you disconnect from your database, the number of hits, misses, and entries in the SQL cache is stored in **SQLReturnData**, as follows:

- **Hits.** The number of times PowerBuilder found a matching statement in the SQL cache.

- **Misses.** The number of times PowerBuilder did not find a matching statement in the cache.

- **Entries.** The total number of statements in the SQL cache. This is determined by your **SQLCache** setting.

Enable Binding

For those DBMSs that support bind variables, PowerBuilder binds input parameters to a compiled SQL statement by default. The **DBParm** parameter **DisableBind** allows you to specify whether or not you want to disable the default binding.

When you set **DisableBind** to 1 to disable the binding, PowerBuilder replaces the input variable with the value entered by the application's user or specified in a script. To disable binding, use the following code:

```
SQLCA.DBParm = 'DisableBind=1'
```

StaticBind

When you retrieve data from a database into a DataWindow, PowerBuilder does not get a result set description to validate your **SELECT** statement against the database before retrieving your data. As a result, the retrieval should be faster, especially when you're accessing the database over a network. If you want to override this default behavior and have PowerBuilder get a description of the result set before retrieving data, set the **DBParm** parameter **StaticBind** to 0. Note that if you set **StaticBind** to 1, your retrieval may become somewhat slower.

System Configuration

Hardware and software configuration can impact the performance of your applications. In many cases, simply giving your users more RAM or upgrading their PCs may help. The following list offers several suggestions that can help improve the performance of your application:

- **Check your RAM.** Your PC might not have enough memory to handle the kind of application you're building. Installing more RAM can help.

- **Get a more powerful PC.** Your PC might not be powerful enough to handle your application.

- **Use disk caching.** You should use disk caching to take advantage of as much memory as possible.

- **Windows 95/NT handles its own virtual memory and swap file.** Check the size of this swap file and, if needed, handle it yourself by increasing its size. (If you're still a Win16 user, you should definitely handle your own swap file. Do not use a temporary swap file.)

- **Defragment the hard drive.** Fragmented hard disks will slow down your system.

- **Use the lowest resolution that meets your needs.** High resolution displays slow down your applications.

- **Avoid running many applications at the same time.** Check your resources and if they are low, avoid running multiple applications simultaneously.

  Note: The tracing and profiling feature of PowerBuilder 6.0 helps you identify areas in your application that you should modify to improve performance. See Chapter 12, "Debugging Your Application," for more information.

Make Your Applications Proactive

Sometimes due to many reasons, you really can't do anything else to improve the performance of your application. If a window takes a long time to open or a DataWindow takes too long to retrieve data, the least you should do is give your users constant feedback. Make your application "proactive." If your application is retrieving but appears to be idle, your users will become impatient and will most certainly complain. To avoid this, the following suggestions may help:

Garbage Collection

Garbage collection is a new feature of PowerBuilder 6.0. In general, PowerBuilder performs garbage collection by periodically checking memory for unreferenced objects and removing them. When a reference is removed from an object, PowerBuilder counts the remaining references to that object. If there are none, that class is removed from memory. Now, if any objects are orphaned in memory, PowerBuilder checks all the reference counts periodically. The garbage collection feature removes unused objects from memory, thus ensuring more efficient memory usage. You can use this feature in the development environment as well as in deployment.

The following subsections describe new functions that allow you to take advantage of garbage collection.

GarbageCollect()

This function allows you to force immediate garbage collection. PowerBuilder makes a pass to identify unused objects, including those with circular references, and then deletes any unused objects. To use this function, you simply call it, like this:

```
GarbageCollect()
```

GarbageCollectSetTimeLimit()

This function specifies the minimum interval between garbage collection passes. Garbage collection passes will not happen before this interval has expired. **GarbageCollectSetTimeLimit()** takes a Long data type argument that's a value in milliseconds set as the minimum period between garbage collection cycles. The return variable from this function is another Long that identifies the interval that existed before this function was called. To set a new interval for garbage collection, use the following code:

```
long ll_newinterval, ll_interval

ll_newinterval = 30000

//set the new interval to 30 seconds
ll_interval = GarbageCollectSetTimeLimit( ll_newinterval )
```

Garbage collection can effectively be disabled by setting the minimum limit to a very large number.

GarbageCollectGetTimeLimit()

This function reads the current minimum period between garbage collection passes. Note that garbage collection will not happen before this interval has expired. **GarbageCollectGetTimeLimit**() returns a Long data type that identifies the current minimum garbage collection interval. Here's an example:

```
long ll_getcollectTime
ll_getcollectTime = GarbageCollectGetTimeLimit()
```

Moving On

For users, performance is the speed with which your application responds to a command. The most common complaint from users involves the speed with which windows are opened and data is retrieved. The issues affecting performance include object instantiation, script execution, data retrieval, and sometimes environment configurations. In this chapter, I offered some solutions and tips for troubleshooting these performance issues. We also talked about PowerBuilder's new garbage collection feature.

In the next chapter, I'll cover the Data Pipeline object. This object is quite useful in administrating data. It allows you to transfer data between objects in the same database, different databases, and even different vendors.

The Data Pipeline

The Data Pipeline object allows you to migrate data between Data objects in a database. The Data Pipeline object makes it easy for you to copy rows from one or more table sources to a new or existing destination table. You can transfer data between objects in the same database or different databases, different servers—and even in different back ends.

The Data Pipeline object can be very useful when it comes to data distribution or synchronization of data among different databases. Although these tasks can also be achieved via other means, using a pipeline eases your workload and makes administration a breeze.

You may never have had to use a data pipeline before, but the day that you do may come sooner than you think. In this chapter, I'll show you how to create a Data Pipeline object and execute it. I'll also cover the object's attributes and methods.

Creating A Data Pipeline Object

Data Pipeline objects are created using the Pipeline Painter. In this section, I'll demonstrate how to migrate a customer table from Sybase SQL Anywhere using ODBC to Sybase SQL Server 11 using the SYC native driver. The first thing to do is to select the datasources, as shown in Figure 27.1.

> **Note:** Your datasource for migrating data can be a predefined query or a stored procedure.

Once you've chosen a source and destination profile, a table listing from the source database's profile is displayed. In this case, select the customer table and then select all the columns to be migrated over. The next screen shows the pipeline's workspace (see Figure 27.2).

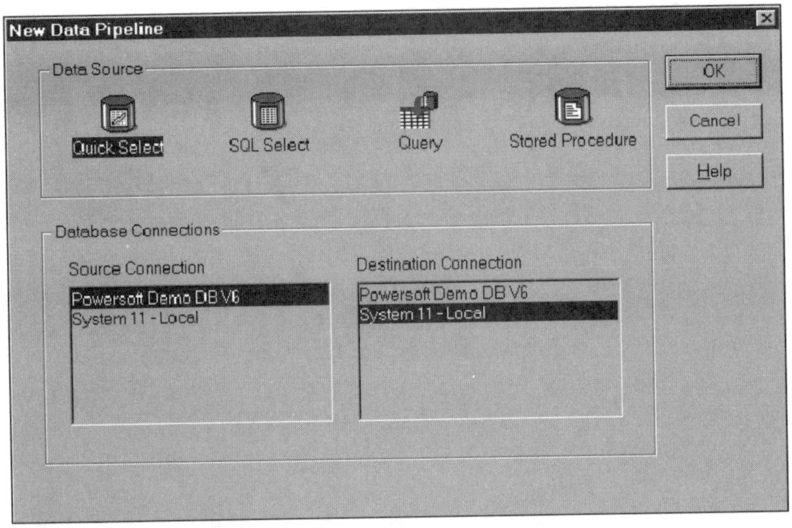

Figure 27.1
Choosing a datasource and destination.

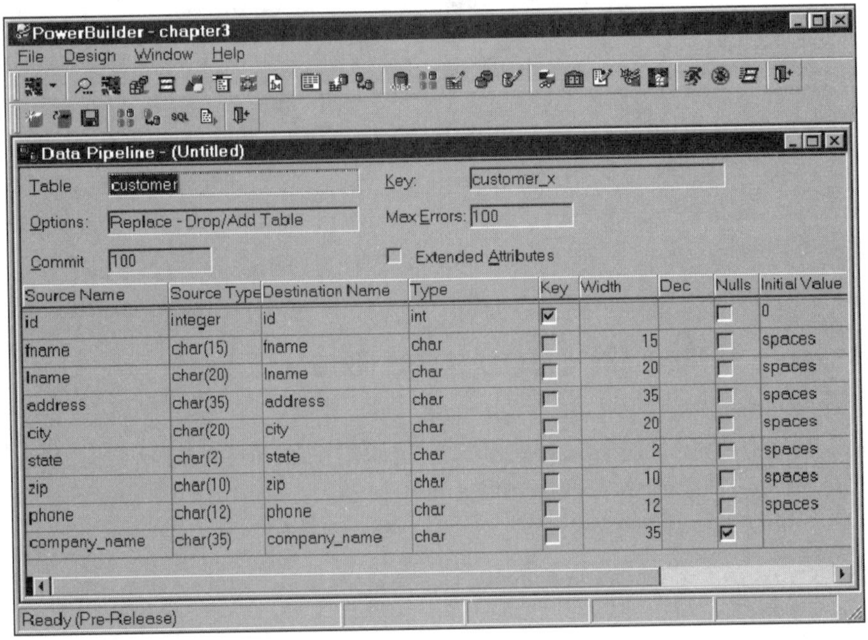

Figure 27.2
The data pipeline's workspace.

Here are some of the characteristics you can define in the pipeline workspace:

- **Source Tables.** You access and retrieve data from these tables.

- **Destination Table.** The table to which you want the data to be pipelined.

- **Piping Operation.** Here are the valid operations:

  - **Create-Add Table.** This option creates a new table in the destination database and copies data from the source table to the newly created table. If the destination table exists, an error will occur.

  - **Replace-Drop/Add Table.** This option drops and re-creates the table in the destination database and copies data from the source data object to the newly created table. No errors will occur if the destination table already exists.

  - **Refresh-Delete/Insert Rows.** This option adds data to the destination table by first deleting all data from the destination table and then copying data from the datasource to the destination table. With this option, the destination object must exist.

  - **Append-Insert Rows.** This option appends data from the source to the destination. Data is not deleted from the destination table before the datasource is inserted, but the destination table must exist first.

  - **Update-Update/Insert Rows.** This last option updates data in the destination table using data from the source table. Any new rows from the source are inserted into the destination, whereas rows from the source that already exist in the destination are updated. With this option, the destination table must exist and the key field must be specified.

- **Frequency Of Commits.** Specifies the frequency of commits during the piping operation. The frequency can be after every x number of rows, after all of the rows are pipelined, or not at all.

- **Number Of Errors.** Specifies the number of errors to allow before the piping operation is terminated.

- **Pipeline Extended Attributes.** Specifies whether or not extended attributes are pipelined to the destination database.

> *Note:* When you define a data pipeline, you can't add Blob columns to it. After a pipeline is defined, however, you can add Blob columns, one at a time, to the pipeline definition. This is done via the Design|Database Blob menu item in the pipeline workspace. This menu item brings up the Blob dialog box (see Figure 27.3), where you specify the source column and table as well as the destination column.

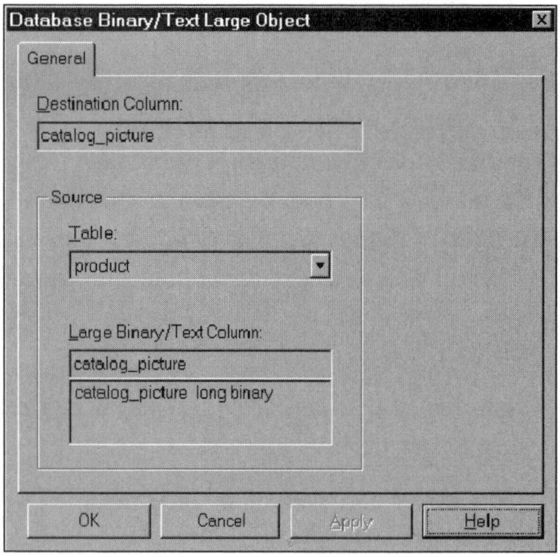

Figure 27.3
Selecting a database Blob column to pipeline.

Finally, you need to execute the pipeline. When the operation is terminated, the status bar will read "Read: 126 Written: 126."

Pipeline In Your Applications

As you can see, using a pipeline in the development environment is not that difficult. However, the Data Pipeline object in the development environment might not support properties and methods that your applications may need in order to handle pipeline execution. To provide the logistical support that your applications can reuse, you must build a User object inherited from the PowerBuilder Pipeline System object. This object contains various properties, events, and functions (all of which are listed in Table 27.1) that enable you to manage a Data Pipeline object during execution of your applications.

Table 27.1 The properties, events, and functions of the Data Pipeline object.

Properties	Events	Functions
DataObject	PipeStart	Start()
RowsRead	PipeMeter	Repair()
RowsWritten	PipeEnd	Cancel()
RowsInError		
Syntax		

The following script creates an instance of the Pipeline User object, assigns a Data Pipeline object to the Pipeline User object's **DataObject** property, and then executes the pipeline. This is basically what was done earlier in the Data Pipeline Painter, but it's the runtime version.

```
//declare your data types
Transaction i_sourcetrans, i_desttrans
PipeLineObject i_myPipe

//create the source transaction
i_sourcetrans = CREATE Transaction
i_sourcetrans.DBMS = "ODBC"
i_sourcetrans.DBParm = "ConnectString = 'DSN=Powersoft " + &
    "Demo DB V6;UID=DBA;PWD=sql'"

//connect to the source transaction
CONNECT USING i_sourcetrans;
IF i_sourcetrans.SQLCode <> 0 THEN
    MessageBox( "Error: " +String(i_sourcetrans.SQLCode), &
        i_sourcetrans.SQLErrText )
    RETURN
END IF

//now create the destination transaction
i_desttrans = CREATE Transaction
i_desttrans.DBMS = "SYC"
i_desttrans.Server = "GORGANI-LAPTOP"
i_desttrans.Database = "dev1"
i_desttrans.LogID = "sa"

//connect to the source transaction
CONNECT USING i_desttrans;
IF i_desttrans.SQLCode <> 0 THEN
    MessageBox( "Error: " +String(i_desttrans.SQLCode), &
        i_desttrans.SQLErrText )
    RETURN
END IF

//now let's create our pipeline
i_myPipe = CREATE u_pipe

i_myPipe.DataObject = "p_pipe"
i_myPipe.Start(i_sourcetrans, i_desttrans, dw_error)
```

Finally, don't forget to destroy your created objects:

```
DESTROY i_sourcetrans
DESTROY i_desttrans
DESTORY i_myPipe
```

> **Note:** When deploying an application that uses Data Pipeline objects, make sure you include your Data Pipeline object in a dynamic library, because an application must always reference its Data Pipeline object dynamically at runtime. You cannot include Data Pipeline objects in an EXE.

Canceling Pipeline Execution

If you need to provide your users with the ability to stop the execution of a pipeline while it's in progress, you have to use the **Cancel()** function. To achieve this, you can provide a function or a command button that lets your users back out from a pipeline operation. Be sure to set the **Commit** property of your Data Pipeline object properly to roll back any changes that have been made to your database. Here's an example:

```
IF i_myPipe.Cancel() = 1 THEN
    MessageBox( "status", "Piping has been stopped!" )
ELSE
    MessageBox( "Status", "Error trying to stop piping!" )
END IF
```

More On Commits

When your Data Pipeline object executes, it commits and updates to the destination table according to the options you've specified. You don't need to write any **COMMIT** statements in your scripts. You may be wondering what happens with committing if your users call the **Cancel()** function to stop a pipeline that's currently executing. In this case, too, the **Commit** property in the Data Pipeline object determines what to do.

If you set the **Commit** value to All, **Cancel()** rolls back every row that was piped by the current **Start()** or **Repair()** function. If you set the **Commit** value to a particular number of rows (for example, 1, 10, or 100), **Cancel()** commits every row that was piped up to the moment of cancellation.

Repairs

When errors have occurred during the pipeline data transfer, the **Start()** function populates its pipeline error DataWindow control with the rows that have caused the errors. Your users or a script that you write can then make corrections to the data. The **Repair()** function is usually associated with a command button that your users can click after correcting data in the pipeline error DataWindow. If errors occur again, the rows that are in error remain in the pipeline error DataWindow. Your users can correct the data again and click the button that calls the **Repair**() function.

The **Repair**() function updates the target database with corrections that have been made in the Pipeline User object's error DataWindow. Here's an example:

```
I_myPipe = Repair( i_desttrans )
```

Moving On

As you can see, the Data Pipeline object is another powerful object that has many potential uses. Using it may save you a lot of time when it comes to moving data back and forth between various tables, databases, and so on.

In the next chapter, I'll cover the Windows Help files. Believe it or not, Help files are very important to your users because they might not be sure about the functionality of a specific part of your application. In order for a deployed application to be complete, it must have a Help file.

Creating Help Files

As a developer, you work quite hard to create a product. As your product is completed, it needs to be deployed to your end users. End users tend to need more than just the application—they need training, documentation, and most definitely online Help.

Unfortunately, documentation is often ignored until the final phase of development. This usually results in the documentation being incomplete or poorly designed. Online Help involves additional effort beyond that required for developing documentation. Therefore, it is sometimes abandoned altogether or is done less adequately than paper documentation.

For your products to be complete, they need proper documentation. If you wish, you can provide your documentation in the form of online Help. It is certainly less expensive to distribute. Also, online Help is rarely misplaced, and, as a result, it is always available to your end users. Online Help provides the ability to hot link and browse, and to search through the documentation much more easily than can be done with conventional documentation. Proper online Help can increase the chances that your end users will actually read your instructions.

If you've ever tried to create Help files, you know what a tedious job it can be. In this chapter, we'll explain the architecture of Help files.

Windows Help Files

A Microsoft Windows Help file (.HLP) is built from several components: a project file, one or more topic files, and an optional contents file. First, let's talk a little about each of these components; then, we'll compile them together.

Project Files

The project file (.HPJ) is an ASCII text file that is used to compile your Help file. The project file contains all the information your compiler needs to combine topic files and other elements into a Help file.

A project file has several sections, and each section in the project file has a different purpose that can be used to improve the effectiveness and usability of your Help file.

[ALIAS]

The [ALIAS] section in your project file associates one set of topic IDs with an alternate set of topic IDs. Alias strings correspond to the IDs assigned by the # footnotes in your topic files. If this section is included, it must precede the [MAP] section in the project file.

Because topic IDs must be unique for each topic and cannot be used for any other topic in the Help project, the [ALIAS] section provides a way to reassign topic IDs that are no longer used or that are invalid. For example, suppose the program defines a context string for each field in a dialog box, but your Help file only provides one topic for all the fields. You can use the [ALIAS] section to map all the program context strings to your one Help topic. In this way, no matter which field the user has selected in the dialog box, Help will display your Help topic when the user requests context-sensitive Help. Here's the syntax:

```
[ALIAS]
context_string = alias-topic_id
```

Context_string specifies the program ID or other topic ID that you want to reassign. *Alias-topic_id* specifies the topic ID that appears in the # footnote of the topic you want Help to recognize. An alias topic ID has the same form and follows the same conventions as a standard topic ID.

[BAGGAGE]

The [BAGGAGE] section lists files that your Help compiler stores within the Help file's internal file system. The files may then be read by a Help DLL. Usually, Help compilers store all file names listed in the [BAGGAGE] section exactly as they are typed. Baggage file names are case-sensitive. To retrieve a baggage file, Help uses the file name without the path. This means that you must specify the file name exactly as it appears in the [BAGGAGE] section.

To access the data from the Help file's internal file system, WinHelp, which runs the Help files, provides callback functions for DLLs so that the DLL can retrieve the appropriate data file from the Help file's [BAGGAGE] section. The {mci} command automatically places its files in the baggage section of the Help file. Here's the syntax:

```
[BAGGAGE]
Filename
```

[BITMAP]

This section is now obsolete and is maintained for backward compatibility only. It's used to specify any bitmaps to be included in your Help files. Here's the syntax:

```
[BITMAP]
Bitmapfilename.bmp
```

[BUILDTAGS]

The [**BUILDTAGS**] section defines the valid build tags for a Help file. Help compilers use the build tags to determine which topics to include or exclude when building the Help file.

This section is used in conjunction with the build tag footnote (*) and the **BUILD** option. The build tag footnote associates a particular build tag with a given topic. If the build tag is included in the [**BUILDTAGS**] section and defined in the **BUILD** expression, Help compilers compile the topic; otherwise, they exclude the topic from the build. Here's the syntax:

```
[BUIDLTAGS]
TAG
```

TAG specifies a build tag consisting of any combination of characters except spaces. Build tags are not case-sensitive, so Help compilers treat uppercase and lowercase characters as the same. Each build tag can have as many as 32 characters.

[CONFIG]

The [**CONFIG**] section contains one or more WinHelp macros that are run when WinHelp opens the Help file. This section can contain macros that carry out actions, such as creating buttons or menus, as well as macros that register routines in external DLLs as WinHelp macros. These routines can then be used the same as WinHelp macros.

When listing macros in the [**CONFIG**] section, include only one macro per line. When a Help file opens, WinHelp runs the macros listed in the [**CONFIG**] section in the order in which they are specified. The following example registers two DLLs, creates a button, and sets the name of the How To Use Help file:

```
[CONFIG]
RegisterRoutine(bmp, CopyBmp, S)
CreateButton(btn_copyart, Copy Art, CopyBmp('pslogo.bmp'))
```

[FILES]

The [FILES] section lists all topic files (.RTF) used to create the Help file. A Help project file must have a [FILES] section. You can create an ASCII text file that contains a list of the topic files you want to include in a build and then use the #include statement in the [FILES] section to specify the ASCII file. Here's the syntax:

```
[FILES]
#include filename
```

[MAP]

The [MAP] section associates topic IDs or aliases with context numbers for context-sensitive Help. The context number corresponds to a value the parent program passes to WinHelp to display a particular topic. Here's the syntax:

```
[MAP]
topic-id          numeric value
```

Topic-id specifies the topic ID of a topic in the Help file. The ID can be any combination of characters (except spaces) and must also be specified in a topic ID footnote (#) in some topic in the Help file. *Numeric value* specifies the context number to associate with the topic ID.

[OPTIONS]

The [OPTIONS] section includes options that control how a Help file is compiled and what feedback the compilation process displays. This section, along with the [FILES] section, is required in all project files. This section should be placed first in the project file so that the options apply during the entire compilation process. Here's the syntax:

```
[OPTIONS]
option
```

Here are the options:

- **BMROOT.** Specifies the folder that contains the bitmap files named in {bmc}, {bml}, and {bmr} references in the topic files

- **BUILD.** Determines which topics to include in the build

- **CHARSET.** Specifies the default character set

- **CITATION.** Adds a citation to the end of any text copied or printed from the Help file

- **COMPRESS.** Specifies how the Help file should be compressed

- **CONTENTS.** Specifies the default topic ID

- **CNT.** Specifies the name of the Help file's contents file

- **COPYRIGHT.** Adds a unique copyright message for the Help file to WinHelp's Version dialog box

- **DBCS.** Specifies whether topic files use a double-byte character set

- **DEFFONT.** Specifies the default font used in WinHelp text boxes

- **ERRORLOG.** Saves compilation messages in a file during the build

- **FORCEFONT.** Forces all authored fonts in topic files to appear in a different font when displayed in the Help file

- **FTS.** Specifies what level of information (if any) to include in the index file for full-text searching

- **HLP.** Specifies the name of the Help file to create

- **INDEX_SEPARATORS.** Specifies the characters WinHelp uses to identify first- and second-level index entries

- **LCID.** Specifies the language of the Help file

- **MAPFONTSIZE.** Maps a font size in the topic file to a different font size in the compiled Help file

- **MULTIKEY.** Specifies an alternate keyword table to use for mapping topics

- **REPLACE.** Specifies a path prefix to replace and its replacement

- **REPORT.** Controls the display of messages during the build process

- **ROOT.** Specifies the folders that contain the topic files listed in the **[FILES]** section

- **TMPDIR.** Specifies the folder in which to place the temporary files that are created while compiling the Help file

- **TITLE.** Specifies the text that appears in the title bar of the Help window when the file is open

[WINDOWS]

The **[WINDOWS]** section defines the size, location, and colors for the primary Help window and any secondary window types used in a Help file. Here's the syntax:

```
[WINDOWS]
window-name="caption", (x, y, width, height), state&buttons, (scrolling-
RGB), (nonscrolling-RGB), state
```

Help Topic

The Help topic is the basic unit of information in your Help file. Topics can range in size from a short example, containing a single picture or word, to a lengthy explanation, involving several graphics and hundreds of words.

A topic contains one or more of the following components:

- **Informational material.** This is usually text, but it can be graphics or multimedia, too.

- **Hotspots.** These are textual or graphical elements that users can click to jump to other topics or to run macros.

- **Footnotes.** These provide instructions to your Help compiler regarding the topic's unique topic ID, the title that will appear in the Topics Found dialog box, keywords that will appear in the index, the position of a topic in a browse sequence, the topic's inclusion in or exclusion from a Help file, and the type of window in which you want the topic to appear.

Topics are stored in topic files and saved in rich text format, one topic to a page. The RTF standard is a method of encoding formatted text and graphics for easy transfer between different programs and different operations. Generally, it's used by all Microsoft Word programs: Word for Windows, Word for the Macintosh, and Word for MS-DOS, for moving word processing documents between different platforms without having to rely on special translation software or conversion utilities. Because the RTF standard provides a format for text and graphics interchange that can be used with different output devices and operating systems, you can use almost any text editor that generates RTF output, including your own custom RTF editor, to create the source files that are built into Help files. You can have any number of topics per topic file, and any number of topic files per Help file.

Software that takes a formatted file and turns it into an RTF file is referred to as an RTF *writer*. Software that translates an RTF file into a formatted file is referred to as an RTF *reader*. An RTF writer separates the program's control information from the actual text and writes a new file containing the text and RTF groups associated with that text. An RTF reader does the converse of this operation. Figure 28.1 illustrates the components of a simple topic file.

Topic IDs

Instructions and commands specific to a topic are inserted as footnote text for that topic. Each footnote is identified by a custom footnote mark, as shown in Table 28.1.

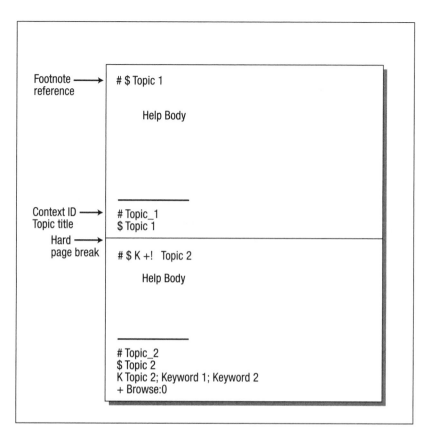

Figure 28.1
A sample topic file.

Table 28.1 Footnote marks representing a Help parameter.

Parameter	Footnote Mark	Description
Topic ID	#	A unique identifier for a topic
Title	$	The title for a topic
Keyword	K	Words used in the index
A-Keyword	A	Words that identify the topic to ALink macros
Browse Code	+	The topic's place in a browse sequence
Entry Macro	!	A macro that runs when the user opens the topic
Build Tag	*	Identifies topics for conditional builds
Window Type	>	Default window type for the topic

Note: Only the topic ID footnote (#) is mandatory. Include the others only if you want the functionality they offer.

Creating A Help File Step By Step

Because I think the process of creating a Help file is somewhat tedious, I'll provide you with step-by-step instructions. This way, you can't go wrong. Follow these steps to create a Help file:

1. Open a new file in a word processor or text editor that can handle rich text format. Write your individual topics, separating each topic with a hard page break.

2. Add appropriate footnotes at the beginning of the file.

3. Save your file in rich text format with the .RTF extension.

Adding A Title Footnote To A Topic

The next thing you want to do is add a title footnote to the topic. To do this, follow these steps:

1. Place the insertion point at the beginning of the topic you want to add a title footnote to.

2. Insert a dollar sign ($) as a footnote mark.

3. Type the title as the footnote text.

Adding A Topic ID To A Topic

1. Place the insertion point at the beginning of the topic you want to add a topic ID to.

2. Insert a number sign (#) as a footnote mark.

3. Type the topic ID name as the footnote text. Please Remember that there are restrictions that you should make a note of:

   • Topic IDs can contain spaces, but avoid leading and trailing spaces.

   • Do not use reserved characters (i.e., # = + @ * % !).

   • 255 characters maximum.

   • Do not begin a topic ID with a number if the ID will also be used in the [**MAP**] section.

Marking A Topic An ALink Target

An ALink macro provides a link to topics by means of keywords listed in topic file and identified by an "A" as the footnote mark. When your users click a hotspot that runs an

ALink macro specifying a keyword, WinHelp jumps to the topic that contains the keyword, or, if more than one topic contains the same keyword, WinHelp displays the Topics Found dialog box listing the titles of the topics. Keywords used in A-footnotes are reserved for use by ALink macros only. To mark a topic as an ALink target, perform the following:

1. Place the insertion point at the beginning of the topic.

2. Insert an A as a footnote mark.

3. Type one or more keywords as the footnote text. Here are some restrictions you should make note of:

    • Separate keywords with a semicolon.

    • Remove spaces before and after keywords.

    • Don't use carriage returns.

    • Don't use more than 255 characters (the maximum) per keyword.

Creating Index Entries For A Topic

To create index entries for a topic, the following steps can be taken:

1. Place the insertion point at the beginning of the topic.

2. Insert a K as a footnote mark.

3. Type a list of keywords as the corresponding footnote text. Here are some restrictions you should make note of:

    • Separate keywords with a semicolon.

    • Remove spaces before and after keywords.

    • Don't use carriage returns.

    • Don't use more that 255 characters (the maximum) per keyword.

Creating A Jump To A Topic Or Pop-Up Topic

To create a jump to a topic or a pop-up topic, the following steps can be taken:

1. Place the insertion point directly after the text or bitmap that you want to be the hotspot; then, type the topic ID of the topic you want to jump to. Do not put a space between the hotspot and the topic ID.

2. Once you've selected the hotspot, apply the double-underline character style if you want another topic to be displayed or apply the single-underline character style if you want a pop-up topic to be displayed.

Adding A Bitmap To A Topic

If you wish to add a bitmap to a topic, follow these steps:

1. Place the insertion point where you want to display the bitmap.

2. To add a single instance of a bitmap, simply copy and paste it.

If you want to use multiple instances of the bitmap, you can create a link to its file by using the following syntax:

```
{bmx filename.bmp}
```

Instead of *x*, specify one or two of the values in the following list:

- **c.** Aligns the bitmap as a text character.

- **l.** Aligns the bitmap with the left margin.

- **r.** Aligns the bitmap with the right margin.

- **t.** Used with any of the above values. Indicates that the white pixels of the bitmap should be converted to the solid color closest to the background color of the window. This can be used only with 16-color bitmaps.

For *filename.bmp*, specify the name of your bitmap file.

Add Video Or Animation To A Topic

Another optional feature that can be added to your Help files is video or animation. To do so, follow these steps:

1. Place the insertion point where you want to add the multimedia file.

2. Type the reference using the following syntax:

   ```
   {mci filename.ext}
   ```

Instead of *filename.ext*, specify the name of the multimedia file you want to add.

The Contents File

The contents (.CNT) file is an ASCII text file that provides the instructions for the Contents tab in the Help Topics dialog box. Also, it directs WinHelp to display the keywords of specified Help files on the Index and Find tabs.

You design your table of contents by specifying the following items in your contents file:

- **Headings.** Represented by book icons and can contain a group of related topics and other headings. Users display the contents of a heading by double-clicking it.

- **Topics.** Represented by page icons and either display a topic or run a macro when a user double-clicks them. Along with the topic title and topic ID, you can specify which Help file a topic is in, as well as which window type you want the topic to appear in.

- **Commands.** Specify the scope and appearance of your table of contents and index, including the name of the default Help file, the title to display in the Help Topics dialog box, and the names of Help files whose keywords you want to include on the Index tab.

Help System Limitations

The 32-bit technology of Windows enables WinHelp version 4.0 to dramatically expand the capability of the Help system you author. Table 28.2 shows the limitations, if any, of WinHelp.

Table 28.2 Data sheet for WinHelp.

Item	Limit
Help file size	2GB
Topics per topic (.RTF) file	No practical limit
Topics per Help file	No practical limit
Topics per keyword	64,000
Topic footnote length	16,383 characters
Keyword length	255 characters
Hotspot hidden text	4,095 characters
Help title string	127 characters
Topic title string	127 characters
Custom window title string	50 characters
Custom window name	8 characters
Copyright string	255 characters
Browse string	50 characters
Referenced bitmaps	65,535 bitmaps per Help file
File name	259 characters
Font name	31 characters
Font ranges	20 ranges
Error log file	No limit
Citation string	2,000 characters

(continued)

Table 28.2 Data sheet for WinHelp *(continued)*.

Item	Limit
Window definitions	255 per Project file
Window caption	50 characters
Contents file entries	No practical limit
Contents headings	9 levels (indented)
Contents topic strings	255 characters
Contents heading text	No practical limit

Context-Sensitive Help

PowerBuilder provides two types of context-sensitive Help: *keyword* and *application*. You should be familiar with keyword Help by now. This Help displays the topic related to a keyword highlighted in the Script Painter. You can develop your own documentation on your specific functions in a Help file and name that Help file USR050.HLP. When a keyword is highlighted and Shift+F1 is pressed, PowerBuilder checks this Help file before using its own Help file.

Your applications can also refer to any Help files that document a PowerBuilder application. These Help files may be context-sensitive and are created like any other Help files, except that the [**MAP**] section contains a list of context IDs that your applications can use as a parameter in its **ShowHelp()** calls. This PowerScript function provides access to the Microsoft Windows Help system that you've created for your applications. When you call **ShowHelp()**, PowerBuilder starts the Windows Help executable and displays the Help file you specify. Here's the general syntax:

```
ShowHelp( helpfile, helpcommand {, typeid } )
```

The arguments for this function are as follows:

- **helpfile.** A string whose value is the name of the file that contains the compiled Help file.

- **helpcommand.** A value for the help command, which is an enumerated type. Here are the values:

  - **Index!.** Displays the top-level contents topic in the Help file. Do not specify a value for **typeid**.

  - **Keyword!.** Goes to the topic identified by the keyword in **typeid**.

  - **Topic!.** Displays the topic identified by the number in **typeid**.

- **typeid.** A number identifying the topic if **helpcommand** is **Topic!** or a string whose value is a keyword of a Help topic if **helpcommand** is **Keyword!**. Do not specify **typeid** when **helpcommand** is **Index!**.

Help Compilers

Use a Help compiler if you can. If you're brave, you can use the Windows SDK to create your Help files. I personally prefer a GUI tool to do the job for me.

A number of good Help compilers that enable you to create Help files quickly are available in the market today. However, you still need to know how to create your .RTF files, and that's where this chapter comes in quite handy.

Here are some of the good Help compilers currently available in the market:

- Doctor Help
- Microsoft Windows Help Compiler
- Microsoft's Help Workshop

Moving On

In this chapter, we discussed Help files. As you can see, documentation completes a deployed application, and this documentation can be in the form of online Help. This chapter has explained the components behind Help files and how they should be constructed.

In the next chapter, I'll cover Distributed PowerBuilder. This feature gives you the ability to partition your applications and run your business logic completely separate from the client piece.

PART VII
The
Comprehensive
Guide

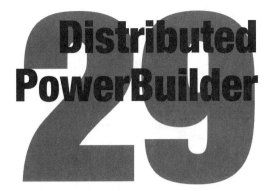

Distributed PowerBuilder

Distributed PowerBuilder was first introduced in version 5 of PowerBuilder. It provides the ability to build applications that can run in a distributed computing environment. You can create objects that contain business rules and distribute them onto one or more application servers that process your client application's requests. This *multitier* environment allows for an unlimited number of application servers.

The distributed features of PowerBuilder 6.0 have been greatly enhanced. It's a joy to build distributed applications because of the many new technologies available. In this chapter, I'll cover distributed PowerBuilder. I'll start with the architecture of distributed computing; then, I'll cover some of PowerBuilder's distributed features, such as various communication drivers, shared objects, asynchronous processing, server push, and proxy library.

The Architecture

Distributed computing is an intrinsic evolution of network computer systems in the client/server architecture. In the client/server environment, the process of developing and deploying business applications presents some difficult problems. The most common problem is the fact that the network computer system does not make it possible to deploy application components in a central location. The business logic required for an application is deployed on the client computer, as shown in Figure 29.1, making maintenance and security difficult. In this model, sometimes called the *two-tier model,* controlling access to information is extremely difficult. Also, when all the business logic for an application is deployed onto the client, the computer's resources seem to disappear quickly, not to mention the fact that this model puts a heavy burden on the amount of network traffic. Sometimes the business logic can be shared with the database server, but not much is gained.

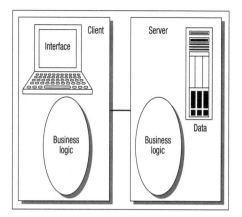

Figure 29.1
The two-tier model.

Distributed computing addresses all these problems by allowing you to partition your application functions between the client and a separate machine called the *application server*. This way, you separate user interface components from the business logic required by your application. By centralizing your business logic on application servers, you can reduce the workload on the client and control access to sensitive information. This approach is called the *three-tier model* and is illustrated in Figure 29.2. PowerBuilder allows you to have many application servers, hence, the *n-tier model*.

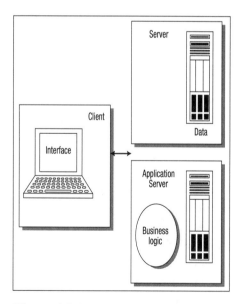

Figure 29.2
The three-tier model.

In a distributed PowerBuilder application, typically you use the services of two separate applications on different machines: a client application and a server application. These two applications work together to fulfill your users' requests. The client application handles all interactions with your users, whereas the server application provides services to the client.

The Client Application

The client applications you build generally contain three main components. The first component is the *user interface*, which handles the interaction with your users. The second component is the *Connection object*, and the third is the *Proxy object*. By now, you should be quite familiar with building a user interface, so let's take a closer look at the last two components.

The Connection Object

The Connection object specifies the parameters that PowerBuilder uses to connect to a server application.

> **Note:** You can customize the Connection object by defining a class User object inherited from the built-in Connection object.

The Connection object has various properties that you must populate before making a connection to your server.

Application
The property of the Connection object specifies the server application to which a client application wants to connect. If you're using a Winsock driver, you can specify the following:

- **The port number for the application.** For example, 13434. Each server application requires a unique port number on the server machine. If you specify a port number, select a number that is greater than 4096. Any number below this number is reserved.

- **The service name for the application.** The service name is an indirect reference to your application's port number. The mapping of the service name to the port number is specified in the TCP/IP services file.

ConnectString
This is the text passed to the **ConnectionBegin** event of the server's Application object at connection time. The text can include application-specific information, such as database connection parameters.

Driver

This is the communications driver that will be used for the connection. Here are the valid values:

- Winsock
- OpenClientServer
- NamedPipes
- Local

ErrCode

This is the code that indicates the success or failure of the most recent operation. Here are the valid values:

- **0.** Success
- **50.** Distributed service error
- **52.** Distributed communications error
- **53.** Requested server not active
- **54.** Server not accepting requests
- **55.** Request terminated abnormally
- **56.** Response to request incomplete
- **57.** Not connected
- **58.** Object instance does not exist
- **62.** Server busy

ErrText

This is the text indicating the success or failure of the most recent operation.

Location

This is the text that specifies the location of the server application. For the Winsock driver, you can specify one of the following values:

- **The host name for the server.** This is specified in your TCP/IP hosts file.
- **The IP address.** For example, 294.99.01.91.
- **LocalHost.** This tells PowerBuilder that the server application resides on the local machine.

Options

This string specifies one or more communications options. If you specify more than one option, you need to separate the options with commas. Note that this option is ignored for NamedPipes and local drivers. For example, you could set **NoDelay=1**, which specifies that each packet is to be sent without delay and corresponds to the **TCP_NODELAY** option. You may want to refer to PowerBuilder's distributed computing manuals for more information on available options. Here's a list of the valid options:

- **BufSize=n.** Sets the buffer sizes used by Windows Sockets.

- **MaxRetry=n.** Specifies how many times the client application will try to connect when the server application's listening port is busy.

- **NoDelay=1.** Specifies that each packet should be sent without delay.

- **PacketSize=n.** Specifies the packet size option used by CT-Lib.

- **RawData=1.** Specifies that raw data should be passed over the network.

Password

This string specifies the password that will be used to connect to the server.

Trace

This string specifies one or more trace options. The trace options are used to troubleshoot client/server connections. If you specify more than one trace option, you need to separate the options with commas. Valid trace options are:

- **Console=1.** Logs all activity to a console window. This option is not supported on the Windows 3.x platform.

- **Level=1.** Enables **Console=1**, **ObjectCalls=1**, and **ObjectLife=1**.

- **Log=filename.** Logs all activity to the specified file.

- **ObjectCalls=1.** Logs each object method call and indicates whether or not the call was successful.

- **ObjectLife=1.** Logs each attempt to create or destroy a remote object and indicates whether or not the operation was successful.

- **ThreadLife=1.** Logs each service thread.

UserID

This string is the name or ID of the user who's connecting to the server. Here are the functions you can use with the Connection object:

- **ConnectToServer()**. Connects your client application to a server application.

- **DisconnectServer()**. Disconnects your client application from a server application.

- **GetServerInfo()**. Allows your client application to retrieve information about its connection to a server.

- **RemoteStopConnection()**. Allows your client application to disconnect another client from a server application.

- **RemoteStopListening()**. Allows your client application to instruct a server application to stop listening for client requests.

In the following example, a client application connects to a server application using the Connection object **myconnect** with the Winsock communications driver:

```
Connection myconnect

myconnect = CREATE Connection
myconnect.Driver = "Winsock"
myconnect.Application = "DemoDPB"
myconnect.Location = "DPBServer"
myconnect.ConnectToServer( )

IF myconnect.ErrCode <> 0 THEN
   MessageBox( "Connection Error", &
      myconnect.ErrText )
   RETURN
END IF

//disconnect and destroy the object
myconnect.DisconnectServer( )
DESTROY myconnect
```

The Proxy Object

Once a connection to a server has been established, the client application can begin using the remote objects provided by the server. The client can call functions associated with remote objects or trigger events defined on those objects.

Each remote object contained in a server application has a corresponding Proxy object in the client application. This Proxy object is a local representation of the remote User object that allows the client application to use the remote object just as if it were a local object. You can create a Proxy object in the Custom Class User Object Painter by right-clicking on the User object and then selecting Set Proxy Name from the pop-up menu and saving your proxy. This proxy is then to be moved to the client application where it can be instantiated and used.

In the previous release of PowerBuilder, to invoke a method of a remote object, you had to use the **CREATE** statement to instantiate a Proxy object. For example, the Proxy object **po_abacus** corresponds to **u_abacus**. To invoke the **uf_add**() method of **po_abacus**, you could use the following code:

```
integer li_result

//create the proxy
po_abacus  myabacus
myabacus = CREATE po_abacus
//connect
myabacus.SetConnect( myconnect )

//call the uf_add function
li_result = myabacus.uf_add( 3, 4 )

DESTROY myabacus
```

> **Note:** The **SetConnect()** function is now obsolete and will be discontinued in future releases. To create an instance of a remote object, use the **CreateInstance()** function instead.

In PowerBuilder 6.0, you can now use the **CreateInstance**() method of the Connection object instead of using the aforementioned method. The **CreateInstance**() function allows you to create an object on your remote server. If you want to create an object locally, you need to use the **CREATE** statement. Let me clarify this a little more. When you deploy a remote object's class definition in a client application, the definition on the client has the same name as the remote object definition deployed in the server application. Variables declared with this type are able to hold either a reference to a local object or a reference to a remote object. Therefore, at execution time, you can instantiate the object locally by using the **CREATE** statement or remotely by using the **CreateInstance**() function. In either case, once you have created the object, its physical location is transparent to client-side scripts that use it. Here's the syntax for using **CreateInstance**():

```
connection.CreateInstance (objectvariable {, objecttypestring })
```

Connection is the name of your Connection object. *Objectvariable* is a variable whose data type is the same class as the object being created or is an ancestor of that class.

Objecttypestring is an optional string that you specify whose value is the name of the class data type to be created.

If **CreateInstance**() succeeds, it returns 0; otherwise, in case of errors, the return codes are as follows:

- **50.** Distributed service error
- **52.** Distributed communications error
- **53.** Requested server not active
- **54.** Server not accepting requests
- **55.** Request terminated abnormally
- **56.** Response to request incomplete
- **62.** Server busy

Assuming that you have the proxy, the following example creates an instance of the **u_abacus** NVO on a remote server and then calls its **uf_add**() method:

```
integer li_result
long ll_rc

Connection myconnect
u_abacus myabacus

ll_rc = myconnect.CreateInstance( myabacus )
//... do error checking ...

IF IsValid(myabacus) THEN
   li_result = myabacus.uf_add( 3, 4 )
END IF
```

The very same object can be instantiated locally, as seen here:

```
integer li_result
long ll_rc

Connection myconnect
u_abacus myabacus

//Create a local object
myabacus = CREATE u_abacus
```

```
IF IsValid(myabacus) THEN
   li_result = myabacus.uf_add( 3, 4 )
END IF
```

You need to use the Project Painter to create a proxy library. Refer to Chapter 24, "Creating A Project," for additional information. You could create a Proxy object for the following reasons:

- To reduce the size of the client application

- To increase security where sensitive code is not delivered to the client

Creating a Proxy object through the Project Painter also reduces the size of the proxy noticeably. For example, if you were to export a Proxy object created via the User Object Painter, you would see this:

```
$PBExportHeader$po_abacus.srx
global type po_abacus from NonVisualObject
   private string ProxyName = "u_abacus"
public:
// public instance variables
// events
end type


forward prototypes
public:
   function long SetConnect (connection theConnection)

   // public scripts from u_abacus
   function integer uf_add (integer ai_var1, integer ai_var2)
   function integer uf_print (datawindow ai_dw)
end prototypes

public function long SetConnect (connection theConnection)
   return theConnection.CreateInstanceFromProxy(this)
end function
```

You would see this export for the very same User object created via the new method through the Project Painter (I'll let you be the judge on this one):

```
$PBExportHeader$u_abacus.srx
global type u_abacus from nonvisualobject
public:
// public instance variables
// events
end type
```

```
forward prototypes
public:
   // public scripts from u_abacus
   function integer uf_add (integer ai_var1, integer ai_var2)
   function integer uf_print (datawindow ai_dw)
end prototypes
```

> **Note:** Before turning your nonvisual objects into Proxy objects, make sure that all instance variables that refer to other nonvisual objects are either private or protected. This results in a smaller Proxy object. And, it also prevents getting compilation errors when compiling the client application.

The Server Application

The server application has two main components: remote objects and the Transport object. Remote objects are nonvisual objects that are contained in an application located on a remote server. The client can invoke methods that are associated with a remote object as if they were defined locally.

To explain the Transport object requires a little more detail. To make your server application function in a distributed environment, you need to use a Transport object to begin listening for client connection requests. The Transport object is a nonvisual object that works like the transaction object in that it's instantiated in a script in the server application. The properties of the Transport object provide information that PowerBuilder needs to process client requests.

The properties of the Transport object are similar to the Connection object, except for the **ErrCode**. Here are the values:

- **0.** Success
- **50.** Distributed service error
- **52.** Distributed communications error
- **55.** Request terminated abnormally
- **56.** Response to request incomplete
- **58.** Object instance does not exist

Here are the two main functions used for the Transport object:

- **Listen().** This function tells a server application to begin listening for client connections.

- **StopListening()**. This function tells a server application to stop listening for client connections.

The following example tells a server application to begin listening for client connections. Note that client applications cannot connect to a server application until the server has executed the **Listen**() function.

```
Transport mytransport

mytransport = CREATE Transport
mytransport.Driver = "Winsock"
mytransport.Application = "DemoDPB"
mytransport.Listen( )

//stop listening & destroy the Transport object
mytransport.StopListening( )
DESTROY mytransport
```

We've now covered both client and server applications. Figure 29.3 shows how these two parts communicate.

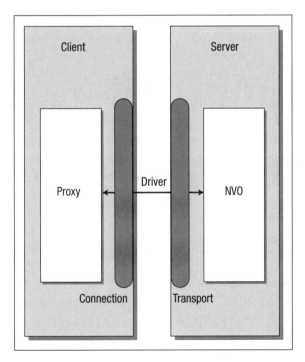

Figure 29.3
Communication between a client and a server application.

Shared Objects

In PowerBuilder version 5.0, when you used distributed functions, you had no way to share memory among clients on a distributed PowerBuilder server. Well, the current version provides support for shared objects. This allows you to work with shared data. *Shared objects* are User objects that can be shared by multiple client connections. Shared objects allow you to provide access to common data that would otherwise need to be retrieved separately by each client connection.

To allow multiple client applications to share a single object, the server application invokes the **SharedObjectRegister**() function to register a named instance of an object. Then, it invokes the **SharedObjectGet**() function to get an object instance that is a reference to that shared object.

The server can perform these operations in its main thread or inside a client session. When the server calls the **SharedObjectRegister**() function, PowerBuilder automatically creates the shared object instance. This eliminates the need for you to issue a **CREATE** statement for the shared object on the server application.

Shared objects are accessible only from the server's main session and from the client sessions created for each client connection on the server. Client applications cannot access a shared object directly. To access a shared object, a client needs to communicate with a remote object that delegates work to the shared object. Often, the remote object has an instance variable that provides a reference to the shared object.

Once the server has registered the shared object instance and has retrieved a reference to the object, client applications can call the methods defined for the shared object by interfacing with the remote object, which in turn passes requests on to the shared object. The methods on remote objects provide indirect access to the methods of the shared object. Typically, these methods have the same names as the methods defined for the shared object. The data types permitted for the arguments and the return value of a shared object method are the same as for a remote object method.

Sessions

At runtime, PowerBuilder creates a separate session for each shared object instance and any objects that the shared object creates. The session for a shared object is created using the Application object definition for the server application.

The shared object session has its own copy of the application's global variables, but the events for the Application object are not triggered. Because of this, if you want your shared object to initialize any variables, you need to code this in the **Constructor** event of the shared object, because the **Open** and **ConnectionBegin** events of the Application object will not be fired.

As other clients make requests for shared object services, these requests are sequentially queued to avoid problems that might arise from concurrent access. This ensures that only one user can modify the contents of a shared object at a time. If an execution time error occurs while a shared object instance is being used, the error is passed back to the client.

Note that a shared object instance is deleted when any of the following events takes place:

- The server application unregisters the object's named instance and no references to the object exist.

- The object is destroyed with a **DESTROY** command.

- The server application has shut down.

> **Note:** A shared object instance is not destroyed when a reference to the shared object is implicitly destroyed by the PowerBuilder garbage collector.

Figure 29.4 illustrates how shared objects are used in a distributed environment.

The following sections describe the functions available for shared objects.

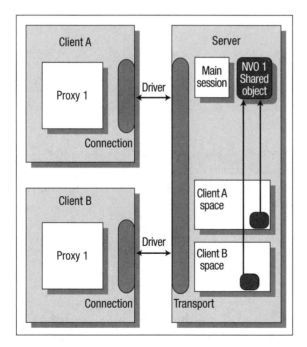

Figure 29.4
Shared objects.

SharedObjectRegister()

As I mentioned earlier, shared objects are only accessible from the server's main session and from the client sessions created for each client connection on the server. Client applications cannot access a shared object directly. Therefore, to register an object to be shared, you need to call the **SharedObjectRegister**() function inside the server's execution context or in a client session on the server. Here's the syntax for calling the **SharedObjectRegister**() function:

```
SharedObjectRegister( classname, instancename )
```

Classname is the name of the User object you want to share. *Instancename* is the name you want to assign to the shared object instance.

The return value from **SharedObjectRegister**() can be one of the following:

- **Success!**. Indicates that your function has succeeded.

- **FeatureNotSupportedError!**. Indicates that the function is not supported on the Windows 3.x and Macintosh platforms (so you shouldn't be calling it).

- **SharedObjectExistsError!**. Indicates that the shared object instance name has already been used.

- **MutexCreateError!**. Indicates that an operating system locking mechanism could not be obtained.

- **SharedObjectCreateInstanceError!**. Indicates that the specified object could not be created.

- **SharedObjectCreatePBSessionError!**. Indicates that a PowerBuilder context session could not be created for the object.

In the following example, the server application registers the User object **u_abacus** so that it can be shared. The name assigned to the shared object instance is "myshare". After registering the object, the server application uses the **SharedObjectGet**() function to store an instance of the object in an object variable.

```
SharedObjectRegister("u_abacus","myshare")
SharedObjectGet("myshare", luo_share )
```

SharedObjectGet()

SharedObjectGet() retrieves a reference to an object that was created with **SharedObjectRegister**(). Once you've obtained the object reference, you can access the object's methods and properties just as you would with any other object. Here's the syntax for using the **SharedObjectGet**() function:

```
SharedObjectGet( instancename, objectinstance)
```

Instancename is the name of a shared object instance. The name you specify must match the name given to the object instance when it was first registered with the **SharedObjectRegister**() function. *Objectinstance* is an object variable in which you want to store an instance of a shared object.

The return value from **SharedObjectGet**() can be one of the following:

- **Success!**. Indicates that your function has succeeded.

- **FeatureNotSupportedError!**. Indicates that the function is not supported on the Windows 3.x and Macintosh platforms.

- **SharedObjectNotExistsError!**. Indicates that the shared object instance name has not been registered.

In the following example, the server application gets a shared object instance from the object registered as **myshare** and stores this instance in the variable **luo_share**. The server application then uses the object instance to call the **uf_add**() function.

```
u_abacus luo_share
integer li_result

SharedObjectGet("myshare", luo_share)
li_result = luo_share.uf_add( 3,4 )
```

SharedObjectUnregister()

To unregister a shared object, you need to call the **SharedObjectUnregister**() function inside the server's execution context or in a client session on the server. Here's the syntax for calling the **SharedObjectUnregister**() function:

```
SharedObjectUnregister ( instancename )
```

Instancename is the name assigned to the shared object instance when it was first registered.

The return value from **SharedObjectUnregister**() can be one of the following:

- **Success!**. Indicates that the function has succeeded.

- **FeatureNotSupportedError!**. Indicates that the function is not supported on the Windows 3.x and Macintosh platforms.

- **SharedObjectNotExistsError!**. Indicates that the shared object instance name has not been registered.

In this example, the server application unregisters the object instance **myshare**:

```
SharedObjectUnregister("myshare")
```

SharedObjectDirectory()

To retrieve the list of registered objects, you need to call the **SharedObjectDirectory**() function inside the server's execution context or in a client session on the server. Here's the syntax for calling the **SharedObjectDirectory**() function:

```
SharedObjectDirectory( instancenames {,classnames} )
```

Instancenames is an unbounded array of type **String** in which you want to store the names of objects that have been registered. *Classnames* is another unbounded array of type **String** in which you want to store the class names of registered objects

The return value from **SharedObjectDirectory**() can be one of the following:

- **Success!**. Indicates that your function has succeeded.

- **FeatureNotSupportedError!**. Indicates that this function is not supported on the Windows 3.x and Macintosh platforms.

In this example, the server application retrieves the list of shared objects and their class names:

```
integer li_rc
string a_instances[]
string a_classes[]

li_rc = SharedObjectDirectory( a_instances, a_classes )
```

> *Note:* You cannot pass a visual object to a shared object. To do so, it must be wrapped in a nonvisual object.

Server Push

Server push is a distributed technique in which the server application can send messages back to the client application. Using Server push is particularly useful when the client application needs to be notified when an asynchronous request has been completed. You will see how this is done in the Chat application on the accompanying CD-ROM.

Now, your server applications can make both synchronous and asynchronous calls against client objects. The client handles server requests the same way the server handles client requests. Asynchronous requests against a client object are queued and processed after all synchronous requests are processed.

To communicate with the client, the server needs to know which client object to communicate with. Because of this, the client must pass an object reference to the server. When the server receives this object reference, it creates a remote reference to the client object and calls functions associated with this object. Function calls made against the remote reference are passed back to the client that contains the object.

> **Note:** *To ensure that messages are actually sent to the client-side object, the client must not pass an autoinstantiated object to the server. Instead, the client must pass a reference to an object that is created with the **CREATE** statement.*

In the following example, the client application makes an asynchronous call to a remote object function. When the server has finished processing, it sends a message back to notify the client that the request has been processed.

```
Connection myconnect

u_abacus  myabacus
u_msgs mymsgs

myconnect.CreateInstance( myabacus )
mymsgs= CREATE u_msgs

myabacus.POST uf_doCalculations( mymsgs )
```

The **uf_doCalculations**() function on the **u_abacus** object takes an argument of type **u_msgs**. Once calculations are done, the server sends an asynchronous message back to the client as seen here:

```
messageobject.POST uf_DisplayCompleted()
```

This request is added to the client's request queue. The **uf_DisplayCompleted**() function on the **u_msgs** object displays a visual text that the calculation is completed.

Asynchronous Processing

In synchronous processing, when a client application makes a request, the server application executes the function immediately and the client has to wait until the server has completed processing the request. When a client application issues an asynchronous call, the server adds the request to a queue and performs the processing at a later point in time. This way, the client can continue to do other processing while the server handles the request.

Asynchronous calls are first queued locally so that the calling function can continue to execute immediately. As each request is pulled off of the local queue, it's sent to the server, where it's added to the client session's asynchronous request queue. Requests are then executed one after another in the order they are received.

If a synchronous call comes in after several asynchronous calls have been made, the synchronous call is executed as soon as possible. Asynchronous requests against a particular object will be processed after all synchronous requests made against this object.

To make an asynchronous function call, you need to call the remote object function with the **POST** keyword. For example, the following script instantiates a remote object on the server and makes an asynchronous call to a function of the remote object:

```
Connection myconnect
u_abacus myabacus

myconnect.CreateInstance( myabacus )
mycustdata.POST uf_add( 3,4 )
```

Note that the following restrictions apply to asynchronous function calls made to remote objects:

- If the function returns a value, the return value will be ignored.

- The client cannot pass parameters by reference in an asynchronous call. Arguments passed by reference will not cause errors at compile time, but they will result in errors at execution time. So be warned!

- The client cannot poll to determine whether or not an asynchronous request has been processed. To notify a client that a request has been processed, the server can send a message back to the client.

- All asynchronous calls are executed in the order they're received. However, the exact timing of function execution cannot be guaranteed.

- If the server or the client crashes, execution of queued asynchronous or synchronous requests cannot be guaranteed. If the server crashes, any queued requests will be lost.

> **Note:** On the accompanying CD-ROM, you'll find a great distributed PowerBuilder chat application. This application uses most of the new distributed features and also follows the object-oriented programming guidelines very closely. Make sure that you read the readme.txt file first and then adjust the INI files and the library search paths as needed. The server runs on one PC, and the clients can run on multiple PCs. The clients send text messages to the server; the server distributes the text messages back to all the clients. Figure 29.5 shows the server.

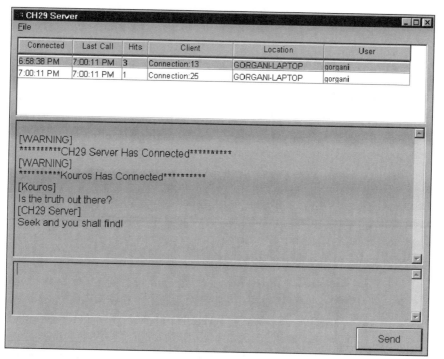

Figure 29.5

The demo chat server application.

DataWindow Synchronization

DataWindow synchronization is the process of managing DataWindow buffers and its status flags in distributed applications that access databases. In a typical client/server application where a single client application performs database updates, PowerBuilder manages the DataWindow state information automatically for you. But, in a distributed application, because your application components are partitioned between the client and the server, you need to write code to manage and synchronize the DataWindow buffers and its status flags on the client with those for the DataStore on the server.

To synchronize a DataWindow control on the client with a DataStore on the server, you need to move the DataWindow data buffers and status flags back and forth between the client and the server whenever changes occur. The procedures for doing this are essentially the same whether the source of the changes resides on the client or the server.

To apply complete state information from one DataWindow or a DataStore to another, you need to follow these steps:

1. Invoke the **GetFullState()** function to capture the current state of the source DataWindow.

2. Invoke the **SetFullState()** function to apply the state of the source DataWindow to the target.

To apply changes from one DataWindow or a DataStore to another, follow these steps:

1. Invoke the **GetChanges()** function to capture the changes from the source DataWindow.

2. Invoke the **SetChanges()** function to apply the changes from the source DataWindow to the target.

When you call **GetFullState()** or **GetChanges()**, PowerBuilder returns DataWindow state information in a Blob. The Blob returned from **GetFullState()** provides everything required to re-create the DataWindow, including the data buffers, status flags, and complete DataWindow specification. The Blob returned from **GetChanges()** provides data buffers and status flags for changed and deleted rows only.

As you know already, the **Update()** function resets the update flags after successfully completing the update. Therefore, when you call the **Update()** function on the server, the status flags are automatically reset for the server DataStore. However, the update flags for the corresponding client DataWindow control are not reset. Therefore, after issuing the **Update()** function on the server DataStore, you need to recapture the status flags for the server DataStore by using **GetChanges()**; then you pass the resulting Blob back to the client and call **SetChanges()** to apply the status flags to the client DataWindow.

The following subsections describe the functions that have been added for DataWindow synchronization.

GetFullState()

GetFullState() retrieves the entire state of a DataWindow or DataStore into a Blob, including the DataWindow object specification, the data buffers, and the status flags. When you set **SetFullState()** to apply the Blob created by **GetFullState()** to another DataWindow, the target DataWindow has enough information to re-create the source DataWindow.

Because the Blob created by **GetFullState()** contains the DataWindow object specification, a subsequent call to **SetFullState()** will overwrite the DataWindow object for the target DataWindow control or DataStore. If the target of **SetFullState()** does not have a DataWindow object associated with it, the Blob will assign one. In this case, **SetFullState()** has the effect of setting the **DataObject** property for the target.

Here's the syntax for using **GetFullState()**:

```
dwcontrol.GetFullState( dwblob )
```

Dwcontrol is the name of the DataWindow control or DataStore for which you want to retrieve state information. *Dwblob* is a Blob into which the returned DataWindow will be placed.

The return value from **GetFullState()** is the number of rows in the DataWindow Blob if it succeeds, and -1 if an error occurs.

The following example retrieves data into a DataStore and uses **GetFullState()** to retrieve the complete state of the DataStore into a Blob:

```
lblob_customer Datastore ids_myds
Long ll_rows

ids_myds = CREATE Datastore
ids_ myds.DataObject = "d_customer"
ids_ myds.SetTransObject( SQLCA )

ids_ myds.Retrieve()

ll_rows = ids_ myds.GetFullState( lblob_customer )
```

SetFullState()

GetFullState() retrieves the entire state of a DataWindow or DataStore into a Blob, including the DataWindow object specification, the data buffers, and the status flags. When you use **SetFullState()** to apply the Blob created by **GetFullState()** to another DataWindow, the target DataWindow has enough information to re-create the source DataWindow.

Here's the syntax for using **SetFullState()**:

```
dwcontrol.SetFullState( dwblob )
```

Dwcontrol is the name of the DataWindow control or DataStore to which you want to apply the Blob. *Dwblob* is a Blob that contains the state information you want to apply to the DataWindow control or DataStore.

SetFullState() returns -1 if an error occurs or one of the following values if it succeeds:

- 1. DataWindow objects match.

- **2.** DataWindow objects do not match.

- **3.** No DataWindow object is associated with the DataWindow control or DataStore; a new one is assigned from the DataWindow Blob.

The following example in a distributed client application calls a remote object function that retrieves database information into a DataStore and puts the contents of the DataStore into a Blob by using **GetFullState()**. After the server passes the Blob back to the client, the client uses **SetFullState()** to apply the Blob to a DataWindow control.

```
Connection myconnect
uo_customer iuo_customer

Blob lblob_customer
long ll_rows

myconnect.CreateInstance( iuo_customer )
iuo_customer.RetrieveData( lblob_customer )

ll_rows = dw_customer.SetFullState( lblob_customer )

IF ll_rows = -1 THEN
    MessageBox( "Error", "SetFullState call failed!" )
END IF
```

GetChanges()

The **GetChanges()** function retrieves changes made to a DataWindow or DataStore into a Blob. **GetChanges()** is used in conjunction with **SetChanges()** to synchronize two or more DataWindows or DataStores. **GetChanges()** retrieves data buffers and status flags for changed rows in a DataWindow or DataStore and places this information in a Blob.

Here's the syntax for calling the **GetChanges()** function:

```
dwcontrol.GetChanges( dwblob {,cookie} )
```

Dwcontrol is the name of the DataWindow control or DataStore for which you want to get changes. *Dwblob* is the Blob into which the returned DataWindow changes will be placed.

Cookie is an optional read-only Blob created by the **GetStateStatus()** function that's compared with *changeblob* to determine the likely success of a subsequent call to **SetChanges()**.

The return code is the number of rows in the DataWindow change Blob if successful, or one of the following if it fails:

- **-1.** Indicates that an internal error has occurred.

- **-2.** Indicates that a conflict exists between the state of the DataWindow change Blob and the state of the DataWindow from which the cookie was created.

- **-3.** Indicates that a conflict exists between the state of the DataWindow change Blob and the state of the DataWindow from which the cookie was created.

The following example uses the **GetChanges()** function to capture changes to a DataWindow control on a client. If **GetChanges()** succeeds, the client calls a remote object function that applies the changes to a DataStore on the server and updates the database.

```
Blob lblob_changes
long ll_rows

ll_rows = dw_customer.GetChanges( lblob_changes )

IF ll_rows = -1 THEN
    MessageBox("Error", "GetChanges call failed!")
ELSE
    iuo_customer.UpdateData( lblob_changes )
END IF
```

SetChanges()

The **SetChanges()** function is used in conjunction with the **GetChanges()** function to synchronize two or more DataWindows or DataStores. **GetChanges()** retrieves data buffers and status flags for changed rows in a DataWindow or DataStore and places this information in a Blob. **SetChanges()** then applies the contents of this Blob to another DataWindow or DataStore.

To determine the likely success of **SetChanges()**, follow these steps:

1. Call the **GetStateStatus()** function of the DataStore on which you want to use **SetChanges()**. **GetStateStatus()** checks the state of the DataStore and makes the state information available in a reference argument called a *cookie*. The cookie is generally much smaller than a DataWindow change Blob.

2. Send the cookie back to the client.

3. Call the **GetChanges()** function on the DataWindow from which you want to apply changes, passing the cookie retrieved from **GetStateStatus()** as a parameter. The return value from **GetChanges()** indicates whether or not any potential conflicts currently exist between the state of the DataWindow Blob and the state of the DataStore.

Here's the syntax for calling the **SetChanges()** function:

```
dwcontrol.SetChanges( dwblob {,resolution} )
```

Dwcontrol is the name of the DataWindow control or DataStore to which you want to apply the changes. *Dwblob* is a read-only change Blob created with **GetChanges()** from which you want to apply changes. *Resolution* is a value of the **dwConflictResolution** enumerated data type indicating how conflicts should be resolved (either by **FailOnAnyConflict!** or by **AllowPartialChanges!**).

The return value from **SetChanges()** can be one of the following:

- 1. Indicates that all changes were applied.
- 2. Indicates that a partial update was successful and that conflicting changes were discarded.
- -1. Indicates a function failure.
- -2. Indicates that a conflict exists between the state of the DataWindow change Blob and the state of the DataWindow.
- -3. Indicates that column specifications do not match.

The following example is a script for a remote object function. The script uses **SetChanges()** to apply changes made to a DataWindow control on a client to a DataStore on a server. The changes made on the client are contained in a change Blob that is passed as an argument to the function. After applying changes to the DataStore, the server updates the database.

```
Datastore ids_myds
long ll_rc

ids_myds.SetChanges( ablob_data )
ll_rc = ids_myds.Update()

IF ll_rc = 1 THEN
    COMMIT
ELSE
    ROLLBACK
END IF

RETURN 1
```

GetStateStatus()

In certain situations in which a single DataStore on a server acts as the source for multiple target DataWindows or DataStores on different clients, you can use the **GetChanges()**

function in conjunction with **GetStateStatus**() to determine the likely success of **SetChanges**(). To determine the likely success of **SetChanges**(), follow these steps:

1. Call the **GetStateStatus**() function of the DataStore on which you want to use **SetChanges**(). **GetStateStatus**() checks the state of the DataStore and makes the state information available in a reference argument called a *cookie*. The cookie is generally much smaller than a DataWindow change Blob.

2. Send the cookie back to the client.

3. Call the **GetChanges**() function on the DataWindow from which you want to apply changes, passing the cookie retrieved from **GetStateStatus**() as a parameter. The return value from **GetChanges**() indicates whether or not any potential conflicts currently exist between the state of the DataWindow Blob and the state of the DataStore.

Here's the syntax for calling the **GetStatus**() function:

```
dwcontrol.GetStateStatus( cookie )
```

Dwcontrol is the name of the DataWindow control or DataStore for which you want to get state status. *Cookie* is a Blob variable in which you want to store a cookie that contains state information for the DataWindow.

The following example is a script for a remote object function using **GetStateStatus**() to capture the state of a DataStore on the server into a cookie. Once the cookie has been created, it's returned to the client.

```
Blob lblob_cookie
long ll_rc

ll_rc = ids_datastore.GetStateStatus(lblob_cookie)

RETURN lblob_cookie
```

Q&A

In this section, I have compiled a few of the most frequently asked questions on distributed processing and their answers. I have also listed solutions to the most common problems with distributed processing.

Where Do I Find the Hosts And Services Files?

In Windows 3.x and Windows 95, you'll find the services and hosts files in your Windows directory. However, in Windows NT, these files are located in the

<win_dir>\system32\drivers\etc directory.

How Do I Update My Host And Services Files?

This is what a services file looks like when opened up:

```
# <service name>   <port number>/<protocol> #<comment>
rscsa           10010/udp
rscsb           10011/udp
qmaster         10012/tcp
qmaster         10012/udp
dpbserv         10013/tcp
```

> **Note:** The services file has to be configured the same on both the server and the client computers. The port numbers must match.
>
> A word of caution: If the service you're adding to your services file is the last entry in the file, make sure you add a blank line after it. Otherwise, your service name will not be recognized for some reason.

The following is a hosts file. This file contains the mappings of IP addresses to host names. Each entry should be kept on an individual line. The IP address should be placed in the first column, followed by the corresponding host name. The IP address and the host name should be separated by at least one space.

```
127.0.0.1       localhost
199.93.178.151  sybaseserver
```

The local host location will allow you to test a distributed PB application via the Winsock protocol without being connected to a network. The 127.0.0.1 address is a special address that works as a loopback within the Winsock driver. An entry must be made in the hosts file for LocalHost.

When Using PFCs With Distributed PowerBuilder, How Do I Use the gnv_app?

In order to use PFC with distributed PowerBuilder, the **gnv_app** User object is required. Because each distributed client connection has its own memory area, the **gnv_app** object needs to be instantiated for each connection. It's recommended that the following code be added to your distributed object:

```
// constructor event:
gnv_app = CREATE n_cst_appmanager
//destructor event:
DESTROY gnv_app
```

Why Do I Get An Error -999?

Error -999, "Listen Not Supported With Local Driver," occurs when you've set the server Transport object driver attribute to "local." The local driver is only valid with the client Connection object and is invalid for the *Transport* object. When a distributed application local is running, no server application is running.

Are ConnectionBegin And ConnectionEnd Events Used In Local Mode?

The answer is Yes. The **ConnectionBegin** and **ConnectionEnd** events reside in the application object. When running in local mode, PowerBuilder only references the client application object. Therefore, any script you place in the server application's **ConnectionBegin** or **ConnectionEnd** events must also reside in the client application object. Because of this, you should limit the size of the scripts in these events.

Why Do I Get An Error 50?

Error 50, "Unable To Setup Runtime Environment," occurs because the compiled server application has not been generated into a dynamic library (PBD/DLL).

Moving On

PowerBuilder's support for distributed computing is a logical extension of its object-oriented architecture. For this reason, a PowerBuilder application that uses object-oriented techniques can be converted to a distributed application with a minimum of difficulty. When you're ready to begin developing a distributed application, you need to package your business logic in custom class User objects. Custom class User objects provide the foundation for any distributed application. Once you've created your nonvisual objects, you can make the adjustments required for client applications to access these objects remotely.

In this chapter, we covered PowerBuilder's distributed capabilities. We first covered the architecture behind distributed PowerBuilder by looking at the components needed for building both client and server applications. We then covered some of the new distributed features of PowerBuilder such as shared objects, asynchronous processing, and DataWindow synchronization. Finally, we touched on some of the commonly asked questions and answers. I'll bet you're all pumped up to begin distributing!

In the next chapter, I'll cover PowerBuilder's Internet application development technology for creating various types of Web applications.

Internet Development

PowerBuilder 6.0 enables you to bring the familiarity and innovation of your PowerBuilder applications to the World Wide Web. One of the main focuses of this version of PowerBuilder is developing Web applications for the Internet and intranets. Sybase calls it being "wired for the Web." To help you become wired for the Web, PowerBuilder provides a set on Internet tools and some new features that you can use to develop applications that can be deployed on Web servers.

In the previous version of PowerBuilder, we were introduced to the Internet Development Toolkit (IDT), which was an additional component from Powersoft. The IDT allowed developers to build on the strength of PowerBuilder's database access technology and scripting language to create business application for the Web. In this latest release, Sybase has bundled the enhanced IDT, now called Internet tools, with PowerBuilder. To provide more Internet capabilities, PowerBuilder 6.0 has many new objects and classes that you can use to build applications for the Web.

In this chapter, I'll cover PowerBuilder's Internet tools and Internet features.

The Internet Tools

The Internet tools are used to create Web-based applications and to make current applications Internet-enabled. The Internet tools consist of the following features:

- **Web.PB.** Brings the distributed computing capabilities of PowerBuilder to the Web.

- **Plug-ins.** Display a PowerBuilder window or DataWindow in an HTML page.

- **WebSite Web server software.** Provides a complete environment for creating, managing, and administering a Web server.

Let me first give you an overall picture of how the Internet tools' architecture works. An Internet application begins with a two-way communication between a Web browser (the client) and a Web server. The client requests an HTML document, and the server simply delivers it. Tags in the document may refer to other resources, such as plug-ins, ActiveX controls, bitmaps, or other programs. When the client encounters these tags, it makes additional requests to the Web server.

Let's take a closer look at each one of these components.

Web.PB

As I mentioned earlier, Web.PB brings the distributed computing capabilities of PowerBuilder to the Web. With Web.PB, you can invoke the services of a PowerBuilder object by using either of the following HTML elements:

- The form element (**<FORM>**)

- The anchor element (**<A>**)

With these elements, you can create Web applications that allow your users to invoke remote object methods either by clicking hypertext links or by entering information in input forms. Web.PB provides support for CGI (Common Gateway Interface), ISAPI (Internet Server API), and NSAPI (Netscape Server) program interfaces.

When a Web browser makes a request that invokes a PowerBuilder object method, the Web server calls Web.PB to service that request. Web.PB passes the request to the server application, which then performs some processing and returns HTML or binary data to the browser. If required, the server application can connect to databases to handle the request. The Web.PB class library provides a session management database that the server can connect to in order to keep track of session and transaction information. This architecture is illustrated in Figure 30.1.

When a Web browser makes a request that invokes a PowerBuilder object method, the Web browser actually calls one of the server's Web.PB program files to service that request. The HTML document that invokes the PowerBuilder method specifies which Web.PB program is called. The Web.PB program file you need to call depends on which interface you use; also, it must reside on the Web server's PC. These interfaces are:

- **PBCGI60.EXE.** Standard CGI

- **PBISA60.DLL.** ISPAI support for the Microsoft Internet Information servers

- **PBNS160.DLL.** NSAPI support for Netscape Commerce and Communication servers.

- **PBNS260.DLL.** NSAPI support for Netscape FastTrack and Enterprise servers

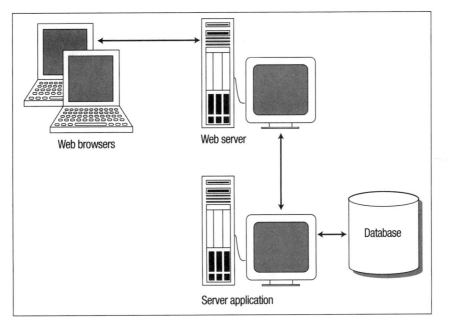

Figure 30.1
Architecture of Web.PB.

Web.PB works with Winsock, NamedPipes, and OpenClientServer drivers. Winsock support is automatically linked with Web.PB.

Server Application

A Web.PB server application is quite similar to a distributed PowerBuilder server application. Their main components are remote objects and the Transport object. Your remote objects are NVOs that have methods that can be called by the Web.PB program. The Transport object makes it possible for the server application to receive client connections and to process client requests for services.

The methods associated with an NVO in a Web.PB server can pass arguments that use any of the standard data types (with the exception of arrays and structures). Your methods can return a String or a Blob.

When Web.PB invokes a method that returns a String, it calls the method once for each program request and returns a single String value. Web.PB inserts a content type TEXT/HTML into the String values that are sent back to the client browser. On the other hand, when Web.PB invokes a method that returns a Blob, it calls the method repeatedly until the method returns a null Blob value. The method must insert the appropriate content type for the data it's returning.

The following example demonstrates how to return an HTML string from a function named **f_get_customer()**. This function is a method of a User object named **u_customer**.

```
Datastore ids_ds
String ls_html
Long ll_rows

String ls_header = "<HTML><HEAD>'
String ls_title = "<TITLE>Customer Listing</TITLE>"
String ls_end = "</HEAD>"
String ls_footer = "</BODY></HTML>"
String ls_head1 = "<BODY><H1>Customer Listing</H1>"

ls_html = ls_header + ls_title + ls_end + ls_head1
ids_ds = CREATE DataStore
ids_ds.DataObjet = "d_customer'
ids_ds.SetTransObject( SQLCA )
ll_rows = ids_ds.Retrieve()

IF ll_rows <> 0 THEN
    ls_html = ls_html + &
        ids_ds.Object.DataWindow.Data.HTMLTable
    ls_html = ls_html + ls_footer
ELSE
    ls_html = "No customers!"
END IF
RETURN ls_html
```

To invoke the **f_get_customers()** function in HTML, you would use the following code:

```
<A HREF= "/Scripts/pbcgi60.exe/DemoPB/u_customers/f_getcustomers">
Customer Listing</A>
```

The Web.PB Class Library

The Web.PB class library contains NVOs that enable you to minimize HTML coding, implement a consistent look and feel, develop distributed applications, and save time.

The Web.PB class library contains two types of objects:

- **HTML generation objects.** These objects contain functions you can use to generate HTML syntax. For example:

  - **U_html_form**

  - **U_html_format**

  - **U_html_template**

- **Session management objects.** These objects contain functions you can use to control session and transactional persistence across a distributed application. For example:

  - **U_session**

  - **U_transaction**

Plug-Ins

HTML forms provide some user interaction via a limited user interface. To get around this and to give you a better user interface, the Internet tools provide you with two plug-ins: the Window plug-in and the DataWindow plug-in.

The Window Plug-In

The Window plug-in lets you display a child window on Web pages viewed in a browser that supports the Netscape plug-ins. The window can include all the controls, including DataWindow and OLE controls. As your users interact with controls in the window, the scripts for the controls' events are executed as if they were in a normal stand-alone application. Database access by the plug-in application happens locally using the client's own database connections.

So, how does the plug-in work? Well, the Window plug-in displays a child window inside a fixed space on the Web page. The user interacts with the controls on the page, and the PowerBuilder scripts for the window and its controls execute the code. When the user switches to another Web page, the window is closed and the DLLs are removed from memory. Figure 30.2 illustrates how the Window plug-in works.

The plug-in is included in the HTML page using the HTML <EMBED> tag. It also names one or more PBDs that contain the PowerBuilder objects and the name of the child window object that's displayed on the page.

The <EMBED> tag is part of the HTML specification for plug-ins. It defines several standard attributes, and PowerBuilder defines additional attributes. The HTML attributes are **SRC** (which is the URL identifying the object), **WIDTH**, and **HEIGHT**. PowerBuilder attributes for the <EMBED> tag let you identify the window object that starts your applications, as well as additional libraries and parameters to pass to your applications. A sample element might look like this:

```
<EMBED SRC=DemoPB.PBD WIDTH=350 HEIGHT=300WINDOW=w_customers>

<HTML>
<HEAD>
<TITLE>Customer Window</TITLE>
</HEAD>
```

```
<BODY>
<IMG SRC="pb6logo.gif" BORDER=0 HEIGHT=40 WidTH=40>
<H1>Customer Lisping in a Window Plug-In</H1>
<P><HR></P>
<P>This Window uses the window plug-in. It retrieves
data into a customer table into d_cutomer DataWindow. </P>
<P>EMBED SRC=DemoPB.PBD WIDTH=350 HEIGHT=300 WINDOW=w_customers></P>
<LI>Back
<A HREF=http://www.sybase.com>HomePage</A></LI>
</BODY>
</HTML>
```

> **Note:** *The server needs the HTML pages and the PBD file names in the **SRC** and **LIBRARY** attributes of the **<EMBED>** tags. The client needs an Internet/intranet connection, a Web browser, the PowerBuilder deployment DLL(s), and the Window plug-in (NPPBA60.DLL).*

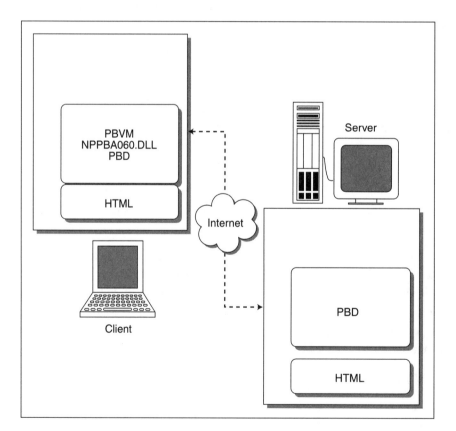

Figure 30.2
How the Window plug-in works.

The DataWindow Plug-In

The DataWindow plug-in lets you display a Powersoft Report (PSR) on a Web page in a browser that supports the Netscape plug-ins. The DataWindow plug-in displays a PSR with the same data and formatting with which it was previewed and saved in the DataWindow or Report Painter, a DataWindow control, or a DataStore. (See Figure 30.3.)

Note: *A PSR cannot have the RichText presentation style.*

The following sample page includes the DataWindow plug-in showing a PSR file:

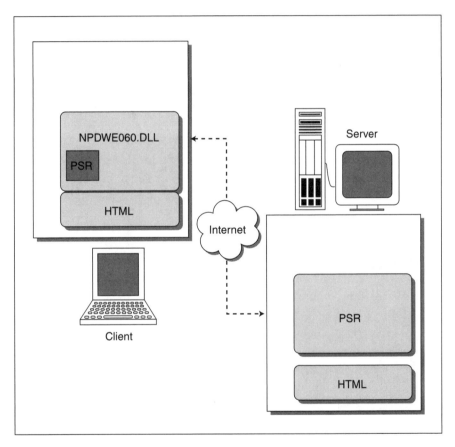

Figure 30.3
How a DataWindow plug-in works.

```
<HTML>
<HEAD>
<TITLE>Customer Report</TITLE>
</HEAD>
<BODY>
<IMG SRC="pb6logo.gif" BORDER=0 HEIGHT=40 WidTH=40>
<H1>Customer Listing</H1>
<P><HR></P>
<p><EBMED SRC=customer.psr WIDTH=600 HEIGHT=30></P>
<LI>Back
<A HREF=http://www.Sybase.com>HomePage</A></LI>
</BODY>
</HTML>
```

> **Note:** You need to copy the PSR and HTML pages to your server. These are PSR file names in the **SRC** attribute of the **<EMBED>** tag. The client needs an Internet/intranet connection, a Web browser, and the DataWindow plug-in (NPDWE60.DLL).

WebSite Web Server

The O'Reilly's WebSite Web Server is bundled with PowerBuilder Enterprise. WebSite is a 32-bit, multithreaded environment for creating, managing, and administering a Web server on the Windows platform. If you need information on installing and using this product, please refer to the WebSite documentation.

Web.PB Wizard

The Web.PB Wizard can be invoked from the PowerBuilder development environment. The Web.PB Wizard is an excellent utility that helps you to generate HTML and Web.PB functions. It also helps you create the HTML elements required to access Web.PB applications.

The wizard solicits the following information from you:

- The User object and function you want to access
- The interface program you use
- The location of the application server

Next, the Web.PB Wizard generates the HTML to create a form or the HTML element required to access the distributed application and then saves it in an HTML file. You can use this file as your Web page or insert it in another file.

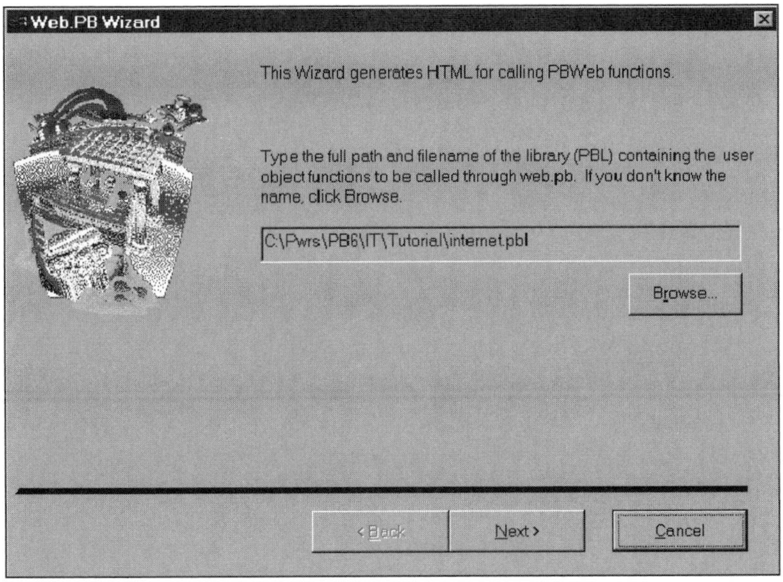

Figure 30.4
The Web.PB Wizard.

The wizard appears as one new system-level toolbar button in the PowerBar, and it also appears on the drop-down panel of the PowerPanel. When you click the button, the applications display as modeless dialog boxes, as shown in Figure 30.4.

To use this feature, add one or both of the following settings to the [**PB**] section of the PowerBuilder initialization file:

```
[PB]
WebPBWizard=html_webpb,<path to pbwizard .PBD>
```

Window ActiveX Control

The Window ActiveX control is a Component object similar to the Window plug-in that can contain PowerBuilder child windows. You can use the PowerBuilder Window ActiveX control to provide a graphical interface inside HTML pages. You can use it with any Web browser that supports ActiveX. This includes Internet Explorer and Netscape Navigator running the ActiveX plug-in. Although the Window ActiveX control is primarily intended for use with Web browsers that support ActiveX, you can display a PowerBuilder window or DataWindow in any application that supports ActiveX.

Note: In addition to providing all the capabilities of the PowerBuilder Netscape plug-ins, the Window ActiveX control features access via JavaScript or VBScript to a subset of the window's events and functions.

The PowerBuilder Window ActiveX control includes functions you can call to invoke methods in the window contained in the control. Additionally, certain events in the control trigger events in the ActiveX container. When an event fires, it first executes any PowerBuilder script for the event and then executes JavaScript or VBScript implemented for the container. A PowerBuilder window displayed in the Window ActiveX control can include all the familiar controls, including DataWindows, OLE objects, and other ActiveX controls. You can also open other windows assuming that they are of type **Popup** or **Response** from the child window. As users interact with controls in the windows, scripts for the controls' events are executed just as they are in stand-alone PowerBuilder applications. Database access by the window occurs locally using the client's defined database connections.

The PowerBuilder Window ActiveX control requires the client workstation to contain the PowerBuilder deployment DLLs as well as a registered version of the PowerBuilder Window ActiveX module—either PBRX60.OCX or PBRXS60.OCX.

To use the PowerBuilder Window ActiveX control, you need to create a PowerBuilder application first. Then, follow these steps:

1. Compile your library to a PBD.

2. Register the PowerBuilder Window ActiveX control on the HTML development workstation.

3. Create an HTML page that includes your PowerBuilder application window. This page can include JavaScript or VBScript that interacts with the window.

4. Configure the Web server by copying the HTML pages, the PowerBuilder Window ActiveX control, and the PBD files for the application to the appropriate directories.

5. On all client workstations, install the PowerBuilder Window ActiveX control and the PowerBuilder deployment DLLs.

   Note: PowerBuilder provides versions of the Window ActiveX control for Windows 95 and Windows NT 4.0. The Window ActiveX control requires the use of a browser that supports ActiveX. Microsoft Internet Explorer version 3.x or higher and Netscape Navigator version 3.x using the NCompass ScriptActive plug-in are two examples.

Functions For The Window ActiveX Control

The following functions are available with the Window ActiveX control:

- **GetArgElement()**. Use this function after calling **InvokePBFunction()** or **TriggerPBEvent()**to access the updated value in an argument passed by reference.

- **GetLastReturn()**. Use this function after calling **InvokePBFunction()** or **TriggerPBEvent()** to access the return value.

- **InvokePBFunction()**. Use this function to invoke a user-defined window function in the child window contained in a PowerBuilder Window ActiveX control.

- **ResetArgElements()**. Use this function after calling **InvokePBFunction()** or **TriggerPBEvent()** to clear the argument list.

- **TriggerPBEvent()**. Use this function to trigger a user event in the child window contained in a PowerBuilder Window ActiveX control.

- **SetArgElement()**. Use this function before calling **InvokePBFunction()** or **TriggerPBEvent()** to specify an argument for the passed function.

Events For The Window ActiveX Control

The Window ActiveX control can respond to certain events occurring within the child window. These are outbound events, which execute first within the PowerBuilder window and then in the Window ActiveX control. You can add JavaScript or VBScript code that responds to these events. Table 30.1 describes the events for the Window ActiveX control.

Table 30.1 Events for the Window ActiveX control.

Event	Description
Activate	Occurs just before the window becomes active.
Clicked	Occurs when the user clicks in an unoccupied area of the window (any area with no visible, enabled object).
Close	Occurs when the window is closed.
Deactivate	Occurs when the window becomes inactive.
DoubleClicked	Occurs when the user double-clicks in an unoccupied area of the window.
Hide	Occurs just before the window is hidden.
Key	Occurs when the user presses a key and the insertion point is not in a line edit.

(continued)

Table 30.1 Events for the Window ActiveX control *(continued)*.

Event	Description
MouseDown	Occurs when the user presses the left mouse button in an unoccupied area of the window.
PBMouseMove	Occurs when the pointer is moved within the window.
PBMouseUp	Occurs when the user releases the left mouse button in an unoccupied area of the window.
RButtonDown	Occurs when the user presses the right mouse button in an unoccupied area of the window.
Resize	Occurs when the user or a script opens or resizes a window.
Show	Occurs when a script executes the **Show()** function for this window. The event occurs just before the window is displayed.
SystemKey	Occurs when the insertion point is not in a line edit and the user presses the Alt key or Alt plus another key.
Timer	Occurs when a specified number of seconds elapses after the **Timer()** function has been called.

How The PowerBuilder Window ActiveX Control Works

The PowerBuilder Window ActiveX control displays a PowerBuilder child window inside a fixed space reserved on the Web page. The user can interact with the controls on the page, and the PowerBuilder scripts for the window and its controls can execute any PowerBuilder code. When the user switches to another Web page, the PowerBuilder window is closed and the PowerBuilder DLLs are unloaded from memory.

The PowerBuilder Window ActiveX control is included on an HTML page using the HTML **<OBJECT>** element. It names one or more PBDs that contain PowerBuilder objects, the name of the child window object that's displayed on the page, and, optionally, the PowerBuilder application object. Tag attributes specify the class ID for the Window ActiveX control, the space allocated for the window, the name of the PBD, and the name of the child window in the PBD.

The following example is a sample **<OBJECT>** tag:

```
<OBJECT NAME="PBRX1" WIDTH=225 HEIGHT=83

CLASSID="CLSID:CEC58653-C842-11CF-A6FB-00805FA8669E">
    <PARAM NAME="_Version" VALUE="65536">
    <PARAM NAME="_ExtentX" VALUE="5962">
    <PARAM NAME="_ExtentY" VALUE="2164">
```

```
    <PARAM NAME="_StockProps" VALUE="0">
    <PARAM NAME="PBWindow" VALUE="w_helloworld">
    <PARAM NAME="LibList" VALUE="http://www.company.com/pbdemo.pbd;">
    <PARAM NAME="PBApplication" VALUE="pbdemo">
</OBJECT>
```

> *Note:* The server needs the HTML page with an *<OBJECT>* tag for the window
> and PBDs containing your child windows and other PowerBuilder objects. The
> client needs the Window ActiveX control installed and registered, the deployment
> DLLs or shared libraries installed, and the directory for the PowerBuilder deploy-
> ment DLLs listed in the system path. The client also needs the Microsoft files
> MFC042D.DLL, MFC42D.DLL, MSVCRTD.DLL, URL.DLL, and URLMON.DLL.

Secure Mode For Plug-Ins And ActiveX

The secure mode helps you to ensure that PowerBuilder applications downloaded over
the Internet do not damage a client system or access information on the client system.
Secure mode restricts activities as follows:

- Calling an external function causes an execution time error.

- Calling a restricted function causes an execution time error.

- Calling functions that result in database access causes an execution time error.

- Applications running in secure mode can only establish an Internet connection to
  the current Web server.

- Calling mail functions causes an execution time error.

- Calling OLE functions causes an execution time error.

- You cannot connect to PowerBuilder application servers.

- Calling DDE functions causes an execution time error.

You implement secure mode by deploying special versions of the PowerBuilder Window
plug-in or PowerBuilder Window ActiveX control, which you deploy on client workstations as appropriate. For example, the default version for a Window plug-in is NPPA60.DLL.
The secure version of this DLL is NPPBS60.DLL. You would use PBRXS60.OCX instead
of PBRX60.OCX, which is the Window ActiveX control.

> *Note:* The DataWindow plug-in displays PSR files only. PSR files are read-only.
> Therefore, a secured version of the DataWindow plug-in (NPDWE60.DLL) does
> not exist.

To use the secured version of the PowerBuilder Window plug-in, copy NPPBS60.DLL to the plug-ins directory on each client's workstation. To use the secured version of the PowerBuilder Window ActiveX control, install and register PBRXS60.OCX on the workstation used for HTML page creation. Use the Class ID for PBRXS60.OCX when specifying the Object element for a secured application. You can also optionally install and register PBRXS60.OCX on all client workstations; however, make sure you use the same Class ID specified in the HTML **<OBJECT>** elements.

The Context Object

The Context object allows your applications to access certain host services that are non-PowerBuilder services. PowerBuilder uses the Context object to provide access to the following services:

- Context information
- Keyword
- Internet

The Context object creates service objects appropriate for the current execution context. This allows your application to take full advantage of the execution environment. For example, in a Window plug-in, your application can access parameters specified in the **<EMBED>** element. Additionally, when running the Window ActiveX control under Internet Explorer, your application can access the ActiveX Automation service, which allows your program to access and control the browser.

By implementing a standard class User object of type **Service** and distributing the PBL and supporting files, Sybase can add support for new contexts at any time.

Before you use a service, you instantiate it by calling the **GetContextService()** function. When you call this function, the Context object returns a reference to the instantiated service. Here's an example:

```
//Declare your variables

ContextInformation    lci_info
ContextKeyword    lck_keyword
Inet    linet_net

//Instantiate the variables

This.GetContextService("ContextInformation",  lci_info)
This.GetContextService("Keyword",      lck_keyword)
This.GetContextService("Internet",      linet_net)
```

Context Information

You can use the Context Information service to obtain information about your application's execution context. That is, the service provides current version information, as well as whether it's running in the PowerBuilder execution environment as a Window plug-in or as a Window ActiveX control. Using this information, you can modify display characteristics and application behavior. For example, you might hide a Close command button when running it as a plug-in or an ActiveX control. Additionally, when running in the Window ActiveX control under Internet Explorer, the Context Information service can return a reference to an ActiveX Automation server object. Your application can use this reference to call functions that control the Web browser.

Using the Context Information service, you can access the following functions that return information:

- **GetName**(). Returns the full context name.

- **GetShortName**(). Returns the abbreviated context name.

- **GetCompanyName**(). Returns the company name.

- **GetVersionNumber**(). Returns the full version number.

- **GetMajorVersion**(). Returns the major version number.

- **GetMinorVersion**(). Returns the minor version number.

- **GetFixesVersion**(). Returns the fix version number.

Keyword

You can use the Keyword service to access environment information for the current context. In the default environment, this service returns host workstation environment variables. When running within the Window plug-in, this service allows you to access parameters specified in the plug-in's **<EMBED>** tag.

To access environment variables, declare an instance or global variable of type **ContextKeyword**. Also, declare an unbounded array of type **String** to contain returned values. Here's an example:

```
ContextKeyword  lck_keyword
String     ls_returnedvalues[]
```

Next, you need to create the context information service by calling the **GetContextService**() function:

```
This.GetContextService("Keyword", lck_keyword)
```

Finally, you need to call the **GetContextKeyword**() function to access the environment variable you want. This example calls the **GetContextKeyword**() function to determine the current application path:

```
lck_keyword.GetContextKeywords("Path", ls_returnedvalues)

//Display the path in a SigleLineEdit
sle_path.text = ls_returnedvalues[1]
```

The following example calls the **GetShortName**() function to determine the current context and the **GetVersionName**() function to determine the current version:

```
String  ls_shortname, ls_versionname
ContextInformation   lci_info

This.GetContextService("ContextInformation", lci_info)
lci_info.GetShortName(ls_shortname)
lci_info.GetVersionName(ls_versionname)
```

Internet

You can use the Internet service to display a Web page in the default browser, to access the HTML for a specified page, and to send data to a CGI, ISAPI, or NSAPI program.

Hyperlinking To A URL

You call the Internet service's **HyperLinkToURL**() function to start the default browser with a specified URL. To hyperlink to a URL, declare a variable of type **Inet**, create the Internet service by calling the **GetContextService**() function, and then call the **HyperLinkToURL**() function, passing the URL of the page to display when the browser starts. Here's an example:

```
Inet  linet_net
GetContextService("Internet", iinet_base)

linet_net.HyperlinkToURL  &
   ("http://www.sybase.com")
```

Getting And Posting To A URL

You call the Internet service's **GetURL**() function to perform an HTTP **Get**, returning raw HTML for a specified URL. To perform an HTTP **Get**, you need to declare a variable of type **Inet**. Also, declare a variable using the descendant InternetResult object as the data type, create the Internet service by calling the **GetContextService()** function, create an instance of the descendant InternetResult object, and then call the **GetURL()** function, passing the URL of the page to be returned and a reference to the instance of the descendant InternetResult object. When the **GetURL()** function completes, it calls the **InternetData()** function defined in the descendant InternetResult object, passing the HTML for the specified URL. Here's an example:

```
Inet  linet_net

//standard class User oject inherited from InternetResult
u_iresult luo_iresult

luo_iresult = CREATE u_iresult

GetContextService("Internet", linet_net)

line_net.GetURL("http://www.mydomain.com", lou_iresult)

DESTROY luo_iresult
```

You call the Internet service's **PostURL()** function to perform an HTTP **Post**, sending data to a CGI, ISAPI, or NSAPI program. The following example posts to a URL:

```
Inet line_net
Blob lblb_urldata
String ls_headers, ls_urlname
Long 11_len

luo_iresult = CREATE u_iresult

ls_urlname = "http://www.mydomain.com"
ls_urlname += "cgi-bin/pbcgi60.exe/"
ls_urlname += "DemoPB/u_customers/f_getcustomers?"
lblb_urldata = Blob ("")
11_len = Len(lblb_urldata)

ls_headers = "Content-Length: " + String(11_len) + "~n~n"

linet_net.PostURL &
   (ls_urlname,lblb_urldata, ls_headers, lou_iresult)

DESTROY lou_iresult
```

Web Jumps

The Web Jumps feature provides up to four links to the World Wide Web from within the PowerBuilder development environment. Use this feature to give yourself easy access to Web pages you use frequently.

You specify the Web pages to link to by using the keys WebLink1, WebLink2, and WebLink3, in the [**PB**] section of your PB.INI file. Here's an example:

```
[PB]

WebLink1=&Sybase,http://www.sybase.com
WebLink2=&Microsoft,http://www.microsoft.com
WebLink3=&Netscape,http://www.netscape.com
```

Choosing A Strategy

Now, for the million dollar question: Which strategy do you choose? Well, I guess you're on your own on this one. You should always match your application requirements with the capabilities and requirements of Internet development components. Ask yourself these questions:

- Is application processing and database access to be centralized?

- Is application processing and database access to occur on the client?

- Does the application require formatted reports that can be prepared ahead of time?

Here are examples for when you should consider Web.PB for centralized data access:

- The server application retrieves browser requests and connects to databases as necessary.

- The browser client requires no extra software.

- The application works with any commercially available browser.

- The database access is centralized on the application server.

- The application server formats results as HTML or some other valid content type, and Web.PB sends it to the client.

Here are examples for when you should consider the Window plug-in for database access on the client:

- Applications beginning with a child window can execute most PowerBuilder functionality.

- The client requires PowerBuilder VM and Window plug-in DLLs (downloaded via synch ActiveX).

- Database access is initiated on the client workstation using client connections.

- The application can display information, accept data input, and update databases.

Here are examples for when you should consider the DataWindow plug-in for preformatted reports:

- To display previously generated reports stored on the Web server

- When the client requires the DataWindow plug-in DLL

- When database access is not necessary

Moving On

Wired for the Web yet? Well, to become wired for the Web, PowerBuilder has given you a set of Internet tools and many new features that you can use to develop Web applications.

In this chapter, we covered PowerBuilder's Internet tools and the new Internet features. We covered the various components of the enhanced IDT, and then we covered some of the new Internet features of PowerBuilder 6.0, such as the Window ActiveX control and secure mode. I am down for the Net!

Now that your applications are on the Internet and available around the globe, in the next chapter, I'll cover internationalization, which discusses having applications available in several languages.

Internationalization

A time may come when you have to write an application that will be deployed overseas, or, perhaps, you may need to write an application for one of your international offices abroad. Corporations today are facing heavy worldwide competition and international business challenges that are prompting developers to create global applications. Therefore, tools are needed to help developers create low-maintenance yet robust applications that are available in more than one language.

In recognizing this urgent need, PowerBuilder 6.0 now includes several new features that enable you to build multilingual applications:

- Support for Unicode character encoding

- Merging of Japanese double-byte character support into the ANSII PowerBuilder 6.0 common code base

- Right-to-left support provided by Hebrew- and Arabic-enabled 32-bit versions of PowerBuilder 6.0

- PowerBuilder 6.0 versions of the Translation Toolkit and localized Powersoft foundation class libraries

- PowerBuilder 6.0 versions of the localized deployment kits

In this chapter, I'll cover these new features and also talk about some of the issues that arise when developing and deploying applications for multiple languages.

Unicode

PowerBuilder for Unicode is a new version of PowerBuilder for the Windows NT 4.x platform that supports the Unicode standard format UTF-16. This is a character encoding system that has the capacity to encode all characters used for written languages through-out the world and uses two full bytes to store each character. You can use Power-Builder for Unicode to develop applications in any of the character sets supported by the Uni-code standard.

In PowerBuilder for Unicode, text in dialog boxes and other built-in objects in the graphical user interface display in English, but everything you type displays in Unicode format. You can migrate applications from the ANSI version of PowerBuilder to the Unicode version. When you open a PBL created in the ANSI version of PowerBuilder, PowerBuilder for Unicode opens a dialog box in which you can specify the library list and the directory where the Unicode version of the application will be saved. Your PBLs will be saved with the extension .PUL (for PowerBuilder Unicode Library) instead of PBL.

A new Migrate menu item appears in the Library Painter in PowerBuilder for Unicode to enable you to migrate applications from Unicode to ANSI. Avoid adding characters that are not supported in the ANSI version, because this may result in strange behavior. You're given two new functions, **ToAnsi**() and **ToUnicode**(), that enable conversion to and from Unicode characters. Note that ANSI string data is stored in a Blob.

To deploy your Unicode applications, you need the 32-bit Unicode deployment DLLs and, once again, Windows NT 4.x, which is the only platform for deployment.

Unicode Vs. DBCS

Unicode is one big character set that supports virtually all the characters used by written languages. A single Unicode PowerBuilder executable file will support multiple languages.

The Japanese double-byte character support (DBCS) is a different character set from Unicode. The Japanese DBCS version of PowerBuilder supports only the Japanese char-acter sets. Both the application displays and user defined text are in Japanese.

The Unicode Standard

The Unicode standard is a new character code designed to encode text for storage in computer files. Unicode goes beyond ASCII's limited capability to encode only the Latin alphabet by providing the capacity to encode all the characters used for written languages throughout the world. The Unicode standard makes it possible to easily exchange text files across languages, and it simplifies the work of computer users who deal with multi-lingual text. In order to accommodate the many thousands of characters used in international text, the Unicode standard uses a 16-bit set instead of ASCII's 7-bit code set. This expansion provides codes for more than 65,000 characters, a huge increase over ASCII's code capacity of 128 characters. To keep character coding simple and efficient, the Unicode standard assigns each character a unique 16-bit value. Also, it doesn't use complex modes or escape codes to specify modified characters or special cases. This simplicity and efficiency make it easy for computers and software to handle Unicode-encoded text files.

Japanese Double-Byte Character Support

PowerBuilder now has DBCS. The Japanese version of PowerBuilder is compiled under the Japanese version of Windows, and it's available as a separate installation for the Japanese versions of Windows 95 and Windows NT. The supported characters sets are Kanji, Hiragana, and Katakana.

You need to use the Japanese version to develop applications in Japanese. These applications can then be deployed in both 16-bit and 32-bit versions of Windows, based on the target you build. Text and everything else you type is displayed in Japanese, and the string-handling functions are double-byte aware. Some of the DBCS-aware string-handling functions are **Fill()**, **Left()**, **LeftTrim()**, **Len()**, **Mid()**, **Pos()**, **Replace()**, **Right()**, **RightTrim()**, and **Trim()**.

These functions are character-based, string-handling functions that have been made double-byte aware, and they replace the single-byte versions in the Japanese products. Two additional forms exist of each function that are bit-based, string-handling functions. These versions of the functions are external functions and must be declared in the Japanese development environment before you can use them in your scripts. The Japanese version of PowerBuilder includes a file that makes declaring these external functions quick and easy.

To deploy applications built with the Japanese DBCS version of PowerBuilder, you need the corresponding deployment DLL. Once again, you can only deploy to Japanese versions of Windows, Windows 95, or Windows NT.

You can migrate applications from the ANSI version of PowerBuilder to the Japanese version, and vice versa. This is done via the Library Painter. Note that if you're going to migrate from Japanese to ANSI, characters that are not supported in the ANSI version will not convert correctly.

Arabic And Hebrew

Arabic- and Hebrew-enabled versions of PowerBuilder are available for Arabic and Hebrew versions of Windows 95 and Windows NT. These versions of PowerBuilder include new functions and a new edit mask character to handle Arabic and Hebrew characters and numbers.

Applications built using the Arabic or Hebrew versions of PowerBuilder must be deployed with the PowerBuilder Arabic or Hebrew deployment DLLs on workstations running the appropriate Arabic or Hebrew version of Windows.

In Arabic and Hebrew, text is displayed in right-to-left order. You can migrate applications from the ANSI version of PowerBuilder to the Hebrew or Arabic versions, and vice versa. Note that right-to-left support is lost when you migrate to the ANSI version.

Functions

Several functions are available to assist you in building Arabic or Hebrew applications. These functions take a string and return a Boolean value indicating that the text is either Arabic or Hebrew. The functions are as follows:

- **IsArabic()**. Takes a character as an argument and returns True if the character is an Arabic character or if it's a number or a neutral character such as a punctuation mark.

- **IsHebrew()**. Takes a character as an argument and returns True if the character is a Hebrew character or if it's a number or a neutral character such as a punctuation mark.

- **IsAllArabic()**. Determines if all characters in the string are Arabic or neutral characters.

- **IsArabicAndNumbers()**. Determines if all characters in the string are Arabic and numbers.

- **IsAnyArabic()**. Determines if any character in the string is an Arabic character.

- **IsAllHebrew()**. Determines if all characters in the string are Hebrew or neutral characters.

- **IsHebrewAndNumbers()**. Determines if all characters in the string are Hebrew and numbers.

- **IsAnyHebrew()**. Determines if any character in the string is a Hebrew character.

- **Reverse()**. Reverses the order of the characters in a string.

  Note: These functions have no effect unless you're using right-to-left versions of PowerBuilder and Windows. If not, these functions return False.

RightToLeft Property

Most objects and controls have a **RightToLeft** property. In general, controls that don't accept input or don't have scrollbars do not have the **RightToLeft** property. For example, drawing objects and static text do not have a "right to left" property. When you set the **RightToLeft** property to True, right-to-left processing is in effect. Table 31.1 lists the behavior of some objects when the **RightToLeft** property is enabled.

Edit Mask

A new mask character (b) in the edit mask control allows the entry of Arabic or Hebrew characters in the Arabic or Hebrew version of PowerBuilder. This mask is generally used when a single letter prefix is required for an ID or when a single character entry is required. The edit mask control does not have a **RightToLeft** property and does not support right-to-left text entry; all text is entered left to right.

Design Issues

When you start developing applications for deployment in multiple languages, you need to be aware of some design issues. Let's go over a few of these issues together:

- The physical design of the your user interface is quite important. Your windows and objects must be flexible to accommodate the different string lengths required when your text in menu items, lists, and labels is translated.

- Your windows and their controls should be designed in such a way that you can use them in both ANSI and right-to-left versions of PowerBuilder.

- Bear in mind the cultural standards of your users. The cultural design of your interface requires you to be aware of what is and isn't acceptable to your users. Beware of colors

Table 31.1 Effect of the RightToLeft property on PowerBuilder objects.

Object	Behavior
Application object	Message boxes display text in right-to-left order and button text displays in the appropriate language (Arabic or Hebrew).
Window object	Scrollbars and menu bars have a right-to-left orientation.
Controls	Text displays in right-to-left order and is right justified. If scrollbars are used, they have a right-to-left orientation.
DataWindow column	Text displays in right-to-left order and is right justified when the cell has focus. If you set the justification of the column to Right, the entire column will be right justified all the time.

that may be offensive to some cultures, or bitmaps that may represent offensive graphics. For example, a bitmap of a "thumbs up" is very offensive in the Arabic world.

PowerBuilder provides localized deployment kits. *Localization* is a process related to internationalization, where the goal is the final customization of a product for use in a particular market. This customization includes the translation of software messages and user interface items as well as product manuals, training materials, and marketing collateral. Localized kits are available in Danish, Dutch, French, German, Italian, Norwegian, Spanish, and Swedish. These localized deployment kits handle language-specific data during execution time. Here are some examples:

- The **DayName()**function returns a name in the language of the deployment kit available on the machine where the application is run.

- When you use the **String()**function to format a date and the month name is displayed as text, the month is in the language of the Deployment Kit.

Translation Toolkit

The Translation Toolkit is a set of tools designed to help you translate any PowerBuilder application to 50 different languages. The Translation Toolkit is a 32-bit application that can only run under Windows 95 or NT. The Translator Tool, which is part of the Translation Toolkit, is also available as a stand-alone application on Windows 95, NT, or 3.1.

When you use the tools in the Translation Toolkit, you work with phrases in an application. These phrases are in the application's object properties, controls, and scripts. With the tools in the Translation Toolkit, you can extract phrases from the project libraries, present the phrases for translation, and substitute translated phrases for the original phrases in the project libraries. Once you use the Translation Toolkit to create a project, a copy of each of your source libraries is created for the project. Your original libraries are not changed.

Currently with version 5.0 of the Translation Toolkit (for PowerBuilder 5.0), you are given five tools (see Figure 31.1). The following three translation tools are available, and each is associated with a phase of a translation project:

- **Phrase Extractor.** Creates the language copies of the source libraries and extracts phrases from these libraries.

- **Translator.** Presents the extracted phrases for translation.

- **Project Translator.** Applies translations to the project by substituting the translated phrases for the original phrases in the copies of the application libraries.

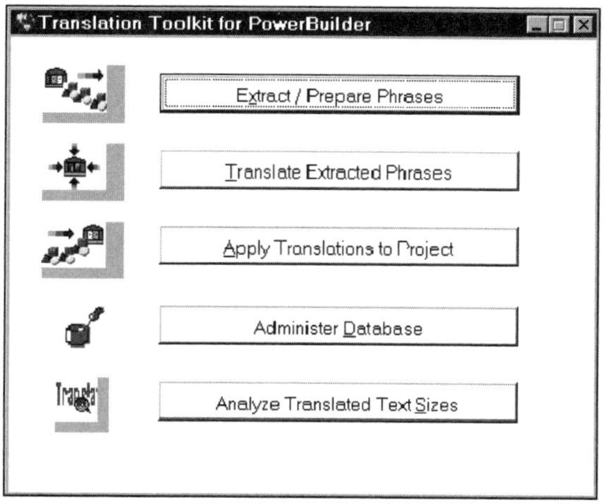

Figure 31.1
Tools in the Translation Toolkit.

Two maintenance tools are also available in the Translation Toolkit:

- **Database Administrator.** This tool is used for importing the Microsoft international glossaries and for displaying and deleting unused images and directory entries. You can also define a new language with the Database Administrator.

- **Text Analyzer.** Saves in the database the size and font adjustments to the controls you resized in PowerBuilder.

The Translation Toolkit for PowerBuilder version 6 will be available three to six months after the release of PowerBuilder 6.0.

Moving On

In recognizing the need for corporations to be successful in the international market, PowerBuilder 6.0 has included several new features that enable you to build multilingual applications. In this chapter, we covered support for Unicode character encoding, Japanese DBCS, Hebrew and Arabic right-to-left support, and the Translation Toolkit. As you can see, Sybase has provided you with all the tools you need to be competitive in foreign industries.

In the next chapter, I'll talk about the PowerBuilder Foundation Class Library (PFCs). The PFC is a set of PowerBuilder objects that you can customize and use to develop class libraries and PowerBuilder applications. It's an interesting topic that has a learning curve, but it isn't steep at all. Once you've mastered it, building future applications will be a breeze.

PowerBuilder Foundation Class Library

The PowerBuilder Foundation Class library (PFC) is a set of PowerBuilder objects and classes that you can use to develop applications, as well as class libraries and frameworks. A *framework* is a set of reusable classes that work together to server as a base for building applications. On the other hand, *class libraries* are utility objects that can be used independently.

PFC incorporates advanced object-oriented coding techniques and service-oriented design into its architecture, which, in turn, encourages you into using object-oriented programming (OOP) in your applications. Using PFC, or following its methodology, is a definite recommendation. This way, you receive all the benefits of our object-oriented religion. You also promote consistency with code standards and naming conventions, and your developments can be standardized. A learning curve is involved, but believe me, the entire PFC architecture is so well thought out that you'll fall in love with it the minute you understand how it's implemented.

In this chapter, I'll cover PFC. However, PFC is such a broad subject that it's almost unfair to try to cover it in one chapter. I'll first give you a brief overview of the PFC architecture and then we'll talk about some of the most common PFC services. Finally, we'll talk about the new 6.0 features of PFC.

The PFC Architecture

PFC is a set of PBLs that contain the ancestor and descendant objects you use to write your applications. It contains over 150 objects and 1,600 methods that you can utilize in your applications. Here are the main objects you use with PFC:

- Windows

- Menus

- DataWindow objects

- User objects

User Objects

The core of the PFC lies in User objects. Both visual and nonvisual User objects (discussed here) are used extensively throughout the PFC:

- **Visual User objects.** Each PFC standard visual User object corresponds to a PowerBuilder window control. These objects include predefined behaviors that provide complete integration with PFC services. PFC also uses custom visual User objects to group window controls.

- **Nonvisual User objects.** The PFC standard class User objects inherit their definitions from built-in PowerBuilder system objects such as Error, Transaction, and all other system objects. The PFC custom class User objects inherit their definition from the PowerBuilder nonvisual object classes. These classes encapsulate data and code used by PFC to implement services and to provide functions that enable instances of these services. PFC also provides *reference variables*, which are pointers to instantiated objects. The reference variables can be used to access an object's instance variables, functions, and events.

PFC does much of its processing through User object functions. Remember that windows, User objects, and controls all have a set of predefined events. PFC extends these events by defining user events for many of its objects. These events accept arguments and return a value.

Object-Oriented Features Of PFC

PFC is quite religious when it comes to object-oriented principles. It uses the following object-oriented features extensively:

- **Inheritance.** Enables objects to be derived from existing objects, with access to their visual components, data, and code. PFC uses inheritance to implement a hierarchy of windows, menus, and User objects.

- **Encapsulation.** Enables an object to contain its own data and code, allowing outside access as needed. Encapsulation is used to separate each object's data and code.

- **Polymorphism.** Provides the ability for functions to exist with the same name but behave differently. Polymorphism is used to provide same-name functions in PFC.

Let's look at some other object-oriented methods that are used extensively throughout PFC.

Services

PFC uses windows and User objects to provide an object-oriented design by separating related types of processing (called *services*). To clarify this a bit more, related sets of functionality are encapsulated into reusable, nonvisual custom classes that act as services for requestor objects. Here are the two types of services in PFC:

- **Instance.** Only one requestor, such as the window or DataWindow, may use it.

- **Application.** One or more instances of any class may use it.

This mechanism can also be called *delegation*. For example, Figure 32.1 shows the DataWindow control as the requestor, making requests for sort, filter, and row services.

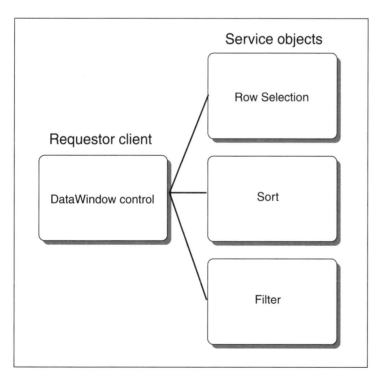

Figure 32.1
The DataWindow control requesting services.

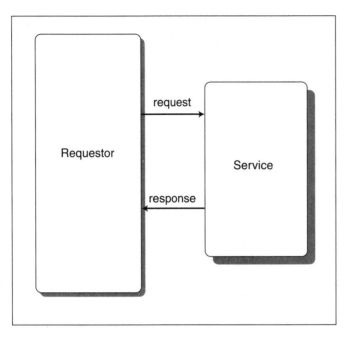

Figure 32.2
Communication between requestors and services.

Requestors can talk to services, and services can talk to requestors. This is illustrated in Figure 32.2.

The requestor classes are service-aware; however, they do not require to know how the service implements its functionality. The requestor has properties defined for various services. For example, the **pfc_u_dw** requestor has the following properties defined:

```
n_cst_dwsrv_sort    inv_sort
n_cst_dwsrv_resize  inv_resize
```

The requestor also has *enabler* functions that automatically handle the creation, destruction, and linkage of service objects. For example, **pfc_u_dw** has the following functions defined:

```
function of_SetSort (boolean)
function of_SetResize (boolean)
```

The service classes have requestor properties and methods to set it. For example, the **pfc_n_cst_dwsrv** service class has the following properties and methods:

```
protected  u_dw  idw_requestor
```

```
//object level function
function of_SetRequestor (u_dw adw_requestor)
```

To enable a service, you have to call an enabler function. For example, the function **of_SetSort**() takes a Boolean argument. When called with False, the service instance is destroyed if it exists; when called with True, if the service is not already instantiated, an instance is created, a reference variable is populated, and, finally, the requestor property is set.

> *Note: PFC automatically destroys all services objects created by your applications.*

The clean up of services is automatic. The enabler functions take care of this task for you. The **Destructor** event of **pfc_u_dw** has the following script:

```
of_SetResize( FALSE )
of_SetSort( FALSE )
```

As I mentioned earlier, PFC is a set of PBLs. These PBLs must be added to your application's library search path in order to be used. The ancestor objects' PBLs include PFC ancestor objects and other objects used by PFC (ancestor object PBLs names start with "PFC"):

- **PFCAPSRV.PBL.** Application manager, application service objects, and the global service objects

- **PFCDWSRV.PBL.** DataWindow services

- **PFCMAIN.PBL.** Basic PFC services

- **PFCWNSRV.PBL.** Window services

- **PFCUTIL.PBL.** Utility services

> *Note: The PFC ancestor objects are not to be modified at all.*

The Extension Level

No class library can completely meet the needs of every application without requiring some modifications. When you're designing class libraries, you have to bear in mind the following factors:

- They must be extendible.

- Specific application functionality may be added.

- Additional base-level functionality may be needed.

- Default behavior may be undesirable.

Lack of extendibility leads to lack of reusable classes. Changes are lost if you upgrade to a new ancestor object. Also, changes impact all other descendants in other applications, which may not require the change. For example, in Figure 32.3, changes made to any functions in **w_ancestor_sheet** are reflected in all applications in which the ancestor sheet is used.

For the ancestor to be extendible, an extension layer is needed to promote the code without affecting the ancestor. By inserting an extension layer, an upgrade path is now available. As illustrated in Figure 32.4, changes made in the extension level do not adversely affect other applications. Also, application-level behavior can be put directly into the extension level. Here are some other benefits of the extension layer:

- You can change PFC behavior without affecting base classes.

- You can add functionality without affecting base classes.

- Maintenance releases can be applied easily.

- Applications are easier to maintain because all customized code exists in the extension layer.

As illustrated in Figure 32.5, PFC implements an extension level in all its inheritance hierarchies where the extension levels can be modified if needed. All extension objects reside in separate PBLs, which are not affected when you upgrade to later releases. Objects in the ancestor libraries contain instance variables, events, and functions as objects in the extension level are unmodified descendants of the objects in the ancestor library.

Note: *You can customize your PFC applications by modifying objects in the extension level.*

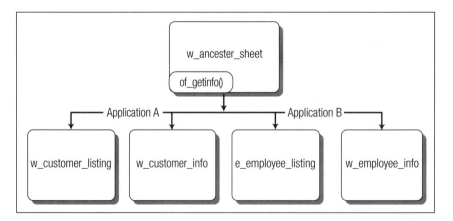

Figure 32.3
Lack of extendibility.

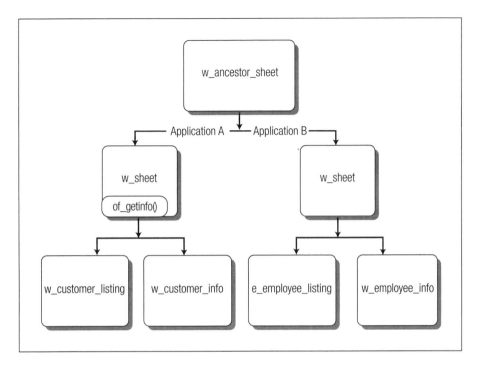

Figure 32.4
Use of extendibility.

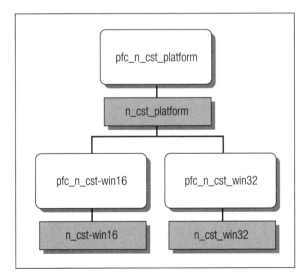

Figure 32.5
Example of the PFC extension level.

The extension PBLs start with "PFE" and correspond to PFC library names. Here's a list of the extensions:

- PFEAPSRV.PBL

- PFEDWSRV.PBL

- PFEMAIN.PBL

- PFEWNSRV.PBL

- PFEUTIL.PBL

Reference Variables

All reference variables in PFC are declared from the extension level. Any new properties or methods in extension level classes are immediately accessible. For example, **u_dw** is an extension class of the **pfc_u_dw** ancestor class.

New properties or methods may be added to the extension class **u_dw**, as seen here:

```
protected boolean  ib_browsemode
function of_GetBrowsemode()
function of_SetBrowsemode()
```

PFC reference variable **idw_active** has immediate access to new methods and properties defined in extension class **u_dw** as illustrated in Figure 32.6. These statements will compile successfully:

```
idw_active.of_GetBrowsemode()
idw_active.of_SetBrowsemode()
```

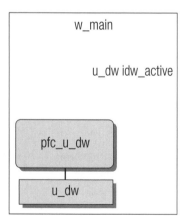

Figure 32.6
Use of reference variables.

Message Router

PFC uses a message router to handle communication between menus and windows. Although the message router is typically used to pass messages from menus to windows, it can be used to communicate between any object and a window. By using the message router, your menu scripts only need to know the user event to call. It does not need to know the current window or the associated window control name. Also, your windows do not need to maintain user events that simply call DataWindow user events.

When your users select a menu item, the item's **Clicked** event calls the menu's **of_SenMessage**() function, passing the name of the user event to be called. This function calls the window's **pfc_MessageRouter** event, which, in turn, calls the specified user event.

Database Access

For database access, PFC uses the **n_tr** User object, which is a custom transaction object inherited from the Transaction System object. The User object **n_tr** includes many instance variables, events, and functions that encapsulate and extend database communication. The **n_tr** object can be used to replace PowerBuilder's SQLCA, or it can be used in addition to SQLCA.

Use **n_tr** functions instead of native SQL transaction management statements. For example, to connect to your database, use **of_Connect**() instead of the **CONNECT** statement.

The Application Manager

The first step in creating an application with PFC is configuring and enabling the application manager, **n_cst_manager**. Within the application manager, you code logic that would otherwise appear in the Application object. The application manager also has instance variables and functions to maintain application attributes, such as the frame window, Application and User INI files, and the application Help file. To emphasize this, let's go through the steps for configuring an application manager:

1. Create a new Application object and add the PFC PBLs to your library search list.

2. If your application connects to a database, change SQLCA to point to **n_tr** instead of transaction. This is done in the Properties page of your Application object.

3. Define a global variable **gnv_app** of type **n_cst_appmanager**:

```
n_cst_app_manager gnv_app
```

*Note: It is a requirement that this variable be named **gnv_app**. All PFC objects, functions, and events require the application manager to be named **gnv_app** of type **n_cst_appmanager**.*

4. Add script to your application's **Open** event to create **n_cst_appmanager** and to redirect all processing from the Application object events to the application manager events:

```
gnv_app = CREATE n_cst_appmanager
gnv_app.Event pfc_open(commandline)
```

5. Add script to your Application object's **Close** event to call the **pfc_Close** event and destroy **n_cst_appmanager**:

```
gnv_app.EVENT pfc_Close()
DESTROY n_cst_appmanager
```

6. Add script to your Application object's **SystemError** event:

```
gnv_app.EVENT pfc_SystemError()
```

7. Add the following script to the **Idle** event:

```
gnv_app.EVENT pfc_Idle()
```

8. Now close your Application object and save it. Next, you need to open up **n_cst_appmanager**, which can be found in PFEAPSRV.PBL. Call functions in the **Constructor** events to initialize instance variables for version, company, and INI files. Here's an example:

```
// The application version
of_SetVersion("Version 6.0")

// The application logo, bitmap file name
of_SetLogo ("tdg.bmp")

// The file name of the application INI file
of_SetAppIniFile ("tdg.ini")
```

9. In the **pfc_Open** event, call functions to enable application services that you want to use. Here are some examples:

- **of_SetDWCache()**. For DataWindow Caching service
- **of_SetError()**. For Error service

- **of_SetTrRegistration()**. For Transaction Registration service

- **of_SetDebug()**. For the Debug service

10. Add code to the **pfc_Open** event to open your application's initial window. You can also call **of_Splash()** to display a splash screen.

```
This.of_Splach( 1 )
Open (w_mdiframe)
```

11. You can write script in the **pfc_Login** event of **n_cst_appmanager** to log your users on to the database. Another alternative is to call the **of_LogonDlg()** function in your frame window's **Open** event.

```
SQLCA.of_SetUser( as_userid, as_password )

IF SQLCA.of_Connect( ) >= 0 THEN
   RETURN 1
ELSE
   MessageBox( is_title, "Connection failed!")
   RETURN -1
END IF
```

12. The last step is to save your application manager.

> **Note:** All other application-level processing should be scripted in the appropriate events in the application manager, **n_cst_appmanager**, not in the Application object. For example, add script to open a frame in the application manager's **pfc_Open** event, not in the Application object's **Open** event.

Programming With PFC

When programming with PFC, every object you create should be inherited from a PFC object instead of created from scratch. Here are some examples:

- **MDI.** Inherit your frame window from **w_frame**, which is found in PFEMAIN.PBL. For your sheets, inherit from **w_sheet**.

- **SDI.** Use **w_main** as the ancestor to your main windows.

- **Menus.** Inherit a menu from **m_master** or **m_frame** in PFEWNSRV.PBL. Customize the menu as needed and associate it with your frame window.

- **Sheets.** Inherit sheets from **w_sheet**, which is found in the PFEMAIN.PBL.

- **Window controls.** Use subclassed PFC User objects on your sheets and avoid using native controls. All PowerBuilder controls are subclassed in PFC. For example, use User object **u_sle** (found in the PFEMAIN.PBL) instead of a standard SingleLineEdit control. Similarly, always use **u_dw** instead of the standard DataWindow control.

Almost all PFC functions are object-level functions. This means they are defined within objects such as windows, menus, or User objects. When you call these functions from outside of the object, you need to use dot notation to qualify the function name. Qualify the function name with the reference variable used to create the object.

To call a PFC object function, you first need to make sure the object has been created. Windows, menus, and visual User objects are created when they are opened. Nonvisual objects have to be created first with the aid of an enabler function. For example, to use the row selection service for a DataWindow, you need to use the **of_SetRowSelect()** function of **u_dw**, which creates the row selection service **n_cst_dwsrv_rowselection** User object and saves a reference to it in the **inv_rowselect** instance variable of **u_dw**. To enable extended row selection, you have to use the **of_SetStyle()** with 2 as its argument:

```
dw_customer.of_SetRowSelect( TRUE )
dw_customr.inv_rowselect.of_SetStyle( 2 )
```

PFC includes precoded events and user events that perform processing to implement PFC services. It also includes empty noncoded user events that allow you to add application-specific code to perform application-specific tasks.

Using PFC Services

PFC provides many services that you can utilize throughout your applications. The PFC services can be categorized as follows:

- Application services
- Window services
- Menu services
- DataWindow services
- Utility services

Going through the various services within each of these categories could occupy an entire book. However, to give you an idea of how powerful these services are and what they can provide for your applications, I'll go through a few examples from some of these categories.

Note: I strongly recommend that you take the time to review the PFC documentation to become familiar with the number of services available. It might save your time in the long run.

Transaction Registration Service

The Transaction Registration service tracks the transaction objects used by your application. This service is for use with the transaction objects based on **n_tr**. Transaction Registration is enabled via the **n_cst_trregistration** User object.

To enable the Transaction Registration service, call the **n_cst_appmanager of_SetTrRegistration**() function:

```
gnv_app.of_SetTrRegistration( TRUE )
```

The application manager destroys the service automatically when the application closes. To register a transaction, you have to call the **of_Register**() function of **n_cst_trregistration**:

```
gnv_app.inv_trregistration.of_Register ( SQLCA )
```

To control whether the transaction registration service commits or rolls back open transactions when it is destroyed, you have to call the **n_tr_of_SetAutoRollback**() function:

```
gnv_app.of_SetAutoRollback( TRUE )
```

Sheet Management Service

The PFC Sheet Management service provides functions that help you manage multiple sheets in your MDI applications. This is done through the **n_cst_winsrv_sheetmanager** User object. To enable the window Sheet Management service, call the **of_SetSheetManager**() function of **w_frame**. This function is available in all windows that are inherited from **w_frame**.

```
This.of_SetSheetManager( TRUE )
```

PFC destroys the service automatically when the frame window closes. To access sheet information, you can call the following functions:

- **of_GetSheetCount**()
- **of_GetSheets**()
- **of_GetSheetsByClass**()
- **of_GetSheetByTitle**()

Sort Service

The DataWindow Sort service allows you to provide easy-to-use sort capabilities in your DataWindows. The Sort service displays a Sort dialog box where your users can select their sort criteria. All you have to do is enable the Sort service and specify its style. You can also allow your users to sort by clicking on column headings. To enable the service for a specific DataWindow control, you first have to enable the Sort service:

```
dw_customer.of_SetSort(TRUE)
```

The service allows you to specify if the user should be presented with the standard PowerBuilder Sort dialog or one of the PFC dialog boxes. The standard PowerBuilder Sort dialog box is used by default. If you want to use one of the PFC Sort dialog boxes, you must specify the sort style. The following script indicates that the PFC drag and drop Sort dialog box should be used with the service:

```
dw_customer.inv_sort.of_SetStyle(1)
```

The DataWindow column names are used within the Sort dialog boxes by default. If you use one of the PFC Sort dialog boxes, you have the choice of using the database column names or the header names instead. It's more user friendly to use the header names, because sometimes the column names are not very meaningful. Here's an example:

```
dw_customer.inv_sort.of_SetColumnNameSource(2)
```

By default, all columns are included in the Sort dialog boxes. If you use one of the PFC Sort dialog boxes, you have the choice of excluding some columns from the dialog box. This is done by passing a string array as the argument of the **of_SetExclude**() function. For example, to exclude the column "fname" from the Sort dialog box, use the following code:

```
String ls_exclude[]
dw_customer.inv_sort.of_SetVisibleOnly(TRUE)
ls_exclude[1] = "fname"
dw_customer.inv_sort.of_SetExclude(ls_exclude)
```

By default, the sort is done on data values and not on display values. To sort on display values, use **of_SetUseDisplay**():

```
dw_customer.inv_sort.of_SetUseDisplay(TRUE)
```

Several different methods are available for sorting the data. Let's take a look at the various sort methods available to you.

Sort By Column Headers

You can allow sorting when the user clicks on a specific column header in the header band of a tabular DataWindow. To enable this service, use the **of_SetColumnHeader**() function:

```
dw_customer.inv_sort.of_SetColumnHeader(TRUE)
```

Once this is done, the DataWindow will be sorted by the column related to the header that the user has clicked. If the user clicks the same column header again, the column will be sorted once again, but in the opposite sort sequence.

Display A Sort Dialog Box With Automatic Sorting

You can trigger the **pfc_SortDlg** event of the DataWindow control to display a Sort dialog box and then automatically sort the DataWindow when the user clicks the OK button. This is done with the following:

```
dw_customer.EVENT pfc_SortDlg()
```

Displaying The Sort Dialog Box Programmatically

Instead of triggering the **pf_SortDlg** event, you can call a set of functions to display the dialog box and then sort:

```
string ls_null

SetNull(ls_null)

//pass a null string to the of_SetSort function
dw_customer.inv_sort.of_SetSort(ls_null)

//sort
dw_customer.inv_sort.of_Sort()
```

To avoid the display of the dialog box, you can directly specify a sort expression instead. Here's an example:

```
dw_customer.inv_sort.of_SetSort("fname A")
dw_customer.inv_sort.of_Sort()
```

> **Note:** Once **of_Sort()** has sorted your DataWindow, the **pfc_RowChanged** event is triggered.

Sort Dialog Box Styles

There are four different Sort dialog boxes you can use with the sort service:

- PowerBuilder Sorting

- Drag & Drop Sorting

- Multi-Column Sorting

- Single-Column Sorting

To specify the sort style, call the **of_SetStyle**() function, specifying the Sort dialog box style as its parameter. The following code sets the Sort dialog box to 1, which is drag and drop.

```
dw_custmer.inv_sort.of_SetStyle( 2 )
```

The Platform Service

The PFC Platform service provides functions that you can call to add platform-specific functionality to your applications. This service is available on multiple platforms without recoding or adding conditional logic that checks the current platform (like we did in Chapter 8, "User Objects").

Getting available memory is a very good example. This function returns the available memory via an external function call, but the external function declaration is different depending on your platform. Let's see how simple this is in PFC:

Declare a variable of type **n_cst_platform** and then call the **of_SetPlatform**() function to create the platform-specific descendant. Next, simply call the **of_GetMemory**() function to get the available memory:

```
//enable the platform service
n_cst_platfrom inv_platform
f_SetPlatform( inv_platform, TRUE )

//call the function
Long ll_memory
ll_memory = inv_platform.of_GetMemory()
```

New PFC 6.0 Features

PowerBuilder 6.0 has enhanced many existing PFC features and has added several new services and functionalities. Most objects now use constants to signify typical return codes. This practice enables you to write more readable code.

The following objects and services are enhancements in PFC 6.0:

- Drop-down calculator and calendar support for **u_dw** and **u_em**

- Window Sheet Manager service

- **pfc_Save** process

- Window Status Bar service

- Error Message service

- DataWindow Caching

- Row Selection service

- Security service

The new PFC 6.0 features can be summarized as follows:

- **Metaclass service.** The PowerBuilder Metaclass is a series of system classes and functions that provide information about class definitions. The PFC Metaclass service complements PowerBuilder's Metaclass, which you can use to look for function and event signatures, variable definitions, and to determine ancestor classes. For example, the following code determines if a function exists and then executes it:

```
n_cst_metaclass lnv_metaclass
powerobject     lpo_obj
string          ls_arg[]

IF lnv_metaclass.of_IsFunctionDefined( &
    lpo_obj.ClassName(), "of_Update", ls_arg) THEN
      lpo_obj.DYNAMIC of_Update()
END IF
```

- **Application Preference service.** Saves and restores application settings. It has INI file and Registry support that you can extend by adding your own settings.

- **Most Recently Used (MRU) service.** Allows you to open the most recently used windows.

- **DataWindow Resize service.** Allows you to register DataWindow columns to be moved or scaled when the actual DataWindow control is resized. For example, the following script registers two columns in the **dw_customer** DataWindow to become scaled right when **dw_customer** is resized:

```
dw_customer.inv_resize.of_Register("custid", &
   inv_resize.SCALERIGHT)

dw_customer.inv_resize.of_Register("fname", &
   inv_resize.SCALERIGHTBOTTOM)
```

- **DataWindow Properties service.** Enables you to view and modify internal Data-Window settings, modify services, and generate code.

- **Drop-down services.** New utilities that jazz up your application by providing calendars and calculators in your DataWindows. These services can be both column-level and standalone controls.

- **Data structures.** Available for linked lists, stacks, queues, and trees.

- **Profiler window.** Tracing and profiling are PowerBuilder system classes and functions that log, model, and analyze various activities that occur when your application is running. The PFC Profiler window assists you in debugging by enabling or disabling trace activities. You can then view the trace file and build various reports.

- **Splitbar control.** Allows you to resize adjacent controls and build Explorer-type windows. It also supports horizontal and vertical alignments. The following code builds an Explorer-type interface:

```
st_splitbar.of_Register(tv_1, st_splitbar.LEFT)
st_splitbar.of_Register(lv_1, st_splitbar.RIGHT)
```

- **Progress Bar control.** A visual indicator for your users during lengthy processes. It supports many styles and is fully configurable.

- **Library Extender.** Creates middle layers in PFC class hierarchies.

    Note: To learn more about these new features, apart from the PFC documentation, I strongly recommend that you take a good look at the PFC code examples installed with the PFC.

Let's take a closer look at a few of these new features.

DataWindow Resize

The DataWindow Resize service resizes or scales registered columns or controls when the actual parent object is resized. Before using the Resize service, you have to enable it. This is done with the **of_SetResize()** function:

```
This.of_SetResize( TRUE )
```

    Note: You cannot use the DataWindow Resize service with DataWindow objects that have the Composite or RichTextEdit presentation style.

Next, you have to call the overloaded **of_Register()** function to register your columns or controls that are to be resized or scaled. Let's go through two examples together. First, let's resize the columns of a DataWindow; then, we'll scale controls on a window.

To resize columns on a DataWindow, you have to call the **of_Register()** function. This function is overloaded, so to resize all columns, you don't need to pass any arguments. However, if you want to resize specific columns, the following arguments are required:

- The object being registered
- The percentage to move the object along the X axis
- The percentage to move the object along the Y axis
- The percentage to scale the object along the X axis
- The percentage to scale the object along the Y axis

The following example registers three columns and resizes them when their parent is resized:

```
IF IsValid(inv_resize) THEN
   This.inv_resize.of_Register("cust_id",0,0,20,0)
   This.inv_resize.of_Register("fname",0,0,20,0)
   This.inv_resize.of_Register("lname",0,0,20,0)
END IF
```

Instead of resizing, you can scale a registered control when its parent object is being resized. For this purpose, once again you need **of_Register()**, but this time, pass it different arguments:

- The object being registered.
- The desired resize/move method. Here are the valid values:
  - **FixedToRight**
  - **FixedToBottom**
  - **FixedToRight&Bottom**
  - **Scale**
  - **ScaleToRight**
  - **ScaleToBottom**
  - **ScaleToRight&Bottom**
  - **FixedToRight&ScaleToBottom**
  - **FixedToBottom&ScaleToRight**

The following script in the **Open** event of a window registers two controls to be scaled when the window is resized:

```
This.inv_resize.of_Register(cb_ok, &
   inv_resize.FIXEDRIGHTBOTTOM)

This.inv_resize.of_Register(dw_customer, &
   inv_resize.SCALERIGHTBOTTOM)
```

Drop-Down Calculator

The Calculator object, **pfc_u_calculator**, found in PFCAPSRV.PBL, is for use with numeric values in DataWindow and EditMask controls. Your users can use the calculator to enter values and calculations, which the object displays in the associated DataWindow column or EditMask control.

The Calculator object is mainly used as a drop-down object, displaying when a DataWindow column gets focus or when your user clicks the drop-down arrow. However, you can also place the Calculator object directly onto a window.

For automatic calculator display, DataWindow columns must use the DropDownListBox edit style; for manual calculator display, DataWindow columns can use the DropDownListBox, Edit, or EditMask edit style. To use this object for DataWindow columns, assign the DropDownListBox, Edit, or EditMask edit style to your required columns. You need to enable the drop-down calculator for your DataWindow by calling the **of_SetDropDownCalculator()** function. The following code can be placed in your DataWindow's **Constructor** event:

```
This.of_SetDropDownCalculator(TRUE)
```

Next, you need to register one or more columns by calling the **of_Register()** function:

```
This.iuo_calculator.of_Register ("commission", &
   This.iuo_calculator.DDLB_WITHARROW))
```

You also need to specify whether the drop-down calculator closes on a single-click or a double-click by calling the **of_SetCloseOnClick()** or **of_SetCloseOnDClick()** function:

```
//close on single click
This.iuo_calculator.of_SetCloseOnClick(FALSE)

//close on double click
This.iuo_calculator.of_SetCloseOnDClick(TRUE)
```

Calendar Object

The Calendar object, **pfc_u_calendar**, found in PFCAPSRV.PBL, is used to provide a drop-down calendar for date values. It can be used with **u_dw**-based DataWindow controls, **u_em**-based EditMask controls, or as a standalone calendar for use with or without an edit mask. Figure 32.7 illustrates a drop-down calendar.

To use this service with DataWindow columns, enable the drop-down calendar by calling the **of_SetDropDownCalendar()** function:

```
This.of_SetDropDownCalendar(TRUE)
```

Next, you need to register columns one by one or all at once. You also need to specify your drop-down style by calling the **of_Register()** function:

```
This.iuo_calendar.of_Register("Startdate", &
    This.iuo_calendar.DDLB)
```

You can also set the font style and color for weekend days:

```
This.iuo_calendar.of_SetSaturdayBold(TRUE)
This.iuo_calendar.of_SetSaturdayColor &
    (RGB(0, 255, 0))

This.iuo_calendar.of_SetSundayBold(TRUE)
This.iuo_calendar.of_SetSundayColor  &
    (RGB(0, 255, 0))
```

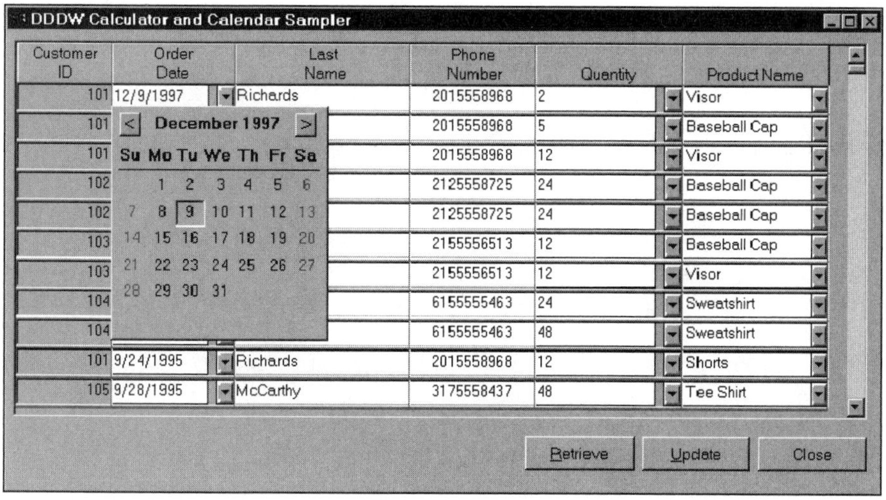

Figure 32.7
A drop-down calendar in a DataWindow.

For further cosmetics, you can set a list of holidays with their font styles and colors as shown in the next example:

```
Date    ld_holidays[11]

ld_97holidays[1] = 1997-01-01
//add more to your list here

This.iuo_calendar.of_SetHoliday(ld_97holidays)
This.iuo_calendar.of_SetHolidayBold(TRUE)
This.iuo_calendar.of_SetHolidayColor( RGB( 0,255,0 ) )
```

As with the Calculator object, the calendar can be closed with a single click or a double-click:

```
//close with a single click
This.iuo_calendar.of_SetCloseOnClick(TRUE)

//close with a double click
This.iuo_calendar.of_SetCloseOnDClick(TRUE)
```

The Library Extender

The PFC Library Extender is just what we've all been waiting for. You can use this tool to automatically create and populate an intermediate extension level between two existing levels, such as the ancestor level and the extension level. To give you a more specific example, you might use the Library Extender to create an intermediate extension level to contain all your organization's corporate-level extensions to PFC. Figure 32.8 shows the main screen of the Library Extender.

Here are the steps to follow to create an extension level:

1. Run the Library Extender and select the library that contains the Application object you want to use in building and populating the new extension level.

2. If you give the Library Extender an Application object, you can adjust the library list. If you build extensions without an application, select the ancestor and extension libraries to use in building the new extension level.

3. Specify the prefix to use for your objects in the new extension level.

4. Specify where to place existing extension-level customizations.

5. Select the objects to be extended.

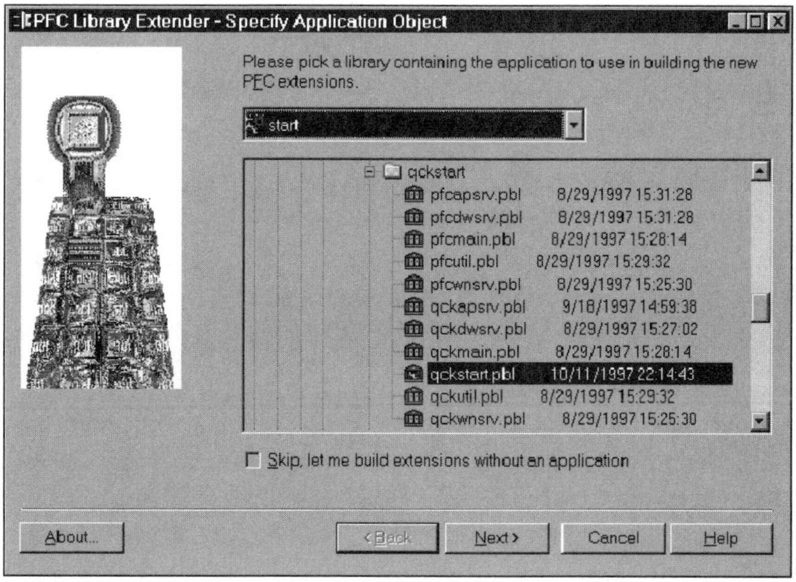

Figure 32.8
The PFC Library Extender.

6. Specify the location of the new PBLs.

7. Specify how to save the new library search path.

Migration

The first step in migrating your PFC applications to any release should be making a full backup of your PFC PBLs and applications. Whenever in doubt on what to do, feel free to contact Sybase technical support for advice or refer to Sybase's technical documents.

If you're using the default extension-level PBLs as your extension level and you have made changes to one or more objects, you must move these PBLs to different locations so that they are not lost when the installation overwrites them. If you're using the QuickStart PBLs, you must move them, too.

Once you've installed the new PFC PBLs, you have to copy new objects to your customized extension PBLs. Make sure you view the newly installed PFC README.TXT file in the PFC's directory. There, you'll find a section on new extension objects that lists any new extension objects and the release in which they were added. Make a note of all extension objects that were introduced in each version that is more current than the PFC version you are using and then copy each of the noted extension objects from the appropriate newly installed PFE PBLs to your corresponding customized extension PBLs.

If you use the default extension-level PBLs, delete the installed extension PFE PBLs and replace them with your customized versions. You can also copy all objects in all your customized extension PBLs to the new extension PBLs that were just installed. This will overwrite the installed extension objects with your changes.

Once this is all done, adjust your application's library paths in PowerBuilder if necessary to include the installed PFC PBLs and the new versions of your customized extension PBLs. Perform a full rebuild on each PFC application that you use. If you previously built an executable for the PFC security scanner, rebuild the scanner executable. If you want to take advantage of the bug fixes, new enhancements, and new features, you should rebuild all your PFC PBLs and update your deployment DLLs.

The PFCOLD.PBL contains PFC obsolete objects. This library is not required for new PFC 6.0 applications but is there for existing PFC applications. If you're migrating, include this library in your search path and then check for user extensions to obsolete objects.

Migration Assistant

The Migration Assistant, a new enterprise tool, illustrated in Figure 32.9, scans your PBLs and highlights usage of obsolete functions and events. Obsolete functions and

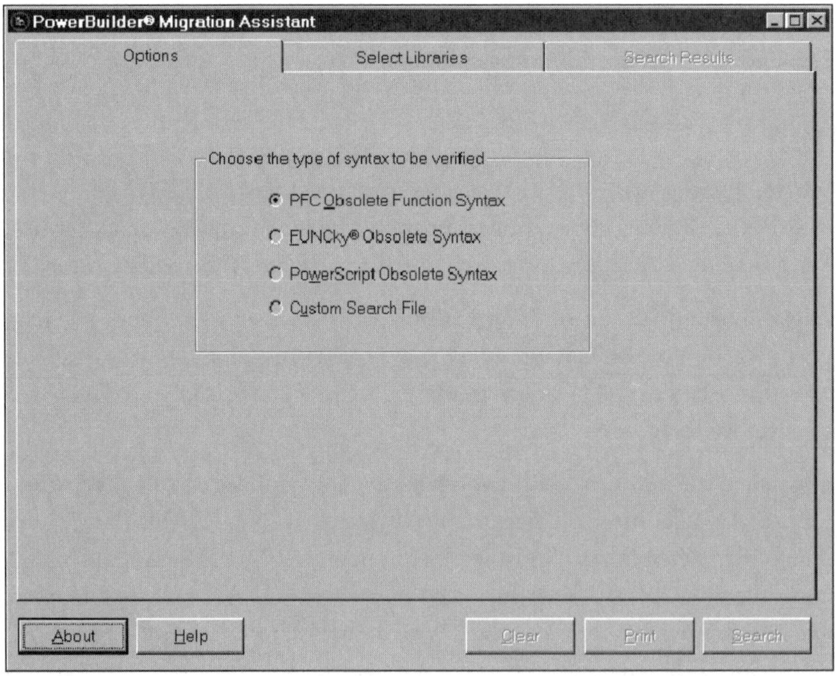

Figure 32.9
The Migration Assistant.

events still work in the current version of PowerBuilder but may not work in future versions. If you plan on maintaining your applications in the future, the recommendation is to use the current syntax and events.

To use the Migration Assistant, first use the Options tab to specify the type of syntax you want to verify; you can check PFC, PowerScript, FUNCky, or your own syntax. Then, use the Select Libraries tab to specify the PBLs to search for obsolete syntax.

Once you've performed a search, use the Search Results tab to see a list of all obsolete functions and events. The next task is modifying your code to use the current syntax. Gook luck!

Moving On

In this chapter, we talked about the PowerBuilder Foundation Class library. What an architecture! The PFC is certainly one of the best things that has happened to PowerBuilder. It uses a service-based architecture that maximizes PowerBuilder's object-oriented capabilities, which gives you the ability to quickly add powerful capabilities to your applications!

I discussed the PFC architecture and the PFC services, and we looked at a few of these services in detail. Finally, I covered some of the new features of PFC 6.0.

In the next chapter, I'll discuss Sybase's CODE partners. As you develop more complex applications, you might require a solution to a specific need. For example, you may be in need of a PFC tool. Well, to facilitate your efforts, Sybase has created partnerships with successful companies known as *CODE partners*. There are many CODE partners with different products and add-ons for the Sybase family of tools. In the next chapter, I'll talk about three in particular and the products they represent.

CODE Partners
33

You can measure the success of a particular development tool by counting the number of third-party vendors building add-on tools for it. As you develop more complex applications, you might require a solution to a specific need. This need could be a number of things—a framework, a class library, an object browser, an object tool, or any other tools that might improve your productivity.

To facilitate you with this need, Sybase has dedicated substantial resources to creating strong, mutually beneficial, noncompetitive partnerships. Client/server Open Development Environment (CODE) is Sybase's strategic framework for protecting existing technology investments and working with emerging client/server technology. CODE extends PowerBuilder's product capabilities and market breadth, both in the richness of its application development functionality and its expanding links to other components of the client/server platform. These include the ongoing development of vendor partnerships that cover the entire enterprise computing environment as well as the expansion of the company's training, consulting, and product support services and alliances.

CODE is also a client/server philosophy that Sybase is advancing to the industry. It seeks to ensure the openness and interoperability of the client/server platform. Because client/server is a market-driven platform, vendors have an obligation to offer products that are competitive within their core technologies, yet provide common interfaces to other product components in the client/server environment. Sybase refers to this principle as building a "community of good client/server citizens."

The list of partners is long, and if you are looking for a solution to a specific problem, Sybase has provided it for you. To serve you better, many successful companies have become partners with Sybase, and with their wide range of products, you'll definitely find the solution you're looking for. For a listing of all of Sybase's CODE partners, visit http://www.sybase.com/partners.

There are three CODE partners that I particularly want to talk about. They are quite successful in what they do, and the products they represent are well known in the PowerBuilder community. Without any further ado, I'd like to introduce these partners and some of the tools they have to offer.

PowerCerv

PowerCerv's mission statement is to be a leader in the delivery of adaptable application solutions to the midtier market. As part of its solutions, PowerCerv provides a suite of client/server tools. In this section, I'll provide you with an overview of these tools. I'll also include a complete feature summary of PFCtool, an easy-to-use class library framework that extends and enhances the functionality of the PFC library.

On the accompanying CD-ROM, you'll find screencams that demonstrate PFCtool in detail. The demos are in the beta version of PFCtool. (Note that the final version will have many more features that were not completed in the beta version.)

For additional information, pricing, and availability, visit PowerCerv's Web site at http://www.powercerv.com.

AppSync 3.0

AppSync is a distribution utility that installs your applications and can automatically synchronize its related files. This utility is customizable and has a scripting language called AppScript that manages your synchronization procedures. With AppSync, you can distribute entire applications and updated versions of your software, as well as plain files of any type using your local area network (LAN), wide area network (WAN), or the Internet.

AppSync deploys files based on date and timestamps, size information, and file type. AppSync also uses dependency checking so that required software packages are installed first.

PADLock 5.0

PADLock (PowerBuilder Application and Data Lock) allows you to secure windows, buttons, DataWindows, and objects in your PowerBuilder applications. PADLock enables your users with appropriate rights to configure applications at runtime according to their organization's business requirements, and it eliminates the need for you to embed client-side security within the application itself. PADLock also allows you to control runtime access to data in DataWindow rows and columns as well as the visibility of windows, controls, and menu items in the application, without the need to modify PowerBuilder code.

FLOWBuilder 4.0

FLOWBuilder is a good tool for enabling workflow in your client/server applications. In other words, with this tool, you can design and develop maintainable systems that cleanly separate an application's business processes from its application-specific logic.

PowerTOOL 5.0

PowerTOOL (PowerBuilder Template Object-Oriented Library) is a standardized PowerBuilder object class library that advances your PowerBuilder development. You can use PowerTOOL and its accompanying methodology to provide a solid foundation for large and small client/server applications. Applications can inherit much of their functionality directly from the PowerTOOL development methodology. This reduces areas of redundant application code and significantly reduces development time, maintenance overhead, and code defects.

Here are some of PowerTOOL's key features, according to PowerCerv:

- Provides a collection of PowerBuilder objects that can immediately be applied to application development, resulting in faster development time.

- Provides standards for application development.

- Supports a user-extensible veneer layer between PowerTOOL core objects and your application. This veneer layer allows you to extend PowerTOOL objects without altering the original ancestors so that the next PowerTOOL upgrade won't overwrite the extensions.

- Incorporates the advanced features of PowerBuilder 5.0. Function overloading, event parameters, dynamic function calls, and new class objects (such as the Tab control, the TreeView control, the ListView control, and the DataStore nonvisual object) are fully supported and extended.

- Allows quick-and-easy creation of both MDI and SDI applications. PowerTOOL provides complete support for MDI frames, sheets, and menus, and it fully supports SDI applications.

- Provides a data-driven navigation facility that allows users to easily move around in large PowerBuilder applications. Applications can be built with or without PowerTOOL's navigation facility.

PFCtool 5.6

In order to reduce the effort involved in creating a PFC application framework, PowerCerv has developed an easy-to-use, PFC-based class library framework called *PFCtool*.

PowerCerv has used its class library development experience to design key components, services, and templates that can help maximize your productivity. PFCtool 5.6 provides the following features:

- **Runtime Configurable Objects (RCO).** These are prebuilt, automated templates that provide dynamic runtime behavior. Each service, object, and RCO behavior can be dynamically configured when the RCO is opened. Support is also provided for dynamic instantiation of a Business Logic Interface object for each visual object and for dynamically changing the associated menu for the RCO.

- **Prebuilt "Save As" templates.** Over 60 different prebuilt templates offer a rich variety of functionality modeled on common information presentation paradigms and service combinations. You can open a template, save it under a different object name, and then uncomment the script for the desired functionality.

The PFCtool 5.6 Sampler provides step-by-step instructions for implementing PFCtool's many objects and services. Also, PFCtool's Parameter wizard provides a structured approach to fully utilizing PFCtool, thus significantly increasing your productivity. In addition, PowerCerv has designed PFCtool to be a true extension of PFC. Other class library architectures insert a layer of objects between the PFC layers. In order to do this, the ancestry must be disassembled and reassembled for each object. This insertion architecture inherently requires the class library vendor to alter native PFC. PowerCerv has built on top of the PFC layers, leaving the PFC ancestors and extension objects untouched. PFCtool ancestor objects inherit from PFC extension objects, not directly from PFC ancestor objects. By truly extending, rather than inserting, PowerCerv does not modify native PFC. Figure 33.1 illustrates how PFCtool is a true extension of PFC.

CYRANO

CYRANO offers a unique integrated set of premier ASQ (Automated Software Quality) products and services that are designed to enable Windows and Open System development teams to address the challenges of automated testing as well as quality and performance management of mission-critical client/server applications. Combining functional and regression testing, unit testing, acceptance testing, load testing, and database testing, the CYRANO suite optimizes the performance and quality of client/server applications or packages during development, before deployment, and during maintenance or a major migration process. For more information on CYRANO's tools, visit its Web site at http://www.cyrano.com.

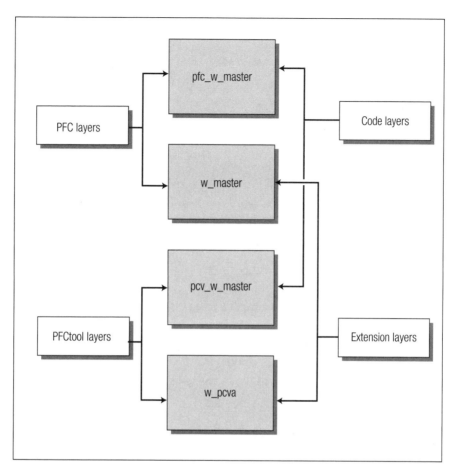

Figure 33.1
PFCtool extending the PFCs.

CYRANO ClientPack

CYRANO ClientPack is a comprehensive, integrated range of industry-leading tools for ensuring the quality of Windows client/server applications.

CYRANO ClientPack assists you in designing and building the client part of a client/server system and in testing the entire enterprise-wide system, end to end. Together, the components of CYRANO ClientPack help ensure that your applications meet the requirements of your users, have quality built in from the beginning, and can easily and automatically be validated for correct functional behavior during development, as well as after any changes have been introduced.

CYRANO ClientPack is comprised of five key products:

- CYRANO Standards
- CYRANO WinScope
- CYRANO Insight
- CYRANO Manager
- CYRANO Robot

On the accompanying CD-ROM, you'll find demos on all of these products. I'm sure you'll enjoy watching the demos as much as I did. The following subsections provide a quick synopsis of these tools.

CYRANO Standards

CYRANO Standards is a conventions and rules manager that enables you to define a complete set of requirements for ensuring quality and performance in the development of client/server applications. Used in conjunction with CYRANO WinScope, CYRANO Standards enables simplified definition of development requirements and automates the checking of your application's compliance to the software standards. Standards that can be defined with CYRANO Standards include the following:

- Naming rules for the naming of every single object
- Graphical rules for the graphical attributes of all visual objects
- Structural rules for the structure of the object and their use in the application
- Coding rules for the way the actual code is written

CYRANO WinScope

CYRANO WinScope is an application development optimizer that enables you to efficiently write client/server software applications that will have increased performance and are easier to maintain. CYRANO WinScope is a companion to the development environment. It also helps you maintain and develop applications to conform to specified development standards and best practices.

CYRANO WinScope also enhances productivity of application development by providing you with a powerful means of navigating applications, including full cross-referencing of every object.

CYRANO Insight

CYRANO Insight is a database client calls analyzer. It enables you to gain an in-depth understanding of every SQL statement or API call issued by the client application to the database server. Also, it helps with dynamic optimization of database calls in any client/server application.

With CYRANO Insight, you can analyze the quality of the transactions in any client/server program simply by running it, even if you don't not have access to the application source code.

CYRANO Insight can be used to assist with your regression testing. When planning to make functional enhancements or bug fixes to the application, you can use CYRANO Insight for validating the changes to the transactions or API calls.

CYRANO Manager

CYRANO Manager lets you plan, manage, and analyze all aspects of Windows NT, Windows 95, and Windows 3.x client/server testing projects. CYRANO Manager is customizable and offers integrated, email-enabled test planning, workflow tracking, and defect management to keep you on top of your project. In addition, CYRANO Manager offers powerful reporting and graphing functions for quick-and-easy analysis of the progress and coverage of your Windows client/server testing project. CYRANO Manager helps keep your entire test team running smoothly.

As per CYRANO Manager's datasheet, the following features are included:

- Stores and organizes test cases and test procedures for integrated, flexible test management

- Imports PowerBuilder library and ASCII text files for automatic generation of test requirements and test procedure names

- Tracks defects along a customizable, rules-based workflow for comprehensive, flexible defect management and tracking

CYRANO Robot

CYRANO Robot enables you to create, modify, and run automated tests on your 32- and 16-bit Windows NT/95 client/server applications and your 16-bit Windows 3.x applications. Integrated with the scaleable CYRANO Test Repository, CYRANO Robot offers object-level support for the 32- and 16-bit versions of applications created with

PowerBuilder and other client/server development tools. CYRANO Robot is a test automation solution that offers reusability and portability of test recordings across Windows platforms to provide one recording that plays back on all Windows platforms.

As per the CYRANO Robot datasheet, the following features are included:

- Delivers object-oriented recording technology to provide fastest, intuitive test creation with a short learning curve.

- Includes an integrated, Visual Basic-compatible scripting environment that delivers the full power of the integrated programming environment for script development.

- A centralized test repository provides easy analysis of test results for improved communication among test team members.

Greenbrier & Russel

Greenbrier & Russel's software products division encompasses two areas: third-party client/server tools and internally developed software. Greenbrier & Russel has formed strategic alliances with leading software vendors to provide productivity enhancement tools for virtually every phase of the development life cycle—from analysis and design through implementation.

Later this year, Greenbrier & Russel plans to offer tools to enhance productivity in the Java development environment. Also, Greenbrier & Russel has prepared a beta version of ObjectSmith 6.0 to be released soon after the release of PowerBuilder 6.0. For additional information on ObjectSmith, such as pricing and availability, visit Greenbrier & Russel's homepage at http://www.gr.com.

ObjectSmith 5.0

ObjectSmith is a PowerBuilder utilities toolset. The new 5.2 release of ObjectSmith provides significantly enhanced functionality over the 5.1 release and works specifically with the previous release of PowerBuilder. This release has been substantially expanded and is divided into four toolsets to meet the needs of different developers and different phases in the development process.

ObjectSmith Developer Toolset

The Developer Toolset, which is a set of tools meant to increase productivity during day-to-day development, includes the following utilities:

- **Object Browser.** This object browser shows all aspects of a PowerBuilder object, including source code for event and function scripts.

- **Script Assistant.** This tool allows you to store standard PowerScript fragments in text files and paste them into the PowerBuilder Script Painter with a single mouse click.

- **Application Archiver.** This tool makes backup copies of all the PowerBuilder libraries in an application and keeps a record of all backups made.

- **Archive Restore.** All ObjectSmith applications that make changes to PBLs or other files automatically keep a backup copy of the files before changes are made. This tool can be used to restore files to their prior state, undoing any changes made by Object-Smith tools. This tool also operates in conjunction with the Application Archiver tool to restore PBLs or other files from the backup repository.

- **Object Finder.** This tool scans all the PBLs on a selected hard drive or network drive looking for objects that match certain user-specified criteria.

- **Reference Finder.** This tool finds all references to a name in one or more selected objects. It can be used to find references to objects, global variables, functions, and so on. References found are reported showing the script context in which they appear.

- **Regenerator.** This tool regenerates selected objects and their ancestors to ensure that interobject references are correctly updated to reflect script changes.

- **Magic Import.** This tool imports a group of objects that have mutual references into a PBL from source text files. Magic Import makes it easier to move a cooperating group of objects from one PBL to another or from one application to another.

- **PB.INI Cleanser.** This tool removes old information from the PowerBuilder INI file to improve performance, reduce confusion, and free wasted space.

- **Object Locator.** The Object Locator is designed to quickly find objects in the current application. This tool accepts an object name in the Search For Object dialog and searches the selected PBLs for matches.

ObjectSmith Professional Toolset

The Professional Toolset is intended for use when editing exported PowerScript code is the only alternative. Here are the tools included in the Professional Toolset:

- **Global Name Changer.** This tool automatically changes all occurrences of one or more object names, function names, event names, or variable names.

- **Inheritance Adjuster.** This tool allows the inheritance hierarchy of PowerBuilder objects to be modified by inserting new layers into an existing hierarchy and by moving objects within the hierarchy.

- **PBL Assistant.** This tool maintains an application profile that is a mapping of PowerBuilder objects to the corresponding source files. It allows one or more selected objects to be rapidly exported to or imported from their source files.

- **PBDebug Viewer.** Allows you to view PBDebug files that are trace files generated by PowerBuilder to help you determine the flow of control through an application.

- **PBR Builder.** This tool identifies all the PowerBuilder resources, such as bitmaps and icons, used in an application and constructs a PBR file containing their references.

- **Archive Restore.** All ObjectSmith applications that make changes to PBLs or other files automatically keep a backup copy of the files before changes are made. This tool can be used to restore files to their prior state, undoing any changes made by ObjectSmith tools.

- **Application Optimizer.** The Application Optimizer allows a group of PBLs to be optimized. It also backs up each PBL into the ObjectSmith archive. This allows PBLs to be restored using the ObjectSmith Archive Restore application. Each PBL is re-created and rewritten so all directory information in the PBL is re-created.

- **Script Assistant.** This tool allows you to store standard PowerScript fragments in text files and paste them into the PowerBuilder Script Painter with a single mouse click.

ObjectSmith Documentation Toolset

The Documentation Toolset is an excellent set of tools for preparing documentation for your applications. It includes the following tools:

- **Source Commenter.** This tool automatically inserts standardized header comments into all event and function scripts as well as variable declaration blocks in selected PowerBuilder objects.

- **Source Documenter.** This tool automatically generates HTML files, RTF files, and Help files describing the variables, attributes, functions, events, and other properties of selected PowerBuilder objects.

- **Source Formatter.** This tool formats PowerScript source code to predetermined publication standards.

- **Source Reporter.** This tool generates a variety of reports concerning PowerBuilder applications and objects.

- **Archive Restore.** All ObjectSmith applications that make changes to PBLs or other files automatically keep a backup copy of the files before changes are made. This tool can be used to restore files to their prior state.

- **Script Commenter.** This application performs commenting of scripts in the Power-Builder development environment.

- **Script Assistant.** This tool allows you to store standard PowerScript fragments in text files and paste them into the PowerBuilder Script Painter with a single mouse click.

The PFC Toolset

The PFC Toolset is designed to assist you with your new PFC applications. It contains the following tools:

- **Application Generator.** This tool generates a fully functional PowerBuilder application based on user-selected options for PFC services and objects to be included.

- **DataWindow Generator.** This tool generates a new user object of type DataWindow that is descended from the PFC base DataWindow control with user-selected DataWindow services automatically enabled.

- **Message Painter.** This tool provides a Painter-style interface for creating and editing messages in PFC's message repository.

- **Level Inserter.** This tool automatically inserts a new customization layer into an existing PFC inheritance hierarchy.

- **Script Assistant.** This tool allows you to store standard PowerScript fragments in text files and paste them into the PowerBuilder Script Painter with a single mouse click.

- **Archive Restore.** All ObjectSmith applications that make changes to PBLs or other files automatically keep a backup copy of the files before changes are made. This tool can be used to restore files to their prior state.

- **MessageBox Painter.** The MessageBox Painter generates messages as source code and pastes them into the active Painter script.

Moving On

In this chapter, I discussed CODE partners, and in particular PowerCerv, CYRANO, and Greenbrier & Russel. The PowerBuilder tools that these partners represent are invaluable. They are all great tools. Which to choose and what to use is your decision!

In the next chapter, I'll talk about some of the design and development tools Sybase has to offer. These tools represent a multiproduct solution and address IT needs your corporation may have. These tools include RAD C++, Java, Web, and 4GL development and are ideal for your next client/server or distributed computing application.

Other Sybase Design And Development Tools

The Sybase design and development tools family represents a multiproduct strategy that addresses the needs of professional application developers like yourself. With tools for RAD C++, Java, Web, and 4GL development, along with the ability to design databases and generate application objects and data-aware components, Sybase tools are ideal for your next client/server or distributed computing application.

Recently, Sybase announced PowerStudio, a combination of various tools bundled together in one complete package along with a component transaction server designed for delivering transactional applications to the Net. No matter what your application requirements are today and where technology moves you tomorrow, it's nice to know that with PowerStudio and Sybase tools, you'll be prepared for it.

In this chapter I'll provide you with an overview of some of these tools. If you require additional information, please feel free to contact Sybase's sales and marketing group or refer to Sybase's Web page at http://www.sybase.com.

Power++

Power++ is the new and continuing version of what was once named Optima++. Comparing Power++ to its competitors, it is the first RAD C++ tool that gives you the performance needed for client/server, distributed, and Internet applications. That's why it has won so many awards in such a short time since its release. Figure 34.1 illustrates Power++'s IDE.

Note that Power++ has three editions—Developer, Professional, and Enterprise. I've based this overview on the Enterprise edition, but for a chart of features for each edition, you can refer to the Sybase Web site at http://www.sybase.com/products/powerpp.

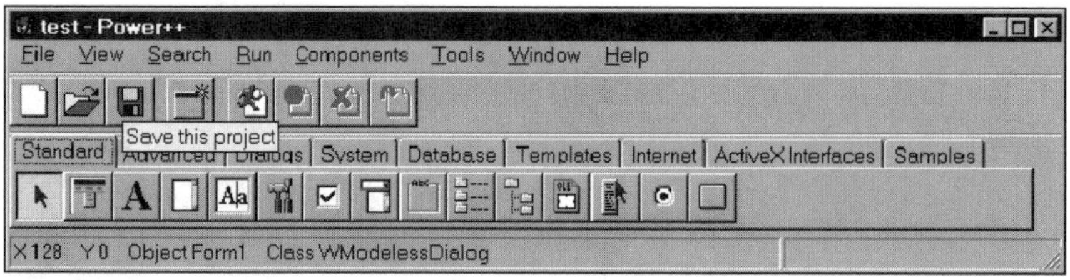

Figure 34.1
The Power++ IDE.

Power++ has many unique and outstanding features. I'll briefly go over a few of them that I think stand out the most:

- **Database Connectivity.** Power++ is an excellent tool for building database applications. The Enterprise version of Power++ is bundled with native database drivers that give you database connectivity to a wide range of datasources such as Sybase SQL Server, Oracle, Informix, DB2, and Microsoft SQL Server. If you're a PowerBuilder developer, you know how valuable these native drivers are. With Power++ Enterprise, you are also given the Sybase DataWindow, the Visual Query Editor, ODBC drivers for many desktop and enterprise DBMSs, and a 3-user Sybase SQL Anywhere server.

- **The DataWindow.** Power++ Enterprise and Professional include the Sybase DataWindow ActiveX control. By now I don't have to tell you about the DataWindow, but just in case, it's a powerful, graphical database control that displays various data-driven presentation styles that range from tabular and grid to crosstab and graphs. Having this technology present is an excellent opportunity to share your DataWindows between Power++ and PowerBuilder.

- **Internet Development.** Developing for the Internet has become the talk of the town these days. Power++ Enterprise and Professional give you Internet support through a collection of controls for Web browsing, Socket services programming, and mail functionality. You can even build Web server extensions using CGI, NSAPI, and ISAPI. The Enterprise edition also gives you Sybase Dynamo, which provides you with the ability to create and manage dynamic, data-driven Web sites. Isn't that great?

As per the Sybase Power++ product information list, the main features of Power++ Enterprise are summarized in the following list:

- Native database drivers for Sybase SQL Server, Oracle, Informix, and Microsoft SQL Server

- The DataWindow ActiveX control

- The ability to build reusable native components and ActiveX Server components
- Multitier support for distributed computing architectures, including Sybase Jaguar CTS and Microsoft Transaction Server
- A Visual Query Editor for creating SQL
- A 3-user Sybase SQL Anywhere server
- Royalty-free Sybase SQL Anywhere runtime engine
- The ability to build Web server extensions using CGI, NSAPI, and ISAPI
- Internet components for building Web applications
- Sybase Dynamo for creating dynamic, data-driven Web sites
- ObjectCycle 2.0 version control system
- The InfoMaker reporting and analysis tool
- InstallShield Express
- Versions of Visual Components, including Formula One and First Impression
- Reference Cards and Parameter Wizards for fast access to native components and ActiveX functionality
- Comprehensive C++ language support, including namespaces and RTTI
- Support for Intel MMX technology

PowerJ

Before getting to PowerJ, let's quickly review Java one more time. We all know that Java is an object-oriented programming language that has become the new buzzword in the computing community. A Java program can run on many different operating systems and hardware platforms, without having to be recompiled or converted in any way. The reason for this is that Java programs are compiled into a platform-independent format called *Java byte code*. This byte code is designed to be executed by a virtual machine called the *Java VM*. Any platform that has an implementation of the Java VM can interpret byte code and therefore run Java programs.

Java is particularly suited for use on the Web, specifically applets, which are designed to be used in Web pages. Sybase's PowerJ is an excellent tool for creating professional Java programs quickly. In my opinion, PowerJ is probably the best thing that has happened to Java. If you're going to be doing any Web or Java development, PowerJ is definitely the tool. For a complete listing of PowerJ features, please refer to Sybase's Web site at http://www.sybase.com/products/powerJ. Here are some features that put PowerJ a step ahead of its competitors:

- **Shorter Java learning curve.** If you haven't had the chance to learn Java yet, PowerJ is designed to assist you with the learning curve of a new programming language. Similar to Power++, the PowerJ development environment, shown in Figure 34.2, gives you drag-and-drop programming as well as reference cards and parameter wizards to allow you to get started quickly. In such a short period of time since its release, PowerJ has won many Editor's Choice awards and has proven to be an excellent Java tool with which to work.

- **Database connectivity.** PowerJ offers database support by providing a set of components that can be used with any JDBC datasource. PowerJ is bundled with the Sybase SQL Anywhere database, but for high-performance data access, PowerJ includes jConnect, a full thin-client JDBC implementation. jConnect gives you Java native database access to the family of Sybase server products, which include Sybase SQL Server, SQL Anywhere, and Sybase IQ, in addition to more than 25 enterprise database servers through the Sybase OmniCONNECT.

- **Support for industry components.** PowerJ also provides support for JavaBeans, ActiveX, and CORBA components. Third-party components can be integrated into PowerJ, and they can be accessible via drag-and-drop programming. This is an excellent feature that allows you to quickly and easily learn the new components. PowerJ also includes a set of built-in JavaBeans components, allowing you to code platform-independent Java applets and applications.

As indicated in the Sybase PowerJ product information list, the main features of PowerJ Enterprise are summarized in the following list:

- Component-based development and deployment system for Java

- Drag-and-drop programming and dynamically generated wizards

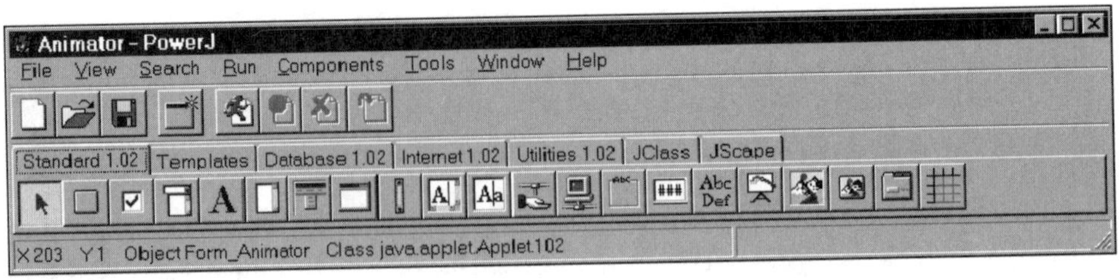

Figure 34.2
The PowerJ IDE.

- Support for JavaBeans, ActiveX, and CORBA

- Class Wizard for creation of reusable Java beans

- Data-aware components, including Grid control and Data Navigator, for use with any JDBC or ODBC datasource or result set

- Client-side caching for high-performance database applications

- Sybase's jConnect for JDBC development seat

- Sybase Jaguar CTS development seat for building and testing OLTP applications for the Web

- In-context debugging

- Support for JDK 1.1 and 1.02

- Open support for Sun and Microsoft VMs

- Power Dynamo development seat for creating and managing dynamic Web sites

- Sybase SQL Anywhere for building and testing your database applications

- ObjectCycle and hooks to other popular version control tools

- Integrated components, classes, and drivers from JScape, KL Group, ObjectSpace, Visigenic, and XDB

- And much more….

PowerDesigner 6.1

The PowerDesigner product family is an integrated design toolset for building databases, data warehouses, data marts, and data-aware components. The PowerDesigner toolset offers an interactive environment that supports all phases of your development cycle, from process modeling to object and component generation. For a complete detailed description and datasheet on PowerDesigner, visit the Sybase Web site at http://www.sybase.com/products/powerdesigner. The PowerDesigner toolset consists of the following tools:

- **ProcessAnalyst.** The PowerDesigner ProcessAnalyst is mainly used for data analysis and gathering information about the data flow of your business applications. Sybase calls this a "data discovery" tool. Great terminology!

- **DataArchitect.** The PowerDesigner DataArchitect is used for what Sybase calls "bi-level conceptual and physical database design and database construction." This tool offers you data modeling capabilities. This includes database design, generation, maintenance, reverse-engineering, and documentation.

- **AppModeler.** The PowerDesigner AppModeler is used for physical database design and application object and data-aware component generation. This tool offers full physical modeling capabilities and allows you to generate objects and components for many development environments such as PowerBuilder 5.0 and 6.0, Visual Basic 3.0, 4.0, and 5.0, Delphi 2.0, and Power++ 2.0. In addition, AppModeler can generate components for creating data-driven Web sites, allowing you to publish live data from a database. AppModeler also offers physical database generation, maintenance, and reporting for more than 30 DBMS vendors and desktop databases.

- **MetaWorks.** The PowerDesigner MetaWorks is used for teamwork environments where model sharing is used. It basically is a tool designed to provide the other tools in the toolset with the ability to share and store data models in a single point of control, called the *MetaWorks Dictionary*.

- **Warehouse Architect.** The PowerDesigner Warehouse Architect is used for data warehouse and data mart modeling and implementation. Warehouse Architect provides full warehousing support for all the major, traditional DBMSs such as Sybase, Oracle, Informix, DB2, and SQL Server, in addition to warehouse-specific DBMSs such as Red Brick Warehouse and Sybase IQ.

- **Viewer.** PowerDesigner Viewer is used for read-only, graphical access to modeling and metadata information. Viewer provides read-only access to all PowerDesigner modeling information, including process, conceptual, physical, and warehouse models. In addition to providing a graphical view into the modeling information, Viewer provides full reporting and documenting capabilities across all models.

Jaguar Component Transaction Server (CTS)

I know that Jaguar CTS probably does not fit into the tools category, but we've all been waiting to migrate applications or develop new and robust applications for the Internet. This task requires dynamic content, secure database access, and large-scale transaction processing. So far, we've only been able to do online transaction processing (OLTP) on corporate LANs or WANs. As a solution for this dilemma, Sybase has introduced Jaguar CTS, a new component transaction server that offers a fast, midtier execution environment that supports multiple component models. Jaguar CTS is also flexible enough to handle both synchronous and asynchronous transactions. Figure 34.3 illustrates the Jaguar server.

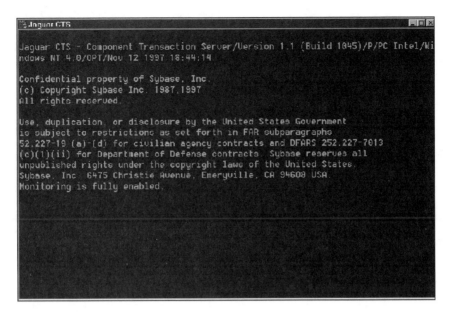

Figure 34.3
The Jaguar server.

For a complete detailed description and datasheet on Jaguar CTS, visit the Sybase Web site at http://www.sybase.com/products/jaguar. Here are a few of the key features of Jaguar CTS:

- **Database connectivity.** Jaguar CTS provides between-the-tiers connectivity to browsers and back-end data stores. It offers multiprotocol support for Net clients such as HTTP, Sybase's TDS, and CORBA's IIOP for release 2. Jaguar CTS offers native, high-speed Java connectivity between applets, servlets, and back-end DBMSs for high-speed result set streaming between all tiers.

- **Transaction management.** Jaguar CTS supports synchronous as well as asynchronous queue-based transaction processing. For synchronous connections, the Jaguar CTS Transaction Manager hides virtually all the complexity of transaction management and coordination from you. Figure 34.4 shows the Jaguar Manager. Jaguar CTS also supports asynchronous processing through dbQ, which is Sybase's database queuing product. dbQ allows NetOLTP business transactions to spawn multiple physical transactions across a variety of systems while securely managing the responses that result.

- **Support for industry components.** Jaguar CTS allows you to execute servlets built according to any popular component model. This includes ActiveX, Java and JavaBeans, C/C++ native objects, and CORBA IDL.

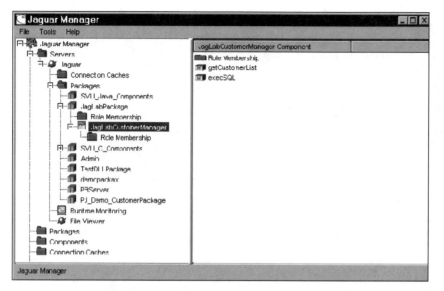

Figure 34.4
The Jaguar Manager.

- **Database Connectivity.** Jaguar provides connectivity to all major DBMSs, including Sybase SQL Server and SQL Anywhere, Oracle7.x, and MS SQL Server via ODBC, JDBC, and Sybase Open Client. Sybase's EnterpriseConnect data access products provide connectivity to mainframe and 20 other datasources. In addition, you get native, high-speed Java connectivity between applets, servlets, and back-end DBMSs.

- **Security.** Security still remains a critical issue in the deployment of Net-based applications. Jaguar CTS Security supports the Internet standard Secure Sockets Layer (SSL) for data encryption. It offers user authentication through SSL public keys as well as application-level security with access control lists (ACLs). It also features a firewall certification program.

Jaguar And PowerBuilder

Jaguar and PowerBuilder are an excellent match. Because of this match, I'll spend a little more time on this topic. We know that Jaguar can host, manage, and execute components. To recap, components are reusable pieces of code that perform a specific functionality or service. For example, components contain business logic, algorithms, and calculations. In Jaguar, these components can be ActiveX programmable objects, Java beans, or C/C++ DLLs.

Before going any further, let's cover some of the Jaguar terms and concepts:

- **Package.** A collection of server components that when combined, form an application.

- **Component.** A collection of methods.

- **Method.** The smallest unit of code written in a specific language.

- **Stub.** A Java class generated by Jaguar Manager that acts as a proxy object for a Jaguar component. This is compiled and linked with your Java applets or applications.

- **Skeleton.** An interface between the Jaguar runtime environment and your code that implements the method. It is mainly used with C/C++ components.

- **Session.** This is kept between your browser and server.

In order to develop a PowerBuilder client application that invokes components running in a Jaguar server, you first need to connect to the server. In general, you create a Jaguar CTS connection in the same way you would define any PowerBuilder datasource, as shown in Figure 34.5. Here are a few things to note:

- Your database driver should be for Sybase System 10/11.

- When you define the server name, you should specify the name given to the Jaguar server in your *sql.ini* file on the Jaguar CTS server machine.

- The name of the database must be specified as *master*.

- The login ID should be a valid user for the defined Jaguar server that you are accessing. The login password should be defined as appropriate for the user under Login ID.

- For DBParm, enter the appropriate host value. Host is the host name defined for your Jaguar CTS server you are accessing.

Here's a sample sql.ini file:

```
[Jaguar]
master=NLWNSCK,Kouros-lab1,7878
query=NLWNSCK, Kouros-lab1,7878
http=NLWNSCK, Kouros-lab1,8080
```

> **Note:** If you have Open Client already installed on your PC as well as Jaguar CTS and the ActiveX Proxy, to avoid a common mistake, ensure that your %SYBASE% environment variable is pointing to the correct sql.ini file.

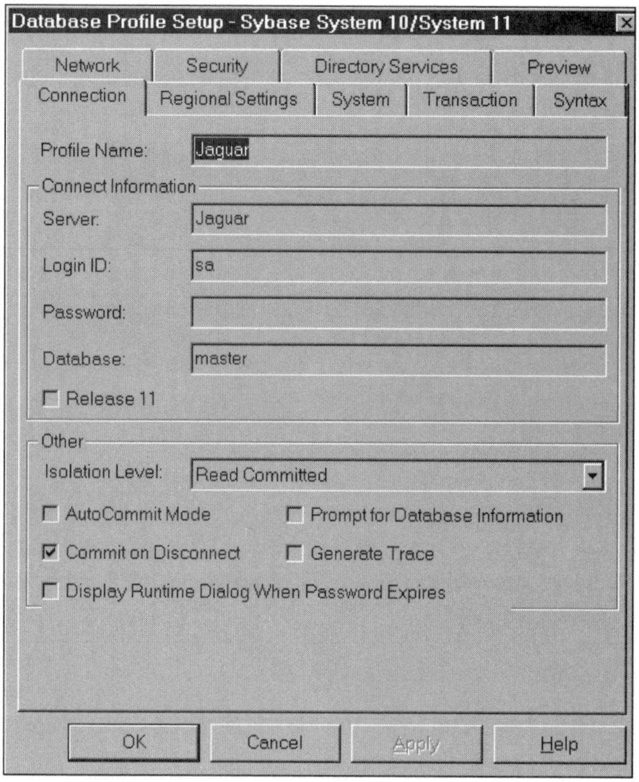

Figure 34.5
The PowerBuilder datasource for a connection to Jaguar CTS server.

There are basically four main approaches to creating a PowerBuilder client to communicate with a Jaguar CTS server:

- DataWindow stored procedure

- Embedded SQL stored procedure

- RPCs

- ActiveX Proxy

Now, let's take a closer look at these approaches.

DataWindow Stored Procedure

The first method involves using a DataWindow stored procedure. This means you create a DataWindow with a stored procedure or, in this case, a Jaguar component as the datasource of your DataWindow. Let's say you've created a Java component named **CustomerInfoImpl** containing a **CustInfo()** method that obtains a result set from a database. If you registered this component with Jaguar under the package CustomerPBPackag, the list of stored procedures will include the entry **CustomerPBPackage.CustomerInfoImpl.CustInfo**.

In PowerBuilder, you need to create a new DataWindow with the datasource being a stored procedure. Once this is done, you'll see a list of all your components to select from. In this case, you use the **CustomerPBPackage.CustomerInfoImpl.CustInfo** procedure to populate the DataWindow you're creating.

> **Note:** The syntax for the **EXECUTE** statement is different than the syntax for a typical Sybase stored procedure. With Jaguar, you don't include **@param_name = ** in the **EXECUTE** statement.

When you connect to the Jaguar server and run the DataWindow application, Jaguar will create the component, invoke the chosen method to obtain a result set, populate the DataWindow with the result set, and then destroy the component instance.

Embedded SQL Stored Procedure

As with all stored procedure DataWindows, the DataWindow object that you create with a Jaguar CTS stored procedure will not be updatable. You need to make the DataWindow object updatable programmatically. An example of what needs to be done is shown here:

```
string ls_return, ls_modify

//Set the DataWindow to be updatable
ls_modify = ls_modify + "DataWindow.Table.UpdateTable='customer' "
ls_modify = ls_modify + "id.Key=Yes "


//Turn on update for customer columns
ls_modify = ls_modify + "fname.Update=Yes "
ls_modify = ls_modify + "lname.Update=Yes "
ls_modify = ls_modify + "city.Update=Yes "


//update DataWindow
ls_return = dw_customer.Modify(ls_modify)
IF ls_return "" THEN
        Messagebox("An Error Has Occurred", ls_return)
END IF

//clear the update flags
dw_customer.ResetUpdate()
```

When your users make changes to the information displayed in the DataWindow, the DataWindow can send these changes back to the Jaguar server. The **SQLPreview** event of the DataWindow generates the appropriate SQL statements such as **DELETE**, **INSERT**, and **UPDATE**. Each time the DataWindow generates one of these statements, it triggers an **SQLPreview** event. To issue an update using component methods on the Jaguar server, you must intercept and write your own **SQLPreview** event. Here's a simple example of code in an **SQLPreview** event:

```
// Stored procedure declaration for Jaguar CTS
DECLARE sp_customer PROCEDURE FOR
PBPackage.PBComponent.setCustomerInfo(:sqlsyntax);

/* Now pass the SQL to the Jaguar CTS method to process
   Call stored procedure to update the database
*/

EXECUTE sp_customer;

// Handle errors if any
IF SQLCA.SQLCode < 0 THEN
    MessageBox ("Error" + String(SQLCA.SQLDBCode), &
        SQLCA.SQLErrText)
END IF

//close the procedure
CLOSE sp_customer;

// Skip the original SQL statements
RETURN 2
```

> **Note:** *You can also use PowerBuilder RPC calls or the ActiveX Proxy interface to update DataWindows from the* **SQLPreview** *event. We'll talk about this in the next section.*

RPCs

You can define PowerBuilder remote procedure calls (RPCs) that map directly to Jaguar CTS component methods. Usually, you create a nonvisual object, inherited from a transaction object, and define your RPCs on this object as local external functions.

To call Jaguar components via RPCs, you create your nonvisual object inherited from the Transaction object and then select the Procedure button, which lists all your Jaguar components in the format *package.component.method.* Once you've selected one, it will appear as a remote procedure.

Note: *The RPC mechanism can only be used to invoke Jaguar CTS component methods that do not return a result set.*

Here's an example of an RPC declaration:

```
SUBROUTINE setCustomerInfo(string sqlsyntax) RPCFUNC ALIAS FOR &
       "PBPackage.PBComponent.setCustomerInfo"
```

In your script, you execute via this:

```
SQLCA.setCustomerInfo(sqlsyntax)
```

ActiveX Proxy

The ActiveX Proxy interface allows you to invoke Jaguar CTS component methods through OLE Automation. Before doing so, remember that the Jaguar CTS ActiveX Proxy must be installed. When the ActiveX Proxy setup program is run, the proxy file JAGPROXY.DLL registers itself on the client. Registry (.REG) and type library (.TLB) files must then be generated and installed on the client for each Jaguar CTS component to be invoked from a PowerBuilder client.

Note: *Using ActiveX Proxy, the component on the Jaguar CTS server stays in memory until you destroy the instance of the OLE object. The stored procedure and RPC interfaces do not keep the server component in memory. They instantiate the component, invoke the method and destroy it.*

When the client script invokes a method on a server component, the client communicates to Jaguar CTS via JAGPROXY.DLL, which uses the Sybase ODBC driver to connect to the Jaguar CTS server. You then use the PowerScript OLE function **ConnectToNewObject**() to invoke the proxy and instantiate the server component.

Let's assume that you have a custom class nonvisual user object named **u_customer** that contains the user object function **uf_getCustomer**(). This function simply retrieves a resultset from the customer table. Once your code is complete, you have to compile your PowerBuilder library into a PowerBuilder dynamic library. Then you use the OLEGenReg (discussed in Chapter 19, "PowerBuilder Automation Server") to create REG and TLB files. Note the ProgID when you create your OLE registration files.

The next step is to create a package in Jaguar Manager. This package can have any name. You then create a new component and give it the name of the ProgID you gave your ActiveX component earlier during the OLEGenReg process. Finally, you import the ActiveX component from the registration (TLB) files you created into Jaguar Manager (see Figure 34.6).

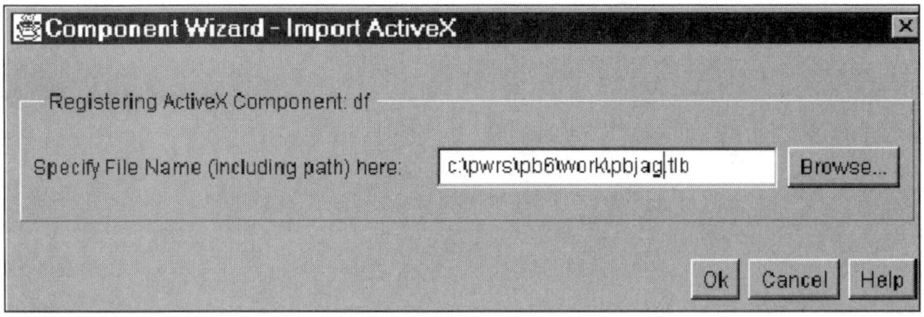

Figure 34.6
Importing an ActiveX component into Jaguar Manager.

Remember that if your method returns a result set, make sure you check the Return Result Set option in the Method Properties of the method within the Jaguar Manager, as shown in Figure 34.7.

Now, your component is ready to be called from a client such as PowerBuilder, PowerJ, or any other tool that can connect to Jaguar. If you want to call your component via ActiveX Proxy, you have to generate TLB/REG files from within the Jaguar Manager, as shown in Figure 34.8.

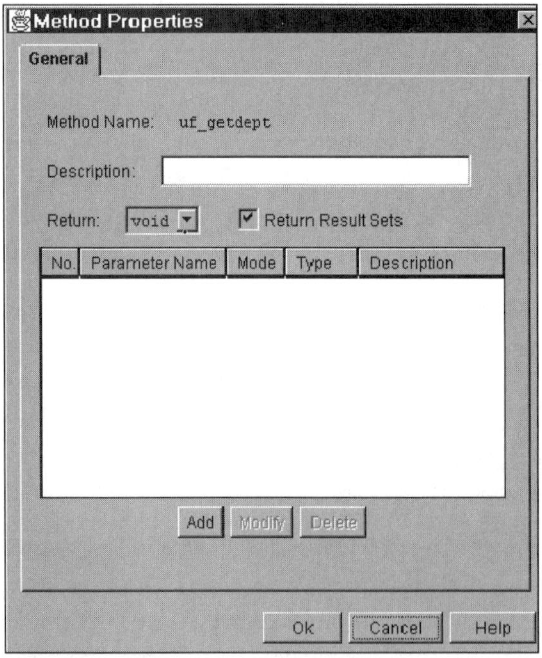

Figure 34.7
Method properties within Jaguar Manager.

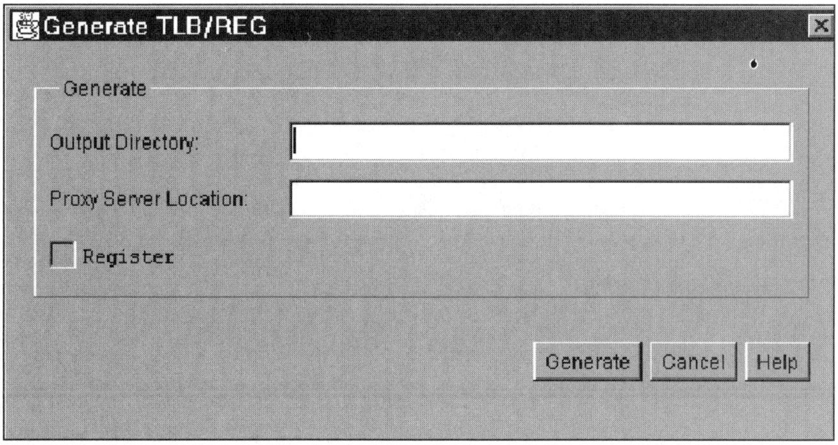

Figure 34.8
Generating TLB/REG files for a Jaguar component.

The TLB/REG files that are generated from the Jaguar Manager have to be run at the client side to be registered with the Registry.

> *Note: Make sure the PowerBuilder runtime DLLs are installed at the server.*

The final step is to code the client application to call the component via ActiveX Proxy. Here's some sample code:

```
integer li_return
OLEObject lole

//create a new OLEObject
lole = CREATE OLEObject
li_return = lole.ConnectToNewObject("PBPackkge.PBComponent")

IF li_return = 0 THEN
       // error processing
       RETURN -1
END IF

//Set up the communication parameters to Jaguar CTS
lole.Username = "jagadmin"    //this must be all lowercase
lole.Password = ""
lole.Host = "Jaguar"

//create the server component:
lole.Initialize()
```

```
//Call component's method on the Jaguar server
lole.getCustomerInfo()

//Destroy the server component instance
DESTROY lole
```

> **Note:** If you are passing a result set back to the client, you could also take advantage of the new DataWindow Synchronization feature or the new DataWindow **GenerateResultSet()** function.

As you can see, Jaguar CTS is truly a powerful tool. What you read in this section was simply the tip of the iceberg. There's a lot more to Jaguar CTS that you'll have to explore for yourself. My recommendation to you is to learn the product well; you will see a lot more of it in the near future.

Other Sybase Design And Development Tools

Sybase offers many other design and development tools as well as middlewares, databases, data warehouses, and more. Here are some of the other tools in the Sybase tools family:

- **InfoMaker.** This is a client/server reporting tool that allows you to build various presentation-style reports from both desktop and large-scale DMBSs through native drivers or ODBC.

- **PowerSite.** A RAD environment for building, managing, and deploying Web applications. PowerSite enables you to create data-driven, thin-client Web applications that can be deployed to Web application servers such as PowerDynamo, Microsoft Active Server Pages, and Netscape LiveWire.

- **PowerDynamo.** An open and scalable Web application server that uses template HTML pages with embedded business logic and database connectivity to give you thin-client Web applications. PowerDynamo's unique feature is the use of the database as a Web repository.

- **ObjectCycle.** This is a great version control tool for managing software components and desktop objects in a team development environment.

Make sure you visit Sybase's Web site at http://www.sybase.com/products for a detailed listing of these products.

Visual Components

The Sybase Visual Components tools are ActiveX controls designed to meet the many programming needs that you may have when developing business applications. These controls include the following:

- dbComplete
- Formula One
- Formula One/NET
- First Impression
- VisualSpeller
- GeoPoint
- WebViewer
- VisualWriter
- System Tools

For a complete listing and detailed description of these components, visit the Visual Components Web site at http://www.visualcomp.com.

Moving On

The Sybase development tools represent a wide range of technologies that address the technology needs of your corporation. In this chapter, I outlined some of the Sybase tools and their main features. The list is long (it can get even longer), and there are many other tools that I have not mentioned. Visit Sybase's Web page, http://www.sybase.com, for a complete listing of the tools that are available to you. The Sybase sales and marketing groups would be more than happy to answer any questions that you may have or provide you with additional information.

The chapters are ending. In the next chapter, being the final chapter, I'll give you my look into the future of the Sybase family of tools, specifically PowerBuilder.

Looking Into The Future

We've finally reached the last chapter in what has been an awesome adventure. Now that this great experience is nearly over, I'll get to the fun part. This is where I reach for my crystal ball and see into the future.

I want to share with you my vision into the future of Sybase design and development tools, specifically PowerBuilder. Now, don't hold me responsible for all that you're about to read here—some features listed in this chapter are from my own personal wish list and are what I would like to see in the next release. However, who knows what the future holds—it's wide open, right?

Future Directions

The industry buzzwords are *multitier*, *Java*, *Dynamic HTML*, *thin clients*, and *components*. Today, when you build enterprise applications, you also face many new challenges for deployment environments, such as three-tier and the Internet. To be successful in these environments, Sybase believes that the software products used to build information technology must meet the following requirements:

- Use standards to promote the building of application logic in the form of standard components.

- Enable rapid application development not only for the client, but for any deployment architecture.

- Deliver data in the right form, to the right place, at the right time.

- Minimize complexity for both end users and developers.

To address all these requirements, Sybase has introduced the Adaptive Component Architecture. This architecture is the result of Sybase's continuing commitment to addressing the real-world needs of information technology professionals and departments. Sybase believes that these departments will derive real, practical benefits from the Adaptive Component Architecture through its primary features, which are:

- The efficiency and flexibility of a single programming model based on standard components.

- The extensibility of specialized data type stores.

- The performance of task-optimized data stores and access methods.

- The reliability of transactions at server and middle-tier levels.

- The continuing reliability of existing systems and applications.

The Adaptive Component Architecture consists of the following components:

- **Adaptive Server.** Supports existing SQL Server applications and their data, component-based logic running on the database server, distributed transactions, multiple-data access methods and stores for relational data, and third-party data stores for specialized data types.

- **Jaguar Component Transaction Server.** Supports distributed transactions, object management, and component-based logic running in the middle-tier server.

- **Data movement and connectivity products.** Products that manage the flow of data required for the various application deployment architectures.

- **Development tools.** Support component creation and rapid application development. Components can be built, debugged, and deployed on a client machine, the database server, or the component transaction server.

Based on my understanding, this architecture is Sybase's future direction. At least that's what I have gathered from reading various magazines and articles on its Web site. You've probably read about it or seen it, too. Now, you might be wondering where PowerBuilder fits into this picture. PowerBuilder is a development tool and is part of the Sybase Design and Development Tools. Starting with version 6.0, PowerBuilder has begun to generate standardized components that can be distributed across multiple platforms. You can now generate C++ and Proxy Library objects as well as application executables. During the lifetime of 6.0, as per Sybase's PowerBuilder product information Web page, we will have component generators that support the creation of standard object types such as Java, COM/DCOM (ActiveX), and CORBA from objects developed in PowerBuilder. As part of the Development Tools, PowerBuilder's primary directive is to commit to object standards and to integrate its development environment features with those of other Sybase tools. This is a must.

Java, Java, And More Java

The industry is demanding Java. As we heard in the 1997 annual Powersoft user conference in Nashville, the next release of PowerBuilder will be able to generate Java code. To what extent, I don't know. However, imagine being able to code in PowerScript but to generate Java. Wow, that will be awesome!

In Nashville, at one of the presentations, we were told that the next release might offer the following features:

- The ability to generate Java code.

- An enhancement of the Library Painter to support first-character recognition.

- The ability to create PBX libraries that are read-only PBDs.

- The ability to copy a database profile.

- Support for DataBlades and cartridges specialty data types.

- Support for OLE DB.

- The ability to see ancestor script in functions.

- Number support in Oracle increased to 38 digits.

- And many more exciting features....

These are all great new features, and I'm sure that there will be many more that we are not aware of yet.

I personally have a wish list, too, that I'd like to see in the new version of PowerBuilder. Well, let's look into the crystal ball. My oh my....I'd like to see a brand new interface in the new release. The current interface is old. PowerBuilder has to become more Windows oriented. Could the new interface be something similar to that of Microsoft Visual Studio? Or, could it go toward the new PowerBuilder Debugger look? (The new debugger looks cool!)

I love the concept of *projects*. I'd like to be able to save my environment, layout, and the application I'm working on in a project. Project A might be an order-entry application, and project B might be an accounting package. Of course, this means that the Project Painter has to be renamed, right?

The PowerBuilder Object Browser is an excellent tool; I use it all the time; I'd like to see this tool enhanced; and I'd like to be able to see and get to much more information from this tool. For example, I'd like to get at my variables or edit my scripts from the browser. Maybe this tool should be combined into the new interface. Wow, that would be cool. Am I asking for too much?

I personally would also like to see an enhanced RichText control in PowerBuilder. I find this control a great addition to PowerBuilder, but it lacks certain capabilities that you'd expect to see, especially if you've ever worked with a major word processor. I would like to see a RichText ActiveX control of some sort with many rich features instead or in addition to the current RichText control.

I have written many PowerBuilder MAPI programs, and I can't wait to do extended MAPI. I would like to see this supported in PowerBuilder one day. If not, I'd like to see an ActiveX of some sort that assists me with this task. Well, I could write my own external DLL, but….

I'd like to see even a thinner client than what we have today. Having worked with many deployment DLLs, PowerBuilder 6.0's new Virtual Machine (VM) is wonderful. However, in my opinion, the PowerBuilder VM should be even smaller than what it is now. I'd like to see more and more distributed and Internet features in the next release. I'd also like to see better integration between the PowerStudio tools.

Well, my own personal wish list is long and what I see in the crystal ball are my own projections. However, if you have an enhancement request, please visit the Web Express Web site available to you from the PowerBuilder Help|Web Express Web Site menu item, and submit your request to Sybase. I am sure it will get looked at by the PowerBuilder product management group. It is nice to know that Sybase cares and does listen to our requests and needs. After all, we are the software industry.

I'm confident that we'll see many great and wonderful new features in the next release. I'm also confident that Sybase will get to the future as fast as we do and will deliver the products and services that will make the paradigm shift as easy as possible.

Moving On

This book has come to an end. It was truly a joy to put it together, and I hope that you've enjoyed reading it. So, where do you go from here? What do you do next?

The future is wide open! Oh, I like this saying. Well, the Sybase Design and Development Tools division has once again taken PowerBuilder to new heights with the release of PowerBuilder 6.0; I'm more impressed than ever. PowerBuilder is once again another step ahead of all its competitors. PowerBuilder is a great tool to work with because it gives you the power to create powerful and robust applications for any environment.

In this book, we covered PowerBuilder and most of the new features in version 6.0. Now, it's to your benefit to put what you've read here to work. One way to do this is to write simple, mini-applications that demonstrate the new features, and then present them to your colleagues.

If you want additional information and material, regularly visiting Sybase's Web site, the PowerBuilder page (http://www.sybase.com/products/powerbuilder) specifically can be quite beneficial. There, you'll find technical documents, educational material, and much more. One important service that you could take advantage of is the PowerBuilder mailing list that can be found at the bottom of that page. Sybase also offers educational courses on PowerBuilder that are very valuable. Attending your local user groups and joining discussions on Sybase's various newsgroups (forums.sybase.com) are two methods for learning more about the technology behind PowerBuilder and other Sybase tools. Reading various PowerBuilder magazines, such as the *PowerBuilder Developers' Journal* or the *PowerStudio Developer's Journal,* is another method for getting more information under your belt.

Now, in order to be recognized in the industry as a PowerBuilder developer, you need to be a Certified PowerBuilder Developer (CPD). I strongly recommend this, as CPDs are highly regarded in the software industry, and developers with this credential are recognized as skilled and preferred resources. Information on this program can be obtained from http://www.sybase.com/services/education/slc.

Good luck to you all, and enjoy being a Power-Builder. It's a great feeling!

Index

* (asterisk), in SELECT statements, 157
[] (brackets), in DataWindow expressions, 44
% (percent), SQL wildcard, 158
? (question marks), in sqlsyntax, 35
_ (underscore), SQL wildcard, 158
64K segment violation error, 414

A

<A> elements, 498
AcceptText function, 40, 43
Access rights, instance variables, 131
Accessing data in DataWindows, 43-45
Action argument, Error event, 46
Actions, Button object, 53-54
ActiveX controls. *See also* OLE.
    deploying applications, 425-426
    inserting, 276, 279-280
    programming, 280
    Window ActiveX control, 505-509
ActiveX technology, defined, 20
Ad hoc polymorphism, 17
Adaptive Component Architecture, 4, 582-583
Adaptive Server. *See* Sybase Adaptive Server.
AddColumn function, 84
AddItem function, 79, 84
Add-ons. *See* CODE.
AddPicture function, 80
Aggregate functions, 158
[ALIAS] section, HELP project files, 454
Aliases, OLE, 275
Ancestor objects, defined, 14
Anchor HTML elements, 498

ANSI character set, database connectivity, 325
Any data type, 31
APIs (application programming interfaces)
    conformance levels (ODBC), 336-341
    DBLib, Sybase SQL Anywhere, 357-358
    SCC API, unable to connect error message,
        203-204
    transaction objects, API calls, 237-240
    Windows API calls, external functions,
        264-269
App Path entries, Registry, 421
Append Row action, Button object, 53
Applets
    Java, 23-24
    JavaBeans, 24
Application development tools
    Sybase tools, 563-579
    third-party add-ons, 551-562
Application manager, PFC library, 533-535
Application Preference service, PFC library, 541
Application Profiler, 191-194
Application programming interfaces. *See* APIs.
Application projects
    creating, 409-412
    machine code vs. Pcode, 412-413
    resources, using, 413-414
    troubleshooting, 414-415
Application property, 471
Application servers, defined, 11
Application tasks, ODBC, 331-332
Application version control
    archived libraries, 202
    benefits of, 197-199

checking in objects, 207-208
checking out objects, 206-207
check-out status
  clearing, 208-209
  viewing, 209-210
for class libraries, 214
for common libraries, 214
configuration file, creating, 204-205
examples, 197-199
libraries
  class, 214
  common, 214
  configuration, 200-203
  restoring, 211-213
new release, creating, 211
PB Native interface, 199-200
registering objects, 205-206
registration directory, viewing, 210
shared libraries, 202-203
support requirements, 213-214
tools, connecting to, 203-204
work library, 200-201
Applications
  executing with external function call, 268-269
  new release, creating, 211
  Sybase SQL Anywhere development
    recommendations, 372-377
AppSync 3.0, CODE partner add-on, 552
Arabic character support, 519-521
Architecture
  Adaptive Component Architecture, 4,
    582-583
  client/server technology, 9-10
  COM, 18-20
  CORBA, 21-23
  DataWindow buffers, 39-40
  distributed computing, 469-471
  menus, 103-104
  ODBC, 330-334
  ODBC drivers, 334-336
  OLE DB, 20-21
  OMA, 22
  PFC library, 525-526
  PowerBuilder 6 components, 4
  Sybase Adaptive Server, 383-387
  Sybase SQL Anywhere, 355-358
Archived libraries, 202
Arguments
  adding to events, 71
  passing to external functions, 258

Arrays
  accessing data, 44
  control array, 78
ASQ (Automated Software Quality) tools, 540
Asterisk (*), in SELECT statements, 157
Asynchronous processing, 485-486
Attributes
  inheritance, 14-15
  window controls, 76-77
AutoCommit, 164, 310, 324-325
AutoInstantiate property, 129
Automated Software Quality tools. See ASQ tools.
Automation. See also Automation servers; OLE.
  deploying applications, 427
  OLE, 273, 282-286
Automation servers
  client code
    named servers, 298-299
    PowerBuilder as server, 292-295
    User object as server, 296-297
  named servers, 297-299
  NVOs
    named servers, 298
    PowerBuilder as server, 292
    User object as server, 296
  PowerBuilder as server, 291-295
  User objects as server, 295-297
  and Windows Registry, 299-303
AVG function, 158

B

B (edit mask character), 521
Back end, defined, 10-11
Background color, changing conditionally, 32
Background processing. See DataStore objects.
[BAGGAGE] section, HELP project files, 454-455
Bands, setting properties conditionally, 32
Base classes, defined, 14
Beans, defined, 24
BETWEEN comparison operator, SQL, 158
Binding
  disabling, 35
  OLE, 275
[BITMAP] section, HELP project files, 455
Brackets ([]), in DataWindow expressions, 44
Breakpoints, setting, 175-176
Browsers. See Internet deployment.
Buffers
  accessing data, 43-45

architecture, 39-40
sharing, 221-223
[BUILDTAGS] section, HELP project files, 455
Business rules, 132, 469. *See also* Distributed
computing.
Button object, 7, 53-55
ButtonClicked event, 37, 52-54
ButtonClicking event, 37, 52-53

C

C++ ClassBuilder, 131-132
C++ data type equivalents, 255-256
C++ projects, 416-417
C++ source, generating, 416-417
Caching DataWindows. *See* DataStore objects.
Calculator object, 544
Calendar object, 545-546
Call graph models, 183
Call Level Interface. *See* CLI.
Call Stack view, 177
Callbacks, external functions, 263-264
Cancel action, Button object, 53
CCUOs (custom class User objects), 128-131
Centralized data access, Internet deployment,
498-501, 504-505, 514
Certified PowerBuilder Developer. *See* CPD.
Change management. *See* Version control.
ChangeMenu function, 104-105
Character sets, database connectivity, 325
Check conditions, Sybase SQL Anywhere, 374
Check In Object(s) dialog box, 207
Check Out Library Entries dialog box, 206-207
CheckBox edit style, 41-42
Checkboxes, centering, 54-55
Checking in objects, 207-208
Checking out objects, 206-207
Check-out status
clearing, 208-209
viewing, 209-210
Child windows, 61
Class identification. *See* CLSID.
Class libraries
defined, 525
version control, 214
Class pools, 6
Class User object type, 115
Class view, 191-192
ClassBuilder, 131-132
Classes, defined, 14

CLI (Call Level Interface), 329
Clicked event
defined, 37
and drag-and-drop, 137
event declaration, viewing, 66-68
MenuItem objects, 103, 108
Client applications
database connectivity, 422-425
distributed computing, 471-478
Internet deployment, 501-503, 514-515
OLE automation servers
named servers, 298-299
PowerBuilder as server, 292-295
User object as server, 296-297
Client process, defined, 10
Client/server Open Development Environment.
See CODE.
Client/server technology
architecture, 9-10
benefits of, 11
client process, 10
defined, 9-10
distributed processing, 12-13
server process, 10-11
Close function, 63
CloseQuery event, 66-67
CloseTab function, 89
CloseWithReturn function, 63
CLSID (class identification), 299
CODE (Client/server Open Development
Environment)
CYRANO tools, 554-558
Greenbrier & Russel tools, 558-561
partners, list of, 551
PowerCerv tools, 552-554
Code reuse. *See* OOP.
Code tables, validating data, 41-42
Color, changing conditionally, 32
Columns
accessing data, 43-44
color, changing conditionally, 32
properties
accessing, 31
setting conditionally, 32
saving, 7
status, getting and setting, 32-33
tags, assigning to, 31
COM (component object model), 18-20
Commands, defined, 14
Commit property, 450

COMMIT SQL statement
  error tests, 49
  transaction objects, 230
CommitOnDisconnect, 322
Common libraries, version control, 214
Common Object Request Broker Architecture.
  See CORBA.
Comparison operators, SQL, 158
Compiler calling conventions, external functions,
  253-254
Component object model (COM). *See* COM.
Component objects, OLE, 274
Components, defined, 120
Composite DataWindows, 47
Composite presentation style, 30
Computer name, obtaining, 264-265
Conditional breakpoints, 176
[CONFIG] section, HELP project files, 455
Configuration file, version control, 204-205
Conformance levels, ODBC, 336-342
Connect dialog box, 203
CONNECT SQL statement
  error tests, 49
  transaction objects, 230, 233
Connection objects, creating, 471-474
ConnectionBegin events, 495
ConnectionEnd events, 495
ConnectString property, 471
ConnectToNewRemoteObject function, 288
ConnectToRemoteObject function, 286-288
Constructor event, 37
Containers, OLE
  accessing objects in, 278-279
  defined, 275
  inserting controls in, 279-280
Context Information service, 511
Context objects
  Context Information service, 511
  Internet service, 512-513
  Keyword service, 511-512
Context-sensitive help, creating, 464-465
Control arrays, 78
Control lists, 78
Controls
  ActiveX. *See also* OLE.
    deploying applications, 425-426
    inserting, 276, 279-280
    programming, 280
    Window ActiveX control, 505-509

DataWindow
  accessing data, 43-45
  buffers, 39-40
  DataObject property, 36-37
  DDDWs, 46-48
  defined, 29, 36
  error handling, 45-46
  events, list of, 37-38
  maximizing, 36-37
  minimizing, 36-37
  and PBR files, 37
  title bar, enabling, 36-37
  transaction objects, setting, 48-49
  validating data, 40-43
drag-and-drop
  events, 137
  functions, 137-138
  properties, 136-137
inheritance, 14
MDI frames, 91-92
OLE, 275-281
window
  attributes, 76-77
  control array, 78
  creating, 79
  DragObject controls, 75
  DrawObject controls, 76
  DropDownListBox, 80-81
  DropDownPictureListBox, 80-81
  events, 76-77
  ListBox control, 79-80
  ListView control, 84-85
  PictureListBox control, 79-80
  RichTextEdit, 85-87
  Tab control, 88-90
  TreeView control, 81-83
Copying data, 45, 160. *See also* Data Pipeline objects.
CopyRTF function, 86
CORBA (Common Object Request Broker
  Architecture), 21-23
COUNT function, 158
CPD (Certified PowerBuilder Developer), 585
CREATE command, 104
Create function, 217-218
CREATE statement, nonvisual objects, 128-129
Crosstab presentation style, 30
Currentrow argument, RowFocusChanging event, 56
Cursor, scrolling options, ODBC, 349-350
CursorLock values, ODBC, 350
Custom class User objects. *See* CCUOs.

Custom controls, OLE, 275
Custom MDI frames, 91
CVUOs (custom visual User objects), 120-124
CYRANO, CODE partner add-ons
  ClientPack, 555-556
  Insight, 557
  Manager, 557
  Robot, 557-558
  Standards, 556
  WinScope, 556

D

Data. *See also* Rows.
  copying, 160
  deleting, 160
  inserting, 160
  modifying, 160-161
  referencing, 161-162
  retrieving, 157-159
Data consumers, defined, 20
Data expressions, 43-45
Data keyword, 44
Data Pipeline objects
  canceling execution, 450
  Commit property, 450
  creating, 445-448
  error handling, 450-451
  events, 448
  functions, 448
  properties, 448
  Repair function, 451
  User objects, creating, 448-450
Data providers, defined, 20
Data types, user-defined, 373
Database administrator (DBA), importance of, 372
Database API, Sybase SQL Anywhere, 357-358
Database connectivity. *See also* Transaction objects.
  about, 48-49
  ANSI character set as default, 325
  AutoCommit, 310, 324-325
  character set, default, 325
  CommitOnDisconnect, 322
  database interface preferences, 312-313
  database profiles
    creating, 316-317
    managing, 314-318
  DBParm property
    DateTimeAllowed parameter, 323-324
    directory services parameters, 319-322

    DisableBind parameter, 314
    FormatArgsAsExp parameter, 324
    PBCatalogOwner parameter, 314, 322
    PWDialog parameter, 323
    Release parameter, 320
    security parameters, 319-322
    setting parameters, 314-318
    string length limit, 322
    Sybase Open Client 11.1 support, 319-322
    UTF8 parameter, 325
  deploying applications, 422-425
  directory services, Sybase Open Client 11.1
    support, 320
  Informix 7.x database driver, 318
  Keep Connection Open preference, 310
  Lock preference, 310-311
  native drivers, 307-309, 318-319
  ODBC 3.0 Driver Manager, 318
  Oracle7.3 database driver, 318-319
  Oracle8.0 database driver, 318-319
  parameters, setting, 314-318
  PFC library, 533
  porting applications, 326-327
  Powersoft database interface, 307-309
  Powersoft repository, 309-310, 322
  preferences, setting, 310-313
  preparation, 309-314
  PRINT statement for debugging, 323
  Read Only preference, 311
  repository tables, 309-310
  scientific notation, converting to, 324
  security services, Sybase Open Client 11.1
    support, 320-322
  Shared Database Profiles preference, 311
  SQL Terminator preference, 311
  SQLCA properties, setting, 317-318
  Sybase Open Client 11.1 support, 319-322
  troubleshooting, 325-326
  Use Powersoft Repository preference, 311-313
  UTF8 character set as default, 325
Database engine, Sybase SQL Anywhere, 356-358
Database files, Sybase SQL Anywhere, 355-356
Database interface preferences, 312-313
Database objects, SQL, 155-156
Database Profile Setup dialog box, 315-316
Database profiles
  creating, 316-317
  managing, 314-318
Database Profiles dialog box, 315
Database servers, defined, 11

Database Tools API, Sybase SQL Anywhere, 358
Database trace, enabling, 181-182. *See also*
    Debugging applications.
Database transactions, defined, 162
Data.HTMLTable property, DataWindows, 50
DataModified! status, 32-33
DataObject property, 36-37
Datasource tasks, ODBC, 333-334
DataStore objects
    about, 224-225
    creating, 226-227
    functions, 225-226
    methods, 225-226
    SaveAs function, 56-57
DataWindow buffers
    accessing data, 43-45
    architecture, 39-40
    sharing, 221-223
DataWindow controls
    accessing data, 43-45
    buffers, 39-40
    DataObject property, 36-37
    DDDWs, 46-48
    defined, 29, 36
    error handling, 45-46
    events, list of, 37-38
    maximizing, 36-37
    minimizing, 36-37
    and PBR files, 37
    title bar, enabling, 36-37
    transaction objects, setting, 48-49
    validating data, 40-43
DataWindow expressions, syntax, 43-45
DataWindow objects
    buffers, sharing, 221-223
    Button objects, 52-54
    caching. *See* DataStore objects.
    CheckBox feature (centering checkboxes), 54-55
    datasources, 29-30
    DataStore objects, 224-227
    defined, 29
    drag-and-drop event parameters, 139-140
    dynamic
        creating, 217-218
        elements, creating, 220
        elements, destroying, 220
        LibraryExport function, 219
        SyntaxFromSql function, 218-219
    Excel format support, 56-57
    GroupBox objects, 54

HTML, generating, 49-52
IntelliMouse support, 55-56
invisible. *See* DataStore objects.
new features, list of, 52-57
performance, 439-442
populating from mail inbox, 245-247
presentation styles, 30-31
print preview mode, scroll bar support, 55
print properties, 147-151
Print Specification tab page, 146-147
printing, 36
properties, accessing, 31-32
query mode, 220-221
result sets, sharing, 221-223
RowFocusChanging event, 56
SaveAs function, 56-57
SaveAsAscii function, 56-57
scroll bar support in print preview, 55
sharing data, 87
source code, obtaining, 217-218
SQL SELECT statement, changing
    dynamically, 223-224
SQL statements, generating, 32-36
status (rows and columns), 32-33
string length limitation, 86
synchronization, 487-493
system events, 37
tab order set to 0, 45
Update properties, setting, 33-34
views, constructing, 35-36
DataWindow plug-in, Internet deployment,
    503-504, 515
DataWindow Resize service, PFC library, 541-544
DataWindowChild objects, 46. *See also* DDDWs.
DataWindows Properties service, PFC library, 542
Date items, getting value, 44
DateTimeAllowed parameter, DBParm property,
    323-324
DBClient, Sybase SQL Anywhere, 357, 378
DBCS (double-byte character support), 519
DBError event, 37, 45
DBLib, Sybase SQL Anywhere, 357-358
Dbo alias, Sybase Adaptive Server, 400-401
DBParm property
    DateTimeAllowed parameter, 323-324
    directory services parameters, 319-322
    DisableBind parameter, 314
    FormatArgsAsExp parameter, 324
    PBCatalogOwner parameter, 314, 322
    PWDialog parameter, 323

Release parameter, 320
security parameters, 319-322
setting parameters, 314-318
string length limit, 322
Sybase Open Client 11.1 support, 319-322
transaction objects, 232
UTF8 parameter, 325
DBTools, Sybase SQL Anywhere, 358
DCOM (distributed COM), 20
DDDW (DropDownDataWindow) objects, 46-48
Debugging applications
about, 171-172
Debug window, 172-178
new features, 6
PBDebug trace, 178-182
PowerBuilder debugger, 171-178
profiling and tracing feature, 182-194
Debugging stored procedures, PRINT statement, 323
Decimal items, getting value, 44
Declaring external functions, 257-258
Default global variables, changing, 128
Delegation, 527
Delete buffers, 40
Delete Row action, Button object, 53
DELETE SQL statement, 33-34, 160
Deleting data, 160
Deploying applications. *See also* Internet deployment.
ActiveX deployment, 425-426
automation, 427
client software, installing, 422-425
Data Pipeline considerations, 450
database connectivity, 422-425
deployment DLLs, 419-421
deployment kit, 419-425
help, where to get, 432
native drivers, 425
ODBC drivers, 422-425
OLE deployment, 425-426
Open Client, installing, 422
PBSync tool, 427-431
Registry, adding App Path entries, 421
synchronization, 427-431
troubleshooting, 431-432
Deploying Sybase SQL Anywhere, 377-378
Descendant objects, 14-15
Describe function, 31, 217-218
Design|Override Ancestor Script option
Powerscript Painter menu, 72
DESTROY statement, nonvisual objects, 128
Destructor event, 38

Development logins, dbo alias, 400-401
Development tools
Sybase tools, 563-579
third-party add-ons, 551-562
Devices, Sybase Adaptive Server, 386-387
Directory, getting current, 265
Directory services, Sybase Open Client 11.1
support, 320
Directory services parameters, DBParm property,
319-322
DisableBind parameter, DBParm, 35, 314
Disabled menu items, 109-110
DISCONNECT SQL statement, 49, 230
Distributed COM. *See* DCOM.
Distributed computing
architecture, 469-471
asynchronous processing, 485-486
client applications, 471-478
Connection objects, creating, 471-474
ConnectionBegin events, 495
ConnectionEnd events, 495
DataWindow synchronization, 487-493
Error -999, 495
Error 50, 495
FAQs (frequently asked questions), 493-495
gnv_app, 494-495
hosts file, 494
Internet deployment, Web.PB, 498-501
Listen Not Supported With Local Driver
error, 495
and PFCs, 494-495
Proxy objects, creating, 415-416, 474-478
remote objects, 474-478
server push, 484-485
services file, 494
sessions (shared objects), 480-481
shared objects, 480-484
troubleshooting, 493-495
Unable To Setup Runtime Environment
error, 495
Distributed processing, defined, 12-13
DllMain function, 252
DLLs (dynamic link libraries). *See also* External
functions.
defined, 251
deployment DLLs, 419-421
synchronizing, 5
Document objects, OLE, 274-275
Documentation, Sybase Adaptive Server, 405-406
Dot notation vs. direct access, 45

Double-byte character support. *See* DBCS.
DoubleClick event, 38
Drag Auto property, 136-137
Drag control, 135
Drag function, 137-138
Drag icon, 136
Drag mode, 135
Drag target, 135
Drag-and-drop
    DataWindow event parameters, 139-140
    defined, 135-136
    events, 137
    example, 138-140
    functions, 137-138
    identifying dragged objects, 138-140
    properties, 136-137
DragDrop event, 38, 138
DragEnter event, 38
DraggedObject function, 138
DragMode data type, actions, 137-138
DragObject controls, 75
DragWithin event, 38
DrawObject controls, 76
Driver manager, ODBC, 332
Driver property, Connection objects, 472
Drivers, ODBC
    architecture, 334-336
    tasks, 333
Drop zone, 135
Drop-down calculator, 544
Drop-down calendar, 545-546
Drop-down lists, 80-81
Drop-down services, 542
Drop-down toolbars, 98-100
DropDownDataWindow objects. *See* DDDW
    objects.
DropDownDataWindow edit style, 41-42
DropDownListBox, 41-42, 80-81
DropDownPictureListBox, 80-81
DWsyntax utility, 31-32
Dynamic libraries, generating, 409-415
Dynamic link libraries. *See* DLLs.
Dynamic SQL, 166-169
Dynamic visual User objects, 124-126
DynamicDescriptionArea (SQLDA), 167
DynamicStagingArea (SQLSA), 166

E

Edit controls, 39-43

Edit masks
    data validation, 43
    internationalization, 521
Edit style, 41-42
Editable drop-downs, 81
EditChanged event, 38, 40
EditMask edit style, 41-42
Educational material, where to find, 585
Elements
    creating, 220
    destroying, 220
Email. *See* MAPI.
<EMBED> tag, 501-502, 504, 511
Embedded SQL, 164-166. *See also* DataStore objects.
Embedding objects, OLE
    defined, 272-273
    Insert Object dialog box, 276
    vs. linking, 277
Empty controls, OLE, 276
Enable property, 103, 108, 111
Encapsulation
    defined, 16
    PFC library, 526
    User objects, 115
Enter key, changing to Tab key, 39
ErrCode property, 472
Error -999, 495
Error 50, 495
Error event, 38, 45-46
Error handling
    Data Pipeline objects, 450-451
    DataWindow controls, 45-46
Error messages
    default, changing, 45
    extracting details, 45
Error Opening DLLs message, 415
ErrorBuffer argument, 218
ErrorLine argument, Error event, 46
ErrorNumber argument, Error event, 46
ErrorObject argument, Error event, 46
ErrorScript argument, Error event, 46
ErrorText argument, Error event, 46
ErrorWindowMenu argument, Error event, 46
ErrText property, Connection objects, 472
Escape sequences, 144
EVENT keyword, 70
Events
    arguments, adding, 71
    calling, 70-71
    custom visual User objects, 121

Data Pipeline objects, 448
DataWindow controls, 37-38
drag-and-drop, 137
encapsulation, 16
executing, 71-72
extending, 15, 72
inheritance, 15
menus, 108-109
OLE, 278
overloading, 18
overriding, 15, 70-71
post-open, 68-69
user-defined, 68-69
  encapsulation, 16
  inheritance, 14
  Window objects, 68-69
viewing, 66-68
window controls, 76-77
vs. window functions, 74
Window objects, list of, 65-66
EVUOs (external visual User objects), 126
Excel format support, 7, 56-57
ExceptionArea type, 46
ExceptionFail! enumerated type, 46
ExceptionIgnore! enumerated type, 46
ExceptionSubstituteReturnValue! enumerated
  type, 46
Executable files, generating, 409-415
Expressions tab page, Properties selection, 32
Extended catalog, 322
Extended MAPI, 242
Extending
  events, 72
  functions, 73-74
  transaction objects, 235-240
Extension levels, PFC library, 529-532, 546-547
External datasource, 30
External functions
  arguments, passing, 258
  callbacks, 263-264
  C/C++ data type equivalents, 255-256
  compiler calling conventions, 253-254
  declaring, 257-258
  defined, 251
  GetComputerName, 264-265
  GetCurrentDirectory, 265
  GetSystemDirectory, 267
  GetUsername, 266-267
  GetWindowsDirectory, 267-268
  GlobalMemoryStatus, 265-266

PlaySound, 268
pointers, 256
structures
  nested, 260-262
  packing, 262-263
  passing, 258-262
Watcom Library Manager, 254-255
Windows API calls, 264-269
WinExec, 268-269
WLIB.EXE, 254-255
writing, 252-255

F

FAQs (frequently asked questions), 493-495. *See
  also* Troubleshooting.
File servers, defined, 11
FileExists event, 86
FileOpen function, 50
[FILES] section, HELP project files, 456
FileWrite function, 50
Filter action, Button object, 53
Filter buffers, 39
Filter function, 46
Filtering, performance considerations, 48
FindItem function, 79
FLOWBuilder 4.0, CODE partner add-on, 553
Fonts, changing, 151-152
Foreign Key Definition dialog box, 161-162
Foreign keys, 161
Foreign languages. *See* Internationalization.
<FORM> elements, 498
Format 1, dynamic SQL, 167
Format 2, dynamic SQL, 167
Format 3, dynamic SQL, 168
Format 4, dynamic SQL, 168-169
FormatArgsAsExp parameter, DBParm
  property, 324
Formatted text, editing, 85-87
Forms, HTML, 50-52, 498
Frames, MDI, 91-93
Frameworks, defined, 525
Freeform presentation style, 30
FROM keyword, 157
Front end, defined, 10
FUNCTION keyword, 257
Functions. *See also* Polymorphism.
  Arabic character support, 520
  calling, 70-71
  Data Pipeline objects, 448

DataStore objects, 225-226
debugging, 186-187, 190-191
declaring in multiple places, 114-115
drag-and-drop, 137-138
encapsulation, 16
executing, 72-74
extending, 15, 73-74
Hebrew character support, 520
inheritance, 14
mailSession object, 244
menus, 108-109
OLE, 278
overriding, 15, 73-74
printing, 142-143
transaction objects, 231-232
user-defined, 69-70
    Sybase SQL Anywhere, 374
    Window objects, 69-70
vs. window events, 74

G

Garbage collection, 443-444
GenerateHTMLForm function, 50-52
Generators
    about, 409
    Application projects, 409-415
    C++ projects, 416-417
    Proxy projects, 415-416
Genericity, 17
GetChanges function, 490-491
GetChild function, 47-48
GetComputerName function, 264-265
GetCurrentDirectory function, 265
GetFocus event, 38
GetFullState function, 488-489
GetItemDate function, 44
GetItemDateTime function, 44
GetItemDecimal function, 44
GetItemNumber function, 44
GetItemStatus function, 33
GetItemString function, 44
GetItemTime function, 44
GetParent function, 90
GetSQLSelect function, 223-224
GetStateStatus function, 492-493
GetSystemDirectory function, 267
GetUsername function, 266-267
GetValidate function, 43
GetWindowsDirectory function, 267-268

Global memory pools, 64
Global variables, changing, 128
Globally unique identifiers. *See* GUIDs.
GlobalMemoryStatus function, 265-266
Gnv_app, 494-495
Graph presentation style, 30
Grayed menu items, 109-110
Greenbrier & Russel, CODE partner, 558-561
Grid presentation style, 30
Group boxes, controls not visible, 54
GROUP BY clause, SQL, 158-159
Group presentation style, 30
GroupBox objects, 7, 54
Grouping data, 158-159
GUIDs (globally unique identifiers), 19, 299

H

Hardware configuration and performance, 442-443
Headers, generating C++, 416-417
Headings, saving, 7
Hebrew character support, 519-521
Help, creating
    context-sensitive help, 464-465
    Help compilers, list of, 465
    Windows Help
        contents file, 462-463
        creating, 460-462
        Help topic files, 458-459
        limitations, 463-464
        project files, 454-457
        topic IDs, 458-459
Help, where to get. *See also* Web sites of interest.
    certification, PowerBuilder, 585
    deploying applications, 432
    educational material, 585
    magazines, 585
    mailing list, 585
    newsgroups, 354, 585
    ODBC, 351
    Sybase Adaptive Server, 405-406
    Sybase SQL Anywhere, 354-355
    technical documents, 585
Help compilers, list of, 465
Help topic files, 458-459
Hierarchical lists, 81-83
.HLP file extension, 453
Hosts file, 494
.HPJ file extension, 454

HTML (HyperText Markup Language). *See also*
  Internet deployment.
  anchor elements, 498
  forms, 50-52, 498
  generating, 49-52
  <OBJECT> elements, 508-509
  SaveAs function, 50
  strings, 50
HyperText Markup Language. *See* HTML.

I

IBM database interface preferences, 312
Icon lists, 84-85
IDT (Internet Development Toolkit). *See* Internet
  deployment.
IIDs. *See* Interface identifiers.
ImportFile function, performance, 48
ImportString function, performance, 48
InfoMaker, Sybase tool, 578
Informix database interface preferences, 312
Informix 7.x database driver, 318
Inheritance
  attributes, 14-15
  controls, 14
  events, 15
  functions, 14
  instance variables, 14
  menus, 14, 107-108, 110
  object-level functions, 14
  and OOP, 14-16
  PFC library, 526
  and polymorphism, 17
  scripts, 14-15
  shared variables, 14
  User objects, 14, 113-114
  user-defined events, 14
  windows, 14, 65
Initialization files, ODBC, 342-346
In-place activation, OLE, 278
Insert Object dialog box, 276
Insert Row action, Button object, 53
Insertable objects, OLE, 275-277
Inserting data, 160
InsertItem function, 79, 81, 84
InsertItemFirst function, 81
InsertItemLast function, 81
InsertItemSort function, 81
INSET SQL statement, 160
Installing Sybase Adaptive Server, 382-383

Instance pools, 64
Instance variables
  controlling access to, 131
  encapsulation, 16
  inheritance, 14
Instances
  creating, 64-65
  defined, 16
Instantiating objects, 79, 436-438
IntelliMouse support, 7, 55-56
Interactivity. *See* ActiveX controls.
Interface identifiers (IIDs), 299
Internationalization
  Arabic support, 519-521
  DBCS (double-byte character support), 519
  design issues, 521-522
  features, list of, 517
  Hebrew support, 519-521
  Japanese double-byte character support, 519
  right-to-left support, 519-521
  Translation Toolkit, 522-523
  Unicode, 517-519
Internet deployment
  centralized data access, 498-501, 504-505, 514
  client data access, 501-503, 514-515
  Context objects, 510-513
  DataWindow plug-in, 503-504, 515
  Internet tools, 5, 497-504
  Java, defined, 23-24
  non-PowerBuilder services, accessing, 510-513
  plug-ins, 501-504, 509-510, 514-515
  preformatted reports, 503-504, 515
  secure mode, 509-510
  strategy, choosing, 514-515
  tools, choosing, 514-515
  Web Jumps feature, 514
  Web.PB, 498-501, 514
  Web.PB Wizard, 504-505
  WebSite Web Server, 504
  Window ActiveX control, 505-510
  Window plug-in, 501-503, 514-515
Internet Development Toolkit. *See* Internet
  deployment.
Internet service, Context objects, 512-513
Interprocess communication, OLE, 275
Intranets. *See* Internet deployment.
Invalid data, preventing. *See* validating data.
Invisible DataWindows. *See* DataStore objects.
Invisible MenuItem, 106, 111
Invisible sheets, 94

IS NULL comparison operator, 158
Isolation levels
    changing (example), 239-240
    ODBC, 348
    Sybase SQL Anywhere, 371-372, 374
    transaction objects, 239-240
ItemChanged event, 38, 40, 43
ItemError event, 38, 40
ItemFocusChanged event, 38
Iunknown interface, 19

J

Jaguar Component Transaction Server (CTS),
    Sybase tool, 568-578
Japanese double-byte character support, 519
Java
    applets, 23-24
    future of, 583
    PowerJ tool, 565-567
Java Virtual Machine, 24
JavaBeans
    applets, 24
    proxy, 5
Joins, SQL, 159
Just-In-Time debugging, 6, 178

K

Keep Connection Open preference, 310
Key columns, WHERE clause, 33-35
Keyword service, Context objects, 511-512

L

Label presentation style, 30
Language support. *See* Internationalization.
Left outer joins, 159
LibMain function, 252
Libraries, OLE, 274
Libraries, version control
    archived, 202
    common, 214
    configuration, 200-203
    restoring, 211-213
    shared, 202-203
    work, 200-201
Library Extender, 542, 546-547
Library File Is Damaged message, 415
LIBRARY keyword, 257

Library Painter
    Source|Check Out, 206
    Source|Clear Check Out Status, 208
    Source|Connect Menu Item, 203
    Source|Create New Release, 211
    Source|Register, 205
    Source|View Check Out Status, 209
LibraryExport function, 219
LIKE comparison operator, 158
Line spacing, changing, 144
Link lists, 103
Linking objects, OLE
    defined, 272-273
    vs. embedding, 277
    Insert Object dialog box, 276
    and naming, 275
ListBox control, 79-80
Listen Not Supported With Local Driver error,
    495
ListView control, 84-85
Local engine deployment, Sybase SQL Anywhere,
    378
Location property, Connection objects, 472
Lock preference, 310-311, 348
Locking, page-level, 387-389
Locking transactions, 369-372
Log file, creating, 232
Logical unit of work, defined, 229
Logins, adding to Sybase Adaptive Server, 400
Logs, Sybase SQL Anywhere, 374-377
Lotus Notes, and MAPI, 250

M

Machine code vs. Pcode, 412-413
Magazines of interest, 585
MailFileDescription object, 243
Mailing list, PowerBuilder, 585
MailMessage object, 243-244
MailRecipient object, 243-244
MailSession object
    functions, 244
    instantiating, 242
Main windows, 60-61
[MAP] section, HELP project files, 456
MAPI (Messaging Application Programming
    Interface)
    about, 241-242
    DataWindows, populating from mail inbox,
        245-247

extended, 242
and Lotus Notes, 250
mailSession object, 242, 244
reading mail, 242-248
sending mail, 248
simple, 242
Margins, changing, 144, 146
Master device, Sybase Adaptive Server, 386-387
MAX function, 158
MDI_1 control, 91-92
MDI (multiple document interface) applications
controls, 91-92
frames, 63, 91-93
menus, 96-97, 109-110
MicroHelp, 97-98
sheets, 94-96
toolbars, 98-100
MdiframeWindow.ArrangeSheets function, 96
MdiframeWindow.GetActiveSheet function, 96
MdiframeWindow.GetFirstSheet function, 96
MdiframeWindow.GetNextSheet function, 96
Media failure, Sybase SQL Anywhere, 374-376
Memory
configuring Sybase Adaptive Server, 389-390
getting status, 265-266
Menu bars, 104-105
Menu class, instantiating, 103-104
Menu objects, 103-104. See also Menus.
MenuID property, 104
MenuItem class, 103
MenuItem objects. See also Menus.
Clicked event, 103, 108
Enable property, 103, 108, 111
invisible, 106, 111
Selected event, 103, 108
Shift Over property, 107-108
Visible property, 103, 108, 111
Menus
architecture, 103-104
encapsulation, 16
events, 108-109
functions, 108-109
grayed menu items, 109-110
inheritance, 14, 107-108
MDI applications, 96-97, 109-110
menu bars, 104-105
performance issues, 111
pop-up menus, 105-106
types of, 104-106
Message objects, 95

Message passing, 16
Message queue processing, 70
Message router, PFC library, 533
Message.DoubleParm property, 95
Message.LongParm property, 100
Message.number event, 37
Message.PowerObjectParm property, 95
Message.StringParm property, 95
Message.WordParm property, 100
Messaging Application Programming Interface.
See MAPI.
Metaclass service, PFC library, 541
Methods, 14, 225-226
MicroHelp, 97-98
Microsoft SQL Server 6.0 database interface
preferences, 312
Migrating applications, 547-549
Migrating data. See Data Pipeline objects.
Migration Assistant, 548-549
MIN function, 158
Modified columns, WHERE clause, 34
Modify function, 31
Modifying data, 160-161
Monikers, OLE, 275
Mouse, IntelliMouse support, 55-56
MouseMove event, 98
MRU (Most Recently Used) service, 541
Multicolumn format, printing, 146-147
MultiLine Edit, populating, 35
Multilingual applications. See Internationalization.
Multiple document interface. See MDI.
Multiple inheritance, 15
Multiple-tier drivers, ODBC, 334-336
Multitier environment, 469

N

Named servers, 297-299
Naming objects, OLE, 275
National languages. See Internationalization.
Native data, OLE, 275
Native drivers, 307-309, 318-319, 425
Nested DataWindows, 48, 51
Nested reports, 47
Nested structures, 260-262
Nested trace tree models, 183, 190
Network communications, configuring Sybase
Adaptive Server, 391
New Project dialog box, 409-412
New release, creating, 211

New release dialog box, 211
New! status, 32-33
NewModified! status, 32-33
Newrow argument, RowFocusChanging event, 56
Newsgroups
    PowerBuilder, 585
    SQL Anywhere, 354
Newspaper-style columns, printing, 146-147
Noneditable drop-downs, 81
Nonexistent objects, referring to, 45
Nonvisual User objects. *See* NVOs.
NotModified! status, 32-33
N-tier model, 470
Null operator, SQL, 158
Numeric items, getting value, 44
N-Up presentation style, 30
NVOs (nonvisual User objects)
    custom class, 128-131
    OLE automation servers
        named servers, 298
        PowerBuilder as server, 292
        User object as server, 296
    PFC library, 526
    standard class, 126-128

O

Object Browser
    MDI_1 properties, 92-93
    OLE, 281
    viewing events, 67
    window controls hierarchy, 76
Object classes, OLE, 273
<OBJECT> elements, 508-509
Object Linking and Embedding. *See* OLE.
Object Management Architecture. *See* OMA.
Object Management Group. *See* OMG.
Object orientation. *See also* OOP.
    defined, 13-18
    and OLE, 273
    PFC library, 526-529
Object ownership, Sybase SQL Anywhere,
    367-369, 372-373
Object request brokers, 22
Object-based encapsulation, 16
ObjectCycle, Sybase tool, 578
Object-level functions
    encapsulation, 16
    inheritance, 14
Object-oriented programming. *See* OOP.

Objects
    creating, 64-65
    defined, 14
    nonexistent, 45
    number of, Sybase Adaptive Server, 391-392
    OLE, 273-276
    profiling and tracing feature, 183-187
Objects in Memory view, 177
ObjectSmith 5.0, CODE partner add-on, 558-561
Occasional breakpoints, 176
OCX deployment, 425-426. *See also* OLE.
ODBC 3.0 Driver Manager, 318
ODBC Driver Manager Trace, 181-182
ODBC (open database connectivity)
    advantages, 329-330
    API conformance levels, 336-341
    application tasks, 331-332
    architecture, 330-334
    conformance levels, 336-342
    cursor, scrolling options, 349-350
    CursorLock values, 350
    database interface preferences, 312
    datasources
        tasks, 333-334
        tracing, 181-182
    driver manager tasks, 332
    drivers
        architecture, 334-336
        deploying applications, 422-425
        Sybase SQL Anywhere, 358
        version, obtaining (example), 238
    help, where to get, 351
    initialization files, 342-346
    isolation levels, 348
    Lock preference, 348
    multiple-tier drivers, 334-336
    ODBC driver tasks, 333
    ODBC.INI initialization file, 344-346
    ODBCINST.INI initialization file, 343-344
    and OLE DB, 20-21
    PBOD6x.INI file, 346-348
    PowerBuilder search algorithms, 346-348
    single-tier drivers, 334-335
    SQL grammar conformance levels, 341-342
    three-tier drivers, 336
    troubleshooting, 350-351
    two-tier drivers, 334-336
ODBC.INI initialization file, 344-346
ODBCINST.INI initialization file, 343-344
Offsite activation, OLE, 278

OLE 2.0
   controls, 276-277
   presentation style, 31
OLE DB architecture, 20-21
OLE (Object Linking and Embedding). *See also* Automation servers.
   about, 271
   ActiveX controls
      inserting, 276, 279-280
      programming, 280
   aliases, 275
   automation, 273, 282-286
   binding, 275
   component objects, 274
   ConnectToNewRemoteObject function, 288
   ConnectToRemoteObject function, 286-288
   containers
      accessing objects in, 278-279
      defined, 275
      inserting controls in, 279-280
   controls, 275-281
   deploying applications, 425-426
   document objects, 274-275
   embedding objects
      defined, 272-273
      Insert Object dialog box, 276
      vs. linking, 277
   empty controls, 276
   events, 278
   functions, 278
   in-place activation, 278
   insertable objects, 275-277
   interfaces, 273-274
   interprocess communication, 275
   libraries, 274
   linking objects
      defined, 272-273
      vs. embedding, 277
      Insert Object dialog box, 276
      and naming, 275
   monikers, 275
   naming objects, 275
   native data, 275
   new features, 284-288
   Object Browser, 281
   and object-oriented design, 273
   objects
      creating, 276
      defined, 274-275
   offsite activation, 278

OLE 2.0 controls, 276-277
   presentation data, 275
   programmable objects, 282-284
   reasons to use, 272
   remote activation, 286-288
   SetAutomationPointer function, 285
   SetAutomationTimeOut function, 286
   and Windows Registry, 299-303
OLEGenReg utility, 300-303
OLEObject objects, 282-284
OLTP (online transaction processing), 11
OMA (Object Management Architecture), 22
OMG IDL (Interface Definition Language), 22
OMG (Object Management Group), 21-22
OMG Object Model, 22-23
Online transaction processing. *See* OLTP.
OOP (Object-oriented programming)
   defined, 13
   delegation, 17
   encapsulation, 16
   function overloading, 18
   inheritance, 14-16
   instantiation, 16
   messages, 14, 16
   objects, 14
   polymorphism, 17-18
   and User objects, 113-115
Open Client, installing, 422
Open database connectivity. *See* ODBC.
Open event, MDI frames, 92-93
Open function, 63-65
OpenSheet function, 63, 94, 109
OpenSheetWithParm function, 63, 95, 109
OpenTab function, 89
OpenTabWithParm function, 89
OpenUserObject function, 125
OpenUserObjectWithParm function, 125
OpenWithParm function, 63
Optima++, 563-565
Options property, Connection objects, 473
[OPTIONS] section, HELP project files, 456-457
Oracle7.3 database driver, 318-319
Oracle8.0 database driver, 318-319
Oracle database interface preferences, 313
Original buffers, 40
Other event, 38
Overriding
   events, 70-71
   functions, 73-74
   SQL statements, 35

P

Pacebase. *See* Sybase SQL Anywhere.

Pack pragma, 262-263

PADLock 5.0, CODE partner add-on, 552

Page First action, Button object, 53

Page Last action, Button object, 53

Page Next action, Button object, 53

Page Prior action, Button object, 53

Page-level locking, Sybase Adaptive Server, 387-389

Paper orientation, 146-147

Paper size, 146-147

Parametric polymorhpism, 17

Parent, menu scripts, 96

ParentWindow property, 96

Partial inheritance, 15-16

Password Expired dialog box, displaying, 323

Password property, Connection objects, 473

Passwords, Sybase Adaptive Server, 399-400

PasteRTF function, 86

Paths, getting
current directory, 265
Windows directory, 267-268
Windows system directory, 267

PB Native interface, 199-200

PBCatalogOwner parameter, 314, 322

/PBDebug command line switch, 179

PBDebug trace
about, 178-179
database trace, enabling, 181-182
runtime trace, enabling, 179-181

PBOD6x.INI file, 346-348

.PBP file extension, 191

PBR files and DataWindow controls, 37

PBSync tool, 5, 427-431

PBTRACE.LOG file, creating, 232

PBUs (PowerBuilderUnits), 77

Pcode vs. machine code, 412-413

Percent (%), SQL wildcard, 158

Performance
DataWindow retrieval, 439-442
executing scripts, 438-439
factors, list of, 435-436
garbage collection, 443-444
hardware configuration, 442-443
ImportFile function, 48
ImportString function, 48
instantiating objects, 436-438
menus, 111
nested DataWindows, 48

SetItem function, 48

software configuration, 442-443

sorting, 48

SQL, 169

system configuration, 442-443

PFC (PowerBuilder Foundation Class) library
application manager, 533-535
Application Preference service, 541
architecture, 525-526
Calculator object, 544
Calendar object, 545-546
database access, 533
DataWindow Resize service, 541-544
DataWindows Properties service, 542
defined, 525
and distributed computing, 494-495
drop-down calculator, 544
drop-down calendar, 545-546
Drop-down services, 542
encapsulation, 526
extension levels, 529-532, 546-547
inheritance, 526
Library Extender, 542, 546-547
message router, 533
Metaclass service, 541
migrating applications, 547-549
Migration Assistant, 548-549
Most Recently Used (MRU) service, 541
new features, 7, 540-541
nonvisual User objects, 526
object-oriented features, 526-529
Platform service, 540
polymorphism, 527
Profiler window, 542
programming objects, 535-536
Progress Bar control, 542
reference variables, 526, 532
services, 527-529, 536-540
Sheet Management service, 537
Sort service, 538-540
Splitbar control, 542
Transaction Registration service, 537
User objects, 526
visual User objects, 526

PFCTool 5.6, CODE partner add-on, 553-554

Physical resources, configuring Sybase Adaptive Server, 391

Picture lists, 79-80

PictureListBox control, 79-80

Pipelines. *See* Data Pipeline objects.

Platform service, PFC library, 540
PlaySound function, 268
Plug-ins, Internet deployment, 501-504,
 509-510, 514-515
Pointers, external functions, 256
PointerX function, 106
PointerY function, 106
Pointing devices, IntelliMouse support, 55-56
Polymorphism
 and inheritance, 17-18
 PFC library, 527
 User objects, 114-115
Pooling transactions, 234-235
PopMenu function, 104, 106
Populating SQLCA, 231-232
Pop-up menus, 105-106
Pop-up windows, 61-62
Porting applications, 326-327
PostEvent function, 70-71, 95
Post-open events, 68-69
Power++, Sybase tool, 563-565
PowerBuilder 6
 certification, 585
 component architecture, 4
 educational material, 585
 future of, 581-584
 history of, 3-4
 Internet deployment, new features, 5
 magazines, 585
 mailing list, 585
 new features, list of, 4-7
 newsgroups, 585
 ODBC search algorithms, 346-348
 as OLE automation server, 291-295
 open technology, new features, 5-6
 productivity, new features, 6-7
 Sybase tools, 563-579
 technical documents, where to find, 585
 third-party add-ons, 551-562
 Web site, 585
PowerBuilder automation server. See Automation
 servers.
PowerBuilder debugger
 about, 171-172
 breakpoints, setting, 175-176
 debug mode, enabling, 176-178
 Debug window, 172-175
 Just-In-Time debugging, 178
PowerBuilder Developer's Journal, 585
PowerBuilder Foundation Class library. See PFC.

PowerBuilder Translation Toolkit Package, 6
PowerBuilder Virtual Machine, 5
PowerBuilder.Applicaiton Registry entry, 291-292
PowerBuilderUnits. See PBUs.
PowerCerv, CODE partner, 552-554
PowerDesigner 6.1, Sybase tool, 567-568
PowerDynamo, Sybase tool, 578
PowerJ, Sybase tool, 565-567
PowerObjects, passing as parameters, 95
Powerscript Painter menu
 Design|Override Ancestor Script option, 72
PowerSite, Sybase tool, 578
Powersoft database interface, 307-309
Powersoft extended catalog, 322
Powersoft repository, 309-310, 322
Powersoft system tables, 322
PowerStudio Developer's Journal, 585
PowerTOOL 5.0, CODE partner add-on, 553
Preformatted reports, Internet deployment,
 503-504, 515
Presentation data, OLE, 275
Presentation styles, DataWindows, 30-31
Preview action, Button object, 54
Preview With Rulers action, Button object, 54
Primary buffers, 39
Primary keys, 161, 373
Print action, Button object, 54
Print area, 141-142
Print cursor, 142
Print dialog box, displaying, 145-146, 149-151
Print function, 143-145
Print preview, scrollable, 7, 55
Print Setup dialog box, displaying, 145, 147
Print Specification page, 146-147
PRINT statement for debugging, 323
PrintClose function, 144
PrintDefineFont function, 151
PrintEnd event, 38, 143
Printers, changing dynamically, 145-146
Printing
 Button object, preventing printing, 54
 canceling, allowing, 143
 columns, newspaper-style, 146-147
 DataWindow objects, 36
 DataWindow print properties, 147-151
 escape sequences, 144
 fonts, changing, 151-152
 functions, list of, 142-143
 line spacing, changing, 144
 manual job management, 143-144

margins, changing, 144, 146
options, setting
  with DataWindow print properties, 147-151
  with Print Specification page, 146-147
paper orientation, selecting, 146-147
paper size, selecting, 146-147
preview, scrollable, 7, 55
print area, 141-142
print cursor, 142
Print dialog box, displaying, 145-146, 149-151
Print function, 143-145
Print Setup dialog box, displaying, 145, 147
printers, changing dynamically, 145-146
titles, 144-145
PrintOpen function, 143
PrintPage event, 143
PrintSend function, 144
PrintSetFont function, 152
PrintSetSpacing function, 144
PrintSetup function, 145
PrintStart event, 38, 143
Private variables, 131
ProfileInt function, 231-232
Profiler window, 542
ProfileString function, 231-232
Profiling and tracing feature
  about, 182-183
  analyzing results, 189-191
  Application Profiler views, 191-194
  collecting data, 187-189
  enabling, 187-189
  functions, list of, 186-187
  objects, list of, 183-187
ProgIDs (programmatic identifiers), 299-300
Programmable objects, OLE, 282-284. *See also*
  Automation servers.
Programmatic identifiers. *See* ProgIDs.
Programming objects, PFC library, 535-536
Progress Bar control, 542
Project files, Windows Help
  [ALIAS] section, 454
  [BAGGAGE] section, 454-455
  [BITMAP] section, 455
  [BUILDTAGS] section, 455
  [CONFIG] section, 455
  [FILES] section, 456
  [MAP] section, 456
  [OPTIONS] section, 456-457
  [WINDOWS] section, 457
Project management. *See* Version control.

Project Painter
  Design|List Objects, 212
  Design|Restore Libraries, 212
Projects. *See also* Applications; Version control.
  Application, 409-415
  C++, 416-417
  Proxy, 415-416
Pronouns, 96
Properties
  Data Pipeline objects, 448
  DataWindow objects
    accessing, 31-32
    Any data type, 31
    dot notation syntax, 31
    DWsyntax utility, 31-32
    getting, 31-32
    setting, 31-32
    strings, 31
    value returned, data type of, 31
    drag-and-drop, 136-137
    names misspelled, 45
    transaction objects, 230-231
Property sheet, Button object, 54-55
Protect attribute, and copying rows, 45
Proxies, defined, 5
Proxy objects, creating, 415-416, 474-478
Proxy projects, 415-416
PWDialog parameter, DBParm property, 323

Q

Query Clear action, Button object, 54
Query datasource, 30
Query mode, DataWindows, 220-221
Query Mode action, Button object, 54
Query Sort action, Button object, 54
Question marks (?), in sqlsyntax, 35
Quick Select datasource, 30

R

RadioButtons edit style, 41-42
RbuttonDown event, 38, 106
Read Only preference, 311
Reading email, 242-248
Recovery
  Sybase Adaptive Server, 392
  Sybase SQL Anywhere, 374-377
REF keyword, 257
Reference variables, 64, 526, 532
Referential integrity, 161-162, 373

Registering objects, version control, 205-206
Registration dialog box, 205-206
Registration directory, viewing, 210
Registration Directory dialog box, 210
Registry
   App Path entries, 421
   CLSIDs, 299
   deployment DLLs, 421
   GUIDs, 299
   IIDs, 299
   and OLE automation servers, 299-303
   OLEGenReg utility, 300-303
   PowerBuilder.Applicaiton entry, 291-292
   profile strings, getting, 266
   ProgIDs, 299-300
   registering objects, 300-303
   UUIDs, 299
RegistryGet function, 232
Release parameter, DBParm property, 320
Remote activation, OLE, 286-288
Remote objects, distributed computing, 474-478
Remote procedure calls, transaction objects, 235-237
Repair function, 451
Report view, enabling, 84
Reports
   Internet deployment, 503-504
   nested, 47
Repository tables, 309-310
Request argument, SQLPreview function, 35
Resize event, 38, 92-93
Response windows, 62
Result sets
   narrowing, 157-158
   sharing, 221-223
Retrieval objects, DDDWs, 47
RetrievalArgument dialog box, avoiding, 47
Retrieve action, Button object, 53
Retrieve function
   performance considerations, 48
   return code, checking, 49
   SQLPreview event, 35
Retrieve (Yield) action, Button object, 53
RetrieveAsNeeded property, 31
RetrieveRow event, 38
RetrieveStart event, 38
Retrieving data, 157-159
RETURN statement, 37
ReturnValue argument, Error event, 46
Rich Text Format. *See* RTF.
RichText presentation style, 31

RichTextEdit, 85-87
RightToLeft property, 521
Right-to-left support, 519-521
Roles, assigning to Sybase Adaptive Server logins, 399
ROLLBACK, 162, 164, 230
Routine view, 192-193
Row argument
   DBError event, 45
   SQLPreview event, 35
RowFocusChanged event, 38
RowFocusChanging event, 7, 38, 56
Row-level triggers, 164
Rows. *See also* Data.
   accessing data, 43-44
   copying, 45
   inserting, 160
   retrieving too many, 49
   status, getting and setting, 32-33
RowsCopy function, 45
RowsDiscard function, 45
RowsMove function, 45
RTF (Rich Text Format), 85-87
Runtime engine deployment, Sybase SQL
   Anywhere, 378
Runtime trace, enabling, 179-181. *See also*
   Debugging applications.

S

Sa logins, Sybase Adaptive Server, 399-400
SaveAs function, 50, 56-57
SaveAsAscii function, 56-57
SaveAsHTMLPage function, 51
SaveRowAs action, Button object, 54
SCC API, unable to connect, 203-204
Scientific notation, converting to, 324
Scripts
   executing, 71-72
   inheritance, 14-15
   performance, 438-439
   triggers, 163-164
   validating data, 43
Scroll bar support in print preview, 55
ScrollHorizontal event, 38
ScrollVertical event, 38
Secure mode, Internet deployment, 509-510
Security
   applets, 23
   DBParm parameters, 319-322
   Java, 23

Sybase Adaptive Server, 398-401
Sybase Open Client 11.1 support, 320-322
Sybase SQL Anywhere, 367-369
SELECT SQL statement, 157-159, 223-224
SELECTBLOB SQL command, 86-87
Selected event, 103, 108
Send To Back property, 54
Sending email, 248
Server process, defined, 10-11
Server push, 484-485
Server-based data validation, 40
Servers
    application, 11
    database, 11
    database interface preferences, 312-313
    file, 11
    Jaguar Component Transaction Server (CTS),
        568-578
    named, 297-299
    in OMG Object Model, 22
    transaction, 11
    WebSite Web Server, 504
Service providers, defined, 20
Services, PFC library, 527-529, 536-540
Services file, 494
Sessions (shared objects), 480-481
SetAutomationPointer function, 285
SetAutomationTimeOut function, 286
SetChanges function, 491-492
SetColumn function, 43, 84
SetConnect function, 475
SetFilter function, 46
SetFullState function, 489-490
SetItem function, 44, 48, 84
SetItemStatus function, 33
SetMicroHelp function, 98
SetRow function, 43
SetSQLSelect function, 223-224
SetTrans function, 48
SetTransObject function, 49
SetTransPool function, 234-235
SetValidate function, 43
Shared Database Profiles preference, 311
Shared libraries, 202-203
Shared objects, 480-484
Shared variables, 14
ShareData function, 222-224
ShareDataOff function, 222-224
SharedObjectDirectory function, 484
SharedObjectGet function, 482-483

SharedObjectRegister function, 482
SharedObjectUnregister function, 483-484
Sheet Management service, PFC library, 537
Sheetrefvar data type, 94
Sheets, MDI, 91, 94-96
Shift Overproperty, 107-108
Simple MAPI, 242
Single-tier drivers, ODBC, 334-335
Software configuration and performance, 442-443
Sort action, Button object, 53
Sort service, PFC library, 538-540
Sorting data, 48, 158-159
Sounds, playing, 268
Source code
    generating C++, 416-417
    obtaining, 217-218
Source control management. *See* Version control.
Source view, 177
Speed. *See* Performance.
Spelling errors, property names, 45
Splitbar control, 542
SQL Anywhere. *See* Sybase SQL Anywhere.
SQL Communications Area. *See* SQLCA.
SQL dialects, 367
SQL grammar conformance levels, 341-342
SQL Painter, 157
SQL Select datasource, 30
SQL Server. *See* Sybase Adaptive Server.
SQL Server Manager (SSM) tool, 404
SQL Server 4.x database interface preferences, 313
SQL (Structured Query Language)
    AutoCommit property, 164
    comparison operators, 158
    database objects, 155-156
    database transactions, 162
    DELETE statement, 160
    dynamic, 166-169
    embedded, 164-166
    INSERT statement, 160
    performance tips, 169
    referential integrity, 161-162
    SELECT statement, 157-159
    SQL Painter, 157
    statements, 32-36, 156-161
    stored procedures, 162-164
    tables, defined, 155
    transactions, 162
    triggers, 163-164
    UPDATE statement, 160-161
SQL Terminator preference, 311

SQLCA (SQL Communications Area)
   populating, 231-232
   properties, setting, 317-318
   transaction object, default, 48, 229
SQLDA (DynamicDescriptionArea), 167
Sqldbcode argument, 45
Sqlerrtext argument, 45
SQLGetConnectAttr function, 239
SQLGetInfo function, 238
SQLPreview event, 35, 38
SQLSA (DynamicStagingArea), 166
SQLSetConnectAttr function, 239
Sqlsyntax argument, 35
Sqltype argument, 35
SSM (SQL Server Manager) tool, 404
Standalone engine deployment, Sybase SQL
   Anywhere, 378
Standard class User objects, 126-128
Standard MDI frames, 91
Standard visual User objects. *See* SVUOs
Statement-level triggers, 164
STATIC|DYNAMIC keyword, 70
Status, rows and columns, 32-33
Step In command, 177
Step Out command, 178
Step Over command, 177
Stored Procedure datasource, 30
Stored procedures
   PRINT statement for debugging, 323
   SQL, 162-164
   Sybase Adaptive Server, 401-404
   Sybase SQL Anywhere, 373-374
Strings
   getting value, 44
   HTML, creating, 50
   length limit, DBParm property, 322
Structured Query Language. *See* SQL.
Structures, external functions
   nested, 260-262
   packing, 262-263
   passing, 258-262
Subclass polymorphism, 17
Subclasses, defined, 14
SUBROUTINE keyword, 257
SUM function, 158
Superclasses, defined, 14
SVUOs (standard visual User objects), 115-120
Sybase Adaptive Server
   architecture, 383-389
   configuring, 389-392

   connecting to database, 392-395
   databases
      architecture, 386-387
      connecting to, 392-395
      creating new, 401
      number of, 392
   dbo alias, 400-401
   development logins (dbo alias), 400-401
   devices, 386-387
   documentation, on CD-ROM, 405-406
   file structure, 383-386
   help, where to get, 405-406
   installing, 382-383
   locking, page-level, 387-389
   logins, adding, 400
   master device, 386-387
   memory, configuring, 389-390
   network communications, configuring, 391
   objects, number of, 391-392
   page-level locking, 387-389
   passwords, 399-400
   physical resources, configuring, 391
   recovery, setting backup interval, 392
   roles, assigning to login, 399
   sa logins, 399-400
   security, 398-401
   SSM (SQL Server Manager) tool, 404
   stored procedures, 401-404
   Sybase Central tool, 404-405
   Sybooks, 405-406
   sybprocs device, 387
   system tables, 396-398
   tools, 404-405
   triggers, 401-404
   tuning, 389-392
   users
      adding, 400
      connections, number of, 391
   versions available, 381
Sybase Central tool, 404-405
Sybase InformationCONNECT DB2 Gateway
   database interface preferences, 313
Sybase Net-Gateway for DB2 database interface
   preferences, 313
Sybase Open Client 11.1 support, 319-322
Sybase SQL Anywhere
   application development recommendations,
      372-377
   architecture, 355-358
   check conditions, 374

configurations
  dynamically started databases, 366-367
  multiple databases, 365
  multiple servers, 365-366
  single database, 365
connecting to
  connection parameters, setting, 358-359
  from ODBC, 360-361
  from SQL Anywhere tools, 362-365
constraints, 374
database API, 357-358
database engine, 356-358
database files, 355-356
Database Tools API, 358
DBA, importance of, 372
DBClient, 357, 378
DBLib, 357-358
DBTools, 358
deploying, 377-378
help, where to get, 354-355
isolation levels, 371-372, 374
local engine deployment, 378
locking transactions, 369-372
logs, 374-377
media failure, 374-376
newsgroups, 354
object ownership, 367-369, 372-373
ODBC driver, 358
optional components, deploying, 378
primary keys, 373
recovery from failure, 374-377
referential integrity actions, 373
requirements, 347-348
runtime engine deployment, 378
security, 367-369
SQL dialects, 367
standalone engine deployment, 378
standards compliance, 354-355
stored procedures
  vs. check conditions, 374
  compiling, 373
system failure, 374-376
transaction log files, 355-356
transaction processing, 369-372
transaction size, 374
triggers
  vs. check conditions, 374
  compiling, 373
troubleshooting, 364-365
user-defined data types, 373

user-defined functions, 374
Sybase SQL Server. *See* Sybase Adaptive Server.
Sybase SQL Server System 10/11 database
  interface preferences, 313
Sybooks, 405-406
Sybprocs device, Sybase Adaptive Server, 387
Synchronization, 5, 427-431. *See also* Data
  Pipeline objects.
SyntaxFromSql function, 218-219
System configuration and performance, 442-443
System events, DataWindows, 37
System failure, Sybase SQL Anywhere, 374-376
System objects, tracing and profiling, 183-186
System Options dialog box
  Enable PBDebug Tracing option, 179
  Enable Tracing, 187-188
  General tab, Enable PBDebug Tracing
    option, 179
  Profiling tab, Enable Tracing, 187-188
System tables, 322, 396-398

T

Tab control, 88-90
Tab key, Enter key acting as, 39
Tab order set to 0, 45
Tabbed pages, 88-90
Tables, SQL, 155
Tabular presentation style, 31
Tag attribute, 98
Target projects
  Application, 409-415
  C++, 416-417
  Proxy, 415-416
Technical documents, where to find, 585
Text lists, 79-80
Third-party add-ons. *See* CODE.
This (menu scripts), 96
Three-tier drivers, ODBC, 336
Three-tier model, 470
Time items, getting value, 44
Title bar, enabling, 36-37
Titles, printing, 144-145
ToolbarMoved event, 99-100
Toolbars, MDI, 98-100
Tools
  Internet tools, 5, 497-504, 514-515
  Sybase Adaptive Server, 404-405
  third-party add-ons, 551-562
Topic IDs, Windows Help, 458-459

Trace blocks, 188
Trace property, 473
Trace view, 193-194
Tracing and profiling. *See* Debugging applications;
    Profiling and tracing.
Tracking changes. *See* Version control.
Transaction log files, Sybase SQL Anywhere, 355-356
Transaction objects. *See also* Database connectivity.
    API calls, 237-240
    COMMIT statement, 230
    CONNECT statement, 230, 233
    connecting to database, 233
    DBParm property, 232
    default, 48, 229
    DISCONNECT statement, 230
    extending, 235-240
    functions, 231-232
    isolation level, changing (example), 239-240
    log file, creating, 232
    logical unit of work, defined, 229
    multiple objects, 233-234
    ODBC driver version, obtaining (example), 238
    pooling transactions, 234-235
    populating, 231-232
    properties, list of, 230-231
    remote procedure calls, 235-237
    ROLLBACK statement, 230
    setting for DataWindows, 48-49
    SQLCA, populating, 231-232
    statements, list of, 230
    transactions, defined, 229
    user-defined, 49
Transaction processing, Sybase SQL Anywhere,
    369-372
Transaction Registration service, PFC library, 537
Transaction servers, defined, 11
Transactions
    defined, 229
    size, Sybase SQL Anywhere, 374
    SQL, 162
Transferring data. *See* Data Pipeline objects.
Translation Assistant, 6
Translation Toolkit, 522-523
Translations requirements. *See* Internationalization.
TreeView control, 81-83
TriggerEvent function, 70-71, 95
Triggers
    SQL (Structured Query Language), 163-164
    Sybase Adaptive Server, 401-404
    Sybase SQL Anywhere, 373-374

Troubleshooting
    Application projects, 414-415
    database connectivity, 325-326
    deploying applications, 431-432
    distributed computing, 493-495
    ODBC, 350-351
    performance
        DataWindow retrieval, 439-442
        executing scripts, 438-439
        factors, list of, 435-436
        garbage collection, 443-444
        instantiating objects, 436-438
        system configuration, 442-443
    Sybase SQL Anywhere, 364-365
Tuning Sybase Adaptive Server, 389-392
Two-tier drivers, ODBC, 334-336
Two-tier model, 469-470
TypeOf function, 138-140
Types, OLE, 273

U

Unable To Locate Source Management DLL, error
    message, 204
Unable To Setup Runtime Environment error, 495
Underscore (_), SQL wildcard, 158
Undoing transactions, 162
Unicode, 517-519
Universally unique identifiers. *See* UUIDs.
Updatable columns, WHERE clause, 33-34
Update action, Button object, 53
Update function
    return code, checking, 49
    SQLPreview event, 35
Update properties, setting, 33-34
UPDATE SQL statement, 33-35, 160-161
UPDATEBLOB SQL command, 86-87
UpdateEnd event, 38
UpdateStart event, 38
Use Powersoft Repository preference, 311-313
User interface. *See* Window objects; Windows.
User name, getting current, 266-267
User objects
    C++ class, 131-132
    CCUOs, 128-131
    creating, 116, 120-121, 128-130, 448-450
    CVUOs, 120-124
    dynamic visual User objects, 124-126
    encapsulation, 16, 115
    EVUOs, 126

inheritance, 14, 113-114
NVOs, 126-131
as OLE automation servers, 295-297
and OOP, 113-115
PFC library, 526
polymorphism, 114-115
Standard class, 126-128
SVUOs, 115-120
types of, 115
User-defined
  data types, 373
  events
    encapsulation, 16
    inheritance, 14
    Window objects, 68-69
  functions
    Sybase SQL Anywhere, 374
    Window objects, 69-70
  transaction objects, 49
User-defined action, Button object, 53
UserID property, 473-474
Users, Sybase Adaptive Server
  adding, 400
  connections, number of, 391
UTF8 character set as default, 325
UTF8 parameter, DBParm property, 325
UUIDs (universally unique identifiers), 299

V

Validating data
  about, 40
  business rules (using NVOs), 132
  with code tables, 41-42
  DataWindow controls, 40-43
  with DDDWs, 46-48
  with edit masks, 43
  with scripts, 43
  server-based validation, 40
  with validation rules, 42-43
Variables
  encapsulation, 16
  window data type, 63-64
Variables view, 177
VCR toolbar, creating, 122-124
Version control
  benefits of, 197-199
  checking in objects, 207-208
  checking out objects, 206-207

check-out status
  clearing, 208-209
  viewing, 209-210
for class libraries, 214
for common libraries, 214
configuration file, creating, 204-205
examples, 197-199
libraries
  class, 214
  common, 214
  configuration, 200-203
  restoring, 211-213
new release, creating, 211
PB Native interface, 199-200
registering objects, 205-206
registration directory, viewing, 210
support requirements, 213-214
tools, connecting to, 203-204
viewing registration directory, 210
Views, constructing, 35-36
Visible property, 94, 103, 108, 110-111
Visual Components, Sybase tool, 579
Visual User objects, 115, 526

W

Watch view, 177
Watcom Library Manager, 254-255
Watcom SQL. See Sybase SQL Anywhere.
.WAV file extension, 268
Waveform files, playing, 268
Web applications. See Internet deployment.
Web browsers. See Internet deployment.
Web Jumps feature, 514
Web pages, creating. See HTML; Internet
  deployment.
Web sites of interest
  CODE partners, list of, 551
  CPDs, 585
  CYRANO, 554
  Greenbrier & Russel, 558
  Jaguar server, 569
  Microsoft, 351
  Power++, 563
  PowerBuilder, 585
  PowerCerv, 552
  PowerDesigner 6.1, 567
  PowerJ, 566
  SQL Anywhere, 354

Sybase, 354
Visual Components, 579
Web-based clients, 5. *See also* Internet deployment.
Web.PB
    about, 498-499
    class library, 500-501
    drivers supported, 499
    interfaces supported, 498
    server application, 499-500
    when to use, 514
Web.PB Wizard, 504-505
WebSite Web Server, 504
Window ActiveX control
    events, 507-508
    functions, 507
    secure mode, 509-510
    usage, 505-506, 508-509
Window controls
    attributes, 76-77
    control array, 78
    creating, 79
    DragObject controls, 75
    DrawObject controls, 76
    DropDownListBox, 80-81
    DropDownPictureListBox, 80-81
    events, 76-77
    ListBox control, 79-80
    ListView control, 84-85
    PictureListBox control, 79-80
    RichTextEdit, 85-87
    Tab control, 88-90
    TreeView control, 81-83
Window data type, 63-64
Window objects. *See also* Windows.
    events
        arguments, adding, 71
        calling, 70-71
        executing, 71-72
        extending, 72
        list of, 65-66
        overriding, 70-71
        post-open, 68-69
        user-defined, 68-69
        viewing, 66-68
        vs. window functions, 74
    functions
        calling, 70-71
        executing, 72-74
        extending, 73-74

        overriding, 73-74
        user-defined, 69-70
        vs. window events, 74
    instantiating, 63-65, 79
Window Painter menu
    Declare|User Events option, 68-69
    Declare|User Events|Args option, 66
    Declare|Windows Functions option, 69
Window plug-in, 501-503, 514-515
Windows
    child, 61
    closing without saving, preventing, 66-67
    control list, 78
    creating, 63-65, 79
    drop-down lists, 80-81
    drop-down toolbars, 98-100
    encapsulation, 16
    formatted text, editing, 85-87
    hierarchical lists, 81-83
    icon lists, 84-85
    inheritance, 14
    inherited, 65
    main, 60-61
    MDI
        defined, 91
        frames, 91-93
        menus, 96-97
        MicroHelp, 97-98
        sheets, 94-96
        toolbars, 98-100
    MDI frame, 63
    menus
        architecture, 103-104
        events, 108-109
        functions, 108-109
        grayed menu items, 109-110
        inheritance, 107-108
        in MDI applications, 109-110
        menu bars, 104-105
        performance issues, 111
        pop-up menus, 105-106
        types of, 104-106
    multiple, 91
    picture lists, 79-80
    pop-up, 61-62
    post-open events, 68-69
    printing
        canceling, allowing, 143
        columns, newspaper-style, 146-147

DataWindow print properties, 147-151
escape sequences, 144
fonts, changing, 151-152
functions, list of, 142-143
line spacing, changing, 144
manual job management, 143-144
margins, changing, 144, 146
options, setting, 146-151
paper orientation, selecting, 146-147
paper size, selecting, 146-147
print area, 141-142
print cursor, 142
Print dialog box, displaying, 145-146, 149-151
Print function, 143-145
Print Setup dialog box, displaying, 145, 147
Print Specification page, 146-147
printers, changing dynamically, 145-146
titles, printing, 144-145
response, 62
tab pages, 88-90
text lists, 79-80
Visible property, 110
Windows API calls, external functions, 264-269
Windows directory, getting path, 267-268
Windows Help
contents file, 462-463
creating, 460-462
Help topic files, 458-459
limitations, 463-464
project files, 454-457
topic IDs, 458-459
Windows messages, trapping, 37
Windows Registry
App Path entries, 421
CLSIDs, 299
deployment DLLs, 421
GUIDs, 299
IIDs, 299
and OLE automation servers, 299-303
OLEGenReg utility, 300-303
PowerBuilder.Applicaiton entry, 291-292
profile strings, getting, 266
ProgIDs, 299-300
registering objects, 300-303
UUIDs, 299
[WINDOWS] section, HELP project files, 457
Windows system directory, getting path, 267
Windowtype data type, 94
WinExec function, 268-269
WLIB.EXE, 254-255
Work library, 200-201
World Wide Web applications. *See* Internet
deployment.